R. Gupta's®

POPULAR MASTER GUIDE

KVS

Kendriya Vidyalaya Sangathan

Librarian

Recruitment Exam

by

RPH Editorial Board

Thoroughly Revised Edition

2027
EDITION

RAMESH PUBLISHING HOUSE, NEW DELHI

Published by
O.P. Gupta *for* Ramesh Publishing House

Admin. Office
12-H, New Daryaganj Road, Opp. Officers' Mess,
New Delhi-110002 ✆ 23275224, 23245124

E-mail: info@rameshpublishinghouse.com
For Online Shopping: www.rameshpublishinghouse.com

Showroom
- Balaji Market, Nai Sarak, Delhi-110006 ✆ 23282525 📱 9354373464
- 4457, Nai Sarak, Delhi-110006

Book Code: R-1630

ISBN: 978-93-5012-409-3

Price: ₹ 390

Printed at: Nidhi Enterprises, Delhi

CONTENTS

Hill Station; National Parks; National Wildlife Sanctuaries; Holy Places in India; Sports; Famous Trophies; Biggest, Largest, Tallest of the World; First in India; Important Days; Parliaments of Important Countries; Mineral Resources of the World; World's Largest Producers; Ten Largest Countries and Their Areas; President of India; Vice-President of India; Prime Ministers of India; The Solar System: Some Facts; The Earth: Facts and Data; Principal Mountain Peaks of the World; Popular Nick Names of Some Famous Personalities; Famous International Organisations, Headquarters and Year of Establishment; Bharat Ratna Award Winners; Art and Culture; Music; Famous International Air Services; Famous Religions, Founders, Holy Books & Places of Worship; Intelligence Agencies of Some Prominent Countries; Some Prominent Races of the World; Famous Straits of the World; Famous Newspapers of the World; Important Boundary Lines; Signals/Signs and Meaning; National Emblems of Important Countries; The Continents of the World; Computer; Defence; Multiple Choice Questions and Answers.

Scheme of Written Examination

Test Duration	180 Minutes	
Total Questions	180 Objective Type Multiple Choice Questions	
Total Marks	180 Marks	
Section Name	**Marks per Question**	**No. of Questions**
Part-I : Proficiency in Languages (30 marks)		
1. General English	01 mark per question	15
2. General Hindi		15
Part-II : General Awareness, Reasoning & Proficiency in Computers (50 marks)		
1. General Knowledge & Current Affairs	01 mark per question	20
2. Reasoning Ability		20
3. Computer Literacy		10
Part-III : Subject-Specific : **Library & Information Science** (100 questions & 100 marks)		
PROFESSIONAL COMPETENCY TEST: 60 MARKS (Demo Teaching-30 marks and Interview-30 marks)		

Previous Years' Paper

Kendriya Vidyalaya Sangathan (KVS)–Librarian

Recruitment Exam – 2023

(Exam held on 06-03-2023)

GENERAL ENGLISH

Directions (Qs. No. 1 & 2): *Rearrange the parts in correct order to make meaningful sentence:*

1. (*a*) is an ennobling form
(*b*) in performing their day-to-day activities
(*c*) helping the elderly
(*d*) of social service
A. (*c*), (*b*), (*a*), (*d*)
B. (*d*), (*a*), (*b*), (*c*)
C. (*b*), (*a*), (*c*), (*d*)
D. (*a*), (*b*), (*c*), (*d*)

2. (*a*) over a long period of time
(*b*) Babu Devaki Nandan Khatri's 'Chandrakanta'
(*c*) was serialised
(*d*) in local Hindi newspapers
A. (*c*), (*b*), (*d*), (*a*)
B. (*a*), (*b*), (*d*), (*c*)
C. (*b*), (*c*), (*d*), (*a*)
D. (*d*), (*a*), (*b*), (*c*)

Directions (Qs. No. 3 & 4): *Change the following sentence from Active Voice to Passive Voice:*

3. Why has the employer sacked the employee?
A. The employer has been sacked by the employee - why?
B. Why has the employee been sacked by the employer?
C. Why the employee has been sacked by the employer?
D. Why is the employee sacked by the employer?

4. The violent thunderstorm frightened the jungle animals.
A. The violent thunderstorm was frightened by the jungle animals.
B. The animals were frightened by the storm.
C. The jungle animals have been frightened by the violent thunderstorm.
D. The jungle animals were frightened by the violent thunderstorm

Directions (Qs. No. 5 & 6): *Fill in the blank with correct preposition.*

5. He is justifiably proud _____ his achievements in sports activities.
A. with
B. of
C. from
D. for

6. All companies should adhere ______ the rules and regulations operating in their fields.
A. of B. with
C. to D. from

1. A	2. C	3. B	4. D	5. B	6. C

Directions (Qs. No. 7 & 8): *Identify the correct tense form of the underlined part in the given sentence.*

7. They have been living in Europe for a long time now.
   A. Present Continuous
   B. Present Perfect Continuous
   C. Present Perfect
   D. Simple Present

8. They had finished eating long before we reached the restaurant.
   A. Simple Present
   B. Present Perfect
   C. Simple Past
   D. Past Perfect

Directions (Qs. No. 9 & 10): *Identify the part which contains on error.*

9. (A) Lata Mangeshkar has sung/ (B) a large number of songs/ (C) in Hindi cinema,/ (D) isn't it?

10. (A) Why can't you/ (B) adjust for/ (C) your parents/ (D) and live with them?

Directions (Qs. No. 11 & 12): *Choose the word nearest in meaning to the given word.*

11. COERCE
    A. shout B. compel
    C. rebuke D. admonish

12. BOISTEROUS
    A. crowded B. illegal
    C. noisy D. chaotic

Directions (Qs. No. 13 & 14): *Choose the word opposite in meaning to the given word.*

13. CURSORY
    A. rapid B. scholarly
    C. intensive D. superficial

14. AVERSION
    A. praise B. worship
    C. indifference D. liking

15. Identify the part of speech of the underlined word.

    There is something endearing about his personality.
    A. Adverb B. Preposition
    C. Conjunction D. Adjective

सामान्य हिन्दी

निर्देशः (प्र.सं. 16 से 20 तक): *निम्नलिखित गद्यांश को ध्यानपूर्वक पढ़िए और उसके आधार पर दिए गए प्रश्न का उत्तर दीजिए:*

कबीर के उद्देश्य काव्य-रचना करना नहीं था। वे तो निर्गुण को वाणी के द्वारा व्यक्त करना चाहते थे। इस कार्य को करते-करते कविता भी अपने आप बन गयी। उनकी वाणी अटपटी कही गयी है। वे भाषा पर शासन करते थे और शब्द को अपना मनचाहा अर्थ देने के लिए विवश कर देते थे। आज हिन्दी के श्रेष्ठ कवियों में उनकी गणना की जाती है और लोग बड़ी श्रद्धा से उनके पद गाते हैं।

16. कबीर की कविता बन गयी:
    A. यात्रा करते-करते
    B. समाज की बुराईयों को देखते-देखते
    C. निर्गुण की अभिव्यक्ति करते-करते
    D. धर्म-प्रचार करते-करते

17. कबीर के उद्देश्य थाः
    A. काव्य रचना
    B. काव्य-प्रचार
    C. निर्गुण की वाणी द्वारा व्यक्त करना
    D. सगुणोपासना

7. B	8. D	9. D	10. B	11. B	12. C
13. C	14. D	15. B	16. C	17. C	

18. कबीर के बारे में कौन-सा कथन सही है?

A. वे रामभक्त कवि कहलाते थे
B. उनके आराध्य दशरथ-पुत्र राम थे
C. उनके पद बड़ी श्रद्धा से गाए जाते हैं
D. उनकी गणना श्रेष्ठ कवियों में कम ही होती है

19. कबीर के बारे में कौन-सा कथन सही है?

A. कबीर सगुणोपासना के समर्थक थे
B. कबीर की आस्था सामाजिक आडंबरों में थी
C. कबीर भाषा पर शासन करते थे
D. कबीर बनारस में दफनाए गए थे

20. भाषा के बारे में कबीर की विशेषता थी:

A. वे केवल राजस्थानी में रचना करते थे
B. वे केवल ब्रजभाषा में रचना करते थे
C. वे शब्द को मनचाहा अर्थ देने के लिए विवश कर देते थे
D. कबीर को निर्गुण कवियों में वह स्थान न मिला

21. निम्नलिखित में भाववाचक संज्ञा शब्द है:

A. मिठास B. परमात्मा
C. सभा D. नदी

22. 'आभ्यांतर' शब्द का विलोमार्थी शब्द है:

A. प्रत्यंतर B. समांतर
C. बाहरी D. बाह्य

23. 'सोना' शब्द का पर्यायवाची शब्द नहीं है:

A. स्वर्ण B. हिम
C. कनक D. हाटक

24. 'तिरंगा' शब्द उदाहरण है:

A. द्विगु समास का
B. कर्मधारय समास का
C. बहुव्रीहि समास का
D. तत्पुरुष समास का

25. व्यंजन संधि वाला शब्द है:

A. उद्गम
B. धनुष्टंकार
C. मनस्ताप
D. निश्चल

26. निम्नलिखित में गुणवाचक विशेषण है:

A. भीतरी
B. बाहरी
C. अधूरा
D. दुबला

27. निम्नलिखित शब्द युग्मों में तत्सम-तद्भव का असंगत युग्म है:

A. कोकिल – कोयल
B. जिह्वा – जीभ
C. क्षार – खार
D. सोना – स्वर्ण

28. निम्नलिखित में एकार्थी शब्द है:

A. अपयश
B. अभिजात
C. अरुण
D. अवधि

29. 'आग उगलना' मुहावरे का सटीक अर्थ है:

A. नाराज होना
B. क्रोधित होना
C. अत्यंत क्रोधित होना
D. लड़ाई करवाना

30. निम्नलिखित में वर्तनी की दृष्टि से शुद्ध शब्द है:

A. छत्रिय
B. मध्यान्ह
C. स्वास्थ
D. माहात्म्य

18. C	**19.** C	**20.** C	**21.** A	**22.** D	**23.** B	**24.** A
25. A	**26.** A, B, D	**27.** D	**28.** A	**29.** C	**30.** D	

GENERAL KNOWLEDGE & CURRENT AFFAIRS

31. Consider the following statements about Indian metallurgy before independence:

(*a*) The sword of Tipu Sultan was made of high carbon silver called Wootz.

(*b*) The Tata Iron and Steel Company (TISCO) was set up in 1912 on the banks of the river Subarnarekha.

(*c*) The legendary scientist Michael Faraday spent four years in early 19th century studying the properties of Indian steel called 'UKKU' in Kannada.

Choose the correct answer from the codes below:

A. Only (*a*) B. Only (*a*) and (*b*)
C. Only (*b*) and (*c*) D. Only (*a*) and (*c*)

32. Which of the following Articles was inserted in Part III (Fundamental Rights) of the Indian Constitution in 1976 but was repealed by the Indian Parliament in 1977?

A. Restriction on Fundamental Rights while Martial Law is in force
B. Saving of laws in respect of anti-national activities
C. Freedom to manage religious affairs
D. Protection against arrest and detention in certain cases

33. Who among the following was a member of the Constituent Assembly of India and the first recepient of the Bharat Ratna?

A. C. Rajagopalachari
B. Zakir Hussain
C. Rajendra Prasad
D. K. Kamraj

34. Which popular uprising in China demanding the establishment of the 'Heavenly Kingdom of Great Peace' coincided with the Revolt of 1857 in India?

A. White Lotus Rebellion
B. Taiping Rebellion
C. Eight Trigrams Uprising
D. Boxer Rebellion

35. At the United Nations Climate Change Conference (COP 26), 2021, India has pledged to reach net zero carbon emission by which year?

A. 2050 B. 2060
C. 2070 D. 2080

36. Who invented 'Cloud Computing' in the 1960s with his work on ARPANET?

A. Joseph Carl Robnett Licklider
B. Lady Ada Lovelace
C. Nicholas Carr
D. Jean-Marie Volland

37. Which among the following is/are example(s) of Temperate grasslands?

(*a*) Prairie (*b*) Steppe
(*c*) Campos

Choose the correct answer from the codes below:

A. Only (*a*)
B. Only (*c*)
C. Only (*a*) and (*b*)
D. Only (*b*) and (*c*)

38. Which among the following independent states were created with the disintegration of Yugoslavia in the early 1990s?

(*a*) Republic of Croatia
(*b*) Republic of Slovenia
(*c*) Republic of Albania

Choose the correct answer from the codes below:

A. Only (*a*) B. Only (*a*) and (*b*)
C. Only (*b*) and (*c*) D. Only (*a*) and (*c*)

31. C **32.** B **33.** A **34.** B **35.** C **36.** A **37.** C **38.** B

39. Which of the following cities is called the 'City of 72 Nations' for its large number of immigrants?

A. Zurich B. Tehran
C. Vienna D. Singapore

40. Which among the following planet(s) has/ have no moons?

(*a*) Mercury
(*b*) Venus
(*c*) Mars

Choose the correct answer from the codes below:

A. Only (*a*) B. Only (*c*)
C. Only (*a*) and (*b*) D. Only (*b*) and (*c*)

41. The process of taking food into the body is called ______.

A. Ingestion
B. Assimilation
C. Absorption
D. Egestion

42. *Cuscuta* is a ______.

A. Parasite B. Insectivorous plant
C. Saprotrophs D. Autotrophs

43. What was the theme of the commemorative postal stamp which was released on the occassion of the 17th Pravasi Bharatiya Divas Convention held in Indore in January 2023?

A. "Ek Bharat Shreshtha Bharat"
B. "Vasudhaiva Kutumbakam"
C. "Atithi Devo Bhava"
D. "Surakshit Jaayen, Prashikshit Jayen"

44. Consider the following statements regarding the All India Presiding Officers' conference (AIPOC) and identify the incorrect statement.

A. The All India Presiding Officers' Conference (AIPOC) is the apex body of the legislatures in India that, completed its hundred years in 2020.
B. The 82nd AIPOC was held in Shimla in 2021.
C. The 83rd AIPOC was held in Jaipur on 11th January, 2023.
D. The first Conference AIPOC was held in 1921 in Shimla.

45. Who among the following is the Gold winner in the 2023 World Habitat in partnership with UN-Habitat, awards?

A. 'Jaga Mission', India
B. 'Homes for Good', Scotland
C. 'Housing Action Group', Namibia
D. 'SIPHO', Spain

46. Digital India Awards, 2022 was given to Government Ministers/Departments/Offices/ Organisations by the Government of India. Which among the following organisation was the winner of 'Platinum' Award under 'Data sharing and use for Socio-Economic Development'?

A. Smart Cities Mission (Ministry of Housing and Urban Affairs)
B. Central Board of Secondary Education (CBSE)
C. Centre for e-governance (Karnataka)
D. Digital Workforce Management System (Kerala)

47. Who among the following authors is the winner of the Nobel Prize in Literature in 2022?

A. Alice Munro
B. Kazuo Ishiguro
C. Annie Ernaux
D. Abdul Razak Gurnah

48. Who among the following is the Prime Minister of Bhutan?

A. Dorji Wangdi
B. Wangchuk Namgyel
C. Yeshey Penjor
D. Dr. Lotey Tshering

39. B	40. C	41. A	42. A	43. D	44. A	45. B	46. A	47. C	48. D

49. Which four teams participated in the semifinals of the FIFA World Cup held in 2022?

A. Argentina, Croatia, Brazil and France
B. France, Argentina, Croatia and Morocco
C. France, Portugal, Argentina and Croatia
D. Argentina, Netherlands, France and Morocco

50. Which among the following is the World's largest river cruise covering a distance of more than 3,200 kilometres?

A. 'Spirit of Ganges'
B. 'Upper Ganges Cruise'
C. 'Ganga Vilas Cruise'
D. 'Lower Ganges Cruise'

REASONING ABILITY

51. There is a certain relation between two given words on left side of :: and one word is given on another side of :: while another word is to be found from the given alternatives, having the same relation with this word as the given pair has. Select the correct alternatives.

Planet : Jupiter :: Island : __?__

A. Ireland B. Netherland
C. Greenland D. Scotland

52. In a certain code language if 'CONSIDER' is written as 'CNOISEDR'. How would 'MANAGERS' be written in that code?

A. MBNBGFST B. NAOAHERT
C. NBOBGDST D. MNAGARES

53. Four words have been given, out of which three are alike in some manner, while the one is different. Choose the odd one.

A. Editor
B. Photographer
C. Reporter
D. Reader

54. Sachit's school bus is facing south when it reaches his school. After starting from his house, it turns left twice and then right before reaching the school. In what direction was the bus facing when it left the bus stop in front of his house?

A. North B. East
C. West D. South

55. In a library, books on the subjects of medicines, cooking and engineering are in yellow cover whereas books on the subjects embroidery and law are in Brown cover. Also the books on the subjects engineering and cooking have new editions whereas books on the subjects medicine, law and embroidery have old editions.

The book on which subject is in yellow colour and has old edition?

A. Law
B. Embroidery
C. Medicine
D. Cooking

56. There are two statements labelled Assertion (A) and Reason (R):

Assertion (A): Weeds should not be allowed to grow along with the crops.

Reason (R): Weeds consume the essential nutrients, which are required by the crops for growth.

Mark your answer as per the codes given below:

A. Both (A) and (R) are true and (R) is the correct explanation of (A).
B. Both (A) and (R) are true and (R) is not the correct explanation of (A).
C. (A) is true, but (R) is false.
D. (A) is false, but (R) is true.

49. B **50.** C **51.** C **52.** D **53.** D **54.** C **55.** C **56.** A

57. A question is given below followed by two statements numbered I and II each containing some information. Decide which of the statements is/are sufficient to answer the question.

Q: How is X related to Lalit?

I: Ravi is brother of Lalit.

II: Father of X is son of Ravi.

A. The statement I alone is sufficient to answer the question while the statement II alone is not sufficient to answer.
B. The statement II alone is sufficient to answer the question while the statement I alone is not sufficient to answer.
C. Both statements I and II together are necessary to answer the question.
D. Both statements I and II together are not sufficient to answer the question.

58. How many even numbers are there which are immediately preceded by an odd number and also immediately followed by an odd number?

4, 7, 3, 8, 3, 5, 5, 3, 4, 9, 8, 6, 7, 2

A. 3 B. 4
C. 2 D. 6

59. The following diagram represents the regions of wheat, gram and rice cultivation.

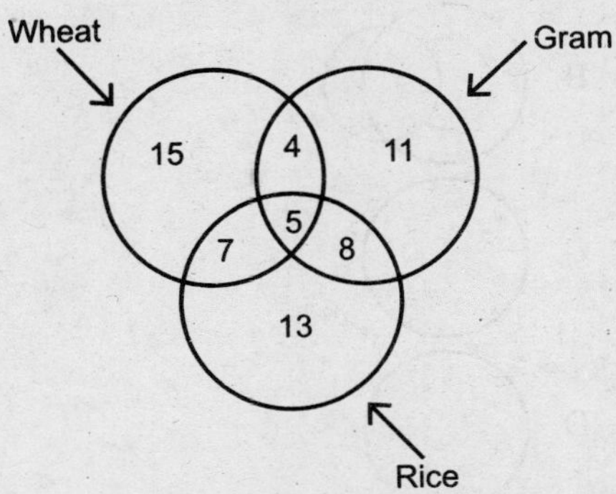

Find the ratio of area which gives the cultivation of all three to the region which does not cultivate Rice?

A. 1 : 4 B. 1 : 5
C. 1 : 6 D. 1 : 7

60. Seven friends A, B, C, D, E, F and G are sitting around a circular table facing the centre. 'C' is the neighbour of 'A' and 'E'. 'G', who is third to the left of 'B', is the neighbour of 'E' and 'F'. 'D' is not neighbour of 'G' and 'C'. 'A' is neighbour of 'B' and 'C'.

Who is sitting between 'D' and 'G'?

A. A B. B
C. E D. F

61. Five men P, Q, R, S and T play a game with ball. The one who has the ball at first gives it to 'R'. The one who has the ball at last had taken from 'P'. 'T' was not the last or first to have the ball. There were two players between 'Q' and 'P'.

Who has the ball at last?

A. P B. Q
C. R D. S

62. In the given letter series, some of the letters are missing which are given in that order as one of the alternatives below it.

Choose the correct alternative.

u w _ _ w v u _ _ u _ v

A. vuwvw B. vwuwv
C. wuvuw D. wvuwv

63. In a certain code language, 'Roses are red' is written as 'Kew xas deko', 'Flowers are beautiful' is written as 'Kew tepo qua' and 'Red flowers' is written as 'deko tepo'. How 'Roses' is written in that language?

A. Kew B. xas
C. deko D. tepo

57. D	58. C	59. C	60. D	61. D	62. A	63. B

64. If $A \leq B$, $A > C$ and $B \leq D$, then which of the following is true?

A. $C \geq B$ B. $C > D$
C. $D = C$ D. $C < D$

65. 'P + Q' means 'P' is son of 'Q', 'P – Q' means 'P' is husband of 'Q', 'P ÷ Q' means 'P' is sister of 'Q' and 'P × Q' means P is mother of 'Q'.

If A ÷ R + C – B, then what is the relation of B with A?

A. Sister B. Mother
C. Daughter D. Aunt

66. Letters of the word given below have been jumbled up, and each letter has been assigned a number. Select the combination of numbers so that the letters arranged accordingly will form a meaningful word.

U	T	R	S	P	I	D
1	2	3	4	5	6	7

A. 4215637 B. 3142567
C. 2134657 D. 7643152

67. Given below are two statements followed by two conclusions numbered I and II. You have to take the given two statements to be true even if they seem to be at variance from commonly known facts. Read the conclusions and then decide which of the given conclusions logically follow(s) from the two given statements, disregarding commonly known facts.

Statements:
All lions are rats.
All rats are ants.

Conclusions:
I. All lions are ants.
II. All ants are lions.

A. Only conclusion (I) follows
B. Only conclusion (II) follows
C. Neither conclusion (I) nor (II) follow
D. Both conclusions (I) and (II) follow

68. A word has been given, followed by four other words, only one of which can be formed by using the letters of the given word. Find that word.

A P P R E C I A T I O N

A. ACTION
B. APPEAL
C. PIECE
D. TREAT

69. Mary is wife of Anil. Nitu is sister of Mayank. Anil is son of Dinesh and Mayank is son of Anil. How is Nitu related to Mary?

A. Sister
B. Daughter
C. Aunt
D. Niece

70. Choose from the following Venn diagrams, the one that best represents the relationship among the three classes given below.

Women, Teachers, Mothers

A. 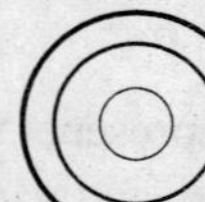

B. 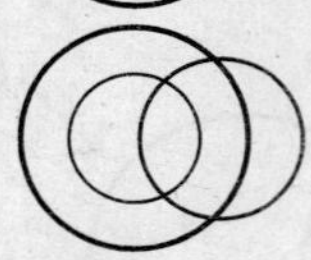

C. 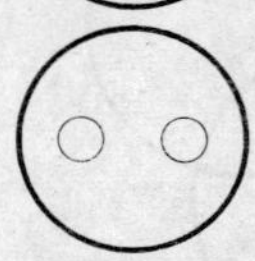

D. 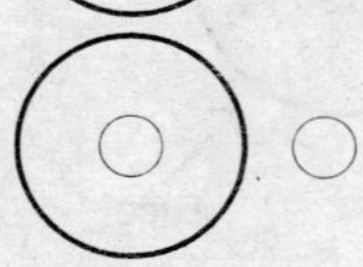

64. D **65.** B **66.** D **67.** A **68.** A **69.** B **70.** B

COMPUTER LITERACY

71. Which of the following is not an input device?
A. Touchpad B. Plotter
C. Joystick D. Barcode Scanner

72. Which of the following is the largest memory unit in the given options?
A. Kilo Byte B. Peta Byte
C. Exa Byte D. Giga Byte

73. Which of the following is not an Operating System?
A. MacOS B. MS Windows
C. Linux D. Mozilla Firefox

74. ______ the company, which does not develop Antivirus software.
A. Norton B. Tally
C. Mcafee D. Kaspersky

75. Abdul Sheikh is interested in making a digital presentation for training his staff using an open source software, which of the following will you suggest for the same?
A. Impress B. Calc
C. Writer D. Powerpoint

76. Gul Patil is planning to buy a new smart-phone, which one of the following aspects should she not be bothered about?
A. Internal Memory B. Camera Pixels
C. Operating System D. Ethernet Port

77. Which of the following ports will be most suitable for connecting High Quality Audio-Video output on a PC/a laptop?
A. USB B. PS2
C. HDMI D. VGA

78. Which of the following is the correct extension of MS Powerpoint file?
A. pptx B. pdocx
C. pwpt D. ppoint

79. ______ is the file extension of an Excel file.
A. excel B. xlsx
C. xcl D. xelx

80. Which of the following is not an example of RDBMS?
A. MySQL B. MS SQL Server
C. MS Word D. IBM DB2

POST SPECIFIC SUBJECT-RELATED QUESTIONS

81. Which of the following is a central nodal agency for 'National Mission on libraries' (NML)?
A. NISCAIR
B. National library of India
C. RRRLF
D. Delhi Public library

82. Who was the first publisher of the 'Five Laws of Library Science of S.R. Ranganathan'?
A. Thomson
B. Edward Goldston
C. Asia Publishing House
D. Oxford

83. In which year, the 'Arunachal Pradesh Public Libraries Act' was enacted?
A. 2003 B. 2006
C. 2009 D. 2011

71. B	**72.** C	**73.** D	**74.** B	**75.** A	**76.** D	**77.** C
78. A	**79.** B	**80.** C	**81.** C	**82.** B	**83.** C	

84. Arrange the following Public Libraries Acts according to the year of enactment of library legislation:

(*i*) Chhattisgarh Public Libraries Act
(*ii*) Gujarat Public Libraries Act
(*iii*) Mizoram Public Libraries Act
(*iv*) Bihar Public Libraries Act

A. (*i*), (*iii*), (*ii*), (*iv*)
B. (*iii*), (*ii*), (*iv*), (*i*)
C. (*ii*), (*iii*), (*i*), (*iv*)
D. (*iii*), (*iv*), (*ii*), (*i*)

85. According to S.R. Ranganathan 'Micro Subject' is a:

A. Subject of small extension and great intention
B. Subject formed by coupling two or more subjects
C. Subject with tiny extension
D. Subject with great extension and very small intension

86. In Cataloguing 'Sino loco' means ______.

A. Without name of author
B. Without year
C. Without place
D. Without class number

87. Which of the following is not a section of a main entry according to Classified Catalogue Code (Ed.5)?

A. Title section   B. Name section
C. Leading section   D. Tracing section

88. Who is the author of book 'Heading and Canons'?

A. B.S. Kesvan
B. Krishna Kumar
C. S.R. Ranganathan
D. P.N. Kaula

89. In Colon Classification, the sequence of 'Specials' in Basic class 'Medicine' is choosen according to the principle of ______.

A. Principle of Later-in-Evolution
B. Principle of Later-in-Time
C. Principle of Spatial Contiguity
D. Principle of Alphabetical Sequence

90. Which of the following Tables is associated with the 'Racial, Ethnic, National Groups', according to DDC (19th Edition)?

A. Table-1   B. Table-2
C. Table-5   D. Table-7

91. "If, in a subject, Facet 'B' is an organ of Facet 'A', then A should preced B" - is related with ______.

A. Cow-Calf Principle
B. Principle of Later-in time
C. Principle of Left to Right
D. Whole-organ Principle

92. According to DDC, 'Unemployed Carpenters' is an example of ______.

A. Simple Subject
B. Complex Subject
C. Compound Subject
D. Complete Subject

93. 'Faceted Application of Subject Terminology' (FAST) is developed by ______.

A. OCLC
B. IFLA
C. ALA
D. CILIP

94. Identify the correct sequence of Facets in main class 'O' Literature in Colon Classification (6th edition):

A. Form, Work, Language, Author
B. Language, Form, Author, Work
C. Form, Language, Author, Work
D. Work, Language, Form, Author

84. B	**85.** A	**86.** C	**87.** B	**88.** C	**89.** A
90. C	**91.** D	**92.** B	**93.** A	**94.** B	

95. Which of the following are related with 'D Space'?

(*a*) Free open software
(*b*) Completely customizable to fit user needs
(*c*) Optimized for google Scholar Indexing
(*d*) Interface available in 51 Languages

A. (*b*), (*c*) and (*d*) are correct
B. (*a*), (*b*) and (*d*) are correct
C. (*a*), (*b*) and (*c*) are correct
D. (*a*), (*c*) and (*d*) are correct

96. A 'Bandwidth in network' is called ______.

A. Size of network.
B. Distance in network.
C. A measure of data transfer rate.
D. A measure of minimum data transfer rate.

97. In which financial estimation method, a minimum amount per head of population is fixed?

A. Per capita method
B. Proportional method
C. Method of details
D. Zero based budgeting method

98. 'ISO 31000' is an International Standard for ______.

A. Library Management
B. Energy Management
C. Space Management
D. Risk Management

99. 'Journal Translation Today' is a publication of ______.

A. NISCAIR
B. National Translation Mission
C. INFLIBNET
D. Commission for Scientific and Technical Terminology

100. 'Conservative, Moderate and Liberal' theories of reference service are propounded by:

A. S.R. Ranganathan
B. Samuel Rothstein
C. James I Wyer
D. Melvil Dewey

101. Who developed the model 'Everyday Life Information Seeking' in Context of Way of life?

A. Sanda Erdelez B. David Ellis
C. Reijo Savolainen D. M.B. Eisenberg

102. In 1949, the Three-Stage user Education Program was proposed by ______.

A. IFLA
B. ALA-Public Library Section
C. UK Library Association's University and Research Section
D. Hopkins

103. Which of the following is not a qualitative research method?

A. Grounded Theory
B. Hermeneutics
C. Experimental
D. Ethnography

104. 'Green Glass' is a service/program of:

A. CILIP B. ALA
C. IFLA D. OCLC

105. Who said that "Librarianship is Salesmanship"?

A. W.C.B. Sayers
B. S.R. Ranganathan
C. Margrette Hutchins
D. William Katz

106. The Three Phase Model of Change Management i.e. Unfreeze, Move or change and Refreeze was formulated by:

A. R.M. Kanter B. Kurt Lewin
C. John Kottler D. Mckinsey

95. C	96. C	97. A	98. D	99. B	100. C
101. C	102. C	103. C	104. D	105. B	106. B

107. Which of the following State Public Libraries Acts have provision of Library cess?

(*a*) Karnataka (*b*) Goa
(*c*) Haryana (*d*) Bihar

Codes:

A. (*a*) and (*c*) are correct
B. (*a*) and (*b*) are correct
C. (*b*) and (*c*) are correct
D. (*a*) and (*d*) are correct

108. Symbol of 'Maharaja of Air India' is a ______.

A. Copyright B. Standard
C. Patent D. Trademark

109. 'National Mission on Libraries' was set up under the chairmanship of ______.

A. Prof. Deepak Pental
B. Shri Sam Pitroda
C. Dr. Jagdish Arora
D. Prof. Subbiah Arunachalam

110. "If the user will not come to the library, the library must go to the users", stated by whom:

A. William A Katz
B. Samuel Rothstein
C. S.R. Ranganathan
D. Margrette Hutchins

111. National Institute of Mental Health and Neurosciences is situated in:

A. Mumbai B. Agra
C. Chennai D. Bangalore

112. 'Application of Ranganathan's Laws to the web' is related to:

A. Meggie Wright B. Alireza Noruzi
C. Michael Gorman D. Talea Anderson

113. As per the Seventh Schedule under Article 246 of Constitution of India, which of the following libraries of National Importance are being financed by Ministry of Culture?

(*a*) Delhi Public Library, Delhi
(*b*) Central Reference Library, Kolkata
(*c*) Parliament Library, Delhi
(*d*) Connemara Public Library, Chennai

Codes:

A. (*a*) and (*d*) are correct
B. (*a*) and (*b*) are correct
C. (*a*) and (*c*) are correct
D. (*b*) and (*d*) are correct

114. IFLA and UNESCO launched an updated Public Library Manifesto in ______.

A. November 2021 B. February 2022
C. June 2022 D. July 2022

115. Which Law of Library Science emphasises most on the enactment of Library Legislation?

A. Second Law B. Third Law
C. Fourth Law D. Fifth Law

116. Under RRRLF Financial Assistance Matching Scheme, assistance is shared on matching basis between RRRLF and developing & Lagging states as per the ratio given below:

A. 60 : 40 B. 90 : 10
C. 70 : 30 D. 50 : 50

117. The concept of 'Ask Library Anything' was originally initiated by ______.

A. IFLA B. SLA
C. ASLIB D. ALA

118. P.V. Verghese Prize is awarded by Indian Library Association for ______.

A. Best Book B. Best Service
C. Best Article D. Best Library

119. 'KZ' which represents the subject 'Animal Husbandary' is an example of ______.

A. Gap device B. Sector Digit
C. Emptying Digit D. Mixed base

107. A	**108.** D	**109.** A	**110.** A	**111.** D	**112.** B	**113.** B
114. D	**115.** A	**116.** A	**117.** D	**118.** C	**119.** C	

120. AACR2(1978) was edited by ______.

(*a*) Eric J. Hunter
(*b*) Michael Gorman
(*c*) Paul W Winkler
(*d*) Joseph Juran

Codes:

A. (*a*) and (*b*) are correct
B. (*b*) and (*c*) are correct
C. (*c*) and (*d*) are correct
D. (*a*) and (*d*) are correct

121. Match the following:

List-I (Classification Scheme)	***List-II (Category)***
(*a*) Subject Classification	I. Almost faceted
(*b*) Colon Classification	II. Purely Enumerative
(*c*) Universal Decimal Classification (UDC)	III. Faceted
(*d*) Library of Congress Classification	IV. Enumerative

	(*a*)	(*b*)	(*c*)	(*d*)
A.	II	IV	III	I
B.	IV	III	II	I
C.	IV	III	I	II
D.	III	IV	I	II

122. Gap Device helps in making classification scheme more ______.

A. Hospitable
B. Faceted
C. Hierarchical
D. Enumerative

123. Identify the symbol of 'Spiritual experience and Mysticism' as given in Colon Classification, 6th Ed.

A. 4
B. MZA
C. Δ
D. Σ

124. Which of the following are included in the primary connectors of a computer system?

(*a*) Power
(*b*) Keyboard
(*c*) Printer
(*d*) Display

Codes:

A. (*a*), (*b*), (*c*) are correct
B. (*a*), (*b*), (*d*) are correct
C. (*a*), (*c*), (*d*) are correct
D. (*b*), (*c*), (*d*) are correct

125. Which programming language is called the mother of Programming languages?

A. C++ B. C
C. Java D. Pascal

126. The term 'communication' was coined by ______.

A. Anthony Oettinger
B. John Bell
C. Ted Off
D. Stuart Murray

127. Which type of Protocol is used by interface for 'Public Data Network' (PDN)?

A. X. 20
B. X. 22
C. X. 25
D. X. 30

128. Identify DTP softwares from the following application softwares.

(*a*) Pagemaker
(*b*) QuarkXPress
(*c*) Freehand
(*d*) Illustrator

Codes:

A. (*b*), (*c*) are correct
B. (*b*), (*d*) are correct
C. (*a*), (*c*) are correct
D. (*a*), (*b*) are correct

120. B **121.** C **122.** A **123.** C **124.** B **125.** B **126.** * **127.** C **128.** D

129. Match the following:

List-I (Field)	List-II (MARC 21 Tag)
(a) Edition	I. 100
(b) Personal Name	II. 250
(c) Uniform Title	III. 130
(d) Physical Description	IV. 300

Codes:

	(a)	(b)	(c)	(d)
A.	II	I	III	IV
B.	I	II	III	IV
C.	I	II	IV	III
D.	II	III	IV	I

130. Which of the following are Library Management softwares:

(a) LIBSYS
(b) KOHA
(c) Dspace
(d) Greenstone

Codes:

A. (a) and (b) are correct
B. (a) and (d) are correct
C. (b) and (d) are correct
D. (b) and (c) are correct

131. Arrange the following Projects of IFLA in chronological sequence:

(a) Functional Requirements for Authority Data (FRAD)
(b) Functional Requirements for Bibliographic Records (FRBR)
(c) Functional Requirements for Bibliographic Records-Object Oriented (FRBROO)
(d) Functional Requirements for Subject Authority Data (FRSAD)

Codes:

A. (a), (b), (d), (c)
B. (b), (c), (d), (a)
C. (b), (a), (d), (c)
D. (a), (d), (b), (c)

132. Which of the following are input devices of a computer?

(a) Optical Character Recognition (OCR)
(b) Scanner
(c) Plotters
(d) Printers

Codes:

A. (b) and (d) are correct
B. (a) and (b) are correct
C. (b) and (c) are correct
D. (a) and (d) are correct

133. ______ is a type of network topology where each device connects one after the other in a sequential chain.

A. Ring Topology
B. Tree Topology
C. Star Topology
D. Linear Bus Topology

134. In the context of Structure the First Component of the MARC Record is ______.

A. Directory
B. Fixed Fields
C. Leader
D. Variable Fields

135. Which of the following are the operating systems?

(a) MPE/ix
(b) Spreadsheet
(c) Linux
(d) MS Word

Codes:

A. (a) and (b) are correct
B. (b) and (d) are correct
C. (a) and (c) are correct
D. (a) and (d) are correct

136. In 1991, HTML Tags were first published on the internet by ______.

A. R. Stout
B. Tim Berners Lee
C. J. Eddings
D. M. Handley

129. A	130. A	131. C	132. B	133. D	134. C	135. C	136. B

137. Which of the following Schools/ Management thoughts are related to Modern Theory of Management?

(*a*) Social System School
(*b*) System School
(*c*) Contingency School
(*d*) Decision Theory School

Codes:

A. (*b*) and (*d*) are correct
B. (*a*) and (*d*) are correct
C. (*a*) and (*b*) are correct
D. (*b*) and (*c*) are correct

138. ______ Principle of Henry Fayol states that there should be only one head and one plan, in order to ensure a coordinated effort.

A. Unity of Direction
B. Unity of Command
C. Esprit de corps
D. Authority and responsibility

139. Arrange the following in alphabetical order as word by word:

(*a*) Singing (*b*) Sing
(*c*) Singer (*d*) Sing at

Codes:

A. (*b*), (*d*), (*c*), (*a*)
B. (*a*), (*d*), (*c*), (*b*)
C. (*d*), (*b*), (*c*), (*a*)
D. (*b*), (*d*), (*a*), (*c*)

140. The concept 'Anomalous State of Knowledge' (ASK) was given by ______.

A. Paul N. Gorman B. N.J. Belkin
C. E.F. Mckechnie D. Krikelas

141. IS 1829 : 1978/1991 is related to:

A. Library Furniture
B. Library Mobile Van
C. Library Building
D. Lightening of Libraries

142. Which of the following budgeting methods combines the functions of Planning activities, Programmes and services, translating them into tangible projects and presents the requirements in budgetary items?

A. Lump Sum Budget
B. Performance Budget
C. Programme Budget
D. Performance Planning and Budgeting System (PPBS)

143. According to Edwin B. Flippo "______ is a statement of the minimum acceptable human qualities necessary to perform a job properly ..."

A. Job Evaluation B. Job Specification
C. Job Analysis D. Job Description

144. Who devised "Browne Charging System"?

A. Vina E. Browne
B. Nina E. Browne
C. H.E. Browne
D. S.D. Browne

145. Find the odd one out:

A. E-PG Pathshala B. Shodhshudhi
C. INFOPORT D. E-Gyankosh

146. 'Demand Theory' of Book selection is suggested by ______.

A. Melvil Dewey
B. Drury
C. S.R. Ranganathan
D. McColvin

147. "Quality in a product or service is not what the supplier puts in. It is what the customer gets out and willing to pay for" said by ______.

A. Philip Crosby
B. Joseph M. Juran
C. Peter Drucker
D. Michael Maccoby

137. D	138. A	139. A	140. B	141. A	142. D
143. B	144. B	145. D	146. D	147. C	

148. Match the following:

List-I (Author)	List-II (Title)
(a) G. Edward Evans	I. Library and Information Centre Management
(b) Edwin B. Flippo	II. Personnel Management
(c) Robert D Stueart and Barbara B. Moran	III. Human Resource and Personnel Management
(d) William B. Werther and Keith Davis	IV. Management Techniques for libraries

Codes:

	(a)	(b)	(c)	(d)
A.	IV	II	I	III
B.	II	IV	I	III
C.	III	II	IV	I
D.	I	IV	II	III

149. 'Indian National Bibliography' is published by ______.

A. UGC
B. RRRLF
C. Central Reference Library, Kolkata
D. National Library of India

150. (NISCPR) National Institute of Science Communication and Policy Research came into existence by merging of which institutions?

(a) CSIR - NISCAIR
(b) CSIR - NPL
(c) CSIR - NISCOM
(d) CSIR - NISTADS

Codes:

A. (b) and (d) are correct
B. (a) and (c) are correct
C. (a) and (b) are correct
D. (a) and (d) are correct

151. 'Science Direct Database' is developed by ______.

A. McGraw Hill
B. Elsevier
C. Thomas Reuters
D. Emerald

152. The online version of "McGraw Hill" Encyclopedia of Science and Technology is ______.

A. McGH online
B. Science online
C. McGraw Hill online
D. Access Science

153. CONTENTdm is a service/programme of ______.

A. IFLA
B. UNESCO
C. OCLC
D. ALA

154. 'Digital Accessible Information System' (DAISY) consortium was founded in ______.

A. Chicago, USA
B. Stockholm, Sweden
C. Hague, Netherland
D. Sydney, Australia

155. Orientation of Library users is a kind of:

A. Current Awareness Service (CAS)
B. Referral Service
C. Reference Service
D. Document Delivery Service (DDS)

156. Match the following:

List-I (Author)	List-II (Book)
(a) William A. Katz	I. Textbook of Information Science
(b) A.J. Walford	II. Introduction to Reference work
(c) C.M. Winchell	III. Guide to Reference Books
(d) P.S. Kawatra	IV. Guide to Reference Material

148. A **149.** C **150.** D **151.** B **152.** D **153.** C **154.** B **155.** C **156.** B

Codes:

	(*a*)	(*b*)	(*c*)	(*d*)
A.	IV	II	III	I
B.	II	IV	III	I
C.	I	IV	II	III
D.	III	IV	II	I

157. Match the following:

List-I (Developer)	***List-II (Model of Information Literacy)***
(*a*) Mike Eisenberg and Bob Berkowitz	I. Sauce
(*b*) Christine Susan Bruce	II. PLUS
(*c*) James Herring	III. Seven Faces of IL
(*d*) Trever Bond	IV. Big 6 Model

Codes:

	(*a*)	(*b*)	(*c*)	(*d*)
A.	II	III	IV	I
B.	IV	III	I	II
C.	III	IV	II	I
D.	IV	III	II	I

158. The '8WS Model' of Information Literacy was formulated by ______.

A. Trevor Bond B. Annette Lamb
C. James Herring D. Mike Eisenberg

159. Who introduced the concept of 'Scientific Management'?

A. Peter Drucker B. F.W. Taylor
C. Henry Fayol D. Peter A. Pyhrr

160. "Facts, concepts or instructions in a formalised manner suitable for communication", is the definition of information given by ______.

A. ALA B. IFLA
C. LA D. UNESCO

161. 'According to UNESCO World Book and Copyright Day' is celebrated every year on:

A. 19th January B. 12th August
C. 23th April D. 14th November

162. 'IASLIC' was founded in the year:

A. 1933 B. 1951
C. 1955 D. 1961

163. The need for librarians to maintain ethical standards was first mentioned in 1903 by:

A. Melvil Dewey
B. D.J. Fasket
C. R. Baker
D. Mary W. Plummer

164. In which year the University of Chicago established the first graduate school of librarianship?

A. 1920 B. 1922
C. 1926 D. 1930

165. ______ Award is given to an individual who has given distinguished service to IFLA as a volunteer engaged in a committee or group.

A. IFLA Best Librarian Award
B. IFLA Medal
C. IFLA Scroll of Appreciation
D. IFLA Dynamic unit and Impact Award

166. How many Metadata Elements are there in the Dublin Core Metadata Element Set Version 1.1?

A. Six B. Nine
C. Fifteen D. Eighteen

167. "Be minute, be minute, be not too minute," is said by ______.

A. Melvil Dewey
B. A.C. Foskett
C. S.R. Ranganathan
D. H.E. Bliss

157. D	**158.** B	**159.** B	**160.** D	**161.** C	**162.** C
163. D	**164.** C	**165.** C	**166.** C	**167.** D	

168. Which of the following Scheme is known for following 'One-Place Theory'?

A. Library of Congress Classification
B. Subject Classification
C. Bibliographic Classification
D. Colon Classification

169. Which of the following are Character User Interface-based (CUI) Operating Systems?

(*a*) LINUX
(*b*) UNIX
(*c*) MS-Windows
(*d*) MS-DOS

Codes:

A. (*a*) and (*b*) are correct
B. (*b*) and (*c*) are correct
C. (*a*) and (*d*) are correct
D. (*b*) and (*d*) are correct

170. 'The study of references, meaning or truth' is called ______.

A. Plagiarism
B. Epidemiology
C. Epistemology
D. Semantics

171. Internet Protocol version 6 (IPv6) was developed by the ______.

A. Internet Engineering Task Force
B. Internet Technical Society
C. Internet Development Task Force
D. Internet Society

172. Which of the following was first proposed by United States Department of Defence (USDoD)?

A. Formula Budgeting
B. Programme Budgeting
C. Performance Budgeting
D. Planning Programming Budgeting System

173. Which of the following is an aim of "One Nation One Subscription" (ONOS) initiative in India?

A. To provide countrywide access to National and International Scientific and Academic Content.
B. To provide countrywide access to International Scientific and Academic Content only.
C. To provide selective access to National Scientific and Academic Content.
D. To provide countrywide access to National Academic Content only.

174. Who among the following has made enormous financial donations for library buildings?

A. Andrew Carnegie
B. Melvil Dewey
C. S.R. Ranganathan
D. T. Wilson

175. 'Choreo Insights' is a product/service of ______.

A. UNESCO
B. ALA
C. OCLC
D. IFLA

176. Which of the following is not a part of Indian National Bibliography?

A. Classified
B. Author and Title Index
C. Publisher Index
D. Subject Index

177. 'INSSPEL' is a ______.

A. Complete index to Information Science Literature only
B. Complete index to Social Security Literature
C. Complete index to Indian Sociology Literature only
D. Complete index to Indian Social Science Literature

168. B **169.** D **170.** D **171.** A **172.** D **173.** A **174.** A **175.** C **176.** C **177.** D

178. Following Definition of 'Information Literacy' is given by:

"Knowledge when and why you need Information, Knowing where to find it and how to evaluate, use and communicate it in an ethical Manner".

A. ASLIB B. ALA
C. IFLA D. CILIP

179. 'Marrakesh VIP Treaty' is related with ______.

A. To facilitate education for all.
B. To facilitate access to published works by visually impaired persons and persons with print disabilities.
C. To facilitate access to all published works by all academicians.
D. To facilitate access to audio-visual material only by visually impaired persons.

180. National Academic Depository (India) is an initiative to provide ______.

A. An online storehouse to all awards
B. An online storehouse to all academic awards
C. An online storehouse to all school education awards only
D. An online repository of all academic articles

EXPLANATORY ANSWERS

1. **(A):** The correct order is option A because it creates a logical and coherent sentence. It starts with the action, "helping the elderly," followed by the purpose or context, "in performing their day-to-day activities." The phrase "is an ennobling form" explains the nature of the action, and "of social service" concludes by classifying the action.

2. **(C):** The correct order is option C because it presents the information in a logical sequence. The subject, "Babu Devaki Nandan Khatri's 'Chandra-kanta'," is introduced first, followed by the action "was serialised." The sentence then provides the location "in local Hindi newspapers" and concludes with the time frame "over a long period of time."

3. **(B):** Why has the employee been sacked by the employer? This option correctly converts the active voice sentence into passive voice while retaining the question format.

4. **(D):** The jungle animals were frightened by the violent thunderstorm. This option correctly transforms the active voice sentence into passive voice and accurately reflects the original meaning.

5. **(B):** "Proud of" is the correct phrase to express pride in someone's achievements. This prepositional phrase is used to express pride or satisfaction in something one has accomplished or is associated with.

6. **(C):** "Adhere to" is used to indicate compliance with rules and regulations. This prepositional phrase means to follow or stick to rules, principles, or standards.

7. **(B):** The sentence "They have been living in Europe for a long time now" uses the present perfect continuous tense to describe an action that started in the past and is still ongoing.

178. D **179.** B **180.** B

8. (D): The sentence "They had finished eating long before we reached the restaurant" uses the past perfect tense to indicate that one action was completed before another action in the past.

9. (D): The correct tag question should be "hasn't she?" since the subject is "Lata Mangeshkar" and the verb is "has sung."

10. (B): The correct phrase should be "adjust to" when referring to adapting or becoming accustomed to a situation or people.

11. (B): "Coerce" means to force or compel someone to do something, so "compel" is the closest in meaning.

12. (C): "Boisterous" describes a lively, noisy, and energetic atmosphere, making "noisy" the nearest in meaning.

13. (C): "Cursory" means superficial or brief, so the opposite would be "intensive," which implies thoroughness and detail.

14. (D): "Aversion" means a strong dislike or opposition, so the opposite is "liking," which signifies a positive feeling or fondness.

15. (B): The underlined word "about" is a preposition. It introduces the prepositional phrase "about his personality," which provides more information regarding the adjective "endearing."

16. (C): प्रस्तुत गद्यांश में कहा गया है कि कबीर मूलतः निर्गुण ब्रह्म के भक्त थे। अपने ब्रह्म की उपासना में वानिया करते थे। उनका उद्देश्य काव्य रचना करना नहीं था, बल्कि भक्ति परक रचना करना था। इसी क्रम में कविता अनायास बनती गई। अतः वे भक्त-कवि थे। इस गद्यांश में यात्रा करना, समाज की बुराइयाँ करने का तथा धर्म के प्रचार का कोई उल्लेख नहीं है।

17. (C): गद्यांश के लेखक का स्पष्ट कहना है कि– कबीर एक भक्त-कवि थे, जिनका उद्देश्य काव्य रचना करना नहीं था, बल्कि वे निर्गुण को वाणी द्वारा व्यक्त करते थे।

18. (C): कबीरदास जी रामभक्त कवि नहीं बल्कि वे ज्ञानाश्रयी धारा के निर्गुण-भक्त कवि थे। उनके आराध्य देव दशरथ-सुत राम नहीं, निर्गुण राम थे। कबीर का मानना है ''दशरथ सुत तिहूँ लोक बखाना, राम नाम का मरम है आना''। कबीरदास जी की वाणी 'बीजक' में सुरक्षित है जिसे आज भी बड़ी श्रद्धा से गाया जाता है। कबीरदास जी की गणना भक्तिकाल ही नहीं अपितु भारतीय भाषा साहित्य के सर्वश्रेष्ठ कवियों में की जाती है।

19. (C): कबीरदास जी निर्गुण भक्त कवि थे। उनकी वाणी अटपटी कही गयी है। वे भाषा पर शासन करते थे। आचार्य हजारी प्रसाद द्विवेदी जी ने उन्हें 'वाणी का डिक्टेटर' कहा है, क्योंकि वे शब्दों को अपना मनचाहा अर्थ देने के लिए विवश कर देते थे। उन्होंने अपनी वाणियों में सामाजिक आंडबरों पर कठोर प्रहार किया है। कबीरदास जी बनारस में नहीं बल्कि मगहर में मृत्यु को प्राप्त हुए।

20. (C): कबीरदास जी की अनुभूति बड़ी गहरी थी जिनके कारण भाषा से मनचाहे तरीके से अपनी बात कहला लेते थे। द्विवेदी जी के शब्दों में ''बन पडा तो सीधे-सीधे, नहीं तो दरेरा देकर''। उनकी भाषा पंचमेल खिचड़ी थी।

21. (A): किसी व्यक्ति, वस्तु, भाव, द्रव्य आदि के नाम को संज्ञा कहते है। इसके पाँच भेद है। 1. व्यक्तिवाचक, 2. जातिवाचक, 3. समूह वाचक, 4. भाववाचक तथा 5. द्रव्य वाचक।

जिस संज्ञा से पदार्थ की अवस्था, गुण-दोष आदि जैसी अमूर्त चीजों का बोध हो। उसे भाववाचक संज्ञा कहा जाता है। जैसे– थकावट, मोटापा, अच्छाई, मिठास, प्यास, भूख आदि।

22. (D): 'आभ्यांतर' का अर्थ अंतरंग, आन्तरिक आदि होता है, जिसका विपरीत शब्द बाहरी, बाह्य आदि होगा।

23. (B): 'सोना' का पर्यायवाची है– स्वर्ण, कंचन, कनक, सुवर्ण, हिरण्य, हेम, हाटक, जातरूप आदि। 'हिम' का अर्थ बर्फ से है।

24. (A): वह समास जिसका पहला पद संख्यावाचक विशेषण होता है तथा समस्त पद किसी समूह का बोध करता है तो वह द्विगु समास कहलाता है। जैसे– पंचमुख, तिरंगा, नवरत्न आदि।

25. (A): 'उद्गम' शब्द का संधि-विच्छेद है– उत् + गम। यह व्यंजन संधि का उदाहरण है। किसी व्यंजन का व्यंजन से अथवा किसी स्वर से मेल होने पर जो परिवर्तन होता है, उसे व्यंजन संधि कहते हैं।

26. (A, B, D): जिस विशेषण से संज्ञा या सर्वनाम के गुण या दोष का पता चलता है, उसे गुणवाचक विशेषण कहते है। जैसे– दुबला, बाहरी, भीतरी, मोटा, काला आदि।

27. (D): तत्सम शब्द हिंदी के ऐसे शब्द है जो संस्कृत के समानार्थक होते है और उन्हें हिंदी में भी उसी रूप में प्रयोग किया जाता है। जैसे– कोकिल, जिह्वा, क्षार, अग्नि, आमलक, उज्जवल आदि।

तद्भव ऐसे शब्द जो मूलतः संस्कृत के नहीं बल्कि संस्कृत से व्युत्पन्न है। जैसे– मुँह, गाँव, अँधेरा, रात, चाँद।

28. (A): एक अर्थ वाले शब्दों को एकार्थी शब्द कहते है। जैसे– अहंकार, अनुग्रह, अस्त्र, आयु, अपयश, अनुराग, आत्मा आदि।

अपयश– स्थायी रूप से दोषी होना।

29. (C): हिंदी मुहावरा 'आग उगलना' का अर्थ– अत्यंत क्रोधित होना है।

30. (D): शुद्ध वर्तनी– माहात्म्य, क्षत्रिय, मध्य, स्वास्थ्य।

31. (C): (*b*) The Tata Iron and Steel Company (TISCO), a pioneering industrial enterprise in India, was founded in 1907 and begin steel production in 1912 on the banks of the Subarnarekha River in Jamshedpur, Jharkhand. This strategic location provided access to vital raw materials, including iron ore, coal, and limestone, which were essential for steel production.

(*c*) Michael Faraday, a renowned English scientist known for his ground-breaking work in electromagnetism and electrochemistry, did study Indian Wootz steel between 1818 and 1822 called UKKU in Kannada.

32. (B): In 1976, during the Emergency period, Article 33A was inserted into Part III (Fundamental Rights) of the Indian Constitution, which allowed for the saving of laws in respect of anti-national activities. However, this article was repealed by the Indian Parliament in 1977 following the end of the Emergency period.

33. (A): C. Rajagopalachari was the member of the Constituent Assembly of India and was the first Indian to receive the Bharat Ratna in 1954. He also served as the last British Governor-General of India and later as the Governor of West Bengal and the Chief Minister of Tamil Nadu.

34. (B): The Taiping Rebellion, which began in 1850 and lasted until 1864, was a major uprising in China led by the Taiping Heavenly Kingdom with the goal of establishing the "Heavenly Kingdom of Great Peace." This rebellion coincided with the Revolt of 1857 in India, both being significant uprisings against established regimes in their respective regions.

35. (C): At the COP 26 climate conference in 2021, India committed to reaching net zero carbon emissions by 2070. This ambitious goal is part of India's broader climate action strategy, which aims to balance economic growth with environmental sustainability. The pledge reflects India's effort to contribute to global climate goals while addressing its developmental needs and responsibilities.

36. (A): Joseph Carl Robnett Licklider, often known as J.C.R. Licklider, was a pioneering figure in the development of computer science and is credited with early concepts related to cloud computing. His work on ARPANET in the 1960s laid the groundwork for network-based computing and the development of ideas that would later evolve into what we now call cloud computing.

37. (C): Temperate grasslands are regions with moderate temperatures and limited precipitation, leading to vast open spaces covered primarily with grasses rather than trees.

(*a*) **Prairie:** This is a type of temperate grassland found in North America, including the Great Plains. Prairies are characterized by their fertile soil and extensive grass coverage, which supports a diverse range of wildlife.

(*b*) **Steppe:** This type of temperate grassland is found in Eurasia, particularly in Russia and Central Asia. Steppes have a similar climate to prairies but are typically more arid and have shorter grasses.

38. (B): In the early 1990s, Yugoslavia experienced a series of conflicts and political changes leading to its disintegration. As a result:

(*a*) **Republic of Croatia:** Declared its independence from Yugoslavia in 1991, becoming one of the new successor states.

(*b*) **Republic of Slovenia:** Similarly declared independence from Yugoslavia in 1991, making it another successor state.

39. (B): Tehran's central position and economic flourishing has attracted great numbers of immigrants from other Iranian cities, justifying the nickname "the city of 72 nations". Tehran is Iran's political and administrative center, a major focal point of the Middle East and a city of international reputation.

40. (C): Mercury and Venus are unique among the planets in our solar system because they do not have any natural satellites or moons.

(*a*) Mercury is the closest planet to the Sun, and its proximity might contribute to its lack of moons, as any potential moons could be pulled away by the Sun's gravity.

(*b*) Venus also lacks moons, which could be due to its dense atmosphere and gravitational interactions.

41. (A): Ingestion is the initial step in the digestive process where food and liquids are taken into the body through the mouth. This process involves the mechanical and chemical breakdown of food, which begins as it is chewed and mixed with saliva. Ingestion is crucial as it provides the necessary nutrients and energy needed for the body to function.

42. (A): *Cuscuta*, or *dodder*, is a parasitic plant that relies on other plants for its nutrition. It attaches itself to the stems or leaves of host plants using specialized structures called haustoria. Unlike autotrophic plants, Cuscuta does not contain chlorophyll and cannot photosynthesize. Instead, it absorbs water and nutrients directly from its host, often weakening or damaging the host plant in the process.

43. (D): The commemorative postal stamp released on the occasion of the 17th Pravasi Bharatiya Divas Convention held in Indore in January 2023 had the theme "Surakshit Jaayen, Prashikshit Jayen". This translates to "Go Safe, go Trained" in English and highlights the importance of safe, legal, orderly, and skilled migration.

44. (A): This statement is incorrect. The AIPOC was actually established in 1921, making it complete its hundred years in 2021. The All India Presiding Officers' Conference (AIPOC) is a significant forum for the presiding officers of various legislative bodies in India. It serves as a platform for them to discuss and address common challenges, share best practices, and promote inter-parliamentary cooperation.

45. (B): The Gold winner in the 2023 World Habitat Awards, in partnership with UN-Habitat, was 'Homes for Good', Scotland. This organization was recognized for its exceptional contributions to providing good-quality, affordable housing to people on low incomes in Scotland. 'Homes for Good' has demonstrated a remarkable commitment to addressing the housing crisis and ensuring that everyone has access to a safe, stable, and affordable home.

46. (A): The 'Platinum' Award under the category of 'Data sharing and use for Socio-Economic Development' was awarded to Smart Cities Mission (Ministry of Housing and Urban Affairs). The Smart Cities Mission, launched by the Government of India in 2015, aims to transform selected cities across the country into smart cities. The mission's focus on data-driven urban development has led to the creation of a vast repository of data, which is being used effectively for various socio-economic development initiatives.

47. (C): Annie Ernaux, a French author, was awarded the Nobel Prize in Literature in 2022 for her courageous and clinically precise explorations of memory and identity. Her work delves deep into the complexities of personal experience, societal norms, and the intersection of the individual and the collective. Ernaux's writing is characterized by its raw honesty, emotional intensity, and unflinching examination of often-taboo subjects.

48. (D): Dr. Lotey Tshering served as Bhutan's Prime Minister from 7 November 2018 to 1 November 2023. As a surgeon and politician, he led the Druk Nyamrup Tshogpa party, focusing on key areas like health, education, and sustainable development during his tenure.

49. (B): The 2022 FIFA World Cup was a thrilling tournament filled with incredible matches and unexpected twists. In the end, it was France, Argentina, Croatia, and Morocco who emerged as the four teams that would compete in the semifinals. These teams demonstrated exceptional skill, determination, and teamwork throughout the tournament, earning their place among the best in the world.

50. (C): The Ganga Vilas Cruise is the world's longest river cruise, covering a distance of more than 3,200 kilometers. This remarkable cruise ship offers a unique opportunity to explore the majestic Ganges River and its tributaries, taking passengers on a journey through India's rich cultural heritage and breathtaking landscapes. The Ganga Vilas Cruise sails from Varanasi to Dibrugarh, traversing through five states and passing through 27 river systems, including the Ganga, Brahmaputra, and Meghna.

51. (C): Jupiter is a planet.

Similary Greenland is an Island

∴ Planet : Jupiter :: Island : **Greenland**.

52. (D): Given,

C	O	N	S	I	D	E	R	=	C	N	O	I	S	E	D	R
1	2	3	4	5	6	7	8		1	3	2	5	4	7	6	8

Similarly,

M	A	N	A	G	E	R	S	=	M	N	A	G	A	R	E	S
1	2	3	4	5	6	7	8		1	3	2	5	4	7	6	8

Therefore, MANAGERS would be written as MNAGARES.

54. (C): Here,

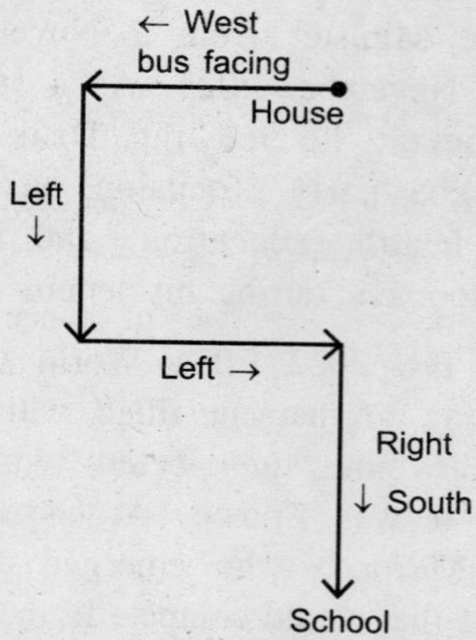

The bus was facing in west direction when it left the bus stop in front of his house.

55. (C): According to question,
Medicines, Cooking, Engineering → Yellow Cover,
Embroidery, Law → Brown Cover,
Engineering, Cooking → New Edition,
Medicine, Law, Embroidery → Old Edition
Therefore, the book of medicine is in yellow colour and has old edition.

57. (D): From statements I and II

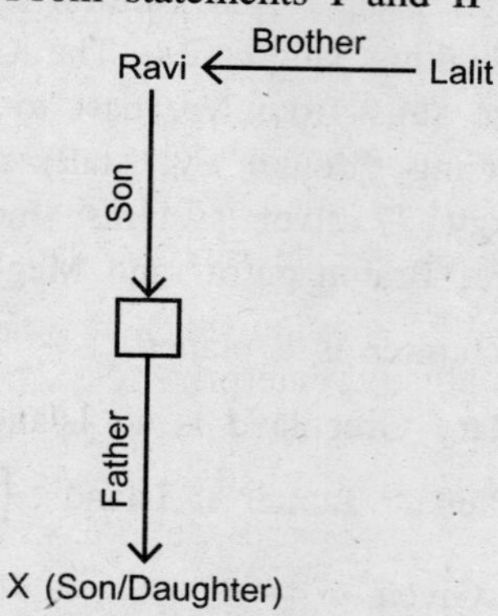

Here, X is Male/Female, It is not clear
So, Both Statements I and II together are not sufficient to answer the question.

58. (C): (3, 8, 3) (3, 4, 9)
There are two even numbers which are immediately preceded by an odd number and also immediately followed by an odd number.

59. (C): From given diagram:
The cultivation of all three region
= 5
and region which does not cultivate rice
= 15 + 4 + 11 = 30
∴ Required Ratio = 5 : 30 = 1 : 6.

60. (D): Given, 7 friends are sitting around a circular table facing the centre.

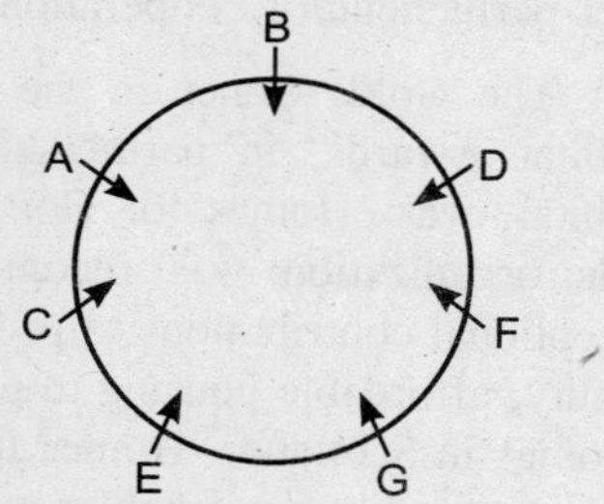

Here, F is sitting between 'D' and 'G'.

61. (D): Given, 5 men play a game with ball.
QRTPS
Here, S has the ball at last.

62. (A): vuwvw
∴ $uw\underline{v}$, $\underline{u}w\underline{v}$, $u\underline{wv}$, $u\underline{w}v$
Here, section uwv is repeated in the given letter series.
∴ Option (A) is the correct alternative.

63. (B): Given,
'Roses are red' = 'Kew xas deko' ...(*i*)
'Flowers are beautiful' = 'Kew tepo qua' ...(*ii*)
'Red flower' = 'deko tepo' ...(*iii*)
from (*i*) and (*ii*)
are = Kew
from (*i*) and (*iii*)
red = deko
∴ from (*i*) Roses = xas
So, 'Roses' is written as xas.

64. (D): Given, $A \le B$, $A > C$ and $B \le D$
$\therefore D \ge B \ge A > C$
$\Rightarrow D > C \Rightarrow C < D$.

65. (B): Given A ÷ R + C – B

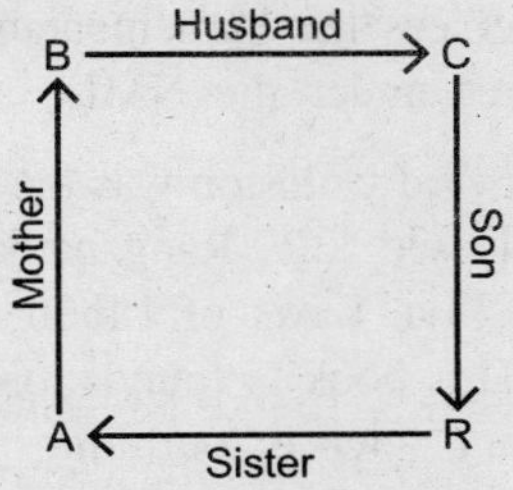

Here, B is the Mother of A.

66. (D): Given, Word:

	U	T	R	S	P	I	D
	1	2	3	4	5	6	7
Meaningful Word:	D	I	S	R	U	P	T
	7	6	4	3	1	5	2

67. (A): From given statements:

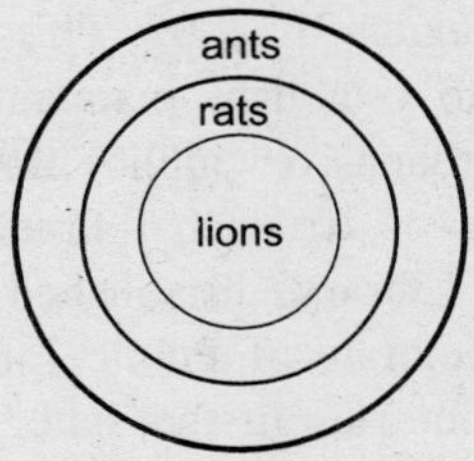

Conclusions:

I. All lions are ants. (true)

II. All ants are lions. (false)

Here, only conclusion I follows.

68. (A): Given, Word: APPRECIATION

Only ACTION can be formed by using the letters of the given word.

69. (B):

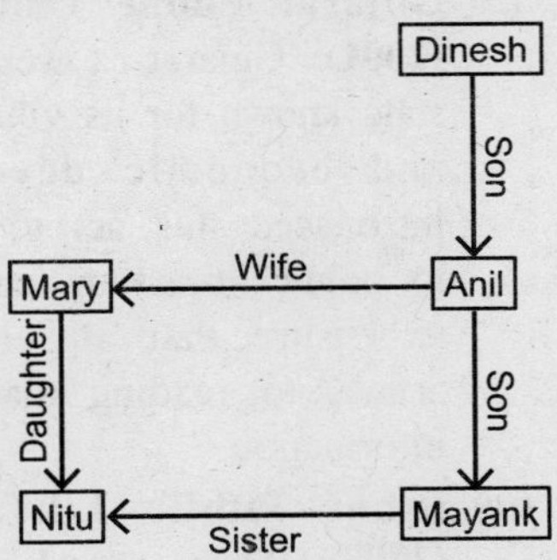

Here, Nitu is the daughter of Mary.

70. (B):

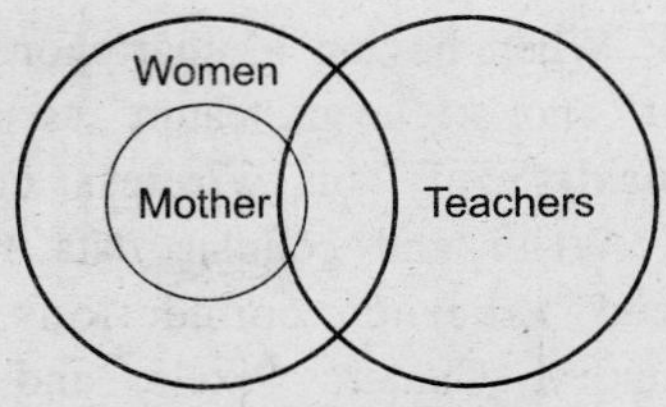

71. (B): Plotter is not an input device. A plotter is an output device used to create hard copies of graphics or images. It works by moving a pen or other writing instrument across a piece of paper to create the desired drawing or image.

72. (C): Among the given options, an exabyte is the largest memory unit. Here's the order from smallest to largest:

- Kilo Byte (KB): 1,024 bytes
- Giga Byte (GB): 1,024 megabytes (MB)
- Peta Byte (PB): 1,024 terabytes (TB)
- Exa Byte (EB): 1,024 petabytes (PB)

An exabyte is larger than a petabyte, gigabyte, or kilobyte.

73. (D): Mozilla Firefox is a web browser used for accessing and navigating the internet, not an operating system. In contrast, MacOS, MS Windows, and Linux are operating systems that manage hardware and software resources on a computer, providing the platform on which applications, including web browsers like Firefox, run.

74. (B): Tally is a company that specializes in accounting and enterprise resource planning (ERP) software, not antivirus software. The other companies listed—Norton, McAfee, and Kaspersky—are well-known for their antivirus and cybersecurity solutions.

75. (A): Impress is the most suitable option for Abdul Sheikh to create a digital presentation using open-source software. Impress is a part of the LibreOffice suite, a free and open-source office productivity software. It offers a wide range of features for creating professional-looking presentations, including templates, slide layouts, animations, and more.

76. (D): When buying a smartphone, Ethernet Port is not a relevant feature, as smartphones typically rely on wireless connections like Wi-Fi and cellular data rather than wired Ethernet connections. Internal Memory, Camera Pixels, and Operating System are important aspects to consider for functionality, performance, and user experience.

77. (C): HDMI (High-Definition Multimedia Interface) is the most suitable port for connecting high-quality audio and video output on a PC or laptop. It supports both high-definition video and multi-channel audio through a single cable. It supports various audio formats and video resolutions, including 4K and 8K.

78. (A): pptx is the correct extension for a Microsoft PowerPoint file. This is the standard extension for PowerPoint presentations created in Microsoft Office 2007 and later versions. It's a more modern format that supports various features and is compatible with other presentation software.

79. (B): XLSX is the file extension for Excel files in the newer XML-based format used by Microsoft Excel since Excel 2007. The other options are not correct extensions for Excel files.

80. (C): MS Word is not an example of a RDBMS (Relational Database Management System). MS Word is a word processing software used for creating and editing documents. It doesn't have the capabilities to store, manage, and retrieve data in a structured relational format like a database.

81. (C): RRRLF (Raja Rammohun Roy Library Foundation) is the central nodal agency for the National Mission on Libraries (NML). RRRLF was established by the Government of India to promote library development and provide support to public libraries across the country. As the nodal agency, it coordinates and oversees the implementation of various initiatives under the NML.

82. (B): Edward Goldston was the publisher who first released S.R. Ranganathan's landmark work, "Five Laws of Library Science," in 1931. This book is foundational in the field of library science, outlining principles that guide library practices and organization. Ranganathan's five laws, which emphasize the importance of providing access to information, are still widely referenced and influential in modern library management.

83. (C): The Arunachal Pradesh Public Libraries Act was enacted in 2009, with the Governor's assent and its effective date both being August 31, 2009. This legislation was passed to establish, maintain, and develop a comprehensive public library system in the state of Arunachal Pradesh. The State Central Library, established in 1956, and the Directorate of Public Libraries manage public libraries in the state.

84. (B): *(iii)* **Mizoram Public Libraries Act (1993):** This pioneering legislation laid the foundation for the development of public libraries in Mizoram, a relatively new state in India. It aimed to provide access to information and knowledge to the people of the state.

(ii) **Gujarat Public Libraries Act (2001):** Gujarat, a western Indian state known for its vibrant culture and economic development, introduced this act to strengthen its public library system. It aimed to ensure that all citizens had access to reading materials and information.

(iv) **Bihar Public Libraries Act (2008):** Bihar, one of India's most populous states, enacted this law

to establish and regulate public libraries within its boundaries. It sought to improve literacy rates and promote education through the provision of library services.

(*i*) **Chhattisgarh Public Libraries Act (2009):** This relatively recent legislation established a framework for public libraries in Chhattisgarh, a central Indian state with a rich cultural heritage. It aimed to promote education, research, and cultural development through libraries.

85. (A): Subject of small extension and great intention is the correct definition of a "Micro Subject" according to S.R. Ranganathan. A micro subject is a highly specific subject with a narrow scope (small extension) but a deep level of detail (great intention). It is often used in specialized fields or research areas where precise and focused information is required.

86. (C): 'Sino loco' (often abbreviated as 's.l.') is a term used in cataloguing to indicate that the place of publication is not known or has not been provided. It originates from Latin, meaning "without place". When cataloguing books or other materials, if the location where the item was published cannot be determined, 's.l.' is used in place of the publisher's city to signify this missing information.

87. (B): The name section is not a section of a main entry in the Classified Catalogue Code (CCC) 5th Edition. The main entry in the CCC is made up of six sections:

- **Leading section:** Contains the document's call number, which is written in pencil
- **Heading section:** Contains the author's name, which can be a single author, multiple authors, a corporation, a pseudonym, or a collaborator
- **Title section:** Starts on the line after the second vertical
- **Note section:** Starts on the line after the second vertical
- **Accession number:** Starts at the first vertical on the bottom line
- **Tracing:** Recorded on the back of the main entry card

88. (C): S.R. Ranganathan is the author of the book "Heading and Canons." This work is a significant contribution to the field of cataloguing and library science, comparing and analyzing various cataloging codes. Ranganathan is a renowned figure in the library world, known for his five laws of library science and his development of the Colon Classification system.

89. (A): The sequence of "Specials" in Basic class "Medicine" in Colon Classification is chosen according to the principle of Principle of Later-in-Evolution. This principle states that subjects that are more complex or evolved should be placed later in the classification scheme. In the case of medicine, the sequence of Specials is arranged based on the complexity or evolution of the medical conditions or treatments.

90. (C): Table-5 in the Dewey Decimal Classification (DDC) 19th Edition is associated with Racial, Ethnic, National Groups. This table provides a hierarchical classification system for these groups, allowing for the systematic organization of information related to race, ethnicity, and nationality.

91. (D): The Whole-organ Principle in classification systems like Colon Classification states that if one facet (Facet 'B') is an organ or part of another facet (Facet 'A'), then the whole (Facet 'A') should precede its parts (Facet 'B') in the arrangement. Therefore, Facet 'A' should be placed before Facet 'B' in the classification scheme.

92. **(B):** In the Dewey Decimal Classification (DDC), 'Unemployed Carpenters' is considered a Complex Subject. This is because it involves multiple concepts: "Unemployed" and "Carpenters," which together describe a specific subject area. Complex subjects are those that require more than one aspect or facet to fully describe the topic.

93. **(A):** OCLC (Online Computer Library Center) is the organization that developed the "Faceted Application of Subject Terminology" (FAST). FAST is a controlled vocabulary that uses a faceted approach to represent subjects, making it easier for users to search for information. It is designed to facilitate the organization and retrieval of library materials by using a faceted approach to subject terminology.

94. **(B):** In the Colon Classification system, specifically for the main class 'O' (Literature), the sequence Language, Form, Author, Work is used. This reflects how facets are prioritized in categorizing literary works. The PMEST formula helps in understanding how different categories like Personality, Matter, Energy, Space, and Time are used to classify subjects. The use of facet analysis and the colon separator are key elements in organizing and breaking down subjects effectively.

95. **(C):** (*a*) **Free open software:** D Space is free to use and open-source, meaning anyone can download, use, and modify it without any licensing costs. This makes it accessible to a wide range of institutions.

(*b*) **Completely customizable to fit user needs:** One of the strengths of D Space is its flexibility. It can be customized to fit the unique needs of an institution, whether that means changing the interface, integrating with other systems, or adjusting the metadata structure.

(*c*) **Optimized for Google Scholar Indexing:** D Space repositories are optimized to make their content discoverable by search engines like Google and Google Scholar. This is important for increasing the visibility of academic and research outputs.

96. **(C):** Bandwidth in a network refers to the maximum rate at which data can be transferred from one point to another over a network in a given amount of time, typically measured in bits per second (bps). It indicates the capacity of the network to handle data, not the size or distance.

97. **(A):** In the Per capita method, a minimum amount of expenditure is fixed per head of the population. This method is often used in budgeting and financial planning, where costs are estimated based on the number of individuals (per person) involved in a specific service or project.

98. **(D):** ISO 31000 is an international standard that provides guidelines and principles for effective risk management. It helps organizations identify, assess, and manage risks in a systematic and structured way across various industries.

99. **(B):** The Journal Translation Today is a scholarly publication focused on translation studies, and it is published by the National Translation Mission (NTM), which operates under the Ministry of Education, Government of India. The mission aims to promote translation in Indian languages and make knowledge resources available in multiple languages.

100. **(C):** James I. Wyer is credited with developing the Conservative, Moderate, and Liberal theories of reference service. Wyer's approach categorizes reference service based on how actively librarians engage with patrons:

Conservative Theory: The librarian takes a passive role, answering only the questions asked and pointing to existing resources.

Moderate Theory: The librarian is more involved, helping users frame their questions and guiding them through the research process.

Liberal Theory: The librarian takes an active role, offering suggestions, providing additional resources, and anticipating user needs.

101. (C): Reijo Savolainen developed the model of Everyday Life Information Seeking (ELIS), which focuses on how people seek information in the context of their everyday activities and way of life. The model examines how individuals search for information outside of professional or academic settings, often influenced by their social and cultural environment.

102. (C): In 1949, the UK Library Association's University and Research Section proposed the Three-Stage User Education Program, which was aimed at providing structured guidance to library users. The three stages typically involved basic library orientation, intermediate training in using library resources, and advanced instruction for specialized research needs.

103. (C): Qualitative research methods focus on understanding phenomena through detailed, non-numeric data, such as interviews, observations, and case studies. Methods like Grounded Theory, Hermeneutics, and Ethnography all fall under qualitative research as they explore concepts, interpretations, and cultural contexts. Experimental research, on the other hand, is a quantitative method that involves manipulating variables and measuring outcomes to establish cause-and-effect relationships. It is typically used in scientific and social science research to test hypotheses under controlled conditions.

104. (D): OCLC is the organization behind the Green Glass service. Green Glass is a data-driven decision support tool designed to help libraries manage their print collections more efficiently and sustainably. It provides insights into collection usage, overlap, and other factors to assist libraries in making informed decisions about weeding, preservation, and shared print initiatives.

105. (B): S.R. Ranganathan, an Indian librarian and educator, is credited with saying "Librarianship is Salesmanship". Ranganathan is considered the father of library science in India and his work had a global impact. He also developed the Five Laws of Library Science, which were first published in 1931.

106. (B): Kurt Lewin developed the Three-Phase Model of Change Management, which includes Unfreeze, Move (or Change), and Refreeze. This model describes the process of managing organizational change by first preparing for change (Unfreeze), implementing the change (Move), and then solidifying and stabilizing the new state (Refreeze).

107. (A): (*a*) **Karnataka:** The Karnataka Public Libraries Act, 1965 includes a provision for a library cess. This cess is collected as a small percentage of the property tax and is used to fund public libraries and support their activities in the state.

(*c*) **Haryana:** The Haryana Public Libraries Act, 2001 also provides for the imposition of a library cess. This cess helps in generating funds specifically for the development and maintenance of public libraries in Haryana.

108. (D): The symbol of the Maharaja of Air India is a trademark. It represents the brand and identity of Air India and is used to distinguish its services from those of other airlines. Trademarks are used to protect brand names, logos, and symbols that are associated with a company's products or services.

109. (A): Prof. Deepak Pental chaired the National Mission on Libraries, a government-backed initiative aimed at advancing and expanding library services throughout India. The mission sought to address various challenges faced by libraries in the country, such as inadequate infrastructure, limited resources, and lack of awareness about library services. Under Pental's leadership, the National Mission on Libraries developed a comprehensive plan to improve the state of libraries in India.

110. (A): William A. Katz (1969) rightly said that "If the users will not come to the library, the Library must go to the users". This can be regarded, indisputably, as the guiding principle of reference service. He also said weeding is one of the best suitable techniques available to ensure the long-range usefulness of library collection.

111. (D): The National Institute of Mental Health and Neurosciences (NIMHANS) is a renowned institute in Bangalore, India, established in 1924. It is recognized for its specialized services in mental health and neurosciences, offering both clinical and research-based expertise. NIMHANS is involved in advanced research and training in the fields of psychiatry, neurology, and related disciplines.

112. (B): Alireza Noruzi is known for his work on the application of S.R. Ranganathan's Laws to the web. His research explores how Ranganathan's principles, originally formulated for traditional library systems, can be adapted to enhance information retrieval and organization on the web.

113. (B): (*a*) **Delhi Public Library (DPL), Delhi:** Established in 1951, the Delhi Public Library is a major public library system in Delhi, India. It serves as a significant cultural and educational resource for the public, offering a wide range of books, periodicals, and digital resources. As a library of national importance, the Delhi Public Library receives funding from the Ministry of Culture, which supports its operations, infrastructure, and development activities.

(*b*) **Central Reference Library, Kolkata:** The Central Reference Library in Kolkata, established in 1951, is one of the premier libraries in India, focusing on providing reference and research services. It has a vast collection of books, periodicals, and reference materials. Like the Delhi Public Library, the Central Reference Library also receives financial support from the Ministry of Culture. This funding helps maintain its extensive collection and support its role as a key resource for research and reference.

114. (D): The International Federation of Library Associations and Institutions (IFLA) and UNESCO launched an updated version of the Public Library Manifesto in July 2022. This updated manifesto outlines the role and importance of public libraries in society, emphasizing their contributions to access to information, education, and community engagement in the modern digital era.

115. (A): The Second Law of Library Science emphasizes most on the enactment of Library Legislation. This law states, "Every Reader His/Her Book." It implies that every reader has the right to access the books they need. To ensure this, the state must establish a robust library system capable of providing adequate library services to all people. This requires appropriate legislation, including provisions for financial support and the establishment of a coordinating authority to oversee the various units within the system.

116. (A): The correct ratio of funding shared between RRRLF and developing & lagging states under the Financial Assistance Matching Scheme is 60:40. This means that for every 60 rupees provided by RRRLF, the developing or lagging state must contribute 40 rupees. This shared funding model aims to ensure that these states receive adequate support for their library infrastructure and services, but also encourages them to participate in the development process.

117. (D): The concept of 'Ask Library Anything' was originally initiated by the American Library Association (ALA). This initiative is designed to encourage library users to ask any questions they have, promoting the idea that libraries are accessible resources for a wide range of inquiries and support.

118. (C): The P.V. Verghese Prize is awarded by the Indian Library Association for the Best Article published in the field of library and information science. This prize honors outstanding contributions to the literature and scholarship in the field, recognizing excellence in writing and research.

119. (C): In the Colon Classification system, 'KZ' for Animal Husbandry is an example of an Emptying Digit. An Emptying Digit in Colon Classification refers to a digit or code that is used to indicate a specific subject or category that is left open or available for further classification within a broader class. This allows for flexibility and expansion within the classification system, accommodating new or emerging topics.

120. (B): Anglo-American Cataloguing Rules, Second Edition (AACR2), published in 1978, is a key set of standards for cataloging library materials. It was created to ensure consistency and comprehensiveness in the bibliographic description of various types of library materials.

(*b*) Michael Gorman was a co-editor of AACR2. He is a prominent figure in library science, known for his contributions to cataloging and library standards. His work on AACR2 helped shape the framework and guidelines used in library cataloging practices.

(*c*) Paul W. Winkler was another co-editor of AACR2. He played a significant role in the development and editing of these cataloging rules. His expertise contributed to the refinement and clarity of the rules set forth in AACR2.

121. (C): (*a*) Subject Classification: IV. Enumerative Classification - Subject Classification systems, such as Dewey decimal classification, primarily use an enumerative approach to organize subjects in a list or hierarchy.

(*b*) Colon Classification: III. Faceted - Colon Classification, developed by S.R. Ranganathan, is a faceted classification system that allows for a detailed breakdown of subjects into multiple facets.

(*c*) Universal Decimal Classification (UDC): I. Almost Faceted- The Universal Decimal Classification is considered almost faceted, providing a comprehensive list of subjects and their subdivisions.

(*d*) Library of Congress Classification: II. Purely Enumerative - The Library of Congress Classification system is often described as Purely Enumerative. It includes some aspects of faceting but is largely enumerative in its structure.

122. (A): A Gap Device in a classification scheme is designed to make the system more hospitable by allowing for the easy integration of new subjects or categories. By creating reserved spaces or gaps in the classification structure, it ensures that the system can accommodate future additions and expansions without disrupting the existing organization. This flexibility helps maintain the system's relevance and adaptability over time.

123. (C): The symbol Δ(Delta) is used to represent 'Spiritual experience and Mysticism' in Colon Classification. This symbol is part of the system's method of using various symbols and letters to categorize subjects, making it easier to classify and retrieve information on specific topics.

124. (B): In a computer system, primary connectors refer to essential components that connect the computer to its core functions:

(*a*) **Power:** This is crucial for supplying electricity to the entire computer system, enabling it to operate.

(*b*) **Keyboard:** This is an input device that allows users to type data and commands into the computer.

(*c*) **Display:** Also known as the monitor, this is an output device that shows the visual output from the computer, including the operating system, applications, and any other content.

125. (B): The C programming language is often referred to as the "mother of all programming languages" due to its significant influence on the development of other programming languages. Developed in the early 1970s by Dennis Ritchie, C has had a profound influence on many other programming languages. Many modern languages, such as C++, Java, Python, and JavaScript, have been inspired by C's syntax, structure, and concepts.

127. (C): X.25 is a protocol used for public data networks (PDN). It is a standard for packet-switched networks, which allows data to be transmitted across a network in small packets. X.25 was widely used for connecting terminals and networks before the advent of more modern protocols like TCP/IP.

128. (D): DTP (Desktop Publishing) software is used for creating and designing printed materials such as brochures, magazines, and books.

(*a*) **Pagemaker:** Developed by Adobe, Pagemaker was one of the first widely used DTP applications. It allows users to design and produce print materials like brochures, newsletters, and magazines with precise control over layout, typography, and graphics. It was particularly popular in the early days of desktop publishing.

(*b*) **QuarkXPress:** QuarkXPress is a professional DTP application known for its powerful layout and design capabilities. It provides tools for creating intricate page layouts, handling text and graphics, and producing high-quality print and digital publications. It has been a staple in the publishing industry for many years.

129. (A): (*a*) Edition is represented by II. 250 in MARC 21. This tag is used to describe the edition of the book or item.

(*b*) Personal Name is represented by I. 100 in MARC 21. This tag is used for the primary personal author or creator of the work.

(*c*) Uniform Title is represented by III. 130 in MARC 21. This tag is used for uniform titles that are used when the title of the work is the same across different editions or formats.

(*d*) Physical Description is represented by IV. 300 in MARC 21. This tag provides information about the physical characteristics of the item, such as pagination, dimensions, and other physical details.

130. (A): LIBSYS and KOHA are examples of Library Management Software:

(*a*) **LIBSYS:** This is a comprehensive library management system used for various library functions, including cataloging, circulation, and acquisitions.

(*b*) **KOHA:** This is an open-source Integrated Library System (ILS) that provides functionalities for cataloging, circulation, and library management. It is widely used by libraries around the world.

131. (C): (*b*) **Functional Requirements for Bibliographic Records (FRBR):** This project was initiated first. FRBR, published by IFLA in 1998, provides a conceptual model for bibliographic records to help in understanding how users interact with bibliographic data.

(*a*) **Functional Requirements for Authority Data (FRAD):** Following FRBR, FRAD was introduced in 2009. It extends the principles of FRBR to authority data, focusing on the functional requirements for authority records, such as personal names and subject headings.

(*d*) **Functional Requirements for Subject Authority Data (FRSAD):** FRSAD, published in 2010, builds on the concepts introduced in FRBR and FRAD but specifically addresses the needs related to subject authority data.

(*c*) **Functional Requirements for Bibliographic Records-Object Oriented (FRBROO):** The Functional Requirements for Bibliographic Records-Object Oriented (FRBRoo) model was published in 2016. The International Federation of Library Associations and Institutions (IFLA) originally designed the FRBRoo model, which is an entity-relationship model.

132. (B): (*a*) **Optical Character Recognition (OCR):** OCR is a technology used to convert different types of documents, such as scanned paper documents or PDF files, into editable and searchable data. While OCR itself is not a physical device, it works with scanners (an input device) to convert printed text into digital text, so it's closely related to input functions.

(*b*) **Scanner:** A scanner is a direct input device that captures images or text from physical documents and converts them into digital formats.

133. (D): In a Linear Bus Topology, devices are connected in a single, straight line, with each device connected to the bus at both ends. Each device is connected to the bus, and data travels in one direction along the bus until it reaches the intended device. This means that data must travel through the entire bus to reach its destination, potentially leading to slower transmission speeds and increased network traffic.

134. (C): In the MARC (Machine-Readable Cataloging) record structure, the first component is the Leader. The Leader is a fixed-length field at the beginning of the MARC record that contains essential information about the record itself, such as its length, type of record, and character encoding.

135. (C): (*a*) **MPE/ix:** This is an operating system developed by Hewlett-Packard for their HP 3000 series of minicomputers. It is a type of operating system.

(*c*) **Linux:** This is a widely used open-source operating system. It is known for its stability and is used in a variety of computing environments, from personal computers to servers.

136. (B): Tim Berners-Lee, a computer scientist, is credited with inventing the World Wide Web. In 1991, he first published the HTML (HyperText Markup Language) and its tags as part of the foundational technology for the web. His work laid the groundwork for creating web pages and linking documents over the internet.

137. (D): (*b*) **System School:** This management thought is part of the Modern Theory of Management. It views organizations as systems composed of interrelated and interdependent parts, which interact with each other and the external environment. The System School emphasizes the holistic nature of organizations and the importance of considering the organization as a whole.

(*c*) **Contingency School:** This school of thought is also associated with Modern Management Theory. It suggests that there is no one-size-fits-all approach to management. Instead, the most effective management strategies depend on the specific circumstances and context in which they are applied. It highlights the importance of adapting management practices to fit different situations.

138. (A): Unity of Direction: This principle, formulated by Henri Fayol, states that there should be a single plan and a single head for each group of activities with the same objective. This principle ensures that all activities directed towards the same goal are coordinated and unified under one plan and leadership.

139. (A): The correct alphabetical order, word by word, is:

(*b*) Sing (*d*) Sing at

(*c*) Singer (*a*) Singing

140. (B): The concept of "Anomalous State of Knowledge" (ASK) was introduced by N.J. Belkin. ASK refers to the situation where an individual encounters a gap in their knowledge and is unable to effectively find or use information to resolve that gap. This concept is important in understanding how people recognize and seek information to address their information needs.

141. (A): IS 1829 : 1978/1991 is related to Library Furniture. It specifies the requirements for library furniture made of timber, including dimensions, materials, and construction standards. This Indian Standard aims to ensure that library furniture is both functional and durable, providing a comfortable and efficient working environment for library users and staff.

142. (D): The Performance Planning and Budgeting System (PPBS) is a budgeting method that combines planning, programming, and budgeting. It translates activities, programs, and services into specific, tangible projects and presents the requirements in budgetary terms. PPBS is designed to link performance and expenditure more closely, providing a systematic approach to budgeting that emphasizes achieving specific objectives and results.

143. (B): According to Edwin B. Flippo, Job Specification is "a statement of the minimum acceptable human qualities necessary to perform a job properly." It outlines the qualifications, skills, and attributes required from individuals to effectively carry out the responsibilities of a particular job. This is distinct from a Job Description, which details the duties and responsibilities of the job itself.

144. (B): Nina E. Browne, a librarian at the Library Bureau in Boston, USA, devised the Browne Charging System in 1895. This innovative system revolutionized library circulation practices at the time by introducing a more efficient and reliable method for tracking borrowed materials. Prior to the Browne Charging System, libraries often used manual methods, such as card catalogs or ledger systems, to track book loans.

145. (D): E-Gyankosh is an initiative specifically for distance education and is a repository for educational content. While it is similar to INFOPORT in that it provides educational resources, it focuses on distance learning materials. The other three (E-PG Pathshala, Shodhshudhi, and INFOPORT) are more broadly oriented towards academic resources and research tracking.

146. (D): Lionel R. McColvin is the proponent of the "Demand Theory" of book selection. This theory emphasizes the importance of selecting books based on the expressed and unexpressed needs of library users. It suggests that books should be chosen to meet the demands of the community, rather than simply because they are available or popular.

147. (C): Peter Drucker, a renowned management consultant and author, is credited with the quote: "Quality in a product or service is not what the supplier puts in. It is what the customer gets out and is willing to pay for." This emphasizes the customer-centric perspective of quality, where the value of a product or service is determined by the customer's perception and willingness to pay, rather than solely by the supplier's efforts.

148. (A): (*a*) G. Edward Evans - IV. Management Techniques for Libraries - G. Edward Evans authored books on various aspects of library management, including techniques specifically tailored for library settings.

(*b*) Edwin B. Flippo - II. Personnel Management - Edwin B. Flippo is renowned for his work on personnel management, focusing on the principles and practices essential for managing human resources effectively.

(*c*) Robert D. Stueart and Barbara B. Moran - I. Library and Information Centre Management - Robert D. Stueart and Barbara B. Moran wrote about library and information center management, covering a broad spectrum of management practices within library environments.

(*d*) William B. Werther and Keith Davis - III. Human Resource and Personnel Management - William B. Werther and Keith Davis addressed human resource and personnel management, providing insights into managing staff and organizational dynamics.

149. (C): The Central Reference Library (CRL) in Kolkata, India publishes the Indian National Bibliography (INB). The CRL is the National Bibliographic Agency of India and is a subordinate organization of the Ministry of Culture. The INB is published monthly and cumulated annually. The INB is published in 14 languages, including English. The INB has been published since 1957. It was first brought out in 1958 during the leadership of Bellary Shamanna Kesavan, the first National Librarian of independent India.

150. (D): The National Institute of Science Communication and Policy Research (NISCPR) was established by merging two key institutions:

(*a*) CSIR - NISCAIR (National Institute of Science Communication and Information Resources): NISCAIR was previously responsible for science communication and the dissemination of scientific information in India. It played a significant role in producing various publications and resources aimed at enhancing the public's understanding of science.

(*d*) CSIR - NISTADS (National Institute of Science, Technology and Development Studies): NISTADS focused on research in the fields of science, technology, and development studies. It contributed to policy research and analysis related to science and technology.

151. (B): Science Direct is a leading full-text scientific database offering journal articles and book chapters from more than 2,500 peer-reviewed journals and more than 11,000 books. It is developed and maintained by Elsevier, a major academic publishing company. It provides access to a vast collection of full-text articles, books, and other scholarly materials from thousands of academic journals and publishers.

152. (D): Access Science is the online platform that hosts the "McGraw Hill Encyclopedia of Science and Technology," offering users access to a comprehensive collection of articles, research, and information across various scientific disciplines. Managed by McGraw Hill, this resource provides in-depth and updated content from the encyclopedia, along with other scholarly materials, making it a valuable tool for researchers, students, and professionals seeking reliable scientific information.

153. (C): CONTENTdm is a digital collection management service provided by OCLC (Online Computer Library Center). It helps libraries and other institutions to manage, preserve, and provide access to their digital collections, such as images, manuscripts, and audio-visual materials. Founded in 1967, OCLC is a member-owned and -governed organization that serves libraries of all sizes and types.

154. (B): The Digital Accessible Information System (DAISY) Consortium was founded in Stockholm, Sweden, in May 1996. It was initially established by talking book libraries to lead the transition from analog to digital talking books. The consortium's goal is to promote the development and use of accessible digital information formats, particularly for people with disabilities.

155. (C): Orientation of library users falls under reference services because it focuses on guiding and educating users about how to navigate and utilize the library's resources effectively. This includes familiarizing them with the library's layout, cataloging system, and various services available, such as research assistance and information retrieval. The goal is to enhance users' ability to independently access and utilize information, improving their overall library experience and effectiveness in finding needed materials.

156. (B): (*a*) **William A. Katz:** Well-known for his contributions to library science, his book "Introduction to Reference Work" is a classic in the field.

(*b*) **A.J. Walford:** Another prominent figure in reference librarianship, his work "Guide to Reference Material" is a widely used resource.

(*c*) **C.M. Winchell:** Her book "Guide to Reference Books" is a standard reference for librarians and researchers.

(*d*) **P.S. Kawatra:** Known for his work in information science, his book "Textbook of Information Science" is a comprehensive guide to the subject.

157. (D): (*a*) Mike Eisenberg and Bob Berkowitz are known for the "Big 6 Model". - Developed by Mike Eisenberg and Bob Berkowitz, the Big 6 Model is a widely recognized framework for information literacy that focuses on six steps: Task Definition, Information Seeking Strategies, Location and Access, Use of Information, Synthesis, and Evaluation.

(*b*) Christine Susan Bruce developed the "Seven Faces of Information Literacy". - Created by Christine Susan Bruce, this model offers a broad perspective on information literacy, outlining seven distinct ways individuals understand and engage with information.

(*c*) James Herring is associated with the "PLUS" model. - Developed by James Herring, the PLUS Model stands for "People, Location, Use, and Search," and it is a practical approach to teaching information literacy, focusing on these key elements to guide users in finding and utilizing information effectively.

(*d*) Trever Bond developed the "Sauce" model. - Trever Bond developed the Sauce Model, which aims to enhance information literacy through a focus on practical skills and strategies. It emphasizes the use of various "ingredients" or approaches to effectively manage and use information.

158. (B): Annette Lamb is the creator of the "8Ws Model" of Information Literacy. This model is a framework designed to guide learners through the process of effectively finding, evaluating, and using information. The eight "W"s of the model are:

- **Watching:** Observing the world around you and identifying information needs.
- **Wondering:** Questioning, brainstorming, and defining the topic or problem.
- **Wiggling:** Exploring different perspectives and considering various possibilities.
- **Webbing:** Searching for information using different resources and connecting ideas.
- **Weaving:** Organizing and synthesizing information into a coherent understanding.
- **Wrapping:** Packaging and presenting findings in a clear and effective manner.
- **Waving:** Sharing information with others and promoting understanding.
- **Wishing:** Reflecting on the learning process and setting new goals.

159. (B): Frederick Winslow Taylor is credited with introducing the concept of Scientific Management. His approach, developed in the early 20th century, focused on improving industrial efficiency through systematic analysis and optimization of workflows, standardization of tasks, and the use of scientific methods to determine the best practices for various operations.

160. (D): UNESCO defines information as "facts, concepts or instructions in a formalized manner suitable for communication." This definition underscores the importance of presenting information in a structured and communicable format, which is crucial for effective dissemination and understanding.

161. (C): UNESCO World Book and Copyright Day is celebrated annually on April 23rd to promote reading, writing, and copyright. It is a day to encourage everyone, especially young people, to discover the pleasure of reading and to support local authors and booksellers.

162. (C): The Indian Association of Special Libraries and Information Centres (IASLIC) was established in 1955 as a professional organization dedicated to advancing the field of special libraries and information centers in India. IASLIC plays a crucial role in promoting the development, growth, and professionalization of these specialized libraries and information centers, which serve a wide range of industries, organizations, and research institutions.

163. (D): Mary W. Plummer, a prominent figure in library science, first emphasized the importance of librarians maintaining ethical standards in her 1903 book "The Profession of Librarianship." She recognized the critical role librarians play in society and the need for them to adhere to a high code of conduct to ensure the integrity and effectiveness of their work.

164. (C): The University of Chicago established the first graduate school of librarianship in 1926. This institution, known as the Graduate Library School, played a significant role in shaping the field of librarianship and setting standards for professional education.

165. (C): The IFLA Scroll of Appreciation is a prestigious award bestowed upon individuals who have demonstrated exceptional dedication, expertise, and service to the International Federation of Library Associations and Institutions (IFLA). These individuals have made significant contributions to IFLA's mission through their voluntary work in committees, groups, or other initiatives.

166. (C): The Dublin Core Metadata Element Set Version 1.1 consists of 15 core elements, which are designed to provide a basic framework for describing digital resources. These elements include:

- Title
- Creator
- Subject
- Description
- Publisher
- Contributor
- Date
- Type
- Format
- Identifier
- Source
- Language
- Relation
- Coverage
- Rights

These elements can be used to describe a wide variety of resources, including web pages, images, videos, and documents.

167. (D): The phrase "Be minute, be minute, be not too minute" is attributed to H.E. Bliss. Bliss suggests that while it's crucial to be precise and detailed (minute) in cataloging and classifying information, one must avoid excessive minutiae that could lead to complexity and inefficiency. It reflects his perspective on the balance between detail and usability in classification systems, emphasizing the need to be thorough but not overly detailed.

168. (B): The 'One-Place Theory' is indeed associated with Subject Classification, particularly with the classification systems that prioritize placing each subject in a single location. This approach helps to maintain a clear and organized structure by ensuring that each subject or concept appears only once, making it easier for users to find and access information.

169. **(D):** UNIX and MS-DOS are both Character User Interface-based (CUI) operating systems.

(*b*) **UNIX:** Known for its powerful command-line interface, UNIX systems allow users to execute commands, scripts, and programs using text input. While UNIX can also support graphical user interfaces (GUIs) like X Window System, its core functionality and many tasks are performed through the command line.

(*d*) **MS-DOS:** This is a purely text-based operating system where users input commands directly into the command prompt. MS-DOS lacks a graphical user interface and relies entirely on textual commands to operate and manage files, directories, and programs.

170. **(D):** Semantics is indeed the study of meaning and reference, particularly in language and logic. It involves analyzing how words, phrases, and sentences convey meaning, and how these meanings relate to the objects or concepts they refer to. Semantics can be applied in various fields, including:

- **Philosophy:** To explore concepts of truth and meaning.
- **Linguistics:** To understand how language structures encode meaning.
- **Computer Science:** To design and interpret programming languages and data structures.

171. **(A):** Internet Protocol version 6 (IPv6) was developed by the Internet Engineering Task Force (IETF). The IETF is responsible for developing and promoting voluntary Internet standards and protocols, including IPv6, which was introduced to address the limitations of the previous version, IPv4, especially regarding the availability of IP addresses.

172. **(D):** Planning Programming Budgeting System (PPBS) was first proposed by the United States Department of Defense (USDoD). PPBS is a budgeting approach that emphasizes planning, programming, and budgeting processes to improve decision-making and resource allocation, integrating financial planning with strategic and operational planning.

173. **(A):** The "One Nation One Subscription" (ONOS) initiative in India aims to provide comprehensive access to both national and international scientific and academic content across the country. This initiative seeks to bridge the digital divide and ensure that researchers, students, and scholars have equitable access to high-quality resources, regardless of their location or institution. By consolidating subscriptions and negotiating favorable terms with publishers, ONOS aims to make these resources more affordable and accessible to a wider audience.

174. **(A):** Andrew Carnegie is renowned for his enormous financial donations for library buildings. He was a Scottish-American industrialist and philanthropist who, in the late 19th and early 20th centuries, funded the construction of thousands of public libraries across the United States and other countries. His contributions had a profound impact on the development of public libraries and access to information.

175. **(C):** Choreo Insights is a library analytics tool that uses WorldCat holdings data to help libraries align their collections with institutional goals and priorities. It is a product of OCLC, a global library cooperative that provides technology and services to libraries worldwide. This service provides analytics and insights to help libraries manage their collections and make data-driven decisions.

176. (C): The Indian National Bibliography (INB) primarily includes key sections such as the Author and Title Index, which help users locate books and materials based on authorship and titles, and the Subject Index, which categorizes items by subject matter. However, it does not include a Publisher Index, which would list publications by their publishers.

177. (D): INSSPEL stands for Indian Social Sciences Periodical Literature. It is a comprehensive bibliographic database that provides access to articles published in Indian social science journals. INSSPEL covers a wide range of disciplines, including sociology, psychology, economics, political science, geography, history, and Indology.

178. (D): The Chartered Institute of Library and Information Professionals (CILIP) has provided the following definition of information literacy: "Knowing when and why you need information, knowing where to find it, and how to evaluate, use and communicate it in an ethical manner." This definition aligns closely with the provided statement and captures the core elements of information literacy.

179. (B): The Marrakesh VIP Treaty, formally known as the Marrakesh Treaty to Facilitate Access to Published Works for Persons Who Are Blind, Visually Impaired, or Otherwise Print Disabled, is an international treaty that aims to address the challenges faced by people with visual impairments or print disabilities in accessing copyrighted material. The treaty allows for the reproduction and distribution of works in accessible formats, such as Braille or audio recordings, without infringing copyright laws.

180. (B): The National Academic Depository (NAD) is an initiative in India designed to create an online storehouse for academic awards, such as degrees and diplomas. It aims to provide a digital repository where academic records can be stored and verified, enhancing the efficiency and reliability of managing academic credentials.

Previous Paper (Solved)

Kendriya Vidyalaya Sangathan (KVS)—Librarian Recruitment Exam - 2018*

GENERAL ENGLISH

1. Select the wrongly spelt word.

A. legal B. levre
C. level D. label

2. Choose the most appropriate option to fill in the blanks.

This winter they are planning .... holiday in Cambodia.

A. the B. no word required
C. a D. an

3. Choose the correct antonym for the given word:

spurious

A. artificial B. useful
C. genuine D. actual

4. Complete the sentence with the correct word/ phrase.

Computer users in my office were warned .... a new virus.

A. off B. about
C. at D. on

5. Choose the correct synonym of the underlined word.

At these sessions, no idea is too <u>preposterous</u> to be thrown on the table.

A. logical B. ridiculous
C. uninteresting D. sensible

6. Select the word with the wrong spelling.

A. shield B. counterfeit
C. conceivable D. frieght

7. In the following question, the given sentence has been divided in three parts. Select the part that has an error. If there is no error, select option No error.

Did you saw/the hockey match/last night?/No error.

A. No error B. last night?
C. the hockey match D. Did you saw

8. Complete the sentence with the correct word/ phrase.

Despite the good advice their parents gave them, the two brothers .... college.

A. quit B. have quitted
C. quitting D. quitted

9. Complete the sentence with the correct word/ phrase.

The questionnaire .... by most of the participants before the workshop began.

A. had completed
B. had been completed
C. has been completed
D. has completed

10. In the following question, the given sentence has been divided in three parts. Select the part that has an error. If there is no error, select option No error.

All fears were forgotten/when the children saw the toys/in a corner of the clinic./No error.

A. when the children saw the toys
B. No error
C. in a corner of the clinic
D. All fears were forgotten

11. Complete the sentence with the correct word/ phrase.

* Online exam held on 22-02-2018.

You don't have to come to see my mother .... you want to.

A. so B. if
C. if not D. unless

12. Complete the sentence with the appropriate article.

We were driving through heavy rain when one of .... windscreen wipers stopped working.

A. No article B. an
C. a D. the

13. Find the most appropriate word that can substitute the following phrase.

Failing to observe the limits of what is permitted or acceptable.

A. unscrupulous B. presumptuous
C. arrogant D. criminal

14. Complete the sentence with the appropriate option.

The vet recognised the bird .... injuries he had healed.

A. whom B. whose
C. who's D. who

15. Complete the sentence with the appropriate option.

Ratan managed to work despite the .... of his computer.

A. unreliably B. unreliable
C. unrelied D. unreliability

16. In the following question, the given sentence has been divided in three parts. Select the part that has an error. If there is no error, select option No error.

She underwent surgery/on the removal/of a cataract in her left eye./No error.

A. She underwent surgery
B. No error
C. on the removal
D. of a cataract in her left eye

Directions (Q.No. 17-20): *Read the passage and answer the questions below.*

On a mid-September day, British climbers Rachel Kelsey and Jeremy Colenso were climbing in the Swiss Alps. They were both experienced climbers and when they started, the weather was good. They reached the Summit but as they started the climb down, an electric storm struck the mountain.

Snow began to fall, making it difficult to see where they could put their hands and feet on the rock. After several frightening minutes, they found a narrow ledge and climbed on to it, hoping the snow would stop and they could climb down.

The snow did not stop and the temperature dropped to –5°C. They decided that they had to get help. Rachel had brought her mobile phone with her. She was unable to contact the mountain rescue service on her mobile phone and the only contact number she had were in London. She sent a text message at 1.30 am to five friends in the UK. It read: 'Need heli rescue off north ridge of Piz Badile, Switz'. They were all asleep.

At 5.00 am Avery Cunliffe got the message. He jumped into action and immediately contacted the rescue services in Geneva. He texted Rachel back saying: 'I'm on the case'. Even then, rescue was impossible because of the treacherous weather and the mountain rescue team had to send a text message to Miss de Kelsey telling her she would have to spend a second night on the mountain. They could reach the stranded couple only at 8.15 am the next day. At about 1.00 pm they were lifted off the mountains in helicopters.

17. What did Rachel do as she was sitting on the ledge?

A. She sent text message to Jeremy Colenso
B. She sent text message to the Mountain Rescue Team
C. She sent text message to friends in Switzerland
D. She send text message to friends in the UK

18. What did Cunliffe mean by 'I'm on the case'?

A. I can't help you
B. I am getting lawyers
C. I am coming to meet you
D. I am doing what needs to be done

19. Rachel and Jeremy could not climb down because:

A. They could not see properly in the snowfall
B. They had forgotten the route

C. It was very cold
D. The mountain was very slippery

20. How long did Rachel and Jeremy spend on the Narrow ledge?

A. About 36 hours
B. Around 12 hours
C. More than 36 hours
D. Almost 24 hours

सामान्य हिन्दी

21. कौन-सा शब्द स्त्रीलिंग है?
A. टिकट B. कपूर
C. अनार D. अवस्था

22. निम्नलिखित में से कौन-सा शब्द अनेकार्थी है?
A. अमर B. आय
C. घन D. विष

23. कौन-सा शब्द एकवचन नहीं है?
A. रात B. गाय
C. सड़क D. बच्चे

24. निम्नलिखित में से कौन-सा शब्द 'वृक्ष' का पर्यायवाची नहीं है?
A. पेड़ B. तरु
C. विटप D. सुमन

25. 'ढोल के भीतर पोल' लोकोक्ति का सही अर्थ होगा :
A. एक से बढ़कर दूसरा चालाक
B. लड़ाई-झगड़े के लिए जिम्मेदार दोनों पक्ष हैं
C. ढोल के भीतर छेद होना
D. केवल दिखावटी शान

26. निम्नलिखित में से कौन-सा शब्द तत्सम है?
A. उँगली B. उल्लू
C. आग D. आम्र

27. कौन-सा शब्द सर्वनाम है?
A. लोहा B. आप
C. पटना D. भारत

28. निम्नलिखित में से कौन-सा शब्द तद्भव है?
A. पुष्प B. मोर
C. भक्त D. प्रिय

29. कौन-सा शब्द विशेषण नहीं है?
A. विद्वान B. सुंदर
C. हम D. दुष्ट

30. कौन-सा अलंकार शब्दालंकार नहीं है?
A. यमक B. श्लेष
C. उपमा D. अनुप्रास

31. 'जन्म' का विलोम होगा :
A. मृत्यु B. जीवित
C. नश्वर D. जय

32. 'जिस शब्द से किसी काम का करना या होना समझा जाए' उसे कहते हैं?
A. संज्ञा B. विशेषण
C. क्रिया D. सर्वनाम

33. 'बिना वेतन के' के लिए एक शब्द होगा :
A. वैयाकरण B. कुबेर
C. अवैतनिक D. याचक

34. 'मनोयोग' में कौन-सी संधि है?
A. विसर्ग B. व्यंजन
C. गुण D. दीर्घ

35. 'सिर मुड़ाते ओले पड़ना' मुहावरे का सही अर्थ होगा :
A. दुःख सह लेना
B. सिर पर ही ओले गिरना
C. होश उड़ जाना
D. काम शुरू होते ही बाधा आना

36. कौन-सा वाक्य अशुद्ध है?
A. रोगी से पानी नहीं पी जाता
B. राम पुस्तक पढ़ रहा था
C. उसकी शोभा देखते ही बनती है
D. बरसात हो रही है

37. निम्नलिखित में से कौन-सा वाक्य वर्तमान काल का है?
A. श्याम खेल रहा था

B. वह गया था

C. वह जाएगा

D. तुम बाजार जाते हो

38. 'गिरीश' में कौन-सी संधि है?

A. दीर्घ B. यण

C. गुण D. वृद्धि

39. 'प्रत्येक' में कौन-सा समास है?

A. कर्मधारय B. अव्ययीभाव

C. द्विगु D. बहुब्रीहि

40. निम्नलिखित में से कौन-सा शब्द विदेशी है?

A. आशा B. अमीर

C. उद्घाटन D. आत्मा

GENERAL AWARENESS

41. What are the colours on the flag of the Communist Party of India?

A. Black & White B. Saffron & White

C. Red & White D. Green & White

42. How is igneous rock formed?

A. Gradual accumulation of sediments

B. Solidification of minerals and application of pressure

C. By varying degrees of pressure and heat

D. Cooling and solidification of magma or lava

43. Which cities does the national highway NH1 connect?

A. Uri—Baramulla—Srinagar—Kargil—Leh

B. Thane—Pune—Banglore—Chennai

C. Delhi—Agra—Allahabad—Kolkata

D. Agra—Indore—Dhule—Mumbai

44. Where is the Amarnath temple located in India?

A. Uttarakhand B. Jammu & Kashmir

C. Sikkim D. Himachal Pradesh

45. When the Women's Cricket Association of India was formed?

A. 1978 B. 1975

C. 1973 D. 1979

46. Where is the Asteroid Belt located?

A. Between Jupiter and Uranus

B. Between Jupiter and Saturn

C. Between Earth and Jupiter

D. Between Mars and Jupiter

47. Who is the founder of the Yogic School of Philosophy?

A. Jamini B. Maharishi Kapil

C. Patanjali D. Aksapada Gautama

48. Which Indian freedom fighter was called the "Iron Man" of India?

A. Vallabhbhai Patel

B. Khan Abdul Ghaffar Khan

C. Lal Bahadur Shastri

D. Dadabhai Naoroji

49. Who presides over the session of the Rajya Sabha?

A. Speaker of India

B. President of the ruling party of India

C. Vice President of India

D. President of India

50. How many representatives are in the Rajya Sabha from the state of Tamil Nadu?

A. 80 B. 20

C. 18 D. 19

51. The Dandi March is also known as:

A. Home Rule Movement

B. Non Co-operation Movement

C. Swaraj Movement

D. Salt Satyagraha

52. Which author created the fictional village called Malgudi?

A. R.K. Narayan B. Girish Karnad

C. W.S. Swaminathan D. Shankar Nag

53. In which of the following does sound travels fastest?

A. Aluminum B. Water

C. Rubber D. Air

54. The design of the court seal of the Supreme Court of India is a reproduction of which famous monument?
A. The wheel of the Sarnath Lion capital of Ashoka
B. The Taj Mahal
C. India Gate
D. The Gateway of India

55. Which phrase has been chosen as the "word of the year 2017" by Collins Dictionary?
A. Fake news
B. My new "Aesthetic"
C. GOAT (Greatest of all time)
D. Keep it 100

56. The maximum age of joining National Pension Scheme—Private Sector has been revised by the PFRDA from 60 years to:
A. 62 years B. 75 years
C. 70 years D. 65 years

57. Where was Mahatma Gandhi born?
A. Porbandar, Gujarat
B. Zeradei, Bihar
C. Nadiad, Gujarat
D. Allahabad, Uttar Pradesh

58. Which ancient city is situated on the banks of the river Sarayu?
A. Ayodhya B. Varanasi
C. Dwarka D. Mathura

59. What is the definition/full form of EMI in economic terms?
A. Equated Monthly Installment
B. Equal Monthly Interest
C. Equal Monthly Increase
D. Equated Monthly Income

60. The bacterial cells that are found in animal and plant cells lack which of the following?
A. Cell walls B. Mobility
C. DNA D. Organelles

61. Who is the author of the book "Interpreter of Maladies"?
A. R.K. Narayan B. Jhumpa Lahiri
C. Vikram Seth D. Rohinton Mistry

62. Who was appointed as Director General of United Nations Educational, Scientific and Cultural Organization (UNESCO) in November 2017?
A. Federico Mayor B. Irina Bokova
C. Audrey Azoulay D. Koichiro Matsuura

63. In the economic jargon, what does the acronym LIBOR stand for?
A. London Interbank Offer Rate
B. Labour Interest Balance Of Revenue
C. Laws In Base Order Rates
D. Liability Induced By Older Rates

64. In economics and finance, the situation where a shock in a particular economy or region spreads out and affects other economies by way of, say, price movements is called as:
A. Clearing price B. Crowding out effect
C. Contagion D. Catch up effect

65. Where does river Krishna originate?
A. Eastern Ghats B. Kashmir
C. Himalayas D. Western Ghats

66. When was the Cripps Mission sent to India?
A. 1910 B. 1932
C. 1942 D. 1915

67. Sushila Chanu Pukhrambam is currently (as of October 2017) the captain of Indian women's national team in which sport?
A. Volleyball B. Football
C. Cricket D. Hockey

68. What is the main function of xylem in plants?
A. Transport water and minerals
B. Derive energy from light
C. Store glucose
D. Exchange Oxygen and Carbon Dioxide

69. What measures, changes in the prices paid by consumers for a basket of goods and services?
A. Consumer Purchase Index
B. Consumer Price Index
C. Index of Consumer Price of Goods and Services
D. Consumed Goods Index

70. Who is Nirad C. Chaudhuri?
A. A famous Indian politician
B. A famous musician
C. An award winning actor
D. A reputed Indian author

REASONING AND NUMERICAL ABILITY

71. Complete the series below with the most appropriate option.

Cow : Leather :: Llama : ?

A. Meat B. Silk
C. Flesh D. Wool

72. Introducing Radhika, Meenu said, "she is the only daughter of my father's only daughter". How is Meenu related to Radhika?

A. Daughter B. Sister
C. Grandmother D. Mother

73. Find the ODD one out:

A. 54-9 B. 36-6
C. 60-12 D. 42-7

74. Identify the next term in the below series:

4D, 6F, 8H, 10J, ...

A. 14K B. 12L
C. 14L D. 12K

75. Which of the following words CANNOT be formed using the letters of the following word using each letter in the word only as many times as if appears in the given word?

NECESSARY

A. RECESS B. ESSAY
C. NEARNESS D. SCENERY

76. Identify the next term in the below series:

BvF, DyJ, FbN, HeR, ...

A. JgH B. JhV
C. JvH D. JuV

77. If WINTER is coded as VIOUER, then the code for SPRING is:

A. RPSNJG B. RPSJNG
C. RSPJNG D. RPQERG

78. Identify the odd option from the below:

A. Hut B. House
C. Palace D. School

79. Three of the given option are similar in a certain way. Select the options that is different from the other three.

A. Dangerous B. Unsafe
C. Hazardous D. Harmless

80. Find the missing term:

376, 184, 88, 40, 16, ..., –2

A. 2 B. 16
C. 4 D. 8

81. If Vincent is the brother of the son of Robert's son, how is Vincent related to Robert?

A. Son B. Grandson
C. Brother D. Uncle

82. Three of the given options are similar in a certain way. Select the option that is different from the other three.

A. Daisy B. Jasmine
C. Orchard D. Lily

83. In the following question, four problem figures have certain common features. Choose a figure from the alternative that has features similar to that of the problem figures.

Problem figures:

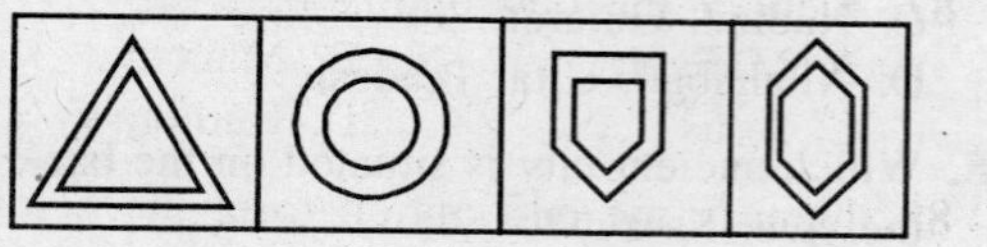

A. 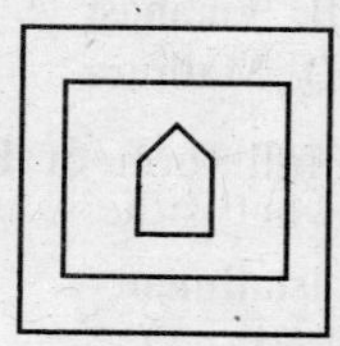 B. 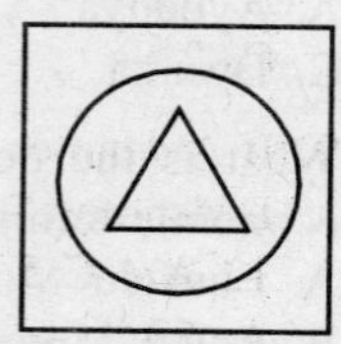

C. 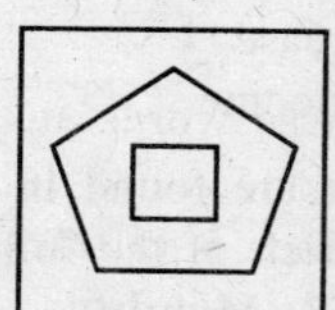 D. 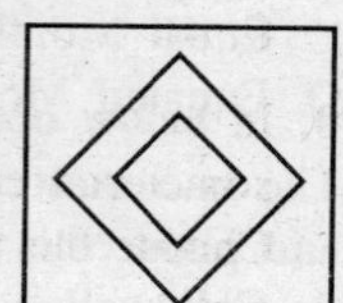

84. In this question, four figures are given. Three of the four figures are similar in a certain way and one is different. Find the figure which is different from the other three.

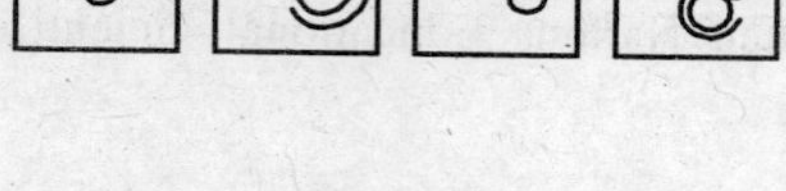

A. 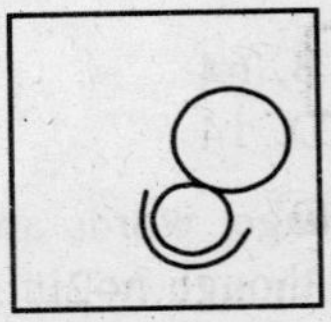 B. 

C. 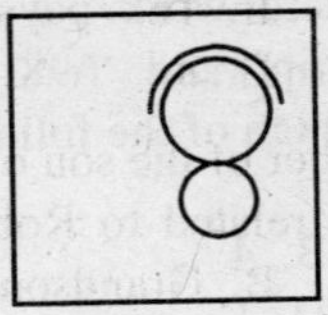 D. 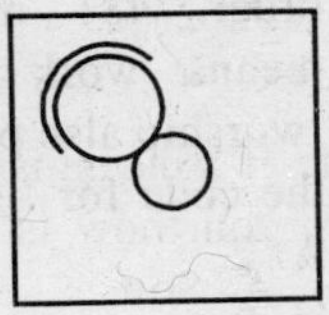

85. Find the missing term:
1000, 1100, 990, 1089, ...
A. 980.1 B. 9801
C. 989.1 D. 999

86. Find such a word from the options that is similar in meaning to the words on both sides of the brackets.
FINAL (.....)ULTIMATE
A. LAST B. END
C. DEAD D. FINISH

87. Identify the odd option out:
A. Mahavir B. Marx
C. Jesus D. Buddha

88. Identify the odd option from the below:
A. 63 B. 17
C. 23 D. 13

89. If A denotes '÷', B denotes '×', C denotes '+' D denotes '–', then what is the value of 18 B 12 A 4 C 5 D 6 = ?
A. 53 B. 35
C. 46 D. 50

90. In below options, three words are similar in some context and one word is different. Choose the word which is different from the rest.
A. Man-House B. Lion-Forest
C. Bird-Nest D. Horse-Stable

91. Find the missing terms in the below number series:
6, 11, 16, 21, ..., ..., 36, 41
A. 26, 30 B. 26, 31
C. 25, 30 D. 25, 31

92. If 23 = 8, 25 = 32, 42 = 16, then 44 = ?
A. 256 B. 250
C. 96 D. 88

93. In the following question, four problem figures have certain common features. Choose a figure from the alternative that has features similar to that of the problem figures.

Problem figures:

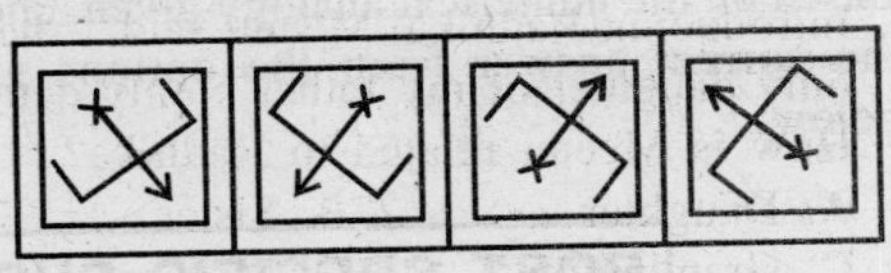

A. 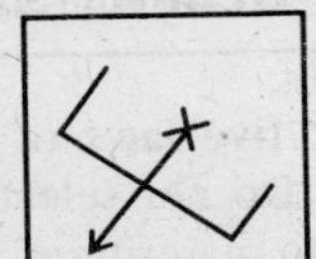 B. 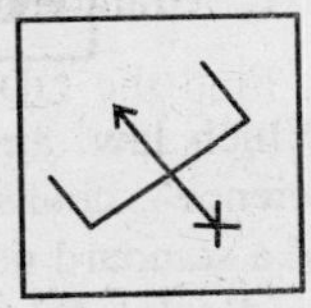

C. 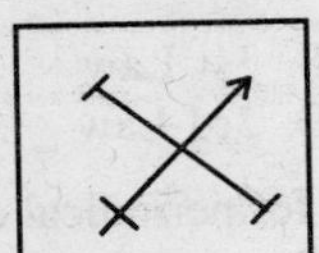 D. 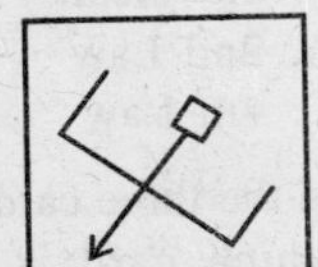

94. Choose the set that is similar to the following set:
(8, 24, 40)
A. (10, 20, 25) B. (7, 13, 29)
C. (6, 12, 20) D. (9, 27, 28)

95. Anil is Balu's brother. "I have as many sisters as brothers", tells Balu to one of his friends. How many brothers and sisters does the family have?
A. 5 sisters & 3 brothers
B. 3 sisters & 4 brothers
C. Data inadequate
D. 4 sisters & 5 brothers

96. If MART is coded as 2179 and SLIT is coded as 8539, how will TRAIL be coded?
A. 97135 B. 97351
C. 97153 D. 91735

97. 'Badminton' is related to 'Court' in the same way as 'Boxing' is related to:
A. Ring B. Arena
C. Pool D. Court

98. Choose the correct option pair that shares the same relationship between the words as shared between the words in the below pair:

Ignite : Light

A. Cling : Attach

B. Attract : Repel

C. Wheel : Car

D. Gain : Lose

99. Based on the numerical analogy given, choose the correct answer from the options given below:

3 : 9 :: 8 : ?

A. 20 B. 64

C. 16 D. 14

100. In a certain code language, words are given specific code numbers, though not in specific order. '481' means 'hard work pays' '246' means 'work is worship' and '698' means 'worship also pays'. Which of the following is the code for 'is'?

A. 2 B. 4

C. 6 D. 1

POST SPECIFIC SUBJECT-RELATED QUESTIONS

101. Which law, among the "five laws of library science", counsels that "Do not select books of a standard not suited to majority of readers in the locality"?

A. 2nd Law B. 1st Law

C. 4th Law D. 3rd Law

102. In the three card system for periodical control, which card is used for recording 'entries relating to the volume, issue and the dates of publication etc.'?

A. Register card

B. Classified card

C. Classified index card

D. Check card

103. In which of the following, the activities are shown as a network of precedence relationships using activity-on-arrow network construction?

A. TQM

B. Decision Tree Analysis

C. CPM

D. PERT

104. Unpublished theses and dissertations are categorised as:

A. Secondary literature

B. Ephemeral literature

C. Tertiary literature

D. Grey literature

105. The shift from print to electronic information resources can be categorised as change under:

A. Socio political environment

B. Economic environment

C. External environment

D. Internal environment

106. When a tear in a page or a tipping on a loose leaf is repaired, it is called as:

A. Re-casing B. Reinforcing

C. Mending D. Re-backing

107. Which of the following is a property of the main memory?

A. It has a very long life

B. It has large capacity

C. It is volatile

D. It is portable

108. Which combination of Boolean operators retrieves more documents?

A. A OR B B. A AND AB NOT B

C. A NOT B D. A AND B

109. What is the essential feature of WORM compared to other optical storage media?

A. It comes on a disk

B. Recording can be digital

C. It has higher storage density

D. Recording once done is irreversible

110. Which of the following is an example of a pointing device?

A. Light pen

B. Punched hole device

C. Keyboard

D. Scanner

111. What is the term of protection of copyright for a literary work in India?
A. 50 years from the year in which the author of the literary work dies
B. 60 years from the year of publication
C. 50 years from the year of publication
D. 60 years from the year in which the author of the literary work dies

112. The UNESCO Public Library Manifesto, renovated in 1994, was prepared in the co-operation with:
A. Library of Congress B. IFLA
C. OCLC D. FID

113. What is the current version of SOUL software?
A. SOUL 4.0 B. SOUL 1.0
C. SOUL 2.0 D. SOUL 3.0

114. The management principle 'Esprit de corps' means:
A. Group spirit
B. Replacing the rule of thumb with science
C. Development of workers
D. Discharge of responsibility

115. Which of the following is the exclusive function of a university library?
A. Providing support to the development of research and publication
B. Extension services
C. Promotion of reading habit
D. Library instruction

116. Which of the following is a book selection tool?
A. Ulrich's International Periodical Directory
B. Indian National Bibliography
C. Universities Handbook
D. World Book Encyclopedia

117. Which budgeting process starts from "scratch" with the proposed activities for the year?
A. Programme budgeting
B. Formula budgeting
C. Performance budgeting
D. Zero-based budgeting

118. Who assigns ISSN for Indian Journals?
A. Centre for Science and Environment, Delhi
B. National Science Library, NISCAIR
C. National Physical Laboratories, New Delhi
D. IISc, Bangalore

119. Which of the following is an indirect method of user study?
A. Analysis of library records
B. Operations research
C. Questionnaire
D. Diary

120. Who among the following was associated in planning Baroda Central Library in 1910?
A. Gopal Rao Ekbote
B. A.A.A. Fyzee
C. Asa Don Dickinson
D. William A Borden

121. Who was the first to give the concept of Selective Dissemination of Information as we understand it today?
A. L.J.S. Strauss
B. E.M. Housman
C. Melvil J. Voigt
D. H. Peter Luhn

122. Which of the following is a viable mean for library resource sharing?
A. Social media B. Blogs
C. Consortium D. RSS

123. Which of the following statistics are the 'most proper form to know the tastes, antipathies and reaction of the readers'?
A. Technical section
B. Circulation section
C. Acquisition section
D. Serial control

124. Who among the following described the 3-fold purpose of reference interview?
A. S.R. Ranganathan B. R.L. Collins
C. William A. Katz D. Robert S. Taylor

125. When did the National Library Week celebration start in India?
A. 1933 B. 1968
C. 1972 D. 1958

126. Which of the following operating systems is machine-independent and open-source?
A. Linux B. IBMZ/VM
C. Apple MAC OS D. MS Windows 7

127. When the user is helped to understand the subject coverage of chemical abstracts, then what it is called as?
A. User orientation B. User advisory
C. User assistance D. User education

128. Who is the author of "Library Buildings: Planning and Design"?
A. Rajwant Singh Chilana
B. S.R. Ranganathan
C. P.N. Kaula
D. B.S. Kesavan

129. What is meant by 'cardinal value' in the context of notation?
A. Type of notation used
B. Concept that refers to semantics
C. Quantitative value that each digit possesses
D. Position of a digit in series

130. Who among the following is the first to outline the objectives and means of cataloguing?
A. S.R. Ranganathan B. Seymour Lubetzky
C. Charles A. Cutter D. Berwick Sayers

131. Which of the following is the "principle of facet sequence"?
A. Cow-Calf principle
B. Principle of literary warrant
C. Principle of earlier in time
D. Principle of later in time

132. In which of the following, a multi-user operating system is used?
A. Servers
B. Hand-held computers
C. Desktop PC's
D. Embedded computers

133. According to staff formula, which section of the university library needs to have "one person for every 50 readers using the library in a day of the year"?
A. Maintenance B. Supervisory
C. Reference D. Circulation

134. In Colon Classification, 'f3' experimenting is a/an:
A. Anteriorising Common Isolate (applicable only after Space facet)
B. Posteriorising Personality Common Isolate
C. Posteriorising Energy Common Isolate
D. Anteriorising Common Isolate (applicable only after Time facet)

135. Which of the "five laws of library science" satisfies the services for differently abled?
A. 5th Law B. 4th Law
C. 3rd Law D. 2nd Law

136. What is meant by 'indent' in the book acquisition work of libraries?
A. List of accessioned items
B. List of approved items
C. List of ordered items
D. List of rejected items

137. Which among the following provides translation service for science and technology documents in India?
A. Centre for Science and Environment, Delhi
B. NISCAIR, Delhi
C. Central Institute of Indian Languages
D. National Library, Kolkata

138. Which of the following is a feature of Web OPAC?
A. It is navigation-based
B. It is phrase-indexed
C. It is command-language-based
D. It is pre-coordinated

139. International Federation of Library Associations and Institutions (IFLA) was established in the year:
A. 1927 B. 1938
C. 1876 D. 1895

140. What type of information service products are the trend reports?
A. Evaluation type B. Location type
C. Condensation type D. Reference type

141. NASSDOC was established in the year:
A. 1967 B. 1953
C. 1969 D. 1970

142. What is the landmark initiative of UGC in the year 1991 for the development of information services for academic libraries?
A. INFONET Consortium
B. INFLIBNET
C. SOUL
D. National Centre for Scientific Information

143. Who has invented the SWOT analysis?
A. Albert S. Humphrey
B. Peter Drucker
C. Peter Pyhrr
D. Philip Kotler

144. Who is the publisher of Statesman's Yearbook 2017?
A. Adam and Charles Black, London
B. Europa Publications, London
C. Oxford University Press
D. Palgrave Macmillan, UK

145. In Classified Catalogue Code, 'specific added class number entry' in a classified catalogue is defined as:
A. Cross reference index entry
B. Class index entry
C. Cross reference entry
D. Book index entry

146. From which year did AGRIS, a global public domain database, became operational?
A. 1975 B. 1964
C. 1971 D. 1967

147. In Dewey Decimal Classification, the number '028' stands for:
A. General libraries
B. Library operations
C. Libraries for specific subject
D. Reading and use of other information media

148. Who has developed the 'Guidelines on information literacy for lifelong learning'?
A. SCONUL B. RUSA
C. ACRL D. IFLA

149. Which of the following network topologies has the cable strung out, but the end of the cable need not be brought back?
A. Mesh B. Bus
C. Star D. Ring

150. As per the classification prescribed by S.R. Ranganathan, 'a record of phenomenon made directly, unmediated by human mind' can be categorised as:
A. Meta-documents B. Conventional
C. Non-conventional D. Neo-conventional

151. The process of placing one or more isolates on the parent basic subject is called as:
A. Denudation B. Agglomeration
C. Lamination D. Fusion

152. Who suggested 'Seven Lamps of conduct' as ethics of librarianship?
A. William B. Paton B. R.L. Mittal
C. B.M. Headicar D. A.K. Mukherjee

153. Which type of fiscal estimation is the Kothari Commission (1964-66) recommendation that a university should spend each year about ₹ 25 for each student and ₹ 300 per teacher.
A. Method of details
B. Per capita method
C. Formula method
D. Method of proportion

154. Which of the following methods is applicable in educating individual user?
A. Lecture method
B. Self-instructional material
C. Guided tour
D. Tutorial

155. Which of the following is a standard for descriptive cataloguing?
A. Z39.50 B. ISO 2709
C. RDA D. OSI

156. What is a shelf list?
A. Catalogue with entries sorted by call number
B. Book order card
C. Copy of main entry card
D. Catalogue entries of special collection

157. Which of the following extension represents uncompressed output of data?
A. .bmp B. .tiff
C. .gif D. .jpg

158. Which of the following TQM techniques prescribes "80/20" rule?
A. Fish bone diagram
B. Pie charts
C. Pareto analysis charts
D. Histogram

159. Which of the following types of programming language is Java?

A. Object-oriented B. Publishing
C. Algorithmic D. Scripting

160. Which university in Maharashtra was the first to start training in Librarianship?

A. R.T.M. Nagpur University, Nagpur
B. University of Pune, Pune
C. University of Mumbai
D. SNDT Women's University, Mumbai

161. Which of the following is a unit for measuring bandwidth?

A. Bits B. Hertz
C. Bauds D. Amplitude

162. Which of the following is a component automated acquisition module?

A. Authority file
B. Customised member card
C. Member category
D. Inter library loan

163. When the user requires almost all relevant literature on a subject, such approach is called as:

A. Exhaustive approach
B. Catching up approach
C. Everyday approach
D. Current approach

164. When a message is transmitted and received over the same channel at the same time, such mode of transmission in network environment is called as:

A. Simple B. Band width
C. Full duplex D. Half duplex

165. Who is the producer of Library Literature and Information Science?

A. Facet Publication
B. H.W. Wilson
C. OCLC
D. American Library Association

166. What does a small circle of a flow chart represent?

A. Process B. Connector
C. Decision D. Terminal

167. In cataloguing, which law directs that, between two or more possible alternative rules bearing on a particular phenomenon, the one leading to overall economy is to be preferred?

A. Law of symmetry
B. Law of parsimony
C. Law of interpretation
D. Law of impartiality

168. According to Delivery of Books and Newspapers (Public Libraries) Act, 1954, India, what is the time limit to deliver books by the publisher to the designated libraries?

A. 30 days B. 15 days
C. 45 days D. 60 days

169. What type of information sources are the indexing and abstracting periodicals?

A. Ephemeral B. Current event
C. Bibliographical D. Ready reference

170. What is a user profile?

A. List of documents required by the user
B. Biodata of a user
C. List of documents retrieved by the user
D. Characteristics that influence user information habits

171. Which type of scheme is the Universal Decimal Classification?

A. Fully faceted
B. Enumerative
C. Almost faceted
D. Almost enumerative

172. Who is the publisher of Indian Library Science Abstracts?

A. IASLIC B. SIS
C. ILA D. IATLIS

173. Which type of service is "Shodh Gangotri: a repository of Indian research in progress"?

A. Alerting service
B. Referral service
C. Document delivery service
D. Review service

174. According to S.R. Ranganathan, the reference service that deals with residual principles and generalities, not readily falling within specific parts, is called as:

A. General help to general reader
B. Initiation of freshman

C. Ready reference service
D. Long range reference service

175. 'Algebra' can be categorised as which type of subject?
A. Complex subject
B. Primary basic subject
C. Non-primary basic subject
D. Compound subject

176. Which of the following organisations provides 'Directory of Public Libraries'?
A. Raja Rammohan Roy Library Foundation (RRRLF), Kolkata
B. Central Reference Library, Kolkata
C. Indian Public Library Movement, Delhi
D. Delhi Public Library System

177. When Sears List of Subject Headings was first published?
A. 1898 B. 1923
C. 1891 D. 1925

178. In which year was the Encyclopedia Britanica last print version of 32 volumes published?
A. 2008 B. 2010
C. 2012 D. 2009

179. In AACR2, in case of works of shared responsibility, the main entry will be prepared under:
A. First two authors B. Title
C. Subject D. First author

180. Which of the following is a feature of DBMS?
A. BIOS
B. GUI
C. Compatibility with SQL
D. Memory management

181. Which of the following features of OPACs has enhanced their use over traditional catalogues?
A. No need for media qualifiers
B. No need for punctuation between elements in bibliographical description
C. Sorting process is static
D. Search facility is available under any element

182. ODLIS stands for:
A. Online Databank of Library and Information Science
B. Online Dictionary of Library and Information Science
C. Open Documents for Library and Information Science
D. Online Directory of Library and Information Science

183. The General Theory of Classification, developed by S.R. Ranganathan, can be categorised as which of the following types?
A. Advanced classification
B. Descriptive theory of classification
C. Dynamic theory of classification
D. Static theory of classification

184. Which of the following elements of catalogue is concerned with pagination, number of volumes, etc.?
A. Collation B. Series
C. Imprint D. Note

185. In which year was the Committee on National Policy on Library and Information System (CONPOLIS) set up by the Govt. of India?
A. 1972 B. 1991
C. 1985 D. 1992

186. As started by J.K. Khanna, the growth of special libraries in India is directly related to:
A. Industrial development
B. Growth of university education
C. Recommendations of Committees/Commissions
D. Independence of India

187. When an individual ought to have information for his/her work or recreation, then what it is called as?
A. Information demand
B. Information need
C. Information want
D. Information requirement

188. Which of the following can be categorised under the fifth generation of computer?
A. Artificial intelligence
B. Transistors
C. VLSI
D. Vacuum tubes

189. Which of the following is a service that helps one with gaining current awareness knowledge?
A. Extracts
B. Digests
C. Indexes
D. Newspaper clippings

190. File management is a function of:
A. Middleware B. GUI
C. Operating system D. Utility software

191. Which of the following characteristics of knowledge is true?
A. Knowledge is dependent
B. Knowledge is complete
C. Knowledge is finite
D. Knowledge is independent

192. Who has developed the episodic model of information seeking behaviour?
A. T.D. Wilson B. Nicholas J. Belkin
C. Elfreda Chatman D. David Ellis

193. Part 3 of Colon Classification is named as:
A. Schedules of Classification
B. Schedules of Classics and Sacred books
C. Rules
D. Index

194. Who among the following was the first to develop UDC?
A. H.E. Bliss B. E.C. Richardson
C. Paul Otlet D. Melvil Dewey

195. Which of the following states has enacted Public Library Act?
A. Meghalaya
B. Chattisgarh
C. Jammu and Kashmir
D. Delhi

196. What type of database is Library Literature and Information Science?
A. Archival B. Abstracting
C. Full-text D. Indexing

197. 'Point system' is associated with which of the following?
A. Job description B. Job performance
C. Job evaluation D. Job specification

198. What is the type of service that actually takes information to the user, preferably before he/she formulates a demand for it?
A. Information dissemination
B. Information and referral
C. Document retrieval
D. Information retrieval

199. In Maharashtra Public Libraries Act, who is the ex-officio President of State Library Council?
A. Director of Education
B. Minister for Education
C. Secretary for Education
D. Director of Public Libraries of the States

200. The catalogue in which some entries are in the form of number entries and some in the form of text entries is called as:
A. Dictionary catalogue
B. Title catalogue
C. Classified catalogue
D. Author catalogue

ANSWERS

1	2	3	4	5	6	7	8	9	10
B	C	C	B	B	D	D	A	B	B
11	**12**	**13**	**14**	**15**	**16**	**17**	**18**	**19**	**20**
D	D	B	B	D	C	D	D	A	C
21	**22**	**23**	**24**	**25**	**26**	**27**	**28**	**29**	**30**
D	C	D	D	D	D	B	B	C	C
31	**32**	**33**	**34**	**35**	**36**	**37**	**38**	**39**	**40**
A	C	C	A	D	A	D	A	B	B
41	**42**	**43**	**44**	**45**	**46**	**47**	**48**	**49**	**50**
C	D	A	B	C	D	C	A	C	C

51	**52**	**53**	**54**	**55**	**56**	**57**	**58**	**59**	**60**
D	A	A	A	A	D	A	A	A	D
61	**62**	**63**	**64**	**65**	**66**	**67**	**68**	**69**	**70**
B	C	A	C	D	C	D	A	B	D
71	**72**	**73**	**74**	**75**	**76**	**77**	**78**	**79**	**80**
D	D	C	B	C	B	B	D	D	C
81	**82**	**83**	**84**	**85**	**86**	**87**	**88**	**89**	**90**
B	C	D	A	A	B	B	A	A	B
91	**92**	**93**	**94**	**95**	**96**	**97**	**98**	**99**	**100**
B	A	A	C	C	A	A	A	B	A
101	**102**	**103**	**104**	**105**	**106**	**107**	**108**	**109**	**110**
D	A	D	D	D	C	C	A	D	A
111	**112**	**113**	**114**	**115**	**116**	**117**	**118**	**119**	**120**
D	B	C	A	A	B	D	B	A	D
121	**122**	**123**	**124**	**125**	**126**	**127**	**128**	**129**	**130**
D	C	B	C	B	A	C	C	C	C
131	**132**	**133**	**134**	**135**	**136**	**137**	**138**	**139**	**140**
A	A	C	B	D	B	B	A	A	A
141	**142**	**143**	**144**	**145**	**146**	**147**	**148**	**149**	**150**
D	B	A	D	C	A	D	D	B	A
151	**152**	**153**	**154**	**155**	**156**	**157**	**158**	**159**	**160**
C	B	B	B	C	A	A	C	A	C
161	**162**	**163**	**164**	**165**	**166**	**167**	**168**	**169**	**170**
A	A	A	C	B	B	B	A	C	D
171	**172**	**173**	**174**	**175**	**176**	**177**	**178**	**179**	**180**
C	A	A	A	C	A	B	B	B	C
181	**182**	**183**	**184**	**185**	**186**	**187**	**188**	**189**	**190**
D	B	C	A	C	A	B	A	D	C
191	**192**	**193**	**194**	**195**	**196**	**197**	**198**	**199**	**200**
A	B	B	C	B	D	C	A	B	C

EXPLANATORY ANSWERS

71. Cow : Leather :: Llama : Wool

As we get leather from cow similarly, we get wool from Llama.

72.

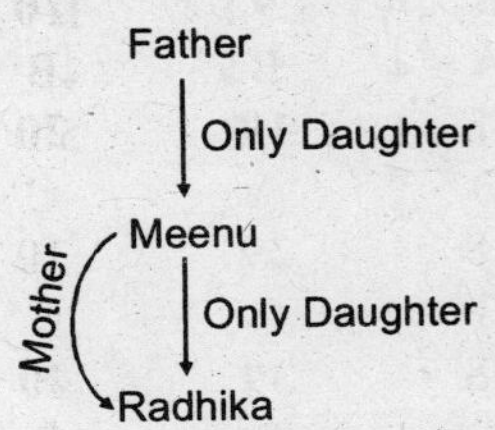

73. $9 \times 6 = 54$

$6 \times 6 = 36$

$12 \times 5 = 60$

$7 \times 6 = 42$

All numbers except 12 are multiplied by 6 to get the other number.

74.

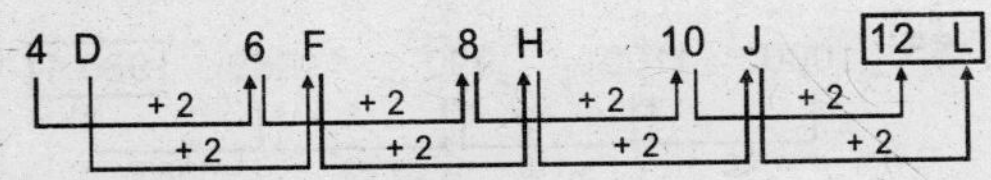

Hence, next term in the series is 12 L.

75. The word NEARNESS cannot form from the given word NECESSARY because N is not two times in the given word.

77. Given

W I N T E R (−1, +1, +1)

V I O U E R

• Similarly,

S P R I N G (−1, +1, +1)

R P S J N G

78. Odd option is (D) school, because all other are used as residences.

79. Harmless is different because all others have the same meaning.

80. 376, 184, 88, 40, 16, [4], −2

(each step ÷ 2 − 4)

Hence, the missing term is 4.

81.

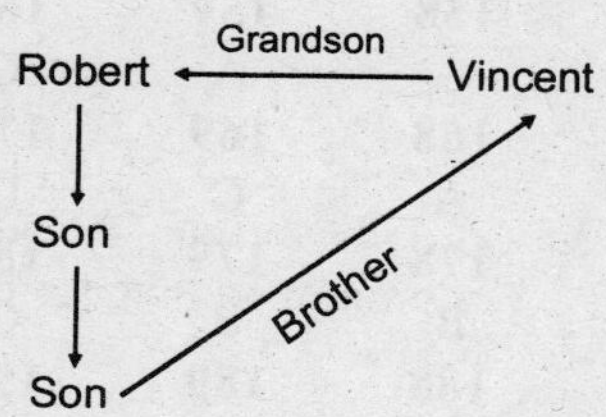

Hence, Vincent is grandson of Robert.

82. An **orchard** is an intentional planting of trees or shrubs that is maintained for food production.

Daisy, Jasmine and Lily are flowers.

Hence, Orchard is different.

83. In the given figures, inner figure is same as outer figure. Hence, option (D) follows the same pattern.

85. 1000, 1100, 990, 1089, [980.1]

(+ 100, − 110, + 99, − 108.9)

Hence, the missing term is 980.1.

87. Except Marx all others are founders of a particular religion.

88. 63 is odd option because all others are prime numbers.

89. Given:

A = ÷

B = ×

C = +

D = −

∴ Value of 18 B 12 A 4 C 5 D 6

$= 18 \times 12 \div 4 + 5 - 6$

$= 18 \times 3 + 5 - 6$

$= 54 + 5 - 6$

$= 59 - 6$

$= 53.$

91. 6, 11, 16, 21, [26], [31], 36, 41

(each step + 5)

Hence, missing terms are 26 and 31 in the given number series.

92. $23 = 8 \Rightarrow 2^3 = 8$

$25 = 32 \Rightarrow 2^5 = 32$

$42 = 16 \Rightarrow 4^2 = 16$

$44 = \mathbf{256} \Rightarrow 4^4 = 256$

96. Given:

M → 2, A → 1, R → 7, T → 9

and

S → 8, L → 5, I → 3, T → 9

Similarly,

T → 7, R → 9, A → 1, I → 3, L → 5

99. 3 : 9 :: 8 : 64

$\because (3)^2 = 9$

$\therefore (8)^2 = 64.$

Previous Paper (Solved)

Kendriya Vidyalaya Sangathan (KVS)—Librarian Recruitment Exam – 2015*

Post Specific Subject-Related Questions

1. In India, Public library developments as a movement was initially started from?
A. Delhi
B. Kolkata
C. Baroda
D. Pune

2. Library grows and grows endlessly' is?
A. First law of library science
B. Fifth law of library science
C. Fourth law of library science
D. Not a law of library science

3. Who is the director of public libraries in India, according to the library legislation of India?
A. Chief Executive at state level
B. Prime minister
C. State governor
D. None of these

4. The number of states in India having library legislation (Presently) is?
A. 11
B. 16
C. 18
D. None of these

5. Indian's first Library Legislation after Independence was enacted in?
A. Bihar
B. Tamil Nadu
C. Maharashtra
D. Punjab

6. In India "Book week" is celebrated in the month of?
A. January
B. November
C. September
D. June

7. In India the Library Science education started at?
A. New Delhi in 1924
B. Baroda in 1911
C. Chennai in 1933
D. None of these

8. American Library Association (ALA) has instituted …….. For promoting love for books and reading?
A. Clarence day Award
B. Carnegie medal
C. Caldcott medal
D. Aurianne medal

9. Open access system of a library is specified in?
A. First law of library science
B. Fifth law of library science
C. Second law of library science
D. Third law of library science

10. Proper organization of reading material and efficient charging system is the implication of?
A. Fourth law of library science
B. Third law of library science
C. Second law of library science
D. None of these

*Held on 06-09-2015.

11. First Indian university that converted the diploma in library science into Bachelor's Degree was?
A. University of Delhi
B. Banaras Hindu University
C. Aligarh Muslim University
D. Panjab University

12. Collection and Provision of Information from Various sources over a period of time is known as?
A. Long range reference service
B. SDI
C. Short range reference service
D. None of these

13. The patents are regarded as?
A. Primary sources
B. Tertiary sources
C. Secondary sources
D. None of these

14. ISSN stands for?
A. Indian Standard Service Number
B. International Standard Serial Number
C. Indian Super Service Number
D. International Super Service Number

15. Which of the following is a technique to train professional staff with in the library?
A. Job Rotation
B. Staff Assessment
C. Conference participations
D. Communicating Job Standards

16. According to Ranganathan the Percentage of total money of the library budget to be spent on the reading materials should be?
A. 10% B. 5%
C. 40% D. 75%

17. The most important aspect of the management is?
A. Performance analysis
B. Budget
C. Cost benefit analysis
D. All these

18. The PPBS technique was developed by?
A. World Bank
B. State Bank of India
C. Rand Corporation
D. RRRLF

19. PERT means?
A. Programme Evaluation Review Technique
B. Programme Evaluation Reverse Technique
C. Post Evaluation Review Technique
D. Postgraduate Evaluation Review Technique

20. The Zero Based Budget was first prepared in?
A. 1947 B. 1950
C. 1970 D. 1965

21. The five step of planning was formulated by?
A. Knoontz and O Donial
B. E. Mayo
C. A. Moslo
D. H. Fayol

22. System analysis of a library is carried out for?
A. Developments of Library routines only
B. Improvement of the functions and services
C. Evaluating the performance
D. All these

23. Thesis is an example of?
A. Micro document
B. Macro document
C. Meta data
D. Conventional document

24. Five Laws of Library Science was first published in?
A. 1925 B. 1930
C. 1931 D. 1933

25. The grant from the UGC for the Academic libraries is called?
A. Regular grant
B. Ad-hoc grant
C. Plan grant
D. Irregular grant

26. The arrangement of main entries in the classified catalogue is?
A. According to the author

B. According to the tile
C. By a classification scheme
D. Alphabetically

27. The indexing periodicals provide us?
A. List of articles
B. List of books
C. Whole bibliographical descriptions of articles
D. List of documents

28. The frequency of Indian National Bibliography (I.N.B.) is?
A. Annually
B. Weekly
C. Monthly
D. Quarterly

29. The number of language books which are covered in Indian National Bibliography (I.N.B.) is?
A. 10 B. 11
C. 14 D. 13

30. The Collection of Maps, Tables and Charts, etc., is called?
A. Globe B. Map
C. Atlas D. Gazetteer

31. Translation of document is?
A. Secondary source
B. Primary source
C. Tertiary source
D. Not a source

32. The sources which are available chiefly in the printed form are called........... sources?
A. Reference
B. Documentary
C. Non-documentary
D. Information

33. In a library scheme of collection, number are devised and maintained by?
A. Reference section
B. Review section
C. Technical section
D. Maintenance section

34. A Database is a collection of?
A. Records in machine readable form
B. Books
C. Journals
D. None of these

35. The e-books means?
A. Book in English
B. Any book available in electronic form
C. Any information available online
D. Any text books

36. In which scheme for classification, the number '999' is free extra-terrestrial subjects?
A.. Colon Classification
B. Dewey Decimal Classification
C. Both A & B
D. None of these

37. A heading which is partly relevant to the subject sought is?
A. Penumbral subject
B. Basic subject
C. Alien subject
D. None of these

38. The catalogue code which provides three level of descriptions is?
A. Classified catalogue code
B. AACR -II
C. Dictionary catalogue code
D. All these

39. Which of the following codes was considered complete codification for subject catalogue?
A. Vatican Code
B. Jewett's Code
C. Ranganathan Code
D. C A Cutter's Code

40. A catalogue of books related to places is?
A. Topographical catalogue
B. Connective catalogue
C. Trade catalogue
D. Serial catalogue

41. A Process of gathering processing representing and storage of information in a database is?
A. Information selectivity

B. Information processing
C. Information retrieval
D. Information representation

42. A sequence of actions which results in obtaining required information is called?
A. Retrieval system
B. Retrieval code
C. Retrieval program
D. Retrieval device

43. The microversion of CDS/ISIS package is written in?
A. C language
B. Fortran language
C. Cobol language
D. Pascal language

44. The vacuum tubes were used in which generation of computers?
A. Second generation
B. Third generation
C. First generation
D. Second and third generation

45. Which of the following type's memory is volatile?
A. ROM B. RAM
C. PROM D. All these

46. The string of 8 bits is called?
A. Byte B. String
C. Character D. Binary

47. Librarians are grouped under which category of library staff according to the? UGC library Committee?
A. Academic
B. Professional
C. Administrative
D. Teaching

48. Surveys of the users are most useful in?
A. Special libraries
B. Public libraries
C. Academic and special libraries
D. University libraries

49. Which of the following is related with library users education?
A. Ranganathan
B. P Knapp
C. M Dewey
D. D M Noris

50. Initiation of the readers means?
A. Orientation
B. Knowledge
C. Beginning
D. Understanding

51. Which Egyptian king called his library "A place of healing for the souls"?
A. Rameses II
B. Seti I
C. Amenmesse
D. Merneptah

52. Open access system was first initiated by?
A. State Lenin Library
B. British Museum
C. Boston Public Library
D. Bibliotheque National

53. How many part are there in 13 digit ISBN number?
A. 07 B. 04
C. 05 D. 02

54. Which of the following service is designated to identify the most suitable documents to a specific user?
A. Internet Link Service
B. Document Delivery Service
C. Selective Dissemination of Information
D. Current Awareness Service

55. Researchers are?
A. Organizers of information
B. Consumers of information
C. Generation of information
D. Both consumers and generators of information

56. Location of Library building is an implication of which Law of Library Science?
A. Fifth B. Third
C. First D. Fourth

57. Author's right to claim ownership of created work is under?
A. Delivery of Books Act
B. Intellectual Property Right
C. Press Act
D. Censorship

58. Indian Science Abstract are published by?
A. ISIC
B. NBT
C. DRTC
D. NISCAIR

59. Raja Ram Mohan Roy Library Foundation (RRRLF) was established to develop?
A. College Libraries
B. Special Libraries
C. University Libraries
D. Public Libraries

60. Universal availability of the publication was launched by?
A. I.F.L.A
B. I.L.A
C. F.I.D
D. I.C.S.U

61. Resources sharing among the libraries was originally known as?
A. Library Distribution
B. Library Cooperation
C. Library Networking
D. Inter Library Loan

62. R.R.L.F is a?
A. Public library
B. Special library
C. Government body for supporting public libraries
D. Trust to support all libraries

63. National policy on library and information system (draft) formulated by?
A. I.L.A
B. R.R.R.L.F
C. IASLIC
D. IATLIS

64. Library Development Plan for India was drafted by?
A. S.R Ranganathan
B. B.S Kesavan
C. P.N Kaula
D. P.B Mangla

65. How many copies of a book should be sent by Publisher under delivery of books Act?
A. 3 Copies
B. 4 Copies
C. 5 Copies
D. 2 Copies

66. The basic information role of a library is to?
A. Collect information in non-print media
B. Collect all information available in print media
C. Collect and dissemination information
D. Give away books to library users

67. Head office of DELNET is located at?
A. Delhi
B. Mumbai
C. Chennai
D. None of these

68. Books for all is variant of?
A. Second law
B. Third law
C. First law
D. None of these

69. A library that is entitled by law to receive a free copy of every book published is?
A. Dormitory library
B. Depository library
C. Deposit library
D. Community library

70. The library which serves all the member of the society without distinction of age sex cast and creed is?
A. Academic library
B. Public library
C. National library
D. Special library

71. The open access to the shelves contributes to the fulfilment of?
A. Third law
B. First law

C. Second law
D. None of these

72. The activity of knowing acquisition organization and use of knowledge is known as?
A. Concept
B. Cognition
C. Perception
D. Appreciation

73. What is the standard size of the catalogue card used in libraries?
A. 12′5 cm
B. 12.5′7.5 cm
C. 5′3 cm
D. 10′8 cm

74. In which state there is no provision of library cess in public library Acts?
A. Tamil Nadu
B. Andhra Pradesh
C. Maharashtra
D. Karnataka

75. Systematic maintenance of the income and expenditure flow on records is called?
A. Funding
B. Marketing
C. Financing
D. Accounting

76. Arrangement of data in predetermined sequence is called?
A. Coding
B. Classifying
C. Processing
D. Sorting

77. In computer terminology and usage 'Bug' stands for?
A. Error in hardware selection
B. Error in software selection
C. Computer virus
D. Programming error

78. The full form of ERNET is?
A. Economic Research Networking
B. Eastern in Region Network
C. Electronic Research Network
D. Education and Research Network

79. MS-Office is?
A. An Operating System
B. A Software
C. The Hardware
D. A Programming language

80. INFLIBNET is proposed to link up mainly?
A. Industrial Libraries
B. Public Libraries
C. R & D Libraries
D. Academic Libraries

81. Which of the following is a multiuser system?
A. DOS
B. UNIX
C. LAN System
D. LAN and UNIX

82. Decimal Fraction Notation was first used by?
A. Richardson
B. Charles Martel
C. Melvil Dewey
D. H P Luhn

83. Canon of modulation falls under?
A. Chain
B. Array
C. Characteristics
D. Success of characteristics

84. A Collection of entities without any special arrangement among them is termed as?
A. Grouping
B. Allocations
C. Aggregate
D. Cluster

85. According to colon classification 'J' is known as?
A. Agriculture
B. Botany
C. Medicine
D. Literature

86. A Scheme for classification that is based on some characteristics of the books, which do

not provide a reliable guidance regarding subject matter is?
A. Artificial classification
B. Form classification
C. Flexible classification
D. Famifying classification

87. In which scheme for classification, provision for arranging both minor and major topic is made by leaving gaps in notation?
A. Library of Congress classification
B. Dewey Decimal Classification
C. Universal classification
D. Colon classification

88. A work which is treated as a subject by itself is?
A. Macro Subject
B. Micro Subject
C. Quasi Subject
D. Spot Subject

89. Detailed classification required for macro documents is known as?
A. Bibliographic Classification
B. Broad Classification
C. Depth Classification
D. Library Classification

90. The suitable reference source to known about the climate of Jaipur (Rajasthan) is?
A. Globe B. Compass
C. Maps D. Gazetteer

91. Which of the following is not a computer programming language?
A. COBOL
B. ASCII
C. BASIC
D. FORTRAN

92. The tracing section helps to identify the?
A. Added entries
B. General subject entry
C. Specific subject entry
D. None of these

93. Catalogue is referred as a?
A. Process B. Tool
C. Method D. Techniques

94. Open journal access system in India is mainly managed by?
A. NIC
B. INFIBNET
C. CSIR
D. ICSSR

95. Information is both product and process statement was given by?
A. J.C. Bradford
B. J. Martin
C. G. Gerbner
D. M. Foucault

96. In MARC 21 subject access field are?
A. 3XX B. 4XX
C. 6XX D. 5XX

97. Digital library function incorporates?
A. Creating and capturing
B. Storage and management
C. Abstracting and reviewing
D. All these

98. Vocabulary in the database is controlled by?
A. Import file
B. Standard files only
C. Authority files only
D. Both standard files and authority file

99. CCF bibliographic record refer to?
A. Data storage
B. Data transfer and standard tags of data indemnification
C. Data storage and formatting of records
D. Formatting of records

100. "Shodhaganga" is repository of?
A. e – journals
B. e – thesis
C. e – books
D. e – resources

*** In addition to these 100 questions, 100 more questions were asked from Hindi, English, Reasoning, Numerical Ability and General Awareness.**

ANSWERS

1	2	3	4	5	6	7	8	9	10
C	B	A	D	B	B	B	C	D	A
11	**12**	**13**	**14**	**15**	**16**	**17**	**18**	**19**	**20**
A	B	A	B	A	C	D	C	A	C
21	**22**	**23**	**24**	**25**	**26**	**27**	**28**	**29**	**30**
D	D	D	C	B	C	C	C	C	C
31	**32**	**33**	**34**	**35**	**36**	**37**	**38**	**39**	**40**
D	B	C	A	B	C	B	D	C	C
41	**42**	**43**	**44**	**45**	**46**	**47**	**48**	**49**	**50**
B	A	D	C	B	A	D	B	B	A
51	**52**	**53**	**54**	**55**	**56**	**57**	**58**	**59**	**60**
C	B	C	C	D	C	B	D	D	A
61	**62**	**63**	**64**	**65**	**66**	**67**	**68**	**69**	**70**
B	C	B	A	B	C	A	A	B	B
71	**72**	**73**	**74**	**75**	**76**	**77**	**78**	**79**	**80**
A	B	B	B	D	C	D	D	B	D
81	**82**	**83**	**84**	**85**	**86**	**87**	**88**	**89**	**90**
C	C	A	D	A	A	B	C	C	D
91	**92**	**93**	**94**	**95**	**96**	**97**	**98**	**99**	**100**
B	A	B	B	B	C	D	D	B	B

Previous Paper (Solved)

Kendriya Vidyalaya Sangathan (KVS)–Librarian Recruitment Exam 2013

PART-1

Directions (Qs. 1 to 3): *Choose the word which best expresses the meaning of the underlined word in the sentence.*

1. He spent his whole life caught up in mundane matters.
A. worldly B. foolish
C. inconsequential D. criminal

2. Smart people are often good at camouflaging their real character.
A. projecting B. displaying
C. hiding D. revealing

3. The old woman lives alone in a dilapidated house.
A. shabby B. decayed
C. ugly D. broken

Directions (Qs. 4 to 6): *Choose the word which is closest to the opposite in meaning of the underlined word in the sentence.*

4. We had a delectable meal yesterday.
A. nice B. tasty
C. heavy D. unsavory

5. Never adopt a callous attitude towards your duties.
A. cooperative B. considerate
C. cautious D. courteous

6. One should not go for a transient solution of a problem.
A. brief B. temporary
C. permanent D. erratic

Directions (Qs. 7 to 9): *Choose the option which best expresses the meaning of the underlined idiom/phrase in the sentence.*

7. Our politicians are often in a Catch-22 situation.
A. absurd B. dangerous
C. hopeful D. depressive

8. One could observe the opposition to the new policy by the rank and file of the government.
A. the majority
B. the special members
C. the official machinery
D. the ordinary members

9. Good politicians are capable of swaying the public opinion with their gift of the gab.
A. flattering words
B. abundance of promises
C. fluency of speech
D. political acumen

Directions (Qs. 10 to 12): *A word has been written in four different ways, out of which only one is correctly spelt. Choose the correctly spelt word.*

10. A. Etiquete B. Ettiquete
C. Etiquette D. Ettiquette

11. A. Diarhoea B. Diarheoa
C. Diarrheoa D. Diarrhoea

12. A. Embarrassment B. Embarassment
C. Embarrasment D. Emberressment

Directions (Qs. 13 to 17): *Each question has a group of sentences marked (1), (2), (3), (4) and (5). Arrange these to form a logical sequence.*

13. 1. According to well known management gurus, these team activities can have unintended consequences for certain employees.
2. I humbly suggest you think again about it.
3. So you believe that office parties are the ultimate team building exercise.
4. Finally, recent research reveals that while social events help homogeneous teams form close bonds, they do not have the same benefits for racially diverse groups of co-workers.
5. Research points out otherwise.

*Held on 14-12-2013.

A. 5 1 4 3 2 B. 3 2 5 1 4
C. 4 1 3 5 2 D. 2 5 1 4 3

14. 1. I have thought about it many times in an objective way.
2. And as a result, I lose my temper often when people goof up or don't deliver.
3. I own a family business with a turnover of over 500 crores.
4. And while my temper has negative results in terms of people getting, I feel it is also a great way to get people to push boundaries.
5. I am very driven and focused on results.
A. 5 1 3 4 2 B. 1 5 4 2 3
C. 3 5 2 1 4 D. 4 3 2 1 5

15. 1. My dream led me to an obsessive interest in design, which slowly opened the door to visual communication.
2. I am so happy that I am now studying design at India's premier institute.
3. Even as a child, I was clear what I wanted to do.
4. However, I was determined that I wanted to join a premier institute or not pursue design at all.
5. I told my parents in class three that I wanted to be an artist.
A. 2 5 1 3 4 B. 1 4 5 3 2
C. 3 5 1 4 2 D. 5 2 1 3 4

16. 1. He will be remembered for many things he did.
2. He was an extremely compassionate and helpful person for all who knew him.
3. One of my mother's uncles died recently.
4. But for me, and many others in our family, he will be remembered for one thing in particular.
5. He had a long and full life, including a distinguished career in the Indian Air Force.
A. 5 3 2 4 1 B. 3 5 1 4 2
C. 2 4 1 3 5 D. 1 4 5 3 2

17. 1. Or you go on a shopping trip with plans to buy certain things but end up buying things you did not need.
2. Thus, there is always a mismatch between our plans and our final outcomes.
3. It has happened to every one of us.
4. And 60 minutes later are left wondering what got into you that you said what you did.
5. you walk into a meeting clear about what you want to say or do.
A. 5 3 2 4 1 B. 2 1 3 5 4
C. 3 5 1 2 4 D. 3 5 4 1 2

Directions (Qs. 18 to 20): *In each question, choose the one word which can be substituted for the given sentence/words.*

18. The school or college in which one has been educated—
A. Alumni B. Alma mater
C. Matinee D. Calvin

19. The period between two reigns—
A. Stasis B. Gap
C. Anachronism D. Interregnum

20. Large scale departure of people—
A. Exodus B. Emigration
C. Migration D. Immigration

निर्देश (प्रश्न 21 एवं 22): *निम्नलिखित विकल्पों में से शुद्ध वर्तनी वाला शब्द छाँटिए—*

21. A. मातृभूमि B. मात्रभूमि
C. मातरभूमि D. मातर्भुमि

22. A. भृष्टाचार B. भ्रषटाचार
C. भ्रष्टाचार D. भ्रष्टचार

निर्देश (प्रश्न 23): *निम्नलिखित वाक्यांश के लिए एक उपयुक्त शब्द चुनिए—*

23. जो व्याकरण का ज्ञाता हो—
A. ज्ञानी B. बुद्धिमान
C. वैयाकरण D. भाषाविद्

निर्देश (प्रश्न 24): *दिए गए शब्द के विभिन्न विकल्पों में से एक शब्द पर्यायवाची (समानार्थक) नहीं है, उसे छाँटिए—*

24. अद्वितीय
A. अपूर्व B. अनुपम
C. श्रेष्ठ D. निरुपम

निर्देश (प्रश्न 25): *दिए गए शब्द का सही विलोम (विपरीतार्थक) चुनिए—*

25. स्वाभाविक
A. कृत्रिम B. कुटिल
C. बनावटी D. नैसर्गिक

निर्देश (प्रश्न 26 एवं 27): *निम्नलिखित में से किस समूह के तीनों शब्द समान लिंग के हैं–*

26. तीनों पुल्लिंग शब्द–
A. रजनी, सरिता, अमरीका
B. बाजरा, डिबिया, नर्मदा
C. भारत, पत्थर, वर्ष
D. अध्यापिका, मास्टर, नागिन

27. तीनों स्त्रीलिंग शब्द–
A. भेड़िया, समाज, छाछ B. अदरक, पनीर, बूँद
C. सुगन्ध, चाबुक, कनस्तर D. घास, पुस्तक, सिगरेट

निर्देश (प्रश्न 28 से 31 तक): *निम्नलिखित शब्दों में आवश्यकतानुसार सन्धि अथवा सन्धि-विच्छेद का विकल्प चुनिए।*

28. विषम
A. विः + सम B. वि + शम
C. वि + सम D. वि + षर्म

29. वयः + वृद्ध
A. वयवृद्ध B. वयःवृद्ध
C. वयोवृद्ध D. वयस्वृद्ध

30. शरत् + चन्द्र
A. शरतेन्द्र B. शरच्चन्द्र
C. शरतचन्द्र D. शरचन्द्र

31. यशोगान
A. यशः + गान B. यश + आगान
C. यश + गान D. यः + शगान

निर्देश (प्रश्न 32 एवं 33): *पदक्रम की दृष्टि से निम्नलिखित विकल्पों में से कौन-सा असंगत है?*

32. A. सौ-पचास B. हीरे-जवाहरात
C. यहाँ-वहाँ D. नाले-नदी

33. A. ऊबड़-खाबड़ B. घास-पात
C. देना-लेना D. भेड़-बकरी

34. निम्नलिखित विकल्पों में से उस विकल्प की पहचान करो जिसमें केवल संज्ञा शब्द हों–
A. हिमालय, कागज, राम B. सुन्दर, शरीफ, ऊँचा
C. चलना, उड़ना, पीना D. आप, मैं, कौन

35. अल्पविराम (,) के सही प्रयोग की दृष्टि से इनमें से कौन-सा विकल्प सही है?
A. महोदय निवेदन है, कि मैं आगे पढ़ना चाहता हूँ
B. महोदय, निवेदन है कि मैं आगे पढ़ना चाहता हूँ
C. महोदय निवेदन है कि मैं, आगे पढ़ना चाहता हूँ
D. महोदय निवेदन है कि मैं आगे, पढ़ना चाहता हूँ

निर्देश (प्रश्न 36 एवं 37): *नीचे दिए गए मुहावरों का सही अर्थ छाँटिए–*

36. चिकनी-चुपड़ी बातें करना–
A. सुन्दर बातें करना B. घी खाकर बातें करना
C. खुशामद करना D. अर्थ स्पष्ट नहीं है

37. आँखों की पुतली होना–
A. बहुत प्यारा होना
B. आँखें पतली होना
C. आँखों से कठपुतली बनाना
D. आँखों में रोग होना

निर्देश (प्रश्न 38 से 40 तक): *निम्नलिखित अनुच्छेदों को ध्यान से पढ़ें और बताएं कि इनमें कितने मुहावरे-लोकोक्ति प्रयुक्त हुए हैं।*

38. "कक्षा में प्रथम आने के कारण मोहन की सारे स्कूल में धाक जम गई। उसने सारे मुहल्ले में अपनी सफलता का ढिंढोरा पीट दिया। उसके माता-पिता का दिल भी बाँसों उछलने लगा। उन्होंने हाथ तंग होने पर भी इस खुशी में एक दावत दी और जी खोलकर खर्च किया। इतने मेहमान आए कि तिल धरने को भी जगह न थी।"
A. छह B. चार
C. तीन D. पाँच

39. "चार पुत्रों की मृत्यु हो जाने के बाद अब रामनाथ ही मेरे अँधेरे घर का उजाला रह गया है। उसे अन्धे की लकड़ी जानकर मैंने उसके पालन-पोषण के लिए आँखों में रातें काटी हैं। उसकी प्रसन्नता के लिए मैंने आसमान के तारे तोड़ने से भी मुँह नहीं मोड़ा। चाँद के टुकड़े-सी बहू से मैंने उसका विवाह किया, लेकिन अब मेरा यही पुत्र सारे समाज में मेरी टोपी उछालता फिरता है।"
A. पाँच B. आठ
C. तीन D. सात

40. "यदि विद्यार्थी पढ़ने में दिन-रात एक कर दें, तो कभी असफल नहीं हो सकते, लेकिन अधिकांश विद्यार्थी टाँगें पसार कर सोते रहते हैं और परीक्षा सिर पर आ जाने पर ही उनकी आँखें खुलती हैं, तब वे कुछ गिने-चुने प्रश्नों को तोते की तरह रट लेते हैं।"

A. तीन B. पाँच
C. सात D. दो

भाग-2

41. The famous 'Lukla airport' situated at the height approximately 2843 meter, also known as 'Tenzing-Hillary airport', in which of the following country this airport is situated?

A. India B. Newzealand
C. Bhutan D. Nepal

42. Malala Yousafzai, a teenager from Pakistan, who addressed the youth assembly in U.N. on her birthday, and she appealed for which of the following services?

A. Free education to all children
B. Security for female labour
C. Free health services for all children
D. Security for girls

43. Which country has closed it's second largest Bank 'Laiki' to save it's Banking system from collapse?

A. Greece B. Turkey
C. Cyprus D. Serbia

44. Who has been selected as Management Director and Chief Executive Officer of National Stock Exchange (NSE) in year 2013?

A. Ravi Narayan
B. Chitra Ramakrishna
C. Naina Lal Kidwai
D. Chanda Kochhar

45. Ministry of Human Resources Development (MHRD) was constituted on September 1985 by .... amendment of 1961 in Charter of India.

A. 170 B. 174
C. 167 D. 163

46. According to the interim census of 2011, which of the following union territories has the highest population?

A. National Capital Region Delhi
B. Daman and Diu
C. Chandigarh
D. Puducherry

47. Who is the author of the book 'Walking with Lions: Tales from Diplomatic Past'

A. Mohammad Hamid Ansari
B. Jaswant Singh
C. K. Natwar Singh
D. Arun Jaitly

48. Which of the following Grand Slam Doubles Competition is won by Leander Paes with Radek Stepanek of Czech Republic in 2013?

A. Australian open B. Wimbledon
C. French open D. American open

49. Which of the following Banks has been fined ₹ 10.5 crore in 2013 for not obeying the KYC norms?

1. Axis Bank 2. HDFC Bank
3. ICICI Bank 4. Yes Bank

A. 1 and 2 B. 2, 3 and 4
C. 1, 2 and 3 D. 1, 3 and 4

50. What is the name of Chinese Table Tennis player, who was famous as "Architect of Ping-Pong Diplomacy" and died in 2013?

A. Xuang Xedong B. Li-ping
C. Li Chong Wei D. Chain-Long

51. An Asteroid (sized 150 feet) that passed at a distance of 27600 km from the earth. What is the name of this Asteroid?

A. 2013 AS15 B. 2012 DA14
C. AS14 2010 D. AT2011 13

52. 'Bihari Puraskar' instituted by K.K. Birla foundation, is given to whom for the year 2012?

A. Sonika Agrawal
B. Hari Ram Meena
C. Praneeta Talukdar
D. G.H. Sankeena

53. On which day the Pie $\left(\frac{22}{7}\right)$ approximation day was celebrated throughout the world in the year 2013?

A. 22 July B. 25 July
C. 5 August D. 9 August

54. In which place the world Swimming competition 2013 was held?

A. Barcelona B. Tokyo
C. London D. Rome

55. In which of the following countries the famous international furniture brand IKEA belongs to?

A. Japan B. U.K.
C. Germany D. Sweden

56. Who is the present Head of National Human Right Commission?

A. M.N. Rao
B. Wajahat Habibullah
C. K.G. Balakrishnan
D. None of the above

57. What is the name of the Indian Advanced Satellite, launched in August 2013 and which is related to the meteorology, discovery and rescue operation services?

A. Insat-3D B. Insat-1B
C. Insat-2A D. Insat-1A

58. What is the difference between male and female literacy rate in India according to the interim census of 2011?

A. 21.59% B. 13.18%
C. 9.10% D. 16.68%

59. Who is the Prime minister of Bhutan?

A. Lyonpo Jigme Y Thinley
B. Shering Tobge
C. Lyonpo Dago Tshering
D. None of the above

60. For Indian Railways the plan expenditure (approx) for the year 2013-2014, in the railway budget of 2013 is—

A. ₹ 43,565 crore B. ₹ 63,363 crore
C. ₹ 75,855 crore D. ₹ 57,320 crore

Directions (Qs. 61 to 64): *Read the given information carefully and answer following questions.*

All the roads of a city either parallel or perpendicular to each other. All the roads are straight. Roads A, B, C, D and E are parallel to each other. Roads C, H, I, J, K, L and M are parallel to each other. Road A is to the east and at a distance of 1 km from the B. Road B is west to the road C and at a distance of $\frac{1}{2}$ km. Road D is west to the road E and at a distance of 1 km. Road G is south to the road H and at a distance of $\frac{1}{2}$ km. Road .... is to the North of road J and 1 km away from each other. Road K is at a distance of 1 km and to the South of road M.

61. If E is between B and C then which of the following statements is false?

A. D is on the west direction of A at a distance of 2 km
B. C is at a distance of less than 1.5 km from the D
C. The sum of distance between E to B and E to C is ½ km.
D. E is at a distance of less than 1 km from A

62. If the road E is between the road B and C, then the distance between A and D is:

A. 1/2 km B. 1 km
C. 1.5 km D. 1.5-2.0 km

63. If K is parallel to I and K is on South direction to the J at a distance of ½ km and is on North direction to the G at a distance of 1 km, then which of the two roads will be ½ km away from each other?

A. I and K B. K and J
C. I and G D. J and G

64. Which of the following statements is necessarily true?

A. E and B crosses each other
B. D is of west direction on the B at a distance of 2 km
C. D is at least 2 km away west direction to A
D. M is on the north direction of L on the 1.5 km away.

Directions (Qs. 65 to 67): *Every question is provided with two statements I and II, there may be a reason and effect relation or may be independent reasons or may be the effects of independent reasons. Read the statements and point your answer as given below:*

A. If statement I is Reason and statement II is it's effect.
B. If statement II is Reason and I is it's effect.
C. If both the statements I and II are effect of independent Reasons.
D. If statement I and II both are effect of several Reasons.

65. Statements

I. University officer has ordered to all his affiliated colleges, to ban all type of phones in the college campus.

II. Maximum teachers of the college have sent their signatured joint petition to complain for the disturbance caused by the ring tone of the cell phones, to the university.

66. Statements

I. In the last examination of class 12th of the government running schools, maximum students have done well.

II. Many teachers of government schools have left their jobs and gone to the public schools.

67. Statements

I. To scatter the illegally gathered people police have taken the help of lathi charge.

II. The mass forum has announced the General strike against the police atrocities.

68. Six students A, B, C, D, E and F are sitting in a field. A and B are from Delhi, while the rests are from Bengaluru D and F are tall while remaining are short in height. A, C and D are girls while remaining are boys. Who is the tall girl from the Bengaluru.

A. F
B. E
C. D
D. C

69. On rearranging the letters of the word 'WONDERFUL' according to the alphabetical order, then the place of how many letters will remain unchanged?

A. Zero
B. One
C. Two
D. Three

70. In a specific code language '123' means 'bright little boy' '145' means 'tall big boy' and '637' means 'beautiful little flower'. In that language, what means for bright?

A. 2
B. 1
C. 4
D. 3

71. Which fraction should be added to $5\frac{3}{4}, 4\frac{4}{5}$ and $7\frac{3}{8}$ to get the result as a whole number?

A. $\frac{1}{40}$
B. $\frac{1}{20}$
C. $\frac{3}{40}$
D. $\frac{1}{10}$

72. On multiplying 11 with a number it will be much greater than 180 as much it was shorter before multiplication. The number is:

A. 25
B. 30
C. 40
D. 45

73. A student has scored 30% marks in physics in the first paper of 180 marks. It is necessary to score minimum 50% marks in two papers for him. Second paper is of 150 marks. In total, which percent marks in second paper he has to obtain to get compulsory average marks.

A. 80%
B. 76%
C. 74%
D. 70%

74. Anna has invested a certain amount in a Bank, which provides simple interest. After two years the amount get increased and became ₹ 2,400. He waited for three years more and finally he got ₹ 3,000, what was the initial amount he had invested earlier?

A. ₹ 2,000
B. ₹ 150
C. ₹ 210
D. ₹ 175

75. Divide ₹ 671 among A, B and C in such manner that, if we increase ₹ 3, ₹ 7 and ₹ 9 respectively in their shares the new amounts should be in ratio of 1 : 2 : 3.

A. ₹ 105, ₹ 223 and ₹ 330
B. ₹ 112, ₹ 223 and ₹ 336
C. ₹ 110, ₹ 220 and ₹ 336
D. None of the above

76. By working 7 hours daily, 30 worker can finish a work in 18 days. How many workers will be required to finish the same work in 30 days if the workers do work 6 hours daily.

A. 15 B. 21
C. 25 D. None of these

77. On increasing denominator by 2 and reducing the nominator by 1 of a rational number it became $\frac{1}{2}$ of the initial. But if the nominator is reduced by 3 and denominator is increased by 5, the rational number became $\frac{1}{4}$ of the initial the number is ....

A. $\frac{7}{8}$ B. $\frac{6}{7}$
C. $\frac{7}{11}$ D. $\frac{5}{10}$

78. Simplify:

$$\sqrt{-\sqrt{3}+\sqrt{3+8\sqrt{7+4\sqrt{3}}}}$$

A. $\sqrt{3}$ B. 5
C. $\sqrt{2}$ D. 2

79. Simplify the following:

$$\frac{0.035\times0.035\times0.035+(0.965)^3}{(0.035)^2-0.035\times0.965+(0.965)^2}$$

A. 5 B. 0.5
C. 1 D. 0.4

80. A number whose sum of fourth and fifth parts is 28 more than third part, the number is:

A. 120 B. 240
C. 220 D. 160

81. Why report cards must be handed over to parents?

A. May be possible that the students would not handed it over to parents guardians
B. Parents/Guardians must have the knowledge of progress of children
C. After that responsibility of teacher is over
D. None of these

82. According to your views, what is the main aim of co-education?

A. To stop the inferiority complex in girls
B. To provide opportunity to boys and girls to know each other
C. To reduce expenses on education
D. To avoid to open the separate schools for girls

83. To promote education of a student which of the following factors is most important?

A. Comprehensive-textbooks
B. Busy schedule of school
C. Concern of parents
D. Motivational environment of study

84. If a student fails to pass an examination continuously for two years, then what will you do?

A. Will tell him to leave the school
B. Will chide him to bring improvement in the grade
C. Will suggest him to search for a job
D. Will try to find out reasons responsible for his failure

85. Which of the following factors is not responsible to keep and develop relish in learning of a student?

A. Ask questions again and again from students
B. Use of means of teaching
C. Telling stories before teaching
D. Developing recreative environment at the time of teaching

86. An easy method to impress the student:

A. Being in touch with principal
B. Making our conduct always better
C. Keeping the students in fear
D. Demonstration of knowledge before students

87. What will the teacher do if the mother, father/guardian does not come to meet him?

A. Will go to meet himself
B. Will punish the student
C. Will write to mother, father/guardians of the student to meet him
D. Will start to ignore him since now

88. Assessment of personality can be done in the best way by using the .... tests.

A. Aptitude B. Projective
C. Survey D. Discoverable

89. Name the educationist who brought forward the idea of five formal stage.

A. J.F. Herbart B. J.J. Rousseau
C. J.A. Comenius D. J.H. Pestalozzi

90. Which of the following factors does not apply to the individualistic system of teaching?

A. Teacher is center of the education
B. Teacher can understand the attitude of student
C. Student gets complete care
D. Student has a chance to work according to his choices

91. What is the main reason to reduce the respect of teachers in our society in present time?

A. Less concern of teachers for the students
B. Indiscipline of students
C. Unnecessary political interruption
D. Teachers' attitude of earning more through tuitions

92. Why should the students with special requirements be taught in unified environment?

A. So that they could feel the sympathy
B. In any way they have to be educated
C. They should learn how to make balance in the common processes of life
D. None of these

93. What is the importance of educational tour for the students?

A. Providing pleasure to students
B. Gain of knowledge from the experience of educational tour
C. To satisfy parents/guardian
D. To reduce the burden of regular classes

94. What is the I.Q. level of a man whose real and mental ages are equal?

A. Zero B. One
C. Hundred D. One Hundred Ten

95. Relation between psychology and education is supposed to be ....

A. Internal
B. Unimportant
C. Non-existence
D. Not much relevant

96. Psycology is a science that is related to ....

A. Behaviour B. Religion
C. Culture D. All of these

97. Motivation/Encouragement is given to get ....

A. Result B. Thinking process
C. Action D. Alienation

98. When the education is given in keeping in mind about attitude; capacity and choices. Then education is called:

A. Goal based teaching
B. Logical teaching
C. Psychological teaching
D. None of these

99. According to the educational scheme of Dalton, which of the following is main?

A. Student B. Teacher
C. Guidance D. None of these

100. The development of .... in the field of education was important work done by F. Fröbel.

A. Latin School
B. Business school
C. Kindergarten
D. Public high school

101. Faculty of INDEST is for ....

A. Social science
B. Humanities
C. Science and technology
D. Art and culture

102. INFLIBNET is an autonomous inter-university centre of ....

A. Science and Technology Department, Govt. of India
B. Cultural Department, Govt. of India
C. National Library Kolkata
D. University Grant Commission (UGC)

103. Whose theory is the *Wall Picture* theory?

A. Face sequence
B. Helping sequence
C. Both A and B
D. None of these

104. Who has got the credit for first library network in India?
A. DELNET B. CALIBNET
C. INFLIBNET D. None of these

105. Which law of library science favours for the open access?
A. First law B. Second law
C. Third law D. Fourth law

106. Which of the following is not a secondary document?
A. Library Herald B. Annual report
C. Atlas D. None of these

107. Who was the chief librarian of independent India?
A. R.K. Dasgupta B. B.S. Kesavan
C. D.R. Kalia D. Y.M. Malay

108. Which of the following states has implemented the public library Act, 2009?
A. Uttar Pradesh B. Rajasthan
C. Arunachal Pradesh D. Haryana

109. .... stages are there of time isolate in the Colon classification.
A. One B. Two
C. Three D. Four

110. In the main class (...........) of the Colon classification, first stage of [P] has been taken from the Geographical part.
A. Fine Arts B. History
C. Law D. All of the above

111. In India, first Ph.D in library science was given by ....
A. Punjab University
B. Delhi University
C. Madras University
D. Kolkata University

112. Which of the following is the permanent record of a library?
A. Library Catalogue
B. Stock register
C. Accession register
D. Shelf list

113. There are .... parts in New Encyclopaedia Britanica.
A. One B. Two
C. Three D. Four

114. What is the edition of British National Bibliography?
A. Weekly B. Monthly
C. Quarterly D. Yearly

115. E-book library software has been developed by ....
A. NIC B. DELNET
C. CALIBNET D. NISCAIR

116. In India N-LIST is developed for the profit of ....
A. Schools B. Colleges
C. Universities D. Industries

117. Information about places and persons is found in ....
A. Encyclopeadia B. Gazetteer
C. Quotations D. Digest

118. Which type of library has the extra source for balance charge income?
A. Academic B. Special
C. Public D. All of above

119. Hypothesis for idea plane, verbal plane, and notational plane was given by ....
A. S.R. Ranganathan B. M.A. Gopinath
C. A Neelameghan D. G. Bhattacharya

120. .... is the part of collection number.
A. Call number B. Book number
C. Class number D. None of these

121. During the British Government the librarian club was established in year .... at ....
A. 1929, Lahore B. 1919, Lucknow
C. 1919, Kolkata D. 1929, New Delhi

122. MALA infozine is a .... of Madras liabrary association
A. Booklet B. Conference work
C. News letter D. Thesis

123. Full name of CILIP is ....
A. Chartered Institute of Library and Information Professionals
B. Chhatrapati institute of library and information professionals
C. Chartered institute of librarians and information professors
D. None of the above

124. Chattopadhyay committee was appointed by ....

A. Raja Ram Mohan Roy Library Foundation
B. Cultural Department, Government of India
C. Indian Library Association
D. National Library, Kolkata

125. After how many years National library mission is reorganized?

A. 3 B. 4
C. 5 D. None of these

126. Library Legislation helps in ....

A. Decorating the Public libraries in better ways
B. Providing better salaries to librarians
C. Saving money of users in purchasing books
D. None of the above

127. Model library bill helps in ....

A. Being familiar with Public libraries in better ways
B. Making amendment in existing library Act
C. Making drafts for library Legislation
D. None of the above

128. Dr. S.R. Ranganathan presented the first library bill in ....

A. All Asia Educational Conference, Banaras
B. All India Library Conference, Kolkata
C. Madras Library Association Conference, Madras
D. Maharashtra Public Library Committee, Mumbai

129. In Independent India first library Legislation was passed in ....

A. Madras state B. Hydrabad state
C. Kolhapur state D. Kolkata state

130. Which of the following Legislation, there is no provision of library cess?

A. Madras public library Act.
B. Andhra Pradesh public library Act.
C. Maharashtra public library Act.
D. None of the above

131. Which of the following states had made necessary the membership of library for the students from class eighth?

A. Arunachal Pradesh B. Uttar Pradesh
C. Chhattisgrah D. None of these

132. Which of the following states department of library is a cell of the education department?

A. Arunachal Pradesh
B. Chhattisgrah
C. Rajasthan
D. Himachal Pradesh

133. To provide .... for the library services is the main work of RRRLF.

A. Helping programme
B. Building facility
C. Human resources
D. None of these

134. Labour Ergonomics is generally known as ......

A. Electrical Engineering
B. Cybernetics
C. Human Factor Engineering
D. Study of economics

135. If the periodic records are kept manually, then these are kept in ....

A. Cardex or line desk
B. Racks
C. Almirahs
D. Lists

136. UNESCO defines a book of .... as 'a compact non-durational publication'.

A. 49 or more pages
B. 100 or more pages
C. 25 or more pages
D. 150 or more pages

137. E-zine is a term used for ....

A. English magazines
B. Engineering magazines
C. Electronic magazines
D. Small magazines and communication letters distributed by any electronic method

138. Newark charging system was started in year ....

A. 1900 B. 1901
C. 1902 D. 1903

139. For the development of employees of a library .... is well defined.

A. Individual and professional development
B. Future

C. Personality development
D. Uninterrupted job

140. Requisite qualities and skills for the staff of a public library is/are ....
A. Ability to communicate with the various members of the society
B. Ability to understand the needs of users
C. Both A and B
D. None of the above

141. Which library works as a 'trustee library' of United Nations Organization?
A. Delhi Public Library
B. Connemara Public Library
C. Kerala State Central Library
D. Karnataka State Central Library

142. National library mission was established in the year ....
A. 2005 B. 2012
C. 2013 D. 2009

143. In how many states of India, Library Bill is applied till July 2013?
A. 12 B. 14
C. 19 D. 9

144. Public library: which of the following description in the guidelines given by Indian Standard Bureau?
A. To provide services to children and backward classes
B. Description for the requirement of place for library
C. Model public library Legislation
D. Public library manifesto

145. To carry out of the library standard is done for the purpose of ....
A. Purchasing of books
B. Preparing the list of magazines
C. Exchange of catalogue record
D. Registration of new members

146. What is the aim of Raja Ram Mohan Roy Library Foundation (RRRLF)?
A. To encourage the partnership of resources
B. To help for the use of technology in libraries
C. To provide financial and other helps for the development of public libraries
D. To improve the status

147. For Public Libraries, it is necessary to fulfill the needs of information about the following:
A. Local Community
B. Business Corporations
C. University Teachers
D. Governmental Organizations

148. The concept of 'Reference Service' was initiated first time by ....
A. S. Parthasarathy B. Melvil Dewey
C. Samuel S. Green D. Justin Vincer

149. The word 'Reference work' was first time published in library magazine in year........... .
A. 1876 B. 1883
C. 1891 D. 1893

150. Library Act is related to the development of ....
A. Public Libraries B. Special Libraries
C. Academic Libraries D. All of these

151. Who is the acting executive head and Ex-officio member secretary of RRRLF?
A. Principal Secretary B. Chairman
C. Director D. Principal

152. Which one of the following is a heritage library?
A. Marwari Library
B. Dayal Singh Public Library
C. Purushottam Das Tandon Library
D. Lalit Kala (Fine art) Library

153. What is the real name of Asiatic Society library at Mumbai?
A. Literary Society
B. Public Library Directorate
C. State Central Library
D. Central Reference Library

154. Mumbai Marathi book Museum was established in which year ....
A. 1893 B. 1895
C. 1898 D. 1891

155. Central library, Baroda is presently a ....
A. State Central Library
B. District Library
C. Public Library
D. Special Library

156. Where is Khuda Baksh Oriental Public Library situated?

A. Rampur B. Lucknow
C. Patna D. Kanpur

157. Maximum public libraries use .... Classification Scheme for the classification of books.

A. Colon B. Dewey Decimal
C. Universal Decimal D. Universal

158. In maximum public libraries service for taking photocopy is a ....

A. Service on cash
B. Free service
C. Financial granted service
D. No service

159. Dictionary and Encyclopaedia are placed at the .... part of library.

A. Rare collection
B. Textbook collection
C. Reference collection
D. None of the above

160. .... service, lies in the area of extension Service.

A. Reference collection
B. Mobile library
C. Related to issue and return of books
D. None of the above

161. .... has made a public library alone in Jaipur without the help of govt. aid and started it. It is popular as Sanmate Pustakalaya.

A. Master Motilalji
B. N.C. Deewanji
C. Motibhai N. Ameen
D. D.R. Kalia

162. Who has said this "as we have tanks and well, we must have libraries in every village".

A. R.K. Das Gupta
B. Chilkamarti Lakshmi Narasimham
C. Wavilal Gopalkrishnaya
D. K.M. Asadullah

163. Who organised library pilgrimage in Andhra Pradesh?

A. Vavilal Gopalakrishnayya
B. Iyyanki Venkata Ramanayya
C. Paturi Nagabhushanam
D. A. Neelameghan

164. 'Delhi Society for promotion of literary and cultural activities' was established in the year ....

A. 1862 B. 1865
C. 1870 D. 1875

165. RRRLF with Nehru Yuva Kendra has initiated to develop ....

A. District youth resource centres (DYRC)
B. Libraries and information centres
C. All village panchayats
D. Village information centres

166. International Serials Data System was established in 1971 by ....

A. FID B. IFLA
C. UNESCO D. UNISIST

167. What is the use of book mark in MS-Word?

A. Easy correction of misspelts
B. To access instantly to a specified document
C. Instant access to the end of document
D. To create a link in document

168. What is the shortcut key for manual break line in M.S. Word document?

A. Ctrl + Enter B. Alt + Enter
C. Shift + Enter D. Space + Enter

169. By which of the following order can you do vertical alignment in a M.S. Word document?

A. File menu to page setup order
B. Format menu to page setup order
C. Format menu to paragraph order
D. Format menu to font order

170. We get how much minimum zoom out percent in MS-Word?

A. 10% B. 15%
C. 25% D. 4%

171. KWIC indexing method is based on which one of the followings?

A. Title B. Citation
C. Abstracts D. Full text

172. In the abbreviated name POSDCORB, CO is stand for what?

A. Cooperation B. Co-ordination
C. Corporation D. Communication

173. Why does accession register prepare in libraries?

A. To register the book

B. To register books and magazines
C. To access the books in the same order as they were received
D. To register every articles brought in library

174. 'Granthalaya Jyoti' is the collection of the articles and speeches given by .... during 1910 to 1966 on library movement.
A. Iyyanki Venkata Ramanayya
B. M.A. Gopinath
C. A Neelameghan
D. Patauri Nagabhushanam

175. 'Saraswati Samrajya Bhavanam' situated at ....
A. Hyderabad B. Chennai
C. Trivandrum D. Vijayawada

176. Which organisation had established CILIP in 2012 in association with library association?
A. Institute of librarianship
B. Institute of documentation
C. Institute of information scientists (IIS)
D. Institute of bibliography

177. When was Indian Library Association established?
A. 1943 B. 1933
C. 1921 D. 1928

178. 'The law of library' or 'Granthalaya Veda' was written by :
A. B.S. Kesavan
B. Iyyanki Venkata Ramanayya
C. S. Parthasarathy
D. Chilakamarti Lakshmi Narasimham

179. Nalanda Database of Indian libraries was developed by ....
A. NISCAIR
B. DRTC
C. ILA
D. National Library Kolkata

180. Recommendations by K.P. Sinha Committee are about .... libraries
A. Special B. Academic
C. Public D. Governmental

181. New name of Association for Information Management is ....
A. ALA B. LA
C. ASLIB D. IASLIC

182. .... is an example of U.D.C.
A. Calculative Scheme
B. Penalised Scheme
C. Sever Penalised Scheme
D. Open Penalised Scheme of Classification

183. Canon of book number in Colon classification consists of .... Elements.
A. Four B. Six
C. Eight D. Ten

184. How many tables are there in the latest edition of D.D.C.?
A. Four B. Five
C. Six D. Seven

185. .... blocks are there in isolate space of Colon classification.
A. Two B. Three
C. Four D. Five

186. According to the sixth edition of Colon classification, the number of tables in classification of books is ....
A. Three B. Five
C. Seven D. Nine

187. The book 'Prolegomena to Classification' was brought out by S.R. Ranganathan in year ....
A. 1928 B. 1937
C. 1950 D. 1960

188. A call number of any document includes ......
A. Accession number
B. Class number
C. Class number, book number and serial number
D. None of these

189. Anglo-American (AA) code was published in the year ....
A. 1876 B. 1908
C. 1949 D. 1961

190. IATLIS is a body of ....
A. Librarians
B. Teachers of Library Science
C. Authors and Publishers
D. Both A and B

191. Work finished in AACR are recorded below ....
A. Editor B. Publication
C. Title of document D. All of the above

192. Library of Congress C.I.P. data is found on the ....
A. Title page of document
B. On the back of title page
C. Back cover of the book
D. The cover of Jacket book

193. According to C.C.C. number of section in main entry is:
A. Four B. Five
C. Six D. Seven

194. In medical libraries prefer to use of .... for subject headings.
A. Sears list of subject headings
B. MeSH
C. LCSH
D. Tough process

195. In India ISSN is distributed by ....
A. CSIR B. NISCAIR
C. ISI D. DRTC

196. Broad System of Ordering (BSO) is a ....
A. Ordering System
B. Classification Scheme
C. Catalogue Code
D. Mean of Management

197. Dr. S.R. Ranganathan has given the details of works completed of any library, in ....
A. Five laws of library science
B. Colon classification
C. Classified catalogue code
D. Library administration

198. The name of advance software for library management developed by INFLIBNET is ....
A. CDS/ISIS B. NETTLIB
C. SOUL D. PMB

199. AGRINDEX is the publication of ....
A. UNO B. ILO
C. ICAR D. FAO

200. In software SOUL, there are .... modules.
A. Four B. Five
C. Six D. Seven

ANSWERS

1	2	3	4	5	6	7	8	9	10
A	C	B	D	D	C	A	D	C	C
11	**12**	**13**	**14**	**15**	**16**	**17**	**18**	**19**	**20**
D	A	B	C	C	B	D	B	D	A
21	**22**	**23**	**24**	**25**	**26**	**27**	**28**	**29**	**30**
A	C	C	C	A	C	D	A	C	B
31	**32**	**33**	**34**	**35**	**36**	**37**	**38**	**39**	**40**
A	D	C	A	B	C	A	A	D	B
41	**42**	**43**	**44**	**45**	**46**	**47**	**48**	**49**	**50**
D	A	C	B	B	A	C	D	C	A
51	**52**	**53**	**54**	**55**	**56**	**57**	**58**	**59**	**60**
B	B	A	A	D	C	A	D	B	B
61	**62**	**63**	**64**	**65**	**66**	**67**	**68**	**69**	**70**
A	A	C	B	A	C	B	C	B	A
71	**72**	**73**	**74**	**75**	**76**	**77**	**78**	**79**	**80**
C	B	C	A	B	B	B	D	C	B
81	**82**	**83**	**84**	**85**	**86**	**87**	**88**	**89**	**90**
B	A	D	D	C	B	C	A	A	A
91	**92**	**93**	**94**	**95**	**96**	**97**	**98**	**99**	**100**
D	C	B	C	A	A	C	C	A	C
101	**102**	**103**	**104**	**105**	**106**	**107**	**108**	**109**	**110**
C	D	A	A	C	A	B	C	B	D

111	112	113	114	115	116	117	118	119	120
B	C	C	A	A	B	D	A	A	A
121	**122**	**123**	**124**	**125**	**126**	**127**	**128**	**129**	**130**
C	C	A	B	A	A	C	B	A	C
131	**132**	**133**	**134**	**135**	**136**	**137**	**138**	**139**	**140**
C	A	A	C	A	A	C	A	A	C
141	**142**	**143**	**144**	**145**	**146**	**147**	**148**	**149**	**150**
A	B	C	B	C	C	A	C	C	A
151	**152**	**153**	**154**	**155**	**156**	**157**	**158**	**159**	**160**
C	D	A	C	A	C	B	C	C	B
161	**162**	**163**	**164**	**165**	**166**	**167**	**168**	**169**	**170**
A	D	B	D	A	C	B	C	A	A
171	**172**	**173**	**174**	**175**	**176**	**177**	**178**	**179**	**180**
D	B	C	A	D	C	B	B	C	C
181	**182**	**183**	**184**	**185**	**186**	**187**	**188**	**189**	**190**
C	C	C	C	A	B	B	B	B	B
191	**192**	**193**	**194**	**195**	**196**	**197**	**198**	**199**	**200**
C	B	C	B	B	B	D	C	D	C

SOME SELECTED EXPLANATORY ANSWERS

68.

	Boys		**Girls**	
	Tall	***Short***	***Tall***	***Short***
Delhi	–	B	–	A
Bangluru	F	E	D	C

Hence, tallest girl is D from Bangluru

69. Given words : W O N D E R F U L

Arrangement in alphabetical series : D E F L N O R U W

Hence, place of 'U' will only unchange.

70.

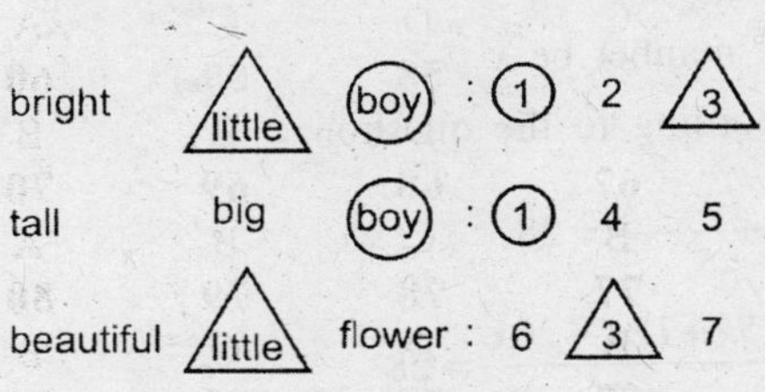

Hence, Code of 'bright' is 2.

72. Let the number be x

According to the question,

$$11x - 180 = 180 - x$$

$$11x + x = 180 + 180$$

$$12x = 360$$

$$x = 30$$

Hence, required number = 30.

73. Marks obtained in first question paper

$$= 180 \times \frac{30}{100} = 54$$

Average of total marks of two papers

$$= \frac{180+150}{2} = 165$$

Required marks obtained in second paper $= 165 - 54 = 111$

Required percentage marks in second paper

$$= \frac{111}{150} \times 100 = 74\%$$

74. Let, Anna deposited ₹ x at the interest rate of $r\%$ per annum

According to the question,

$$2400 = x + \frac{x \cdot r \times 2}{100} \qquad ...(i)$$

and $3000 = x + \frac{x.r.5}{100}$ ...(ii)

From equations (i) and (ii)

$$\frac{5x.r}{100} - \frac{x.r}{100} = 3000 - 2400$$

$$\frac{3x.r}{100} = 600$$

$$x.r = 20000$$

Putting the value of $x.r = 20000$ in (i) then we get

$$2400 = x + \frac{20000 \times 2}{100}$$

$$x = 2400 - 400 = ₹\ 2000$$

75. $3 + 7 + 9 = 19$

When total amount is $= 671 + 19 = 690$

then, A : B : C = 1 : 2 : 3

$$A = 690 \times \frac{1}{6} = 115$$

$$B = 690 \times \frac{2}{6} = 230$$

$$C = 690 \times \frac{3}{6} = 345$$

∴ Actual amount of A = 115 − 3 = ₹ 112

Actual amount of B = 230 − 7 = ₹ 223

Actual amount of C = 345 − 9 = ₹ 336

77. Let the fraction be $\frac{x}{y}$

According to the question,

$$\frac{x-2}{y+1} = \frac{1}{2} \Rightarrow 2(x-2) = y + 1$$

$$2x - y = 5 \quad ...(i)$$

Again $\frac{x-3}{y+5} = \frac{1}{4}$

$$4(x-3) = y + 5$$

$$4x - y = 17 \quad ...(ii)$$

From equations (i) and (ii),

$$4x - 2x = 17 - 5$$

$$2x = 12$$

$$x = 6$$

When $x = 6$, then

$$4 \times 6 - y = 17$$

$$24 - y = 17$$

$$y = 24 - 17 = 7$$

Hence, fraction $\frac{x}{y} = \frac{6}{7}$

78. $\sqrt{-\sqrt{3} + \sqrt{3 + 8\sqrt{7 + 4\sqrt{3}}}}$

$$= \sqrt{-\sqrt{3} + \sqrt{3 + 8\sqrt{(2+\sqrt{3})^2}}}$$

$$= \sqrt{-\sqrt{3} + \sqrt{3 + 8(2+\sqrt{3})}}$$

$$= \sqrt{-\sqrt{3} + \sqrt{16 + 8\sqrt{3}}}$$

$$= \sqrt{-\sqrt{3} + \sqrt{(4+\sqrt{3})^2}}$$

$$= \sqrt{-\sqrt{3} + 4 + \sqrt{3}}$$

$$= \sqrt{4} = 2$$

79. From formulae, $a^3 + b^3 = (a + b)(a^2 - ab + b^2)$

Here $a = 0.035$, $b = 0.965$

$$\therefore (0.035)^3 + (0.965)^3$$

$$= (0.035 + 0.965)\{(0.35)^2 - 0.035 \times 0.965 + (0.965)^2\}$$

$$\frac{(0.035)^2 + (0.965)^3}{\{(0.035)^2 - 0.035 \times 0.965 + (0.965)^2\}}$$

$$= 0.035 + 0.965$$

$$= 1$$

80. Let, number be x

According to the question,

$$= \frac{x}{4} + \frac{x}{5} - \frac{x}{3} = 28$$

$$= \frac{15x + 12x - 20x}{60} = 28$$

$$= \frac{7x}{60} = 28$$

$$x = \frac{28 \times 60}{7} = 240.$$

ENGLISH LANGUAGE

1. Comprehension Passages

ENGLISH LANGUAGE COMPREHENSION

The objective of language comprehension test is to ascertain the ability of the candidates to understand the passage properly. Therefore candidates are required to take notice of the following points:

1. Read the full passage very attentively and intelligently.
2. Try to comprehend the gist of it.
3. Make a mental note of all the important details and points given in the passage.
4. Read the passage for the second time in case you have not been able to understand it satisfactorily.
5. Divide the time proportionately for all the passages.
6. Answer the questions on the basis of facts, as given in the paragraph.
7. Don't waste much time in answering the questions of any one passage.
8. Check all the answers once again, very carefully, to see whether any question is left unanswered by mistake.

MODEL QUESTIONS (FOR PRACTICE)

Directions: *Each of the following passages is followed by five questions. Read the passage carefully and then answer the questions that follow each. For each question, four probable answers A, B, C and D are given. Only one out of these is correct. Choose the correct answer.*

PASSAGE-1

The use of words like 'welcome', 'thank you', 'please', etc., at the right moment reflects a polite nature. The civic sense also lies within the scope of good manners. We should not shout or talk loudly in public places like hospitals and libraries and create disturbance. We should not cheat people or make fun of them. Cleanliness is also necessary. We must not throw the waste on roads and make use of dustbins. We should not harm the public property as it belongs to all of us. While in a queue, discipline should be maintained. We must give fair chance to others.

1. Expressions like 'welcome' 'thank you' and 'please' reflect
   A. happiness B. discipline
   C. civic sense D. polite nature
2. While in a library, we should
   A. respect others B. avoid arguments
   C. talk in low tone D. be courteous
3. A public property belongs to
   A. nobody
   B. all of us
   C. government
   D. one who maintains it

4. Discipline is
   A. the rule of proper conduct or action
   B. the rule of road sense
   C. making use of dustbins
   D. forming a queue
5. The most appropriate title for this passage would be
   A. Polite Nature
   B. Courtesy
   C. Good Manners
   D. Civic Sense

PASSAGE-2

There is an old proverb 'Early to bed and early to rise makes a man healthy and wise.' I am in the habit of getting up early in the morning and have formed the habit of taking long morning walks in the past two years. It is a light exercise and best for physical fitness. The morning air which is fresh and pure is beneficial for the lungs. The early rays of the rising sun are good for healthy skin. 'Health is wealth' and doctors also recommend morning walk to their patients for gaining sound health and freshness of energy.

1. What is good for lungs?
   A. Sunrays B. Fresh air
   C. Sound sleep D. Light exercise
2. What is a light exercise?
   A. Early to bed
   B. Early to rise
   C. Morning walk
   D. Gaining sound health
3. What is good for skin?
   A. Fresh air
   B. Morning air
   C. Morning walk
   D. Rising sun's rays
4. What is best for physical fitness?
   A. Light exercise
   B. Long morning walk
   C. Early to rise
   D. Fresh and pure air
5. Long morning walk
   A. bring sound sleep
   B. ensures physical fitness
   C. ensures healthy skin
   D. keeps healthy, wealthy and wise

PASSAGE-3

Mahatma Gandhi lived a splendid long life and has set great moral standards before us. He showed to the world the true way to peace. He wished to see India prosper but he became a martyr for the noble cause of Hindu-Muslim unity at the time of partition when a religious fanatic, Nathuram Godse, shot him dead on January 30, 1948. His last words were 'Hey Ram'. He lived and died for his country and countryman.

1. Mahatma Gandhi showed the world the true way to
   A. prosperity B. love
   C. truth D. peace
2. Mahatma Gandhi became a martyr for the noble cause of
   A. truth
   B. non-violence
   C. freedom of India
   D. Hindu-Muslim unity
3. Mahatma Gandhi was shot dead
   A. before India achieved independence
   B. by a mad man
   C. by an intolerant religious person
   D. by a non-religious person
4. Mahatma Gandhi set great moral standards. It means
   A. he was a great religious teacher
   B. he was a great moralist
   C. he made India morally stronger
   D. moral was everything to him
5. Gandhiji lived and died for his country and countryman. It means
   A. he was born in India and died in India
   B. he was a patriot
   C. he was a great moralist
   D. he sacrified his life for India and her people

PASSAGE-4

On one hot day a crow felt very thirsty. He flew from one place to another in search of water. After long hours of labour he found a pitcher. Eagerly, he perched on the mouth of the pitcher. He found that the water was at the bottom of the vessel. He tried his best to dip his beak but did not succeed. He did not know what to do. Suddenly some pebbles lying nearby gave him an idea. One by one he dropped the pebbles with his beak into the pitcher. The level of water slowly came up to the mouth of the pitcher. The crow then drank the water and quenched his thirst.

1. The crow found a pitcher
   A. as it flew
   B. after many hours of labour
   C. full of water
   D. which was empty
2. What is the moral of the passage?
   A. No pains, no gains
   B. God helps those who help themselves
   C. Necessity is the mother of invention
   D. Try and try again, you will succeed at last
3. The crow flew from place to place
   A. in search of pitcher
   B. in search of pebbles
   C. in search of water
   D. in search of a vessel
4. The pitcher, the crow found
   A. was full of water
   B. was dry
   C. had little water in the bottom
   D. had water up to its mouth
5. As the crow dropped pebbles into the pitcher, what happend?
   A. The pitcher broke down
   B. The water leaked one of the pitcher
   C. The level of water into the pitcher rose up slowly
   D. Water level immediately rose to the mouth of the pitcher

PASSAGE-5

Once upon a time a crane and a fox lived in a forest. They were good friend. One day the fox invited the crane to a feast. He made a tasty food and served it before the crane on a plate. The crane could not eat anything because of the long beak. But the fox licked all his food. The crane felt insulted. He decided to teach the fox a lesson. Next day he invited the fox. He prepared the same tasty food and placed it in front of the fox inside a narrow glass. The crane ate easily while the fox looked on. Now, it was the fox's turn to remain hungry.

1. What is the moral of the passage?
   A. Beware of the wicked
   B. One good turn deserves another
   C. Be contented with what you have
   D. Tit for tat
2. The crane could not eat tasty food because the
   A. food was served in a shallow plate
   B. food was very hot
   C. food was served in a long jar
   D. crane was not hungry
3. The fox had to remain hungry because
   A. the food served was not enough in quantity
   B. the food was served inside a narrow glass
   C. the food served was not tasty
   D. the food was all liquid
4. Why did the crane feel insulted?
   A. Because he was invited to feast but he could not eat anything
   B. Because the food was served in a shallow plate and he could not eat
   C. Because the food was too hot
   D. Because the fox gulped all the food quickly
5. The crane successfully taught a lesson to the fox when he invited the fox to a feast and served the food
   A. in a narrow glass
   B. in a large plate
   C. in a broken plate
   D. in a long jar

PASSAGE-6

The family set down at the table and began to talk about the summer holidays. They had to decide a place to visit during the vacation. Should they go to their village or to a hill station? The parents preferred the village while the children wished to go the hill station. After few moments of discussion the elders decided to visit both the places. First they shall go to the village for a week and then stay at the hill station for the remaining days. For the first time the family shall be together during the holidays. The children were happy with the holiday plan.

1. The purpose for which the family set down at the table was
A. to decide a place to visit during the vacation
B. to educate the children how to carry articles during a visit to a hill station
C. to decide the date when they should start their journey
D. to tell the children that they will visit a hill station during this vacation

2. The final plan was to visit
A. their village
B. a hill station
C. their village as well as a hill station
D. their home town

3. The final decision was made by
A. the boys B. the girls
C. the women D. the elders

4. They decided first to go to their village and stay there for
A. a day B. a week
C. ten days D. a fortnight

5. Why were children happy?
A. Because a hill station was included in their holiday plan
B. Because a visit to their village was excluded from their holiday plan
C. Because their choice prevailed
D. Because they were going all alone to the hill station

PASSAGE-7

Once Govind intended to go on pilgrimage with his family. He asked Mirind to accompany. But for his trade's reason, he did not go with him. So Govind thought it safe to leave the box of his jewellery with him, as it was dangerous to leave it in a lone house or take it on the journey. So he went to him with the box. He took him to a lonely place under a tree and handed it over to him. He told Mirind, "Keep it safe with you. I shall return from the journey after six month then I shall take it back from you." Mirind said, "Don't worry, I shall keep it as safe as own."

1. Govind intended to go
A. for a business trip
B. to a hill station
C. on a long journey to a sacred place
D. to his home town for a long period

2. Why did Govind leave his box of jewellery with Mirind?
A. Because it was not safe to take the box with him on a long journey
B. Because Mirind was his fast friend
C. Because the box was very heavy
D. Because his house was unsafe

3. Why did Govind take Mirind to a lonely place?
A. To tell him that the box contained valuable jewellery
B. So that no third person could see box
C. To show him what was within the box
D. To tell him that the box will remain with him

4. Where did Govind hand over the box of jewellery to Mirind?
A. At Mirind's house
B. At his own house
C. In a lonely place
D. In a lonely place under a tree

5. It was not safe to leave the box in a lone house. Here the word 'lone house' means
A. a house in a deserted place
B. a house where none lives
C. a house without door and lock
D. a house near the forest

PASSAGE-8

Zahir-ud-din Babar was the first Mughal emperor of India. A descendent of Timur on father's side and Changez Khan on his mother's side, Babar was a brave warrior. After defeating Ibrahim Lodhi in the First Battle of Panipat in 1526 he entered Delhi and soon gained control over Agra. After many more battles with Rajputs he extended his empire over Punjab, Uttar Pradesh and north Bihar. He died at a young age of 48 years in 1530 at his capital Agra without getting much time to consolidate his victories.

1. Zahir-ud-din Babar was the first
   A. Muslim ruler of India
   B. Mughal ruler of India
   C. Afghan ruler of India
   D. Turk ruler of India
2. Babar was born in the years
   A. 1480 B. 1482
   C. 1492 D. 1962
3. Babar first occupied
   A. Punjab B. Agra
   C. Delhi D. Panipat
4. Babar was a brave warrior. Here brave warrior means
   A. courageous soldier
   B. a kind hearted soldier
   C. a clever fighter
   D. a victorious general
5. Babar extended his empire over Punjab and Uttar Pradesh after many more battles with the
   A. Afghans B. Rajputs
   C. Mughals D. Lodhies

PASSAGE-9

Our National Flag is tricolour. It has three equal horizontal strips. The strip at the top is saffron, in the middle is white and at the bottom is green. The ratio of width to length of the flag is 2 : 3. In the centre of the white strip is a wheel in navy blue. The wheel represents the *chakra.* Its design is similar to the wheel which appears on the abacus of the Sarnath Lion Capital of Ashoka. Its diameter approximates to the width of the white strip. The wheel has 24 spokes. It was adopted by Constituent Assembly on July 22, 1947. We love our national flag. We respect it. We are ready to sacrifice our life to protect its honour. It represents the nation. So it is a symbol of national honour.

1. In our national flag the wheel is located in the centre of
   A. saffron strip B. white strip
   C. green strip D. blue strip
2. In our national flag which of the strips is at the bottom in our national flag
   A. blue C. saffron
   B. white D. green
3. Why do we love our national flag?
   A. Because it is tricolour
   B. Because it has three strips
   C. Because it has a wheel at the centre
   D. Because it is a symbol of national honour
4. Our national flag was approved by
   A. President
   B. Lok Sabha
   C. Parliament
   D. Constituent Assembly
5. The diameter approximates to the width of the white strip. Here the word 'approximates' means
   A. is more or less equal
   B. is exactly equal
   C. is not equal
   D. is related

PASSAGE-10

Distance in large cities are long. All the people do not have their own means of transport. They have to depend upon the state or private buses. The number of bus users is very large. Every bus stop is, therefore, crowded. The number of buses is not adequate. Thus people suffer the torture of long wait at the bus stop. Some bus stops are quite orderly. People form queues and get into the buses turn by turn. However, often this order is forgotten and confusion spreads when the bus comes and the law of jungle prevails.

1. Why are the bus stops crowded?
   A. Because they are small is size
   B. Because the number of passengers is very large
   C. Because they are situated at some busy centre
   D. Because people do not form queues
2. Long wait at the bus stop is the result of
   A. over-crowding in the buses
   B. late running of buses
   C. shortage of buses
   D. slow speed of buses
3. Some bus stops are quite orderly where
   A. there is no crowd
   B. the number of buses is adequate

C. people do not have to wait for long
D. people form queues and enter the buses one by one

4. Most of the people who travel by buses are
A. non-working
B. do not have their own vehicles
C. have to go a long distance
D. live in large cities

5. What happens when people do not have their own transport?
A. They have to wait for a bus at a bus stop
B. They have to depend upon the state or private buses
C. They have to travel long distances
D. They form queues and get into buses one by one

PASSAGE-11

A certain king once fell ill and doctors said that only a sudden fright would restore his health but the king was not a man for anyone to play tricks on, except his fool. One day, when the fool was with him in his boat he cleverly pushed the king into water but he was rescued and put to bed. The fright, the bath and bed cured the diseased king, but he was so angry with the fool that he turned him out of the country.

1. What did the doctor say about the king?
A. Only a sudden fright would restore the king's health
B. Only fool would cure the king
C. Only a boat trick could cure the king
D. The king had suffered a sudden fright

2. He cleverly pushed the king into water but *he* was rescued and put to bed. In this sentence *he* refers to
A. the king B. the fool
C. the doctor D. the river

3. When the fool pushed the king into water they were
A. in the palace B. in the bed
C. in the garden D. in a boat

4. Who played the trick on the king?
A. The doctor B. The boatman
C. The fool D. The fright

5. The fool who cured the king was
A. rewarded
B. thrown into water
C. turned out of the country
D. put into jail

ANSWERS

	1	2	3	4	5
Passage 1.	D	C	B	A	C
Passage 2.	B	C	D	B	B
Passage 3.	D	D	C	B	D
Passage 4.	B	C	C	C	C
Passage 5.	D	A	B	B	A
Passage 6.	A	C	D	B	A
Passage 7.	C	A	B	D	B
Passage 8.	B	B	C	A	B
Passage 9.	B	D	D	D	A
Passage 10.	B	C	D	B	B
Passage 11.	A	A	D	C	C

2. English Grammar

PARTS OF SPEECH

Part of speech	Definition or Function	Examples
Noun	Name of a person, place, animal, quality or thing	Ram, boy, dog pen, sun, Delhi, truth, honesty
Pronoun	Used in place of a noun	I, you, he she, they
Articles & Determiners	Points out indefinite and definite nouns	a, an, the, few, some
Adjective	Describes a noun or pronoun	big, honest, wooden valuable, quiet, deep, soft, narrow
Adverb	Describes a verb, an adjective or another adverb	silently, widely, softly, quietly, very, carefully
Verb	Tells about action or state of something or someone	is, am, was, have, do, like, walk, work, make, throw, tell
Conjuction	Joins words, clauses or sentences	and, but, when, yet, while, else
Preposition	Links a noun or pronoun to another word	at, to, after, on for, under, over, with
Interjection	Expresses sudden feelings or emotions	Ah!, Alas!, oh!, ouch!, hi!, well!, Hurrah!

NOUNS

A word which denotes a person, a thing, an animal or a place is said to be a noun.

There are two noun numbers in English — the *Singular* and the *Plural*.

Singular Numbers : A noun that denotes one person or one thing, is said to be in the Singular number. For example — book, pencil, bird, dog, hen etc. are in singular number.

Plural Number : A noun that denotes more than one person or one thing is said to be in plural number. For example — boys, pens, lions, girls, men etc. are in plural number.

REMEMBER

Singular	*Plural*
Cat	Cats
Book	Books
Pen	Pens
Room	Rooms
Tree	Trees
Bus	Buses
Bush	Bushes
Box	Boxes
Glass	Glasses
Dish	Dishes
Judge	Judges
Tax	Taxes
Watch	Watches
Calf	Calves
Thief	Thieves
Knife	Knives

Singular	*Plural*
Scarf	Scarves
Wife	Wives
Leaf	Leaves
Wolf	Wolves
Half	Halves
Monarch	Monarchs
Roof	Roofs
Hoof	Hoofs
Gulf	Gulfs
Staff	Staffs
Radio	Radios
Bamboo	Bamboos
Folio	Folios
Hero	Heroes
Volcano	Volcanoes
Mango	Mangoes
Potato	Potatoes
Photo	Photos
Piano	Pianos
Baby	Babies
Fly	Flies
Country	Countries
Lady	Ladies
Boy	Boys
Monkey	Monkeys
Ox	Oxen
Child	Children
Man	Men
Woman	Women
Tooth	Teeth
Axis	Axes
Basis	Bases
Foot	Feet
Goose	Geese
Englishman	Englishmen
Radius	Radii
Vertex	Vertices
Stimulus	Stimuli

1. Note the plurals of the following nouns:

Singular	*Plural*	*Singular*	*Plural*
copy	copies	cry	cries
baby	babies	duty	duties
body	bodies	country	countries
family	families	diary	diaries
fly	flies	fairy	fairies
city	cities	spy	spies
army	armies	storey	storeys
bay	bays	monkey	monkeys

2. The following nouns do not undergo any change in plural form, in general.

Singular	*Plural*	*Singular*	*Plural*
deer	deer	sheep	sheep
thousand	thousand	pair	pair
hundred	hundred	score	score
dozen	dozen	gross	gross

Note: We can write—

(*a*) thousands of men; (*b*) two pairs of shoes; (*c*) dozens of mangoes; (*d*) scores of people etc.

But—

(*a*) two thousand rupees; (*b*) three hundred men; (*c*) five dozen eggs, etc.

3. The following nouns are usually used in plural forms. They take a plural verb after them—

eatables	fetters	surroundings
riches	alms	spectacles
trousers	pants	scissors
premises	thanks	annals
congratulations	goods	shorts
tongs	pains	arms
breeches	(for troubles)	

4. The following are the nouns which are plural in appearance but are usually used in singular number. They are followed by a singular verb—

news	politics	physics
mathematics	economics	ethics
politics	classics	gallows
statistics	athletics	innings
mechanics	summons	mumps

5. Collective nouns often used as plurals—

public	police	cattle
audience	clergy	folk
people	poultry	nation
elite	gentry	glitterati

6. The nouns that are usually used in singular forms—

advice	hair	rice
fuel	alphabet	machinery
offspring	issue	furniture
mischief	stationery	luggage
bedding	information	abuse

7. Material nouns are always used in singular number—

gold copper milk
water silk wool

Note: They may be used in plural with a different meaning.

copper coins (coppers), chains or fetters (irons), cans made of tin (tins).

GENDERS

The difference in sex is denoted by Gender in grammar. The various genders are as follows :

1. **Masculine Gender :** A noun that denotes a male is said to be of the masculine gender, as man, uncle, ox, boy etc.
2. **Feminine Gender :** A noun that denotes a female is said to be of feminine gender, as woman, aunt, princess, cow etc.
3. **Common Gender :** Nouns which denote both males and females are said to be of the common gender, as friend, cousin, person, parent, baby etc.
4. **Neuter Gender :** A noun that denotes the name of object without life is said to be of neuter gender, as file, table, pencil.

REMEMBER

Masculine	*Feminine*
Boy	Girl
Son	Daughter
Brother	Sister
Murderer	Murderess
Sorcerer	Sorceress
Son-in-law	Daughter-in-law
Father-in-law	Mother-in-law
Man-servant	Maid-servant
Land-lord	Land-lady
Bachelor	Maid
Gentleman	Lady
Monk	Nun
Earl	Countess
Lad	Lass
Sir	Madam
Duke	Dutchess
Emperor	Empress
Milk-man	Milk-maid
Pea-cock	Pea-hen

Masculine	*Feminine*
Step-father	Step-mother
Hero	Heroine
Viceroy	Vicerine
Mr.	Mrs.
Governor	Governess
Master	Mistress
Wizard	Witch
Heir	Heiress
Host	Hostess
Lion	Lioness
Mayor	Mayoress
Actor	Actress
Buck	Doe
Colt	Filly
Dog	Bitch
Horse	Mare
Count	Countess
Hunter	Huntress
Prince	Princess
Abbot	Abbess
God	Goddess
Author	Authoress
Ox	Cow
Widower	Widow
Grand-father	Grand-mother
He-goat	She-goat
Milk-man	Milk-woman
Bridegroom	Bride
Tiger	Tigress
Priest	Priestess
Poet	Poetess
Shepherd	Shepherdess
Nephew	Niece
Stag	Hind

PRONOUNS

The repetition of a noun in a sentence or a set of sentences is really boring. So, instead of repeating the noun, we can use a word (for that noun) called the pronoun.

"A pronoun is a word that we use instead of a noun".

Example:
This is *Sachin. He* plays cricket.
Note: *He* is the pronoun used in place of *Sachin.*

Kinds of Pronouns

1. **Personal pronouns :** A pronoun which is used instead of the name of a person is known as a 'Personal Pronoun'. A list of the 'Personal pronouns' is listed below :

I, my, mine, me, we (First Person)
You, your, yours (Second Person)
He, his, him, she, her, hers, it, its, they, their, theirs, them (Third Person)

2. **Demonstrative, Indefinite and Distributive Pronouns :**

(a) Demonstrative Pronouns : Pronouns used to point out the objects to which they refer are called Demonstrative Pronouns.

Examples :

(i) *This* is a present from my uncle.
(ii) *These* are merely excuses.
(iii) Bembay mangoes are better than *those* of Bangaluru.

(b) Indefinite Pronouns : All pronouns which refer to persons or things in a general way and do not refer to any particular person or thing are called Indefinite Pronouns.

Examples :

(i) *Somebody* has stolen my watch.
(ii) *Few* escaped unhurt.
(iii) Did you ask *anybody* to come?

(c) Distributive Pronouns : Each, either, neither are called distributive pronouns because they refer to persons or things one at a time. For this reason they are always singular and followed by the verb in singular.

Examples :

(i) *Each* of the men received a reward.
(ii) *These* men received *each* a reward.
(iii) *Either* of you can go.

3. **Relative Pronouns :** A relative pronoun refers or relates to some noun going before, which is called its Antecedent.

Examples :

(i) I met Hari *who* used to live here.
(ii) I have found the pen *which* I had lost.
(iii) Here is the book *that* you lent me.

4. **Interrogative Pronouns :** These pronouns, are used for asking questions.

Examples :

(i) *Whose* book is this?
(ii) *What* will all the neighbours say?
(iii) *Which* do you prefer, tea or coffee?

Note : Interrogative pronouns can also be used in asking indirect questions. Consider the following examples :

(i) I asked *who* was speaking.
(ii) Tell me *what* you have done.
(iii) Say *which* you would like best.

Behaviour of the Pronouns

1. If three pronouns are used together in the same sentence they are arranged in the following order :

2	+	3	+	1
↓		↓		↓
Second Person		Third Person		First Person

Examples :

I, you and he must help *that* poor man. (Incorrect)

You, he and I must help *that* poor man. (Correct)

2. When two or more singular nouns are joined by and, the pronoun used for them should be plural.

Examples :

Mohan and Sohan are friends. *They* play football. *They* live at Lajpat Nagar.

3. But if these nouns joined by and refer to the same person or thing, the pronoun used should be singular.

Examples :

(i) Delhi, the beautiful city and the capital of India, is famous for *its* historical monuments.
(ii) The manager and owner of the firm expressed *his* views on the demands of the workers.

4. When two nouns are used with as well as, the pronoun agrees with the first subject.
Examples :
(a) Mohan as well as his friends is doing *his* work.
(b) The students as well as their teachers are doing *their* work.

5. When two singular nouns joined by 'and' are preceded by *each* or *every,* the pronoun used must be singular and should agree in gender with the second noun.
Examples :
(a) Every man and every woman will do *her* best for the nation.
(b) Each boy and each girl went to *her* house.

6. When two nouns are joined by using 'with', the pronoun agrees with the noun coming before 'with'.
Examples :
(a) The boy with *his* parents has gone to see a movie.
(b) The children with *their* parents have gone to picnic.

7. When two different nouns are joined by either.......... or; neither .... nor, the pronoun is used according to the number and gender of the second noun.
Examples :
(a) Either your sister or you have done *your* work.
(b) Neither the students nor the teacher was in *his* class.

8. The pronoun coming after '*than*' must be in the same case as that coming before '*than*'.
Examples :
(a) She plays better than *me*. (Incorrect)
She plays better than *I*. (Correct)
(b) His elder brother is more intelligent than *him*. (Incorrect)
His elder brother is more intelligent than *he*. (Correct)

9. 'Many a' always takes a singular pronoun and singular verb.
Example :
Many a soldier has met *his* death in the battle field.

10. 'Who', 'Whose', 'Whom' are used only for persons.
Examples :
(a) *Who* is knocking at the door?
(b) *Whose* pen is this?
(c) *What* do you want?

11. 'Which' is used for things.
Example :
Which game do you like?

MULTIPLE CHOICE QUESTIONS

Directions: *In the following questions choose the correct options to fill the blanks.*

1. The place was so dirty that ..... wished to run away from there.
A. everybody B. anybody
C. few D. some

2. ..... was there to help me.
A. Somebody B. Anything
C. Anybody D. Nobody

3. Is there .... to eat?
A. some B. something
C. any D. few

4. ..... of the students were making a great noise.
A. Anyone B. Somebody
C. Many D. Nobody

5. ..... of the students can solve this sum.
A. Someone B. Anybody
C. Somebody D. None

6. ...... of us should try our best to make India a heaven.
A. Any B. Somebody
C. Anybody D. All

7. ...... of us do not know the real meaning of our lives.
A. Any B. Something
C. Several D. Many

8. My .... black.
A. hairs are B. hair is
C. hairs shall D. hair will

9. She saw two .... on the last Sunday.
A. thiefs B. theifs
C. thieves D. theives

10. My sister is a ....
A. bacheloress B. bachelor
C. unmaried D. spinster

11. One is supposed to do ....
A. our duty B. their duty
C. one's duty D. his duty

12. Take anything .... you want.
A. that B. which
C. than D. then

13. I cannot tolerate ....
A. separated you
B. your separation
C. separation from you
D. you separated

14. He is .... faithful partner.
A. Yours B. You
C. Your D. Your's

15. Ajay is more smart than ....
A. her B. hers
C. herself D. she

16. Vivek works harder than ....
A. me B. I
C. her D. his

17. They should help ....
A. the poor people B. the poor
C. the poor persons D. the poor peoples

18. .... are mad.
A. All his sons B. His all sons
C. Sons all his D. All sons his

19. The poor fellow .... to fate.
A. resigned
B. resigned himself
C. resigned itself
D. resigned themselves

20. Nobody will help you but ....
A. I B. me
C. ours D. his

21. It is a good chance, You must avail .... this opportunity.
A. of B. yourself of
C. for D. from

22. The person who is elected .... my relative.
A. is B. he is
C. his D. him

23. He made ....
A. yours mention B. mention of you
C. mention for you D. mention about you

24. .... I know, he is quite faithful.
A. As far as B. So far as
C. So far this D. So far so

25. It is a duty of a person to take .... for his family.
A. pain B. pains
C. pain-killers D. pained

26. She does not love .... husband.
A. his B. her
C. its D. their

27. Let .... work together.
A. him and me B. he and I
C. he and him D. I and me

28. Copper, Silver and Gold ....
A. each will do B. either will do
C. any one will do D. any will do

29. Jessica and Roma are very irregular .... habits.
A. in her B. in their
C. in its D. in every

30. One likes to enjoy .... who was a great poet.
A. The sonnets of Shakespeare
B. Shakespeare's sonnets
C. Sonnets
D. Shakespeare

31. That is the boy .... everybody loves.
A. whom B. who
C. that D. whose

32. That is the girl .... won the first prize.
A. whom B. who
C. whose D. which

33. That is the man .... purse was lost.
A. who B. whom
C. whose D. their

ANSWERS

1	2	3	4	5	6	7	8	9	10
A	D	B	C	D	D	D	B	C	D
11	**12**	**13**	**14**	**15**	**16**	**17**	**18**	**19**	**20**
C	A	C	C	D	B	B	A	B	B
21	**22**	**23**	**24**	**25**	**26**	**27**	**28**	**29**	**30**
B	A	B	A	B	B	A	C	B	A
31	**32**	**33**							
A	B	C							

ARTICLES

The family of the articles has only three members. They are : A, An and The. However, they fall under two groups :

(a) Definite Article *(b)* Indefinite Article

'The' is known as definite article whereas 'a' and 'an' are known as indefinite articles.

Use of the Definite Article 'The'

'The' is used before

1. The superlative degree :
   He is the ablest man of the town.
   (ablest is a superlative degree)
2. The name of states, countries etc. having a descriptive name :
   (i) The J & K is a small state. (J & K is a descriptive name)
   (ii) He lives in the U.S.A. (U.S.A. is a descriptive name)
   (But the Delhi and the America are wrong because neither Delhi nor America is a descriptive name)
3. The names of the scriptures :
   The Gita is a holy book. (Gita is a scripture)
4. Name of newspapers :
   The Tribune is published from Chandigarh.
5. Name of rivers, canals, seas, oceans, bays, gulfs, groups of islands etc. :
   (i) The Ganga is a holy river.
   (ii) The Indian Ocean is the deepest ocean.
   (iii) The Persian Gulf is a narrow gulf.
6. The name of famous buildings :
   The Taj is one of the best buildings in India.
7. The names of nationals, sects and communities:
   (i) The English defeated the Germans in the World War.
   (ii) The rich should help the poor.
   (iii) The Hindus believe in the caste system.
8. Proper nouns used as common nouns :
   (i) Kalidas is the Shakespeare of India.
   (ii) Delhi is the London of India.
9. Famous historical events :
   The Industrial Revolution changed the face of England.
10. The directions and the celestial bodies:
    The sun rises in the east.
11. Titles :
    Akbar, the Great was loved by his subjects.

Do not use 'the'

1. Before languages :
   The English is an international language. (Incorrect)
   English is an international language. (Correct)
2. Before the names of games :
   The hockey is a popular game. (Incorrect)
   Hockey is a popular game. (Correct)

Use of the Indefinite Articles 'A' and 'An'

'A' is used before :

1. All singular common nouns beginning with a consonant :
   (i) A boy sings a song.

(ii) A black and a white cow were grazing in the field.

2. If a word begins with a vowel but gives the sound of a consonant, 'a' should be used before it :
   (i) He was helped in his work by a European.
   (ii) He is a one-eyed man.
   (iii) It is a useful work.

'An' is used as follows :

1. All singular common nouns beginning with a vowel (*i.e.*, a, e, i, o, u) :
   (i) He is an artist.
   (ii) He is an old man.
   (iii) I intend to buy an umbrella.
2. If a word starts with a consonant but gives the sound of a vowel, "an" should be used before it :
   (i) Brutus is an honourable man.
   (ii) He is an honour to his profession.
   (iii) He is an L.L.B.
   (iv) He is an M.A.
   (v) You will reach there in an hour.

Demonstratives, that, these and those

1. The demonstrative adjectives and pronouns are for objects nearby the speaker:
   this (singular) those (plural)
   and for objects far away from the speaker.
   That (singular) those (plural)
2. Demonstratives are the only adjectives that agree in number with their nouns.
   That hat is nice.
   Those hats are nice.
3. When there is the idea of selection, the pronoun "one" (or "ones") often follows the demonstrative.
   I want a book. I'll get this (one).
   If the demonstrative is followed by an adjective, "one"(or "ones") must be used.
   I want a book. I'll get this big one.

MULTIPLE CHOICE QUESTIONS

Directions: *In the following questions choose the correct options to fill the blanks.*

1. .... will have to be paid for this material.
A. Half rupee B. Half a rupee
C. A half rupee D. An half rupee

2. .... is taking keen interest in India.
A. The USA B. USA
C. An USA D. A USA

3. Only .... can save our country.
A. the Hitler B. a Hitler
C. Hitler D. an Hitler

4. I can run for ....
A. hundred miles B. the hundred miles
C. a hundred miles D. an hundred miles.

5. .... man-eater has been killed.
A. The B. A
C. An D. Either A or B

6. What .... fine idea!
A. the B. an
C. a D. No article

7. .... earth is moving around the sun.
A. An B. A
C. The D. No article

8. This is .... first example while I got.
A. the B. a
C. an D. No article

9. This is .... house which was built during earthquake.
A. a B. an
C. the D. No article

10. .... America is a rich country.
A. The B. An
C. A D. No article

11. .... U.S.A. is a developed country.
A. A B. An
C. The D. No article

12. .... Bible is a holy book.
A. A B. The
C. An D. No article

13. .... rich should help the poor.
A. The B. A
C. An D. No article

14. .... Gold is a costly metal.
A. The B. A
C. An D. No article

15. Kalidas is .... Shakespeare of India.
A. a B. an
C. the D. No article

16. I cannot do .... difficult work.
A. a such B. the such
C. such the D. such a

17. How foolish .... plan it is!
A. a B. an
C. the D. No article

18. An ink is .... useful article.
A. an B. a
C. the D. No article

19. There are .... husband and wife.
A. a B. an
C. the D. No article

20. He is learning .... French
A. the B. a
C. an D. No article

ANSWERS

1	2	3	4	5	6	7	8	9	10
B	A	B	C	D	C	C	A	C	D
11	**12**	**13**	**14**	**15**	**16**	**17**	**18**	**19**	**20**
C	B	A	D	C	D	A	B	D	D

ADJECTIVES & ADVERBS

An Adjective is a word which adds something to the meaning of a noun or a pronoun.

Mridula is an *intelligent* girl.
He has a *black* goat.
He is a *brilliant* student.
She is a *clever* girl.
It is a *beautiful* picture.

In the sentences given above, the words in italics are adjectives.

An Adverb is a word which qualifies the meaning of a Verb, an Adjective or another Adverb.

(*i*) He talks *slowly.*
(*ii*) He is a *very* good student.
(*iii*) He talks *very* slowly.

In sentence (*i*), *slowly* qualifies the verb *talks.*

In sentence (*ii*), *very* qualifies the adjective *good.*

In sentence (*iii*), *very* qualifies the adverb *slowly.*

Adjectives have three degrees of comparison :

1. **Positive Degree :** It expresses the common form of an adjective.
   Example :
   Ram is a *tall* boy.
   In the above sentence *tall* is an adjective and expresses the common form.
2. **Comparative Degree :** It expresses the more of the same form.
   Example :
   Ram is *taller* than Mahesh.
   In the above sentence *taller* is an adjective that expresses the more of the common form of the adjective *tall.*

"When and How to Use" Comparative Degree?

(a) Comparative Degree is used when two persons or two groups of persons or things are compared.
Examples :
(a) He is *wiser* than his younger brother.
(b) This glass is *cleaner* than the other.

(b) When two different qualities in the same person are compared, more is used instead of 'er' to form the comparative. The formula used in this case should be :
More + Positive Degree
She is *fairer* than polite. (Incorrect)
She is *more fair* than polite. (Correct)

(c) When selection of one out of two persons or things is meant, the degree of comparison is followed by of and *the* is used before it.
Example :
Zia is abler of *the* two sisters.

(d) If two comparatives are used in the same sentence to impress upon an idea, both should be preceded by the definite article.

Examples :

(i) The higher you go, the cooler it is.

(ii) The more we get, the more we desire.

(e) When one person or thing is compared with another of the same kind, other is used after the comparative degree. In such sentences other is normally preceded by any or all.

Examples :

(i) Kalidas is greater than any dramatist. (Incorrect)

Kalidas is greater than any other dramatist. (Correct)

(ii) Lead is heavier than all metals. (Incorrect)

Lead is heavier than all other metals. (Correct)

(f) Senior, junior, superior, inferior, prior, anterior (earlier than) and posterior (later than) are always followed by 'to'.

Examples :

(i) Ram is senior *to* Mohan by three years.

(ii) That pen is inferior *to* that.

(iii) He is junior *to* me in rank.

(iv) This event was posterior *to* that.

Note: Never use *than* after the above mentioned adjectives.

Important Information

(a) 'Preferable' is also used as an adjective of the comparative degree. As such, it is always followed by *to* and not *a*.

Death is preferable than dishonour. (Incorrect)

Death is preferable *to* dishonour. (Correct)

(b) To intensify the Degree of comparison, we use *far* or *much* before the comparative.

Examples :

(i) This book is *far* better than that.

(ii) His performance was *much* better than Mohan's.

Warning : Always avoid the use of double comparatives.

Don't say : Ram is more cleverer than his younger brother.

Say: Ram is cleverer than his younger brother.

3. **Superlative Degree :** It expresses the most of the common form of an adjective.

Example :

He is the ablest man of the town.

How and when to use the Superlative Degree?

(a) The Superlative Degree is used when more than two persons or things are compared.

(b) The Superlative Degree is generally preceded by 'the' and followed by 'of' in most of the cases or otherwise.

(c) When an adjective of the superlative degree is preceded by a Possessive Adjective or a Noun in the Possessive case, 'the' should not be used before it.

Example :

Which is Kalidas' best play?

It will be a blunder to use 'the' before the Superlative Degree in such cases.

Don't say : Which is Kalidas' the best play.

(d) To intensify the degree of comparison, *by far* is used before the superlative degree.

Example :

India is *by far* the most beautiful country of the world.

Note: Always avoid the use of double superlatives.

Don't say : He is the most strongest boy in the class.

Say : He is the strongest boy in the class.

Use of some Important Adjectives

1. (a) **'Some'** is used as follows :

(i) With countable nouns where it means—a little, a small quantity.

(ii) In a question which shows some request.

Examples :

(i) There is some water in the bottle.

(ii) Some of the students were absent yesterday.

(iii) Will you have some milk?

(iv) Will you buy some fruit for me?

(b) **'Any'** is used as follows :

(i) In negative sentences.

(ii) In interrogative sentences.

(iii) After 'Hardly', 'Scarcely' and 'Barely'.
(iv) After 'If'.

Examples :

(i) There is not any sugar in the pot.
(ii) We haven't any rice in the house.
(iii) I have hardly any money.
(iv) There are scarcely any plants in this field.
(v) If there is any danger, blow the whistle.

2. (a) **Older :** Older (and oldest) are used for persons animals and things. But 'Older' and 'Oldest' refer to the persons who do not belong to the same family.

Examples :

(i) Radha is older than Shyama.
(ii) John is the oldest member of the staff. 'Older' and 'Oldest' refer to the persons who do not belong to the same family.

(b) **Elder** (and **eldest**) are used in respect of the members of the same family like sons, daughters, brothers, sisters.

Examples :

(i) My elder sister is a lecturer.
(ii) Meenakshi is the eldest of the three sisters.

Note :

(i) 'Elder' is not followed by 'than'.
(ii) 'Elder' and 'Eldest' cannot be used for things.

3. (a) **'Few'** is negative and is the opposite of 'Many'. It means 'not many'.

(b) **'A few'** is positive and means 'some at least'. It is the opposite of 'None'.

(c) **'The few'** means 'minority' and suggests 'whether there is'.

Examples :

(i) We have few holidays in school.
(ii) Only a few boys will fail in the examination.
(iii) The few poems that he wrote are very popular.

4. (a) **Further** means 'something additional'.

(b) **Farther** means 'a greater distance'.

Examples :

(i) Further discussion will be held in the office of the principal.
(ii) Amritsar is farther from Delhi than Ambala.

5. (a) **Little** is negative. It means, 'not much', or 'hardly any'.

(b) **A little** is positive. It means 'some quantity'.

(c) **The little** denotes quantity. It means, 'not much but all that is, or whatever quantity there is'.

Examples :

(i) There is little hope of his success.
(ii) He knows a little of everything.
(iii) I have spent the little money I had.
(iv) The little knowledge of shoe-making proved very useful to me.

6. (a) **'Much'** expresses 'quantity'.

(b) **'Many'** expresses 'number'.

(c) **'Many a'**—'Singular noun' and 'Singular verb' are used with 'many a'.

Examples :

(i) There is not *much* water in the jug.
(ii) *Many* boys are absent today.
(iii) *Many* a battle has been fought on the soil of India.

7. (a) **'Less'** denotes 'in a small degree'.

(b) **'Fewer'** denotes 'number'.

Examples :

(i) He devotes less time to his studies.
(ii) There are no fewer than ten chairs in this room.

8. (a) **'Each'** is used for a single number of 'two persons' or 'things'.

(b) **'Every'** is used for a single number of 'many persons' or 'things'.

Examples :

(i) Each boy must take part in games.
(ii) There are only two poets. Each poet recited his poem.
(iii) Every man dies in this world.
(iv) Every man is expected to do his duty.

9. (a) **'Either'** means one of the two or both.

(b) **'Neither'** is negative of the either.

Examples :

(i) You may buy either of these two chairs.
(ii) Neither of them could speak on the stage.

10.(a) '**Later**' expresses 'late in time'.

(b) '**Latter**' means 'second in position or order'.

Examples :

(i) My father reached later than I expected.

(ii) The latter position was better than the former.

Use of some Important Adverbs

1. (a) Also, too, enough:

(i) He taught English. Also, he edited the school magazine

(ii) He is a writer and also he is a painter.

(iii) He is too obstinate to listen to any reason.

(iv) This is too difficult a piece for the junior students.

(v) Sarla was kind enough to help the poor.

(vi) He is brave enough to help the truth.

Note: 'Too' is used in a negative sense, but enough is used in a positive sense.

(b) Fairly and rather: Both suggest the meaning 'moderately'. But, mainly 'fairly' is used with the words that denote a positive meaning and rather is used with the words that denote a negative meaning:

(i) Rita did fairly well in that competition, but her performance was rather poor in sports.

(ii) Mona is fairly rich, but she is rather stingy.

Note: 'Rather' can also be used in a positive sense.

(i) This is a rather interesting job.

(ii) That boy is rather smart.

(c) Hardly, barely, scarcely: These words mostly convey the negative suggestions and are almost similar.

(i) I have hardly any strength now.

(ii) There was barely any supply to the township,

(iii) There were scarcely a hundred guests present.

Note: With slight variance in the meaning, the words given above convey the idea of 'very little', 'not enough', 'lack of quantity and number'.

(d) Yet, Still: These adverbs can often be used to connect the sentence units:

(i) He has been defeated many times in the contest; still he wants to be a competitor.

(ii) Mona was sick; yet she went on doing her work.

(e) Alone:

(i) He alone (none else) is capable of handling that fire,

(ii) He hunted all alone in the forest. (not in any company)

Special Note:

(a) Apart from their conventional positions the adverbs might be used in different positions with different meanings and angles.

(i) He had only four books.

(ii) John only contacted his friend in need.

(iii) He greeted me only.

(iv) Only he greeted me there.

(b) Inversion: Some adverbs can be inverted *i.e.* placed in the beginning of the sentence and then be followed by an interrogative form. The most common of these adverb are: so, seldom, never, nowhere, under no circumstances, hardly, scarcely etc.

(i) So big was the bus that it could not enter the narrow lane.

(ii) Hardly had he reached the station when he received the message.

MULTIPLE CHOICE QUESTIONS

Directions: *In the following questions choose the correct options to fill the blanks.*

1. The girl whom you met is the .... sister of Ravi.

A. eldest B. elder

C. older D. oldest

2. The historical place is ....

A. seeing worth

B. worthy of seeing
C. worth seeing
D. worthy seeing

3. These flowers smell ....
A. sweet B. sweetly
C. more sweetly D. sweetest

4. .... aspirant cannot pass the entrance examination.
A. Each B. Every
C. All D. No

5. Harivansh Rai .... second Shakespeare.
A. is a B. is
C. is the D. is an

6. .... student in the class got prizes.
A. Each and every B. Every and each
C. Every D. Never

7. It is .... picture than the one we saw last Monday.
A. interesting B. much interesting
C. more interesting D. most interesting

8. She is clever ....
A. that her mother is
B. as her mother is
C. to her mother is
D. than her mother is

9. They will get ....
A. Red, green and black paper
B. Red, green black paper
C. Red and green and black paper
D. Red green black paper

10. Health is .... wealth.
A. preferable to
B. more preferable than
C. more preferable to
D. most preferable then

11. .... water that was in the jug evaporated.
A. Little B. The little
C. Small D. A small

12. He has not sung .... songs.
A. much B. most
C. more D. many

13. Srishti has searched .... office.
A. whole the B. the whole
C. a whole D. some whole

14. Premchand was .... best and .... famous writer.
A. a, the most B. the, a most
C. the, more D. the, the most

15. William Shakespeare is famous as ....
A. a poet and a dramatist
B. a poet and dramatist
C. the poet and the dramatist
D. a poet and the dramatist

16. What does .... leader suggest?
A. other B. another
C. others D. anothers

17. He .... money.
A. has few B. have few
C. has little D. have little

18. The .... boys are rewarded.
A. first two B. two first
C. firsts two D. two's first

19. He is .... brave.
A. stronger than
B. stronger then
C. more strong then
D. more strong than

20. No sooner said ....
A. so done B. and done
C. then done D. but done

21. She returned .... than I had thought.
A. quickly B. more quicker
C. more quickly D. quicker

22. He is .... foolish person.
A. rather the B. a rather
C. rather a D. rather

23. This pen .... rupees.
A. costs twenty
B. twenty costs only
C. costs only twenty
D. only costs twenty

24. It is .... pride.
A. nothing else but
B. nothing else than
C. else nothing than
D. but

25. This tea is .... to drink.
A. too hot B. very hot
C. enough hot D. much hot

ANSWERS

1	2	3	4	5	6	7	8	9	10
A	C	A	B	A	C	C	C	A	A
11	**12**	**13**	**14**	**15**	**16**	**17**	**18**	**19**	**20**
B	D	B	D	B	B	C	A	D	C
21	**22**	**23**	**24**	**25**					
C	C	C	A	A					

DETERMINERS

Determiners are actually Adjectives. They are always followed by nouns.

Determiners are of the following kinds:

1. Demonstrative Determiners
this, that, these, those

2. Possessive Determiners
my, our, your, his, her, its, their

3. Quantitative Determiners
some, any, much, enough, sufficient, whole, a little, the little, little, all, both

4. Numerical Determiners
a few, some, few, the few, any, several, many, no, etc.

One, two, three ... (Cardinals)

First, second, third ... (Ordinals)

5. Distributive Determiners
either, neither

6. Articles

Indefinite: a, an

Definite: the

MULTIPLE CHOICE QUESTIONS

Directions: *In the following questions choose the correct options to fill the blanks.*

1. Give me .... rice.
A. some B. few
C. a few D. any

2. .... sheep grazing on the slope of the hill had gone away.
A. Any B. The few
C. This D. Much

3. Have you got .... magazines to read?
A. all B. much
C. some D. little

4. I have .... money that I want to spend on shares.
A. any B. much
C. less D. some

5. There is .... owl on the branch of the tree.
A. a B. the
C. an D. some

6. My brother is .... MBA.
A. a B. an
C. the D. any

7. Have you got .... cheese?
A. some B. many
C. a few D. few

8. No, I have not got .... cheese.
A. many B. few
C. any D. some

9. There is only .... milk left in the bottle.
A. enough B. few
C. much D. a little

10. There is .... hope of his recovery.
A. any B. little
C. many D. few

11. .... dogs were barking at the strangers.
A. Some B. Any
C. Much D. Less

12. The girl bought her father .... juice.
A. few B. some
C. any D. many

13. You should take .... honey everyday.
A. any B. many
C. a little D. a few

14. .... boy was punished by the teacher.
A. Either B. All
C. Any D. Many

15. .... girl was asked to join the army.
A. None B. Neither
C. All D. Any

16. .... water in the jug has been drunk by Mohan.
A. The little B. The few
C. A few D. Few

17. I shall play .... piano at the party.
A. some B. any
C. the D. few

18. .... labourers were found dead in the mine.
A. Any B. Fewer
C. Many D. Less

19. Could I borrow .... umbrella?
A. our B. your
C. yours D. my

20. My brother is standing in the .... row.
A. any B. many
C. some D. first

ANSWERS

1	2	3	4	5	6	7	8	9	10
A	B	C	D	C	B	A	C	D	B
11	**12**	**13**	**14**	**15**	**16**	**17**	**18**	**19**	**20**
A	B	C	A	B	A	C	C	B	D

THE VERB

A Verb is a word that tells something about the action or state of or happenning to a person or thing.

A Verb tells the following:

1. What a person or thing does.
Sachin goes to school daily.
The bell *rang* loudly.
Many birds fly in the sky.
She *sang* a song.

2. What a person or thing is.
India *is* the biggest democracy in the world.
Ram Mehar *is* very rich.
They *are* happy.

3. What is done to a person or thing.
You *are liked* by all.
Two thieves *were arrested.*
Four students *were punished* by the teacher.

4. What happens to a person or thing.
His maternal uncle *died* last week.
Two ships *sank* yesterday.
Leaves *turn* yellow in autumn.

5. What a person or thing has, had, and so on.
I *have* a new car.
He *had* a scooter last year.
He *has* several cows and goats.

It goes without saying that a verb is the most important part of a sentence. No sentence is complete without a Verb.

Important Information

1. If two or more singular nouns are joined by 'and' the verb used will be plural.

   Example:
   (i) He and I were going to the market.
   (ii) Ram and Mohan are friends.

2. If two singular nouns joined by 'and' points out to the same thing or person, the verb used must be singular.

   Example:
   (i) Rice and curry is the favourite food of the Punjabis.
   (ii) The Collector and District Magistrate is away.

3. In case two subjects are joined by 'as well as' the verb agrees with the first subject.

   Example :
   (i) Kanta as well as her children is playing.
   (ii) Children as well as their mother are playing.

In the case of first sentence the verb (is) agrees with Kanta and in the case of second sentence the verb (are) agrees with the children.

4. 'Neither', 'Either', 'Every', 'Each', 'Everyone', and 'Many a' are followed by a singular verb.
   Example :
   (i) Either of the plans is to be adopted.
   (ii) Neither of the two brothers is sure to pass.
   (iii) Every student is expected to be obedient.
   (iv) Everyone of them desires this.
   (v) Many a person is drowned in the sea.
5. If two subjects are joined by 'Either .... or' / 'Neither .... nor', the verb agrees with the subject near to it.
   Example :
   (i) Either my brother or I am to do this work.
   (ii) Neither he nor they are prepared to do this work.
6. 'A great many' is always followed by a 'plural noun' and a 'plural verb'. For example : A great many students have been declared successful.
7. Similarly if two subjects are joined by 'with', 'together with', 'no less than', in addition to 'and not', etc. the verb agrees with the first subject.
   Example :
   (i) The boy with his parents has arrived.
   (ii) He, no less than I, is to blame.
8. Nouns, plural in form, but singular in meaning, take a singular verb.
   Example :
   This news was broadcast from television yesterday.

MULTIPLE CHOICE QUESTIONS

Directions: *In the following questions choose the correct options to fill the blanks.*

1. The bus with all its passengers .... lost.
A. were B. was
C. are D. would

2. You as well as I .... responsible for this work.
A. am B. are
C. was D. is

3. Raghava like all his companions .... a spoiled child.
A. are B. were
C. is D. will be

4. Pen and ink .... required for me.
A. are B. were
C. is D. has required

5. Every girl and every boy .... attended the seminar.
A. have B. has
C. is D. are

6. Not only she but all her sisters ...... been married.
A. has B. have
C. is D. are

7. There .... nothing but miseries in life.
A. is B. are
C. were D. will be

8. Neither prose nor poem .... given.
A. were B. was
C. has D. have

9. Either he or I .... wrong.
A. is B. are
C. am D. were

10. Either Sulekha or Rekha .... coming here.
A. are B. is
C. were D. have

11. .... the child or his parents to blame?
A. Is B. Are
C. Were D. Has

12. You and I .... neighbours.
A. am B. are
C. was D. has

13. The house with all its belongings ..... sold away.
A. were B. are
C. was D. must

14. Either water or juice .... required.
A. is B. are
C. were D. has

15. There were not as many tables as .... required.
A. was B. were
C. is D. are

16. They each .... a book.
A. have B. are
C. has D. is

17. He and I .... class friends.
A. is B. am
C. was D. are

18. She as well as I .... guilty.
A. is B. are
C. am D. must be

19. Purushottam .... not read more on this chapter.
A. needs B. has been need
C. need D. had been need

20. He came .... to his aunt.
A. run B. running
C. to run D. in run

21. She dislikes .... meat.
A. eat to B. to eat
C. eating D. to eating

22. He likes ....
A. sing to B. singing
C. to sing D. to singing

23. We are ready .... the match.
A. play to B. to playing
C. playing D. to play

24. .... is injurious to health.
A. Smoking B. To smoke
C. To smoking D. Smoke to

25. He loves .... raw vegetables.
A. eaten B. eating
C. to eating D. eat to

26. He seemed .... finished his homework.
A. have to B. to have
C. having D. to having

ANSWERS

1	2	3	4	5	6	7	8	9	10
B	B	C	C	B	B	A	B	C	B
11	**12**	**13**	**14**	**15**	**16**	**17**	**18**	**19**	**20**
A	B	C	A	B	A	D	A	C	B
21	**22**	**23**	**24**	**25**	**26**				
C	B	D	A	B	B				

CONJUNCTIONS

A conjunction is a word which connects words, clauses or sentences.

Look at the following sentences.

(i) He bought apples *and* mangoes.
(ii) God made the country *and* man made the town.
(iii) The door was open *but* there was no one in the house.
(iv) He knows that I am here *and* that I want to see him.

In the sentence (i), *and* connects two words—*apples* and *mangoes.*

In the sentence (ii), *and* connects two sentences—*God made the country* and *man made the town.*

In the sentence (iii), *but* connects two sentences—*The door was open* and *there was no one in the house.*

In the sentence (iv), *and* connects two clauses—*that I am here* and *that I want to see him.*

The main coordinating conjunctions are: and, but, for, or, nor, also, either ..... or, neither ..... nor.

There are some conjunctions which are used in pairs. They are:

either .... or, ... neither .... nor, both .... and, though .... yet, whether .... or, not only .... but also.

Example: *Either* take it *or* leave it.

It is *neither* useful *nor* ornamental.

They *both* like *and* respect me.

Though he is suffering from high fever, *yet* he does not cry.

He does not care *whether* you go *or* stay.

He is *not only* doltish, *but also* obstinate.

The conjunctions which are used in pairs in this way, are called correlative conjunctions, or merely correlatives.

Use of Important Conjunctions

1. **As soon as :** As soon as denotes simultaneous time.
   Example : As soon as he saw his enemy, he took to his heels.
2. **No sooner .... than :**
   (a) 'No sooner' is always followed by 'than'.
   (b) Please remember that 'No sooner' is always followed by do/does/did. As such only first form of the verb should be used after the subject.
   Example :
   No sooner did he see his enemy than he took to his heels.
3. **Hardly :** Hardly is followed by when.
   Examples :
   (i) Hardly had I left the house when it started raining.
   (ii) We had hardly come into the room when his father began chastising him.
   Note :
   A. Hardly is never followed by than.
   B. 'Scarcely' can also be used in the sense and manner of 'Hardly'.
4. **Lest :** Lest is used in the sense of so that .... not. It is always followed by should. Lest is negative in sense. Hence 'not' should never be used with it.
   Example :
   Work hard lest you should fail.
   Note : 'Lest' is always followed by 'should' and not 'may'.
5. **Unless :** Unless expresses condition. It is also used in the negative sense. Use of 'not' is not allowed with unless because unless is already in the negative sense.
   Example :
   Unless you labour hard you will not pass.
6. **Until :** 'Until' expresses time. It means 'till not'.
   Example :
   Wait here until I return.
   Note : Until is in the negative sense. So 'not' should not be used with it. Example :
   Wait here until I do not return. (Incorrect)
   Wait here until I return. (Correct)
7. **As well as :** When two subjects are joined by 'as well as', the verb always agrees with the first subject.
   Examples :
   (i) The teacher as well as students is playing.
   (ii) Students as well as the teacher are playing.
   Note : 'Both' and 'as well as' cannot be used together in the same sentence.
   Examples :
   Both Sita as well as Kanta are beautiful. (Incorrect)
   Sita as well as Kanta is beautiful. (Correct)
   Both Sita and Kanta are beautiful. (Correct)
8. **As if :** 'As if' is used in the sense of pretension. While using 'as if' in a sentence, we should see that even the third person singular subject gets 'were'.
   Example :
   He talks as if he were mad.
9. **Till :** Till expresses time. Till is always used in the affirmative.
   Example :
   We did not come back till sunset.
10. **Rather than :** 'Rather than' is used in the sense of 'preference'. 'Rather' is always followed by 'than'.
    Example :
    I would rather die than submit.
11. **As long as/so long as :** Both express time during which an action or event takes place.
    Example :
    As long as there is life, there is hope.
12. **However :** It is both a subordinate and co-ordinate clause.
    Examples :
    (a) Mala worked hard, she however, failed.
    (b) However hard he may work, he cannot pass.
13. **Such as :** 'Such as' gives us the sense of 'like'. Such is always followed by 'as'.
    Example :
    Life is such a puzzle as cannot be solved.

MULTIPLE CHOICE QUESTIONS

Directions: *In the following questions choose the correct options to fill the blanks.*

1. Neither he .... his friend is good.
A. or B. and
C. but D. nor

2. The officer asked the peon .... why he was late.
A. that B. if
C. but D. No word needed

3. Both Ajay .... Vijay are intelligent.
A. or B. nor
C. and D. No word needed

4. No Sooner did the thief see the public .... he ran away.
A. then B. and
C. but D. than

5. Abhinav .... his brothers was going to Mumbai.
A. but B. yet
C. No word needed D. together with

6. He behaves .... he were the captain of the team.
A. as if B. as
C. No word needed D. that

7. Either Rupali .... Sonali is going to attend the meeting.
A. and B. but
C. nor D. or

8. Neither Nirmal .... Ashwinee is going to listen the speech.
A. and B. but
C. nor D. or

9. Ravi .... Prakash are going to Kolkata.
A. or B. nor
C. but D. and

10. Rice .... curry is my usual breakfast.
A. and B. but
C. then D. than

11. Hardly had he left .... his brother came.
A. then B. than
C. when D. that

12. I would rather have a copy .... a book.
A. then B. than
C. when D. that

13. He is no other .... my friend.
A. then B. than
C. when D. but

14. He saw a snake ....he awoke.
A. then B. when
C. than D. No word needed

15. Ten years have passed .... my grandmother died.
A. since B. when
C. then D. than

16. She is .... good .... bad.
A. either, not B. neither, or
C. neither, nor D. neither, than

17. The cellphone is both cheap .... best.
A. than B. and
C. then D. or

18. No sooner did the rogue see the police .... he disappeared.
A. then B. than
C. so D. because

19. Srishti will go .... Sanju goes.
A. if B. than
C. then D. although

20. She is wise .... timid.
A. and B. yet
C. but D. however

21. Make hay .... the sun shines.
A. though B. while
C. after D. before

22. He is so weak .... he cannot walk.
A. but B. that
C. then D. so

23. Although he is rich, ... he is unhappy.
A. but B. yet
C. so D. still

24. Wait here .... I come back.
A. till B. until
C. before D. after

25. He is my friend .... I shall help him.
A. so
B. hence
C. that is why
D. therefore

26. He must go away .... he will be beaten.
A. otherwise B. and
C. or D. else

27. God loves good men .... good men love God.
A. and B. or
C. that D. those

28. He was late .... he was not punished.
A. but B. yet
C. still D. therefore

29. Walk slowly ...., you may fall.
A. and B. or
C. so D. otherwise

30. Work hard, ... you will fail.
A. and B. or
C. otherwise D. else

ANSWERS

1	2	3	4	5	6	7	8	9	10
D	D	C	D	D	A	D	C	D	A
11	**12**	**13**	**14**	**15**	**16**	**17**	**18**	**19**	**20**
C	B	B	B	A	C	B	B	A	C
21	**22**	**23**	**24**	**25**	**26**	**27**	**28**	**29**	**30**
B	B	B	A	B	C	A	C	D	D

PREPOSITIONS

A *Preposition* is a word which is placed before a noun or a pronoun to show its relation to some other word in the sentence.

1. I saw a goat *in* the field.
2. I am fond *of* hot coffee.

In sentence 1, the word *in* shows the relation between two things—*goat* and *field.*

In sentence 2, the word *of* shows the relation between the attribute expressed by the adjective *found* and *tea.*

The words *in* and *of* are here used as prepositions.

The noun or pronoun which is used with a preposition is called its object. The noun or pronoun is in the objective case. It is governed by the preposition. Now it is absolutely clear that in sentence 1, the noun *field* is in the objective case. The word *field* is governed by the preposition *in.*

A preposition may have two or more objects.
The road runs over *hill* and *plain.*
Here, the words *hill* and *plain* are used as objects.

Use of Important Prepositions

1. Among, Between

'**Among**' is used for more than two persons or things; '**Between**' is used only for two.

Examples :

(i) Distribute these sweets *among* the poor students of the class.
(ii) Distribute these books *between* Ram and Shyam.

2. Among, In

'**Among**' is used before collective plural nouns. '**In**' is used before collective singular nouns.

Examples :

(i) I found him standing *among* the crowd.
(ii) I saw him in the crowd.

3. Beside, Besides

'**Beside**' means 'by the side of'. '**Besides**' means 'in addition to'.

Examples :

(i) The daughter was sitting *beside* her mother.
(ii) *Besides* his relatives, he invited his friends also.

4. In, Within

'**In**' means at the expiry of a period of time in future, '**Within**' means before the expiry of a period of time in any tense.

Examples :

(i) She will return *in* a week.

(ii) I shall finish my work *within* a weak.

5. On, Upon

'**On**' is used for things at rest; '**Upon**' is used for things in motion.

Examples :

(i) He is sitting *on* the floor.

(ii) The dog sprang *upon* the table.

6. By, With

'**By**' denotes the agent or doer, **'With'** denotes the instrument with which anything is done.

Examples :

(i) The bird was killed *by* the hunter with an arrow.

(ii) He beat the dog *with* a stick.

(iii) I shall reach here *by* five o'clock.

7. After, In

'**After**' means at the end of a period of time in the past. '**In**' means at the end of a period of time in future.

Examples :

(i) I shall return your book *in* a week.

(ii) He returned the book *after* a week.

8. For, From, Since

'**For**' is used before a noun denoting a period of time with all the tenses. '**From**' is used before a noun or phrase denoting a point of time, it is used in all the tenses. '**Since**' is used before a noun or phrase denoting some point of time and is always produced by a verb in the perfect continuous tense or third form of a verb.

Examples :

(i) We have been playing cards *for* two hours.

(ii) She stayed with her uncle *from* the 15th of March to the 15th of May.

(iii) I have been reading this book *since* morning.

9. Above, Over

'Above' means 'higher from', **Over** is used in the following four senses :

(i) In the sense of 'above' :
At noon, the sun is *over* our heads.

(ii) In the sense of 'beyond' :
I cannot get *over* my disappointment.

(iii) In the sense of 'Superiority' :
God *over* all blesses for ever more.

(iv) In the sense of 'Conclusion' :
It is all *over* with me.

10. At, Towards

'**At**' denotes the idea of aim, **'Towards'** denotes the idea of destination.

Examples :

(i) He threw the stone *at* the cat.

(ii) He went *towards* the house.

11. At, In, On

'At' is used as follows :

(i) **'At'** is used with small towns and villages.

Examples :

(a) He was born *at* Sonepat.

(b) He lives *at* village Bangra. (Bangra is a village)

(ii) **'At'** is used before a noun denoting a definite point of time.

Example :

He called on me *at* 9 p.m. yesterday.

'In' is used as follows :

(iii) '**In**' is used with the names of big cities, provinces and countries.

Examples :

(a) His father lives *in* England.

(b) His younger brother lives *in* Calcutta.

(iv) '**In**' is used before the names of months and years.

Example :

His elder sister was born *in* 1972 *in* the month of May.

'On' is used with dates and names of days.

Examples :

(a) I joined college *on* the 26th April.

(b) He will leave for Kolkata *on* Wednesday next.

Important Information

1. '**In**' is also used in the following phrases : In the morning; In the evening, In winter, In summer.

2. '**In**' also denotes a place inside anything. He travelled *in* a crowded bus.
3. '**At**' is used in the following phrases : *At* home, *At* the station, *At* work, *At* play.

12. Below, Beneath

Below means 'of lower level in position, dignity and expectation' etc. *Beneath* means 'under'.

Examples :

(i) It is *below* my dignity to talk to her.

(ii) They rested *beneath* the shade of a tree.

13. In, Into, To

'**In**' expresses Rest or Motion inside anything. '**Into**' expresses Motion towards the inside of anything or change from one medium to another. '**To**' denotes motion from one place to another.

Examples :

(i) The boys are *in* the room.

(ii) Translate this passage from English *into* Hindi.

(iii) Every morning he goes *to* the temple.

14. Till, By, Of, Off

- 'Till' means upto or not earlier than.
- 'By' means not later than.
- 'Of' shows cause, source, separation, quality, contents, possession, apposition, point of reference, space in time etc.
- 'Off' shows separation at a near distance, and detached condition.

Consider the following examples:

(i) I shall work *till* 5 a.m.

(ii) Madhu died *of* cancer.

(iii) The nib *of* the pen is made *of* gold.

(iv) He presented me a bottle *of* perfume.

(v) Our principal is a man *of* principle.

(vi) He lived in the house *of* his friend.

(vii) *By* this time tomorrow, I'll have finished my job.

(viii) My house is *off* the road.

(ix) The book fell *off* the table.

MULTIPLE CHOICE QUESTIONS

Directions: *Tick the correct preposition for the blank in each of the following sentences.*

1. He applied ...... the manager.

A. for B. to
C. with D. by

2. Trust ...... God and do the right.

A. in B. for
C. to D. with

3. She is worthy ...... a prize.

A. with B. for
C. to D. of

4. Mr. Gomes has no taste ...... music.

A. of B. for
C. with D. to

5. You are hard ...... hearing.

A. at B. of
C. with D. for

6. He is sure ...... his success

A. for B. with
C. on D. of

7. Preeti was warned ...... the danger ahead.

A. for B. at
C. of D. about

8. I am thankful ...... you for a good advice.

A. for B. with
C. to D. of

9. Deepak would not surrender ...... the police.

A. with B. to
C. for D. on

10. The small plant in your lawn is very sensitive ...... touch.

A. on B. with
C. to D. about

11. Divya was sure to succeed ..... the examination.

A. for B. in
C. to D. with

12. Geeta was jealous ...... Ravina's beauty.

A. to B. with
C. for D. of

13. He was ignorant .... what was happening there.
A. for B. of
C. to D. with

14. Your pen is inferior ...... mine.
A. than B. with
C. from D. to

15. Reenu is no match ...... Meenu.
A. to B. for
C. with D. upon

16. It is necessary ...... you to apply for this job.
A. on B. with
C. for D. to

17. Be loyal ...... your country.
A. for B. to
C. on D. with

18. Mukesh is junior ...... me.
A. than B. to
C. from D. of

19. Deepika was innocent ...... the crime.
A. of B. with
C. from D. to

20. I am desirous.... joining the Indian cricket team.
A. for B. of
C. to D. on

ANSWERS

1	2	3	4	5	6	7	8	9	10
B	A	D	B	B	D	D	D	B	D
11	**12**	**13**	**14**	**15**	**16**	**17**	**18**	**19**	**20**
B	D	B	D	B	D	B	B	A	B

SYNONYMS

A synonym is a word which conveys a meaning similar to the given word.

REMEMBER

Words	*Synonyms*
Add	Increase
Adequate	Enough
Adjust	Adapt
All	Aggregate
Allow	Permit
Abode	Dwelling
Apt	Proper
Assess	Appraise
Accuse	Calumniate
Abashed	Timid
Annoy	Displease
Ample	Enough, Sufficient
Amplify	Increase
Apathetic	Unenthusiastic
Accost	Address
Authentic	True
Adjust	Fit
Approve	Assent, Allow, Accept
Adapt	Conform
Adversary	Opponent, Rival, Competitor
Beat	Whack
Benign	Kind
Breeze	Zephyr
Baffle	Puzzle
Booty	Spoil
Beauty	Charm
Beast	Animal
Bandit	Robber
Blaze	Shine
Bond	Tie
Bend	Twist
Bate	Diminish
Beg	Plead
Barbaric	Wild, Savage
Bashful	Shy, Reserved

Words	Synonyms	Words	Synonyms
Begin	Start	Dwell	Live, Dilate
Blend	Mix, Mingle	Declare	Pronounce
Bizarre	Funny	Drunk	Flushed
Below	Under	Deficient	Lacking
Bedevil	Confuse	Damn	Condemn, Curse
Bemoan	Lament	Decrease	Diminish
Babble	Nonsense	Destruction	Devastation
Blame	Fault	Efficient	Competent
Behaviour	Demeanour	Ethnic	Racial
Call	Accost	Enthral	Enslave
Copy	Imitate	Earnest	Serious
Close	Shut	Envious	Jealous
Caress	Love	Ending	Final
Camp	Stay	Egg	Incite
Connect	Attach	Extempore	At once
Cut	Injure, Curtail	Extensive	Far-ranging
Cling	Stick	Extra	Surplus
Conical	Funny	Existence	Life
Convey	Carry	Exceed	Overstep
Conspicuous	Prominent	Enormous	Vast
Cheerful	Happy, Pleasant	Excessive	Superfluous
Curtail	Decrease	Free	Unhindered
Cheerless	Sad, Dejected	Frigid	Cold
Curious	Strange	Feed	Cater
Circumstance	Factor, Situation, Condition	Fame	Reputation
		Frame	Make
Competent	Capable	First	Initial
Congruent	Overlapping	Frighten	Terrorise, Intimidate
Cope	Deal, Endure	Fervent	Fervid
Confident	Sure	Fall	Decline
Complex	Intricate	Feeble	Frail
Cajole	Coax, Flatter	Fickle	Changeable
Cunning	Crafty	Finish	Conclude
Delectable	Joyful, Delightful	Fraud	Deception
Devilish	Diabolical	Forgiving	Placable
Delicate	Soft	Grow	Develop
Devil	Fiend	Greed	Avidity
Delay	Postpone	Greet	Welcome
Dislike	Repugnance	Grave	Serious
Destroy	Ruin	Group	Constellation

Words	Synonyms
Given	Bestowed
Gratitude	Thankfulness
Have	Possess
Hire	Rent
Hit	Strike
Handsome	Beautiful
Hinder	Prevent
Heap	Pile
Hope	Expect
Hard	Harsh
Help	Aid
Hymn	Song
Henpecked	Enslaved
Hoodwink	Mystify, Cheat
Humble	Polite, Urbane, Modest
Harass	Vex, Trouble
Impart	Instil
Intact	Untouched
Instal	Establish
Indict	Impeach
Imitate	Ape
Instigate	Incite
Initiate	Start, Introduce
Inimical	Unfriendly
Insufferable	Intolerable
Impartiality	Justice
Jolly	Merry
Joyful	Delectable
Join	Conjoin
Kind	Benign
Kill	Murder
Kindred	Similar
Kinship	Relationship
Keen	Sharp
Knowledge	Scholarship
Lazy	Slothful
Large	Substantial, Gargantuan
Listless	Careless, Lackadaisical
Lax	Loose
Little	Small
Lifelike	Realistic

Words	Synonyms
Lofty	High
Lenient	Soft, Gentle
Lacking	Deficient, Wanting
Lessen	Decrease
Middleclass	Bourgeois
Mitigate	Lessen, Abate
Modesty	Humility, Lowliness
Mix	Mingle, Blend
Mixture	Mingling
Mixed	Assorted
Modify	Decrease
Mean	Imply
Multifarious	Varied
Miscarry	Abort
Note	Notice
Noble	Stately
Native	Indigenous
Needful	Necessary
Notify	Declare
Nervous	Shaky, Tremulous, Timid
Natural	Spontaneous
Near	Close
Normal	Natural
Offend	Displease
Oppress	Persecute, Tyrannize
Opponent	Adversary
Obstruct	Hinder, Check
Offence	Fault
Offender	Villain
Overstep	Exceed
Overlapping	Congruent
Occult	Mystic
Profane	Unholy
Patience	Forbearance
Pornographic	Obscene
Plenitude	Abundance
Prominent	Important
Prodigal	Spender
Procrastinate	Postpone
Promote	Develop, Honour
Persecute	Tyrannise

Words	Synonyms
Profess	Claim
Pliant	Flexible
Plebian	Common
Polished	Sophisticated
Quake	Shake
Quit	Leave
Queer	Eccentric
Quell	Suppress
Quantify	Allot
Reply	Answer
Relinquish	Retire
Read	Peruse
Relation	Reference
Render	Do
Remainder	Residuals
Repeat	Reiterate
Repentant	Contrite
Retaliative	Retaliatory
Rumour	Hearsay
Reveal	Divulge
Ritualistic	Ceremonious
Soft	Delicate
Sort	Kind, Choose, Select
Selfish	Egoistic
Sensual	Earthly
Suppress	Quell, Check
Stimulate	Provoke
Tasteless	Insipid
Travel	Journey
True	Authentic, Faithful, Truthful
Turbulence	Turmoil
Tragedy	Calamity
Tasteful	Tasty, Delicious
Touching	Painful
Thankful	Grateful
Tremendous	Great, Huge
Tough	Strong
Terminate	Conclude, End
Theory	Doctrine
Tell	Relate
Tremble	Shake, Shiver
Urge	Spur

Words	Synonyms
Unbeaten	Unsubdued
Use	Utilize, Practise
Underhand	Unfair, Undue
Unfair	Unjust
Unravel	Reveal, Divulge
Unimportant	Common
Unconcerned	Apathetic
Unimitated	Inimitable
Unfortunate	Unlucky
Understand	Perceive, Comprehend
Vain	Proud, Haughty, Conceited, Shameless
Vale	Valley, Dale, Dell
Vice	Fault
Virtue	Quality
Veracity	Reality
Value	Price, Prize
Vex	Tease
Vibrate	Quiver, Shake
Violent	Excessive
Vivid	Clear, Lucid
Victory	Triumph
Vulgar	Indecent
Virtuous	Honest
Variegated	Varied, Multifarious
Well	Good
Yell	Cry, Shout
Yonder	There
Yearn	Wish, Desire
Yoke	Slavery
Zest	Earnestness, Enthusiasm
Zealous	Earnest

ANTONYMS

A antonym is a word which conveys a meaning opposite to the given word.

REMEMBER

Words	Antonyms
Abhor	Love
Abnormal	Normal
Able	Unable
Acceptable	Unacceptable
Adequate	Inadequate
Amusing	Boring

Words	*Antonyms*	*Words*	*Antonyms*
Angry	Calm	Hard	Soft
Apex	Bottom	Hate	Love
Attract	Repel	Honest	Dishonest
Bad	Good	Idle	Busy
Barren	Fertile	Immoral	Moral
Beautiful	Ugly	Include	Exclude
Bitter	Sweet	Incorrect	Correct
Brave	Cowardly	Intelligent	Unintelligent
Brief	Lengthy	Kind	Cruel
Bright	Dull	Like	Dislike
Calm	Violent	Long	Short
Careful	Careless	Lucid	Vague
Clear	Vague, Cloudy	Major	Minor
Cold	Hot	Naive	Experienced
Cruel	Kind	Nadir	Apex
Dear	Cheap	Neat	Clumsy
Deep	Shallow	Obedient	Disobedient
Difficult	Easy	Obscure	Clear
Direct	Indirect	Oppose	Support
Dishonest	Honest	Optimistic	Pessimistic
Disobey	Obey	Out	In
Encourage	Discourage	Patience	Impatience
Enormous	Tiny	Peaceful	Belligerent
Excellent	Bad	Pious	Impious
Expensive	Cheap	Polite	Impolite
Eat	Fast	Potent	Impotent
Fair	Unfair	Prominent	Unimportant
Fake	Authentic	Proper	Improper
False	True	Pure	Impure
Famous	Notorious	Quick	Slow
Fool	Genius	Quiet	Disturbance
Generous	Miserly	Real	False, Unreal
Genius	Fool	Reject	Select, Choose
Genuine	Unauthentic	Reliable	Unreliable
Gigantic	Tiny	Respect	Disrespect
Glad	Depressed	Right	Wrong
Good	Bad	Robust	Feeble, Weak
Great	Little	Sad	Happy
Happy	Sad		

Words	Antonyms
Secret	Open
Sensible	Insensible
Severe	Mild
Sharp	Blunt
Simple	Complex
Sociable	Unsociable
Tall	Short
Tidy	Untidy
Uncanny	Canny
Violent	Calm
Vivid	Vague

Words	Antonyms
Strong	Weak
Big	Small
Easy	Difficult
Fast	Slow
High	Low
Catchy	Unattractive
Ugly	Handsome, Beautiful, Tidy
Tasty	Insipid
Sonorous	Harsh

MULTIPLE CHOICE QUESTIONS

Directions (Qs. 1 to 20): *In the following questions choose the word which best expresses the meaning of the given word.*

1. ABSURD
A. Foolish B. Simple
C. Courageous D. Silly

2. ABANDON
A. Lose B. Profit
C. Vacate D. Foil

3. CAJOLE
A. Pause B. Lenient
C. Blast D. Lure

4. COMBAT
A. Fight B. Conflict
C. Shoot D. Quarrel

5. LAMENT
A. Condone B. Console
C. Complain D. Contribution

6. DEBACLE
A. Disgrace B. Defeat
C. Collapse D. Decline

7. SHIVER
A. Fear B. Tremble
C. Shake D. Ache

8. TORTURE
A. Terror B. Harassment
C. Torment D. Tranquility

9. LAUDABLE
A. Lovable B. Commendable
C. Profitable D. Oblivious

10. FIXED
A. Sterile B. Static
C. Stubborn D. Parennial

11. QUEER
A. Unfamiliar B. Cute
C. Curious D. Strange

12. SUFFICIENT
A. Fit B. Proper
C. Adequate D. Vast

13. GLOSS
A. Brightness B. Soothing
C. Rubbing D. Miracle

14. LONGING
A. Prune B. Apathy
C. Curtail D. Craving

15. JEER
A. Applaud B. Magnanimity
C. Avoid D. Scoff

16. ZENITH
A. Minimum B. Nadir
C. Plant D. Peak

17. GARB
A. Distort B. Dress
C. Trivial D. Rage

18. ABHOR
A. Rude
B. Reconcile
C. Crave
D. Detest

19. YIELD
A. Shum
B. Incisive
C. Retain
D. Surrender

20. YOKE
A. Twist
B. Release
C. Link
D. Extra

Directions (Qs. 21 to 38): *In the following questions choose the word which best expresses the opposite of the given word.*

21. TRAGIC
A. Dramatic
B. Strong
C. Gentle
D. Comic

22. ORAL
A. Verbal
B. Sane
C. Minor
D. Written

23. ADMIRE
A. Hate
B. Unlike
C. Dislike
D. Enough

24. VIOLENT
A. Gentle
B. Savage
C. Haughty
D. Decline

25. ADVERSITY
A. Windfall
B. Inprosperity
C. Prosperity
D. Slave

26. GENUINE
A. Spurious
B. Obscure
C. Countless
D. Apathetic

27. GRUDGE
A. Essence
B. Guile
C. Goodwill
D. Ill-will

28. STIFF
A. Soft
B. Courteous
C. Lively
D. Flexible

29. VANITY
A. Conceit
B. Pride
C. Ostentious
D. Humility

30. FRONT
A. Upper
B. Unusual
C. Back
D. Rear

31. ATTRACT
A. Lured
B. Longing
C. Repel
D. Disguise

32. COMFORT
A. Discomfort
B. Discontent
C. Uncomfort
D. Miscomfort

33. WELCOME
A. Repel
B. Accept
C. Resist
D. Fight

34. TACTFUL
A. Naive
B. Loose
C. Strict
D. Uncivilized

35. DUTIFUL
A. Harmful
B. Watchful
C. Forgetful
D. Remiss

36. RIGID
A. Flux
B. Adoptable
C. Yielding
D. Adaptable

37. RARE
A. Petty
B. Poor
C. Small
D. Common

38. ZEAL
A. Despair
B. Calmness
C. Passiveness
D. Indifference

ANSWERS

1	2	3	4	5	6	7	8	9	10
D	C	D	A	C	C	B	C	B	B
11	**12**	**13**	**14**	**15**	**16**	**17**	**18**	**19**	**20**
D	C	A	D	D	D	B	D	D	C
21	**22**	**23**	**24**	**25**	**26**	**27**	**28**	**29**	**30**
D	D	C	A	C	A	C	D	D	D
31	**32**	**33**	**34**	**35**	**36**	**37**	**38**		
C	A	C	A	D	D	D	D		

3. Sentence Completion

It is such an exercise which starts with the primary schools and continues in the highest level of competitive examinations. One must practise it regularly to score well.

Directions (Qs. 1 to 15): *Pick out the most effective word(s) from the given words to fill in the blanks to make the sentence meaningfully complete.*

1. The student ...... that book from the library to study at home.
A. issued B. borrowed
C. hired D. lent

2. I wish I ...... a king.
A. was B. am
C. should be D. were

3. He ...... to listen to my arguments and walked away.
A. denied B. disliked
C. objected D. refused

4. The flow of blood was so ...... that the patient died.
A. intense B. adequate
C. profuse D. extensive

5. When I met her yesterday, it was the first time I ...... her since Christmas.
A. saw B. have seen
C. had seen D. have been seing

6. Can you pay ...... all these articles?
A. for B. of
C. off D. out

7. I ...... you to be at the party this evening.
A. expect B. hope
C. look forward to D. desire

8. ...... being a handicapped person, he is very cooperative and self-reliant.
A. Because B. Although
C. Since D. Despite

9. The child broke ...... from his mother and ran towards the painting.
A. away B. after
C. down D. with

10. With his ...... income, he finds it difficult to live a comfortable life.
A. brief B. sufficient
C. meagre D. huge

11. He could ...... a lot of money in such a short time by using his intelligence and working hard.
A. spend B. spoil
C. exchange D. accumulate

12. Though the brothers are twins, they look ......
A. alike B. handsome
C. indifferent D. different

13. Unfavourable weather conditions can ..... illness.
A. cure B. detect
C. treat D. enhance

14. No sooner did the bell ring, ... the actor started singing.
A. when B. than
C. after D. before

15. If I ...... realised it, I would not have acted on his advice.
A. was B. had
C. were D. have

Directions (Qs. 16 to 25): *In each question, an incomplete statement (Stem) followed by four fillers* *is given. Pick out the best one which can complete the incomplete stem correctly and meaningfully.*

16. Unless you work harder you will fail, means .....
A. if you fail you will work harder.
B. you must at least plan well than you will not fail.
C. hardly you will fail if you do not desire so.
D. if you do not put more efforts, then you will fail.

17. Even if it rains I shall come, means .....
A. if I come it will not rain.
B. if it rains I shall not come.
C. I will certainly come whether it rains or not.
D. whenever there is rain I shall come.

18. Dinesh is as stupid as he is lazy means .....
A. Dinesh is stupid because he is lazy.
B. Dinesh is lazy because he is stupid.
C. Dinesh is either stupid or lazy.
D. Dinesh is equally stupid and lazy.

19. He is so lazy that he .....
A. cannot depend on others for getting his work done.
B. cannot delay the schedule of completing the work.
C. can seldom complete his work on time.
D. dislike to postpone the work that he undertakes to do.

20. He always stammers in public meetings, but his today's speech .....
A. was fairly audible to everyone present in the hall.
B. was not received satisfactorily.
C. could not be understood properly.
D. was free from that defect.

21. In order to raise the company's profit, the employees .....
A. demanded two additional increments.
B. decided to go on paid holidays.
C. requested the management to implement new welfare schemes.
D. offered to work overtime without any compensation.

22. Although, he is reputed for making very candid statements, ...
A. his today's speech was not fairly audible.
B. his promises had always been realistic.
C. his speech was very interesting.
D. his today's statements were very ambiguous.

23. I felt somewhat more relaxed .....
A. but tense as compared to earlier.
B. and tense as compared to earlier.
C. as there was already no tension at all.
D. and tension-free as compared to earlier.

24. With great efforts his son succeeded in convincing him not to donate his entire wealth to an orphanage .....
A. and lead the life of a wealthy merchant.
B. but to a home for the forsaken children.
C. and make an orphan of himself.
D. as the orphanage needed a lot of donations.

25. Even though it is a very large house, ...
A. there is a lot of space available in it for children.
B. there is hardly any space available for children.
C. there is no dearth of space for children.
D. the servants take a long time to clean it.

ANSWERS

1	2	3	4	5	6	7	8	9	10
B	D	D	C	C	A	A	D	A	C
11	**12**	**13**	**14**	**15**	**16**	**17**	**18**	**19**	**20**
D	D	D	B	B	D	C	D	C	D
21	**22**	**23**	**24**	**25**					
D	D	D	C	B					

4. Spotting Errors

The most common errors in English are of spellings, grammar and usage of words. By regular practice, the errors can be easily spotted and minimised.

MULTIPLE CHOICE QUESTIONS

Directions: *In the following questions some of the sentences have errors and some are correct. Find out which part of a sentence has an error, the number of that part is your answer. If a sentence is free from errors, then your answer is D i.e., No error.*

1. (A) Either Ram or/(B) you is responsible/(C) for this action./(D) No error.
2. (A) The student flatly denied/(B) that he had copied/(C) in the examination hall./(D) No error.
3. (A) By the time you arrive tomorrow/(B) I have finished/(C) my work./(D) No error.
4. (A) The captain with the members of his team/ (B) are returning/(C) after a fortnight./(D) No error.
5. (A) After returning from/(B) an all-India tour/ (C) I had to describe about it./(D) No error.
6. (A) The teacher asked his students/(B) if they had gone through/(C) either of the three chapters included in the prescribed text./(D) No error.
7. (A) Do you know/(B) how old were you/(C) when you came here?/(D) No error.
8. (A) Beware of/(B) a fair-weather friend/(C) who is neither a friend in need nor a friend indeed./ (D) No error.
9. (A) Copernicus proved/(B) that Earth/(C) moves round the Sun./(D) No error.
10. (A) The property/(B) was divided/(C) among the two brothers./(D) No error.
11. (A) I am quite certain/(B) that the lady is not only greedy/(C) but miserly./(D) No error.
12. (A) The brilliant success in the examination/ (B) as well as his record in sports/(C) deserves high praise./(D) No error.
13. (A) I cannot find/(B) where has he gone/(C) though I have tried may best./(D) No error.
14. (A) If I was/(B) the Prime Minister of India/(C) I would work wonders/(D) No error.
15. (A) If it weren't/(B) for you,/(C) I wouldn't be alive today./(D) No error.
16. (A) He looked like a lion/(B) baulked from/ (C) its prey./(D) No error.
17. (A) Widespread flooding/(B) is affecting/(C) large areas of the villages./(D) No error.
18. (A) If we really set to/(B) we can get the whole house/(C) cleaned in an afternoon./(D) No error.
19. (A) It's arrogant for you/(B) to assume you'll/ (C)win every time./(D) No error.
20. (A) The two books are the same/(B) except for the fact that this/(C) has an answer in the back./(D) No error.

21. (A) Your husband doesn't/(B) believe that you are older/(C) than I./(D) No error.

22. (A) I could not/(B) answer to/(C) the question./(D) No error.

23. (A) Two years passed/(B) since/(C) my cousin died./(D) No error.

24. (A) I am learning English/(B) for ten years/(C) without much effect./(D) No error.

25. (A) Ramesh has agreed/(B) to marry with the girl/(C) of his parent's choice./ (D) No error.

26. (A) When he was arriving./(B) the party was/(C) in full swing./(D) No error.

27. (A) The most studious boy/(B) in the class/(C) was made as the captain./(D) No error.

28. (A) I am participating/(B) in the two-miles race/(C) tomorrow morning./(D) No error.

29. (A) When the boy committed a mistake/(B) the teacher made him to do/(C) the sum again./(D) No error.

30. (A) Whenever a person lost anything/(B) the poor folk around/(C) are suspected./(D) No error.

ANSWERS

1	2	3	4	5	6	7	8	9	10
B	D	B	B	C	C	D	D	B	C
11	**12**	**13**	**14**	**15**	**16**	**17**	**18**	**19**	**20**
C	D	B	A	C	C	C	A	A	C
21	**22**	**23**	**24**	**25**	**26**	**27**	**28**	**29**	**30**
C	B	A	A	B	A	C	B	B	A

EXPLANATORY ANSWERS

1. Replace 'is' by 'are'.
2. No error.
3. Replace 'have' by 'would have'.
4. Replace 'are' by 'is'.
5. Replace 'had to describe' by 'described'.
6. Replace 'either' by 'any'.
7. No error.
8. No error.
9. Omit 'that'.
10. Replace 'among' by 'between'.
11. Add 'also'.
12. No error.
13. Replace 'has he' by 'he has'.
14. Replace 'was' by 'were'.
15. Replace 'wouldn't be' by 'would not have been'.
16. Replace 'its' by 'his'.
17. Replace 'areas' by 'area'.
18. Replace 'set to' by 'set on'.
19. Replace 'for' by 'of'.
20. Replace 'in' by 'on'.
21. Replace 'I' by 'me'.
22. Omit 'to'.
23. Replace 'passed' by 'have passed'.
24. Replace 'am' by 'have been'.
25. Omit 'with'.
26. Replace 'was arriving' by 'arrived'.
27. Omit 'as'.
28. Replace 'in' by 'at'.
29. Omit 'to'.
30. Replace 'lost' by 'loses'.

5. One Word Substitution

There are many single words in English language which can be perfectly used for a number of words. These words help in expressing ideas in a short and correct manner for the right occasion. Such words not only increase the vocabulary but also enable you to economise in the use of words to a great extent.

Multiple Word Expression	***Substitution***
One who always looks towards the bright side of things	Optimist
One who always looks towards the dark side of things	Pessimist
The time when one develops from a child into an adult	Adolescence
The process of growing more plants in order to form a forest.	Afforestation
The science which deals with farming	Agriculture
From some other country or place etc.	Alien
A term, etc. giving more than one meaning	Ambiguous
A vehicle which is used to carry sick persons	Ambulance
An animal which can live both in water and on land	Amphibian
A lawless situation when there is no government	Anarchy
Belonging to the history of thousands of years old	Ancient
Once a year	Annual
A very old object but still valuable	Antique
Words of opposite meanings	Antonyms
Words of similar meanings	Synonyms
Signatures of a famous person	Autograph
A government led by one person with absolute authority	Autocracy
A written work of one's own life history	Autobiography
A person who has never been married	Bachelor
A person usually having no hair on his head	Bald
A place where one can deposit money and get interest	Bank
A person who cuts our hair	Barber
A building/group of buildings where soldiers live	Barracks
A person who makes buns and biscuits	Baker
A person who lives by asking people for food and money without doing any useful job	Beggar
The crime of having married to two persons at the same time	Bigamy
The branch of science which deals with the study of plants	Botany
Able to speak two languages	Bilingual

Multiple Word Expression	*Substitution*
Able to speak more than two languages	Polyglot
The branch of science which deals with the living organisms	Biology
A powerful snow storm	Blizzard
A great successful book or movie	Blockbuster
A short news on the radio or TV	Bulletin
A system in which the most important works are organised by the government officials	Bureaucracy
A person who has no vision in his eyes	Blind
A page or a series of pages on which the information of days, weeks, months, etc. is given	Calendar
A person who eats human flesh	Cannibal
A complete list of items often arranged alphabetically	Catalogue
A sudden disaster	Catastrophe
A period of 100 years	Century
A branch of science which deals with chemicals	Chemistry
A printed leaf usually issued by banks that we sign to carry certain financial deal	Cheque
A person who makes or mends shoes	Cobbler
A group of people who has been chosen by others to make decisions on their own	Committee
A building in which nuns live	Convent
An animal which feeds on other animals	Carnivorous
A person who does criticism	Critic
A person who cannot hear	Deaf
A condition in which one loses a lot of water from one's body because of vomiting, etc.	Dehydration
A system of government in which the people cast their votes to elect their leaders	Democracy
The study of skin problems	Dermatology
A long piece of land covered with sand	Desert
The art of managing relationships between countries	Diplomacy
A piece of information about the words in a book form	Dictionary
A piece of information about the telephone numbers of the people in a book from	Directory
A person in charge of a newspapers, magazine etc.	Editor
A person who thinks he is better than the others	Egoist
To leave your country and settle in some other country	Emigrate
A book or series of books giving almost all knowledge about an area or some persons etc.	Encyclopaedia
Study of insects	Entomology
Time when day and night are of the same duration	Equinox
To sell things out of the country	Export
To purchase things from some other country	Import
A plant or animal no longer in existence	Extinct
A situation when there is a shortage of food for a long period of time	Famine
An amount of money that we pay for some action or services	Fee
Related to women	Feminine
An animal strong and aggressive	Ferocious

Multiple Word Expression	*Substitution*
A piece of land where plants grow easily from the soil that is favourable to them	Fertile
A work of literature having some imaginary events	Fiction
A large amount of water covering certain area	Flood
A person who sells flowers	Florist
A religious ceremony for burying or cremating a dead person	Funeral
A substance which kills fungus	Fungicide
A person studying or having studied the diseases and the related things of female reproductory system	Gynaecologist
The murder of the person of the same group race or country	Genocide
A substance which kills germs	Germicide
A situation in which many people die because of fire during war	Holocaust
The act of killing a person deliberately	Homicide
A word having the pronunciation as the other one does but it differs in meaning	Homophone
A word having the same spelling as the other one does but it is pronounced in some other way	Homonym
A person who is attracted towards the person of the same sex	Homosexual
Go across and parallel to the ground	Horizontal
A substance which kills the insects	Insecticide
That cannot be corrected	Incorrigible
That cannot be defeated	Invincible
That cannot be eaten	Inedible
That cannot be seen	Invisible
A place in a school or college where books are kept for the benefit of students, teachers etc.	Library
A place in a school or college where scientific experiments are performed	Laboratory
An official who is a judge in the lowest court	Magistrate
A piece of music or a book before it is printed	Manuscript
Related to men	Masculine
One who believes in the existence of God	A theist
One who does not believe in the existence of good	An atheist
That can be believed	Credible
That cannot be believed	Incredible
That which dissolves in a solvent	Soluble
That which does not dissolves in a solvent	Insoluble
Hard writing that can be read	Legible
Hard writing that cannot be read	Illegible
A person who does jobs beneficial to mankind	Philanthropist
A person who goes on foot	Pedestrian
A person who fights for his own country	Patriot
An act of killing oneself	Suicide
A woman whose husband is dead	Widow
A man whose wife is dead	Widower
A person who eats vegetarian and non-vegetarian diets	Omnivorous

Multiple Word Expression	*Substitution*
Something which is everywhere at the same time	Omnipresent
One who knows everything	Omniscient
A child who does not have parents	Orphan
An award etc. given after the death of the person	Posthumous
The place where animals are kept for amusement and to increase the knowledge of the public	Zoo
The science which deals with the study of animals	Zoology

MULTIPLE CHOICE QUESTIONS

Directions: *In questions given below, out of the four alternatives, choose the one which can be substituted for the given words/sentences.*

1. Something that relates to everyone in the world
A. General B. Common
C. Usual D. Universal

2. An expression of mild disapproval
A. Warning B. Denigration
C. Impertinence D. Reproof

3. One who is not easily pleased by anything
A. Maiden B. Medieval
C. Precarious D. Fastidious

4. Murder of a king
A. Infanticide B. Matricide
C. Genocide D. Regicide

5. A remedy for all diseases
A. Stoic B. Marvel
C. Panacea D. Recompense

6. A dramatic performance
A. Mask B. Mosque
C. Masque D. Mascot

7. Study of birds
A. Orology B. Optology
C. Ophthalmology D. Ornithology

8. Ready to believe
A. Credulous B. Credible
C. Creditable D. Incredible

9. Incapable of being seen through
A. Ductile B. Opaque
C. Obsolete D. Potable

10. One who eats everything
A. Omnivorous B. Omniscient
C. Irresistible D. Insolvent

11. A place where bees are kept is called
A. An apiary B. A mole
C. A hive D. A sanctuary

12. One who cannot be corrected
A. Incurable B. Incorrigible
C. Hardened D. Invulnerable

13. One who is in charge of a museum
A. Curator B. Supervisor
C. Caretaker D. Warden

14. Continuing fight between parties, families, clans, etc.
A. Enmity B. Feud
C. Quarrel D. Skirmish

15. A voice loud enough to be heard
A. Audible B. Applaudable
C. Laudable D. Oral

16. A paper written by hand
A. Handicraft B. Manuscript
C. Handiwork D. Thesis

17. Habitually silent or talking little
A. Serville B. Unequivocal
C. Taciturn D. Synoptic

18. To slap with a flat object
A. Chop B. Hew
C. Gnaw D. Swat

19. A person who speaks many languages
A. Linguist B. Monolingual
C. Polyglot D. Bilingual

20. A light sailing-boat built specially for racing
A. Canoe B. Yacht
C. Frigate D. Dinghy

21. A fixed orbit in space in relation to earth
A. Geological B. Geo-synchronous
C. Geo-centric D. Geo-stationary

22. A style in which a writer makes a display of his knowledge
A. Pedantic B. Verbose
C. Pompous D. Ornate

23. A religious discourse
A. Preach B. Stanza
C. Sanctorum D. Sermon

24. A place that provides refuge
A. Asylum B. Sanatorium
C. Shelter D. Orphanage

25. Detailed plan of a journey
A. Travelogue B. Travelkit
C. Schedule D. Itinerary

26. A person who insists on something
A. Disciplinarian B. Stickler
C. Instantaneous D. Boaster

27. A drawing on transparent paper
A. Red print B. Blue print
C. Negative D. Transparency

28. One who believes that all things and events in life are predetermined is a
A. Fatalist B. Puritan
C. Egoist D. Tyrant

29. A school boy who cuts classes frequently is a
A. Defeatist B. Sycophant
C. Truant D. Martinet

30. The act of violating the sanctity of the church is
A. Blasphemy B. Heresy
C. Sacrilege D. Desecration

31. A place where monks live as a secluded community
A. Cathedral B. Diocese
C. Convent D. Monastery

32. One who is fond of fighting
A. Bellicose B. Aggressive
C. Belligerent D. Militant

33. Tending to move away from the centre or axis
A. Centrifugal B. Centripetal
C. Axiomatic D. Awry

34. Words inscribed on tomb
A. Epitome B. Epistle
C. Epilogue D. Epitaph

35. Leave or remove from a place considered dangerous
A. Evade B. Evacuate
C. Avoid D. Exterminate

36. Original inhabitants of a country
A. Abroge B. Aborger
C. Aborgory D. Aborigins

37. Government by the officials
A. Theocracy B. Plutocracy
C. Bureaucracy D. Democracy

38. Incapable of being exhausted
A. Inexhaustible B. Inaexhaustible
C. Exhaustable D. Non-tired

39. A person of good understanding, knowledge and reasoning power
A. Expert B. Intellectual
C. Snob D. Literate

40. One absorbed in his own thoughts and feelings rather than in things outside
A. Scholar B. Recluse
C. Introvert D. Intellectual

ANSWERS

1	2	3	4	5	6	7	8	9	10
D	D	D	D	C	C	D	A	B	A
11	**12**	**13**	**14**	**15**	**16**	**17**	**18**	**19**	**20**
A	B	A	B	A	B	C	D	A	B
21	**22**	**23**	**24**	**25**	**26**	**27**	**28**	**29**	**30**
D	A	D	A	D	B	D	A	C	C
31	**32**	**33**	**34**	**35**	**36**	**37**	**38**	**39**	**40**
D	A	A	D	B	B	C	A	B	C

6. Spelling Errors

There are thousands of words in English language. It is difficult to remember the spellings and meanings of all at once. Try to learn as many as you can. Use a dictionary regularly.

Directions: *Find the correctly spelt words.*

1. A. Damage B. Dammage C. Damaige D. Dammege
2. A. Efficiant B. Effecient C. Efficient D. Eficient
3. A. Schedule B. Schdule C. Schedale D. Schedeule
4. A. Occurad B. Occurred C. Ocurred D. Occured
5. A. Grieff B. Grief C. Grieef D. Grrief
6. A. Guarantee B. Garuntee C. Guaruntee D. Gaurantee
7. A. Meddicine B. Medicine C. Medicene D. Medicinne
8. A. Benefeted B. Benefitted C. Benifited D. Benefited
9. A. Acommodation B. Acomodation C. Accomodation D. Accommodation
10. A. Querrelsome B. Quarrelsame C. Quarrelsome D. Querralsome
11. A. Sympathetic B. Smypathetic C. Sympothetic D. Sympethetic
12. A. Prograssive B. Progressive C. Progresive D. Prograsive
13. A. Uncivilized B. Uncevilized C. Uncivillized D. Uncevelized
14. A. Extravagant B. Extreragent C. Extreregant D. Extravegent
15. A. Missunderstood B. Miesunderstood C. Misunderstood D. Misunderstod
16. A. Belligerent B. Beligirent C. Belligarant D. Belligerrent
17. A. Astonished B. Astronished C. Astoneshed D. Asstonished
18. A. Sincerely B. Sencerely C. Sincerelly D. Sincerrely
19. A. Rigourous B. Rigerous C. Rigorous D. Regerous
20. A. Satellite B. Sattellite C. Satelite D. Sattelite
21. A. Pesanger B. Passenger C. Pessenger D. Pasanger
22. A. Humurous B. Humorous C. Humoreus D. Humorrous
23. A. Exeggerate B. Exaggerate C. Exadgerate D. Exagerate
24. A. Fariegn B. Forein C. Foriegn D. Foreign
25. A. Excesive B. Excessive C. Exccessive D. Exccesive
26. A. Forcaust B. Forcast C. Forecast D. Forecaste
27. A. Paralleted B. Paralelled C. Parralleled D. Parallelled

28. A. Ocasion B. Occassion
C. Occasion D. Ocassion

29. A. Boquet B. Bouquet
C. Bouquete D. Bouquette

30. A. Chettering B. Chaterring
C. Chattering D. Chatering

31. A. Discourage B. Disscourage
C. Discourege D. Discaurage

32. A. Curageous B. Courageous
C. Courrageous D. Couregeous

33. A. Abandon B. Abanddon
C. Abendon D. Abbandon

34. A. Embarassment
B. Emberrassement
C. Embarrassment
D. Embbaresment

35. A. Eccintric B. Eccentrie
C. Eccentric D. Eccintrie

36. A. Occasional B. Occassional
C. Occesional D. Occessional

37. A. Querrel B. Querral
C. Quarrel D. Quarel

38. A. Contrebution B. Contribution
C. Contributtion D. Conterbution

39. A. Desgrace B. Disgrece
C. Disgrice D. Disgrace

40. A. Harassment B. Herassment
C. Harasment D. Harassmient

41. A. Imaginative B. Imeginative
C. Imagenative D. Imaginetive

42. A. Suficient B. Suficiant
C. Sufficient D. Sufficiant

43. A. Adequate B. Edequate
C. Adaquete D. Edaquete

44. A. Exparienced B. Experianced
C. Experienced D. Experrienced

45. A. Flatering B. Fletering
C. Flattering D. Fletaring

46. A. Cuttiveted B. Culltrivated
C. Cultivated D. Caltivated

47. A. Praiceworthy B. Peiseworthy
C. Praiseworthy D. Praisaworthy

48. A. Profesional B. Professionel
C. Professional D. Profissional

49. A. Ameteur B. Amateur
C. Amataur D. Amateor

50. A. Unfevourable B. Unfevaurable
C. Unfavourable D. Unfivourable

ANSWERS

1	2	3	4	5	6	7	8	9	10
A	C	A	B	B	A	B	B	D	C
11	**12**	**13**	**14**	**15**	**16**	**17**	**18**	**19**	**20**
A	B	A	A	C	A	A	A	C	A
21	**22**	**23**	**24**	**25**	**26**	**27**	**28**	**29**	**30**
B	B	B	D	B	C	A	C	B	C
31	**32**	**33**	**34**	**35**	**36**	**37**	**38**	**39**	**40**
A	B	A	C	C	A	C	B	D	A
41	**42**	**43**	**44**	**45**	**46**	**47**	**48**	**49**	**50**
A	C	A	C	A	C	C	C	B	C

सामान्य हिंदी

व्याकरण

व्याकरण वह शास्त्र है जिसके द्वारा किसी भी भाषा के शब्दों और वाक्यों के शुद्ध स्वरूपों एवं शुद्ध प्रयोगों का ज्ञान कराया जाता है।

व्याकरण के चार अंग हैं : (i) वर्ण विचार (ii) शब्द विचार (iii) पद विचार और (iv) वाक्य विचार

भाषा : भाषा अभिव्यक्ति का एक ऐसा साधन है जिसके द्वारा मनुष्य अपने विचारों को दूसरों पर प्रकट कर सकता है और दूसरों के विचार जान सकता है। भाषा के दो रूप हैं–(i) मौखिक और (ii) लिखित।

बोली : भाषा का क्षेत्रीय रूप बोली कहलाता है।

लिपि : किसी भी भाषा के लिखने की विधि को लिपि कहते हैं।

वर्ण : हिन्दी भाषा में प्रयुक्त सबसे छोटी ध्वनि वर्ण कहलाती है। जैसे–अ, आ, ई, क्, ख्, आदि

वर्णमाला : वर्णों के समुदाय को वर्णमाला कहते हैं। हिन्दी वर्णमाला में 44 वर्ण हैं। जिनमें 11 स्वर तथा 33 व्यंजन हैं।

स्वरवर्ण : उन वर्णों को कहते हैं, जिनका उच्चारण बिना किसी दूसरे वर्ण की सहायता से होता है। हिन्दी में 11 स्वर हैं–अ, आ, इ, ई, उ, ऊ, ए, ऐ, ओ, औ, ऋ।

व्यंजन वर्ण : उन वर्णों को कहते हैं, जिनका उच्चारण स्वर वर्णों की सहायता के बिना नहीं हो सकता है। इनकी संख्या 33 है–

क ख ग घ ड़ च
छ ज झ ञ ट ठ
ड ढ़ ण त थ द
ध न प फ ब भ
म य र ल व श
ष स ह।

वर्ण : एक या अधिक वर्णों से बनी हुई स्वतन्त्र सार्थक ध्वनि शब्द कहलाती है।

शब्दों को तत्सम, तद्भव, देशज और विदेशी भागों में बाँटा जाता है।

तत्सम : जो शब्द संस्कृत भाषा से हिन्दी में बिना किसी परिवर्तन के लिए जाते हैं वे तत्सम कहलाते हैं, जैसे– अग्नि, क्षेत्र, मित्र, नासिका आदि।

तद्भव : उन शब्दों को कहते हैं, जो संस्कृत से ही लिए गए हैं, परन्तु हिन्दी में आने पर जिनका रूप बदल गया है। जैसे–आग, खेत, रात आदि।

देशज : उन शब्दों को कहते हैं, जो बोलचाल तथा देश की अन्य भाषाओं से लिए गए हैं। जैसे–कटोरा, झंझत, डिबिया, लोटा आदि।

विदेशज या विदेशी : उन शब्दों को कहते हैं, जो किसी विदेशी भाषा से आए हैं।

जैसे–स्कूल, कार, कमरा, खुदा, जोश, सरकार आदि।

शब्द सम्पदा

तत्सम शब्दों के तद्भव रूप

तत्सम	तद्भव	तत्सम	तद्भव
अग्नि	आग	अद्य	आज
अष्ट	आठ	अंक्षि	आँख
अर्ध	आधा	अस्थि	हड्डी
अश्रु	आँसू	आम्र	आम

तत्सम	तद्भव	तत्सम	तद्भव
ग्राम	गाँव	गर्दभ	गधा
गृध्र	गीध	गौर	गोरा
गृह	घर	घट	घड़ा
धातु	धात	धृत	घी

तत्सम	तद्भव	तत्सम	तद्भव
लक्ष	लाख	सप्त	सात
त्वम्	तुम	दुग्ध	दूध
रत्न	रतन	वर्ष	बरस
भक्त	भगत	मर्कट	बन्दर
रात्रि	रात	उलूक	उल्लू
अन्धकार	अन्धेरा	क्षीर	खीर
निद्रा	नींद	पृष्ठ	पीठ
ज्येष्ठ	जेठ	स्वर्ण	सोना
श्वास	साँस	काक	काग
कार्य	काज	कर्ण	कान
पाद	पाँव	हस्त	हाथ
नासिका	नाक	कंटक	काँटा
दश	दस	दधि	दही
दीप	दीया	निद्रा	नींद
नव	नौ	पत्र	पत्ता

तत्सम	तद्भव	तत्सम	तद्भव
प्रस्तर	पत्थर	जिह्वा	जीभ
हस्ती	हाथी	दन्त	दाँत
क्षेत्र	खेत	नृत्य	नाच
सूचिका	सूई	स्वर्णकार	सुनार
लोक	लोग	पर्यड़्क	पलंग
स्वप्न	सपना	कातर	कायर
पुत्र	पूत	मानव	मनुष्य
शत	सौ	पुष्प	फूल
पक्व	पक्का	कृषक	किसान
कर्म	कार्य	आम्र	आम
कर्ण	कान	अष्ट	आठ
घंटिका	घंटी	चन्द्र	चन्द
यव	जौ	धूम्र	धुआँ
भ्रमर	भँवर		

विराम चिह्न

विराम का अर्थ रुकना। अपने विचारों को ठीक ढंग से प्रकट करने के पढ़ते अथवा लिखते समय हमें कुछ रुकना पड़ता है। इस प्रकार के रुकने को विराम कहते हैं। प्रत्येक-विराम के लिए अलग-अलग चिह्न हैं–

पूर्ण विराम	[।]
अल्प विराम	[,]
अर्ध विराम	[;]
प्रश्न बोधक	[?]
विस्मयादि बोधक	[!]
योजक	[–]
उद्धरण	[“ ”]

कारक

कारक शब्द उस रूप को कहते हैं, जिससे संज्ञा या सर्वनाम वाक्य के साथ सम्बन्ध जाना जाता है।

जैसे–शीला कलम **से** लिखती है।

यह सीमा **की** पुस्तक है।

कारक के भेद विभक्ति चिह्नों सहित

कारक	विभक्ति
कर्त्ता	ने
कर्म	को
करण	से
सम्प्रदान	के लिए
अपादान	से
सम्बन्ध	का, के, की
अधिकरण	में, पर
सम्बोधन	हे, अरे!

पर्यायवाची शब्द

जिन शब्दों से एक समान अर्थ का बोध होता है, उन्हें पर्यायवाची या समानार्थी शब्द कहते हैं।

कुछ पर्यायवाची शब्दों के उदाहरण निम्नलिखित हैं–

आग – अग्नि, अनल, पावक, हुताशन, ज्वाला।

आकाश – नभ, आसमान, गगन, लोभ।

असुर – राक्षस, दानव, निशाचर, दैत्य।

अमृत – अभिय, पीयूष, सुधा, सोम।

अन्धकार – अन्धेरा, तिमिर, तम, तमिस्त्र।

आँख – नेत्र, नयन, लोचन, चक्षु, दृग।

कमल – जलज, पंकज, नीरज, राजीव।

इन्द्र – सुरपति, देवेन्द्र, सुरेन्द्र, देवेश।
ईश्वर – प्रभु, भगवान, जगदीश, दीनबन्धु।
पक्षी – खग, विहग, चिड़िया, नभचर।
बादल – घन, जलधर, वारिद, नीरद।
गंगा – सुरसरि, जाह्नवी, त्रिपथगा, देवनदी, विष्णुपदी।
चन्द्रमा – शशि, मयंक, निशाकर, सुधाकर, सुधांशु, सोम हिमांशु, राकेश।
जल – पानी, नीर, लोभ, अम्बु, सलिल, क्षीर, वारि।
फूल – पुष्प, कुसुम, सुमन, प्रसून, सारंग।
पृथ्वी – भू, भूमि, धरा, वसुन्धरा, वसुधा, धरती क्षमा, लोक।
कपड़ा – पट, वस्त्र, चीर, अम्बर, दुकूल।
घर – गृह, गेह, निकेतन, आलय, निलय, भवन, शाला, धाम, सदन।
जंगल – वन, कानन, अरण्य, विपिन।
तालाब – सरोवर, ताल, जलाशय, तड़ाग।
दिन – दिवस, वासर, वार।
पहाड़ – गिरि, पर्वत, गूधर, नग, महीधर, मेरू।
पत्थर – पहाड़, प्रस्तर, पाहन।
पवन – वायु, समीर, हवा, मारुत, अनिल।
पुत्र – सुत, तनय, पूत, आत्मज।
बिजली – तड़ित, चपला, दामिनी।
वृक्ष – तरू, रूख, विटप, पेड़।
मनुष्य – नर, मानव, मनुज, आदमी।
हाथी – करि, हस्ती, गज।
मित्र – सखा, मीत, सहचर, दोस्त।
राजा – नरेश, नृप, महीप, भूप।
समुद्र – सागर, सिन्धु, जलधि, नीरधि।
सरस्वती – शारदा, वागेश्वरी, भारती, महाश्वेता।
साँप – पन्नग, सर्प, विषधर, अहि, व्याल।

सूर्य – दिनकर, दिवाकर, रवि, भानु, भास्कर।
स्त्री – नारी, महिला, दारा, वामा।
शरीर – देह, तन, काया, गात, बदन।
गणेश – गजानन, गणपति, विनायक, एकदन्त, गजवदन लम्बोदर, विघ्न नाशक।
घोड़ा – तुरंग, बाजि, हय, अश्व, घोटक।
युद्ध – समर, रण, संग्राम।
सिंह – केसरी, मृगराज, केहरी।
शत्रु – अरि, रिपु, बैरी।
विष्णु – हरि, कमलेश, रमापति, चक्रपाणि, केशव, माधव, पीताम्बर।
कोष – खजाना, भण्डार, निधि।
धन – दौलत, द्रव्य, मुद्रा।
तलवार – कृपाण, असि, खड्ग।
अंग – भाग, हिस्सा, अवयव।
चोर – तस्कर, दस्यु, रजनीचर।
पत्नी – भार्या, दारा, गृहिणी।
पुत्र – तनय, सुत, लड़का, बेटा।
पुत्री – तनया, सुता, लड़की, बेटी।
माता – जननी, अम्बा, अम्बिका, अम्मा, माँ, धात्री।
मोर – शिखी, नीलकण्ठ, मयूर।
मृत्यु – मौत, काल, देहान्त।
रक्त – रुधिर, शोणित, खून, लहू।
विष – जहर, हलाहल, गरल।
सोना – कंचन, स्वर्ण, कनक।
हृदय – उर, छाती, वक्ष, वक्षस्थल, हिय, हिया।
सभा – अधिवेशन, परिषद्, बैठक, महासभा, समागम, समिति, सम्मेलन।
यमुना – कालिन्दी, कृष्णा, जमुना, रविसुता तरणि-तनुजा।

विलोम-शब्द

शब्दों के अपने निश्चित अर्थ होते हैं। उन अर्थों के विपरीत अर्थ देने वाले शब्द को विलोम-शब्द कहते हैं।

शब्द	विलोम	शब्द	विलोम	शब्द	विलोम	शब्द	विलोम
अमृत	विष	उदार	संकीर्ण	आदि	अन्त	उत्थान	पतन
अनुकूल	प्रतिकूल	अनुराग	विराग	इच्छा	अनिच्छा	उचित	अनुचित

शब्द	विलोम	शब्द	विलोम
अल्पायु	दीर्घायु	अनुज	अग्रज
उन्नति	अवनति	आकाश	पाताल
अधिक	न्यून	आयात	निर्यात
एक	अनेक	अन्धकार	प्रकाश
अर्थ	अनर्थ	उदय	अस्त
परकीया	स्वकीया	जड़	चेतन
जय	पराजय	अनिवार्य	वैकल्पिक
नकद	उधार	अपेक्षा	उपेक्षा
उपस्थित	अनुपस्थित	आदर	अनादर
अन्धेरा	उजाला	अपना	पराया
उत्तम	अधम	आय	व्यय
सुपुत्र	कुपुत्र	स्वाधीन	पराधीन
आहार	निराहार	कठोर	कोमल
दाता	याचक	दोषी	निर्दोषि
खेद	प्रसन्नता	धनी	निर्धन
निकट	दूर	चर	अचर
देव	दानव	खरा	खोटा
गरीब	अमीर	प्रेम	घृणा
जीवन	मृत्यु	बुरा	भला
सजीव	निर्जीव	मित्र	शत्रु
सुगन्ध	दुर्गन्ध	मौखिक	लिखित
संक्षेप	विस्तार	कटु	मधुर
आरम्भ	अन्त	कड़वा	मीठा
कृतज्ञ	कृतघ्न	दिन	रात
साक्षर	निरक्षर	पवित्र	अपवित्र
पाप	पुण्य	जल	थल
धीर	अधीर	निर्मल	मलिन
गुण	अवगुण	नश्वर	अनश्वर
निन्दा	स्तुति	भारी	हल्का
मनुष्यता	पशुता	सरस	नीरस
मान	अपमान	क्रय	विक्रय

शब्द	विलोम	शब्द	विलोम
धर्म	अधर्म	गहरा	उथला
गुरु	शिष्य	पक्ष	विपक्ष
जन्म	मृत्यु	बन्धन	मुक्ति
यश	अपयश	ज्ञान	अज्ञान
आदर	अनादर	पूर्ण	अपूर्ण
सफल	असफल	शान्त	अशान्त
कीर्ति	अपकीर्ति	वादी	प्रतिवादी
आस्तिक	नास्तिक	स्वदेश	परदेश
सज्जन	दुर्जन	राग	द्वेष
ऊसर	उर्वर	उदार	कृपण
अगला	पिछला	अगम	सुगम
अग्नि	जल	अति	अल्प
अर्थ	अनर्थ	अतल	वितल
अत्यधिक	स्वल्प	अधः	उपरि
अधिकतम	न्यूनतम	अतिवृष्टि	अनावृष्टि
अनाथ	सनाथ	ईश्वर	जीव
अनुलोम	विलोम	अर्पण	ग्रहण
अवनि	अम्बर	अस्त	उदय
आकर्षण	विकर्षण	आगे	पीछे
आजाद	गुलाम	आदान	प्रदान
आधुनिक	प्राचीन	आना	जाना
आय	व्यय	आयात	निर्यात
आवश्यक	अनावश्यक	आशा	निराशा
आस्था	अनास्था	इहलोक	परलोक
उच्च	निम्न	उत्थान	पतन
उपकार	अपकार	उपयोग	दुरुपयोग
एकता	अनेकता	कल	आज
कृत्रिम	प्राकृत	कृष्ण	शुक्ल
कपूत	सपूत	कोमल	कठोर
गगन	धरा	ज्ञान	अज्ञान
झूठ	सच		

लिंग

लिंग का अर्थ है 'चिह्न'। लिंग शब्द उस चिह्न को कहते हैं जिससे वस्तु के पुरुष या स्त्री होने की कल्पना हो। लिंग दो प्रकार के होते हैं—(1) पुल्लिंग (2) स्त्रीलिंग

पुल्लिंग—पुल्लिंग संज्ञा के उस रूप को कहते हैं जिससे उसके पुरुष होने का ज्ञान होता है। जैसे—राम, श्याम, घोड़ा, हाथी, कुत्ता आदि। **स्त्रीलिंग**—स्त्रीलिंग संज्ञा के उस रूप को

कहते हैं जिससे उसके स्त्री होने का ज्ञान हो। जैसे–भैंस, गाय, बकरी, सीता, रमा इत्यादि।

पुल्लिंग	स्त्रीलिंग	पुल्लिंग	स्त्रीलिंग
इन्द्र	इन्द्राणी	मेहतर	मेहतरानी
नौकर	नौकरानी	जेठ	जेठानी
देवर	देवरानी	सेठ	सेठानी
पण्डित	पण्डिताइन	ओझा	ओझाइन
बनिया	बनियाइन	दुबे	दुबाइन
हलवाई	हलवाइन	चौबे	चौबाइन
गुरु	गुरुआइन	लड़का	लड़की
दास	दासी	कबूतर	कबूतरी
हिरण	हिरणी	क्षत्रिय	क्षत्राणी
मुगल	मुगलानी	हिन्दू	हिन्दुआनी
चौधरी	चौधरानी	भव	भवानी
लाला	ललाइन	पण्डा	पण्डाइन
ठाकुर	ठकुराइन	बाबू	बबुआइन
घोड़ा	घोड़ी	गूँगा	गूँगी
बच्चा	बच्ची	चाचा	चाची
बकरा	बकरी	मामा	मामी
मुर्गा	मुर्गी	साला	साली
चींटा	चींटी	रस्सा	रस्सी
देव	देवी	ब्राह्मण	ब्राह्मणी
बेटा	बेटी	बूढ़ा	बुढ़िया
चूहा	चुहिया	डिब्बा	डिबिया
गुड्डा	गुड़िया	कुम्हार	कुम्हारिन
सुनार	सुनारिन	नाती	नातिन
जुलाहा	जुलाहिन	दर्जी	दर्जिन
पापी	पापिन	हाथी	हथिनी
पिता	माता	बैल	गाय
कवि	कवयित्री	विधुर	विधवा
बाप	माँ	बादशाह	बेगम

पुल्लिंग	स्त्रीलिंग	पुल्लिंग	स्त्रीलिंग
नर	मादा	मर्द	औरत
युवक	युवती	वर	वधू
सम्राट्	सम्राज्ञी	साढू	साली
फूफा	बुआ	पुत्र	पुत्री
पहाड़	पहाड़ी	गोप	गोपी
गधा	गधी	तरुण	तरुणी
नर्तक	नर्तकी	बेटा	बिटिया
बछड़ा	बछिया	चिड़ा	चिड़िया
बन्दर	बन्दरिया	कुत्ता	कुतिया
नाई	नाइन	धोबी	धोबिन
ग्वाला	ग्वालिन	भंगी	भंगिन
स्वामी	स्वामिनी	विद्वान्	विदुषी
साधु	साध्वी	पुरुष	स्त्री
पति	पत्नी	वीर	वीरांगना
साहब	मेम	सास	ससुर
मियाँ	बीबी	राजा	रानी
बिलाड़	बिल्ली	अनुज	अनुजा
छात्र	छात्रा	महोदय	महोदया
प्रिय	प्रिया	मामा	मामी
लोटा	लुटिया	मोर	मोरनी
शेर	शेरनी	जाट	जाटिन
डाक्टर	डाक्टरनी	मालिक	मालकिन
माली	मालिन	बाघ	बाघिन
हाथी	हथिनी	स्वामी	स्वामिनी
बालक	बालिका	धनवान	धनवती
धावक	धाविका	नेता	नेत्री
गुणवान	गुणवती	नर	मादा
अभिनेता	अभिनेत्री	प्राचार्य	प्राचार्या
प्रबन्धकर्ता	प्रबन्धकर्ती	दाता	दात्री
ननदोई	ननद	अध्यापक	अध्यापिका

वचन

शब्द के जिस रूप से उसके एक अथवा अनेक होने का बोध हो, उसे वचन कहते हैं।

हिन्दी में दो वचन होते हैं–

(1) एकवचन और (2) बहुवचन

एकवचन–शब्द के जिस रूप से एक ही वस्तु का बोध हो, उसे एकवचन कहते हैं। जैसे–लड़का, गाय, बकरी, घोड़ा, राम, सीता आदि।

बहुवचन–शब्द के जिस रूप से अनेकता का बोध हो उसे बहुवचन कहते हैं। जैसे–लड़के, कपड़े, गायें आदि।

एकवचन	बहुवचन	एकवचन	बहुवचन
लड़का	लड़के	कौवा	कौवे
बेटा	बेटे	कमरा	कमरे
कपड़ा	कपड़े	बहन	बहनें
चीज	चीजें	गधा	गधे
रुपया	रुपये	घोड़ा	घोड़े
नहर	नहरें	रात	रातें
बात	बातें	सड़क	सड़कें
दाना	दाने	लोटा	लोटे
पैसा	पैसे	पुस्तक	पुस्तकें
कन्या	कन्याएँ	वधू	वधुएँ
नारी	नारियाँ	लड़की	लड़कियाँ
मुर्गा	मुर्गे	घण्टा	घण्टे
गद्दा	गद्दे	हीरा	हीरे
बच्चा	बच्चे	प्याला	प्याले
छाता	छाते	गाय	गायें
कथा	कथाएँ	कविता	कविताएँ
बहू	बहुएँ	टोपी	टोपियाँ
नाली	नालियाँ	बेटा	बेटे
ताला	ताले	जूता	जूते

एकवचन	बहुवचन	एकवचन	बहुवचन
डिबिया	डिबियाँ	नाक	नाकें
पूँछ	पूँछें	मूँछ	मूँछें
चिड़िया	चिड़ियाँ	सरिता	सरिताएँ
बालिका	बालिकाएँ	चाभी	चाभियाँ
कहानी	कहानियाँ	दरवाजा	दरवाजे
कलम	कलमें	कुटिया	कुटियाँ
रानी	रानियाँ	नाई	नाइयों
माता	माताएँ	बाल	बालों
हाथ	हाथों	मुख	मुख
कोट	कोट	दाँत	दाँतों
नाखून	नाखूनों	पैर	पैरों
बैल	बैलों	माली	मालियों
राजा	राजाओं	पिता	पिता
चन्द्रमा	चन्द्रमा	कवि	कवियों
मुनि	मुनियों	कौआ	कौए
छात्रा	छात्राएँ	सेना	सेनाएँ
दिशा	दिशाएँ	गुड़िया	गुड़ियाँ
मेज	मेजें	भैंस	भैंसें
अंगूर	अंगूरों	समुद्र	समुद्र
केला	केले	पत्ता	पत्ते

अनेक शब्दों के लिए एक शब्द

जिसकी कोई उपमा न हो : **अनुपम**
तेज बुद्धि वाला : **कुशाग्रबुद्धि**
कल्पना से परे हो : **कल्पनातीत**
जो उपकार नहीं मानता है : **कृतघ्न**
जो उपकार मानता है : **कृतज्ञ**
किसी की हँसी उड़ाना : **उपहास**
ऊपर कहा हुआ : **उपर्युक्त**
ऊपर लिखा हुआ : **उपरलिखित**
जिस पर उपकार किया गया हो : **उपकृत**
इतिहास का ज्ञाता : **इतिहासज्ञ**
आलोचना करने वाला : **आलोचक**
ईश्वर में आस्था रखने वाला : **आस्तिक**
बिना वेतन का : **अवैतनिक**
जो कहा न जा सके : **अकथनीय**
जो गिना न जा सके : **अगणित**

जिसका कोई शत्रु ही न जन्मा हो : **अजातशत्रु**
जिसके समान कोई दूसरा न हो : **अद्वितीय**
जो परिचित न हो : **अपरिचित**
आकाश में उड़ने वाला : **नभचर**
जो टुकड़े-टुकड़े हो गया हो : **खण्डित**
मछली की तरह आँखों वाली : **मीनाक्षी**
मयूर की तरह आँखों वाली : **मयूराक्षी**
बच्चों के लिए काम की वस्तु : **बालोपयोगी**
जिसकी बहुत अधिक चर्चा हो : **बहुचर्चित**
जिस स्त्री को कभी सन्तान न हुई हो : **बन्ध्या (बाँझ)**
फेन से भरा हुआ : **फेनिल**
प्रिय बोलने वाली स्त्री : **प्रियम्वदा**
जिसकी उपमा न हो : **निरुपम**
जो थोड़ी देर पहले पैदा हुआ हो : **नवजात**
जिसका कोई आधार न हो : **निराधार**

नगर में वास करने वाला	: **नागरिक**
रात में घूमने वाला	: **निशाचर**
ईश्वर में विश्वास न रखने वाला	: **नास्तिक**
माँस न खाने वाला	: **निरामिष**
बिल्कुल बर्बाद हो गया	: **ध्वस्त**
जिसकी धर्म में निष्ठा हो	: **धर्मनिष्ठ**
देखने योग्य	: **दर्शनीय**
बहुत तेज चलने वाला	: **द्रुतगामी**
जो किसी पक्ष में न रहे	: **तटस्थ**
तत्त्व को जानने वाला	: **तत्त्वज्ञ**
तप करने वाला	: **तपस्वी**
जिसे देखकर डर लगे	: **डरावना**
जो जन्म से अन्ध हो	: **जन्मान्ध**
जीने की प्रबल इच्छा	: **जिजीविषा**
जिसने इन्द्रियों को जीत लिया हो	: **जितेन्द्रिय**
चिन्ता में डूबा हुआ	: **चिन्तित**
जो बहुत समय तक ठहरे	: **चिरस्थायी**
जिसकी चार भुजाएँ हों	: **चतुर्भुज**
जिसके हाथ में चक्र हों	: **चक्रपाणि**
जिससे घृणा की जाए	: **घृणित**
जिसे गुप्त रखा जाए	: **गोपनीय**
गणित ज्ञाता	: **गणितज्ञ**
आकाश को चूमने वाला	: **गगनचुम्बी**
जिसका आदि न हो	: **अनादि**
जो कुछ न जानता हो	: **अज्ञ**
जो अनुकरण करने योग्य हो	: **अनुकरणीय**
जिसका अन्त न हो	: **अनन्त**
जो कभी न मरे	: **अमर**
जो कम बोलता हो	: **अल्पभाषी**
जिसका इलाज न हो	: **लाइलाज**
जिसका कोई नाथ न हो	: **अनाथ**
कम जानने वाला	: **अल्पज्ञ**
जहाँ जाना सम्भव न हो	: **अगम**
बड़ा भाई	: **अग्रज**
कम खाने वाला	: **अल्पाहारी**
जो बात पहले कभी न हुई हो	: **अभूतपूर्व**
दूसरों के पीछे चलने वाला	: **अनुचर**
जो पहले न पढ़ा हो	: **अपठित**
जिसके आर-पार दिखाई देता हो	: **पारदर्शी**
आज्ञा पालन करने वाला	: **आज्ञाकारी**
काम से जी चुराने वाला	: **कामचोर**
प्रतिदिन होने वाला	: **दैनिक**
जिसका कोई अर्थ न हो	: **निरर्थक**
हाथ से लिखा हुआ	: **हस्तलिखित**
आँखों के सामने होने वाला	: **प्रत्यक्ष**
जिसका आचरण अच्छा हो	: **सदाचारी**
वह पुरुष जिसकी पत्नी मर गई हो	: **विधुर**
वह स्त्री जिसका पति मर गया हो	: **विधवा**
जिसका रूप अच्छा न हो	: **कुरूप**
सदा सत्य बोलने वाला	: **सत्यवादी**
बड़ी इमारत के टूटे-फूटे भाग	: **खण्डहर**
प्रशंसा के योग्य	: **प्रशंसनीय**
जहाँ अनाथ रहते हों	: **अनाथालय**
प्रत्येक मास होने वाला	: **मासिक**
जहाँ पानी के जहाज आकर रुकते हैं	: **बन्दरगाह**
प्रत्येक सप्ताह होने वाला	: **साप्ताहिक**
प्रत्येक वर्ष होने वाला	: **वार्षिक**
जो कठिनाई से मिले	: **दुर्लभ**
जिसका आकार हो	: **साकार**
जिसका आकार न हो	: **निराकार**
जो कभी बूढ़ा न हो	: **अजर**
बहुत बोलने वाला	: **वाचाल**
पृथ्वी पर रहने वाला	: **थलचर**
जल में रहने वाला	: **जलचर**
नभ में विचरण करने वाला	: **नभचर**
जल-थल दोनों में रहने वाला	: **उभयचर**
जिसमें रस न हो	: **नीरस**
पढ़ने वाला	: **पाठक**
जो भाषण देता हो	: **वक्ता**
जो साथ में पढ़ता हो	: **सहपाठी**
जिसके नीचे रेखा खींची हो	: **रेखांकित**
जानने की इच्छा रखने वाला	: **जिज्ञासु**
जिसकी कोई सन्तान न हो	: **निःसन्तान**
जिसका कोई मूल्य न हो	: **अमूल्य**
जो वन में घूमता हो	: **वनचर**
जो इस लोक के बाहर की बात हो	: **अलौकिक**

जो इस लोक की बात हो	: **लौकिक**	सब कुछ जानने वाला	: **सर्वज्ञ**
जिसका सम्बन्ध पश्चिम से हो	: **पाश्चात्य**	जो स्वयं पैदा हुआ हो	: **स्वयंभू**
जो स्थिर रहे	: **स्थावर**	जो शरण में आया हो	: **शरणागत**
दुःखान्त नाटक	: **त्रासदी**	जिसका वर्णन न किया जा सके	: **वर्णनातीत**
ज्ञान देने वाली	: **ज्ञानदा**	व्याकरण जानने वाला	: **वैयाकरण**
भूत, वर्तमान भविष्य को देखने वाला	: **त्रिकालदर्शी**	रचना करने वाला	: **रचयिता**
जो क्षमा के योग्य हो	: **क्षम्य**	खून से रंगा हुआ	: **रक्तरंजित**
हिंसा करने वाला	: **हिंसक**	अत्यन्त सुन्दर स्त्री	: **रूपसी**
हित चाहने वाला	: **हितैषी**	कीर्तिमान पुरुष	: **यशस्वी**

महत्त्वपूर्ण शब्दों की भाववाचक संज्ञा

शब्द	भाववाचक संज्ञा	शब्द	भाववाचक संज्ञा	शब्द	भाववाचक संज्ञा	शब्द	भाववाचक संज्ञा
दास	दासता	क्षत्रिय	क्षत्रियत्व	अहं	अहंकार	अपना	अपनापन
पशु	पशुता	बालक	बालकपन	व्यक्ति	व्यक्तित्व	मीठा	मिठास
बन्धु	बन्धुत्व	मित्र	मित्रता	गरीब	गरीबी	सफल	सफलता
बूढ़ा	बुढ़ापा	सती	सतीत्व	बुरा	बुराई	स्वस्थ	स्वास्थ्य
सेवक	सेवा	शिशु	शैशव	सरल	सरलता	कंजुस	कंजुसी
अपना	अपनत्व	पराया	परायापन	कमजोर	कमजोरी	हरा	हरियाली
सर्व	सर्वस्व	मम	ममत्व	गर्म	गर्मी	मोटा	मोटाई
पण्डित	पाण्डित्य	पुरुष	पुरुषत्व	चालाक	चालाकी	गम्भीर	गम्भीरता
ब्राह्मण	ब्राह्मणत्व	बच्चा	बचपन	पढ़ना	पढ़ाई	लिखना	लिखाई
प्रभु	प्रभुता	नारी	नारीत्व	थकना	थकावट	लिखना	लिखावट
देव	देवत्व	लड़का	लड़कपन	लूटना	लूट	लड़ना	लड़ाई
मनुष्य	मनुष्यता	दानव	दानवता	हँसना	हँसी	आप	अपनत्व
निज	निजता	स्व	स्वत्व				

महत्त्वपूर्ण शब्दों के विशेषण

शब्द	विशेषण	शब्द	विशेषण	शब्द	विशेषण	शब्द	विशेषण
अंक	अंकित	अर्थ	आर्थिक	तीन	तीसरा	झगड़ा	झगड़ालू
इतिहास	ऐतिहासिक	उदासी	उदास	ठण्ड	ठण्डा	जाति	जातीय
कलंक	कलंकित	कुसुम	कुसुमित	काँटा	कँटीला	विदेश	विदेशी
जटा	जटिल	भार	भारी	रोज	रोजाना	भूगोल	भौगोलिक
बनारस	बनारसी	बाजार	बाजारू	पीड़ा	पीड़ित	पुत्र	पुत्रवान
प्यास	प्यासा	पुराण	पौराणिक	आलस्य	आलसी	अंतर	आंतरिक
पंक	पंकित	पक्ष	पाक्षिक	ईर्ष्या	ईर्ष्यालु	कर्म	कर्मठ
धन	धनी	दो	दूसरा	करुणा	कारुणिक	कृपा	कृपालु

शब्द	विशेषण	शब्द	विशेषण	शब्द	विशेषण	शब्द	विशेषण
गुण	गुणी	जल	जलमय	फ्रांस	फ्रांसीसी	बाहर	बाहरी
जीव	जैविक	तट	तटस्थ	भय	भयभीत	मधु	मधुर
तर्क	तार्किक	धर्म	धार्मिक	मौन	मौनी	मन	मानसिक
नमक	नमकीन	पत्थर	पथरीला	मानव	मानवीय	रक्षा	रक्षक
पल्लव	पल्लवित	पान	पनवाड़ी	रघु	राघव	रोग	रोगी
मुख	मुखर	मिठास	मीठा	वर्ष	वार्षिक	शक्ति	शक्तिशाली
मास	मासिक	मद	मादक	श्रम	श्रमिक	अंत	अंतिम
रक्त	रक्तिम	रस	रसीला	कागज	कागजी	मर्म	मार्मिक
वन	वन्य	विष्णु	वैष्णव	शब्द	शाब्दिक	अज्ञान	अज्ञानी
शहर	शहरी	तप	तपस्वी	गुलाब	गुलाबी	प्रकृति	प्राकृतिक
जापान	जापानी	तेज	तेजस्वी	परिचय	परिचित	पूजा	पुजारी
तत्त्व	तात्त्विक	दया	दयालु	रोग	रोगी	ग्राम	ग्रामीण
देव	दैविक	निंदा	निंदक	सुगंध	सुगंधित	मैं	मेरा
नव	नवीन	पोषण	पोषक	जो	जैसा	आप	आप-सा
पेट	पेटू	पाप	पापी	तुम	तुम्हारा	कौन	कैसा
पूजा	पूज्य	भूख	भूखा	वह	वैसा	पढ़ना	पढ़ाकू
फेन	फेनिल	भारत	भारतीय	गाना	गायक	बेचना	बिकाऊ
माया	मायावी	रंग	रंगीन	भागना	भगोड़ा	वन्द	वन्दनीय
विष	विषैला	श्री	श्रीमान	चलना	चलती	घूमना	घुमक्कड़
सुर	सुरीला	विवाह	वैवाहिक	चलना	चालू	मरना	मरियल
आदर	आदरणीय	ऋण	ऋणी	भूलना	भुलक्कड़	पीछे	पिछला
किताब	किताबी	क्रम	क्रमिक	भीतर	भीतरी	नीचे	निम्न
ग्राम	ग्रामीण	घर	घरेलू	अणु	आणविक	अधिकार	आधिकारिक
चतुर	चतुरता	जहर	जहरीला	अनुभव	अनुभवी	अन्याय	अन्यायी
सप्ताह	साप्ताहिक	अनुभव	अनुभवी	अपमान	अपमानित	अभ्यास	अभ्यासी
ओज	ओजस्वी	कल्पना	काल्पनिक	अवश्य	आवश्यक	आदि	आदिम
कुल	कुलीन	गाँव	गँवार	आयु	आयुष्मान्	उदय	उदित
चमक	चमकीला	चाचा	चचेरा	उपज	उपजाऊ	एकता	एक
दीन	दीनता	नगर	नागरिक	अंत	अंतिम	कुल	कुलीन
नागपुर	नागपुरी	परिवार	पारिवारिक	खर्च	खर्चीला	खून	खूनी
पुष्प	पुष्पित	पिता	पैतृक	गुण	गुणी		

श्रुतिसम भिन्नार्थक शब्द

शब्द	अर्थ	शब्द	अर्थ	शब्द	अर्थ	शब्द	अर्थ
आदि	आरम्भ	आदी	अभ्यस्त	अरि	शत्रु	अरी	सम्बोधन
कुल	वंश	कूल	किनारा	अगम	दुर्गम	आगम	शास्त्र

शब्द	अर्थ	शब्द	अर्थ	शब्द	अर्थ	शब्द	अर्थ
अयश	अपकीर्ति	अयस्क	लोहा	पुर	नगर	पूर	बाढ़
अपेक्षा	चाहना, तुलना में	उपेक्षा	निरादर	भवन	महल	भुवन	संसार
अनिल	हवा	अनल	आग	लक्ष्य	उद्देश्य	लक्ष	लाख
अवधि	काल, समय	अवधी	अवध की भाषा	सर	तालाब	शर	बाण
आयात	बाहर से आना	आयत	एक आकृति	सर्ग	अध्याय	स्वर्ग	एक लोक
चिर	पुराना	चीर	कपड़ा	कर्म	कार्य	क्रम	सिलसिला
तनु	पतला	तनू	पुत्र, गाय	चिता	शव जलाने के लिए लकड़ियों का ढेर	चीता	बाघ
तरंग	लहर	तुरंग	घोड़ा				
दारा	स्त्री	द्वार	दरवाजा	शव	लाश	शब	रात
दूत	संदेशवाहक	द्यूत	जुआ	शस्त्र	हथियार	शास्त्र	ग्रन्थ
जलद	बादल	जलज	कमल	श्रवण	सुनना	श्रमण	बौद्ध संन्यासी
प्रदीप	दीपक	प्रतीप	उल्टा	मत	विचार	मत्त	मस्त
प्रसाद	कृपा	प्रासाद	महल	शोक	दु:ख	शौक	चाव
पास	निकट	पाश	बन्धन	ग्रह	नक्षत्र	गृह	घर
द्विप	हाथी	द्वीप	टापू	कपट	धोखा	कपाट	दरवाजा
देव	देवता	दैव	भाग्य	उपयुक्त	ठीक	उपर्युक्त	ऊपर कहा गया
नीर	जल	नीड़	घोंसला	सुत	बेटा	सूत	धागा
पवन	वायु	पावन	पवित्र	शूर	वीर	सूर	अंधा
बन्द	खुला नहीं	बद	बुरा	श्याम	कृष्ण	शाम	संध्या
पथ	रास्ता	पथ्य	रोगी का भोजन	दिन	वार	दीन	गरीब
				कटिबद्ध	तैयार रहना	करबद्ध	हाथ जोड़ना

अनेकार्थक शब्द

शब्द	विभिन्न अर्थ	शब्द	विभिन्न अर्थ
अंक	संख्या, गोद	जड़	मूर्ख, मूल
अक्षर	वर्ण, ईश्वर	कल	मशीन, आनेवाला कल, चैन
पानी	जल, प्रतिष्ठा	सुर	देवता, स्वर
अचल	पवर्त, स्थिर	द्विज	पक्षी, ब्राह्मण
आम	फल, सामान्य	तीर	किनारा, बाण
अंबर	वस्त्र, आकाश	प्रकृति	स्वभाव, कुदरत
अवस्था	आयु, दशा	पत्र	चिट्ठी, पत्र
उत्तर	दिशा, जबाव	पद	पैर, उपाधि
विधि	तरीका, भाग्य	फल	परिणाम, फल
कर	हाथ, टैक्स	तनु	पतला, कोमल
कनक	सोना, धतुरा	वर्ण	रंग, जाति
गुरु	श्रेष्ठ, शिक्षक	हल	समाधान, खेत जोतने का साधन
हान	भारी हथौड़ा, बादल	अशोक	राजा, वृक्ष

शब्द	विभिन्न अर्थ	शब्द	विभिन्न अर्थ
आभीर	अहीर, एक राग	घट	घड़ा, हृदय
एकाक्ष	काना, कौआ	जलज	कमल, मछली
खल	दुष्ट, खलिहान	हेम	सोना, जल

सामान्य अशुद्धियाँ

अशुद्ध	शुद्ध	अशुद्ध	शुद्ध	अशुद्ध	शुद्ध	अशुद्ध	शुद्ध
दुनियां	दुनिया	श्रीमति	श्रीमती	शताब्दि	शताब्दी	लड़ायी	लड़ाई
सामिग्री	सामग्री	वापिस	वापस	स्थाई	स्थायी	लिखायी	लिखाई
प्रदर्शिनी	प्रदर्शनी	द्वारिका	द्वारका	अलोकिक	अलौकिक	कृप्या	कृपया
ऊत्थान	उत्थान	दुसरा	दूसरा	गंवार	गँवार	असोक	अशोक
प्रशाद	प्रसाद	अमावश्या	अमावस्या	दुस्कर	दुष्कर	मूल्यावान	मूल्यवान्
वसंत	वसंत	बर्ष	वर्ष	नवम्	नवम	क्षात्र	छात्र
विना	बिना	बन	वन	छमा	क्षमा	प्रन्तु	परन्तु
दाइत्व	दायित्व	सम्वाद	संवाद	प्रीक्षा	परीक्षा	मरयादा	मर्यादा
कुन्डली	कुण्डली	मॉसिक	मानसिक	दुदर्शा	दुर्दशा	विषेश	विशेष
कन्ठ	कण्ठ	अगामी	आगामी	उज्वल	उज्ज्वल	आल्हाद	आहलाद्
सप्ताहिक	साप्ताहिक	संसारिक	सांसारिक	महत्व	महत्त्व	उपलक्ष	उपलक्ष्य
आधीन	अधीन	हस्ताक्षेप	हस्तक्षेप	लीये	लिये	पिओ	पियो
बरात	बारात	क्षत्रीय	क्षत्रिय	हुये	हुए	कवित्री	कवयित्री
तिथी	तिथि	कालीदास	कालिदास	प्रमात्मा	परमात्मा	घनिष्ट	घनिष्ठ
पुर्ती	पूर्ति	अतिथी	अतिथि	यथेष्ठ	यथेष्ट	पियास	प्यास
नीती	नीति	ग्रहणी	गृहिणी	व्यस्क	वयस्क	त्यौहार	त्योहार
क्यूँ	क्यों	साधू	साधु	मुसलिम	मुस्लिम	ऐैनक	ऐनक
वधु	वधू	रेणू	रेणु	नोकरी	नौकरी	कल्यान	कल्याण
नुपुर	नूपुर	निर्वान	निर्वाण	पाणी	पानी	आसा	आशा
जादु	जादू	द्रश्य	दृश्य	हृदय	हृदय	घ्रणा	घृणा
अनुग्रहीत	अनुगृहीत	बृज	ब्रज	श्रंगार	शृंगार	हिन्दुस्थान	हिन्दुस्तान
बनस्पति	वनस्पति	श्राप	शाप	प्रशन	प्रश्न	ग्यान	ज्ञान
सैना	सेना	सेनिक	सैनिक	अन्धेरा	अँधेरा	पेड	पेड़
इतिहासिक	ऐतिहासिक	प्रथक	पृथक	महयान्ह्न	मध्यान्ह	मेंहदी	मेहंदी
सम्पति	सम्पत्ति	कृतघन	कृतघ्न	शमशान	श्मशान	चिन्ह	चिह्न
बिमारी	बीमारी	व्यक्तिक	वैयक्तिक	कुंज	कुञ्ज	ग्रहस्थ	गृहस्थ
वितीत	व्यतीत	निस्वार्थ	निःस्वार्थ	अजोध्या	अयोध्या	अनधिकार	अनाधिकार
परिस्थित	परिस्थिति	रचियता	रचयिता	अनिष्ठा	अनिष्ट	अनुकुल	अनुकूल
मैथिलिशरण	मैथिलीशरण	आर्शिवाद	आशीर्वाद	अनुसंगिक	आनुषंगिक	अनुशरण	अनुसरण
निरिक्षण	निरीक्षण	पत्नि	पत्नी	अभिसेक	अभिषेक	अरमाण	अरमान

अशुद्ध	शुद्ध	अशुद्ध	शुद्ध	अशुद्ध	शुद्ध	अशुद्ध	शुद्ध
अहिल्या	अहल्या	आदरनीय	आदरणीय	सम्राज	साम्राज्य	सविनयपूर्वक	सविनय
आविस्कार	आविष्कार	उँचाई	ऊँचाई	सिंदुर	सिंदूर	स्त्रवण	श्रवण
उतरदाई	उत्तरदायी	उपर	ऊपर	हरीश्चन्द्र	हरिश्चन्द्र	हिन्दु	हिन्दू
उपरोक्त	उपर्युक्त	उश्रृंखल	उच्छृंखल	हिन्दूस्तान	हिन्दुस्तान	बुद्धिवान	बुद्धिमान्
कलस	कलश	कल्यान	कल्याण	भाग्यमान	भाग्यवान	विद्वान	विद्वान्
गनित	गणित	जबाब	जवाब	श्रीमान	श्रीमान्	आंख	आँख
तत्व	तत्त्व	तलाब	तालाव	ऊंट	ऊँट	कंगना	कँगना
तिरष्कार	तिरस्कार	त्रिवार्षिक	त्रैवार्षिक	गँगा	गंगा	गांधी	गाँधी
दिपिका	दीपिका	देहिक	दैहिक	जांच	जाँच	तांगा	ताँगा
द्वन्द	द्वन्द्व	नरायन	नारायण	दांत	दाँत	मंहगा	महँगा
निरव	नीरव	निरोग	नीरोग	मांस	माँस	मुंह	मुँह
पुष्टी	पुष्टि	पुस्प	पुष्प	सांप	साँप	सांस	साँस
पेत्रिक	पैतृक	प्रनय	प्रणय	हुँकार	हुंकार	निर्पेक्ष	निरपेक्ष
प्रनाम	प्रणाम	प्रयाप्त	पर्याप्त	भाप्कर	भास्कर	सन्मुख	सम्मुख
प्रसंशा	प्रशंसा	प्रांगन	प्रांगण	माताहीन	मातृहीन	विद्यार्थि	विद्यार्थी
प्रान	प्राण	पृष्ट	पृष्ठ	गुणि	गुणी	द्वैवाषिक	द्विवार्षिक
ब्रत	व्रत	भगीरथी	भागीरथी	पूज्यनीय	पूजनीय	अकाश	आकाश
भरथ	भरत	भष्म	भस्म	इद	ईद	इसलाम	इस्लाम
मंत्रीमंडल	मंत्रिमण्डल	रसायण	रसायन	ऐसा	ऐसा	दोसरा	दूसरा
राज्यमहल	राजमहल	रामायन	रामायण	पुत्रि	पुत्री	प्रस्तूत	प्रस्तुत
वनोवास	वनवास	वानी	वाणी	हरयाली	हरियाली	दिवाली	दीवाली
वाल्मीकी	वाल्मीकि	वास्प	वाष्प	राष्ट्रिय	राष्ट्रीय	एकहरा	इकहरा
व्योहार	व्यवहार	सन्यासी	संन्यासी	एतबार	इतबार		

वाक्यगत अशुद्धियाँ

अशुद्ध	शुद्ध	अशुद्ध	शुद्ध
हम अच्छी भाषण दिए थे।	हमने अच्छा भाषण दिया था।	राम और सीता आयी थी।	राम और सीता आए थे।
आप खाए कि नहीं?	आपने खाया कि नहीं?	भाई-बहन जा रही हैं।	भाई-बहन जा रहे हैं।
वह मुझे देखा तो घबरा गया।	उसने मुझे देखा तो घबरा गया।	वह लड़की को बुलाओ।	उस लड़की को बुलाओ।
मैं किताब पढ़ा हूँ।	मैंने किताब पढ़ी है।	मेरे लिए पढ़ता हूँ।	अपने लिए पढ़ता हूँ।
मैं सारी पुस्तक पढ़ डाली।	मैंने सारी पुस्तक पढ़ डाली।	सीता राम की आज्ञाकारी पत्नी थी।	सीता राम की आज्ञाकारिणी पत्नी थीं।
सीता भात खायी।	सीता ने भात खाया।		
राम रोटी खाया।	राम ने रोटी खायी।	देरी न करना।	देर न करना।
लड़की ने दही गिरा दी।	लड़की ने दही गिरा दिया।	उसे मृत्युदण्ड की सजा मिली।	उसे मृत्युदण्ड मिला।
शुद्ध गाय की घी दो।	गाय का शुद्ध घी दो।	हमारे शिक्षक प्रश्न पूछते हैं।	हमारे शिक्षक प्रश्न करते हैं।
तुम, मैं और वह चलेगा।	तुम, वह और मैं चलूँगा।	कै बजे? तीन बजा।	कितना बजा? तीन बजे।

अशुद्ध	शुद्ध	अशुद्ध	शुद्ध
उसका प्राण उड़ गया।	उसके प्राण उड़ गये।	मेरे को मत मारो।	मुझे मत मारो।
मैंने आँख से देखा।	मैंने आँखों से देखा।	मोहन ने पत्र को पढ़ा।	मोहन ने पत्र पढ़ा।
अपन को पढ़ना है।	मुझे पढ़ना है।	पुस्तक पर नहीं लिखो।	पुस्तक पर मत लिखो।
पुस्तक फट गया।	पुस्तक फट गई है।	वह सज्जन पुरुष है।	वह सज्जन है।
घोड़ी तेज दौड़ता है।	घोड़ी तेज दौड़ती है।	आप हमारे घर आओ।	आप हमारे घर आइए।
मेरा प्रणम स्वीकार करो।	मेरा प्रणाम स्वीकार करो।	हम आपसे कुछ कहे थे।	हमने आपसे कुछ कहा था।
दो बालक खेलता है।	दो बालक खेलते हैं।	मकान की दायीं ओर सड़क है।	मकान के दायीं ओर सड़क है।
ये सब मेरा पुस्तक है।	ये सब मेरी पुस्तकें हैं।	पिताजी घर नहीं हैं।	पिताजी घर पर नहीं हैं।
सूरज पूरब में उगते हैं।	सूरज पूर्व में उगता है।	घर पर सब कुशल हैं।	घर में सब कुशल हैं।
वह लौट आए।	वे लौट आए।	उसे भारी दुःख हुआ।	उसे बहुत दुःख हुआ।
वहाँ अनेकों लोग थे।	वहाँ अनेक लोग थे।	सड़क में मत खेलो।	सड़क पर मत खेलो।

मुहावरे तथा लोकोक्तियाँ

- अँगूठी का नगीना—अत्यन्त महत्त्वपूर्ण।
- अंधा दरबार—न्यायहीन स्थान।
- अंधेर नगरी—न्याय का अभाव।
- अक्ल का दुश्मन—मूर्ख।
- अक्ल का दुम—मूर्ख।
- आँख का तारा—अतिप्रिय।
- ईद का चाँद—बहुत दिनों के बाद दिखाई देना।
- कछुआ चाल—धीमी गति।
- काला नाग—दुष्ट आदमी।
- किताबी कीड़ा—सदैव कुछ-न-कुछ पढ़ना।
- किस्मत का मारा—भाग्य का मन्द।
- कोल्हू का बैल—बहुत कठिन परिश्रम करनेवाला।
- कोड़ी का तीन—तुच्छ।
- खाली हाथ—पैसे का अभाव।
- गाजर-मूली—अशक्त।
- गुलर का फूल—दुर्लभ वस्तु।
- गोबर-गणेश—निरामूर्ख।
- घर का उजाला—कुल-दीपक।
- घड़ियाली आँसू—बनावटी शोक।
- चलता-पुरजा—चालाक।
- चाँद का टुकड़ा—परम सुन्दर वस्तु या व्यक्ति।
- चाँदी का जूता—रिश्वत।
- चार दिन की चाँदनी—थोड़े समय का सुख।
- जलती आँख—क्रोधाभिभूत।
- जीभ का पतला—लालची।
- टेढ़ी खीर—विकट काम।
- ठिकाने की बात—न्यायसंगत बात।
- अढ़ाई दिन की हुकूमत—थोड़े समय का ऐश्वर्य।
- तकदीर का सिकन्दर—भाग्य का बलवान्।
- थाली का बैंगन—मत बदलते रहना।
- दाँत कटी रोटी—घनिष्ठता।
- दाहिना हाथ—सहायक।
- दिल का बादशाह—बहुत बड़ा उदार।
- दूध का दूध और पानी का पानी—उचित न्याय।
- दूध का धोआ—निर्दोष।
- दो दिन का मेहमान—बहुत थोड़े समय ठहरने वाला।
- धरती का फूल—ऐसा व्यक्ति जो हाल में अमीर हुआ है।
- धोबी का कुत्ता—निकम्मा।
- नसीब का मारा—बुरे दिन देखनेवाला।
- निन्यानबे का फेरा—धन बढ़ाने की चिन्ता।
- पत्थर का कलेजा—हर दुःख सहने की शक्ति।
- पत्थर की लकीर—चिरस्थायी सदा सत्य।
- फूलों की सेज—आनन्ददायक कार्य।
- बगुला-भगत—कपटी व्यक्ति।
- बच्चों का खेल—साधारण काम।
- बलि का बकरा—निःसहाय व्यक्ति।

- बरसाती बादल–अस्थायी।
- बात का पक्का–सत्यवादी।
- बायें हाथ का खेल–सरल काम।
- बिन बादल बरसात–असमय लाभ।
- बे-पेंदी का लोटा–बे ठिकाने का आदमी।
- भागीरथ प्रयत्न–अत्यधिक परिश्रम।
- भीष्म प्रतिज्ञा–दृढ़ संकल्प।
- मक्खी चूस–कंजूस।
- मिट्टी के मोल–बहुत सस्ता।
- मोटा असामी–मूर्ख मालदार।
- राम कहानी–आत्मवृतान्त।
- लँगोटिया यार– बचपन का मित्र।
- हवाई महल–कोरी कल्पना।
- आँख लगना–नींद आना।
- आँख खुलना–होश में आना।
- आँखें दिखाना–क्रोध से घूरना।
- आँसू पोंछना–धैर्य बँधाना।
- अन्धे की लकड़ी–एकमात्र सहारा।
- कान भरना–चुगली करना।
- कान पर जूँ न रेंगना–कोई असर न होना।
- नाक कटना–प्रतिष्ठा खत्म होना।
- नाक रगड़ना–दीनता दिखाना।
- नाकों चने चबवाना–खूब सताना।
- मुँह की खाना–बुरी तरह हारना।
- आस्तीन का साँप–विश्वासघाती मित्र।
- कन्धे से कन्धा मिलाना–पूरा सहयोग करना।
- ईंट से ईंट बजाना–पूरी तरह नष्ट कर देना।
- नौ दो ग्यारह होना–भाग जाना।
- दाँत खट्टे करना–बुरी तरह हराना।
- हाथ मलना–पछताना।
- खून का प्यासा–जानी दुश्मन।
- घी के दिए जलाना–खुशी मनाना।
- चार चाँद लगाना–प्रतिष्ठा बढ़ाना।
- तीन तेरह होना–अलग-अलग होना।
- पानी फेर देना–नाश कर देना।
- गाल बजाना–डींगे मारना।
- जान से हाथ धो बैठना–मारा जाना।
- पानी-पानी होना–बहुत लज्जित होना।
- फूला न समाना–बहुत प्रसन्न होना।
- अपना उल्लू सीधा करना–अपना मतलब निकालना।
- आँखें चुरा लेना–अनदेखा कर देना।
- अन्धे की लाठी–एकमात्र सहारा।
- आसमान पर चढ़ना–बहुत अभिमान करना।
- आँखें खुलना–होश आना।
- चोरी और सीना जोरी–दोषी होकर धमकाना।
- आग में घी डालना–क्रोध को भड़काना।
- अँगुली पर नचाना– अच्छी तरह वश में करना।
- एक आँख से देखना–समान दृष्टि से देखना।
- एक ही थैले के चट्टे-बट्टे–एक जैसे।
- ओखली में सिर देना–जान-बूझकर आपत्ति मोल लेना।
- कलेजा मुँह को आना–बहुत दुःखी होना।
- कफन बाँधकर चलना–मौत से न घबराना।
- काँटे बिछाना–बाधा डालना।
- कलेजा ठण्डा होना–सन्तोष होना।
- कमर कसना–तैयार होना।
- खून खौलना–जोश में आना।
- खाक छानना–मारे-मारे फिरना।
- गागर में सागर भरना–थोड़े शब्दों में बहुत कुछ कह देना।
- घाव पर नमक छिड़कना–दुखी को अधिक दुखी करना।
- घी के दिए जलाना–खुशी मनाना।
- घोड़े बेचकर सोना–गहरी नींद में सोना।
- चल बसना–परलोक सिधारना।
- छठी का दूध याद आना–भारी संकट में पड़ना।
- छाती पर साँप लोटना–बहुत ईर्ष्या होना।
- जमीन पर पैर न रखना–अधिक घमण्ड होना।
- झक मारना–व्यर्थ समय खोना।
- टेढ़ी खीर–कठिन काम।
- डींग मारना–अपनी झूठी प्रशंसा करना।
- डूब मरना–बहुत लज्जित होना।
- तलवे चाटना–चापलूसी करना।
- ताक में रहना–मौका ढूँढ़ते रहना।
- दंग रह जाना–आश्चर्य में पड़ जाना।
- दाल न गलना–वश न चलना।
- दाल में काला होना–संदेह होना।
- पीठ दिखाना–हारकर भागना।
- मुँह तोड़ उत्तर देना–खरा उत्तर देना।

वस्तुनिष्ठ प्रश्न

अभ्यास-1

निर्देशः *नीचे प्रत्येक शुद्ध शब्द की वर्तनी के लिए चार विकल्प दिए गए हैं। आपको सही विकल्प का चयन करना है।*

1. A. ऋषि B. ऋषी C. रिषी D. ऋसि

2. A. विषेसन B. विशेषण C. विसेशन D. विशेशन

3. A. दुशासन B. दुसाशन C. दूशाषण D. दुःशासन

4. A. संस्कृति B. संसकृति C. संष्कृति D. संस्कृती

5. A. दूनियां B. दुनियां C. दुनिया D. दूनिआ

6. A. टिपनी B. टिप्पणि C. टिप्पणी D. टिप्पनी

7. A. शाषण B. साशन C. शासन D. शाशन

8. A. किसमस B. किरसमस C. क्रिसमस D. कृसमस

9. A. अनुग्रहित B. अनुग्रहीत C. अनुगृहीत D. अनुग्रहित

10. A. पराकम B. प्राक्रम C. पराक्रम D. प्राकर्म

11. A. नायका B. नाइका C. नाइक D. नायिका

12. A. समरिधी B. समद्धी C. समृद्धि D. समरिद्धि

13. A. युधिष्ठर B. यूधिष्ठर C. युधिष्ठिर D. युधिष्टर

14. A. वाल्मीकि B. बाल्मीकि C. बालमीकि D. बाल्मिक

15. A. परलोकिक B. प्रलौकिक C. पारलौकिक D. परलौकिक

16. A. त्रितीय B. तर्तीय C. तृतीय D. तिरतीय

17. A. व्योहार B. व्यौहार C. व्यवहार D. ब्यवहार

18. A. अहिल्या B. अहल्या C. अहिलया D. अहीलया

19. A. आदरनीय B. आदरणीय C. आदरनीया D. आदरणीया

20. A. आर्द B. आद्र C. आर्द्र D. आर्दृ

21. A. आधीन B. अधिन C. अधीन D. अधीम

22. A. आविस्कार B. आविष्कार C. आवीस्कार D. आविश्कार

23. A. आसा B. आषा C. आशा D. अशा

24. A. उज्वल B. उजज्ज्वल C. उजज्वल D. उज्ज्वल

25. A. उन्नती B. उन्नित C. उन्नति D. उन्नती

26. A. कलस B. कलष C. कलश D. कलशा

27. A. गनीत B. गनित C. गणीत D. गणित

28. A. तलाव B. तालाव C. तलाब D. तालाब

29. A. दुष्ट B. दूष्ट C. दुस्त D. दुश्त

30. A. निरोग B. निररोग C. नीरोग D. नीरोगी

उत्तरमाला

1. A	2. B	3. D	4. A	5. C
6. C	7. C	8. C	9. C	10. C
11. D	12. C	13. C	14. A	15. C
16. C	17. C	18. B	19. B	20. C
21. C	22. B	23. C	24. D	25. C
26. C	27. D	28. D	29. A	30. C

अभ्यास-2

निर्देशः *नीचे कुछ शब्द दिए गए हैं। प्रत्येक के पर्यायवाची के चार विकल्प दिए गए हैं। इनमें से एक विकल्प सही पर्यायवाची है, उसका चयन कीजिए :*

1. अग्नि
A. अनिल B. अनल
C. गर्म D. ताप

2. अमृत
A. पीयूष B. गरल
C. सरस D. जीवनदायनी

3. आँख
A. लोचन B. आस्थि
C. वदन D. जलज

4. आकाश
A. अनन्त B. पाताल
C. वितल D. तल

5. कपड़ा
A. परिधान B. पटिका
C. पीताम्बर D. लँहगा

6. कमल
A. सरोज B. सरोवर
C. पंक D. पुष्प

7. गंगा
A. पाताल नदी B. हिमनदी
C. भागीरथ D. त्रिपथगा

8. चाँद
A. मयंक B. भानु
C. दिनकर D. रवि

9. नदी
A. सरिता B. प्रवाह
C. धारा D. जलधर

10. पर्वत
A. पत्थर B. चट्टान
C. शिखर D. मेरू

11. पवन
A. अनिल B. अनल
C. अग D. विहग

12. पति
A. साजन B. प्रिया
C. भार्या D. दारा

13. पानी
A. मही B. मेदिनी
C. अम्बु D. तरणी

14. पुत्र
A. आत्मज B. तनया
C. सुता D. आत्मजा

15. पुत्री
A. सुता B. सुत
C. आत्मज D. नन्दन

16. फूल
A. बहार B. मधु
C. माधव D. सुमन

17. वृक्ष
A. विटप B. अभ्र
C. प्रसून D. रसा

18. बादल
A. अज B. व्यामोह
C. नीरद D. मधुप

19. बिजली
A. चंचला B. खटका
C. त्रास D. संत्रास

20. माता
A. धात्री B. धरणी
C. धरित्री D. श्यामा

21. घोषणा
A. आवाज B. पुकारना
C. ऐलान D. ललकारना

22. उत्कर्ष
A. आकर्षण B. विकर्षण
C. उन्नति D. निष्कर्ष

23. उदय
A. अन्त B. विकास
C. प्रगट D. व्यस्त

24. दक्ष
A. निपुण B. समर्थ
C. कर्मठ D. मेहनती

25. संवाद
A. विवाद B. झगड़ा
C. सम्बोधन D. वार्तालाप

उत्तरमाला

1. B	2. A	3. A	4. A	5. A
6. A	7. D	8. A	9. A	10. D
11. A	12. A	13. C	14. A	15. A
16. D	17. A	18. C	19. A	20. A
21. C	22. C	23. C	24. A	25. D

अभ्यास-3

निर्देशः *नीचे चार-चार शब्दों के समूह दिए गए हैं। प्रत्येक समूह में एक शब्द बेमेल है तथा शेष तीन शब्द पर्यायवाची हैं, आपको उस शब्द का चयन करना है, जो बेमेल है :*

1. A. तम B. अंधकार
   C. तिमिर D. अंश
2. A. अनल B. आग
   C. दहन D. तमिस्त्रा
3. A. अतुल B. अद्वितीय
   C. अनुपम D. शुष्मा
4. A. अहं B. अहंकार
   C. दर्प D. निराला
5. A. पता B. खोज
   C. जाँच D. शोध
6. A. गरल B. पीयूष
   C. सुधा D. सोम
7. A. कानन B. जंगल
   C. पादप D. वन
8. A. अश्व B. गज
   C. घोड़ा D. तुरंग
9. A. दानव B. मानव
   C. दैत्य D. राक्षस
10. A. आँख B. चक्षु
    C. नयन D. मुख
11. A. अन्तरिक्ष B. वसुन्धरा
    C. आसमान D. गगन
12. A. इच्छा B. अभिलाषा
    C. कामना D. प्रयोजन
13. A. कपड़ा B. चीर
    C. वसन D. पोशाक
14. A. अब्ज B. कमल
    C. राजीव D. आम्र
15. A. कोयल B. पिक
    C. काग D. वनप्रिय
16. A. गंगा B. देवनदी
    C. गोदावरी D. भागीरथी
17. A. गणेश B. एकदन्त
    C. देवराज D. गणपति
18. A. घर B. निलय
    C. निकेतन D. झोपड़ी
19. A. चाँद B. हिमांशु
    C. विनायक D. सुधांशु
20. A. नदी B. तरणी
    C. तटिनी D. सरिता
21. A. पक्षी B. चिड़िया
    C. सुमन D. विहग
22. A. पवन B. अचला
    C. वात D. वायु
23. A. समीर B. पृथ्वी
    C. भू D. भूमि
24. A. पानी B. समीर
    C. अम्बु D. जल
25. A. पुत्र B. तनया
    C. तनय D. सुत
26. A. पुत्र B. तनया
    C. सुता D. कन्या
27. A. गृहिणी B. आदमी
    C. पुरुष D. नर
28. A. मधु B. फूल
    C. पुष्प D. सुमन
29. A. माधव B. तरु
    C. पेड़ D. वृक्ष
30. A. माता B. अम्बु
    C. अम्मा D. जननी

उत्तरमाला

1. D	2. D	3. D	4. D	5. A
6. A	7. C	8. B	9. B	10. D
11. B	12. D	13. D	14. D	15. C
16. C	17. C	18. D	19. C	20. B
21. C	22. B	23. A	24. B	25. B
26. A	27. A	28. A	29. A	30. B

अभ्यास-4

निर्देशः *गहरे काले शब्द के विलोम शब्द का चयन कीजिए:*

1. उसे हर काम में **सफलता** मिल रही है।
A. असफलता B. सफल
C. कुशलता D. निपुणता

2. कभी किसी की **निन्दा** नहीं करनी चाहिए।
A. गुणगान B. स्तुति
C. प्रशंसा D. यशोगान

3. आलस्य व्यक्ति का सबसे बड़ा **दुश्मन** है।
A. शत्रु B. घातक
C. मित्र D. सहायक

4. वे बुढ़ापे से **दुखी** हैं।
A. अप्रसन्न B. सुखी
C. खुश D. नाराज

5. यहाँ उसकी **चतुराई** नहीं चली।
A. चालाकी B. बहादुरी
C. निपुणता D. मूर्खता

6. शहद की **मिठास** कम नहीं होती।
A. मीठा B. तीखा
C. कड़ुवा D. खहा

7. साहसी के **साहस** को देखकर मैं चकित रह गया।
A. हिम्मत B. बहादुरी
C. निडर D. भय

8. फिल्मोत्सव में सर्वश्रेष्ठ **अभिनेता** को पुरस्कार प्रदान किया गया।
A. हीरोइन B. नेत्री
C. मीनाक्षी D. अभिनेत्री

9. नाटक में नायक और **नायिका** की भूमिका महत्वपूर्ण होती है:
A. हीरो B. नायक
C. नेत्र D. नेता

10. कवि-सम्मेलन में एक कवि और एक **कवयित्री** को आमंत्रित किया गया था।
A. लेखक B. सम्पादक
C. नेता D. कवि

11. विद्यालय के वार्षिकोत्सव के लिए नेता और एक **नेत्री** को आमंत्रित किया गया।
A. अभिनेता B. विद्वान्
C. विदुषी D. नेता

12. मोहन बहुत **चतुर** है।
A. निपुण B. तेज
C. सुस्त D. मूर्ख

13. सोहन अब पूर्ण **स्वस्थ** है।
A. प्रसन्न B. खुश
C. अस्वस्थ D. अप्रसन्न

14. पक्षी **आकाश** में उड़ते हैं :
A. गगन B. नभ
C. धरती D. पाताल

15. वह विद्यालय में देर से आया और **अनुपस्थित** हो गया।
A. पूर्व B. उपस्थित
C. प्रवेश D. समयपूर्व

16. **बालक** चाँद की ओर देख रहा है।
A. बालिका B. लड़का
C. बच्चा D. बच्ची

17. मैं उसके विचार से बिल्कुल **सहमत** नहीं हूँ।
A. समर्थन B. सहमति
C. असहमत D. प्रशंसक

18. उसकी हालत **अधिक** खराब है।
A. बहुत B. कम
C. ठीक D. कुशल

19. **धर्म** की सर्वत्र विजय होती है:
A. अधर्म B. ज्ञान
C. भक्ति D. ईमानदारी

20. अच्छे चरित्र के बिना जीवन **निरर्थक** है:
A. व्यर्थ B. अर्थपूर्ण
C. सार्थक D. कुशल

21. **ईमानदारी** बड़ी दुर्लभ वस्तु है:
A. सच्चाई B. भलाई
C. बेइमानी D. परोपकारी

22. एवरेस्ट संसार का सबसे **ऊँचा** पर्वत है:
A. नीचा B. वितल
C. पाताल D. मध्यम

23. वह विश्वास के **योग्य** नहीं है:
A. काबिल B. विश्वासी
C. अयोग्य D. बेकार

24. क्या वह इतना **मूर्ख** है?
A. चालाक B. विद्वान्
C. बुद्धिमान D. धूर्त

25. कितना सुहावना **दृश्य** है!
A. अदृश्य B. दर्शनीय
C. सुन्दर D. व्यर्थ

उत्तरमाला

1. A	2. C	3. C	4. B	5. D
6. C	7. D	8. D	9. B	10. D
11. D	12. D	13. C	14. D	15. B
16. A	17. C	18. B	19. A	20. C
21. C	22. A	23. C	24. C	25. A

अभ्यास-5

निर्देश: नीचे प्रत्येक **काले गहरे शब्द** के चार विलोम दिए गए हैं। इनमें सही विलोम का चयन कीजिए :

1. **अग्नि**
A. आग B. अनल
C. दहन D. जल

2. **अग्रज**
A. अनुज B. भ्राता
C. भाई D. अम्बा

3. **अच्छा**
A. बुरा B. खराब
C. गंदा D. भ्रष्ट

4. **अंत**
A. प्रारम्भ B. समाप्त
C. शेष D. अल्प

5. **अचल**
A. विचल B. वितल
C. सजल D. चल

6. **अति**
A. अधिक B. बहुत
C. अल्प D. कम

7. **अत्यधिक**
A. अल्प B. अधिक
C. स्वल्प D. न्यूनतम

8. **अंधकार**
A. अंधेरा B. प्रकाश
C. रात्रि D. दिन

9. **अतिवृष्टि**
A. अनावृष्टि B. वृष्टि
C. वर्षा D. वर्षण

10. **अनाथ**
A. नाथ B. स्वामी
C. मासिक D. सनाथ

11. **अनुकूल**
A. मनोकूल B. प्रतिकूल
C. अनुकरण D. मनस्वी

12. **अनुराग**
A. राग B. विराग
C. विग्रह D. स्नेह

13. **अन्त**
A. श्री गणेश B. आदि
C. शुरुआत D. समाप्त

14. **अपना**
A. अपनत्व B. पराया
C. मित्र D. शत्रु

15. **अपमान**
A. मान B. सम्मान
C. वर्तमान D. स्वाभिमान

16. **अपेक्षा**
A. इच्छा B. स्वेच्छा
C. प्रविच्छा D. उपेक्षा

17. **अमर**
A. मर्त्य B. मृत्यु
C. सुधा D. गरल

18. **अल्पायु**
A. चिरायु B. उमरदराज
C. नश्वर D. सनातन

19. **अस्त**
A. उदय B. विकास
C. निर्माण D. सृष्टि

20. **आकर्षण**
A. प्रतिकर्षण B. विकर्षण
C. सम्मोहन D. विरत

21. **आकाश**
A. गगन B. नभ
C. वसुन्धरा D. पाताल

22. **आगे**
A. पीछे B. पूर्व
C. पृष्ट D. पृष्ठ

23. **आजाद**
A. स्वतंत्र B. स्वतंत्रतता
C. परतंत्र D. गुलाम

24. **आदान**
A. आयात B. निर्यात
C. प्रदान D. निदान

25. **आधुनिक**
A. अर्वाचीन B. नूतन
C. प्राचीन D. वर्तमान

उत्तरमाला

1. D	**2.** A	**3.** A	**4.** A	**5.** D
6. D	**7.** C	**8.** B	**9.** A	**10.** D
11. B	**12.** B	**13.** A	**14.** B	**15.** B
16. D	**17.** A	**18.** A	**19.** A	**20.** B
21. D	**22.** A	**23.** D	**24.** C	**25.** C

अभ्यास-6

नीचे कुछ शब्द दिए गए हैं प्रत्येक शब्द के चार ाक अर्थ दिए गए हैं। सही अर्थ का चयन कीजिए :

. **सुरक्षित**
A. कुशल B. घटना
C. दुर्घटना D. बचाव

2. **प्रतिभाशाली**
A. सज्जन B. कुशाग्र
C. विद्वान् D. वैभवशाली

3. **आत्मसमर्पण**
A. अपने आप को सौंपना B. समर्पण
C. अर्पण D. त्यागज

4. **सिद्धहस्त**
A. निपुण B. कर्मठ
C. मेहनती D. परिश्रमी

5. **सुशोभित**
A. मजेदार B. सुस्वागतम्
C. अच्छा D. शोभा पाना

6. **स्वादिष्ट**
A. मजेदार B. बेकार
C. मीठा D. तीखा

7. **स्वावलम्बी**
A. निर्भर B. परालंबी
C. आत्मनिर्भर D. अतिथि

8. **उपकरण**
A. साधन B. युक्ति
C. यंत्र D. मशीन

9. **कीमत**
A. क्रय B. विक्रय
C. मूल्य D. बिक्री

10. **संगठन**
A. एकता B. अनेकता
C. समूह D. संस्था

11. **विपत्ति**
A. दुख B. विपदा
C. मुसीबत D. सुख

12. **तृण**
A. तिनका B. धूल
C. धूप D. लकड़ी

13. **आश्चर्य**
A. निरीक्षण B. दृष्टिगोचर
C. हैरानी D. थकावट

14. **हार्दिक**
A. हृदय से B. शरीर से
C. मन से D. मस्तिष्क से

15. **नियति**
A. भाग्य B. किनारा
C. समय D. पवित्र

16. **सुगन्धित**
A. दुर्गन्ध B. खुशबू वाला
C. फूल D. कमल

17. **उत्साह**
A. होश B. हवास
C. जोश D. हिम्मत

18. **सहयोग**
A. मिलन सार B. मेहनती
C. परोपकारी D. आपसी सहायता

19. **मुसीबत**
A. विपत्ति B. सुशोभित
C. सहायता D. मदद

20. **निरक्षर**
A. साक्षर B. दर्शनीय
C. पठनीय D. अनपढ़

21. **उपवन**
A. वन B. तीर
C. जंगल D. बाग

22. **मेघ**
A. बादल B. पंकज
C. राजीव D. मेघनाद

23. **आधुनिक**
A. प्राचीन B. पुरातन
C. भूतकाल D. आज का

24. **तीर**
A. वाण B. धनुष
C. किनारा D. नदी

25. **परीक्षण**
A. जाँच B. पड़ताल
C. परीक्षा D. इम्तहान

26. **अभिवादन**
A. नमस्ते B. प्रणाम
C. बधाई D. शुभकामना

27. **सर्वत्र**
A. नश्वर B. सजीव
C. ईश्वर D. सभी जगह

28. **हलवाहा**
A. चरवाहा B. किसान
C. मजदूर D. हल चलाने वाला

29. **शिखर**
A. पर्वत B. पहाड़
C. टीला D. चोटी

30. **भयानक**
A. डरावना B. भयभीत
C. डरना D. खूँखार

उत्तरमाला

1. D	2. B	3. A	4. A	5. D
6. A	7. C	8. C	9. C	10. A
11. C	12. A	13. C	14. A	15. A
16. B	17. C	18. D	19. A	20. D
21. D	22. A	23. D	24. A	25. A
26. B	27. D	28. D	29. D	30. A

अभ्यास-7

निर्देशः *नीचे कुछ शब्द दिए जा रहे हैं। प्रत्येक शब्द के* **उपसर्ग** *के सन्दर्भ में चार विकल्प दिए गए हैं। आपको सही विकल्प का चयन करना है :*

1. अलबत्ता
A. अ B. अल
C. लब D. त्ता

2. अलगरज
A. अल B. लग
C. गर D. रज

3. कमसिन
A. क B. कम
C. सि D. सिन

4. अनमोल
A. अ B. अन
C. मो D. मोल

5. अनजान
A. अ B. अन
C. जा D. जान

6. अनपढ़
A. अ B. पढ़
C. प D. अन

7. अधखिला
A. अ B. अध
C. ला D. खिला

8. अधजला
A. अ B. ज
C. अध D. ला

9. अधपका
A. अ B. अध
C. पका D. का

10. अधखिला
A. अ B. अध
C. खिला D. ला

11. उन्नीस
A. उन B. उन्
C. नीस D. स

12. उनसठ
A. उ B. उन
C. सठ D. ठ

13. दुकाल
A. द B. दुक
C. दु D. काल

14. दुबला
A. दब B. दुब
C. ला D. दु

15. निकम्मा
A. नि B. निक
C. कम्मा D. मा

16. निर्लज्ज
A. निर B. निल
C. नि D. लज्ज

17. बिनब्याहा
A. बि B. बिन
C. ब्याहा D. हा

18. भरपेट
A. भर B. पेट
C. पे D. ट

19. भरपाई
A. भ B. र
C. पा D. भर

20. कुपात्र
A. कु B. कुप
C. पा D. पात्र

21. सुजान
A. सु B. सुज
C. सुजा D. जान

22. गैर कानूनी
A. गै B. गैर
C. कानु D. नुनी

23. गैरसरकारी
A. गैर B. सर
C. का D. कारी

24. अपमान
A. अ B. अप
C. मा D. मान

25. अनुशासन
A. अ B. शासन
C. सन D. अनु

26. अविनीत
A. अवि B. अ
C. नी D. नीत

27. अभिमान
A. अभि B. अ
C. मा D. मान

28. अभियान
A. अ B. मान
C. यान D. अभि

29. अध्ययन
A. अध् B. अधि
C. यन D. न

30. निश्चल
A. नि B. निर
C. निस D. चल

उत्तरमाला

1. B	**2.** A	**3.** B	**4.** B	**5.** B
6. D	**7.** B	**8.** C	**9.** B	**10.** B
11. A	**12.** B	**13.** C	**14.** D	**15.** B
16. A	**17.** B	**18.** A	**19.** D	**20.** A

21. A	22. B	23. A	24. B	25. D
26. B	27. A	28. D	29. B	30. A

अभ्यास-8

निर्देशः *निम्नलिखित शब्दों में प्रयुक्त प्रत्यय सम्बन्धी चार विकल्प दिए गए हैं, सही विकल्प का चयन कीजिए :*

1. भलाई
A. ई B. लाई
C. आई D. भला

2. चतुराई
A. चतु B. रा
C. ई D. आई

3. भूखा
A. भू B. भूख
C. खा D. आ

4. भिड़न्त
A. भिड़् B. भि
C. न्त D. अन्त

5. प्यासा
A. आस B. सा
C. आसा D. सा

6. बिकाऊ
A. बिक B. काऊ
C. आऊ D. ऊ

7. तैराक
A. तै B. तैर
C. राक D. आक

8. सन्नाटा
A. सन् B. सन्ना
C. नाटा D. आटा

9. लोहार
A. लोह B. आरा
C. आरी D. आर

10. मिलान
A. आना B. आने
C. आनी D. आन

11. चढ़ाव
A. चढ़ B. चढ़ा
C. आव D. व

12. लगाव
A. लग B. अव
C. आव D. गाव

13. लिखावट
A. लिख B. लिखा
C. वट D. आवट

14. मिलावट
A. मिल B. वट
C. आवट D. ट

15. मिठास
A. मिठ B. ठास
C. आस D. स

16. चिकनाहट
A. चिक B. नाह्ट
C. हट D. आहट

17. सड़ियल
A. सड़ B. यल
C. ड़ियल D. इयल

18. मरियल
A. मर B. यल
C. मरि D. इयल

19. गड़रिया
A. गड़ B. इया
C. रिया D. या

20. सजीला
A. ईला B. इला
C. ला D. स

21. लुटेरा
A. लुट B. एरा
C. ऐरा D. रा

22. लठैत
A. ए B. ऐ
C. ऐत D. त

23. भगोड़ा
A. ओ B. ओड़ा
C. ड़ा D. भगो

24. खपत
A. ख B. प
C. त D. पत

25. जीवट

A. व B. अट

C. जीव D. जी

उत्तरमाला

1. C	2. D	3. D	4. D	5. D
6. C	7. D	8. D	9. D	10. D
11. C	12. C	13. D	14. C	15. C
16. D	17. D	18. D	19. B	20. A
21. B	22. C	23. B	24. C	25. B

अभ्यास-9

निर्देशः *नीचे कुछ मुहावरे दिए गए हैं। प्रत्येक के अर्थ के लिए चार विकल्प दिए गए हैं। आपको सही विकल्प का चयन करना है :*

1. **अक्ल पर पत्थर पड़ना**

A. बुद्धि काम न करना B. दुविधा होना

C. संकट में होना D. परेशान होना

2. **अपना उल्लू सीधा करना**

A. अवसर देखना B. काम निकालना

C. मतलब साधना D. मूर्ख बनाना

3. **अपने मुँह मियाँ-मिट्ठू बनना**

A. मिठाई खाना

B. प्रशंसा करना

C. निंदा करना

D. अपनी प्रशंसा स्वयं करना

4. **अपने पाँव पर आप कुल्हाड़ी मारना**

A. हानि पहुँचाना B. खेद होना

C. अपना पैर काटना D. अपनी हानि स्वयं करना

5. **आँखें चुरा लेना**

A. भाग जाना B. छिप जाना

C. अनदेखा करना D. मिल जाना

6. **अक्ल का दुश्मन**

A. मित्र होना B. शत्रु होना

C. महामूर्ख D. महाविद्वान्

7. **अंधे की लाठी**

A. एक मात्र सहारा B. मित्र होना

C. शत्रु होना D. दुख पहुँचाना

8. **आकाश-पाताल एक करना**

A. भाग-दौड़ करना B. परेशान होना

C. थक जाना D. कठिन परिश्रम करना

9. **घड़ों पानी पड़ना**

A. लज्जित होना B. तुच्छ समझना

C. लाभ होना D. थकावट

10. **अगर-मगर करना**

A. नुकसान करना B. बहाने बनाना

C. बदनाम करना D. कपट करना

11. **मुँह की खाना**

A. गिर जाना B. हार जाना

C. भाग जाना D. व्यर्थ होना

12. **आस्तीन का साँप होना**

A. शत्रु B. मित्र

C. कपटी मित्र D. दयालु

13. **एक आँख से देखना**

A. बुरा व्यवहार B. समान व्यवहार

C. कपट करना D. लज्जित होना

14. **बाल-बाँका न होना**

A. घायल होना B. साफ़ बच जाना

C. क्रोधित होना D. स्वस्थ होना

15. **दाँतों तले उँगली दबाना**

A. उँगली काटना B. चिंतित हो जाना

C. चकित रह जाना D. प्रसन्न हो जाना

16. **जान के लाले पड़ना**

A. मरने का खतरा होना B. भाग जाना

C. हार जाना D. मुश्किल में पड़ना

17. **बोली मारना**

A. ताना देना B. सताना

C. मजाक करना D. याद दिलाना

18. **अंधों में काना राजा**

A. मूर्खों में अल्पज्ञ को विद्वान् माना जाना

B. सबको मूर्ख समझना

C. अत्यधिक महत्त्वपूर्ण

D. काना राजा

19. **अक्ल के घोड़े दौड़ाना**

A. बुद्धि लड़ाना

B. कल्पना करना

C. तरह-तरह के उपाय सोचना

D. ज्ञान-प्राप्त करना

20. पानी उतर जाना
A. शर्म करना B. लज्जित न होना
C. भाग जाना D. इज्जत करना

21. तीन-पाँच करना
A. तितर-बितर करना
B. वचन देकर फिर जाना
C. घुमा-फिरा कर बातें करना
D. परेशान करना

22. हथियार डाल देना
A. हार जाना B. जीत जाना
C. धोखा देना D. विजय होना

23. आँख खुलना
A. होश में आना B. अत्यन्त प्यार होना
C. उल्टा काम करना D. क्रोध करना

24. कमर सीधी करना
A. थक जाना B. थकावट दूर करना
C. काम करना D. परिश्रम करना

25. पगड़ी रखना
A. चैन की सांस लेना
B. अपमान करना
C. दया की भीख माँगना
D. अपमान होना

26. लोहा मानना
A. संघर्ष करना
B. विजय होना
C. श्रेष्ठता स्वीकार करना
D. खुशामद करना

27. काठ मार जाना
A. दुःखी होना B. चुप होना
C. सफल होना D. मर जाना

28. चाँद पर थूकना
A. अपमान करना
B. बढ़कर बातें करना
C. महान पुरुष पर लांछन लगाना
D. महत्त्वाकांक्षी होना

29. उगल देना
A. अपराध स्वीकार कर लेना
B. सच बोलना
C. उल्टी करना
D. अनपच होना

30. हाथ मलना
A. पश्चाताप करना B. सर्दी मिटाना
C. दुख करना D. तैयार होना

उत्तरमाला

1. A	**2.** C	**3.** D	**4.** D	**5.** C
6. C	**7.** A	**8.** D	**9.** A	**10.** B
11. B	**12.** C	**13.** B	**14.** B	**15.** C
16. D	**17.** A	**18.** A	**19.** A	**20.** B
21. C	**22.** A	**23.** A	**24.** B	**25.** C
26. C	**27.** B	**28.** C	**29.** A	**30.** A

अभ्यास-10

निर्देशः *नीचे कुछ वाक्य खण्ड दिए गए हैं, पूरे वाक्य खण्ड के लिए एक शब्द का चयन कीजिए।*

1. जिसका आदि न हो
A. अनंत B. अमर
C. शाश्वत D. अनादि

2. जो कुछ न जानता हो
A. मूर्ख B. महामूर्ख
C. ज्ञानी D. अज्ञ

3. जो अनुकरण करने योग्य हो
A. अनुकरणीय B. अद्वितीय
C. आदरणीय D. अगम

4. जिसका अंत न हो
A. अनंत B. अनादि
C. आदि D. परलोक

5. जो कभी न मरे
A. मर्त्य B. मुर्त्त
C. अर्मुत्त D. अमर

6. जिसके समान दूसरा न हो
A. अनुकूल B. प्रतिकूल
C. कृतज्ञ D. अद्वितीय

7. जो कम बोलता हो
A. मृदुभाषी B. वाचाल
C. अल्पभाषी D. अल्पज्ञ

8. जिसका इलाज न हो

A. मरणशील B. अमरत्व

C. बिमारी D. लाइलाज

9. जिस का विश्वास न किया जा सके

A. विश्वसनीय B. अविश्वसनीय

C. विश्वासी D. धूर्त्त

10. जिसका कोई नाथ न हो

A. सनाथ B. स्वामी

C. नाथ D. अनाथ

11. कम जानने वाला

A. अल्पज्ञ B. अज्ञ

C. विद् D. विद्वान

12. जहाँ जाना संभव न हो

A. दुर्गम B. अगम

C. तल D. वितल

13. कम खाने वाला

A. बहुभोजी B. पेटु

C. कंजूस D. अल्पाहारी

14. जो बात पहले कभी न हुई हो

A. भूतपूर्व B. अभूतपूर्व

C. प्राचीन D. अर्वाचीन

15. जिस स्त्री के सन्तान न हों

A. बाँझ B. कुलटा

C. पतिता D. विधवा

16. जो कहा न जा सके

A. अकथनीय B. अकथ्य

C. करणीय D. सम्भव

17. एहसान न मानने वाला

A. कृतज्ञ B. कृतघ्न

C. आस्तिक D. विश्वासी

18. जिसने देश के साथ विश्वासघात किया हो

A. विश्वासघाती B. द्रोही

C. आतंकवादी D. देश द्रोही

19. जिसने राष्ट्र के हित में अपना जीवन बलिदान कर दिया हो

A. देशभक्त B. शहीद

C. राष्ट्रभूत D. भारतपुत्र

20. वह जमीन जिसमें कुछ भी पैदा न हो

A. ऊसर B. बंजर

C. उर्वर D. पथरीला

21. वह वस्तु जिसकी चाह हो

A. श्रेष्ठ B. आवश्यक

C. इच्छित D. अभीष्ट

22. दूसरों के पीछे चलने वाला

A. अनुयायी B. अनुज

C. अनुचर D. अनुकरणीय

23. जो पहले न पढ़ा हो

A. पठित B. अपठित

C. पठनीय D. अपठनीय

24. जिसके आर-पार दिखाई देता हो

A. अपारदर्शी B. गम्य

C. अगम्य D. पारदर्शी

25. आज्ञा पालन करने वाला

A. शिष्य B. शिष्या

C. अनुचर D. आज्ञाकारी

26. काम से जी चुराने वाला

A. कामचोर B. आलसी

C. कर्मठ D. परिश्रमी

27. प्रतिदिन होने वाला

A. दैनिक B. शाश्वत

C. सनातन D. अमर

28. जिसका कोई अर्थ न हो

A. सार्थक B. निरर्थक

C. आर्थिक D. अनार्थिक

29. उपकार मानने वाला

A. कृतज्ञ B. कृतघ्न

C. विश्वासी D. अनुयायी

30. हाथ से लिखा हुआ

A. पठनीय B. अपठनीय

C. स्पष्ट D. हस्तलिखित

उत्तरमाला

1. D	**2.** D	**3.** A	**4.** A	**5.** D
6. D	**7.** C	**8.** D	**9.** B	**10.** D
11. A	**12.** A	**13.** D	**14.** B	**15.** A
16. A	**17.** B	**18.** D	**19.** B	**20.** A
21. C	**22.** C	**23.** B	**24.** D	**25.** D
26. A	**27.** A	**28.** B	**29.** A	**30.** D

अभ्यास-11

निर्देशः *नीचे कुछ संज्ञा शब्द दिए जा रहे हैं। प्रत्येक के संज्ञा-भेद के लिए चार विकल्प दिए गये है। सही विकल्प का चयन कीजिए :*

1. तुलसीदास
   A. जातिवाचक B. भाववाचक
   C. व्यक्तिवाचक D. समूहवाचक
2. यमुना
   A. व्यक्तिवाचक B. जातिवाचक
   C. समूहवाचक D. भाववाचक
3. बच्चा
   A. जातिवाचक B. समूहवाचक
   C. भाववाचक D. व्यक्तिवाचक
4. मानवता
   A. भाववाचक B. जातिवाचक
   C. द्रव्यवाचक D. समूहवाचक
5. हिमालय
   A. व्यक्तिवाचक B. जातिवाचक
   C. भाववाचक D. समूहवाचक
6. भारत
   A. जातिवाचक B. भाववाचक
   C. व्यक्तिवाचक D. समूहवाचक
7. एशिया
   A. व्यक्तिवाचक B. भाववाचक
   C. द्रव्यवाचक D. समूहवाचक
8. महाराष्ट्र
   A. जातिवाचक B. व्यक्तिवाचक
   C. समूहवाचक D. द्रव्यवाचक
9. सूर सागर
   A. व्यक्तिवाचक B. भाववाचक
   C. द्रव्यवाचक D. समूहवाचक
10. सोमवार
   A. जातिवाचक B. व्यक्तिवाचक
   C. द्रव्यवाचक D. समूहवाचक
11. खटमल
   A. जातिवाचक B. व्यक्तिवाचक
   C. द्रव्यवाचक D. समूहवाचक
12. मैना
   A. जातिवाचक B. व्यक्तिवाचक
   C. द्रव्यवाचक D. समूहवाचक
13. चाँदी
   A. द्रव्यवाचक B. समूहवाचक
   C. भाववाचक D. व्यक्तिवाचक
14. अच्छाई
   A. भाववाचक B. समूहवाचक
   C. जातिवाचक D. व्यक्तिवाचक
15. पीतल
   A. द्रव्यवाचक B. भाववाचक
   C. व्यक्तिवाचक D. जातिवाचक
16. वीरता
   A. भाववाचक B. जातिवाचक
   C. द्रव्यवाचक D. समूहवाचक
17. रूस
   A. जातिवाचक B. व्यक्तिवाचक
   C. भाववाचक D. द्रव्यवाचक
18. लम्बाई
   A. भाववाचक B. समूहवाचक
   C. द्रव्यवाचक D. व्यक्तिवाचक
19. दल
   A. जातिवाचक B. व्यक्तिवाचक
   C. समूहवाचक D. द्रव्यवाचक
20. मार्च
   A. समूहवाचक B. व्यक्तिवाचक
   C. द्रव्यवाचक D. जातिवाचक
21. झुण्ड
   A. समूहवाचक B. जातिवाचक
   C. व्यक्तिवाचक D. द्रव्यवाचक
22. टोली
   A. जातिवाचक B. व्यक्तिवाचक
   C. समूहवाचक D. द्रव्यवाचक
23. सुभाष चौक
   A. जातिवाचक B. समूहवाचक
   C. व्यक्तिवाचक D. भाववाचक
24. संघ
   A. जातिवाचक B. द्रव्यवाचक
   C. समूहवाचक D. भाववाचक
25. गिरोह
   A. समूहवाचक B. द्रव्यवाचक
   C. जातिवाचक D. भाववाचक

उत्तरमाला

1. C	2. A	3. A	4. A	5. A
6. C	7. A	8. B	9. A	10. B
11. A	12. A	13. A	14. A	15. A
16. A	17. B	18. A	19. C	20. B
21. A	22. C	23. C	24. C	25. A

अभ्यास-12

निर्देश: *नीचे दिए गए वाक्य में रिक्त स्थान है। प्रत्येक वाक्य के नीचे कारक चिह्न दिए गए हैं। रिक्त स्थान की पूर्ति के लिए उपयुक्त कारक चिह्न का चयन कीजिए :*

1. निम्नलिखित शब्दों........अर्थ बताइए
A. का B. के
C. से D. पर

2. सरकार मुझे नौकरी........मत निकालिए
A. पर B. में
C. से D. को

3. इस कथन........पुष्टि कीजिए
A. को B. से
C. की D. ने

4. छात्र-छात्राएँ राष्ट्र........सम्पत्ति और उसके भावी कर्णधार होते हैं
A. के B. की
C. को D. में

5. प्रत्येक प्रश्न........चार सम्भावित उत्तर दिए गए हैं
A. के लिए B. में
C. के D. से

6. माता बच्चे........पढ़ाती है
A. को B. के
C. की D. से

7. गुरुजी........सबसे छोटे लड़के को एक नारंगी दी
A. ने B. को
C. से D. के लिए

8. मोहन सोहन से मिलने........गया है
A. से B. के
C. को D. के लिए

9. उसने कलम........लिखा
A. के B. में
C. पर D. से

10. मैं ड्राइवर........गाड़ी चलवाता हूँ
A. के B. पर
C. में D. से

11. शिक्षक छात्रों........पुस्तक पढ़वाते हैं
A. के लिए B. मैं
C. पर D. से

12. मैंने दाढ़ी........उसे मुसलमान समझ लिया
A. से B. के
C. को D. के लिए

13. श्याम अपने भाई हरि........आम लाया है
A. के B. के लिए
C. का D. पर

14. मोहन घर........आता है
A. में B. पर
C. से D. का

15. उसे पाँच दिनों........मूर्च्छा आया करती है
A. पर B. से
C. के D. को

16. मेधावी छात्र परीक्षा........चोरी नहीं करते
A. में B. पर
C. से D. के लिए

17. अच्छे आदमी........पहचान क्या है?
A. के B. का
C. की D. के लिए

18. परिश्रम........सफलता निश्चित है
A. से B. के
C. को D. के लिए

19. शूर्पणखा........नाक और कान काटे गए
A. का B. की
C. के D. से

20. युद ने राधा........तीन संतरे दिए
A. से B. के
C. के लिए D. को

उत्तरमाला

1. A	2. C	3. C	4. B	5. C
6. A	7. A	8. D	9. D	10. D
11. D	12. A	13. B	14. C	15. B
16. D	17. C	18. A	19. B	20. D

गद्यांश (अपठित-बोध)

गद्यांश 1

यदि हम निरन्तर प्रयत्न करेंगे तो निश्चय ही अपने सभी लक्ष्यों को प्राप्त कर लेंगे, किन्तु प्रायः देखा जाता है कि अधिक-आशावादी लोग थोड़ा सा प्रयत्न करके अधिक फल की कामना करने लगते हैं और मनोवांछित फल प्राप्त न होने पर निराश हो जाते हैं। अतः जीवन में सफलता प्राप्त करने के लिए परिस्थितियों के समक्ष घुटने न टेकें, बल्कि दृढ़ता से उनका मुकाबला करें। याद रखें, जितना कठोर हमारा परिश्रम होगा उसका फल भी उतना ही मीठा होगा।

उपर्युक्त गद्यांश को ध्यानपूर्वक पढ़ें और निम्न प्रश्नों के उत्तर के लिए सही विकल्प को चुनें:

1. फल न मिलने पर कौन निराश हो जाते हैं?
   A. आशावादी लोग B. कम आशावादी लोग
   C. अधिक आशावादी लोग D. निराशावादी लोग
2. लक्ष्य प्राप्ति के लिए क्या किया जाना चाहिए?
   A. फल की कामना
   B. हिम्मत से मुकाबला
   C. निरन्तर प्रयत्न
   D. परिस्थितियों से मुकाबला
3. आशावादी शब्द का विलोम शब्द है:
   A. निराश B. निराशावादी
   B. दुखी D. अप्रसन्न
4. मनोवांछित शब्द का क्या अर्थ है?
   A. इच्छित B. परीक्षित
   C. लाभदायक D. मन को खुश करने वाले
5. परिश्रम शब्द का अर्थ है:
   A. साहस B. हिम्मत
   C. काम D. कठिन मेहनत

गद्यांश 2

पन्द्रह अगस्त 1947 को हमारा देश स्वतंत्र हुआ। स्वतन्त्रता प्राप्ति के बाद विश्व के दूसरे देशों के साथ भारत के राजनयिक एवं सांस्कृतिक सम्बन्ध जुड़े। पर्यटकों के साथ-साथ राजनीतिज्ञों और साहित्यकारों को भी विदेश यात्रा के पर्याप्त अवसर मिले। विभिन्न प्रकार की छात्रवृत्तियों के माध्यम से बहुत से लोग विदेशों में पढ़ने गए। बहुत से लोगों ने विदेशों में उपलब्ध आजीविका के अवसरों का लाभ उठाया। इन सबके परिणामस्वरूप प्रचुर मात्रा में यात्रावृत्तांत लिखे गए। विदेश-विषयक यात्रावृतांत्तों में रूस और स्वदेश-विषयक यात्रावृतांत्तों में लेखकों की दृष्टि कश्मीर से कन्याकुमारी तक व्याप्त हुई।

उपर्युक्त गद्यांश को ध्यानपूर्वक पढ़ें और निम्नलिखित प्रश्नों के उत्तर के लिए सही विकल्प को चुनें:

1. भारत कब स्वतंत्र हुआ?
   A. 15 अगस्त 1947
   B. 15 अगस्त 1946
   C. 15 अगस्त 1948
   D. 15 अगस्त 1949
2. स्वतंत्र भारत के अन्य देशों के साथ किस प्रकार के संबंध जुड़े?
   A. राजनीतिक
   B. राजनयिक
   C. धार्मिक
   D. राजनयिक एवं सांस्कृतिक
3. आजीविका का क्या अर्थ है?
   A. उपार्जन B. वेतन
   C. मेहनत D. रोजगार
4. यात्रा-वृत्तांत का क्या अर्थ है?
   A. भ्रमण B. पर्यटन
   C. सफरनामा D. विदेशभ्रमण
5. स्वतंत्र का विलोम शब्द है:
   A. परतंत्र B. आजाद
   C. गुलामी D. मुक्ति

गद्यांश 3

युवा वर्ग का मस्तिष्क नई-नई बातों की ओर ज्यादा तेज दौड़ता है। उसमें अन्य वर्ग के व्यक्तियों से अधिक आवेश और शक्ति होती है। इस अवस्था में यदि सही शिक्षा और

उचित मार्ग-दर्शन न मिले तो यही शक्ति प्रेरणा और निर्माण के स्थान पर विनाश की ओर ले जाती है। बिगड़ने और बनने की यही आयु होती है। दुर्भाग्य से हमारे देश में शिक्षा पद्धति केवल उपाधि बाँटने का काम ही करती है। एक सम्पूर्ण व्यक्तित्वपूर्ण मनुष्य बनाना आज की शिक्षा पद्धति के लिए मुश्किल है।

उपर्युक्त गद्यांश को ध्यानपूर्वक पढ़ें और निम्नलिखित प्रश्नों के उत्तर के लिए सही विकल्प को चुनें।

1. निर्माण का विलोम शब्द क्या हैं?

A. रचना B. बनावट
C. विनाश D. सृजन

2. मार्ग-दर्शन का क्या अर्थ है?

A. उपाधि B. रास्ता
C. उद्देश्य D. रास्ता दिखलाना

3. शक्ति विनाश की ओर कब अग्रसर होती है?

A. अधिक आवेश और शक्ति के अभाव में
B. सही शिक्षा और उचित मार्ग दर्शन के अभाव में
C. दुर्भाग्यपूर्ण शिक्षा पद्धति के कारण
D. इनमें से कोई नहीं

4. हमारे देश की शिक्षा पद्धति क्या कार्य करती है?

A. मार्ग-दर्शन B. शक्ति प्रेरणा
C. उपाधि देना D. उपर्युक्त सभी

5. दुर्भाग्य का विपरीत शब्द हैः

A. भाग्य B. सौभाग्य
C. भाग्यशाली D. भाग्यवान

गद्यांश 4

भिखारी की भाँति गिड़गिड़ाना प्रेम की भाषा नहीं है। यहाँ तक कि मुक्ति के लिए भगवान् की उपासना करना भी अधम उपासना में गिना जाता है। प्रेम कोई पुरस्कार नहीं चाहता। प्रेम सर्वथा प्रेम के लिए ही होता है। भक्त इसलिए प्रेम करता है कि बिना प्रेम किए वह रह ही नहीं सकता। जब तुम किसी मनोहर प्राकृतिक दृश्य को देखकर उस पर मोहित हो जाते हो तो तुम किसी फल की याचना नहीं करते और न वह दृश्य ही तुमसे कुछ माँगता है। फिर भी उस दृश्य का दर्शन तुम्हारे मन को आनंद से भर देता है।

उपर्युक्त गद्यांश को ध्यानपूर्वक पढ़ें और निम्नलिखित प्रश्नों के उत्तर के लिए सही विकल्प का चयन करें:

1. प्रेम का उद्देश्य क्या होता है?

A. मुक्ति B. उपासना
C. भक्ति D. प्रेम

2. मुक्ति का अर्थ हैः

A. आजादी B. स्वतंत्रता
C. परतंत्र D. निर्वाण

3. कैसी उपासना अधम मानी गई है?

A. प्रेम की उपासना
B. भगवान की उपासना
C. मुक्ति की उपासना
D. भक्ति की उपासना

4. मनोहर शब्द हैंः

A. विशेषण B. संज्ञा
C. सर्वनाम D. अव्यव

5. प्राकृतिक शब्द का अर्थ हैः

A. ईश्वरीय B. मानव संबंधी
C. प्रकृति संबंधी D. प्रेम संबंधी

गद्यांश 5

कुछ लोग भाग्यवादी होते हैं और सब-कुछ भाग्य के सहारे छोड़कर कर्म से विरत हो जाते हैं। ऐसे लोग समाज के लिए बोझ हैं। वे कभी कोई बड़ा काम नहीं कर पाते। बड़ी-बड़ी खोज, बड़े-बड़े आविष्कार और बड़े-बड़े निर्माण कार्य कर्मशील लोगों के द्वारा ही संभव हो सके हैं। हम अपनी बुद्धि और प्रतिभा तथा कार्य-क्षमता के बल पर सही मार्ग पर चल सकते हैं, किन्तु बिना कठिन श्रम के अपने लक्ष्य तक नहीं पहुँच सकते। कठिन परिश्रम करने के बाद पाई गई सफलता हमारे मन को अलौकिक आनंद से भर देती है। यदि हम अपने कार्य में अपेक्षित श्रम नहीं करते तो हमारा मन ग्लानि का अनुभव करता है।

उपर्युक्त गद्यांश को ध्यानपूर्वक पढ़ें और निम्नलिखित प्रश्नों के उत्तर के लिए सही विकल्प चुनें:

1. ''आविष्कार'' शब्द का अर्थ है :

A. अनुसंधान B. खोज
C. निर्माण D. विनाश

2. अलौकिक शब्द का क्या अर्थ है?
A. संसारिक B. भौतिक
C. अमानुषी D. प्राकृतिक

3. सफलता का विलोम क्या है?
A. सफल B. असफल
C. सफलतापूर्वक D. असफलता

4. परिश्रम करने और न करने से हमारे जीवन पर क्या प्रभाव पड़ता है?
A. लोग भाग्यवादी बन जाते हैं
B. कर्म से विरत हो जाते हैं
C. मन में ग्लानि का अनुभव होता है
D. इनमें से कोई नहीं

5. किस प्रकार के लोग समाज के लिए बोझ हैं?
A. भाग्यवादी B. कर्मठ
C. परिश्रमी D. प्रतिभाशाली

गद्यांश 6

वैदिक काल से हिमालय के पहाड़ बहुत पवित्र माने जाते हैं। इसमें कोई सन्देह नहीं कि हिमालय के पहाड़ों का दृश्य अति सुन्दर है। उसकी विशालता को देखकर मन में आनन्द और कृतज्ञता की लहर उठती है। ऐसा लगता है कि यह विशाल सृष्टि प्रभु की अनुपम देन है। सारी सृष्टि के प्रति समभाव जाग्रत होता है। वस्तुतः यह दृष्टि कोरी कल्पनात्मक या आध्यात्मिक नहीं है। देखा जाए तो सारे भारत की जलवायु का समतोल करने वाले यह हिमालय के पहाड़ हैं, विशेषकर उत्तरी भारत को वर्षा और पानी देने वाले ये ही हैं। गंगोत्री, यमुनोत्री, बद्री, केदार को तीर्थ माना जाता है, जो व्यर्थ कल्पना नहीं है। उन स्थानों से निकलने वाली पवित्र नदियाँ ही वास्तव में हमारी प्राणदात्री रही हैं।

उपर्युक्त गद्यांश को ध्यानपूर्वक पढ़ें और निम्नलिखित प्रश्नों के उत्तर के लिए सही विकल्प चुनें :

1. हिमालय के पर्वत बहुत पवित्र कब से माने जाते हैं?
A. पाषाण काल से B. वैदिक काल से
C. प्राचीन काल से D. आधुनिक काल से

2. विशालता शब्द है :
A. जातिवाचक B. भाववाचक
C. विशेषण D. सर्वनाम

3. भारत की जलवायु को समतोल कौन करता है?
A. गंगोत्री B. यमुनोत्री
C. केदार D. हिमालय

4. सृष्टि का समानार्थक शब्द है :
A. सृजन B. रचना
C. प्रकृति D. संसार

5. प्राणदात्री का क्या अर्थ है?
A. गंगोत्री
B. यमुनोत्री
C. प्राणसंचार करने वाली
D. समभाव जाग्रत करने वाली

गद्यांश 7

सच्चा मित्र एक शिक्षक की भाँति होता है। जिस प्रकार शिक्षक अपने छात्र को सन्मार्ग की ही ओर अग्रसर करता है, उसी प्रकार एक सच्चा मित्र अपने मित्र को पाप के गर्त में गिरने से बचाता है। मानव-जीवन अधिक रहस्यपूर्ण है। कभी-कभी जीवन में ऐसे अवसर उपस्थित हो जाते हैं, जब मनुष्य की धर्मबुद्धि नष्ट हो जाती है और उसका मन द्रुत गति से पाप की ओर दौड़ता है। ऐसे समय में मित्र का ही उपदेश अधिक कल्याणकारी सिद्ध होता है। मित्र के उपदेश का जितना प्रभाव हृदय पर पड़ता है, उतना और किसी का नहीं पड़ता है।

उपर्युक्त गद्यांश को ध्यानपूर्वक पढ़ें और निम्नलिखित प्रश्नों के उत्तर के लिए सही विकल्प चुनें :

1. सच्चा मित्र किस प्रकार का होता है?
A. विपत्ति में सहायता देने वाला
B. गलत मार्ग पर चलमे से रोकने वाला
C. शिक्षक के भाँति
D. धार्मिक गुरु की तरह

2. सन्मार्ग शब्द का विपरीत शब्द है :
A. अग्रसर B. कुमार्ग
C. सुमार्ग D. मार्गदर्शक

3. व्यक्ति को पाप के गर्त्त में गिरने से कौन बचाता है?
A. शिक्षक B. भाई
C. पिता D. सच्चा मित्र

4. मानव पाप की ओर कब दौड़ता है?
A. जब स्वार्थी बन जाता है
B. जब धर्म-बुद्धि नष्ट हो जाती है
C. जब सच्चामित्र साथ छोड़ देता है
D. जब धनवान बन जाता है

5. उपदेश में कौन-सा उपसर्ग है?
A. उ B. उप
C. दे D. देश

गद्यांश 8

सब तरह के भावों को प्रकट करने की योग्यता रखने वाली और निर्दोष होने पर भी यदि कोई भाषा अपना निज का साहित्य नहीं रखती, तो वह रूपवती भिखारिन की तरह कदापि आदरणीय नहीं हो सकती। उनकी शोभा, उसकी बड़ी सम्पन्नता, उसकी मान-मर्यादा उसके साहित्य पर ही अवलम्बित रहती है। उसके विचारों और राजनैतिक स्थितियों का प्रतिबिम्ब देखने को यदि कहीं मिल सकता है, तो उसके ग्रन्थ साहित्य में मिल सकता है। सामाजिक शक्ति या सजीवता, सामाजिक अशक्ति या निर्जीवता और सामाजिक सभ्यता तथा असभ्यता का निर्णायक एकमात्र साहित्य है।

उपर्युक्त गद्यांश को ध्यानपूर्वक पढ़ें और निम्नलिखित प्रश्नों के उत्तर के लिए सही विकल्प चुनें :

1. साहित्य विहीन भाषा किस प्रकार की होती है?
A. आदरणीय B. भिखारिन
C. रूपवती D. रूपवती भिखारिन

2. रूपवती का पुल्लिंग रूप है:
A. रूपवान B. सुन्दर
C. सुन्दरी D. रूपवत

3. भाषा की मान मर्यादा किस पर निर्भर करती है?
A. लिपि पर B. साहित्यकार पर
C. भक्ति पर D. साहित्य पर

4. "सम्पन्नता" शब्द का विपरीत शब्द है:
A. गरीबी B. विपन्न
C. अमीर D. विपन्नता

5. राजनैतिक, सामाजिक शक्ति का दर्शन हमें किसमें मिलता है?
A. समाज B. राज्य
C. नेता D. साहित्य

गद्यांश 9

स्वतंत्र भारत का सम्पूर्ण दायित्व आज विद्यार्थियों के ही ऊपर है, क्योंकि आज जो विद्यार्थी हैं, वे ही कल स्वतंत्र भारत के नागरिक होंगे। भारत की उन्नति, उसका उत्थान उन्हीं की उन्नति और उत्थान पर निर्भर करता है। अतः विद्यार्थियों को चाहिए कि वे अपने भावी जीवन का निर्माण बड़ी सतर्कता और सावधानी के साथ करें। उन्हें प्रत्येक क्षण अपने राष्ट्र, अपने समाज, अपने धर्म, अपनी संस्कृति को अपनी आँखों के सामने रखना चाहिए, जिससे उनके जीवन से राष्ट्र को कुछ बल प्राप्त हो सके। जो विद्यार्थी राष्ट्रीय दृष्टिकोण से अपने जीवन का निर्माण नहीं करते, वे राष्ट्र और समाज के लिए भार-स्वरूप हैं।

उपर्युक्त गद्यांश को ध्यानपूर्वक पढ़ें और निम्नलिखित प्रश्नों के उत्तर के लिए सही विकल्प चुनें :

1. भारत की उन्नति किस पर निर्भर करती है?
A. युवाओं पर B. नेताओं पर
C. साहित्यकारों पर D. विद्यार्थियों पर

2. **उन्नति** का समानार्थक शब्द है :
A. पतन B. उत्थान
C. विकास D. उदय

3. **उत्थान** का विपरीत शब्द है :
A. उदय B. पतन
C. पराजय D. हार

4. किसे अपने जीवन का निर्माण सतर्कता और सावधानी से करना चाहिए?
A. युवाओं को B. नेताओं को
C. बच्चों को D. विद्यार्थियों को

5. धर्म, संस्कृति तथा समाज का रक्षक कौन है?
A. नागरिक B. ग्रामीण
C. विद्यार्थी D. युवा

गद्यांश 10

हास्य एक ऐसा माध्यम है, जो नीरस-जीवन को भी सुखद बना देता है। हास्य का जादू इतना प्रभावशाली होता है कि वह छूत के रोग की तरह चारों ओर फैल जाता है। जिसने कभी हँसना नहीं सीखा, सचमुच उसने जीना नहीं सीखा। सामान्यतः मनुष्य को जीवन में इतनी मुसीबतें झेलनी

पड़ती हैं कि वह अपने जीवन को पहाड़ समझने लगता है। ऐसे दूभर जीवन को यदि जीने योग्य बनाना हो तो उसके लिए आवश्यक है कि जीवन में हँसने की गुंजाइश हो। हँसी के सहारे मनुष्य अपने कष्टों को भुलाने का प्रयत्न करता है। संघर्ष, तनाव, व्यस्तता, घुटन यदि आज के जीवन की सहज देन हैं, तो इनसे बचने के लिए यह आवश्यक है कि हम हँसना सीखें।

उपर्युक्त गद्यांश को ध्यानपूर्वक पढ़ें और निम्नलिखित प्रश्नों के उत्तर के लिए सही विकल्प चुनें :

1. नीरस जीवन को कौन सुखद बना देता है?
   A. संगीत B. गीत
   C. आमोद प्रमोद D. हास्य
2. **नीरस** का संधि विच्छेद है :
   A. नी + रस B. नि + रस
   C. निः + रस D. नीः + रस
3. किसका जीवन व्यर्थ है?
   A. जिसने रोना नहीं सीखा
   B. जिसने हँसना नहीं सीखा
   C. जिसने गाना नहीं सीखा
   D. इनमें से कोई नहीं
4. **हँसना** शब्द है :
   A. संज्ञा B. विशेषण
   C. क्रिया विशेषण D. क्रिया
5. तनाव और घुटन से बचने के लिए क्या करना चाहिए?
   A. रोना चाहिए B. गाना चाहिए
   C. हँसना चाहिए D. काम करना चाहिए

गद्यांश 11

किसी पुस्तक को पढ़ने में जल्दी नहीं करनी चाहिए, जो कुछ लेखक कहता है, उसे समझने की चेष्टा करनी चाहिए। प्रत्येक शब्द का अर्थ समझने की चेष्टा करनी चाहिए। यदि लेखक योग्य है, तो दूसरी बार वह पुस्तक और अधिक आनन्द देगी और तीसरी बार और अधिक। प्रत्येक बार अध्ययन करने पर आपको नवीन सुन्दर और नए विचार मिलेंगे और उसे आप जितना ही पढ़ेंगे, उतना ही स्नेह करने लगेंगे। सहस्रों व्यक्तियों ने गीता और रामायण तथा कुरान और बाइबिल को बार-बार पढ़ा है। उनका अनुभव है कि प्रत्येक बार उन्हें नई सूझ और नए विचार मिलते गए। कुछ लोग तो इस बात पर गर्व करते हैं कि उन्होंने अमुक पुस्तक को अनेक बार पढ़ा है, उन्हें कंठस्थ हो गई है।

उपर्युक्त गद्यांश को ध्यानपूर्वक पढ़ें और निम्नलिखित प्रश्नों के उत्तर के लिए सही विकल्प चुनें :

1. किसे समझने की चेष्टा करनी चाहिए?
   A. पुस्तक B. रामायण
   C. महाभारत D. गीता
2. पुस्तक की सजीवता किस पर निर्भर करती है?
   A. लेखक B. प्रकाशक
   C. पाठक D. चिन्तक
3. **आनन्द** का विपरीत शब्द है :
   A. शोक B. दुख
   C. संताप D. खुशी
4. नवीन, सुन्दर और नए विचार हमें कहाँ से प्राप्त होता हैं?
   A. पुस्तक को बार-बार पढ़कर
   B. सुनकर
   C. भाषण से
   D. अच्छे व्यक्तियों से मिलने पर
5. **कंठस्थ** शब्द का शब्दार्थ है :
   A. कंठ में स्थित B. सुंदर कंठ
   C. जबानी याद D. पंडित जी

गद्यांश 12

अहिंसा परम धर्म है और हिंसा आपद् धर्म। मनुष्य बराबर अहिंसा की ओर चलना चाहता है, किन्तु परिस्थितियाँ उससे हिंसा कराती है, अर्थात् परमधर्म की रक्षा के लिए आदमी बराबर आपद्धर्म से काम लेता रहा है। भारत अपनी सेनाओं को विघटित कर दे, तब भी उसका अपमान उससे अधिक होने वाला नहीं, जितना नेफा में हुआ। किन्तु परमधर्म पर टिकने की सामर्थ्य अगर भारत में नहीं है, तो आपद्धर्म पर उसे आना चाहिए। व्यवहारतः आपद्धर्म परमधर्म का विरोधी नहीं, उसका रक्षक है।

उपर्युक्त गद्यांश को ध्यानपूर्वक पढ़ें और निम्नलिखित प्रश्नों के उत्तर के लिए सही विकल्प चुनें :

1. **परमधर्म** का विपरीत शब्द है :
   A. महान धर्म B. आपद्धर्म
   C. सच्चाधर्म D. इनमें से कोई नहीं
2. आपद्धर्म किसे कहा जाता है?
   A. अहिंसा B. सत्याग्रह
   C. विपत्ति D. हिंसा
3. मानव से हिंसा कौन करवाती है?
   A. लोभ B. स्वार्थ
   C. द्वेष D. परिस्थितियाँ
4. **सामर्थ्य** का शब्दार्थ है :
   A. संघर्ष B. परिश्रम
   C. शक्ति D. पराक्रम
5. **परमधर्म** की रक्षा कौन करता है?
   A. अहिंसा B. हिंसा
   C. आपदधर्म D. युद्ध

गद्यांश 13

वर्तमान काल विज्ञापन का युग माना जाता है। समाचार-पत्रों के अतिरिक्त रेडियो और टेलीविजन भी विज्ञापन के सफल साधन हैं। विज्ञापन का मूल उद्देश्य उत्पादक और भोक्ता में सीधा सम्पर्क स्थापित करना होता है। जितना अधिक विज्ञापन किसी पदार्थ का होगा, उतनी ही उसकी लोकप्रियता बढ़ेगी। इन विज्ञापनों पर धन तो अधिक व्यय होता है, पर इनसे बिक्री बढ़ जाती है। ग्राहक जब इन आकर्षक विज्ञापनों को देखता है तो वह उस वस्तु-विशेष के प्रति आकृष्ट होकर उसे खरीदने को बाध्य हो जाता है।

उपर्युक्त गद्यांश को ध्यानपूर्वक पढ़ें और निम्नलिखित प्रश्नों के उत्तर के लिए सही विकल्प चुनें :

1. वर्तमान को किसका युग माना जाता है?
   A. फैशन B. विज्ञापन
   C. संगीत D. धन
2. उत्पादक तथा भोक्ता के बीच कौन संबंध स्थापित करता है?
   A. टेलीविजन B. समाचार-पत्र
   C. रेडियो D. विज्ञापन
3. **वर्तमान** शब्द का विपरीत शब्द है :
   A. अर्वाचीन B. आधुनिक
   C. आजकल D. प्राचीन
4. **आकर्षक** का शब्दार्थ है :
   A. विकर्षक B. सुन्दर
   C. मनमोहक D. आश्चर्यजनक
5. भोक्ता किस कारण वस्तुओं को खरीदने के लिए बाध्य हो जाता है?
   A. विज्ञापन
   B. आकर्षक विज्ञापन
   C. लोकप्रियता के कारण
   D. आसानी से उपलब्ध होना

गद्यांश 14

लगभग दो सौ वर्ष की गुलामी ने भारत के राष्ट्रीय स्वाभिमान को पैरों से रौंद डाला, हमारी संस्कृति को समाप्त कर दिया, हमारे विश्वासों को हिला दिया और हमारे आत्मविश्वास को चकनाचूर कर दिया, किन्तु अपने इस बूढ़े देश से प्यार करने वाले, इसके एक सामान्य संकेत पर प्राण न्यौछावर करने वाले दीवानों का अभाव न था। एक आवाज उठी और देखते ही देखते राष्ट्र का दबा हुआ आत्माभिमान उन्मत्त हो उठा। इतिहास साक्षी है जाने और अनजाने सहस्त्रों देशभक्त स्वतंत्रता की अनमोल निधि को पाने के लिए शहीद हो गए।

उपर्युक्त गद्यांश को ध्यानपूर्वक पढ़ें और निम्नलिखित प्रश्नों के उत्तर के लिए सही विकल्प चुनें :

1. **स्वाभिमान** का संधि विच्छेद है:
   A. स्वा + भिमान B. स्वः + अभिमान
   C. स्व + अभिमान D. स्वा + अभिमान
2. भारत का राष्ट्रीय स्वाभिमान किस कारण समाप्त हो गया था?
   A. लम्बे गुलामी से B. निरंकुश शासक से
   C. स्वार्थी मानव से D. धर्म के विनाश से
3. **आत्मविश्वास** का शब्दार्थ है
   A. घमण्ड B. गर्व
   C. अपने पर विश्वास D. अभिमान
4. भारत की अनमोल निधि को पाने के लिए कौन शहीद हो गए?
   A. देशभक्त B. नेता
   C. युवा D. युवती

5. **अनमोल निधि** का शब्दार्थ है:

A. अनन्त खजाना B. अमूल्य खजाना

C. बहुमूल्य D. स्वतंत्रता

गद्यांश 15

दुनिया के विभिन्न देशों के विकास पर विहंगम दृष्टि डालने से यह स्पष्ट हो जाता है कि आज जिस देश ने वैज्ञानिक उपलब्धियों के सहारे अपना औद्योगीकरण कर लिया, उसी को उन्नत देश कहा जाता है। जिस देश में औद्योगीकरण का स्तर नीचा है, वह पिछड़ा हुआ देश कहा जाता है। वैज्ञानिक आविष्कारों और औद्योगीकरण के आधार पर ही किसी देश की प्रगति को आँका जाता रहा है। विज्ञान ने मानव को पूरी तरह बदल दिया है।

उपर्युक्त गद्यांश को ध्यानपूर्वक पढ़ें और निम्नलिखित प्रश्नों के उत्तर के लिए सही विकल्प चुनें :

1. **विहंगम दृष्टि** का क्या अर्थ है?

A. एक झलक B. गहन दृष्टि

C. गहन चिन्तन D. इनमें से कोई नहीं

2. **विकास** का विपरीत शब्द है :

A. उत्थान B. उदय

C. पतन D. विनाश

3. **वैज्ञानिक** शब्द में कौन-सा प्रत्यय हैं?

A. निक B. वै

C. ईक D. इक

4. मानव जीवन को किसने बदल दिया है :

A. विकास B. वैज्ञानिक

C. विज्ञान D. उद्योग

5. किसी भी देश की स्तर को किससे नापा जाता है?

A. उपलब्धियों पर

B. औद्योगीकरण से

C. वैज्ञानिकों से

D. आविष्कारों से

गद्यांश 16

विश्व का वर्तमान उन्नत रूप मानव-श्रम की ही कहानी कह रहा है। गगन चुंबी अट्टालिकाएँ, लंबी-चौड़ी सड़कें, बड़े-बड़े विशाल नगर आकाश में उड़ते वायुयान तथा मानव-जीवन को सुखी और समृद्ध बनाने में योगदान करने वाले ज्ञान-विज्ञान के अनन्त रूप-ये सभी मनुष्य के श्रम का जयघोष करते हैं। स्पष्ट है कि मनुष्य और उसका शरीर विधाता की अनुपम रचना है जो निश्चय ही महान उद्देश्यों की संपूर्ति के लिए दिया गया है। इस दुर्लभ तन को यदि हम आलस्य, प्रसाद अथवा घटिया कामों में गँवा देते हैं तो उस विधाता के प्रति अन्याय करते हैं।

उपर्युक्त गद्यांश को ध्यानपूर्वक पढ़ें और निम्नलिखित प्रश्नों के उत्तर के लिए सही विकल्प चुनें :

1. विश्व का वर्तमान रूप किसका उद्योतक है?

A. चिन्तक का B. नेता का

C. वैज्ञानिक का D. मानव श्रम

2. **गगन चुंबी अट्टालिकाएँ** का अर्थ है :

A. आकाश में उड़ने वाला

B. आकाश को छूने वाला

C. बहुमंजिली इमारत

D. इनमें से कोई नहीं

3. आकाश का समानार्थक शब्द है :

A. वसुन्धरा B. धरा

C. पयोद D. गगन

4. **सुखी** का विपरीत शब्द है :

A. प्रसन्न B. अप्रसन्न

C. दुखी D. उदासी

5. विधाता की अनुपम रचना क्या है?

A. मानव शरीर B. समुद्र

C. वन D. पृथ्वी

गद्यांश 17

हमारे देश में एक ऐसा भी युग था जब नैतिक और आध्यात्मिक विकास ही जीवन का वास्तविक लक्ष्य माना जाता था। अहिंसा की भावना सर्वोपरि थी। आज पूरा जीवन दर्शन ही बदल गया है। सर्वत्र पैसे की हाय-हाय तथा धन का उपार्जन ही मुख्य ध्येय हो गया है, भले ही धन-उपार्जन के तरीके गलत ही क्यों न हों? इन सबका असर मनुष्य के प्रतिदिन के जीवन पर पड़ रहा है। समाज का वातावरण दूषित हो गया है-

बाह्य वातावरण तो दूषित है ही, आज सब जानते हैं पर्यावरण की समस्याएँ कितनी चिन्तनीय हो उठी है। इन

सबके कारण मानसिक और शारीरिक तनाव-खिंचाव और व्याधियाँ पैदा हो रही हैं।

उपर्युक्त गद्यांश को ध्यानपूर्वक पढ़ें और निम्नलिखित प्रश्नों के उत्तर के लिए सही विकल्प चुनें :

1. भारत का प्राचीन आदर्श था :
A. सत्य और अहिंसा
B. नैतिक और आध्यात्मिक विकास
C. धन उपार्जन
D. इनमें से कोई नहीं

2. **अहिंसा** का विपरीत शब्द है :
A. हिंसा B. सत्याग्रह
C. विनम्रता D. नैतिकता

3. जीवन दर्शन क्यों बदल गया है?
A. हिंसा के कारण
B. अहिंसा के कारण
C. धन लिप्सा के कारण
D. आध्यात्मिक विकास के कारण

4. समाज का वातावरण दूषित क्यों हो गया है?
A. शारीरिक तनाव
B. मानसिक व्याधियाँ
C. पर्यावरण की समस्याएँ
D. धन उपार्जन के गलत तरीके

5. **पर्यावरण** का शब्दार्थ है:
A. जलमंडल B. स्थलमंडल
C. वायुमंडल D. वातावरण

गद्यांश 18

राजा राम मोहन राय में "होनहार बिरवान के होत चीकने पांत" वाली कहावत पूरी तरह चरितार्थ हुई। बाल्यकाल में उनकी बुद्धि कितनी कुशाग्र थी, इसकी अनेक कहानियाँ सुनी जाती हैं। उनके पिता ने उनकी पढ़ाई का समुचित प्रबन्ध किया। गाँव की पाठशाला में उन्होंने बंगला सीखी। उन दिनों कचहरियों में फारसी का बोलबाला था। अतः उन्होंने घर पर ही मौलवी से फारसी पढ़ी। नौ वर्ष की उम्र में वे अरबी की उच्च शिक्षा के लिए पटना भेजे गये। पटना उस समय भारतवर्ष में इस्लामी संस्कृति का केन्द्र था। पटना में वे तीन वर्ष तक रहे। उन्होंने कुरान का मूल अरबी में अध्ययन किया। चार वर्ष तक काशी में संस्कृत का अध्ययन किया। उपनिषदों के अद्वैतवाद का उनपर पूरा प्रभाव पड़ा। फलतः उन्हें निराकार ईश्वर पर विश्वास हुआ।

उपर्युक्त गद्यांश को ध्यानपूर्वक पढ़ें और निम्नलिखित प्रश्नों के उत्तर के लिए सही विकल्प चुनें :

1. राजा राममोहन राय ने बंगला कहाँ सीखी?
A. पटना B. काशी
C. कलकत्ता D. गाँव की पाठशाला

2. अरबी की शिक्षा उन्होंने कहाँ पाई?
A. काशी B. पटना
C. ईरान D. ईराक

3. संस्कृत साहित्य का अध्ययन उन्होंने कहाँ किया?
A. पटना B. काशी
C. इलाहाबाद D. कलकत्ता

4. **कुशाग्र** शब्द का अर्थ है :
A. तेज B. बुद्धिमान
C. होनहार D. विद्वान्

5. निराकार शब्द का विलोम है :
A. साकार B. आकार
C. विशाल D. मूर्ति

गद्यांश 19

मोती राजा साहब की सवारी का खास हाथी था। यों तो वह बहुत सीधा और समझदार था, पर कभी-कभी उसका मिजाज गर्म हो जाता था। एक बार पागलपन में उसने अपने महावत को मार डाला। राजा साहब ने यह खबर सुनी, तो उन्हें बहुत क्रोध आया, मोती की पदवी छिन गई। उसे राजा साहब की सवारी से निकाल दिया गया। कुलियों की तरह उसे लकड़ियाँ ढ़ोनी पड़ती, पत्थर लादने पड़ते और शाम को वह पीपल के नीचे मोटी जंजीरों से बाँध दिया जाता।

उपर्युक्त गद्यांश को ध्यानपूर्वक पढ़ें और निम्नलिखित प्रश्नों के उत्तर के लिए सही विकल्प चुनें :

1. राजा साहब की सवारी के हाथी का क्या नाम था?
A. सोना B. मोती
C. हीरा D. ऐरावत

2. किसने महावत को मार डाला था?
A. राजा B. हाथी
C. मोती D. दरबारी

3. **मिजाज** शब्द का शब्दार्थ है :

A. विचार B. ध्यान

C. मन D. दिल

4. किसकी पदवी छिन गई थी?

A. महावत की B. राजा की

C. मोती की D. हाथी की

5. समझदार और सीधा कौन था?

A. राजा साहब B. महावत

C. मोती D. इनमें से कोई नहीं

गद्यांश 20

मनुष्य का यह दावा है कि वह सक्षम है, समर्थ है। हिमालय की तराई में घने जंगलों के बीच में बना एक छोटा-सा स्टेशन, जो दोपहर के बाद वाली ढ़लती धूप में भी बुरी तरह जल रहा था, मानो मनुष्य के इस दावे का प्रमाण था। प्रकृति इस मनुष्य के वश में है, वह इस प्रकृति को मनचाहा नवीन रूप देता है। वह इस प्रकृति के साथ न जाने कितने खिलवाड़ करता है। तराई का वह जंगल भी तो उसी प्रकृति का एक भाग था।

उपर्युक्त गद्यांश को ध्यानपूर्वक पढ़ें और निम्नलिखित प्रश्नों के उत्तर के लिए सही विकल्प चुनें :

1. **सक्षम** शब्द समानार्थक शब्द है :

A. समर्थ B. शक्तिशाली

C. कायर D. निर्माता

2. सक्षम और समर्थ होने का दावा कौन करता है?

A. प्रकृति B. मानव

C. दानव D. पशु

3. छोटा-सा स्टेशन कहाँ स्थित है?

A. घने जंगलों में B. हिमालय की तराई में

C. नदी के किनारे D. नगर में

4. प्रकृति के साथ कौन खिलवाड़ करता है?

A. मानव B. वैज्ञानिक

C. नेता D. युवा

5. **नवीन** का विपरीत शब्द है :

A. पुराना B. नूतन

C. नवनीत D. अतीत

गद्यांश 21

पता नहीं जंगल में भी प्राण होते हैं या नहीं। वैसे जन्म लेना, मरना, शैशव, युवावस्था और वृद्धावस्था, जीवन के सब चिह्न जंगल में होते हैं। न जाने कितने पशु-पक्षी इन जंगलों की गोद में आश्रय लिए हुए हैं। कभी भयानक रूप से क्रुद्ध और उबलते हुए और कभी निष्प्राण से सुखे हुए नदी-नाले। ये सब जंगल के भाग हैं और जंगल के अन्दर इन अनगिनत प्राणियों में जीवन-मरण का संघर्ष चला करता है। रोज ही जन्म होते हैं, रोज ही मृत्यु के फेरे लगते हैं। जीवन-मरण की सीमाओं में बद्ध जो प्रकृति का क्रम है। वह तो चलता ही रहता है।

उपर्युक्त गद्यांश को ध्यानपूर्वक पढ़ें और निम्नलिखित प्रश्नों के उत्तर के लिए सही विकल्प चुनें :

1. जीवन के सब चिह्न किसमें होते है?

A. जंगल में

B. मानव में

C. पशु में

D. पादप में

2. **शैशव** का शब्दार्थ है :

A. युवा B. बुढ़ापा

C. बचपन D. नश्वर

3. जंगलों में कौन आश्रय लेता है :

A. पशु-पक्षी B. जन्तु

C. पादप D. मानव

4. **निष्प्राण** का समानार्थक शब्द है :

A. सजीव B. निर्जीव

C. शाश्वत D. नश्वर

5. **जीवन** का विपरीत शब्द है :

A. मरण B. अमर

C. प्राण D. नश्वर

गद्यांश 22

यह आदान-प्रदान ही मानव-सभ्यता का मूल स्रोत है; इस आदान-प्रदान के लिए ही मुनष्य ने पहाड़ों को लाँघकर और सागरों को पार करके दुनिया के हर-एक कोने का पता लगाया। इस आदान-प्रदान की क्रिया-प्रतिक्रिया के रूप में न जाने कितने युद्ध लड़े गए, न जाने कितने देश बरबाद किए गए, न जाने कितनी सभ्यताएँ नष्ट की गई और यह आदान-प्रदान चल रहा है।

उपर्युक्त गद्यांश को ध्यानपूर्वक पढ़ें और निम्नलिखित प्रश्नों के उत्तर के लिए सही विकल्प चुनें :

1. मानव-सभ्यता का मूल स्रोत क्या है?
A. आदान B. प्रदान
C. आदान-प्रदान D. इनमें से कोई नहीं

2. मानव का विपरीत शब्द है :
A. नर B. मनुष्य
C. दानव D. दुष्ट

3. दुनिया के हर एक भाग का पता किसने किया है?
A. मानव B. खोजकर्ता
C. आविष्कारक D. दानव

4. युद्ध क्यों लड़े गए थे :
A. क्रिया-प्रतिक्रिया के कारण
B. आदान-प्रदान के कारण
C. स्वार्थ के कारण
D. धन उपार्जन के कारण

5. आदान-प्रदान शब्द है :
A. विपरीत शब्द
B. क्रिया विशेषण
C. पर्यायवाची शब्द
D. सहचर-शब्द

उत्तरमाला

गद्यांश 1
1. C **2.** D **3.** B **4.** A **5.** D

गद्यांश 2
1. A **2.** D **3.** D **4.** C **5.** A

गद्यांश 3
1. C **2.** D **3.** B **4.** C **5.** B

गद्यांश 4
1. D **2.** D **3.** C **4.** A **5.** C

गद्यांश 5
1. B **2.** D **3.** D **4.** C **5.** A

गद्यांश 6
1. B **2.** B **3.** D **4.** A **5.** C

गद्यांश 7
1. C **2.** B **3.** D **4.** B **5.** B

गद्यांश 8
1. D **2.** A **3.** D **4.** D **5.** D

गद्यांश 9
1. D **2.** B **3.** B **4.** D **5.** C

गद्यांश 10
1. D **2.** C **3.** B **4.** D **5.** C

गद्यांश 11
1. A **2.** A **3.** A **4.** A **5.** C

गद्यांश 12
1. B **2.** D **3.** D **4.** C **5.** C

गद्यांश 13
1. B **2.** D **3.** D **4.** C **5.** B

गद्यांश 14
1. C **2.** A **3.** C **4.** A **5.** B

गद्यांश 15
1. A **2.** D **3.** C **4.** C **5.** B

गद्यांश 16
1. D **2.** C **3.** D **4.** C **5.** A

गद्यांश 17
1. B **2.** A **3.** C **4.** D **5.** D

गद्यांश 18
1. D **2.** B **3.** B **4.** A **5.** A

गद्यांश 19
1. B **2.** C **3.** C **4.** C **5.** C

गद्यांश 20
1. A **2.** B **3.** B **4.** A **5.** A

गद्यांश 21
1. C **2.** C **3.** A **4.** B **5.** A

गद्यांश 22
1. C **2.** C **3.** A **4.** B **5.** D

❑❑❑

GENERAL INTELLIGENCE AND REASONING

SERIES

Directions : *In each of the following series determine the order of the letters. Then from the given options select the one which will complete the given series.*

1. BMK, DLM, FKO, HJQ, ?

A. JIR B. JIT
C. JHS D. JIS

2. A, CD, FGH, ?

A. IJKL B. KLMN
C. JKLM D. LMNO

3. BXJ, ETL, HPN, KLP, ?

A. PHR B. NIR
C. NHR D. MHR

4. PUF, QVG, RWH, ?

A. SXI B. SYZ
C. SXJ D. SVI

5. DEF, HIJ, MNO, ?

A. RTV B. STU
C. PTU D. SRU

Directions : *Which of the following groups of letters will complete the given series?*

6. ab---b-bbaa-

A. babba B. abaab
C. abbab D. baaab

7. aa-ab--aaa-a

A. baaa B. abab
C. aaab D. aabb

8. -baa-aab-a-a

A. baab B. abab
C. aaba D. aabb

9. -a cca-ccca-acccc-aaa

A. ccaa B. acca
C. caac D. caaa

10. c-bbb--abbbb-abbb-

A. abccb B. bacbb
C. aabcb D. abacb

Directions : *In the following questions, select the number(s) from the given options for completing the given series.*

11. 3, 9, 27, 81, 243, ?

A. 486 B. 729
C. 972 D. 359

12. 1, 6, 12, 19, 27, ?

A. 38 B. 35
C. 36 D. 54

13. 2, 6, 14, 30, 62, ?

A. 126 B. 128
C. 120 D. 130

14. 8, 48, 16, 96, 32, ?

A. 192 B. 150
C. 64 D. 288

15. 2, 8, 14, 24, 34, 48, ?

A. 66 B. 62
C. 58 D. 64

Directions : *In the given series find the number which is wrong.*

16. 5, 25, 120, 625, 3125, 15625

A. 15625 B. 625
C. 120 D. 5

17. 4, 8, 11, 22, 18, 36, 24, 50

A. 8 B. 22
C. 36 D. 24

18. 2, 4, 12, 24, 72, 142, 432

A. 432 B. 12
C. 142 D. 72

19. 2, 3, 4, 4, 6, 8, 9, 12, 16

A. 3 B. 9
C. 6 D. 12

20. 97, 91, 86, 83, 79, 77, 76, 76

A. 86 B. 76
C. 91 D. 83

ANSWERS

1	2	3	4	5	6	7	8	9	10
D	C	C	A	B	D	C	B	D	A
11	**12**	**13**	**14**	**15**	**16**	**17**	**18**	**19**	**20**
B	C	A	A	B	C	D	C	B	D

SOME SELECTED EXPLANATORY ANSWERS

1. The letters in one group correspond to the letters in the next group in the manner +2, –1, +2 respectively.

BMK DLM FKO HJQ JIS

+2 +2 +2 +2

–1 –1 –1 –1

+2 +2 +2 +2

2. The letters are in natural sequence and from one group to the next one letter is dropped. Also the number of letters in groups is increased by one.

A CD FGH JKLM

↓ ↓ ↓

B E I

3. The letters in one group correspond to the letters in the next group in the manner +3, – 4, +2 respectively, *i.e.*,

BXJ ETL HPN KLP NHR

+3 +3 +3 +3

–4 –4 –4 –4

+2 +2 +2 +2

4. The three letters in each group are moved one step forward.

PUF QVG RWH SXI

+1 +1 +1

+1 +1 +1

+1 +1 +1

5. The letters are in natural order. The number of letters dropped in between the groups is increased by one at each step.

DEF HIJ MNO STU

↓ ↓ ↓

G KL PQR

6. The series is abbaab, abbaab

7. The series is aaaaba, aaaaba

8. The series is aba, aba, aba, aba

9. The series is c,a,cc,aa, ccc, aaa, cccc, aaaa

10. The series is cabbbb, cabbbb, cabbbb

11. The numbers in the series are multiplied by 3 to get the next numbers.

12. The difference between the numbers in the series increases by 1, after beginning from 5, *i.e.*,

1 6 12 19 27 36

+5 +6 +7 +8 +9

13. The difference between the numbers in the series doubles each time, after beginning from 4, *i.e.*,

2 6 14 30 62 126

+4 +8 +16 +32 +64

14. *Explanation I* : The sequence in the series is × 6, ÷ 3 which is repeated.

8 48 16 96 32 192

×6 ÷3 ×6 ÷3 ×6

Explanation II : There are two alternate series and the numbers are multiplied by 2.

×2 ×2

8 48 16 96 32 192

×2 ×2

Series I : 8, 16, 32

Series II : 48, 96, 192

15. The sequence in the series is :

2 8 14 24 34 48 62

+6 +6 +10 +10 +14 +14

The difference increases by 4 at alternate step.

16. The numbers in the series are multiplied by 5 to get the next number.

∴ 125 should be in place of 120.

17. Two numbers form a pair. The first number increases by 7 for the next pair and the second number is the double of first number.

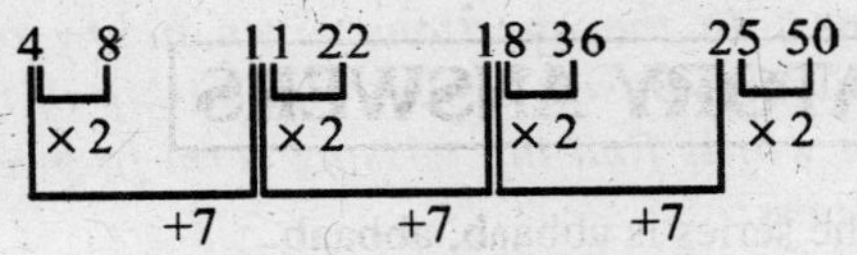

∴ 25 should be in place of 24.

18. There are two alternate series and in each series, the numbers are multiplied by 6 to get the next number.

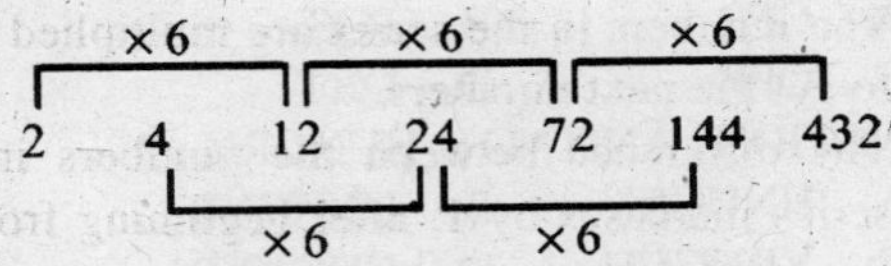

∴ 144 should be in place of 142.

19. There are three alternate series and in each series, the numbers are multiplied by 2 to get the next number.

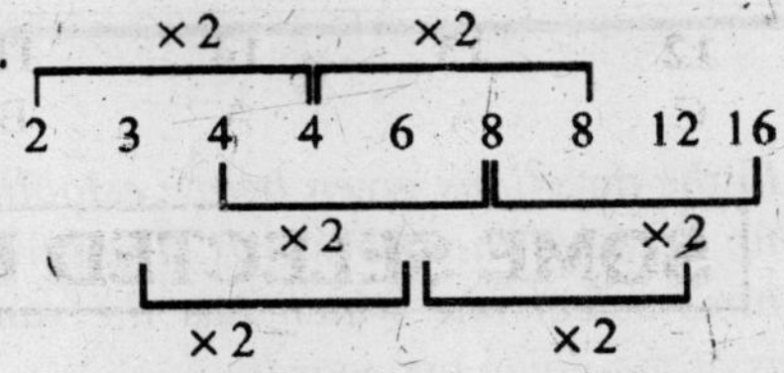

Series I : 2, 4, 8

Series II : 3, 6, 12

Series III : 4, 8, 16

∴ 8 should be in place of 9.

20. The difference between the consecutive numbers in the series decreases by 1 at each step.

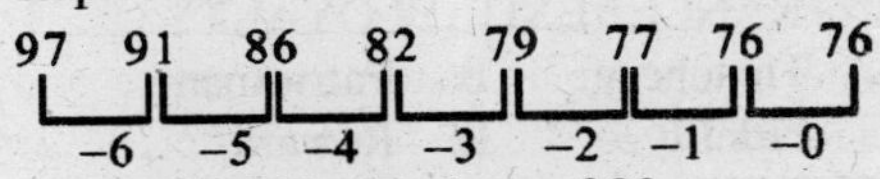

∴ 82 should be in place of 83.

ANALOGIES OR RELATIONSHIPS

Directions : *In the questions given below establish the relationship between the two words. Then from the given options select one which has the same relationship as of the given two words.*

1. ADULT : BABY : : FLOWER : ?
A. Seed B. Bud
C. Fruit D. Butterfly

2. WRITER : READER : : PRODUCER : ?
A. Creator B. Contractor
C. Creature D. Consumer

3. ENTRANCE : EXIT : : LOYALTY : ?
A. Treachery B. Patriotism
C. Fidelity D. Reward

4. MOTHER : MATERNAL : : FATHER : ?
A. Eternal B. Detrimental
C. Paternal D. Formidable

Directions : *In the questions given below one term is missing. Based on the relationship of the two given words find the missing term from the given options.*

5. GFC : CFG : : RPJ : ?
A. JRP B. JPR
C. PJR D. RJP

6. BCF : DEG : : MNQ : ?
A. OPR B. PQS
C. OPP D. QRT

7. NATION : ANITNO : : HUNGRY : ?
A. HNUGRY B. UNHGYR
C. YRNGUH D. UHGNYR

8. SSTU : MMNO : : AABC : ?
A. GGHH B. IJKK
C. XXYZ D. NOOP

ANSWERS

1	2	3	4	5	6	7	8
B	D	A	C	B	A	D	C

SOME SELECTED EXPLANATORY ANSWERS

1. The youngone of an adult is a baby and that of a flower is a bud.

2. A writer aims to please the readers by his writings, a producer aims to please the consumers by his products.

3. The related words are opposites.

4. Relations on the mother's side are maternal and on the father's side paternal.

5. The letters of the first group are reversed.

GFC : CFG : : RPJ : JPR

6. The three letters are moved 2, 2 and 1 steps forward respectively.

BCF : DEG : : MNQ : OPR

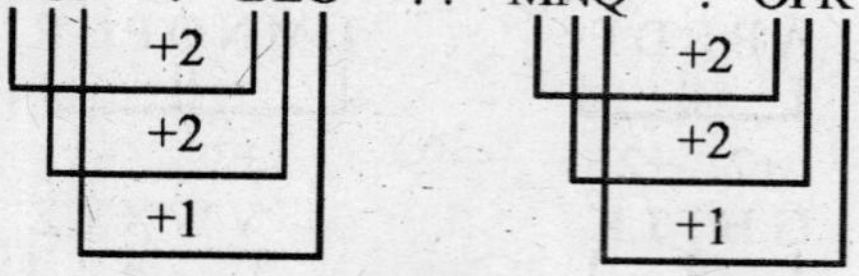

7. The word is divided in sections of two letters and the letters are reversed.

NATION : ANITNO : : HUNGRY : UHGNYR

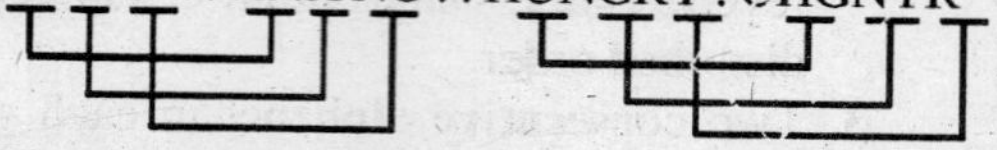

8. The first letter in each group is repeated and followed by two consecutive letters.

ODD ONE OUT

Directions : *Three of the following four in each question are alike in a certain way and so form a group. Select the group of letters that does not belong to that group.*

1. A. ACE B. LOR
   C. GIK D. VXZ
2. A. TSR B. LKJ
   C. PQO D. HGF
3. A. EF LM B. KJ SR
   C. XW HG D. ED YX
4. A. JOPK B. BOPC
   C. QOPR D. TOPS
5. A. DfH B. MoQ
   C. UwY D. InO
6. A. JKkL B. OPpQ
   C. DEEf D. VWwX
7. A. BdfH B. FHJL
   C. RTvX D. uVwX
8. A. DFHEG B. TWXUV
   C. OQSPR D. JLNKM
9. A. FEUV B. DCXW
   C. BAZY D. HGTS
10. A. UTSR B. XYZW
    C. ONML D. IHGF

ANSWERS

1	2	3	4	5	6	7	8	9	10
B	C	A	D	D	C	D	B	A	B

SOME SELECTED EXPLANATORY ANSWERS

1. The sequence in each group is +2. Only option B has sequence in +3, *i.e.*,

   ABCDE: A→C +2, C→E +2 LMNOPQR: L→O +3, O→R +3

   GHIJK: G→I +2, I→K +2 VWXYZ: V→X +2, X→Z +2

2. The sequence of alphabet in each group is in reverse order. Only option C has sequence in disturbed order.
3. Two consecutive alphabet in each group are in reverse sequence (–1), *i.e.*,

   KJ (–1) SR (–1); XW (–1) HG (–1); ED (–1) YX (–1)

   Only in option (A) the sequence is in natural order (+1), *i.e.*,

   EF (+1) LM (+1)

4. In each group, letters 'OP' are common. The two corner alphabet are in natural order (+1); *i.e.*,

   JOPK (+1); BOPC (+1); QOPR (+1)

   Only in option (D) they are in reverse order (–1); *i.e.*,

   TOPS (–1)

5. In other groups, only the alphabet in the centre is of lower case. In this option letter 'L' on the left is also in lower case.
6. In other groups, the third letter which is a repeat of the second alphabet is in lower case.
7. In each group, the sequence of the alphabet, irrespective of the case, is +2; *i.e.*,

   B D f H ; F H J L ; R T v X

   +2 +2 +2   +2 +2 +2   +2 +2 +2

   Only in option (D) the sequence is in natural order (+1), *i.e.*,

   u V w X

   +1 +1 +1
8. In each group: the alphabet at positions-first, fourth, second, fifth and third, form a natural sequence.
   In option (B), the alphabet at positions first, fourth, fifth, second and third, form the natural sequence.
9. In each group, two alphabets in the corner and two alphabets in the centre correspond to their reverse order positioned alphabet. *i.e.*,

natural order → A B C D E F G H I J K L M
reverse order → Z Y X W V U T S R Q P O N
natural order → N O P Q R S T U V W X Y Z
reverse order → M L K J I H G F E D C B A

   As such—
   D corresponds with W and
   C corresponds with X.
   B corresponds with Y and
   A corresponds with Z.
   H corresponds with S and
   G corresponds with T.

   Similarly,
   F should correspond with U and
   E should correspond with V;
   i.e. letters 'UV' should be written as 'VU'
10. In each group, the alphabet are in reverse order. In option (B), the order is disturbed.

CODING AND DECODING

Directions : *In the following questions select the right option which indicates the correct code for the word or letter given in the question.*

1. If CHAIR is coded as FKDLU then RAID is coded as :

A. ULGD B. ULKG
C. ULDG D. UDLG

2. If CONDEMN is coded as CNODMEN, then TEACHER is coded as :

A. TEACHER B. TAEECHR
C. TCAEEHR D. TAECEHR

3. In a code language COME is written as XLNV and ABLE as ZYOV. How will MOLLY be written in that code?

A. NLOBO B. NLBOO
C. LNOOB D. NLOOB

4. In a certain code PROFESSION is written as EFORPNOISS. In the same code DICTIONARY will be written as :

A. YRANOITCID
B. ITCIDYRANO
C. ITCIDYRNAO
D. ITCDIYARNO

5. JUNE is coded as NXPF, how will STAY be coded in the same manner?

A. WWCZ B. WVCZ
C. WWDB D. VWZC

Directions : *In the following questions study the coded patterns and then select the right option from the given alternatives.*

6. In a certain language, (a) 'go ju mi' stands for 'plenty of money'; (b) pao ju go nei vu' for 'money creates lots of problems'; (c) 'kol vu nei' for 'problems create tension'; and (d) 'sol tun ju haw' for 'still money is needed'. Which of the following words stand for 'money'?

A. nei B. ju
C. haw D. go

7. In a certain language, (a) 'FOR' stands for 'old is gold'; (b) 'ROT' stands for 'gold is pure'; (c) 'ROM' stands for 'gold is costly'. How will 'pure old gold is costly' be written?

A. TFROM B. FOTRM
C. FTORM D. TOMRF

8. In a certain code '415' means 'milk is hot'; '18' means 'hot soup'; and '895' means 'soup is tasty'. What number will indicate the word 'tasty'?

A. 9 B. 8
C. 5 D. 4

9. In a certain code '643' means 'she is beautiful', '593' means 'he is handsome', and '567' means 'handsome meets beautiful'. What number will indicate the word 'meets'?

A. 5 B. 3
C. 7 D. 6

10. In a certain code language, (a) 'dugo hui mul zo' stands for 'work is very hard'; (b) 'hui dugo ba ki' for 'Bingo is very smart'; (c) 'nano mul dugo' for 'cake is hard', and (d) 'mul ki qu' for 'smart and hard'. Which of the following words stand for 'Bingo'?

A. jalu B. dugo
C. ki D. ba

ANSWERS

1	2	3	4	5	6	7	8	9	10
D	D	D	B	A	B	A	A	C	D

SOME SELECTED EXPLANATORY ANSWERS

2. In this word, the second and third letters interchange their places and the fifth and sixth letters do the same. Other letters retain their position.

CONDEMN .... CNODMEN

TEACHER .... TAECEHR

3. The letters of the word are coded by their represented letters in the reverse series.

C O M E → letters in natural series
X L N V → letters in reverse series
↓ ↓ ↓ ↓
3rd 15th 13th 5th → position of letters
A B L E → letters in natural series
Z Y O V → letters in reverse series
↓ ↓ ↓ ↓
1st 2nd 12th 5th → position of letters

Similarly,

M O L L Y → letters in natural series
N L O O B → letters in reverse series
↓ ↓ ↓ ↓ ↓
13th 15th 12th 12th 25th → position of letters

4. The word is divided into two equal parts and the letters of each part are written backwards.

PROFE SSION .... EFORP NOISS

Similarly,

DICTI ONARY .... ITCID YRANO

5. The word is coded by moving the letters +4, +3, +2, and +1 steps respectively.

JUNE .... NXPF
+4
+3
+2
+1

Similarly,

STAY .... WWCZ
+4
+3
+2
+1

6.

	Code	Sentence
1.	go *ju* mi	plenty of *money*
2.	pao *ju* go nei vu	*money* creates lots of problems
3.	kol vu nei	problems create tension
4.	sol tun *ju* haw	still *money* is needed

In 1st, 2nd and 4th codes and their sentences the word 'ju' is repeated and so is 'money'.

8.

	Code	Sentence
1.	415	milk is hot
2.	18	hot soup
3.	895	soup is *tasty*

From 3rd code and its sentence neither number '9' is repeated nor the word 'tasty'.

9.

	Code	Sentence
1.	643	she is beautiful
2.	593	he is handsome
3.	567	handsome *meets* beautiful

From 3rd code and its sentence, neither number '7' nor the word 'meets' is repeated.

10.

	Code	Sentence
1.	*dugo hui* mul zo	work *is very* hard
2.	*hui dugo* **ba** *ki*	**Bingo** *is very smart*
3.	nano mul *dugo*	cake is *hard*
4.	mul *ki* qu	*smart* and hard

From 2nd code and its sentence, neither 'ba' nor 'Bingo' is repeated.
(Words repeated are in italics)

STATEMENT ANALYSIS

1. Among five friends, A is heavier than B; C is lighter than D; B is lighter than D but heavier than E. Who among them is the heaviest?
   A. B B. C
   C. A D. Can't say
2. Pune is bigger than Jhansi, Sitapur is bigger than Chittor. Raigarh is not as big as Jhansi, but is bigger than Sitapur. Chittor is not as big as Sitapur. Which is the smallest?
   A. Jhansi B. Pune
   C. Chittor D. Sitapur
3. Ajay works more than Ram. Alok works as much as Raju. Pankaj works less than Alok. Ram works more than Alok. Who works the most of all?
   A. Ajay B. Ram
   C. Alok D. Raju
4. Vipul is taller than Hans. Hans is taller than Anand. Alok is taller than Ashok. Ashok is taller than Hans. Who among them is the tallest?
   A. Vipul
   B. Alok
   C. Ashok
   D. Cannot be determined
5. Pramod is taller than Gopal. Gopal is shorter than Madhu. To find out who among them is the tallest, which of the following further informations is necessary?
   A. Madhu is taller than Gopal.
   B. Madhu is shorter than Pramod's brother
   C. Pramod is taller than Madhu.
   D. Pramod is taller than Madhu's brother.
6. Among five friends P, Q, R, S and T, who is the youngest? To arrive at the answer which of the following information given in the statements (*a*) and (*b*) is sufficient?
   (*a*) R is younger than P and T.
   (*b*) S is younger than Q.
   A. Only (*a*) alone is sufficient
   B. Either (*a*) or (*b*) is sufficient
   C. Both (*a*) and (*b*) together are needed
   D. Both (*a*) and (*b*) together are not sufficient
7. Sushma is richer than Rashmi whereas Anand is richer than Priya. Arun is as rich as Rashmi. Shoba is richer than Sushma. Which of the following statements is correct according to the above propositions?
   A. Rashmi is poorer than Priya.
   B. Priya is richer than Arun
   C. Arun is poorer than Sushma.
   D. Anand is richer than Rashmi
8. A is elder to B while C and D are elder to E who lies between A and B. If C be elder to B, which one of the following statements is necessarily true?
   A. E is elder to B
   B. A is elder to C
   C. C is elder to D
   D. D is elder to C
9. Vikram is taller than Rajan but shorter than Annie. Jamal is taller than Annie. Sita is taller than Vikram. Rajan is shorter than Sita. Who is the shortest of all in the group?
   A. Sita
   B. Rajan
   C. Vikram
   D. Cannot be determined
10. Suresh is as much older than Kamal as he is younger than Prabodh. Navin is as old as Kamal. Which of the following statements is wrong?
    A. Suresh is older than Navin
    B. Kamal is younger than Suresh
    C. Prabodh is not the oldest
    D. Navin is younger than Prabodh

ANSWERS

1	2	3	4	5	6	7	8	9	10
D	C	A	D	C	D	C	A	B	C

SOME SELECTED EXPLANATORY ANSWERS

1. The five friends in descending order of weight are : A/D, B/C, E or A/D, B, C/E. Either A or D is the heaviest.

2. The order of cities in descending order of size is : Pune, Jhansi, Raigarh, Sitapur, Chittor.

3. On the basis of doing work, the descending order will be : Ajay, Ram, Alok/Raju, Pankaj.

4. On the basis of height, the descending order will be Vipul/Alok, Ashok, Hans, Anand. Either Vipul or Alok is the tallest.

5. According to the information both Pramod and Madhu are taller than Gopal. Option (c) decides who is the tallest.

6. Statements are not inter-related.

7. On the basis of wealth, the descending order will be :

1. Shobha, Sushma, Rashmi/Arun
2. Anand, *and* Priya

(The two statements are not inter-related.)

8. The order in descending seniority will be : A/C/D, E, B.

9. On the basis of height the descending order will be :

Jamal/Sita, Annie, Vikram, Rajan.

or

Jamal, Sita/Annie, Vikram, Rajan.

10. On the basis of age the descending order will be : Prabodh, Suresh, Kamal/Navin.

PLACE ARRANGEMENT

Directions : *In the following questions, understand the arrangement pattern and then select the right answer from the given options :*

1. Five boys are sitting in a row. Raghu is not adjacent to Shyam or Amit. Ajay is not adjacent to Shyam. Raghu is adjacent to Mayank. If Mayank is at the middle in the row, then Ajay is adjacent to whom out of the following?

A. Amit B. Raghu
C. Mayank D. Shyam

2. Mini is to the right of Rajni but to the left of Ananta. Saya is to the right of Mini but to the left of Jaya. Who is on the extreme left if all the girls are facing North?

A. Jaya B. Mini
C. Rajni D. Saya

3. Kittu is in-between Mohan and Sohan. Raju is to the left of Sohan and Shyam is to the right of Mohan. If all of the friends are sitting facing South, then who is on their extreme right?

A. Mohan B. Sohan
C. Kittu D. Shyam

4. A, B, C, D and E are running one behind the other. C is not near E and A is not near D. B is next to A and E is not near D. Who is in the middle?

A. B B. E
C. A D. Cannot be said

5. O, P, Q, R, S and T are standing on a bench according to their height. P is taller than O but shorter than S. Only S is taller than T. R is shorter than P but taller than Q. Who is the shortest?

A. O B. Q
C. P D. Cannot be said

ANSWERS

1	2	3	4	5
B	C	D	A	D

SOME SELECTED EXPLANATORY ANSWERS

1. The order of sitting is :
Amit, Shyam, Mayank, Ajay, Raghu
or
Ajay, Raghu, Mayank, Amit, Shyam

2. The order in which the girls are positioned is :
Rajni, Mini, Ananta, Saya, Jaya
or
Saya, Jaya, Ananta
or
Saya, Ananta, Jaya

3. The order of sitting while facing South is:
Shyam, Mohan, Kittu, Sohan, Raju.

4. The positions while running behind the other is :

E / A / B / C / D *or* E / A / B / D / C

5. In descending order of height, the standing positions are :

S / T / P / R / O / Q *or* S / T / P / R / Q / O

Either O or Q is the shortest. The information given is not enough to clarify the answer.

DIRECTION SENSE

Directions : *In the following questions, select the right answer from the given options to depict the correct direction/distance.*

1. Kittu walks towards East and then towards South. After walking some distance he turns towards West and then turns to his left. In which direction is he walking now?

A. North B. South
C. East D. West

2. A person is driving towards West. What sequence of directions should he follow so that he is driving towards South?

A. left, right, right B. right, right, left
C. left, left, left D. right, right, right

3. Richa drives 8 km to the South, turns left and drives 5 km. Again, she turns left and drives 8 km. How far is she from her starting point?

A. 3 km B. 5 km
C. 8 km D. 13 km

4. Dingi runs 40 km towards North then turns right and runs 50 km. He turns right and runs 30 km, and once again turns right and runs 50 km. How far is he from his starting point?

A. 90 km B. 50 km
C. 10 km D. 5 km

5. Debu walks towards East then towards North and turning 45° right walks for a while and lastly turns towards left. In which direction is he walking now?

A. North B. East
C. South-East D. North-West

ANSWERS

1	2	3	4	5
B	D	B	C	D

SOME SELECTED EXPLANATORY ANSWERS

1. 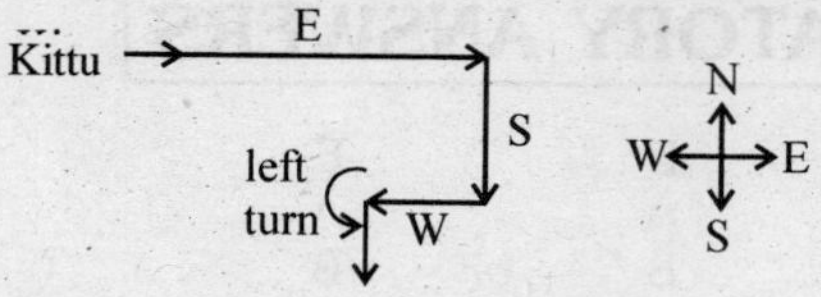

2. 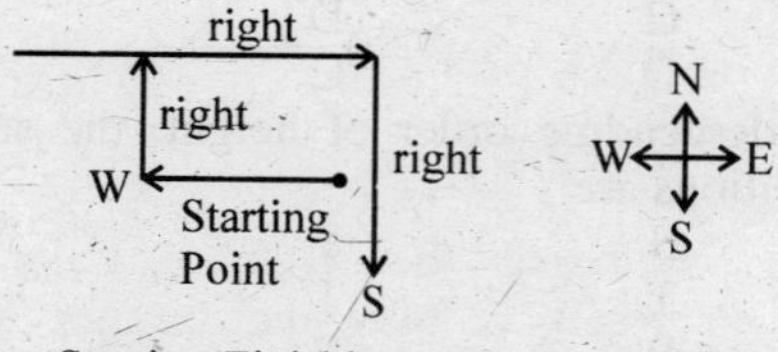

3. 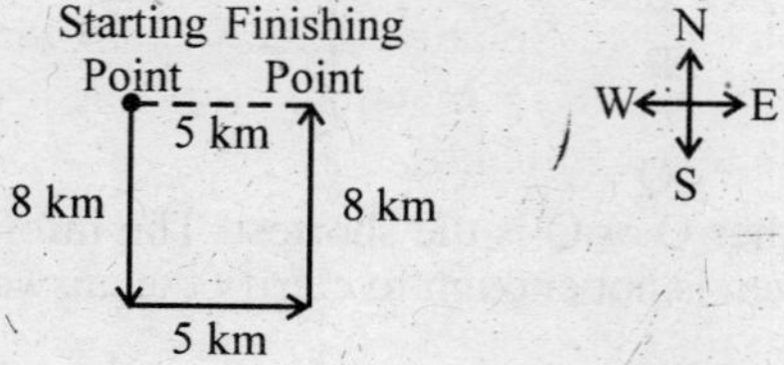

4. 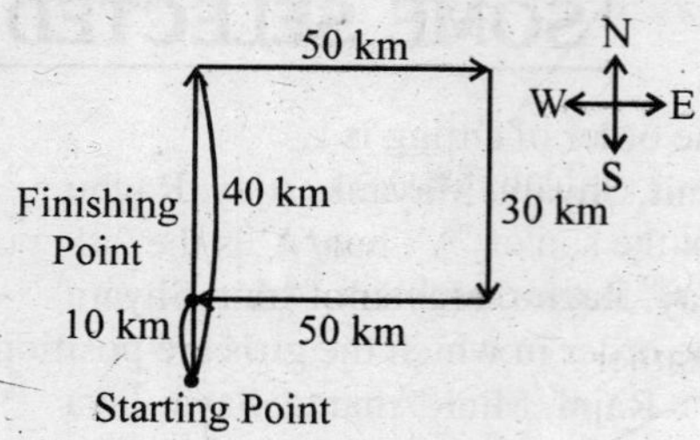

5. 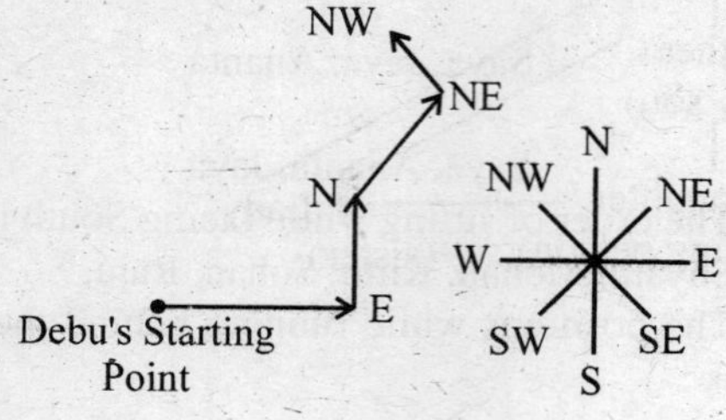

BLOOD RELATIONSHIPS

Directions : *In each of the following questions keenly study the relationship mentioned between the persons, and then from the given options select the right relationship as the answer.*

1. 'A' is the father of 'B' and 'C'. 'B' is the son of 'A' but 'C' is not the son of 'A'. What is 'C's' relation with 'A'?

A. Daughter B. Son
C. Niece D. Nephew

2. A lady said, "The person standing there is my grandfather's only son's daughter". How is the lady related to the standing person?

A. Sister B. Mother
C. Aunt D. Cousin

3. Ravi is the brother of Amit's son's son. What is Amit's relation to Ravi?

A. Cousin B. Father
C. Grandfather D. Son

4. Mayank said, "My mother is the sister of Rajat's brother." What is Rajat's relation with Mayank?

A. Cousin B. Maternal uncle
C. Uncle D. Brother-in-law

5. Introducing Lily, Raghav said, "Her father is my mother's only son". How is Lily related to Raghav?

A. Aunt B. Daughter
C. Mother D. Sister

ANSWERS

1	2	3	4	5
A	A	C	B	B

SOME SELECTED EXPLANATORY ANSWERS

1.

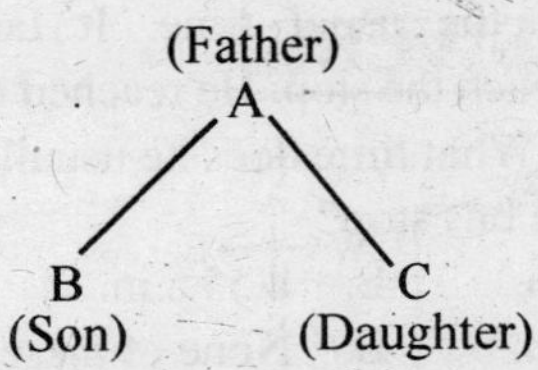

'C' is not the son of 'A', but 'A' is the father of 'C'. So, 'C' is the daughter of 'A'.

2.

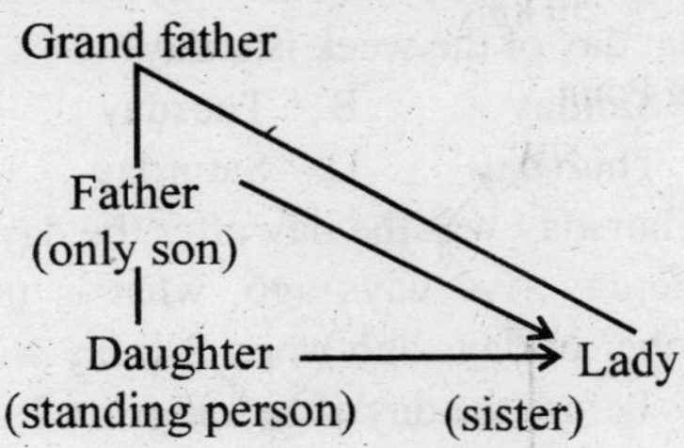

Lady's grandfather's son is lady's father and father's daughter will only be lady's sister.

4.

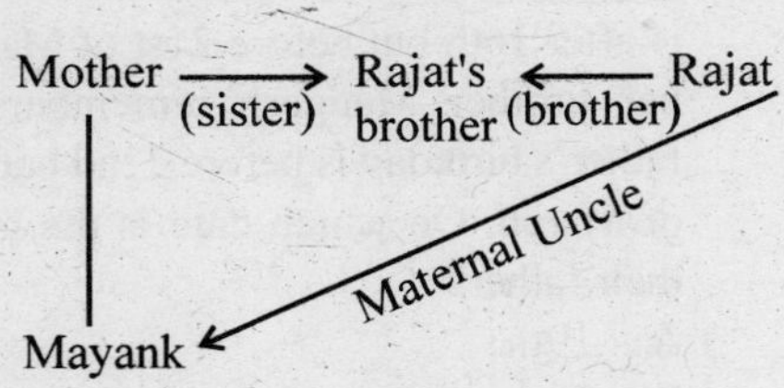

Mayank's mother is the sister of Rajat's brother. So Rajat is also the brother of Mayank's mother. Relation of the brother with his sister's child is maternal. So Rajat is Mayank's maternal uncle.

CALENDAR, CLOCK, TIME, DISTANCE

1. If the day before yesterday was Thursday, when will Sunday be?
   A. Tomorrow B. Day after tomorrow
   C. Today D. Two days after today
2. There are twenty people working in an office. The first group of five works between 8:00 A.M. and 2:00 PM. The second group of ten works between 10:00 AM to 4:00 PM. And the third group of five works between 12 noon to 6:00 PM. There are three computers in the office which all the employees frequently use. During which of the following hours the computers are likely to be used most?
   A. 1:00 PM - 3:00 PM
   B. 12 noon - 2:00 PM
   C. 2:00 PM - 4:00 PM
   D. 10:00 AM - 12 noon
3. If the seventh day of a month is three (3) days earlier than Friday, what day will it be on the nineteenth day of the month?
   A. Sunday B. Monday
   C. Wednesday D. Friday
4. Radha remembers that her father's birthday is after 16th but before 21st of March, while her brother Mangesh remembers that his father's birthday is before 22nd but after 19th of March. On which date is the birthday of their father?
   A. 19th
   B. 20th
   C. 21st
   D. Cannot be determined
5. A man is three (3) years older than his wife and four (4) times as old as his son. If the son attains an age of fifteen (15) years after three (3) years, what is the present age of the mother?
   A. 60 years B. 51 years
   C. 48 years D. 45 years
6. A clock is so placed that at 12 noon its minute hand points towards north-east. In which direction does its hour hand point at 1.30 P.M.?
   A. East B. West
   C. North D. South
7. If in the above question clock is turned through an angle of 135° in an anticlockwise direction, in which direction will its minute hand point at 8.45 P.M.?
   A. East B. West
   C. North D. South
8. A couple married in 1980 had two children, one in 1982 and the other in 1984. Their combined ages will equal the years of the marriage in?
   A. 1986 B. 1985
   C. 1987 D. 1988
9. Manoj left home for the bus stop 15 minutes earlier than the usual time. It takes 10 minutes to reach the stop. He reached the stop at 8.40 a.m. What time does he usually leave home for the bus stop?
   A. 8.30 a.m. B. 8.55 a.m.
   C. 8.45 p.m. D. None of these
10. Mamuni went to the movies nine days ago. She goes to the movies only on Thursday. What day of the week is today?
    A. Sunday B. Tuesday
    C. Thursday D. Saturday
11. If Thursday was the day after the day before yesterday five days ago, what is the least number of days ago when Sunday was three days before the day after tomorrow?
    A. Two days ago
    B. Three days ago

C. Four days ago
D. Five days ago

12. 1.12.91 is the first Sunday. Which is the fourth Tuesday of December 91?
A. 31.12.91 B. 24.12.91
C. 17.12.91 D. 26.12.91

13. If the third day of a month is Monday, which of the following will be the fifth day from 21st of that month?
A. Tuesday B. Monday
C. Wednesday D. Thursday

14. Keshav runs a factory in three shifts of eight hours each with 210 employees. In each shift minimum of 80 employees are required to run the factory effectively. No employee can be allowed to work for more than 16 hours a day. At least how many employees will be required to work for 16 hours every day?
A. 30
B. 60
C. Data inadequate
D. None of these

15. If 15 horses eat 15 bags of gram in 15 days, in how many days will one horse eat one bag of grain?
A. 15 days B. 1/15 days
C. 1 day D. 30 days

16. A century leap year is divisible by :
A. 4 B. 16
C. 40 D. 400

17. If the fifth day of a month is Friday, which of the following will be the Seventh day from 10th of that month?
A. Tuesday B. Monday
C. Wednesday D. Thursday

18. Day after tomorrow is my birthday. On the same day next week falls 'Holi'. Today is Monday. What will be the day after 'Holi'?
A. Wednesday B. Thursday
C. Friday D. Saturday

19. A clock shows the time as 3 : 30 p.m. If the minute hand gains 2 minutes every hour, how many minutes will the clock gain by 4 a.m.?
A. 23 Minutes B. 24 Minutes
C. 25 Minutes D. 26 Minutes

20. Two brothers were expected to return home on the same day. Rajat returned 3 days earlier but Rohit returned 4 days later. If Rajat returned on Thursday, what was the expected day when both the brothers were to return home and when did Rohit Return?
A. Wednesday, Sunday
B. Thursday, Monday
C. Sunday, Thursday
D. Monday, Friday

ANSWERS

1	2	3	4	5	6	7	8	9	10
A	B	A	B	A	A	D	A	D	D
11	**12**	**13**	**14**	**15**	**16**	**17**	**18**	**19**	**20**
A	B	C	D	A	D	C	B	C	C

SOME SELECTED EXPLANATORY ANSWERS

1. Thursday —Day-before-yesterday
Friday —Yesterday
Saturday —Today
Sunday — Tomorrow

2. 1. 5 people work between 8 a.m. to 2 p.m.
2. 10 people work between 10 a.m. to 4 p.m.
3. 5 people work between 12 noon to 6 p.m.

So, computers are used most between 12 noon to 2 p.m.

3. 7th day is 3 days earlier than Friday so, 10th day is Friday, so also is 17th.

∴ 19th day will be 2nd day ahead of Friday, *i.e.,* Sunday.

4. Father's birthday

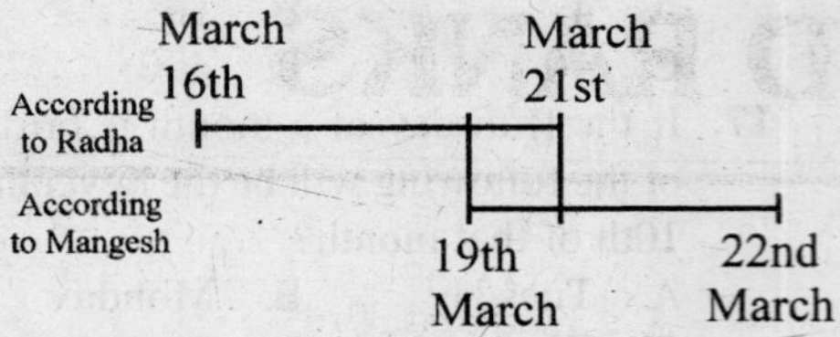

∴ Their father's birthday is on 20th March.

5. Present age of son is 15 – 3 = 12 years. Age of the man is 4 times the age of son, *i.e.*,
12 × 4 = 48 years
Man is 3 years elder to his wife/son's mother.
So Age of the mother is 48 – 3 = 45 years

6.

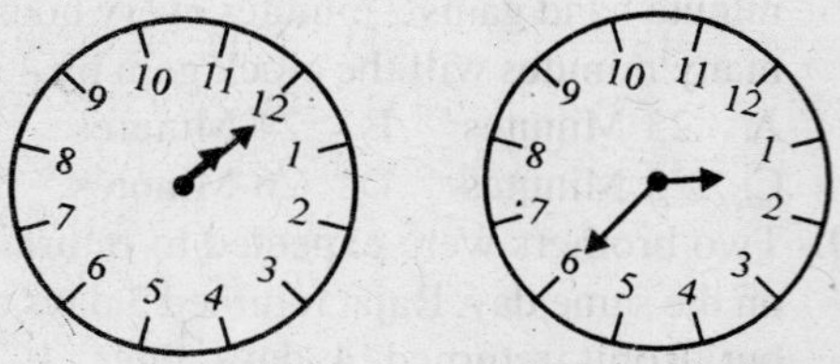

At 12 noon

At 1.30 p.m. the hour hand will point towards East.

7.

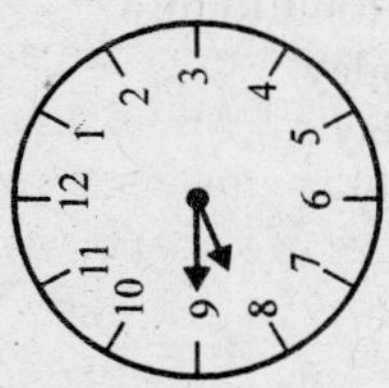

After rotating the clock in earlier question, its minute hand will point towards South at 8:45 p.m.

8. 1982 — 2 years later — 1st child
1984 — 4 years later — 2nd child
Total age of children — 2 years.
1985 — 5 years later — Total age of children: 4 years.
1986 — 6 years later — Total age of children : 6 years.

9. Manoj reached the bus stop at 8.40 a.m. He left his home at 8:40 – 10 minutes = 8:30 a.m. He left 15 minutes earlier than usual, so his actual time of leaving home is 8:30 am + 15 minutes = 8:45 a.m.

10. Mamuni goes to the movies on Thursday, so nine days ago was Thursday.
∴ Two days ago was also Thursday. So, today is Saturday.

11. Day after the day-before-yesterday five days ago is the 6th day which is Thursday. And so, the 3rd day will be Sunday. Three days before the day-after-tomorrow is Yesterday which is the 1st day of the five days. So, two days ago was Sunday.

12. First Sunday is on 1st December
First Tuesday is on 3rd December
3 weeks later, Fourth Tuesday will be on 3 + (7 × 3) = 24th December.

13. 3rd day of the month is Monday
5th day from 21st is 26th
26 – 3 = 23 days
23 days later, 23/7 leaves 2 days.
So, two days ahead of Monday will be Wednesday.

14. 80 employees are required for double shift.

15. 15 horses eat 15 bags of grain in 15 days
15 horses eat 1 bag of grain in 1 day
1 horse eats 1 bag of grain in 15 days

16. A leap year is divisible by 4 and a century leap year is divisible by 400.

17. Seventh day from 10th is 17th.
5th day is Friday. Next Friday is on 12th, 17 – 12 = 5, 5 days ahead of Friday will be Wednesday. So, 17th is Wednesday.

18. Today is Monday
Day-after-tomorrow is Wednesday
Next week 'Holi' is also on Wednesday
So, Day after Holi is Thursday.

19. Hours between 3:30 p.m. and 4 a.m. are — 12½ hours. Number of minutes gained will be 12½ × 2 = 25 minutes.

20. Rajat returned on Thursday. 3 days later was the day of expected return, *i.e.*, Sunday. Rohit returned 4 days after Sunday, *i.e.*, Thursday.

ROWS AND RANKS

1. In a row of trees, one tree is fifth from either end of the row. How many trees are in the row?
   A. 11 B. 8
   C. 10 D. 9
2. Jaya ranks 5th in a class of 53. What is her rank from the bottom in the class?
   A. 49th B. 48th
   C. 47th D. 50th
3. Mohan ranks twenty-first in a class of sixty-five students. What will be his (Mohan's) rank if the lowest candidate is assigned rank 1?
   A. 44th B. 45th
   C. 46th D. Data inadequate
4. If Rahul finds that he is 12th from the right in a line of boys and 4th from the left, how many boys should be added to the line such that there are 28 boys in the line?
   A. 12 B. 14
   C. 20 D. 13
5. In a row of boys, Rajan is tenth from the right and Suraj is tenth from the left. When Rajan and Suraj interchange their positions, Suraj will be twenty-seventh from the left. Which of the following will be Rajan's position from the right?
   A. Tenth
   B. Twenty-sixth
   C. Twenty-ninth
   D. None of these
6. Mahesh and Suresh are ranked 11th and 12th respectively from the top in a class of 41 students. What will be their respective ranks from the bottom?
   A. 32nd and 33rd
   B. 29th and 30th
   C. 30th and 31st
   D. 31st and 30th
7. Uma ranked 8th from the top and 37th from bottom in a class. How many students are there in the class?
   A. 47 B. 46
   C. 45 D. None of these
8. In a queue, Sadiq is 14th from the front and Joseph is 17th from the end, while Jane is in between Sadiq and Joseph. If Sadiq be ahead of Joseph and there be 48 persons in the queue, how many persons are there between Sadiq and Jane?
   A. 5 B. 6
   C. 7 D. 8
9. Rohan ranked eleventh from the top and twenty-seventh from the bottom among the students who passed the annual examination in a class. If the number of students who failed in the examination was 12, how many students appeared for the examination?
   A. 48
   B. 49
   C. 50
   D. Cannot be determined
10. Some boys are sitting in a row. P is sitting fourteenth from the left and Q is seventh from the right. If there are four boys between P and Q, how many boys are there in the row?
    A. 19 B. 21
    C. 25 D. 23

ANSWERS

1	2	3	4	5	6	7	8	9	10
D	A	B	D	D	D	D	C	B	C

SOME SELECTED EXPLANATORY ANSWERS

1. 

Total number of trees in the row are :
(5 + 5) – 1 = 9

2. 

Jaya's rank from the bottom is :
(53 – 5) + 1 = 49th.

3. 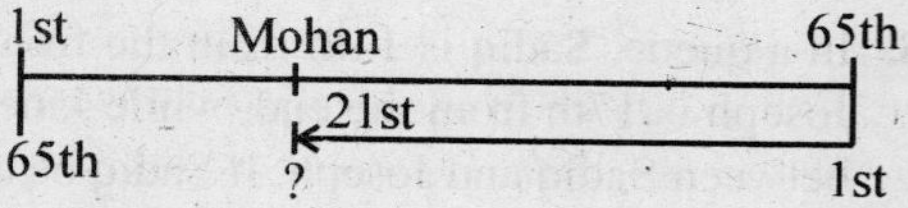

Note : Mohan's rank from the last or the question asked means the same.

Mohan's rank is (65 – 21) + 1 = 45th

4. 

The number of boys in the line are :
(4 + 12) – 1 = 15
To make a line of 28 boys, (28 – 15) *i.e.* 13 more boys are needed.

5. 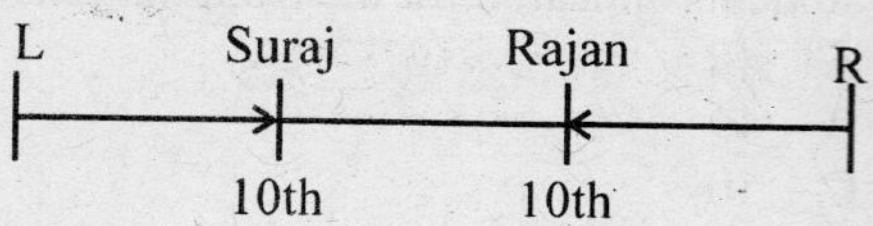

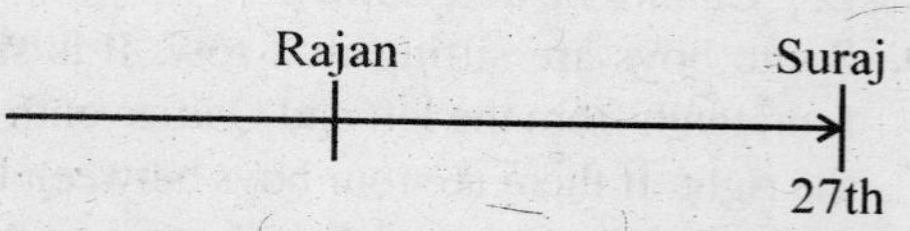

As the position of boys is equal from both ends, Rajan will also be 27th from the right after changing positions.

6. 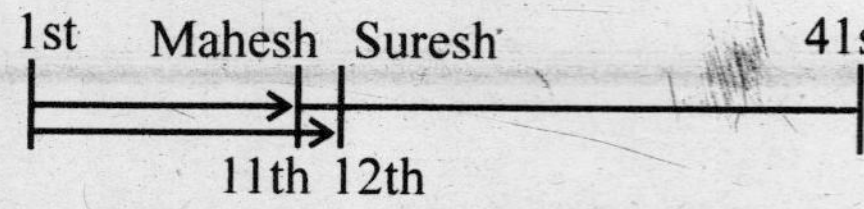

Mahesh's position from bottom is :
(41 – 11) + 1 = 31st
Suresh's position from bottom is :
(41 – 12) + 1 = 30th

7. 

Total number of students in the class are :
(8 + 37) – 1 = 44

8. 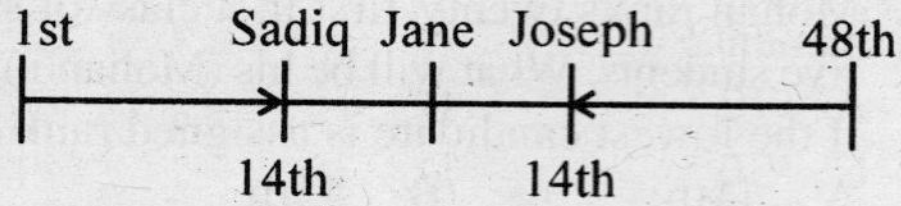

Sadiq's position from last is :
(48 – 14) + 1 = 35th
Number of persons between Sadiq and Joseph are (35 – 17) – 1 = 17
Jane is in-between Sadiq and Joseph *i.e.*, she's at 9th position from both the boys.
∴ there are 8 persons between Sadiq and Jane.
Note : (8 + 8) – 1 = 17

9. 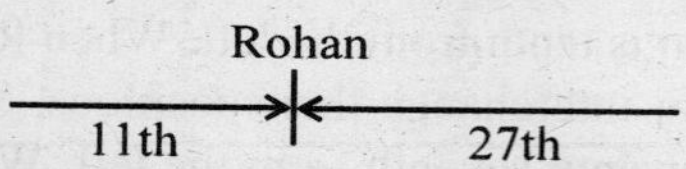

Number of students who passed the examination (11 + 27) – 1 = 37
Those who failed = 12
Total number of students who appeared in the examination = 37 + 12 = 49.

10. 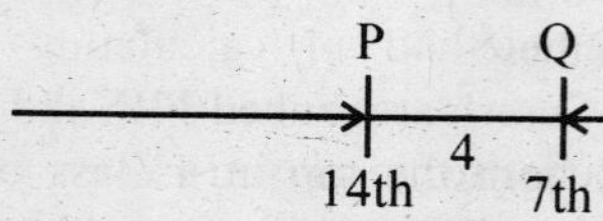

The number of boys in the row are :
(14 + 4 + 7) = 25

NUMBER PROBLEMS

1. How many 6's are there in the following series of numbers which are preceded by 7 but not immediately followed by 9?
6 7 9 5 6 9 7 6 8 7 6 7 8 6 9 4 6 7 7 6 9 5 7 6 3
A. One B. Two
C. Three D. Four

2. In a chess tournament each of six players will play every other player exactly once. How many matches will be played during the tournament?
A. 12 B. 15
C. 30 D. 36

3. How many 4's are there in the following series which are preceded by 7, but are not preceded by 8?
3 4 5 7 4 3 7 4 8 5 4 3 7 4 9 8 4 7 2 7 4 1 3 6
A. 1 B. 2
C. 3 D. 4

4. How many even numbers are there in the following series of numbers, each of which is immediately preceded by an odd number, but not immediately followed by an even number?
5 3 4 8 9 7 1 6 5 3 2 9 8 4 3 5
A. Nil B. 1
C. 2 D. 3

5. If all the numbers from 1 to 51 which are exactly divisible by 3 are arranged in descending order, which of the following numbers will come at the seventh and tenth places from the top?
A. 33 & 27 B. 33 & 21
C. 21 & 30 D. 33 & 24

ANSWERS

1	2	3	4	5
C	B	D	C	D

SOME SELECTED EXPLANATORY ANSWERS

1. 6 7 9 5 6 9 $\underset{1}{\underline{7 6 8}}$ $\underset{2}{\underline{7 6 7}}$ 8 6 9 4 6 7 7 6 9 5 $\underset{3}{\underline{7 6 3}}$

2. When all the players have to play with each other then the method of calculating the number of matches to be played is $\frac{n(n-1)}{2}$ where '*n*' is the number of players playing the match. So, the number of matches played will be :
$(6 \times 5) \div 2 = 30 \div 2 = 15$

3. 3 4 5 $\underset{1}{\underline{7 4}}$ 3 $\underset{2}{\underline{7 4}}$ 8 5 4 3 $\underset{3}{\underline{7 4}}$ 9 8 4 7 2 $\underset{4}{\underline{7 4}}$ 1 3 6

4. 5 3 4 8 9 7 $\underset{1}{\underline{1 6 5}}$ $\underset{2}{\underline{3 2 9}}$ 8 4 3 5

5. The numbers divisible by 3 in descending order are :
51, 48, 45, 42, 39, 36, 33, $\underset{7th}{\underline{30}}$, 27, $\underset{10th}{\underline{24}}$, 21, 18, 15, 12, 9, 6, 3.

SYMBOL SUBSTITUTION

1. If "+" means "–"; "–" means "×"; "×" means "÷" and "÷" means "+", then

$15 \times 5 \div 10 + 5 - 3 = ?$

A. 9.5 B. 0
C. – 2 D. 24

2. If "+" means "–"; "–" means "×"; "×" means "÷" and "÷" means "+", then

$15 \times 3 \div 15 + 5 - 2 = ?$

A. 0 B. 10
C. 20 D. 6

3. If "+" means "÷"; "×" means "–"; "÷" means "+" and "–" means "×", then

$16 \div 8 \times 6 - 2 + 12 = ?$

A. 22 B. 24
C. 23 D. 20

4. If "+" means "×"; "–" means "÷"; "÷" means "+" and "×" means "–", then what will be the value of $20 \div 40 - 4 \times 5 + 6 = ?$

A. 60 B. 1.67
C. 150 D. 0

5. If "+" means "×"; "–" means "÷"; "×" means "–" and "÷" means "+", then

$5 + 8 - 4 \times 2 \div 9 = ?$

A. 15 B. 13
C. 17 D. 11

ANSWERS

1	2	3	4	5
C	B	C	D	C

SOME SELECTED EXPLANATORY ANSWERS

1. $15 \div 5 + 10 - 5 \times 3$

$3 + 10 - 15 = -2$

2. $15 \div 3 + 15 - 5 \times 2$

$5 + 15 - 10 = 10$

3. $16 + 8 - 6 \times 2 \div 12$

$16 + 8 - 1 = 23$

4. $20 + 40 \div 4 - 5 \times 6$

$20 + 10 - 30 = 0$

5. $5 \times 8 \div 4 - 2 + 9$

$10 - 2 + 9 = 17$

MISSING NUMBERS

Directions : *In each question given below which one number can be placed at the sign of interrogation?*

1.

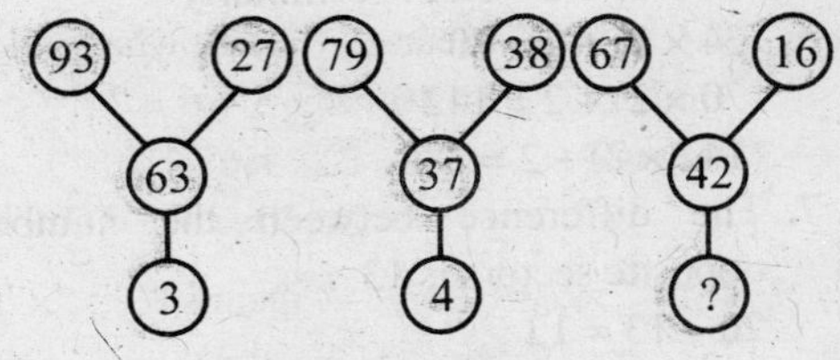

A. 5 B. 6
C. 8 D. 9

2.

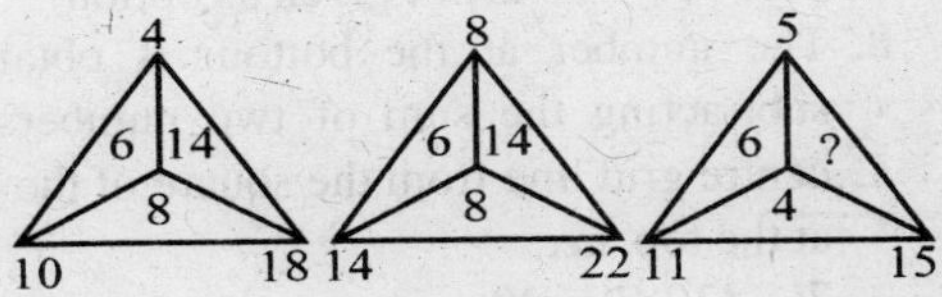

A. 8 B. 14
C. 10 D. 6

3.

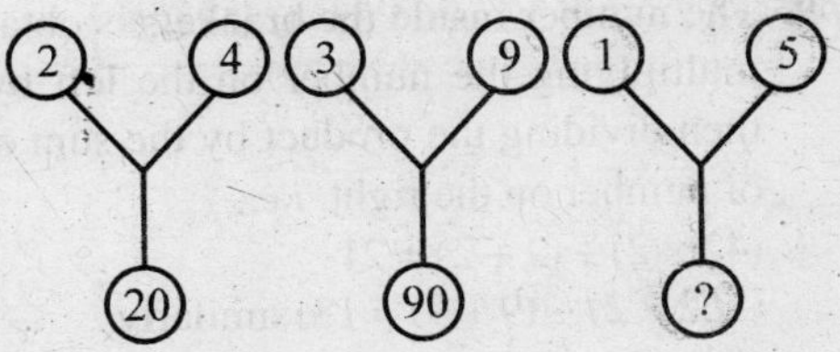

A. 20 B. 25
C. 26 D. 75

4.

27	22	50
13	12	26
9	2	?

A. 12 B. 39
C. 18 D. 24

5.

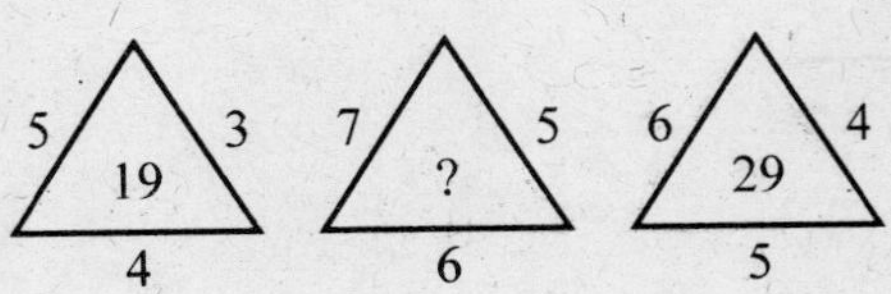

A. 25 B. 47
C. 37 D. 41

6.

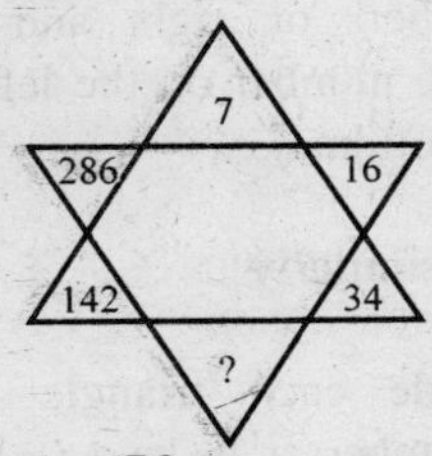

A. 70 B. 68
C. 56 D. 92

7.

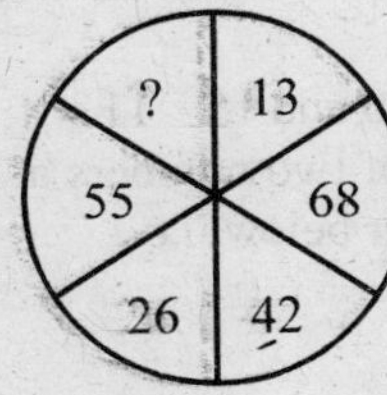

A. 41 B. 37
C. 29 D. 25

8.

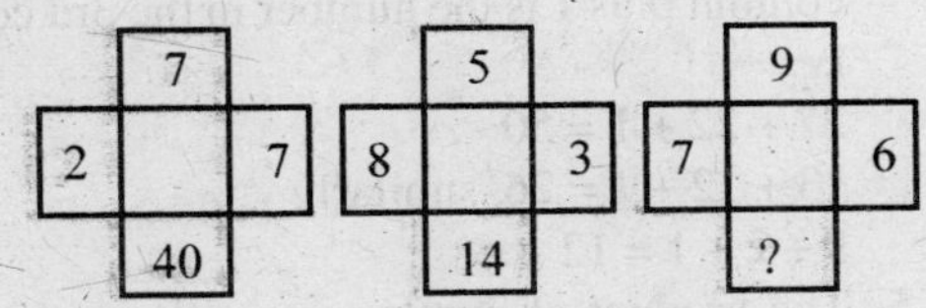

A. 72 B. 68
C. 82 D. 96

9.

42	(21)	22
78	(?)	84
162	(18)	99

A. 12 B. 13
C. 60 D. 72

10.

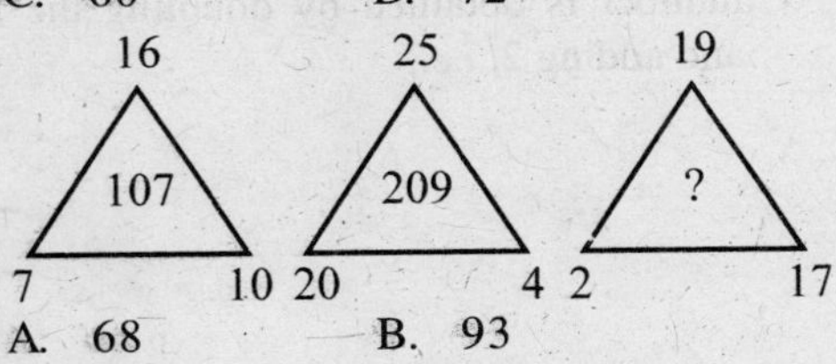

A. 68 B. 93
C. 175 D. 217

ANSWERS

1	2	3	4	5	6	7	8	9	10
D	C	C	A	D	A	C	B	B	A

SOME SELECTED EXPLANATORY ANSWERS

1. The sum of numbers on right and centre subtracted from the number on the left gives the number at the bottom, *i.e.*,
$93 - (27 + 63) = 3$
$79 - (38 + 37) = 4$, similarly
$67 - (16 + 42) = 9$

2. The number inside each triangle is the difference of the numbers at its base *i.e.*
$10 - 4 = 6$, $18 - 4 = 14$ and $18 - 10 = 8$
$14 - 8 = 6$, $22 - 8 = 14$ and $22 - 14 = 8$, similarly
$11 - 5 = 6$, $15 - 5 = 10$ and $15 - 11 = 4$.

3. The sum of squares of two numbers at the top gives the third number below, *i.e.*,
$2^2 + 4^2 = 20$
$3^2 + 9^2 = 90$, similarly
$1^2 + 5^2 = 26$

4. The sum of numbers in 1st and 2nd column plus 1 is the number in the 3rd column, *i.e.*,
$27 + 22 + 1 = 50$
$13 + 12 + 1 = 26$, similarly
$9 + 2 + 1 = 12$

5. The product of numbers on either side of the triangle plus the number at the base is the number inside the triangle, *i.e.*,
$(5 \times 3) + 4 = 19$
$(6 \times 4) + 5 = 29$, similarly
$(7 \times 5) + 6 = 41$

6. Clockwise starting from number 7, the next number is obtained by doubling the number and adding 2, *i.e.*,
$(7 \times 2) + 2 = 16$
$(16 \times 2) + 2 = 34 \ldots$, similarly
$(34 \times 2) + 2 = 70$
$(70 \times 2) + 2 = 142$
$(142 \times 2) + 2 = 286$

7. The difference between the numbers in opposite sectors is 13, *i.e.*,
$26 - 13 = 13$
$68 - 55 = 13$, similarly
The missing number is $42 - 13 = 29$
($42 + 13 = 55$ is not given as option)

8. The number at the bottom is obtained by subtracting the sum of two numbers in the centre grid line from the square of the number at the top, *i.e.*,
$7^2 - (2 + 7) = 40$
$5^2 - (8 + 3) = 14$, similarly
$9^2 - (7 + 6) = 68$

9. The number inside the brackets is obtained by multiplying the number on the left by 2 and then dividing the product by the sum of digits of number on the right, *i.e.*,
$(42 \times 2) \div (2 + 2) = 21$
$(162 \times 2) \div (9 + 9) = 18$, similarly
$(78 \times 2) \div (8 + 4) = 13$

10. Subtracting the sum of squares of two numbers at the base from the square of number at the apex gives the number inside the triangle, *i.e.*,
$16^2 - (7^2 + 10^2) = 107$
$25^2 - (20^2 + 4^2) = 209$, similarly
$19^2 - (2^2 + 17^2) = 68$

ALPHABET PROBLEMS

Directions : *The following questions are based on alphabet series in natural or reverse order and the combinations that can be made by changing the position of alphabet in given words.*

1. Which alphabet comes immediately before the sixth alphabet from the left extreme in alphabetical series?

A. U B. E
C. F D. V

2. Which letter is midway between G and S?

A. L B. N
C. M D. No letter

3. Which letter should be ninth letter to the left of ninth letter from the right if the first half of the alphabet is reversed?

A. I B. D
C. F D. E

4. If the alphabet is in reverse order, which letter will be eighth letter to the left of the seventh letter counting from the right end?

A. O B. P
C. N D. Q

5. What will be the fifth letter to the right of the thirteenth letter from the right?

A. R B. S
C. I D. O

ANSWERS

1	2	3	4	5
B	C	D	A	B

SOME SELECTED EXPLANATORY ANSWERS

1.

Sixth letter from left is 'F' and letter immediately before 'F' is 'E'.

2.
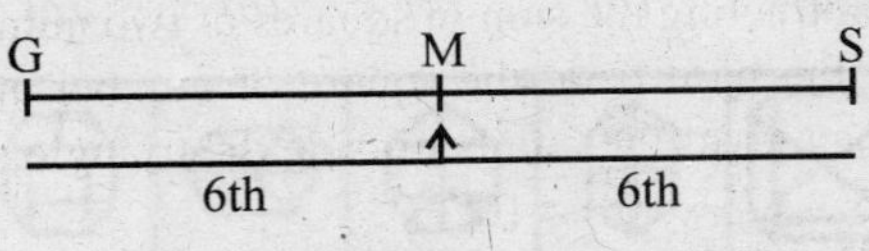

'M' is midway between G and S.

3. MLKJIHGFEDCBANOPQRSTUVWXYZ
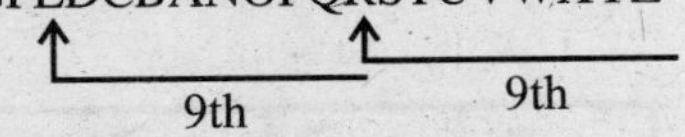

4. ZYXWVUTSRQPONMLKJIHGFEDCBA
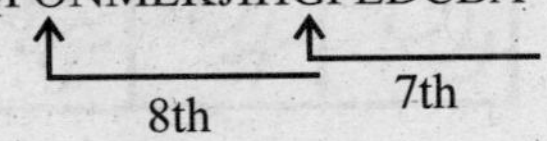

5.
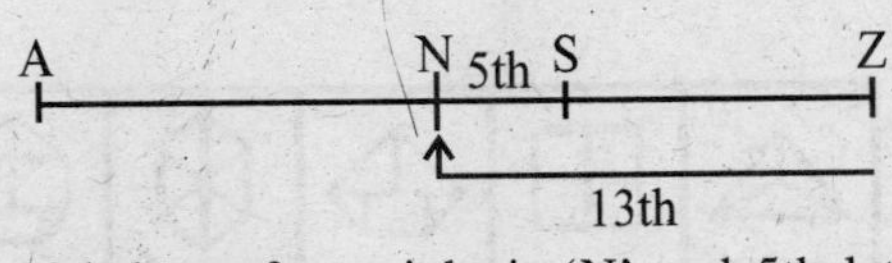

13th letter from right is 'N' and 5th letter to the right of 'N' is 'S'.

NON-VERBAL SERIES

Directions (Q. 1–10) : *In each of the following questions which one of the five answer figures given below should come after the problem figures if the sequence are continued?*

Problem Figures | **Answer Figures**

1. 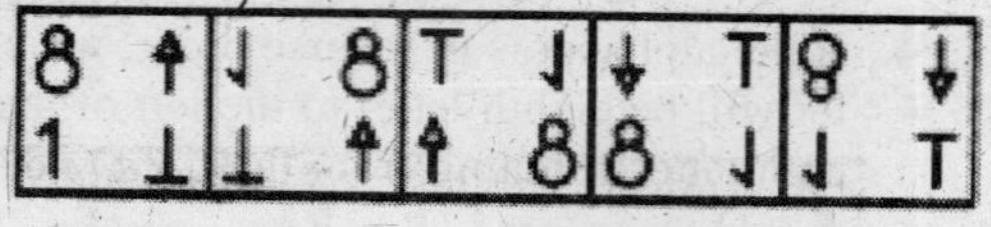 

(a) (b) (c) (d) (e)

2. 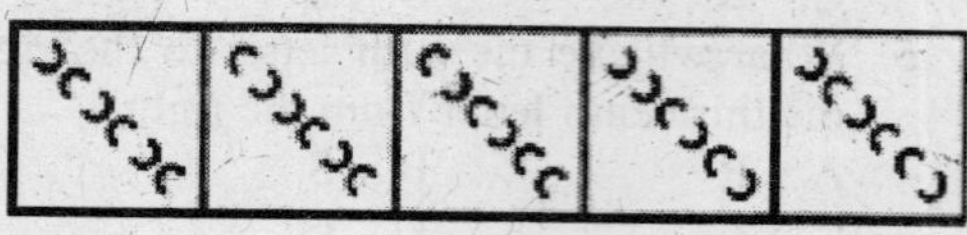 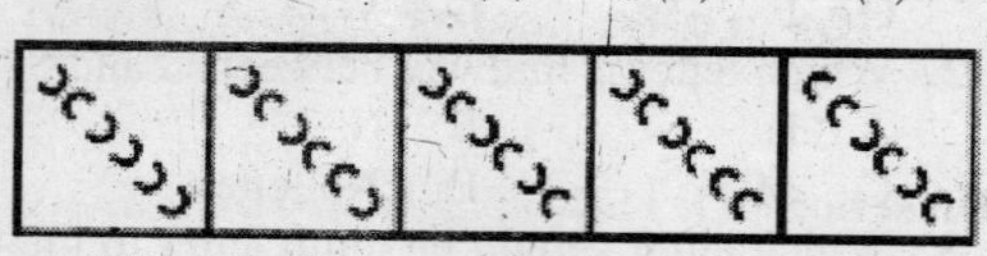

(a) (b) (c) (d) (e)

3.  

(a) (b) (c) (d) (e)

4.  

(a) (b) (c) (d) (e)

5.  

(a) (b) (c) (d) (e)

6.  

(a) (b) (c) (d) (e)

7.  

(a) (b) (c) (d) (e)

Problem Figures **Answer Figures**

8. 

(a) (b) (c) (d) (e)

9. 

(a) (b) (c) (d) (e)

10. 

(a) (b) (c) (d) (e)

Directions (Q. 11-20) : *In each of these questions, a series begins with an unmarked figure on the extreme left in the row of figures. One and only one of the five lettered figures in the series does not fit into the series. The two unmarked figures, one on the extreme left and the other on the extreme right fit into the series. Take as many aspects into account as possible of the figures in the series and find out the one and only of the five marked figures which does not fit into the series. The letter of that figure is the answer.*

11. 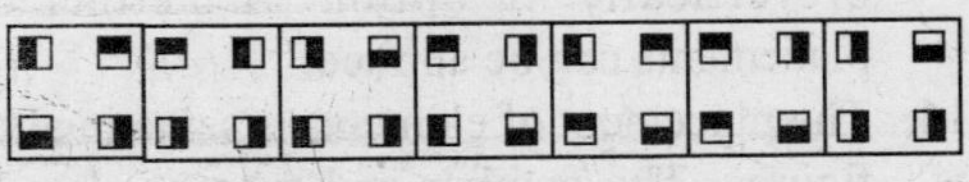

(a) (b) (c) (d) (e)

12. 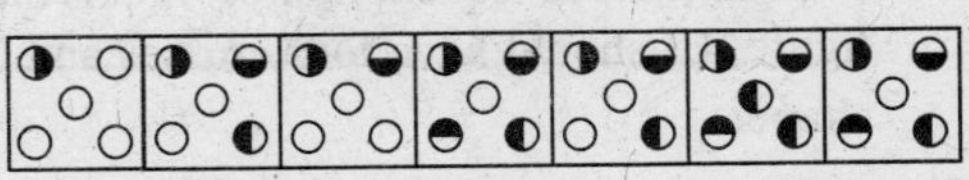

(a) (b) (c) (d) (e)

13. 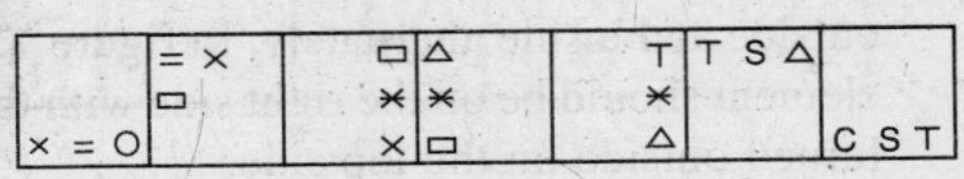

(a) (b) (c) (d) (e)

14. 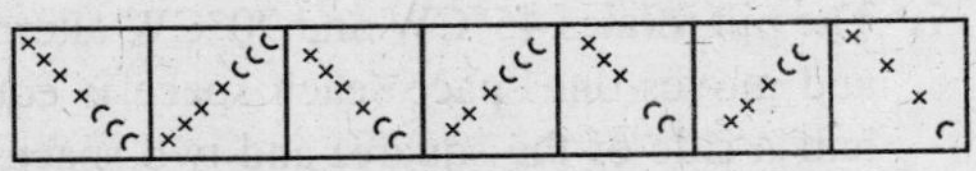

(a) (b) (c) (d) (e)

15. 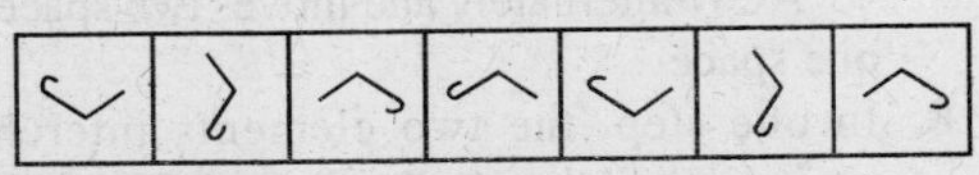

(a) (b) (c) (d) (e)

16. 

(a) (b) (c) (d) (e)

ANSWERS

1	2	3	4	5	6	7	8	9	10
D	C	D	A	C	E	C	E	C	B
11	**12**	**13**	**14**	**15**	**16**				
A	E	A	C	C	E				

SOME SELECTED EXPLANATORY ANSWERS

1. In each step, all the elements move to the adjacent corner (of the square boundary) in a CW direction and the element that reaches the upper-left corner gets vertically inverted.
2. We can label the arcs as shown . The arcs get inverted in the sequence (1 & 2), (3, 4 & 5), (6 & 1), (2, 3 & 4), (5 & 6), ...
3. All the elements move half-a-side of the square boundary in ACW direction in each step. Also, first, third and fifth elements are replaced by new elements in one step and second, fourth and sixth elements are replaced by new elements in the next step. The two steps are repeated alternately.
4. In each step, the dot moves one space CW and the arrow moves two spaces CW.
5. One arc and four arcs get inverted alternately.
6. The number of parts increases by one along with the number of sides in the figure.
7. The pin rotates 45°CW and 90°CW alternately and moves one space (each space is equal to half-a-side of the square) and two spaces CW alternately. The arrow rotates 90°ACW and 45°ACW alternately and moves two spaces and one space.
8. In one step, the two elements interchange positions and the smaller element gets enlarged while the larger element gets reduced in size. In the next step, the smaller element is replaced by a new small element and the larger element is replaced by a new large element.
9. In each step, the elements move in the order .
10. The upper-left element gets laterally inverted in first, third, fifth. .... steps; the upper-right element gets rotated through 180° is first, fourth, seventh,.... steps; the lower-left element gets laterally inverted in second, fourth, sixth, ... steps; the lower-right element gets rotated through 180° in third, sixth,... steps and the pin at the middle-right position gets laterally inverted in every second step.
11. The shade in the top left square is moved one step clockwise till figure B and then reversed, the process is repeated. The shade in the top right square is moved one step anticlockwise till figure D and then reversed. The shade in the bottom left square is moved one step clockwise in alternate figures and the shade in bottom right square is moved one step clockwise after two figures. In figure 'A' the rule is isolated by the shade in the bottom left square.
12. In alternate figures a new circle is shaded clockwise. The pattern of the shade is also moved clockwise. In figure 'E' right half of the circle in the centre should have been shaded.
13. The three elements are placed either horizontally or vertically. In option 'A' neither of the placements can be applied.
14. The placement of elements is same in alternate figures. The number and type of elements is same in two subsequent figures. In this manner, figure 'C' should have four crosses and two C shapes.
15. *(c)*: The element is moved one step anticlockwise and the arc at one end is turned outside and inside alternately. In figure 'C' the element should be on the right side with the arc turned outside on the top side.
16. The left most element, line segment with the dot is moved one step towards right till figure C where it reaches the extreme right position. This process is repeated from figure D where the element on the extreme left, line segment with a circle, is moved. In figure 'E' the placement of the elements does not follow the rule of the series.

KNOWLEDGE OF COMPUTER

A Brief History of Computers

INTRODUCTION OF COMPUTER

Computer is the most amazing machine man has ever created. Today computers are used in almost all walks of life: bank, hospitals, schools, publishing, manufacturing, entertainment, shops, libraries, factories, games, elections, security services etc. A computer is basically a programmable computing machine. In this chapter we will discuss the various parts of the computer which make the fast and better computation. We will provide a better solution to the problems related to the organization of computer.

GENERATIONS OF COMPUTERS

The first Generation: Vacuum Tubes

ENIAC

The ENIAC (Electronic Numerical Integrator And Computer), designed by and constructed under the supervision of John Mauchly and John Presper Eckert at the University of Pennsylvania, was the world's first general-purpose electronic digital computer. The project was a response to U.S. wartime needs. Mauchly, a professor of electrical engineering at the University of Pennsylvania and Eckert, one of his graduate students, proposed to build a general-purpose computer using vacuum tubes. In 1943, this proposal was accepted by the Army, and work began on the ENIAC. The resulting machine was enormous, weighing 30 tons, occupying 15,000 square feet of floor space, and containing more than 18,000 vacuum tubes. When operating, it consumed 140 kilowatts of power. It was also substantially faster than any electronic-mechanical computer, being capable of 5000 additions per second.

The ENIAC was decimal rather than a binary machine. That is, numbers were represented in decimal form and arithmetic was performed in the decimal system. Its memory consisted of 20 "accumulators", each capable of holding a 10-digit decimal number. Each digit was represented by a ring of 10 vacuum tubes. At any time, only one vacuum tube was in the ON state, representing one of the 10 digits. The major drawback of the ENIAC was that it had to be programmed manually by setting switches and plugging and unplugging cables.

The ENIAC was completed in 1946, too late to be used in the war effort. Instead, its first task was to perform a series of complex calculations that were used to help determine the feasibility of the H-bomb. The ENIAC continued to be used until 1955.

The Von Neumann Machine

The programming process could be facilitated if the program could be represented in a form suitable for storing in memory alongside the data. Then, a computer could get its instructions by reading them from memory, and a program could be set of altered by setting the values of a portion of memory.

This idea, known as the Stored-program concept, is usually attributed to the ENIAC designers, most notably the mathematician John Von Neumann, who was a consultant on the ENIAC project. The idea was also developed at about the same time by Turing. The first publication of the idea was in a 1945 proposal by Von Neumann for a new computer, the EDVAC (Electronic Discrete Variable Computer).

In 1946, von Neumann and his colleagues began the design of a new stored-program computer, referred to as the IAS computer, at the Princeton

Institute for Advanced Studies. The IAS computer, although not completed until 1952, is the prototype of all subsequent general-purpose computers. Figure below shows the general structure of the IAS computer. It consists of:

- A main memory, which stores both data and instructions.
- An arithmetic-logical unit (ALU) capable of operating on binary data.
- A control unit, which interprets the instructions in memory and causes them to be executed.
- Input and output (I/O) equipment operated by the control unit.

Commercial Computers

The 1950's saw the birth of the computer industry with two companies, Sperry and IBM, dominating the marketplace.

In 1947, Eckert and Mauchly formed the Eckert-Mauchly Computer Corporation to manufacture computers commercially. Their first successful machine was the UNIVAC I (Universal Automatic Computer), which was commissioned by the Bureau of the Census for the 1950 calculations. The Eckert-Mauchly Computer Corporation became part of the UNIVAC division of Sperry-Rand Corporation, which went on to build a series of successor machines.

The UNIVAC II, which had greater memory capacity and higher performance than the UNIVAC I, was delivered in the late 1950's and illustrates several trends that have remained characteristic of the computer industry. First, advances in technology allow companies to continue to build larger, more powerful computers. Second, each company tries to make its new machines upward compatible with the older machines. This means that the programs written for the older machines can be executed on the new machine. This strategy is adopted in the hopes of retaining the customer base; that is, when a customer decides to buy a newer machine, he is likely to get it from the same company to avoid losing the investment in programs.

The UNIVAC division also began development of the 1100 series of computers, which was to be its bread and butter. This series illustrates a distinction that existed at one time. The first model, the UNIVAC 1103, and its successors for many years were primarily intended for scientific applications, involving long and complex calculations. Other companies concentrated on business applications, which involved processing large amounts of text data. This split has largely disappeared but it was evident for a number of years.

IBM, which was then the major manufacturer of punched-card processing equipment, delivered its first electronic stored-program computer, the 701, in 1953. The 701 was intended primarily for scientific applications. In 1955, IBM introduced the companion 702 product, which had a number of hardware features that suited it to business applications. These were the first of a long series of 700/7000 computers that established IBM as the overwhelmingly dominant computer manufacturer.

The Second Generation: Transistors

The first major change in the electronic computer came with the replacement of the vacuum tube by the transistor. The transistor is smaller, cheaper, and dissipates less heal than a vacuum tube but can be used in the same way as a vacuum tube to construct computers. Unlike the vacuum tube, which requires wires, metal plates, a glass capsule, and a vacuum, the transistor is a solid-state device, made from silicon. The transistor was invented at Bell Labs in 1947 and by the 1950's had launched an electronic revolution. It was not until the late 1950s, however, that fully transistorized computers were commercially available. IBM again was not the first company to deliver the new technology. NCR and more successfully RCA were the front-runners with some small transistor machines. IBM followed shortly with the 7000 series.

The use of the transistor defines the second generation of computers. It has become widely accepted to classify computers into generations based on the fundamental hardware technology employed. Each new generation is characterized by greater processing performance, larger memory capacity, and smaller size than the previous one.

The Third Generation: Integrated Circuits

A single, self-contained transistor is called a discrete component. Throughout the 1950s and early 1960s, electronic equipment was composed largely of discrete components—transistors, resistors, capacitors, and so on. Discrete components were manufactured separately, packaged in their own containers, and soldered or wired together onto circuit boards, which were then installed in computers, oscilloscopes, and other electronic equipment. Whenever an electronic device called for a transistor, a little tube of metal containing a pinhead-sized piece of silicon had to be soldered to a circuit board. The entire manufacturing process, from transistor to circuit board, was expensive and cumbersome.

These facts of life were beginning to create problems in the computer industry. Early second-generation computers contained about 10,000 transistors. This figure grew to the hundreds of thousands, making the manufacture of newer, more powerful machines increasingly difficult. In 1958 came the achievement that revolutionized electronics and started the era of microelectronics: the invention of the integrated circuit. It is the integrated circuit that defines the third generation of computers. Perhaps the two most important members of the third generation are the IBM System/360 and the DEC PDP-8.

Later Generations

Beyond the third generation there is less general agreement on defining generations of computers. There have been a fourth and a fifth generation, based on advances in integrated circuit technology. With the introduction of large-scale integration (LSI), more than 1000,000 components can be placed on a single integrated circuit chip.

The Summary of Generations of Computer

- Vacuum tube - 1946-1957
- Transistor - 1958-1964
- Small scale integration: 1965

Up to 100 devices on a chip

- **Medium scale integration: -1971**

100-3,000 devices on a chip

- **Large scale integration :1971-1977**

3,000 - 100,000 devices on a chip

- **Very large scale integration: 1978 -1991**

100,000 - 100,000,000 devices on a chip

- **Ultra large scale integration : 1991**

Over 100,000,000 devices on a chip

FUNCTIONAL UNITS OF COMPUTER

Computer allocates the task between its various functional units. The computer system is divided into three separate functional units for its operation. They are:

- Central Processing Unit (CPU)
- Arithmetic Logical Unit (ALU)
- Control Unit (CU)

Central Processing Unit (CPU)

The ALU and the CU of a computer system are jointly known as the Central Processing Unit. You may call CPU as the brain of any computer system. It is just like brain that takes all major decisions, makes all sorts of calculations and directs different parts of the computer functions by activating and controlling the operations.

Arithmetic Logical Unit (ALU)

After you enter data through the input device it is stored in the Primary storage unit. The actual processing of the data and instruction are performed by Arithmetic Logical Unit. The major operations performed by the ALU are addition, subtraction, multiplication, division, logic and comparison. Data is transferred to ALU from storage unit when required. After processing the output is returned back to storage unit for further processing or getting stored.

Control Unit (CU)

The next component of computer is the Control Unit, which acts like the supervisor seeing that things are done in proper fashion. The control unit determines the sequence in which computer programs and instructions are executed. Things like processing of programs stored in the main memory, interpretation of the instructions and issuing of signals for other units of the computer to execute them. It also acts as a switch board operator when several users access the computer simultaneously. Thereby it coordinates the activities of computer's peripheral as they perform the input and output.

PARTS OF THE COMPUTER

There is basically two parts of the computer:

(a) Hardware
(b) Software

(a) Hardware

Hardware is best described as a device that is physically connected to your computer or something that can be physically touched. A CD-ROM, Monitor, Printer, and video card are all examples of computer hardware. Without any hardware your computer would not exist and software would have nothing to run on. The image to the right is of a web cam, an example of an external hardware peripheral that allows users to make basic videos, transmit videos of themselves over the Internet, and take pictures.

Computer hardwares are:

- **Central Processing Unit (CPU):** The "microprocessor" brain of the computer system is called the central processing unit. Everything that a computer does is overseen by the CPU.
- **Memory:** This is very fast storage used to hold data. It has to be fast because it connects directly to the microprocessor. There are several specific types of memory in a computer.
- **RAM (Random Access Memory):**It is used to temporarily store information that the computer is currently working with.
- **ROM (Read Only Memory):** A permanent type of memory storage used by the computer for important data that does not change.
- **Keyboard:** Generally used to type or select an option on the screen. It is an input device.
- **Mouse:** It is an input device which is used to point and select some option on VDU.
- **VDU (Visual Display Unit):** It is an output device where the output of any command is displayed *i.e.*, The screen.
- **Printer:** It is the output device. Different types of printer are:
  1. Dot matrix printer
  2. Inkjet Printer
  3. Laser Printer etc.
- **Floppy Disk Drives:** It is a common form of removable storage. Floppy disk are extremely inexpensive and easy to save information.
- **Scanner:** It is an input device. A scanner scans an image and transform the image to ASCII Graphics. These codes can be edited, manipulated & then printed.
- **CD-ROM Drive:** It is an input device. To read a CD-ROM disk a CD-ROM drive is required. One can only read from it and cannot write on it.
- **DVD-ROM:** DVD-ROM is similar to Cd-Rom but is capable of holding much more information.
- **CD-Writer:** It is input device. To write from other CD to your CD, writer is used.

(b) Software

Software is a collection of commands that help users to communicate with the computer or help the computer perform specific tasks for them. Without any type of software the computer would be of no use.

Examples of software **programs** or **applications** would be the **Operating System** (DOS, Windows, UNIX, MacOS and various others), **Wordprocessor** (typing letters), **Spreadsheet** (financial info), **Database** (inventory control and address book), **Graphics program**, **Internet Browser**, **Email** and many others.

Software is capable of performing specific tasks, as opposed to hardware which only perform mechanical tasks that they are mechanically designed for. Practical computer systems divide software systems into three major groups:

System Software

System software is a program that manages and supports the computer resources and operations of a computer system while it executes various tasks such as processing data and information, controlling hardware components, and allowing users to use application software. That is, systems software functions as a *bridge* between computer system hardware and the application software. System software is made up of many control programs, including the operating system, communications software and database manager. Computer software includes operating systems, device drivers, diagnostic tools and more.

Systems software consists of three kinds of programs. The system management programs, system support programs, and system development programs. These are explained briefly.

System Management Programs

These are programs that manage the application software, computer hardware, and data resources of the computer system. These programs include operating systems, operating environment programs, database management programs, and telecommunications monitor programs. Among these, the most important system management programs are operating systems. The operating systems are needed to study more details. There are two reasons. First, users need to know their functions first. For the second, there are many kinds of operating systems available today.

Telecommunications monitor programs are additions of the operating systems of microcomputers. These programs provide the extra logic for the computer system to control a class of communications devices.

System Support Programs

These are the programs that help the operations and management of a computer system. They provide a variety of support services to let the computer hardware and other system programs run efficiently. The major system support programs are system utility programs, system performance monitor programs, and system security monitor programs (virus checking programs).

System Development Programs

These are programs that help users develop information system programs and prepare user programs for computer processing. These programs may analyze and design systems and program itself. The main system development programs are programming language translators, programming environment programs, computer-aided software engineering packages.

Programming Software

Software that assists a programmer in writing computer programs.

Application Software

Allows users to accomplish one or more tasks. Application software utilizes the capacities of a computer directly for a dedicated task. Application software is able to manipulate text, numbers and graphics. It can be in the form of software focused on a certain single task like word processing, spreadsheet or playing of audio and video files. Here, we look at the application software types along with some examples of application software of each type.

Different Types of Application Software

- **Word Processing Software:** This software enables users to create and edit documents. The most popular examples of this type of software are MS-Word, WordPad and Notepad among other text editors.
- **Database Software:** Database is a structured collection of data. A computer database relies on database software to organize data and enable database users to perform database operations. Database software allows users to store and retrieve data from databases. Examples are Oracle, MSAccess, etc.

- **Spreadsheet Software:** Excel, Lotus 1-2-3 and Apple Numbers are some examples of spreadsheet software. Spreadsheet software allows users to perform calculations using spreadsheets. They simulate paper worksheets by displaying multiple cells that make up a grid.
- **Multimedia Software:** They allow users to create and play audio and video files. They are capable of playing media files. Audio converters, audio players, burners, video encoders and decoders are some forms of multimedia software. Examples of this type of software include Real Player and Media Player.
- **Presentation Software:** The software that is used to display information in the form of a slide show is known as presentation software. This type of software includes three functions, namely, editing that allows insertion and formatting of text, methods to include graphics in the text and a functionality of executing slide shows. Microsoft PowerPoint is the best example of presentation software.
- **Enterprise Software:** It deals with the needs of organization processes and data flow. Customer relationship management or the financial processes in an organization are carried out with the help of enterprise software.
- **Information Worker Software:** Individual projects within a department and individual needs of creation and management of information are handled by information worker software. Documentation tools, resource management tools and personal management systems fall under the category of this type of application software.
- **Educational Software:** It has the capabilities of running tests and tracking progress. It also has the capabilities of a collaborative software. It is often used in teaching and self-learning. Dictionaries like Britannica and Encarta, mathematical software like Matlab and others like Google Earth and NASA World Wind are some of the well-known names in this category.
- **Simulation Software:** It is used to simulate physical or abstract systems. Simulation software finds applications in both, research and entertainment. Flight simulators and scientific simulators are examples of simulation software.
- **Content Access Software:** It is used to access content without editing. Common examples of content access software are web browsers and media players.
- **Application Suites:** An application suite is an important type of application software. It consists of a group of applications combined to perform related functions. OpenOffice.org and Microsoft Office are the best examples of this type of application software. These application suites, as you know, come as bundles of applications like word processors, spreadsheets, presentation software, etc. Applications in the suite can work together or operate on each other's files.

Utility Software

Utility software is system software designed to help analyze, configure, optimize or maintain a computer. A single piece of utility software is usually called a utility or tool.

Utility software usually focuses on how the computer infrastructure (including the computer hardware, operating system, application software and data storage) operates. Due to this focus, utilities are often rather technical and targeted at people with an advanced level of computer knowledge - in contrast to application software, which allows users to do things like creating text documents, playing games, listening to music or viewing websites.

Utility Software Examples

- **Anti-virus** utilities scan for computer viruses.
- **Backup** utilities can make a copy of all information stored on a disk, and restore either the entire disk (e.g. in an event of

disk failure) or selected files (e.g. in an event of accidental deletion).

- **Data compression** utilities output a shorter stream or a smaller file when provided with a stream or file.
- **Disk cleaners** can find files that are unnecessary to computer operation, or take up considerable amounts of space. Disk cleaner helps the user to decide what to delete when their hard disk is full.
- **Disk compression** utilities can transparently compress/uncompress the contents of a disk, increasing the capacity of the disk.
- **Disk defragmenters** can detect computer files whose contents are broken across several locations on the hard disk, and move the fragments to one location to increase efficiency.
- **Disk partitions** can divide an individual drive into multiple logical drives, each with its own file system which can be mounted by the operating system and treated as an individual drive.
- **Disk space analyzers** for the visualization of disk space usage by getting the size for each folder (including sub folders) & files in folder or drive, showing the distribution of the used space.
- **Archive** utilities output a stream or a single file when provided with a directory or a set of files. Archive utilities, unlike archive suites, usually do not include compression or encryption capabilities. Some archive utilities may even have a separate un-archive utility for the reverse operation.
- **File managers** provide a convenient method of performing routine data management tasks, such as deleting, renaming, cataloging, uncataloging, moving, copying, merging, generating and modifying data sets.
- **Memory testers** check for memory failures.
- **Network utilities** analyze the computer's network connectivity, configure network settings, check data transfer or log events.
- **Registry cleaners** clean and optimize the Windows registry by removing old registry keys that are no longer in use.
- **Screensavers** were desired to prevent phosphor burn-in on CRT and plasma computer monitors by blanking the screen or filling it with moving images or patterns when the computer is not in use. Contemporary screensavers are used primarily for entertainment or security.

Firmware

Firmware is a program for the hardware. It is an embedded coded (program) for the hardware. So, it can perform its function specifically for which device is made. Every device has inbuilt firmware that gives the device ability to perform its work. There are lots of devices that use a screen and buttons. The device consists of firmware that instruct the device to perform certain functions on given command. Examples are a video card and sound card.

COMPUTER FUNDAMENTAL

COMPUTER

Computer is an advanced electronic device that takes raw data as input from the user and processes these data under the control of set of instructions (called program) and gives the result (output) and saves output for the future use. It can process both numerical and non-numerical (arithmetic and logical) calculations.

A computer has four functions:

(*a*) accepts data **Input**
(*b*) processes data **Processing**
(*c*) produces output **Output**
(*d*) stores results **Storage**

Input (Data)

Input is the raw information entered into a computer from the input devices. It is the collection of letters, numbers, images etc.

Process

Process is the operation of data as per given instruction. It is totally internal process of the computer system.

Output

Output is the processed data given by computer after data processing. Output is also called as Result. We can save these results in the storage devices for the future use.

COMPUTER SYSTEM

All of the components of a computer system can be summarized with the simple equations.

COMPUTER SYSTEM = HARDWARE + SOFTWARE + USER

Hardware = Internal Devices + Peripheral Devices

All physical parts of the computer (or everything that we can touch) are known as Hardware.

Software = Programs

Software gives "intelligence" to the computer.

USER = Person, who operates computer.

PROCESSOR

The main unit inside the computer is the CPU. This unit is responsible for all events inside the computer. It controls all internal and external devices, performs arithmetic and logic operations. The CPU (Central Processing Unit) is the device that interprets and executes instructions.

SOFTWARE

Software, simply are the computer programs. The instructions given to the computer in the form of a program is called Software. Software is the set of programs, which are used for different purposes. All the programs used in computer to perform specific task is called Software.

Types of Software

1. System software

(a) Operating System Software: Operating system is an example of system software, which provide the platform to the application softwares.

DOS, Windows XP, Windows Vista, Unix/Linux, MAC/OS X etc.

(b) Utility Software: Windows Explorer (File/ Folder Management), Windows Media Player, Anti-Virus Utilities, Disk Defragmentation, Disk Clean, BackUp, WinZip, WinRAR etc...

2. Application software

(a) Package Software: MS Office 2003, MS Office 2007, Macromedia (Dreamweaver, Flash, Freehand), Adobe (PageMaker, PhotoShop)

(b) Tailored or Custom Software: SAGE (Accounting), Galileo/Worldspan (Travel) etc.

COMPUTER LANGUAGES & SCRIPTING

Low Level Language

(*i*) Machine Level Language

(*ii*) Assembly Language

Machine language

These language instructions are directly executed by CPU. It is in the form of '0' and '1' means in binary language.

Assembly language

The endeavor of giving machine language instructions a name structure that means bit strings of instructions of machine language are given name here.

- **High Level Language:** The user friendly language ...more natural language than assembly language. Like C++, Java etc.
- **Assembler:** It is a program written in a computer language which convert assembly language into machine language.
- **Compiler:** It is also a program written in a computer language, which convert high level language to machine language.

High Level Language

COBOL (Common Business Oriented Language), FORTRAN (Formula Translation), BASIC (Beginner's All-purpose Symbolic Instruction Code), C, C++ etc. are the examples of High Level Language.

TYPES OF COMPUTER

On the Basis of Working Principle

(a) **Analog Computer:** An analog computer (spelt analogue in British English) is a form of computer that uses *continuous* physical phenomena such as electrical, mechanical, or hydraulic quantities to model the problem being solved.

(b) **Digital Computer:** A computer that performs calculations and logical operations with quantities represented as digits, usually in the binary number system.

(c) **Hybrid Computer (Analog + Digital):** A combination of computers those are capable of inputting and outputting in both digital and analog signals. A hybrid computer system setup offers a cost effective method of performing complex simulations.

COMPUTER TYPES ON THE BASIS OF SIZE

(a) Super Computer

The fastest type of computer. Supercomputers are very expensive and are employed for specialized applications that require immense amounts of mathematical calculations. For example, weather forecasting requires a supercomputer. Other uses of supercomputers include animated graphics, fluid dynamic calculations, nuclear energy research, and petroleum exploration.

The chief difference between a supercomputer and a mainframe is that a supercomputer channels all its power into executing a few programs as fast as possible, whereas a mainframe uses its power to execute many programs concurrently.

(b) Mainframe Computer

A very large and expensive computer capable of supporting hundreds, or even thousands, of users simultaneously. In the hierarchy that starts with a simple microprocessor (in watches, for example) at the bottom and moves to supercomputers at the top, mainframes are just below supercomputers. In some ways, mainframes are more powerful than supercomputers because they support more simultaneous programs. But supercomputers can execute a single program faster than a mainframe.

(c) Mini Computer

A midsized computer. In size and power, minicomputers lie between *workstations* and *mainframes*. In the past decade, the distinction between large minicomputers and small mainframes has blurred, however, as has the distinction between small minicomputers and workstations. But in general, a minicomputer is a multiprocessing system capable of supporting from 4 to about 200 users simultaneously.

(d) Micro Computer

(*i*) **Desktop Computer:** A personal or micro-mini computer sufficient to fit on a desk.

(*ii*) **Laptop Computer:** A portable computer complete with an integrated screen and keyboard. It is generally smaller in size than a desktop computer and larger than a notebook computer.

(*iii*) **Palmtop Computer/Digital Diary/ Notebook/PDAs:** A hand-sized computer. Palmtops have no keyboard but the screen serves both as an input and output device.

(e) Workstations

A terminal or desktop computer in a network. In this context, workstation is just a generic term for a user's machine (client machine) in contrast to a "server" or "mainframe."

BOOTING

The process of loading the system files of the operating system from the disk into the computer memory to complete the circuitry requirement of the computer system is called booting.

Types of Booting

There are two types of booting:

- **Cold Booting:** If the computer is in off state and we boot the computer by pressing the power switch 'ON' from the CPU box then it is called as cold booting.
- **Warm Booting:** If the computer is already 'ON' and we restart it by pressing the 'RESET' button from the CPU box or CTRL, ALT and DEL key simultaneously from the keyboard then it is called warm booting.

COMPUTER HARDWARE

HARDWARE

The **hardware** are the parts of the computer itself including the Central Processing Unit (CPU) and related **microchips** and **micro-circuitry**, keyboards, monitors, case and drives (hard, CD, DVD, floppy, optical, tape, etc...). Other extra parts called **peripheral components** or **devices** include mouse, printers, modems, scanners, digital cameras and cards (sound, colour, video) etc... Together they are often referred to as a **personal computer**.

Central Processing Unit

Though the term relates to a specific chip or the **processor** a CPU's performance is determined by the rest of the computer's **circuitry** and **chips**.

Currently the Pentium chip or processor, made by Intel, is the most common CPU though there are many other companies that produce processors for personal computers. Examples are the CPU made by Motorola and AMD.

With faster processors the **clock speed** becomes more important. Compared to some of the first computers which operated at below 30 **megahertz** (MHz) the Pentium chips began at 75 MHz in the late 1990's. Speeds now exceed 3000+ MHz or 3 **gigahertz** (GHz) and different chip manufacturers use different measuring standards (check your local computer store for the latest speed). It depends on the **circuit board** that the chip is housed in, or the **motherboard**, as to whether you are able to upgrade to a faster chip. The motherboard contains the circuitry and connections that allow the various components to communicate with each other.

Though there were many computers using many different processors previous to this I call the 80286 processor the advent of home computers as these were the processors that made computers available for the average person. Using a processor before the 286 involved learning a proprietary system and software. Most new software are being developed for the newest and fastest processors so it can be difficult to use an older computer system.

Keyboard

The keyboard is used to type information into the computer or **input** information. There are many different keyboard layouts and sizes with the most common for Latin based languages being the QWERTY layout (named for the first 6 keys). The standard keyboard has 101 keys. Notebooks have embedded keys accessible by special keys or by pressing key combinations (CTRL or Command and P for example). **Ergonomically** designed keyboards are designed to make typing easier. Hand held devices have various and different keyboard configurations and **touch screens**.

Some of the keys have a special use. They are referred to as command keys. The 3 most common are the Control (CTRL), Alternate (Alt) and the Shift keys though there can be more (the Windows key for example or the Command key). Each key on a standard keyboard has one or two characters. Press the key to get the lower character and hold Shift to get the upper.

Removable Storage and/or Disk Drives

All disks need a **drive** to get information off - or **read** - and put information on the disk - or **write**. Each drive is designed for a specific type of disk whether it is a CD, DVD, hard disk or floppy. Often the term 'disk' and 'drive' are used to describe the same thing but it helps to understand that the disk is the **storage device** which contains computer files - or software - and the drive is the mechanism that runs the disk.

Digital flash drives work slightly differently as they use **memory cards** to store information so there are no moving parts. Digital cameras also use Flash memory cards to store information, in this case photographs. **Hand held devices** use digital drives and many also use removable or built in memory cards.

Mouse

Most modern computers today are run using a mouse controlled pointer. Generally if the mouse has two buttons the left one is used to **select** objects and text and the right one is used to **access menus**. If the mouse has one button (Mac for instance) it controls all the activity and a mouse with a third button can be used by specific software programs.

One type of mouse has a round ball under the bottom of the mouse that rolls and turns two wheels which control the direction of the pointer on the screen. Another type of mouse uses an optical system to track the movement of the mouse. **Laptop** computers use touch pads, buttons and other devices to control the pointer. Hand helds use a combination of devices to control the pointer, including touch screens.

Note: It is important to clean the mouse periodically, particularly if it becomes sluggish. A ball type mouse has a small circular panel that can be opened, allowing you to remove the ball. Lint can be removed carefully with a tooth pick or tweezers and the ball can be washed with mild detergent. A build up will accumulate on the small wheels in the mouse. Use a small instrument or finger nail to scrape it off taking care not to scratch the wheels. Track balls can be cleaned much like a mouse and touch-pad can be wiped with a clean, damp cloth. An optical mouse can accumulate material from the surface that it is in contact with which can be removed with a finger nail or small instrument.

Monitors

The monitor shows information on the screen when you type. This is called **outputting** information. When the computer needs more information it will display a message on the screen, usually through a **dialog box**. Monitors come in many types and sizes. The resolution of the monitor determines the sharpness of the screen. The resolution can be adjusted to control the screen's display..

Most desktop computers use a monitor with a **cathode tube** or **liquid crystal display**. Most notebooks use a liquid crystal display monitor.

To get the full benefit of today's software with full colour graphics and animation, computers need a colour monitor with a display or **graphics** card.

Printers

The printer takes the information on your screen and transfers it to paper or a **hard copy**. There are many different types of printers with various levels of quality. The three basic types of printer are; **dot matrix**, **inkjet**, and **laser**.

- Dot matrix printers work like a typewriter transferring ink from a ribbon to paper with a series or 'matrix' of tiny pins.
- Ink jet printers work like dot matrix printers but fire a stream of ink from a cartridge directly onto the paper.

- Laser printers use the same technology as a photocopier using heat to transfer toner onto paper.

Modem

A modem is used to translate information transferred through telephone lines, cable, satellite or line-of-sight wireless.

The term stands for **modulate and demodulate** which changes the signal from **digital**, which computers use, to **analog**, which telephones use and then back again. **Digital modems** transfer digital information directly without changing to analog.

Modems are measured by the speed that the information is transferred. The measuring tool is called the **baud rate**. Originally modems worked at speeds below 2400 baud but today analog speeds of 56,000 baud are standard. Cable, wireless or digital subscriber lines can transfer information much faster with rates of 300,000 baud and up.

Modems also use **Error Correction** which corrects for transmission errors by constantly checking whether the information was received properly or not and Compression which allows for faster data transfer rates. Information is transferred in **packets**. Each packet is checked for errors and is re-sent if there is an error.

Anyone who has used the Internet has noticed that at times the information travels at different speeds. Depending on the amount of information that is being transferred, the information will arrive at it's destination at different times. The amount of information that can travel through a line is limited. This limit is called **bandwidth**.

There are many more variables involved in communication technology using computers, much of which is covered in the section on the Internet.

Scanners

Scanners allow you to transfer pictures and photographs to your computer. A scanner 'scans' the image from the top to the bottom, one line at a time and transfers it to the computer as a series of bits or a bitmap. You can then take that image and use it in a paint program, send it out as a fax or print it. With optional **Optical Character Recognition** (OCR) software you can convert printed documents such as newspaper articles to text that can be used in your word processor. Most scanners use **TWAIN** software that makes the scanner accessable by other software applications.

Digital cameras allow you to take digital photographs. The images are stored on a memory chip or disk that can be transferred to your computer. Some cameras can also capture sound and video.

Case

The case houses the microchips and circuitry that run the computer. Desktop models usually sit under the monitor and tower models beside. They come in many sizes, including desktop, mini, midi, and full tower. There is usually room inside to expand or add components at a later time. By removing the cover off the case you may find plate covered, empty slots that allow you to add cards. There are various types of slots including IDE, ASI, USB, PCI and Firewire slots.

Depending on the type notebook computers may have room to expand. Most Notebooks also have connections or ports that allows expansion or connection to exterior, peripheral devices such as monitor, portable hard-drives or other devices.

Cards

Cards are components added to computers to increase their capability. When adding a peripheral device make sure that your computer has a slot of the type needed by the device.

Sound cards allow computers to produce sound like music and voice. The older sound cards were 8 bit then 16 bit then 32 bit. Though the human ear can't distinguish the fine difference between sounds produced by the more powerful sound card they allow for more complex music and music production.

Colour cards allow computers to produce colour (with a colour monitor of course). The first colour cards were 2 bit which produced 4 colours [CGA]. It was amazing what could be done with those 4 colours. Next came 4 bit allowing for 16

[EGA and VGA] colours. Then came 16 bit allowing for 1064 colours and then 24 bit which allows for almost 17 million colours and now 32 bit and higher allow monitors to display almost a billion separate colours.

Video cards allow computers to display video and animation. Some video cards allow computers to display television as well as capture frames from video. A video card with a digital video camera allows computers users to produce live video. A high speed connection is required for effective video transmission.

Network cards allow computers to connect together to communicate with each other. Network cards have connections for cable, thin wire or wireless networks for more information.

Cables connect internal components to the **Motherboard**, which is a board with series of electronic path ways and connections allowing the CPU to communicate with the other components of the computer.

Memory

Memory can be very confusing but is usually one of the easiest pieces of hardware to add to your computer. It is common to confuse **chip memory** with disk storage. An example of the difference between memory and storage would be the difference between a table where the actual work is done (memory) and a filing cabinet where the finished product is stored (disk). To add a bit more confusion, the computer's hard disk can be used as **temporary memory** when the program needs more than the chips can provide.

Random Access Memory or **RAM** is the memory that the computer uses to temporarily store the information as it is being processed. The more information being processed the more RAM the computer needs.

One of the first home computers used 64 kilobytes of RAM memory (Commodore 64). Today's modern computers need a minimum of 64 Mb (recommended 128 Mb or more) to run Windows or OS 10 with modern software. RAM memory chips come in many different sizes and speeds and can usually be **expanded**. Older computers came with 512 Kb of memory which could be expanded to a maximum of 640 Kb. In most modern computers the memory can be expanded by adding or replacing the memory chips depending on the processor you have and the type of memory your computer uses. Memory chips range in size from 1 Mb to 4 Gb. As computer technology changes the type of memory changes as well making old memory chips obsolete. Check your computer manual to find out what kind of memory your computer uses before purchasing new memory chips

MULTIPLE CHOICE QUESTIONS

1. Android is a mobile operating system designed primarily for touchscreen mobile devices such as smartphones and tablets. Which among the following was the first Android Operating System?

A. Cupcake B. Alpha
C. Gingerbread D. Doughnut
E. Eclair

2. Which among the following key combinations can be used to search in Windows Explorer?

A. Ctrl + F B. Ctrl + S
C. Ctrl + G D. Alt + S
E. None of the above

3. A router is a networking device that forwards data packets and is connected to two or more data lines from different networks. Which among the following was the earliest device which had almost the same functionality as that of a router?

A. Interface Delay Device
B. Interface Traffic Manager
C. Interface Routing Processor
D. Interface Message Processor
E. Interface Data Manager

4. A vacuum tube (also called a VT, electron tube or, in the UK, a valve) is a device sometimes used to amplify electronic signals. Vacuum Tubes were used in which generation of Computers?

A. 1st Generation B. 2nd Generation
C. 3rd Generation D. 4th Generation
D. 5th Generation

5. In Computer programming API is a set of subroutine definitions, protocols, and tools for building software and applications. Which among the following is an application programming interface for the programm-ing language Java, which defines how a client may access a database?

A. J2EE B. JDK
C. JAVA SE D. JDBC
E. JSX

6. Which of the following errors occurs when software tries to access protected memory?

A. Segmentation Fault
B. Displaytime Error
C. IO Error
D. Runtime Error
E. Zero Division Error

7. Which among the following is a term representing unit of data storage in computer memory?

A. Pixel B. Decimal
C. Octet D. Point
E. Fragment

8. Microsoft PowerPoint is a slide show presentation program for use on both Microsoft and Apple Macintosh operating systems. In MS PowerPoint Broadcast is a feature available in which tab?

A. File B. View
C. Slide Show D. Transitions
E. Review

9. Which among the following carries signals that control the actions of the computer?

A. Control Bus B. Data Bus
C. Memory Unit D. NIC
E. Address Bus

10. Which among the following is not a secondary memory?

A. Cache B. Pen Drive
C. Hard Disk D. Memory Card
E. Memory Stick

11. Which among the following is a cloud computing platform and infrastructure created by Microsoft?

A. Simple Storage Service
B. Atmos
C. Openstack Swift
D. OceanStore
E. Azure

12. After a credit card transaction has been authorized by the issuing bank by sending an authorization code to the merchant, the settlement stage of the process begins. Which of the following is a system type used to process such statements?

A. Multi-tasking B. Memory Processing
C. Level Processing D. Batch Processing
E. Online Processing

13. Assembly is a _______ based low-level language replacing binary machine-code instructions, which are very hard to remember, it is the classic and uncontroversial example of a low level language.

A. Memory B. High Level
C. Key D. Mnemonic
E. FORTRAN

14. China now has more of the world's fastest supercomputers than other countries. Which among the following is a Chinese super-computer?

A. BlueGene/Q system
B. Cray XC30
C. Shaheen II
D. Fujitsu's K
E. Tianhe-2

15. Which among the following is an important circuitry in a computer system that does the arithmetic and logical processing?

A. Memory B. ALU
C. Flag Register D. CU
E. Calculator

16. Which among the following is not a mobile Operating System?
A. Bada B. Safari
C. Symbian D. MeeGo
E. WebOS

17. Which among the following key can be used as a shortcut to rename a folder in Microsoft Windows 8 and higher versions?
A. F2 B. F4
C. F6 D. F9
E. F11

18. AT & T designed its first commercial modem, specifically for converting digital computer data to analog for transmission across its long distance network. What is the name of the modem?
A. Telex B. Memex
C. CompuServe D. Bell 103 dataset
E. Dataphone

19. Integrated Chips or IC's were started to be in use from which generation of computers?
A. 1st Generation B. 2nd Generation
C. 3rd Generation D. 4th Generation
E. 5th Generation

20. In Computer programming there is a set of subroutine definitions, protocols, and tools for building software and applications. Which among the following is a term for sets of requirements that govern how one application can talk to another?
A. UPS B. API
C. CGI D. J2EE
E. OLE

21. When you first turn on a computer, the COU is preset to execute instructions stored in ....
A. RAM B. Flash memory
C. ROM D. The CD-ROM
E. The ALU

22. Which of the following is **not** a function of the control unit?
A. Read instructions
B. Interpret instructions
C. Execute instructions
D. Direct operations
E. Provide control signals

23. What are .bas, .doc, .htm examples of in computing?
A. Extensions
B. Protocols
C. Databases
D. Other than those given as options
E. Domains

24. Documents converted to .... can be published to the web.
A. a doc file
B. http
C. Other than those given as options
D. machine language
E. HTML

25. What kind of software would you most likely use to keep track of a billing account?
A. Web authoring
B. electronic publishing
C. spreadsheet
D. word processing
E. Power point

26. A computer virus normally attaches itself to another computer program known as a ....
A. host program
B. target program
C. backdoor program
D. Bluetooth
E. Trojan horse

27. When a file contains instructions that can be carried out by the computer. It is often called a(n) .... file.
A. Other than those given as options
B. information
C. application
D. executable
E. data

28. Data duplication wastes the space, but also promotes a more serious problem called ....
A. Isolated data
B. Data inconsistency
C. Other than those given as options
D. Program dependency
E. Separated data

29. Which of the following is **not** a version of the Windows operating system software for the PC?

A. ME B. 98
C. XP D. 10
E. 95

30. The main directory of a disk is called the .... directory.

A. network B. folder
C. root D. File
E. Other than those given as options

31. Which of the following is **not** an example of application software?

A. Word processing software
B. Spreadsheet software
C. Operating system software
D. Database software
E. Graphics software

32. Which of the following is **not** true about RAM?

A. RAM is the same as hard disk storage
B. RAM is a temporary storage area
C. RAM is volatile
D. RAM is a primary memory
E. All are true

33. The data storage hierarchy consists of ....

A. Bits, Bytes, Records, Fields, files and databases
B. Characters, fields, records, files and databases
C. Bytes, bits, fields, records, files and databases
D. Bits, bytes, fields, records, files and databases
E. Other than those given as options

34. = Sum (B1 B0) is an example of a ....

A. function B. cell address
C. formula D. value
E. Other than those given as options

35. .... are often delivered to a PC through an email attachment and are often designed to do harm.

A. Portals
B. Spam
C. Viruses
D. Other than those given as options
E. E-mail messages

36. Decreasing the amount of space required to store data and programs is accomplished by ....

A. Crashing B. Disk caching
C. RAID D. file compression
E. Other than those given as options

37. What is the difference between a CD-ROM and CD-RW?

A. They are the same –just two different terms used by different manufacturers
B. A CD-Rom can be written to and a CD-RW cannot
C. Other than those given as options
D. A CD-ROM holds more information than a CD-RW
E. A CD-RW can be written to but a CD-ROM can only be read from

38. Computer program are written in a high-level programming language, however, the human readable version of a program is called ....

A. word size B. source code
C. instruction set D. Read & Write code
E. None of these

39. The clock rate of a processor is measured in ....

A. megabytes or gigabytes
B. milliseconds
C. megahertz or gigahertz
D. nanoseconds
E. micro hertz

40. When cutting and pasting, the item cut is temporarily stored in the ....

A. dashboard B. ROM
C. hard drive D. Diskette
E. clipboard

41. Copying the Excel 2007 formula = SUM (A1:A5) from cell A6 to cell B6 will result in what formula for cell B6?

A. = SUM (B6:A6)
B. < SUM (A1:B6)
C. = SUM (B1:A5)

D. > SUM (B1:B5)
E. Other than those given as options

42. RAM is used as a short memory because it—
A. has small capacity B. is very expensive
C. is programmable D. volatile
E. not very useful

43. The Num Lock Key and Caps Lock Key are considered .... because their function changes each time you press them.
A. toggle B. dual
C. function D. cursor control
E. control

44. OLE stands for—
A. Offline Linking and Embedding
B. Online Link Emulation
C. Object Link Export
D. Object Linking and Embedding
E. Online Link Embedding

45. Microsoft Word is an example of—
A. Application software
B. An input device
C. System software
D. A processing system
E. An operating system

46. Which of the following is not an example of an output device?
A. Speaker B. Plotter
C. Microphone D. Printer
E. Monitor

47. The digital telecommunications, termed as ISDN is an abbreviation for—
A. Interactive Standard Dynamic Networks
B. Integrated Standard Digital Networks
C. Internet Services Data Network
D. International Services Data Network
E. Integrated Services Digital Network

48. Which of the following places the common data elements in order to the smallest from the largest?
A. Character, file, field, record, database
B. Character, field, record, file, database
C. Character, record, field, database, file
D. Character, file, record, field, database
E. Character, field, record, database, file

49. Software made freely available to the public by the publisher is called—
A. Fair use
B. Compact disc
C. Freeware
D. Process ware
E. Copyright

50. A web site's own unique Internet address that no other web site can use is its—
A. Search Engine B. FTP
C. URL D. WWW
E. IP v 6

51. The windows shortcut to delete an item permanently is—
A. Shift + Delete B. Shift + F1
C. Ctrl + F1 D. Ctrl + F2
E. Shift + F2

52. WAN is a type of computer network. It stands for—
A. Wireless Array Network
B. Wild Area Network
C. Wide Access Network
D. Wide Area Network
E. Wireless Area Network

53. Which of the following is a type for intercepting computer communications?
A. Hacking B. Sniffing
C. Pretexting D. Spoofing
E. Phishing

54. Which key allows movement from one cell of a table to the next?
A. Shift B. CTRL
C. Esc D. Tab
E. ALT

55. Pressing the .... key will make the number pad act as directional arrows.
A. Caps lock B. Arrow lock
C. Shift D. Esc
E. Num lock

56. The most widely used device in communication is a —
A. Coprocessor B. Channel
C. Bus D. Modem
E. Scanner

57. Codes consisting of light and dark marks which may be optically read is known as—
A. Mnemonics B. Stripe-code
C. Decoder D. Special-code
E. Bar code

58. Which of the following is not a type of data storage media?
A. Magnetic Tape B. A Database
C. Hard Disc D. Optical Disc
E. Magnetic Disc

59. Compiler means—
A. A program which translates source code into object program
B. Keypunch Operator
C. A person who compiles source programs
D. The same thing as a programmer
E. Computer data operator

60. Which of the following is operating system software?
A. Microsoft Access
B. Microsoft Windows
C. Microsoft Power Point
D. Microsoft Excel
E. Microsoft Word

61. Reusable optical storage will typically have the acronym ....
A. CD B. DVD
C. ROM D. RW
E. None of these

62. .... is processed by the computer into information.
A. Data B. Numbers
C. Alphabets D. Pictures
E. None of these

63. A .... is an electronic device that process data, converting it into information.
A. computer B. processor
C. case D. stylus
E. None of these

64. File extensions are used in order to
A. name the file
B. ensure the filename is not lost
C. identify the file
D. identify the file type
E. None of these

65. The most common type of storage devices are ....
A. persistent B. optical
C. magnetic D. flash
E. None of these

66. "GUI" stands for ....
A. Gnutella Universal Interface
B. Graphical User Interface
C. Graphic Uninstall/Install
D. General Utility Interface
E. None of these

67. A .... is a design tool that graphically shows the logic in a solution algorithm.
A. flowchart B. hierarchy chart
C. structure chart D. context diagram
E. None of these

68. A file that contains definitions of the paragraph and character styles for your document and all things you customised toolbars and menus is called a ....
A. guide B. pattern
C. base document D. template
E. None of these

69. Programs designed specifically to address general-purpose applications and special-purpose applications are called ....
A. operating system
B. system software
C. application software
D. Management information systems
E. None of these

70. A .... contains buttons and menus that provide quick access to commonly used commands.
A. toolbar B. menu bar
C. window D. find
E. None of these

71. .... has invented the mechanical calculator for adding numbers
A. Charles Babbage B. Newton
C. Pascal D. Peano
E. E.F. Codd

72. A unit of hardware used to monitor the computer processing
A. Terminal B. Console

C. CPU D. Server
E. Client

73. Which of these is not a feature of a reentrant procedure
A. multiple users can share a single copy of a program during the same period
B. The program code can modify itself
C. The local data for each user process must be stored separately
D. the permanent part is the code
E. the temporary part is the pointer back to the calling program and local variables used by that program

74. What is the split-MAC architecture
A. The split-MAC architecture uses MAC addresses to create a forward/filter table and break up broadcast domains
B. The split-MAC architecture uses MAC addresses on the wireless network and IP addresses on the wired network
C. The split-MAC architecture allows the splitting of 802.11 protocol packets between the AP and the controller to allow processing by both devices
D. The split-MAC architecture uses MAC addresses to create a forward/filter table and break up collision domains
E. All of these

75. In .... normal form, all non-key fields of data structure are dependent on the whole key
A. First B. Second
C. Third D. Fourth
E. Fifth

76. For selecting or highlighting, which of the following is generally used?
A. Icon B. Keyboard
C. Mouse D. Floppy Disk
E. None of these

77. What does storage unit provide?
A. Place for typing data
B. Storage for information and instruction
C. Place for printing information
D. All of the above
E. None of these

78. Which type of memory is closely related to processor?
A. Main Memory
B. Secondary Memory
C. Disk Memory
D. Tape Memory
E. None of these

79. Which device is used to access your computer by other computer or for talk over phone?
A. RAM B. CD ROM Drive
C. Modem D. Hard Drive
E. None of these

80. Permanent Memory in computer is called
A. RAM B. ROM
C. CPU D. CD ROM
E. None of these

81. .... allows users to upload files to an online site so they can be viewed and edited from another location.
A. General-purpose application
B. Microsoft Outlook
C. Web-hosted technology
D. Office Live
E. None of these

82. What feature adjusts the top and bottom margins so that the text is centered vertically on the printed page?
A. Vertical justifying
B. Vertical adjusting
C. Dual centering
D. Horizontal centering
E. Vertical centering

83. Which of these is **not** a means of personal communication on the internet?
A. chat B. instant messaging
C. instanotes D. electronic mail
E. None of these

84. What is the overall term for creating, editing, formating, storing, retrieving, and printing a text document?
A. Word processing
B. Spreadsheet design
C. Web design
D. Database management
E. Presentation generation

85. Fourth-generation mobile technology provides enhanced capabilities allowing the transfer of both .... data, including full-motion video, high-speed internet access, and video-conferencing.
A. video data and information
B. voice and nonvoice
C. music and video
D. video and audio
E. None of these

86. .... is a form of denial of service attack in which a hostile client repeatedly sends SYN packets to every port on the server using fake IP addresses.
A. Cybergaming crime
B. Memory shaving
C. Syn flooding
D. Software piracy
E. None of these

87. Which of these is a point-and-draw device?
A. mouse B. scanner
C. printer D. CD-ROM
E. keyboard

88. The letter and number of the intersecting column and row is the—
A. cell location
B. cell position
C. cell address
D. cell coordinates
E. cell contents

89. A set of rules for telling the computer what operations to perform is called a—
A. procedural language
B. structures
C. natural language
D. command language
E. programming language

90. A detailed written description of the programming cycle and the program, along with the test results and a printout of the program is called—
A. documentation B. output
C. reporting D. spec sheets
E. Directory

91. Forms that are used to organize business data into rows and columns are called—
A. transaction sheets B. registers
C. business forms D. sheet-spreads
E. spreadsheets

92. In Power Point, the Header & Footer button can be found on the Insert tab in what group?
A. Illustrations group B. Object group
C. Text group D. Tables group
E. None of these

93. A(n) .... is a set of programs designed to manage the resources of a computer, including starting the computer, managing programs, managing memory and coordinating tasks between input and output devices.
A. application suite
B. compiler
C. input/output system
D. interface
E. operating system (OS)

94. A typical slide in a slide presentation would **not** include—
A. photo images charts and graphs
B. graphs and clip art
C. clip art and audio clips
D. full-motion video
E. content templates

95. The PC productivity tool that manipulates data organized in rows and columns is called a—
A. spreadsheet
B. word processing document
C. presentation mechanism
D. database record manager
E. EDI creator

96. In the absence of parentheses, the order of operation is —
A. Exponentiation, addition or subtraction, multiplication or division
B. Addition or subtraction, multiplication or division, exponentiation
C. Multiplication or division, exponentiation, addition or subtraction
D. Exponentiation, multiplication or division, addition or subtraction
E. Addition or subtraction, exponentiation, Multiplication or division

97. To find the Paste Special option, you use the Clipboard group on the ...... tab of PowerPoint.
A. Design B. Slide Show
C. Page Layout D. Insert
E. Home

98. Which view display miniature images of photographs within a folder?
A. Tiles view and Icons view
B. Thumbnails view and Filmstrip view
C. Details view and List view
D. All views display a miniature image
E. None of these

99. Usually downloaded into folders that hold temporary internet files, ... are written to your computer's hard disk by some of the Web sites you visit.
A. anonymous files B. behaviour files
C. banner ads D. large files
E. cookies

100. What is the easiest way to change the phrase, revenues, profits, gross margin, to read revenues, profit and gross margin?
A. Use the insert mode, position the cursor before the g in gross, then type the word and followed by a space
B. Use the insert mode, position the cursor after the g in gross, then type the word and followed by a space
C. Use the overtype mode, position the cursor before the g in gross, then type the word and followed by a space
D. Use the overtype mode, position the cursor after the g in gross, then type the word and followed by a space
E. None of these

101. A program, either talk or music, that is made available in digital format for automatic download over the internet is called a —
A. wiki B. broadcast
C. vodcast D. blog
E. podcast

102. Which PowerPoint view displays each slide of the presentation as a thumbnail and is useful for rearranging slides?
A. Slide Sorter B. Slide Show
C. Slide Master D. Notes Page
E. Slide Design

103. Different components on the motherboard of a PC unit are linked together by sets of parallel electrical conducting lines. What are these lines called?
A. Conductors B. Buses
C. Connectors D. Consecutives
E. None of these

104. What is the name given to those applications that combine text, sound, graphics, motion video, and/or animation?
A. motionware B. anigraphics
C. videoscapes D. multimedia
E. maxomedia

105. A USB communication device that supports data encryption for secure wireless communication for notebook users is called a—
A. USB wireless network adapter
B. wireless switch
C. wireless hub
D. router
E. None of these

106. A(n) .... language reflects the way people think mathematically.
A. cross-platform programming
B. 3GL business programming
C. event-driven programming
D. functional
E. None of these

107. When entering text within a document, the Enter key is normally pressed at the end of every—
A. Line B. Sentence
C. Paragraph D. Word
E. File

108. When a real-time telephone call between people is made over the Internet using computers, it is called—
A. a chat session
B. an e-mail
C. an instant message
D. Internet telephony
E. None of these

109. Which of the following is the first step in sizing a window?
A. Point to the title bar
B. Pull down the View menu to display the toolbar
C. Point to any corner or border
D. Pull down the View menu and change to large icons
E. None of these

110. Which of the following software could assist someone who **cannot** use their hands for computer input?
A. Video conferencing
B. Speech recognition
C. Audio digitizer
D. Synthesizer
E. None of these

111. .... a document means the file is transferred from another computer to your computer.
A. Uploading
B. Really Simple Syndication (RSS)
C. Accessing
D. Downloading
E. Upgrading

112. Which computer memory is used for storing programs and data currently being processed by the CPU?
A. Mass memory
B. Internal memory
C. Non-volatile memory
D. PROM
E. None of these

113. Computers that control processes accept data in a continuous—
A. data traffic pattern
B. data highway
C. infinite loop
D. feedback loop
E. slot

114. What refers to a set of characters of a particular design?
A. keyface B. formation
C. calligraph D. stencil
E. typeface

115. .... is used by public and private enterprises to publish and share financial information with each other and industry analysts across all computer platforms and the Internet.
A. Extensible Markup Language (EML)
B. Extensible Business Reporting Language (XBRL)
C. Enterprise Application Integration (EAI)
D. Sales Force Automation (SFA) software
E. None of these

116. Which part of the computer is used for calculating and comparing?
A. ALU B. Control unit
C. Disk unit D. Modem
E. None of these

117. The method of Internet access that requires a phone line, but offers faster access speeds than dial-up is the .... connection.
A. cable access
B. satellite access
C. fibre-optic service
D. Digital Subscriber Line (DSL)
E. modem

118. .... software creats a mirror image of the entire hard disk, including the operating system, application, files and data.
A. Operating system B. Backup software
C. Utility programs D. Driver imaging
E. None of these

119. What is a URL?
A. a computer software program
B. a type of programming object
C. the address of a document or "page" on the World Wide Web
D. an acronym for Unlimited Resources for Learning
E. a piece of hardware

120. What is the significance of a faded (dimmed) command in a pull-down menu?
A. The command is not currently accessible
B. A dialog box appears if the command is selected
C. A Help window appears if the command is selected

D. There are no equivalent keystrokes for the particular command
E. None of these

121. Your business has contracted with another company to have them host and run an application for your company over the Internet. The company providing this service to your business is called an —
A. Internet service provider
B. Internet access provider
C. Application service provider
D. Application access provider
E. Outsource agency

122. A(n) .... allows you to access you e-mail from anywhere.
A. Forum
B. Webmail interface
C. Message Board
D. Weblog
E. None of these

123. Which of the following would you find on Linkedln?
A. Games B. Connections
C. Chat D. Applications
E. None of these

124. .... is a technique that is used to send more than one call over a single line.
A. Digital transmission
B. Infrared transmission
C. Digitizing
D. Streaming
E. Multiplexing

125. The Search Companion can —
A. Locate all files containing a specified phrase
B. Restrict its search to a specified set of folders
C. Locate all files containing a specified phrase and restrict its search to a specified set of folders
D. Cannot locate all files containing a specified phrase or restrict its search to a specified set of folders
E. None of these

126. Which of the following **cannot** be part of an e-mail address?
A. Period (.) B. At sign (@)
C. Space ( ) D. Underscore (_)
E. None of these

127. Which of the following must be contained in a URL?
A. a protocol identifier
B. the letters, www.
C. the unique registered domain name
D. www. and the unique registered domain name
E. a protocol identifier, www. and the unique registered domain name

128. Which of the following information systems focuses on making manufacturing processes more efficient and of higher quality?
A. Computer-aided manufacturing
B. Computer-integrated manufacturing
C. Computer-aided software engineering
D. Computer-aided system engineering
E. None of these

129. A mistake in an algorithm that causes **incorrect** results is called a—
A. logical error B. syntax error
C. procedural error D. compiler error
E. machine error

130. Unsolicited e-mail is known as—
A. spam B. bologna
C. RAMJAM D. ham
E. None of these

131. To change selected text to all capital letters, click the change case button, then click ....
A. UPPERCASE B. UPPER ALL
C. CAPS LOCK D. Lock Upper
E. Large Size

132. A person who used his or her expertise to gain access to other people's computers to get information illegally or do damage is a ....
A. hacker
B. analyst
C. instant messenger
D. programmer
E. spammer

133. A device that connects to a network without the use of cables is said to be ....
A. distributed B. free
C. centralized D. open source
E. None of these

134. Reusable optical storage will typically have the acronym ....
A. CD B. DVD
C. ROM D. RW
E. ROS

135. The most common type of storage devices are ....
A. persistent B. optical
C. magnetic D. flash
E. steel

136. Codes consisting of lines of varying widths or lengths that are computer-readable are known as–
A. an ASCII code
B. a magnetic tape
C. an OCR scanner
D. a bar code
E. None of these

137. A Web site's main page is called its–
A. Home Page
B. Browser Page
C. Search Page
D. Bookmark
E. None of these

138. Part number, part description, and number of parts ordered are examples of–
A. control B. output
C. processing D. feedback
E. input

139. To access properties of an object, the mouse technique to use is–
A. dragging B. dropping
C. right-clicking D. shift-clicking
E. None of these

140. Computers use the .... number system to store data and perform calculations.
A. binary B. octal
C. decimal D. hexadecimal
E. None of these

141. .... are attempts by individuals to obtain confidential information from you by falsifying their identity.
A. Phishing trips B. Computer viruses
C. Spyware scams D. Viruses
E. Phishing scams

142. Why is it unethical to share copyrighted files with your friends?
A. It is not unethical, because it is legal.
B. It is unethical because the files are being given for free.
C. Sharing copyrighted files without permission breaks copyright laws.
D. It is not unethical because the files are being given for free.
E. It is not unethical—anyone can access a computer.

143. Which of the following can be used to select the entire document?
A. CTRL + A B. ALT + F5
C. SHIFT + A D. CTRL + K
E. CTRL + H

144. To instruct Word to fit the width of a column to the contents of a table automatically, click the .... button and then point to AutoFit Contents.
A. Fit to Form B. Format
C. Autosize D. Contents
E. AutoFit

145. The simultaneous processing of two or more programs by multiple processors is–
A. multiprogramming B. multitasking
C. time-sharing D. multiprocessing
E. None of these

146. A disk's content that is recorded at the time of manufacture and that cannot be changed or erased by the user is–
A. memory-only B. write-only
C. once-only D. run-only
E. read-only

147. What is the permanent memory built into your computer called?
A. RAM B. Floppy
C. CPU D. CD-ROM
E. ROM

148. The default view in Excel is .... view.
A. Work B. Auto
C. Normal D. Roman
E. None of these

149. What displays the contents of the active cell in Excel?
A. Namebox B. RowHeadings
C. Formulabar D. Taskpane
E. None of these

150. In Word you can force a page break–
A. By positioning your cursor at the appropriate place and pressing the F1 key
B. By positioning your cursor at the appropriate place and pressing Ctrl+Enter
C. By using the Insert/Section Break
D. By changing the font size of your document
E. None of these

151. Grouping and processing all of a firm's transactions at one time is called–
A. a database management system
B. batch processing
C. a real-time system
D. an on-line system
E. None of these

152. Help Menu is available at which button?
A. End B. Start
C. Turn off D. Restart
E. Reboot

153. You can keep your personal files/folders in–
A. My Folder B. My Documents
C. My Files D. My Text
E. None of these

154. A central computer that holds collections of data and programs for many PCs, work-stations, and other computers is a(n) –
A. supercomputer B. minicomputer
C. laptop D. server
E. None of these

155. When you save to this, your data will remain intact even when the computer is turned off–
A. RAM
B. motherboard
C. secondary storage device
D. primary storage device
E. None of these

156. The .... folder retains copies of messages that you have started but are not yet ready to send.
A. Drafts B. Outbox
C. Address Book D. Sent Items
E. Inbox

157. You can..........a search by providing more information the search engine can use to select a smaller, more useful set of results.
A. refine B. expand
C. load D. query
E. slowdown

158. The contents of .... are lost when the computer turns off.
A. storage B. input
C. output D. memory
E. None of these

159. The .... enables you to simultaneously keep multiple Web pages open in one browser window.
A. tab box B. pop-up helper
C. tab row D. address bar
E. Esc key

160. A DVD is an example of a(n) –
A. hard disk
B. optical disc
C. output device
D. solid-state storage device
E. None of these

161. The basic unit of a worksheet into which you enter data in Excel is called a ....
A. tab B. cell
C. box D. range
E. None of these

162. .... is the process of dividing the disk into tracks and sectors.
A. Tracking
B. Formatting
C. Crashing
D. Allotting
E. None of these

163. Which ports connect special types of music instruments to sound cards?
A. BUS B. CPU
C. USB D. MIDI
E. MINI

164. The process of transferring files from a computer on the Internet to your computer is called ....
A. downloading B. uploading
C. FTP D. JPEG
E. downsizing

165. In Excel, ... allows users to bring together copies of work books that other users have worked on independently.
A. Copying B. Merging
C. Pasting D. Compiling
E. None of these

166. If you want to connect to your own computer through the Internet from another location, you can use–
A. e-mail B. FTP
C. instant message D. Telnet
E. None of these

167. To reload a Web page, press the .... button.
A. Redo B. Reload
C. Restore D. Ctrl
E. Refresh

168. Mobile Commerce is best described as–
A. The use of Kiosks in marketing
B. Transporting products
C. Buying and selling goods/services through wireless handheld devices
D. Using notebook PC's in marketing
E. None of the above

169. Video processors consist of .... and .... , which store and process images.
A. CPU and VGA B. CPU and memory
C. VGA and memory D. VGI and DVI
E. None of these

170. ...., are words that a programming language has set aside for its own use.
A. Control words B. Control structures
C. Reserved words D. Reserved keys
E. None of these

171. What is the process of copying software programs from secondary storage media to the hard disk called?
A. configuration B. download
C. storage D. upload
E. installation

172. This first step in the transaction processing cycle captures business data through various modes such as optical scanning or at an electronic commerce website–
A. Document and report generation
B. Database maintenance
C. Transaction·processing start-up
D. Data Entry
E. None of these

173. When the pointer is positioned on a ...., it is shaped like a hand.
A. Grammar error B. Formatting error
C. ScreenTip D. Spelling error
E. Hyperlink

174. The computer abbreviation KB usually means–
A. Key Block B. Kernel Boot
C. Key Byte D. Kit Bit
E. Kilo Byte

175. Which of the following are advantages of CD-ROM as a storage media?
A. CD-ROM is an inexpensive way to store large amount of data and information
B. CD-ROM disks retrieve data and information more quickly than magnetic disks do
C. CD-ROMs make less errors than magnetic media
D. All of the above
E. None of the above

176. A(n) ....is a special visual and audio effect applied in PowerPoint to text or content.
A. animation B. flash
C. wipe D. dissolve
E. None of these

177. Which of the following is a storage device that uses rigid, permanently installed magnetic disks to store data/information–
A. floppy diskette B. hard disk

C. permanent disk D. optical disk
E. None of these

178. The piece of hardware that converts your computer's digital signal to an analog signal that can travel over telephone lines is called a–
A. red wire B. blue cord
C. tower D. modem
E. None of these

179. Personal computers can be connected together to form a–
A. server B. supercomputer
C. network D. enterprise
E. None of these

180. A .... is the term used when a search engine returns a Web page that matches the search criteria.
A. blog B. hit
C. link D. view
E. success

181. What type of resource is most likely to be a shared common resource in a computer network?
A. Printers
B. Speakers
C. Floppy disk drives
D. Keyboards
E. None of these

182. Example of non-numeric data is ....
A. Employee address B. Examination score
C. Bank balance D. All of these
E. None of these

183. ....represents raw facts, whereas .... is data made meaningful.
A. Information, reporting
B. Data, information
C. Information, bits
D. Records, bytes
E. Bits, bytes

184. A word in a web page that, when clicked, opens another document ....
A. Anchor B. URL
C. Hyperlink D. Reference
E. None of these

185. A computer cannot "boot" if it does not have the ....
A. Compiler B. Loader
C. Operating System D. Assembler
E. None of these

186. What characteristic of read-only memory (ROM) makes it useful?
A. ROM information can be easily updated
B. Data in ROM is nonvolatile, that is, it remains there even without electrical power
C. ROM provides very large amounts of inexpensive data storage
D. ROM chips are easily swapped between different brands of computers
E. None of these

187. Which of the following refers to a small, single-site network?
A. LAN B. DSL
C. RAM D. USB
E. CPU

188. Which keystroke will take you at the beginning or the end of a long document?
A. Ctrl + PageUp and Ctrl + PageDown
B. Shift + Home and Shift + End
C. Ctrl + Home and Ctrl + End
D. The only way is by using the right scroll bar
E. None of these

189. Coded entries which are used to gain access to a computer system are called ....
A. Entry codes B. Passwords
C. Security commands D. Code words
E. None of these

190. In Word you can force a page break ....
A. By positioning your cursor at the appropriate place and pressing the F1 key
B. By using the Insert/Section Break
C. By positioning your cursor at the appropriate place and pressing Ctrl+Enter
D. By changing the font size of your document
E. None of these

ANSWERS

1	2	3	4	5	6	7	8	9	10
B	A	D	A	D	A	C	C	A	A
11	12	13	14	15	16	17	18	19	20
E	D	D	E	B	B	A	E	C	B
21	22	23	24	25	26	27	28	29	30
C	D	A	E	C	E	D	B	A	C
31	32	33	34	35	36	37	38	39	40
C	A	D	C	C	D	E	B	C	E
41	42	43	44	45	46	47	48	49	50
A	D	A	D	A	C	E	B	C	C
51	52	53	54	55	56	57	58	59	60
A	D	B	D	B	D	E	B	A	B
61	62	63	64	65	66	67	68	69	70
D	A	A	D	B	B	A	D	C	A
71	72	73	74	75	76	77	78	79	80
C	B	B	D	D	C	B	A	C	B
81	82	83	84	85	86	87	88	89	90
C	E	C	A	B	C	A	C	E	A
91	92	93	94	95	96	97	98	99	100
E	C	E	E	A	D	E	B	E	A
101	102	103	104	105	106	107	108	109	110
E	A	B	D	A	D	C	D	C	B
111	112	113	114	115	116	117	118	119	120
D	B	D	E	B	A	D	B	C	A
121	122	123	124	125	126	127	128	129	130
E	B	B	E	C	C	C	B	A	A
131	132	133	134	135	136	137	138	139	140
A	A	E	B	C	D	A	E	C	A
141	142	143	144	145	146	147	148	149	150
A	C	A	A	D	E	E	C	C	B
151	152	153	154	155	156	157	158	159	160
C	B	B	D	D	A	A	B	C	B
161	162	163	164	165	166	167	168	169	170
B	B	C	A	B	D	E	C	C	C
171	172	173	174	175	176	177	178	179	180
E	D	C	E	D	A	B	D	C	C
181	182	183	184	185	186	187	188	189	190
A	A	B	C	C	B	A	A	B	C

●●●

LIBRARY AND INFORMATION SCIENCE

FUNDAMENTALS OF LIBRARY AND INFORMATION SCIENCE

LIBRARY SCIENCE

Library and Information Science is an "interrelated science that deals with the properties and behaviour of information and controls the flow and use of information, of processing information for maximum storage, retrieval and dissemination." It is related with maths, psychology, information science, arts, management and other subjects.

Library Science and Information Science all are mainly connected with processing of information for storage, retrieval and dissemination. It is changing according to the needs of library users and the library management has to adopt new technologies to satisfy the users.

In America, the term Documentation was replaced by Information Science in mid seventies. In several countries, the library science and information science are treated as independent subjects for studying and understanding. But in India, we study library science and information science as one subject.

Concept parallelism between Library Science & Information Science:

Concept	Library Science	Information Science
1. Unit	Library Centre	Information Centre
2. Medium	Book	Data Base
3. User	Reader	Recipient
4. Staff	Librarian	Information Officer
5. Service	On Demand	As & When needed
6. Tool	Catalogue	Controlled Vocabulary

INFORMATION SOCIETY

The world has seen three main important revolutions. These are as follows:

(1) Agricultural; (2) Industrial;
(3) Technological or Informational.

These three revolutions brought splendid changes in the physical, social and economical environment and behaviour of human society.

With the help of Agricultural revolution, human society became the master of agriculture and their social life began to grow. With Industrial revolution, the human society got more unbanisation and mass production and importantly economical changes in the world.

INFORMATION AS A RESOURCE

Information is regarded as a national "resource" like energy, water, air etc., and an important 'thing' for the progress of a nation. The impact of fast, reliable and inexpensive information will be as great as that of electricity in national and international economy. IBM, the computer company says that the information is like an inexhaustible and renewable source of energy.

It is also regarded as a "commodity" because continuum ranging from raw data to finished information, its regulation will be affected in the future by the value of information as it is taken by tax authorities. It may be expensive or cheap like any other commodity.

ROLE OF INFORMATION

1. It is used in research and development with the help of information, R&D saves time, money and research potential.
2. It helps in Industries and Business by Telemarketing, Customer Service, Product Development, Identification of products, materials etc.

3. Planning Commission and Policy making are greatly depend upon the availability of information for planning and policy making.
4. Information provides a means of improving the management of enterprises and services of all kinds. Such as Data Base Management System (D.B.M.S.), M.I.S. provide help in decision making.

COLLECTION & STORAGE

After being generated, the information must be collected in any form for future use. Collection of Information is mainly depends on whether it is print material or non print material.

But in recent days, collection of information is done as follows:

1. **Libraries** are the oldest institutions charged with the responsibility of collecting information. The invention of printing by movable types of Johannes Guntenberg and large scale production of printed books enabled and libraries to change their attitude from prerservation, collection to use.
2. **Documentation centres** are evolved with the increasing research, scientific periodicals gained importance. A new set of techniques like indexing, abstracting, union catalogues etc. are developed. In addition translation, micro-photography etc. are also adopted to meet the needs of the specialist users. Efforts are started to collect information as micro-literature. Automation and computerisation are initiated. These new activities are given a new name called ***Documentation***.
3. **Information centres** are developed for collecting and storing of information resulted in the development and use of new tools, techniques and services. Use of computers, networking, online retrieval, compact disc storage etc. are the new tools & techniques pressed into use. Computerised collection & storage, machine indexing and abstracting, computerised databases, online search facilities etc. are introduced.
4. **New services** are modified, diversified and developed to meet the special needs of the users. Selective Dissemination of Information (S.D.I.), a service designed to identify the most suitable documents to a specific user.

The Present Information Chain:

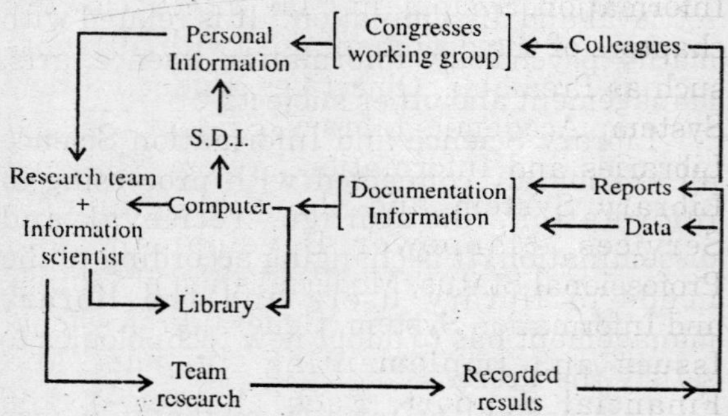

LIBRARY & INFORMATION POLICY AT THE NATIONAL LEVEL: INDIAN SCENARIO

National Information Policy is a set of decisions taken by a government, through set laws and regulations, to orient the development of information transfer activities in order to satisfy the information needs of the country. It needs necessary instruments such as financial, personnel, institutional, for concrete implementation.

FOCUS ON A NATIONAL LIBRARY AND INFORMATION POLICY

Professional Associations like the Indian Library Association (ILA), the Indian Association of Special Libraries and Information Centres (IASLIC), the Society for Information Science (SIS), have been urging the government to initiate efforts towards formulating a National Information Policy, through a number of seminars and conferences. Separate draft policy statements were prepared by ILA and The Raja Rammohan Roy Library Foundation and submitted to the Government of India in 1984. As s consequence, the Department of Culture set up a Committee in October 1985 under the chairmanship of Professor D.P. Chattopadhyay for the formulation of a National Policy on Library and Information System.

After considerable efforts, the Committee submitted a Draft Policy on Library and Information System in May 1986. The ten chapters of the document deal with elements such as Preamble, Objectives, Public Library System, Academic Library System, Special Libraries and Information System, National Library System and the Bibliographical Services, Manpower Development and Professional Status, Modernisation of Library and Information System, General Professional Issues and Implementing Agencies and Financial Support. Each chapter makes specific recommendations with reference to upgrading and coordinating the existing library and information systems and services and initiating new programmes relevant to our national needs, using Information Technology.

LIBRARY & INFORMATION SCIENCE EDUCATION IN INDIA

With the education of Library Science, we can make an educated world or society for enhancing Library and Information services. For a well organised and better services of Library, all the workers, Astt. Librarian and Librarian must have the knowledge & proper education of Library Science.

First of all, *Sir Morris Gayer* approved the Library Science education in India at University of Delhi, because he thought without Library services and Library education, no society could attain its social development.

AIMS AND NEED OF LIBRARY & INFORMATION SCIENCE EDUCATION

Library is an important institution. It needs special workers to maintain it and it can be preserved and developed with the help of Library and Information science education. Library Science education is a technical subject and librarianship is its service.

Library and Information science education has two main aims:

A. General aim applies on every level of its education. These are as follows:

1. Training for technical service of libraries.
2. Preparation of desired workers for libraries for maintaining.
3. Giving knowledge of other subject other than library techniques.
4. Training for working librarians.

B. Special aim applies to special levels of its education. In India, mainly there are three courses in Library & Information science education except research (Ph.D.):

1. Certificate/Diploma of Library & Information Science (C.Lib./D.Lib)

In this course, the students get the knowledge and training about basic element and rules of library. Its eligibility condition is 10th/12th with 45% from recognised board (Regular/ Distance mode).

2. Bachelor of Library & Information Science (BLI Sc. or B.Lib.):

In this course, knowledge of basic rules are given and its understanding; training of cataloguing, classification, techniques used in libraries and modern situation of library science are given. To take admission in it, the eligibility criteria is any Graduation degree with 50% or D.Lib with 50% + 12th (in any stream).

3. Master of Library & Information Science (M.Lib./MLI Sc.)– In this course, following knowledge & training are given:

(a) Development & Evolution of Information science.
(b) Research methodology & practice.
(c) Writing of catalogue.
(d) Classification writing style.
(e) Administration of Libraries.
(f) Library automation.

Its eligibility criteria is any Graduation degree + B.lib/BLISc. with 50% in both.

HISTORY OF LIBRARY & INFORMATION SCIENCE EDUCATION IN INDIA

Firstly, Library Science education started in Baroda in 1911 (unofficially). The king of Baroda invited a student of Melvil Dewey, William A. Borden to establish a library and to give library science education. On other hand, Punjab university also invited a student of Melvil Dewey, Asa Dew Dickenson from America to open a Library Science College in 1915 at Punjab. It gave the education upto 1947.

Bengal Library Assiciation also started a Library Science education camp from 1935-1945.

In India, the actual step was taken by Dr. S.R. Ranganathan. He was the Secretary of Madras Library Association and he started the education of Library Science in 1929 with the help of Madras University.

In 1931, Madras University started with certificates given to students after the completion of course. It was of 3 months duration course. In 1937, this was converted into Post Graduate with 1 year duration. In 1941, Banaras Hindu University started "Post Graduate Diploma in Library Science". The year in which these courses started in other universities are:

	University	*Year*
1.	University of Delhi	1947
2.	University of Maharashtra (Mumbai/Pune)	1944
3.	University of Kolkata	1946
4.	Aligarh Muslim University	1951
5.	University of Baroda	1956
6.	Nagpur University	1957

The higher education i.e., M.lib, M.Phil. and Ph.D. first of all have been started by University of Delhi. Dr. S.R. Ranganathan requested the Vice-Chancellor of that time Sir Morris Gayer to start Master of Library Science in 1948. In 1964, several other universities had started these courses.

Mr. D.B. Krishna Rao was the first person to get Ph.D. in Library & Information Science from University of Delhi in 1957.

PRESENT SCENE

Now, it has became a professional course for the students and this education is getting more attention of the parents and students.

Several other central and state universities are running courses like B.Lib; M.Lib; M.Phil and Ph.D. of duration one year for B.Lib, M.Lib, M.Phil and 3-5 years for Ph.D. depends on research area selected. There is separate department of Library and Information Science in all universities. Several Universities have started programmes to give practical knowledge to teachers of Library Science to train students for enhancing the Library services in India.

The review committee of University Grants Commission in 1965 proposed that there must be one teacher for ten students for B.Lib. course and one teacher for fifteen students for M.Lib. course. There must be one Reader and two Lecturers for B.Lib course and one Professor, two Readers and four Lecturers for M.lib. course". The committee also proposed the infrastructure of Library & Informaiton department as below–

1. Two Lecturer room; 2. One Practical room; 3. One Reading room; 4. Separate room for every teacher; 5. One seminar room; 6. One presentation room; 7. An Administration room; 8. And a grant of Rupees one lakh in every sixth month.

The list of some universities of India is given, which are running courses of Library & Information Science education.

COURSES

	University	C.Lib	B.Lib.	M. Lib	M.Phil.	Ph.D.
1.	Agra		✓	✓		
2.	Aligarh		✓		✓	
3.	Andhra Pradesh	✓	✓	✓	✓	
4.	Annamallai		✓	✓		
5.	B.H.U.		✓	✓		
6.	Bangalore		✓	✓		
7.	Baroda		✓	✓		
8.	Bahrampur		✓	✓		
9.	Bhagalpur		✓	✓		
10.	Bardwan		✓	✓		
11.	Calicat		✓	✓		
12.	Delhi		✓	✓	✓	✓
13.	Gujarat		✓			
14.	Guwahati		✓	✓		
15.	Gulberg		✓	✓		
16.	I.G.N.O.U.		✓	✓		✓
17.	I.S.I; Bangalore	✓				
18.	Manipur		✓			
19.	Madurai		✓	✓		
20.	Magdh		✓			
21.	Mysore		✓	✓		
22.	Punjab		✓	✓		
23.	Pune		✓	✓		
24.	Rajasthan		✓	✓		
25.	Rajkot		✓			
26.	Mumbai		✓	✓		
27.	Udaipur		✓	✓		
28.	Tirupati		✓	✓		
29.	J.N.U.		✓	✓	✓	✓
30.	Jamia		✓			

Several State Library Associations and Indian Library Association are running Certificate and Diploma courses in Library & Information Science to enhance and develop more manpower for Library services in India.

MULTIPLE CHOICE QUESTIONS

1. Study of interrelated science that deals with the properties and behaviour of information and controls the flow and use of information, of processing information for maximum storage, retrieval and dissemination is—

A. Information Technology
B. Information Science
C. Library Science
D. Computer Science

2. Which of the following term may replace the term Documentation?

A. Information Science
B. Computer Science
C. Production System
D. Document Delivery

3. In Library science, the medium is book. What is the medium in Information Science?

A. Information B. Data base
C. Knowledge D. All of these

4. Informatics is—

A. Information Science
B. Information Technology
C. Information Cycle
D. None of these

5. The main components of Information Technology are—

A. Computer and Communication Technology
B. Reprographic Technology and Micrographic Technology
C. Both of above
D. None of above

6. Integrated Services Digital Network (I.S.D.N.) is an example of—

A. Computer technology
B. Communication technology
C. Reprographic technology
D. None of above

7. Document Delivery Service (DDS) is depends on—
A. Micrographic technology
B. Reprographic technology
C. Computer technology
D. Internet

8. Which statement/s is/are correct?
1. Information is regarded as a commodity.
2. It is like an inexhaustible and renewable source of energy.
A. Only 1 B. Only 2
C. Both 1 & 2 D. None of these

9. Information is generated by—
A. Surveys and Censuses
B. Research and Development
C. Government Activities
D. All the above

10. Large scale use of information has converted the present knowledge society into—
A. Information age
B. Information society
C. Information explosion
D. Only A & B

11. Collection of information is done in—
A. Libraries
B. Documentation centres
C. Information
D. All of these

12. In the scientific field, books are known as—
A. Micrographs B. Reprographs
C. Monographs D. All of these

13. Which of the following services is designated to identify the most suitable documents to a specific user?
A. Document Delivery Serivce
B. Selective Dissemination of Information
C. Internet Link Service
D. Any of the above

14. The service of providing urgent and quick information to a user is—
A. Selective Dissemination of Information
B. Current Awareness services
C. Document Delivery Services
D. Any of the above

15. The barrier/s to communication of informaton is/ are —
A. Institutional and Financial
B. Technical and Linguistic
C. Social and Administrative
D. All of the above

16. The set of decisions taken by Government, through set laws and regulations, to orient and development of information transfer activities in order to satisfy the information needs of the country is—
A. National Information Policy
B. National Curriculum
C. Annual Policy
D. Internatioanl Organisational Policy

17. The reason/s to go for National Information Policy is/ are—
A. Information may be used as wealth
B. Different categories in information transfer
C. Information revolution has come
D. All of the above

18. A.A. Code of 1908 (Cataloguing) was compiled by—
A. ALA B. LC
C. ILA D. None of the above

19. BSO was drafted in the year—
A. 1970 B. 1971
C. 1980 D. 1981

20. Who was the Chairman of formulation committee for National Policy for Library and Information Science in 1985?
A. Prof. D.P. Chattopadhyay
B. Prof. K.N. Raj
C. Dr. S. Swaminathan
D. Dr. N.R. Subramanium

21. UNESCO attemped to make user education programmes through—
A. NISSAT B. UNISIST
C. INIS D. AGRIS

22. Resource sharing eliminated duplication of money, manpower and—
A. language B. material
C. religion D. time

23. The Headquarters of _____ is located at Chicago—
A. FID B. AIM
C. ALA D. IFLA

24. IFLA's headquarters is Located at—
A. Paris B. Chicago
C. London D. The Hague

25. PRECIS was developed by Derek Austin for use in the—
A. BNB B. INB
C. ISBN D. ISBD

26. Subject heading list and thesauri are two types of _____ indexing language.
A. natural B. free
C. Controlled D. none of these

27. PRECIS and POPSI are the examples of _____ indexing model.
A. post-coordinate B. Pre-coordinate
C. natural D. free

28. Computer Aided Subject System was introduced for _____ in 1991.
A. INB B. ABPR
C. BNB D. Bolles in Print

29. The world Cat Services is provided by —
A. LC B. WLN
C. OCLC D. RLIN

30. Which is the world's largest and most comprehensive bibliographic database?
A. First search
B. OCLC Access service
C. World Cat
D. Prompt Cat

31. Many times the term information is synonymously used with other terms like _____ knowledge etc.
A. news B. library
C. data D. intelligence

32. The human activities result in _____ of information.
A. dissemination B. generation
C. storage D. retrievel

33. _____ are used for handling large mass of information and for quick retrieval of the desired items from it.
A. Book stacks B. Computers
C. Books shops D. Libraries

34. According to definition of Unesco document, _____ is made up of symbolic elements, communicating scientific and technical knowledge irrespective of their nature (numerical, textual, graphic etc.), material carrier and form of presentation.
A. information B. data
C. intelligence D. books

35. The term 'news', 'data', and 'knowledge' are related to the concept of and synonymous with _____
A. advice B. facts
C. information D. wisdom

36. The term 'data' may be described as discrete and _____ piece of information.
A. organised B. unorganised
C. systematised D. processes

37. When some existing exchange control regulation are amended, the notifications are published regularly in Reserve Bank of India Bulletin. This is an example of _____
A. data B. information
C. knowledge D. news

38. The analysed information in social science maybe categorised into statistical information, descriptive information and _____
A. Discrete information
B. unorganised information
C. analytical information
D. societal information

39. The review literature type of document is an example of _____ information.
A. statistical B. descriptive
C. analytical D. documentary

40. The national income statistics data when collected, described, analysed or interpreted is known as _____ information.
A. analytical B. descriptive
C. statistical D. collected

41. Knowledge is an organised body of _____
A. facts B. data
C. intelligence D. information

42. The progress of a nation is often judged by the percentage of _____ income spent on R&D.
A. individual B. educational
C. national D. local

43. Industrial revolution took place in
A. late 18th century
B. late 19th century
C. middle of 20th century
D. early 19th century

44. The large scale growth in the organised body of information and continuous addition of output of current research activities characterises the phenomenon _____
A. explosion of books
B. explosion of research
C. explosion of organized body
D. information explosion

45. Office of the Registrar of India conducts _____ censuses to collect population data of the country.
A. annual B. biennial
C. triennial D. decennial

46. Researchers are _____ of information.
A. generators
B. consumers
C. organizers
D. both consumers and generators

47. _____ need information for imparting education.
A. Researchers
B. Students
C. Medical practioners
D. Teachers

48. Government officials need information for _____.
A. Keeping up with current development
B. decision making
C. solving technical snags on shop floor
D. identifying gaps in the existing knowledge

49. Information and knowledge are the central instruments of change in—
A. Industrial society
B. Information society
C. Agricultural society
D. Business society

50. The structure of US-MARC format comprises _____ components.
A. 2 B. 3
C. 4 D. 8

ANSWERS

1	2	3	4	5	6	7	8	9	10
B	A	B	A	C	B	B	C	D	D
11	12	13	14	15	16	17	18	19	20
D	C	B	B	D	A	D	A	B	A
21	22	23	24	25	26	27	28	29	30
B	B	C	D	A	C	A	B	C	B
31	32	33	34	35	36	37	38	39	40
C	B	B	A	C	B	B	C	B	C
41	42	43	44	45	46	47	48	49	50
D	C	C	A	D	D	D	B	B	B

LIBRARY SCIENCE LAWS AND NETWORKING

INTRODUCTION

The five Laws of Library Science were enunciated in 1928 by the Dr. S.R. Ranganathan, the Librarian of the University of Madras. Their first formal exposition occurred at the Provincial Educational Conference held at Chidambaram in December that year. Dr. Ranganathan, after his education in Librarianship in the University of London, School of Librarianship in 1924 and his observation of the working of several libraries in England, has been struggling to discover whether the principles and practices that he observed could be generalised and reduced to certain cardinal principles. In other words, he was in search of some principles which could tell us what should be done in the library field to make library organisation, management and operation efficient and universalise its services. These basic principles may also contain, in a latent form, many other practices not known now and which may surface later. The outcome of this line of thinking of Ranganathan was the formal enunciation of the Five Laws of Libarary Science. These laws are:

(i) ***Books are for use***
(ii) ***Every reader his/ her book***
(iii) ***Every book its reader***
(iv) ***Save the time of the reader***
(v) ***The library is a growing organism***

Every activity relating services has a rationale in one or another of these laws or in all of them collectively. Also, we can examine whether there is anything left undone in a library out of those covered by the laws. The laws, therefore, constitute the philosophical basis for all library work, programs, activities and services.

It is significant to note that these laws are valid and could be seen as governing every activity concerning modern information systems and services. When Ranganathan used the expressions "books" and "readers", he naturally meant that books stand for knowledge and information and readers stand for users of library and information services. In modern studies on knowledge and information and all other related expressions, it must be remembered that the carriers and channels of information and knowledge have changed from print to other forms, but all the services are revolving round information and users. The dimensions of services now have expanded widely in scope but the basic philosophy of the service remains very much unchanged.

Therefore, these five laws can be restated to suit modern developments in information and library systems to suit the changed contexts. The restated laws are:

- **Documents/ informations are for use**
- **Every user his/ her document/ information**
- **Every document/ information its user**
- **Save the Time of the user**
- **Documentation/ information system is a growing organism**

LIBRARY SCIENCE AND NETWORKING

In the present day context, no single library could think of organizing library services entirely based on its own collection. It has, to certain extent, depend on resources external to its collections. The reason for this dependency is ascribed to the rising cost of journals, the growing pressures on library space and the cost of processing and maintaining large collections. In essence, these factors call for effective cooperation among different libraries.

DEVELOPMENTS IN INDIA

The need for networking of libraries with the objective of resource sharing was felt in the 1980s after witnessing a great deal of progress made by the developed countries in this direction. The 'Working Group' of the planning commission on libraries and informatics headed by Dr. N.Seshagiri recommended the need for modernisation of library service and inter-linking of library system during the 7th plan period (1985-1990).

In 1985 NISSAT conveyed a meeting under the chairmanship of Director-General, CSIR. One of the recomendations of this meeting was establishment of a Science and Technology library in Calcutta and the promotion of automation and networking in the city. CMC Ltd. was commissioned by NISSAT to prepare the feasibility report on the Calcutta Network (CALIBNET). The report was completed and published in 1989. In the meanwhile, in January 1988, India International Centre, New Delhi with the support of NISSAT began the work on Delhi Library Network (DELNET) as a project of the centre. In July 1992, it was registered as a society under the registration Act of 1860.

The recommendation of the working group on modernisation of library service and informatics headed by Dr. Seshagiri, paved the way for the establishment of an information and library network (INFLIBNET). The report of INFLIBET was published in 1989. In 1991, INFLIBNET opened its office at Ahmedabad as soon as funds became available under the Eighth Plan, INFLIBNET began its work.

In the meantime proposals were made regarding the establishment of more networks in cities like Chennai, Pune, Mumbai and Bangalore. Therefore, besides CALIBNET, DELNET and INFLIBNET the library networks started in one form or the other in Mumbai, Bangalore, Chennai, Pune and Ahmedabad.

In the following discussion, account of CALIBNET, DELNET and INFLIBNET is presented. These form some selected examples of case studies.

1. CALIBNET

CALIBNET was sponsored by NISSAT which initiated the action for the preparation of a feasibility report by CMC. According to the feasibility report, CALIBNET was to be a network of 40 libraries. It was to be developed in two phases. NISSAT provided funds for the development of software package (MAITRAYEE) based on INGRESS 502 for CALIBNET. The package was developed by CMC Ltd.

Details regarding the total quantity of machine-readable date produced by different participation libraries using MAITRAYEE package of software are not totally available. It is understood that CALIBNET is providing access to INTERNET and is offering CD-ROM databases searching facility. Whether CALIBNET has started the creation of a union catalogue for the books available in the participating libraries is not known.

It appears that CALINBNET has not yet developed itself into a resource sharing network of libraries in Kolkata as was envisaged. A full picture of CALIBNET and the value-added products it has developed so far to aid the resource sharing activity by libraries in Kolkata has yet to emerge. Only then, its achievements can be evaluated critically in the real sense.

2. DELNET

DELNET was originally started as a project of India International Centre (IIC) New Delhi, with the financial support from NISSAT. The financial support continued for the period 1988 to 1992. It became a registered society in

March 1992. Some of the salient features of the network are:

1. It has 67 institutional libraries as its members (the membership is on the increase from year to year).
2. In order to promote resource sharing among member libraries DELENT has, so far, created the following:
   (a) Union catalogue of books available in the member libraries in computer-readable form (1068 lakh records).
   (b) Union list of periodicals (116 libraries) *(i)* Union list of scientific and technical periodicals (7,811 records); *(ii)* Union list of social science periodicals (6919 records); *(iii)* Union list of periodicals in humanities (1178 records).
   (c) Specialists database (1,200 specialists)
   (d) Database of articles (50,000 records)
   (e) Union catalogue of periodicals (2391 records)
   (f) Database of language publication (sample database)
3. **DELSIS**, the networking software based on BASIS plus which can accommodate and retrieve millions of bibliographic and full text records was developed by DELNET itself.
4. **INTERNET** access and E-mail facilities are provided for its members and access to INTERNET is available at DELNET headquarters. Also, DELNET has created a Home page on www. It can be accessed on INTERNET at the following address: HYPERLINK http://www.nic http:// www.nic in/delnet:
5. It is claimed by DELNET that it has saved nearly Rs.1 crore on the part of participating libraries and providing them an exposure to the application of modern technology.
6. **DELNET** has been arranging training programmes for the staff members of the participating libraries and providing them an exposure to the application of modern techology.

It may be stated that DELNET has made a break-through in resource sharing activities and has thus become the first operational library network in India. It is on the path of enlarging its activities and is contemplating to develop an on-line database of 'Books in Print: New Titles', with the cooperation of some renowned publishers.

3. INFLIBNET

The INFLIBNET programme was conceptualised by the then Chairman of UGC Prof. Yash Pal. It was his belief that a library and information network of the magnitude of INFLIBNET is very essential for the country in the present context of computer and communications technologies making a great impact on the provision of library and information services in the developed world. The entire programme envisaged for INFLIBNET has neen described and discussed along with operational details in the document "Development of an Information and Network—Report of the Inter-Agency Working Group UGC, 1988".

Objectives: The objectives of the creation of INFLIBNET as recommended were:

1. to evolve a national network, interconnecting various libraries and information centres in the country and to improve the capability in information handling and service;
2. to provide access to document collection of libraries by creating on-line union catalogue of monographs, serials, and non-book materials;
3. to provide improved access to bibliographic numerical and factual databases with particular emphasis on those databases created indigenously by the Sectoral Information Centres of NISSAT and UGC Information centres;
4. to establish gatways for on-line accessing of information;

5. to provide document delivery service by enriching information sources of libraries having rich collection in specific areas;
6. to implement computerisation of operations and services in libraries and information centres following uniform standards;
7. to enable users disbursed all over the country to have access to information regarding books, monographs, serials, and non-book materials by locating the sources where available, and to obtain them through the facilities of new technologies and union catalogue of documents;
8. to encourage cooperation among libraries, documentation centres, information centres in the country, so that the resources can pooled for the benefit of weaker resource centres by the stronger ones;
9. to develop suitable professional manpower of appropriate quality to establish and manage and sustain the INFLIBNET and;
10. to evolve standards and uniform guidelines in techniques, methods, procedures, hardware and software, and services and so on, and promote adoption in actual practice by all libraries in order to facilitate exchange of resources towards optimisation.

INFLIBNET SERVICES

INFLIBNET is planned and designed as a multiple function/service network. It is expected to provide the following services:

1. Catalogue based service
2. Database services
3. Document supply service
4. Collection development (helping different participants in acquisition, and procurement)
5. Communication based services

CATALOGUE BASED SERVICES

Catalogue service comprise of shared cataloguing of monographs, serials and non-book materials, complication of union catalogue of books, serials and non-book materials, provision of on-line access for shared cataloguing and location identification, assisting in catalogues production in card, book, magnetic tape/floppy, etc.

DATA BASE SERVICES

These include searching of databases for current as well as retrospective services, provision of computer-based SDI and provision of non-bibliographic information such as on-going and completed projects, institution and specialist by compiling, maintaining and searching such non-bibliographic databases.

Document supply services include inter-library loan services and document delivery services through fax/non-fax etc.

Collection development services is basically intended to help the member libraries in selection, acquisition and procurement aspects.

COMMUNICATION BASED SERVICES

These are of different types such as:

- Referral services
- Electronic mail services
- Bulletin Board-view/update bulletin board
- Academic communication through electronic mail, file transfer, computer/ audio/ video conferencing, etc.

INFLIBNET is conceived as a cooperative venture and its resources strength is expected to depend on its participting members and their resources. It is expected that 200 university libraries, 400 special libraries of the R&D organisation and 500 college libraries would form the members of this network.

INFLIBNET intends to provide access to the vast information resources available in the country. The access to information is intended to be provided to all those who might need it. This could become possible only when modern technologies are utilised for the purpose. Hence, the working group report emphasised the use of computers, communications and document delivery technology for data capture, data preparation, information processing and its transfer and delivery.

Due to non-availability of funds, the INFLIBNET is not fully operational but it has been registered as a project under IUCCA and its head office is located at Ahmedabad. The present services are limited to training of manpower, preparation of guidelines for data capturing, encouraging library automation activities, developments of suitable software and implementing at some libraries. It is involved in the organization of seminars and conferences relating to application of information technology. It must be mentioned here that the progress is rather slow. Although automation process was started by funding 54 university libraries, only 17 libraries could only acquire hardware till now. Now achievements could be made in the resource sharing among university libraries during the period 1991-1996, while the working group report envisaged it to be completed by 1994, and end users were supposed to be served by collecting documents from 400 nodes in the county and were likely to get offered modern services. Even the other targets set by the Working Group could not be achieved. The Review Committee report of 1996 mentions the following as achievements of INFLIBNET:

(a) Compilation of a union catalogue (machine-readable) with 5000 records,
(b) Databases of theses/dissertation (65,000 records).
(c) Serials database which contains about 30,000 records.

INFLIBNET Review Committee under the chairmanship of Dr. S. Venkateswaran submitted its report in September, 1996 and inter-alia recommended a revised set of objectives for INFLIBNET. It also emphasised adequate representation of library experts in the Management Board and Council. It remains to be seen how soon UGC accepts INFLIBNET Review Committee recommendations and what follow up action it would take to translate these recommendations into an action plan.

It must be mentioned here that the other library networks such as MALIBNET, BONET etc have not made much progress. It might take a long time for all these networks to become functional and service oriented in the real sense.

LIBRARY LEGISLATION AND MOVEMENT IN INDIA

The public library should serve as a local information centre making the sources of knowledge readily available to the public. Public libraries should stimulate neo-literates, semi-literates, non users to become readers, and serve the population with knowledge and information.

LIBRARY LEGISLATIONS IN INDIA

Ten States of India have put into state book their Public Libraries Act. The chronological sequence is as follows:

(i) **Tamil Nadu:** (Then called Madras Public Libraries Act, 1948)
(ii) **Andhra Pradesh:** (The Hyderabad Public Libraries Act, 1955, as a result of States reorganisation, merged in Andhra Pradesh Public Libraries Act, 1960).
(iii) **Karnataka:** (The Karnataka Public Libraries Act, 1965)
(iv) **Maharashtra:** (The Kolhapur Public Libraries Act was passed in 1945. After States reorganisation, this State of Kolhapur was merged with Maharashtra State. The Maharashtra Public Libraries Act, 1967.)
(v) **Manipur:** (Manipur Public Libraries Act, 1988)
(vii) **Kerala:** (Kerala Public Libraries Act, 1989)
(viii) **Haryana:** (Haryana Public Libraries Act, 1989)
(ix) **Mizoram:** (Mizoram Public Libraries Act, 1993)
(x) **Goa:** (Goa Public Libraries Act, 1994)

(xi) **Pondicherry:** The basic provision of the public library system as depicted in these Acts are discussed here. As stated earlier, library legislation should take care of the following five aspects:

(a) Accessibility of information to all sections of the people.

(b) An establishment of institutional newtork to provide care and preserve documents.

(c) Establishment of committees to provide guidelines in relation to policy-making , decision-making and implementation of service.

(d) Provision of finances and the *modus operandi* for expenditure.

(e) Arrangement of a reporting system of the activities of various public libraries.

We shall discuss these features in each of the ten Acts in the following sections, delineating the provisions made for public library services.

LIBRARY AND INFORMATION SCIENCE PROFESSION

Library associations are learned societies. They promote development of the library movement in a country. They strive for better provision of library and information services. In this process, library associations also strive for advancement of the profession and the professionals.

Professional associations are made up of, by and for the professionals the fields concerned e.g. librarians, library staff members, library science teachers, users of libraries and library associations.

All these sectors are eligible for membership of library association. An associations is what its members make of it by their active collaboration and participation in its programmes and activities. As a fresh entrant to the profession, it is worthwhile for you to know how you can participate in the activities of the professional associations to serve their ultimate cause.

LIBRARY ASSOCIATIONS, SYSTEMS AND PROGRAMMES

Now as a participant in this programme, you are aspiring to qualify yourself to become a library and information professional. You should know your responsibilities and obligations to the profession, i.e. striving for improvement of library and information systems and services and advancement of library and information science. After all, the image of a profession is built up by its members. Qualitative performance of duties and adherence to ethical principles and standards are essential to bring credibility, and to hold the status of the profession high.

PROFESSION, PROFESSIONALS, PROFESSIONALISM

In order to understand properly the technical words relating to professional ethics, we shall study their meanings and contents in this section.

The Random House Dictionary of English Language (RDH) defines:

A Profession, as an occupation, especially that one requiring extensive education in branch of science or the liberal arts; or the body of persons engaged in such an occupation. Synonymous with 'profession' are words such as vocation, employment, occupation, business, trade—all refer to the activity to which a person regularly devotes himself, especially his regular work, or means of getting a living. Whereas 'occupation' is the general word to indicate an activity in which a person is engaged for his living, 'profession' implies an occupation requiring special knowledge and training in some field of science or learning.

A Professional is one who is engaged in an activity as a means of livelihood or for a gain or pertaining to or connected with as profession. For example: a professional tennis player; a researcher; a musician who are all competent experts in their respective occupations.

Professionalism is the professional character, spirit or methods, the standard practices of a professional as distinguished from an amateur. An expertise is expected of professionals with full involvement in and commitment to those who receive services from them.

The age-old professions are agriculture, medicine, education, fine arts (painting, sculpture, music) and such other established occupations, recognized and respected by society, not necessarily measured by the monetary earnings of these professionals. With industrialisation, economic and social growth, many new professions have sprung up in the last two hundred years. More particularly the 20th century has witnessed the growth of hundreds of new professions Librarianship is one such profession that emerged in the 19th/20th Century when corpus of knowledge multiplied geometrically requiring rapid expansion in its nature of work and services of knowledge organisation, retrieval and dissemination.

LIBRARIANSHIP AS A PROFESSION

A Code of Professional Ethics for Librarians describes that "The goal of librarianship is to mediate between humanity and humanity's store of recorded knowledge and information; to encourage an informed, enlightened and empowered citizenry; and to join with others in the fight for intellectual freedom and access to information." To build up this image for the library and information profession, and to establish quality, a set of ethical codes has to be formulated and is to be practised by librarians and information professionals. But before we get to discuss these codes, we shall see to what extent librarianship can be deemed to be a profession.

US SITUATION

Despite all these problems and difficulties, attempts have been made to design a code of ethics for the lirbrary and information profession. The American Library Association, after prolonged debates and discussions, adopted a professional ethical code in 1938.

The ALA Ethical code attempted to define and regulate the rlations of librarians to

(a) the governing authority;
(b) their constituency;
(c) their fellow employees within the library;
(d) their profession; and
(e) society.

The national debate, however, on the articles relating to the above stated areas went on in the next decades. In 1975 ALA adoped a new Statement of Professional Ethics which replaced the 1938 code. The same year, the ALA Council instituted and authorised a Standing Committee on professional ethics to augment the Statement on Professional Ethics by explanatory interpretations and additional statements. At the ALA membership meeting in 1981, the Code of Ethics was officially adopted. Responding to numerous criticisms on the 1981 code, the ALA Standing Committee on Professional Ethics decided to proceed towards further revision.

In 1990, the American Association for Information Science (ASIS) also, published a draft of the ASIS Code of Ethics for Information professionals in the August/ September 1990 issue of the Bulletin of the ASIS. This Code comprised a preamble and four categories of ethical responsibilites to:

(a) individual persons,
(b) society,
(c) the sponsor,
(d) the client or employer, and
(e) the profession.

The ASIS Code of Ethics for Informational Professionals has, however, remained in draft form pending acceptance by the Association's Board of Directors.

UK SITUATION

In 1978 the Working Party on Professional Ethics was established within the United Kingdom's Library Association to develop a draft code of ethics. A draft was prepared for discussion and debate in 1980; the final version of the code, the Code of Professional Conduct was adopted by the Council of the UK Library Association at its 100th Annual General Meeting in 1983. The Code includes the procedures and regulatory actions that will follow a breach of the code by a member of the Library Association. A unique feature of the LA's code of Professional Conduct is its implementation mechanism that involves sanctions imposed by the LA's Disciplinary Committee on those who ignore the professional conduct set by the Code.

The features of the Code relate to:

(a) the competency of the librarian;
(b) the question of discretion and respect of a client's privacy;
(c) professional independence and intellectual freedom;
(d) the integrity of members.

INDIAN SITUATION

Indian adventure of designing a professional code of ethics have remained at the level of efforts to survey literature on professional ethics and no more. Mention has already been made about discussions at a national conference of IASLIC in 1984. The subject of professional ethics has been dealt with in AK Mukherjee's book, *Librarianship—Its Philosophy and History* (1966) and RL Mittal's, *Library Administration* (1964).

Two articles by Meganand in *Indian Librarian in* 1962 and literature survey by Amitabh Chatterji appearing in IASLIC Bulletin in September 1965 are additional literature references.

The only effort to consider this subject seriously in a professional forum appears to be at the IASLIC conference in 1984. There were ten papers presented at the Conference, five of these give a good overview of professional ethics, four on professional ethics for person working in university, special and other institutional libraries, and another on Ranganathan's Five Laws vis-a-vis professional ethics with special reference to a research library. All these papers have a good number of references which would facilitate further readings on the subject.

Johan Bekker, a leading authority on ethics in librarianship, has suggested a few broad principles for designing a code.

1. Librarians should exercise their best professional judgement on behalf of users. They should therefore provide the highest level of service, not only complying with requests, but also anticipating needs; consider the needs of users the central focus of their work; assist actively in preventing incompetence and misconduct in their profession and in encourageing adherence to this code and other standards; protect each users right to privacy.
2. Librarians should strive to improve libraries and library services. They should therefore; be active members of local and national professional associations; pursue continuing education in order to improve their skills, knowledge and qualification; protect and enhance the reputation of libraries by exemplary professional conduct and service; involve themselves in research and other systematic efforts to understand and improve library service; avoid situations that could compromise professional judgement or provide personal benefits at the expense of the library and its users.
3. Librarians should be sensitive to the conditions under which learning and scholarship can flourish; freedom of inquiry and of thought and its expression. They should therefore, ensure the free

flow of information between libraries; allow access to the library holdings and services to everyone in need of information; avoid bias in the acquisition and presentation of information; resist efforts to censor library materials or restrict intellectual freedom.

4. Librarians should be sensitive to the concerns of the large society of which they are a part. They should therefore, protect and preserve sources of information for future use; assure that confidential and proprietary information is safeguarded; avoid transformation into the practice of other professions; take care that the access to information provided to users is not misused to curtail the freedom of others.

   This type of code attempts to present, both to those who work in libraries and to those who use libraries, an indication of what it is that librarians and the public to take such statements seriously and to see that breaches of the code do not occur.

PROGRAMMES AND ACTIVITIES OF LIBRARY ASSOCIATIONS

Library associations undertake all or some of the programmes and activities mentioned below, depending upon their stage of development. These associations interact with conceived governments from time to time, using every conceivable opportunity for sound development of a library system in the country. These tasks are done by advising, representing and helping in drafting of legislation, formulation of policy statements, guidance, etc.

1. Conferences
2. Library publicity
3. Service conditions
4. Education
5. Publications
6. Standards, services, research
7. Cooperation

LIBRARY ASSOCIATIONS OF INDIA

We have historical records of early library associations in India such as Baroda Library Association (1910), Andhra Desa Library Association (1914), Bengal Library Association (1927) and Madras Library Assocation (1937). The India Library Association was founded in 1933. The post-independece period has witnessed an increase in the number of library associations.

We have at present, many national and state level library associations. There are also associations devoted to special categories of libraries, subjects, fields and the special interests. For example, the Govt. of India Libraries Association, (GILA), Indian Assocation of Teachers of Library and Information Science (IATLIS), Micrographic Congress of India (MIC), Society for Information Science etc.

INDIAN LIBRARY ASSOCIATION (ILA)

The Indian Library Association was founded in 1933 at Calcutta. It is a registered society, with headquarters now located at Delhi. It is the premier national association representing the entire library profession in the country.

The birth of the Association can be traced to the holding of an All India Library Conference at Calcutta in September 1933. All leading librarians of that period were instrumental in organising the conference, whose main aim was to form the Indian Library Association. Between 1933 and 1947, seven all-India Library Conferences were held in different parts of the country. Publications of ILA included two editions of the Directory of Indian Libraries and an quarterly journal entitled Library Bulletin, as an official organ. After Independence, the Association witnessed both hectic and lean periods of active.

Until 1983, when ILA completed fifty years, 22 more All- India Library Conferences were held. The growth over the period was steady but not spectacular. Some initiatives taken by the ILA can be said to have had an impact over library development in the country. For instance, in 1992, the ILA successfully organized an Indian Federation of Library Associations (IFLA) conference at Delhi. However, the expectations of the library profession have all along been far more than what was achieved. At the present time, the library profession is keen to make ILA strong and effective and there are signs of some progress.

INDIAN ASSOCIATION OF SPECIAL LIBRARIES AND INFORMATION CENTRES (IASLIC)

Address: P-29/- CIT Scheme 6 M, Kankurgachi, Kolkata 700054. The Indian Association of Special Libraries and Information Centres (IASLIC) was founded in 1955. It is a registered society, with headquarters located in Kolkata. It was formed with the aim of having an association in India similar to the Association for Information Management in the UK and the Special Libraries Association in the USA.

At a largely attended meeting of librarians held at Calcutta on 25 June 1955 under the Chairmanship of Dr. S.L. Hora, the idea of starting an all India association devoted to the progress of special libraries and information centres was motted. Following this initiative another meeting held on 3 September 1955 formalized the decision to establish the Indian Association of Special Libraries and Information Centres (IASLIC). The spontaneous cooperation and enthusiasm shown by professionals in the formative period as well as dedicated efforts of some founding members have helped in laying a firm foundation for the association. Over a period of forty years and more, IASLIC has grown in stature and in range of activities and has been contributing in many ways to the improvement of special libraries and information centres in the country. It has earned recognition for its regular and systematic work all these years.

A. OBJECTIVES

IASLIC has the following major objectives:

(i) to encourge and promote the systematic acquisition, organization and dissemination of knowledge;

(ii) to improve the quality of library and information service and dissemination work:

(iii) to coordinate the activities and foster mutual cooperation and assistance among special libraries, information centres, etc.

(iv) to act as a centre for research in special library and documentation techniques;

(v) to act as a centre for information in scientific technical and other fields;

(vi) to take such action as may be incidental and conductive to the attainment of the objects of the Association.

B. ORGANIZATION

The membership of IASLIC consists of honorary members, donors, life and ordinary members and institutional members. The General Body elects, for a two year term, a President, six vice-Presidents, a General Secretary, a Treasurer, two Joint Secretaries, two Assistant Secretaries, a Librarian and 25 Council Members. The council appoints from among its members the Executive and Finance Committees. The work of the Association is distributed among six divisions with specific responsibilities assigned to them.

C. ACTIVITIES

(i) Meeting IASLIC hold a biennial seminar and a conference in alternate years in different parts of the country at the venue of host organizations who are usually unversity libraries/ departments of library and information science, institutions, associations, etc. It has recently formed special interest groups

devoted to areas like Industrial Information, Social Science Information, Computer Application and Humanities. They meet at the time of the annual conference/ seminar to discuss problems of common interest. IASLIC organizes from time to time adhoc seminars, lectures, exhibitions, etc. It has study circles at Kolkata and other cities. The meetings of the study circles are held every month, wherein technical issues are discussed.

(ii) **Publication:** The serial publications of IASLIC are IASLIC Bulletin (quarterly) established in 1956, annual subscription Rs.300/- It is the official organ and carries learned articles in library and information science. There is the IASLIC Newsletter (monthly) which diss-eminates information about the activities of the Association as well as other news of professional interest; and the Indian Library Science Abstracts (annual). It brought out the second edition of the Directory of Special and Research Libraries in India in 1985. It has brought out some monographs and one each of a manual, code and glossary. The Association brings out regularly its Annual Report and Statement of Accounts and Membership List. IASLIC gives best Librarian of the year and best Article in IASLIC Bulletin awards every years.

(iii) **Education and Training:** In the past, IASLIC used to conduct regular training courses in foreign languages and in library science at graduate level. Now, it is engaged in a continuing education programme on topics like Computer Application, Indexing, CDS/ISIS. It conducts short term training workshops for the benefit of working professionals at Calcutta and at othe places. Every year 3-4 workshops are being organized.

(iv) **Bibliography and Translation Services:** IASLIC offers translation and bibliography compilation services to individuals and institutions on a profit basis. It maintains a library devoted to library and information science literature.

(v) **Professional Issues:** The Association strives to improve the standards of service in special libraries and information centres. In this connection, it has made attempts to evolve a code of ethics for librarianship. It brings to the attention of authorities issues which call for improvement and corrective measures. It concerns itself in sound planning and development of library and information system and promotes suitable measures in this regard. It has taken measures like drafting an inter library loan code for library cooperation. It has been quite responsive to the need for securing better salary scales, service conditions and status for library professionals. It brings together library and information professionals at all levels and speaks for them as a sole on professional issues.

(vi) **Relations with other Bodies:** IASLIC maintains a healthy relationship with the Indian Library Association and other library associations. It has taken a leading part in the formation of the Joint Council for Library Associations in India. (JOCLAI). It takes an active interest in implementing the common programmes of this Joint Council for Library Associations in India. IASLIC is cooperating with the National Information System for Science and Technology (NISST) by taking up specific assignments and projects. It is represented in Indian Standards Institution, Documentation and Information Committee (ISI/EC2) (now known as Bureau of India Standards).

(vii) **Perspective for Future:** IASLIC has had satisfying accomplishments in play-

ing a leader/ coordinator role in the special library and information field in the country. It is now poised for assured growth and development in the period ahead for serving the cause of special librarianship in India.

MULTIPLE CHOICE QUESTIONS

1. The restated fifth law of Library Science in the changing world is ——— a growing organism.
   A. Information System
   B. Public Library
   C. Learning System
   D. College Library
2. Location of library building is an implication of which Law of Library Science?
   A. Fourth B. First
   C. Third D. Fifth
3. A variant to the second Law of Library Science is —
   A. Closed access
   B. Open access
   C. Books for all
   D. Books for limited users
4. Who proposed the "Five Laws of Library Science"?
   A. Thomas Bray
   B. Paul Otlet
   C. Grogan
   D. Dr. S.R. Ranganathan
5. Author's right to claim ownership of a created work is —
   A. Intellectual Property right
   B. Delivery of Books Act
   C. Censorship
   D. Press Act
6. I.B.M. is —
   A. International Bibliographic Method
   B. International Business Machines
   C. International Book Market
   D. Indian Business Machines
7. Information infrastructure is also called as —
   A. Information product
   B. Information provider
   C. Information industry
   D. Information superhighway
8. The British Library Act came into operation in —
   A. 1953 B. 1983
   C. 1993 D. 1973
9. Public Library Development in India as a movement was initially started from —
   A. Baroda B. Pune
   C. Kolkata D. Ahmedabad
10. In which year, the first general library law was enacted in U.S.A. at national level?
    A. 1946 B. 1956
    C. 1966 D. 1976
11. Fourth Law of Library Science has direct implication on —
    A. Library building
    B. Library staff
    C. Classification & cataloguing
    D. Library building
12. The National Union Catalogue of scientific serials is complied and maintained by —
    A. INALIS
    B. Library of Congress
    C. National Library Kolkatta
    D. INSDOC
13. Karnataka Public Library Act was enacted in the year —
    A. 1965 B. 1975
    C. 1969 D. 1970
14. Which Public Library Act provides an independent Ministry for library services?
    A. Kerala B. West Bengal
    C. Mizoram D. Manipur

15. Indian Science Abstracts is published by —
A. DRTC B. ISIC
C. NISCAIR D. NBT

16. UNESCO attempted to make user education programme through—
A. NISSAT B. PRECIS
C. AGRIS D. UNISIST

17. Resources sharing eliminated duplication of money, manpower and —
A. material B. language
C. time D. religion

18. Which is one of the traditional way of sharing resources among libraries?
A. Library Association
B. Inter-Library Loan
C. Library Conference
D. Purchase of Computer

19. Which association prepared a feasibility report for CALIBNET?
A. NISCAIR B. NASSDOC
C. NISSAT D. NIC

20. The process of supplying the relevant documents on a specific topic to the user is —
A. Indexing Service
B. Literature Supply
C. Abstracting Services
D. Document Delivery Service

21. Which is considered as the image, status culture or practice of an occupation?
A. Professional ethics
B. Library staff
C. Library standards
D. Library motivation

22. Which one was founded in 1933?
A. Information Service Society
B. Indian Library Association
C. Association for Government Libraries
D. Union Public Services Commission

23. P.V. Verghese Prize is awarded by Indian Library Association for —
A. Best Library B. Best Service
C. Best Article D. Best Book

24. Directory of Special & Research Libraries in India was brought in 1985 by —
A. INSP B. NASSDOC
C. FID D. IASLIC

25. The headquarters of American Library Association is at —
A. Chicago B. Hague
C. New York D. California

26. Journal of Librarianship is published by —
A. ASIS
B. The Library Association
C. ILA
D. ALA

27. "Federation of International Documentation" was founded by —
A. Paul Otlet
B. Henri La Fontaine
C. Both of these
D. S. Maitrayee

28. The headquarter of IFLA is located at —
A. California B. Sydney
C. Paris D. The Hague

29. Which association sponsored AGRIS?
A. FAO B. UNO
C. ICAR D. NASSDOC

30. Which institution is a spectral centre of NISSAT in marine science?
A. Central Maritime Institute
B. National Maritine Institute, New Delhi
C. Nation Institute of Archaeology & Muesology, N. Delhi
D. National Institute of Oceanography, Goa.

31. Ranganathan's five Laws of Library Science are a set of norms for good —
A. Librarianship
B. Documentation
C. Information System
D. Information Service

32. The second law of Library Science emphasises on —
A. Currency of library service
B. Democratisation of library service
C. Dissemination of library service
D. Aristocracy of library service

33. According to which Law of Library Science "Library grows & grows endlessly"?
A. First B. Second
C. Fifth D. Third

34. The acronym for Association for Information Management is —
A. IAMA B. AFIM
C. AIM D. ASLIB

35. NAPLIS was prepared by —
A. Department of Information Technology
B. Department of Education
C. Department of Culture
D. None of the above

36. Librarian of Library of Congress is appointed by —
A. President of L.C.
B. President of USA
C. Chairmain, Parliamentary Council
D. Any of the above.

37. Building a good image of the library & information profession in society contributes to professional ethics in —
A. Public Library staff
B. Library service
C. Librarianship
D. Library management

38. The Library Association is involved in promoting library interests in —
A. Canada B. Australia
C. India D. Great Britain

39. Indian Library Association has created a database of libraries is —
A. NALANDA B. SOUL
C. OASIS D. ISIS

40. American Library Association has started an award for creative professional achievement, which is —
A. Grogan Award
B. Melvil Dewey Award
C. E.P. Dutton Award
D. Melvil Calvin Award

41. ASLIB's Headquarters is located at —
A. Rome B. Paris
C. London D. Washington

42. Food and Agriculture Organisation sponsored the —
A. UNO B. NISSAT
C. RRRLF D. AGRIS

43. It consists of print and non-print materials as well as human resources that are eligible to be shared in ways that enhance the quality of service —
A. Library Resources
B. Library Staff
C. Library Management
D. Networking

44. The main objective/s of resource sharing in libraries is/are —
A. reduction in all round cost
B. avoidance of unnecessary duplication of information resources & their processing and maintenance costs.
C. development of specialised areas of collection building, each library concentrating on areas of its own concern.
D. All of the above

45. Which is/are important in Resource sharing system?
A. Record keeping
B. Acquisitions policy
C. Loan transaction
D. All of the above

46. Resource sharing requires on reach an agreement on —
A. type of material to share & acquisition policy
B. circulation policy and co-operative cataloguing & their maintenance.
C. production of union catalogue with uniformity and standardisation of bibliographic control
D. All of the above

47. What is the philosophy behind the concept of resource sharing in libraries?
A. "Access" to information resources available in the libraries.
B. "Equivalence" which means libraries should not only receive but should also give
C. Both of the above
D. None of the above

48. A library activity which lends on loan documents required by other library users is —
A. Inter-Library Loan (ILL)
B. Document Delivery Service (DDS)
C. Management Information Service (MIS)
D. OPAC

49. It is an automated catalogue system stored in machine readable form & accessed on-line by the library clientele-via-a V.D.U. employing a user-friendly software is —
A. On-line Public Access Catalogue (OPAC)
B. Inter Library Loan (ILL)
C. Resource sharing
D. Library Union Catalogue (LUC)

50. Who was the head of Working Group of Planning Commission on Libraries & Informatics for the modernisation of library services and inter-linking of library systems (1985-1990)?
A. Dr. S.R. Ranganathan
B. Dr. N. Seshagiri
C. Dr. A.P.J. Abdul Kalam
D. Dr. S. Ramachandran

51. Which was originally started as a project of India International Centre (IIC), New Delhi with the financial support from NISSAT?
A. DELNET B. NASSDOC
C. UGC D. CALIBNET

52. DELNET became a registered society in the year —
A. September, 1973
B. March, 1992
C. April, 2000
D. October, 1995

53. Which is the networking software based on *BASIS* plus which can accommodate and retrieve millions of bibliographic & full text records was developed by DELNET itself?
A. DELSIS B. HYPERIS
C. AGRIS D. IIC

54. INFLIBNET programme was the concept of —
A. Prof. Yash Pal
B. Prof. B.N. Shina
C. Prof. S.R. Ranganathan
D. Dr. R.R. Shaw

55. The service/s that are rendered by INFLIBNET is/are —
A. Catalogue based services
B. Database services & Communication based services
C. Document supply services
D. All of the above

56. Which is <u>not</u> a objective of INFLIBNET?
A. to establish gateways for on-line accessing of information
B. to optimise information resource utilisation through resource sharing
C. to evolve national network of libraries.
D. reference, legal and maintenance services

57. The communication based service/s of INFLIBNET is/are—
A. Referral services & e-mail services
B. Academic Communication
C. Bulletin board
D. All of the above

58. The main important achievement/s of INFLIBNET from 1988 to 2003 is/are —
A. Compilation of Union Catalogue (machine-readable) with 7500 records
B. Database of these and dissertation with 1 lakh records
C. Serial database which contains about 550,000 records
D. All of the above

59. Who was the chairman of INFLIBNET Review Committee?
A. Dr. S. Venkateswaran
B. Dr. S.R. Ranganathan
C. Prof. S.S. Sinha
D. Dr. S. Seshwari

60. Calcutta Library Network (CALIBNET) was sponsored by —
A. CMC Ltd.

B. NISSAT
C. MAITRAYEE
D. None of the above

61. The process of supplying the relevant documents on a specific topic to the user —
A. Electronic mail
B. Document Delivery Service
C. OPAC
D. Resource sharing

62. The reason/s for library legislation is/are —
A. it will maintain standards in library service
B. it will provide a steady & permanent source of finance
C. it will constitute a proper administrative and supervisory body with executive powers
D. All of the above

63. A Public Library is the —
A. "People's University"
B. Institution of Nation
C. "Adhoc University"
D. All of the above

64. According to the Library Legislation of India, who is the Director of Public Libraries?
A. President of India
B. Chief Executive at State Level.
C. Chief Minister
D. Governor of state

65. The salient features of Model Union Libraries Act is/are —
A. Constitution of a National Library Authority
B. National Copyright Library
C. Constitution of a National Library Fund
D. All of the above

66. Who initiated the Model Library Act during All Asia Educational Conference held at Varanasi in 1930?
A. Dr. S.R. Ranganathan
B. Sir Morris
C. Lord Curzon
D. Dr. S. Sheshgiri

67. National seminar on Library Legislation held in 1990 at —
A. New Delhi
B. Kolkata
C. Chenni
D. Mumbai

68. Model Library & Information Services Act was drafted by —
A. Dr. S.R. Ranganathan
B. Dr. S. Sheshgiri
C. Dr. Venkatapaiah
D. Prof. Yashpal

69. A document prepared for the guidance to prepare a Bill for placing before the Assembly is —
A. Act B. Patent
C. Nodes D. Model Bills

70. How many states presently in India have library legislation?
A. 11 B. 12
C. 13 D. 27

71. The Library Legislation should take care of the following point/s —
A. Accessibility of information to all sections of the people and provision of finances and the *modus operandi* for expenditure.
B. Arrangement of a reporting system of the activities of various public libraries.
C. An establishment of institutional network to provide care & preserver-documents.
D. All of above

72. The Madras Public Libraries Act was enacted in the year —
A. 1948 B. 1960
C. 1965 D. 1933

73. The first amendment of Andhra Pradesh Public Libraries Act, 1960 was done in—
A. 1964 B. 1969
C. 1987 D. 1989

74. The important feature/s of Karnataka Public Libraries Act, 1965 is/are —
A. Constitution of Local Library Authorities for the cities & districts
B. Provision for creating an independent

Department of Public Libraries, with a professional as its head
C. Provision for Copyright Collection of state
D. All of the above

75. Maharashtra Public Libraries Act was enacted in —
A. 1960 B. 1964
C. 1967 D. 1970

76. Goa Public Libraries Act was enacted in —
A. 1989 B. 1992
C. 1993 D. 1994

77. Manipur Public Libraries Act was enacted in —
A. 1980 B. 1988
C. 1992 D. 1933

78. Which states' Public Libraries Act is an unique and famous for its democratic & more decentralised pattern?
A. Goa B. Pondicherry
C. Kerala D. Manipur

79. Haryana Public Libraries Act was enacted in the year —
A. 1989 B. 1994
C. 1992 D. 1988

80. Which states levy library cess on either property tax or house tax?
A. Goa B. Mizoram
C. West Bengal D. Haryana

81. Which statehas largest number of libraries?
A. Maharashtra B. Tamil Nadu
C. West Bengal D. Andhra Pradesh

82. The helpful factor/s of Library Cess is/are —
A. Library Cess makes it imperative on the government to actively consider the establishment and maintenance of libraries
B. The provision for library cess has a greater impact as a democratic right of citizens to contribute to the development as well as to get access to library facilities
C. It gives provision for financial management
D. A & B only

83. Which state's entire technical staff of the public libraries comes under the cadre of "Library Service"?
A. Karnataka B. New Delhi
C. West Bengal D. Manipur

84. Which state has largest number of readers of Public libraries?
A. West Bengal
B. Karnataka
C. Tamil Nadu
D. Madhya Pradesh

85. The first conference of Indian Library Association was organised —
A. on October 13, 1933
B. in 1976
C. on September 12, 1933
D. in 1971

86. Library Legislation was firstly enacted in the state —
A. Delhi B. Goa
C. Kolkata D. Chennai

87. Dr. S.R. Ranganathan completed his librarianship studies at —
A. University of London in 1924
B. University of Annamalai in 1924
C. University of Madras in 1933
D. University of London in 1933

88. Which is **not** a implication of fourth law of library science?
A. Location of library
B. Staff of Library
C. Cataloguing
D. A & B only

89. Which is a implication of Vth law of library science?
A. Book Stock B. Readers
C. Modernisation D. All of these

90. The criteria fulfilled by a librarian to deem librarianship as profession is —
A. service orientation
B. Expertise in tools & technique
C. Altruistic motivation & self motivation
D. All of the above

91. Indian Association of Special Libraries & Information Centre (IASLIC) was

founded in 1955. Its headquarters is located at —
A. Delhi B. Kolkata
C. Chennai D. Mumbai

92. NALANDA is a database of libraries, containing —
A. Academic Libraries
B. Public Libraries
C. Special Libraries
D. All of the above

93. ASLIB is —
A. Association for special Libraries & Information Bureau)
B. Association for School Libraries Information Bureau.
C. Academic & Special Libraries Information Branch
D. Academic & School Libraries & Information Branch

94. Which international association promote international contact among library associations & librarians?
A. International Federation of Library Association & Institution
B. International Federation of Documentation
C. UNESCO (NISCAIR)
D. RRRLF

95. Which was founded by International Institute of Bibliography in 1895?
A. IFLA B. FID
C. UNESCO D. UGC

96. Which association was founded by Department of Culture, Govt. of India in May 1972?
A. University Grants Commission
B. Raja Ram Mohan Roy Library Foundation
C. INSDOC (NISCAIR)
D. DRDO

97. International Nuclear Information System (INIS) founded in 1970. Its headquarters is at —
A. Mysore B. Chicago
C. Vienna D. Hague

98. National Information System for Science & Technology (NISSAT) works for —
A. the development of National Information System
B. the Education & Training
C. sponsoring DELNET, MYLIBNET
D. All of the above

99. Bibliography on India in 2000 A.D. is a publication of —
A. NASSDOC
B. INSDOC (NISCAIR)
C. DESIDOC
D. RRRLF

100. Who designated Dr. S.R. Ranganathan as the "Father of Library Science" of India?
A. Sir Morris Gayer
B. Pt. Jawahar Lal Nehru
C. Abul Kalam Azad
D. Dr. Zakir Hussain

101. "Book Week" in India celebrated every year in the month of —
A. November B. December
C. June D. September

102. Commonwealth Library Association's headquarters is located at —
A. Nigeria B. New Delhi
C. Hauge D. Chennai

103. Who opened the first "School of Library Economy"
A. S.R. Ranganathan
B. Melvil Dewey
C. D.N. Marshal
D. A.S. Dickenson

104. "School of Librarianship" is situated at—
A. New Delhi B. London
C. New York D. Los Angeles

105. The Library Science education in India is started in —
A. Baroda, (1911)
B. New Delhi, (1924)
C. Madras (1924)
D. None of the above

106. In which year, the University of Delhi started the course of library science?
A. 1944 B. 1945
C. 1946 D. 1947

107. Who got the first Doctor of Philosophy (Ph.D.) degree from University of Delhi?
A. D.B. Krishnarao (1957)
B. S.K. Venkataraman (1947)

C. William Bordon (1907)
D. D.N. Marshal (1946)

108. Who was the president of "Library Development Committee", Mumbai?
A. A.A.A. Fauji
B. D.N. Marshal
C. S.R. Ranganathan
D. Sir Morris Gayer

109. Match the following:—

	Column A		Column B
1.	Study of acquisition, handling & communication of information	a.	Intellectual property
2.	Author's right to claim ownership of a created work	b.	Documentation
3.	Information stored on computer files, & accessible via a remote terminal & telecommunication link.	c.	Databate

Codes :-
A. 1–a, 2–b, 3–c B. 1–b, 2–a, 3–c
C. 1–c, 2–a, 3–b D. 1–b, 2–c, 3–a

110. Match the following:—

	Column A		Column B
1.	A packaged carrier of information & knowledge	a.	Book
2.	A recorded message, irrespective of physical form or content	b.	Information
3.	Organised information irrespective of physical form	c.	Knowledge
		d.	User

Codes :-
A. 1–a, 2–b, 3–c B. 1–d, 2–c, 3–a
C. 1–a, 2–b, 3–d D. 1–b, 2–c, 3–a

ANSWERS

1	2	3	4	5	6	7	8	9	10
A	B	C	D	A	B	C	D	A	B
11	**12**	**13**	**14**	**15**	**16**	**17**	**18**	**19**	**20**
C	D	A	B	C	D	A	B	C	D
21	**22**	**23**	**24**	**25**	**26**	**27**	**28**	**29**	**30**
A	B	C	D	A	B	C	D	A	D
31	**32**	**33**	**34**	**35**	**36**	**37**	**38**	**39**	**40**
A	B	C	D	A	B	C	D	A	B
41	**42**	**43**	**44**	**45**	**46**	**47**	**48**	**49**	**50**
C	D	A	D	D	D	C	A	A	B
51	**52**	**53**	**54**	**55**	**56**	**57**	**58**	**59**	**60**
A	B	A	A	D	D	D	D	A	B
61	**62**	**63**	**64**	**65**	**66**	**67**	**68**	**69**	**70**
C	D	A	B	D	A	A	C	D	A
71	**72**	**73**	**74**	**75**	**76**	**77**	**78**	**79**	**80**
D	A	A	D	C	D	B	C	A	D
81	**82**	**83**	**84**	**85**	**86**	**87**	**88**	**89**	**90**
A	D	A	B	C	D	A	D	D	D
91	**92**	**93**	**94**	**95**	**96**	**97**	**98**	**99**	**100**
B	D	A	A	A	B	C	D	A	A
101	**102**	**103**	**104**	**105**	**106**	**107**	**108**	**109**	**110**
A	A	B	B	A	D	A	A	B	A

INFORMATION SOURCES OF LIBRARY SCIENCE

THE REFERENCE SOURCES

A basic question arises then when we start discussing reference books, that is what books and other materials a reference library should stock and how they should be organised so as to constitute a reference collection.

The reference collection should include three classes of materials:

- reference books such as, Dictionaries, Encyclopaedias, Bibliographies, Yearbooks, Directories, Biographies;
- standard works of information such as Gazetteers, Atlases, etc.;
- all such materials that cannot be lent for home reading such as indexing and abstracting periodical, statistical sources; and

REFERENCE QUERIES

The most important aspect in the reference work relates to the reference questions with their corresponding reference sources. You are aware that for the majority of the questions asked in the libraries, reference sources are the most logical starting point for searching information. Much of the reference work involves the knowledge of the reference books and matching the questions to their sources.

The different categories of queries received in the libraries relate to:

- Author/ title queries;
- Directional and administrative enquiries;
- Fact-finding queries;
- Material-finding queries; and
- Research queries.

Given below are some reference questions and the types of reference sources:

The reference librarians should be able to look analytically at all the questions that are put to them, analyse them and then only provide the required reference sources.

ROLE OF COMPUTERS

As you are aware, the introduction of computers in the libraries has brought about sea-change in the various services provided by modern libraries. The use of computers has also tremendously enhanced the image of the reference SCI vice of the libraries. Presently, computer has been taken for granted as an important component of reference work. Computer searching has now become an essential part of reference work in most of the large libraries.

The use of information technology can be envisaged as a two-way process, the organization of internal information sources in any electronic format and an external tool to access information sources in any format. This helps in forming a basis for future resource sharing and helps in skillful processing, analysis and supply of information so as to effectively use the valuable resources.

The reference environment is affected by the growth of information technology. The various areas influenced are listed below:

***(a)* Electronic Dictionaries:** Several language dictionaries have been made available in CD-ROM (Compact Disc - Read Only Memory) format which have made searches very easy and much more user-friendly. A dictionary in CD-ROM can combine text, images and sound

Type of questions	Corresponding examples of queries	Types of reference source
Current awareness	Where can I find all latest papers published in chemistry?	Indexing/Abstracting Serials on the subject
Language	How can I find the meaning of the word 'unobtrusive'?	Dictionary
Trend	What developments took place in computer industry during last year?	Yearbook
Book	Where can I find a list of all books on the subject of 'Information Technology'?	Bibliography/Trade Catalogue
Background	How can I get brief information on Australia or Olympics?	Encyclopaedia
Institutions/Organizations	Please give me the names and address of Engineering Colleges in India	Directory/Handbook
Biography	Biography of K.R. Narayanan, President of India	

in one package and make cross-referencing a very simple process. Example: Encyclopaedia Britannica.

***(b)* Online Databases:** Source and reference databases have been at the forefront of the electronic publishing industry and will continue to be there in the years to come.

Some very popular databases that can be searched online are:

(a) MEDLARS DATABASE

(b) DIALOG: Online Computer Library Centre (OCLC) etc.

***(c)* Teletex and Videotext Systems:** Libraries in the developed countries offer reference services using the broadcast teletex systems like the ORACLE and CEEFAX covering a variety of topics such as news, advertisements, teleshopping and entertainment. Private cable television companies can also access these systems by dialling the required codes.

***(d)* Online Catalogues:** The Online Public Access Catalogues (OPAC) supplement the existing card catalogues and can be consulted for comprehensive searches. Here the users have the choice for searching materials available in more than one place. Most of the OPACs are very user-friendly and are helpful to natïve users who have no idea about searching materials in the libraries. The user after having access to such catalogues usually become self sufficient and seldom require are services or help of the reference staff while using libraries or accessing information.

REFERENCE AND INFORMATION ACCESS TOOLS

Man has been communicating over the centuries through various media and formats on a variety of subjects. All this eventually led to finding of information when it was wanted from various forms of materials. There is a large quantity of printed material available throughout the world today. Librarians and the library users have always put up with the problems posed by the printed literature as it is very much scattered not only in literacy forms but also in various physical forms. The whole of available literature has been classified into three broad categories by several experts into-primary, secondary and territory sources of information. Knowing about primary, secondary and tertiary sources is very useful as they indicate the relative currency and relative accuracy of the materials.

The primary sources are most original and current sources of information often not seen by anyone else before publication. These are in the form of journal articles, books or monographs, reports, dissertations, pamphlets, conference papers, etc. Very often the primary source contains the research findings of a scientist. In order to control or use primary sources in the library, we make use of the reference works referred to as secondary sources like the indexes.

An index is a secondary source if it is used to locate primary sources. A secondary source, thus, has information about original or primary information which is usually rearranged and modified for use by users. Thus, any work reporting about findings of others becomes a secondary source.

The tertiary sources consist of information which is collection of primary and secondary sources of information. Any sources not falling in the category of primary and secondary is a tertiary source. The tertiary sources usually list all kinds of secondary sources.

There are another type of information source which provides information of a particular query wherein specific answer is required, for example, address, telephone number of a person or institution. This is referred to as reference sources.

In reference work, access to various information and access sources is very important. The reference and information access sources are encyclopaedias, dictionaries, biographical sources, geographical sources, fact finding sources, etc. All these are based on most of the information otherwise available but in a scattered way and thus fall in the category of secondary sources.

The various reference sources have been prepared and published keeping in mind the various types of reference queries.

In the subsequent sections we will study about the various kinds of reference sources which will provide answers to various type of questions related to books, facts, some organisations, places, trends, current awareness, background information, spellings, meanings, statistic, etc.

DOCUMENTARY REFERENCE SOURCES

1. Dictionaries
2. Encyclopaedias
3. Bibliographies
4. Biographical Sources
5. Geographical Sources
6. Ready Reference Sources
7. Government Publications
8. Indexing and Abstracting Sources
9. Patents and Standards
10. Reference Sources for Current Events

DICTIONARIES

A Dictionary is a book explaining the words of a language, or the terms of a subject, arranged in some definite order, usually arranged in alphabetical order, with explanation of their meanings and use. It also usually gives the orthography, pronunciation, usage and meaning of each word. A dictionary is mostly compiled from the written and spoken words as its sources. Later on new words and new meanings, when occur, are added.

The science of compiling a dictionary is called Lexicography. Lexicographers adopt many innovative techniques and compile dictionaries of varied aspects of languages, linguistics and several disciplines.

ALTERNATE NAMES FOR DICTIONARIES

There are some reference books, which also deal with words but are known by various other names. They have identical purpose with a slight difference in scope. They are known as:

(a) Glossary *(b) Lexicon*
(c) Thesaurus *(d) Vocabulary*

***(a)* Glossary:** The word 'glossary' originates from the Latin word 'glossarium' meaning 'a collection of words peculiar to a field of knowledge'. Each entry in a glossary is known as a 'gloss' meaning 'a word', 'a comment', 'an explanation' or 'an interpretation'. It is an alphabetical list of terms and explanations often of specialised or technical nature (such as a glossary of computer terms). Sometimes it is linked with a particular text (such as Glossary of Indian terms in an English novel). Glossaries typically appear at the end of book as appendices. The person who compiles glossary is a glossarist. The Central Hindi Directorate has brought out a large number of glossaries.

***(b)* Lexicon:** It is derived from a Greek word 'Lexicon', meaning 'dictionary'. Each entry in the Lexicon is known as 'Lexis' meaning 'a word'. Lexicon is a dictionary of words of a language, arranged alphabetically giving meaning in another language. It is chiefly applied to dictionaries of Greek, Syrian, Arabic, Latin and Hebrew languages.

In recent years, the scope of a lexicon has been widened. There are two types of lexicon:

1. The lexicon of a language of dialect and
2. The lexicon of writers or individual works.

***(c)* Thesaurus:** The term 'thesaurus' also has its origin in Greek. It means 'a storehouse' or 'treasury' or 'a repository'. Peter Mark Roget was the first person to use 'thesaurus' for English dictionary in 1852. The term is now used in two different senses.

Roget's International Thesaurus. Ed.3. New Delhi: Oxford and IBH, 1978.

Longman Pocket Roget's Thesaurus. Harlow: Longman, 1986.

The Oxford Children's Thesaurus. Oxford: Oxford University Press, 1986.

In recent years, the word 'thesaurus' has undergone 8 changes. Now, thesauri, are compiled in various subjects which resemble synonym dictionaries. They are compiled *(a)* to provide subject headings list for indexers and searchers and *(b)* to provide an effective language interface between people and manual or computer data storage systems. They are useful to the libraries in information retrieval.

UNESCO: IBE Education Thesaurus. Ed.5. Paris : UNESCO, 1991.

***(d)* Vocabulary:** The name 'vocabulary' originates from a medieval Latin word 'vocabularium'. It is often used for a stock of words and phrases with brief explanations and meanings restricted to a single work or author. The entries are usually arranged in alphabetical order.

It encompasses:

(i) words of a language, e.g., vocabulary of basic Hindi.

(ii) words available to or used by an individual, e.g., vocabulary of Shakes-peare.

(iii) words appropriate to a subject or occupation, e.g., vocabulary of Commerce.

(iv) word list developed for a particular purpose e.g., an international vocabulary of technical theatre terms.

(v) a list or set of code words, gestures, symbols, style or colours.

An International Vocabulary of Technical Theatre Terills in 8 languages. (American, Dutch, English, French, German, Italian, Spanish, Swedish). New York: Theatre Arts Books, 1959.

Consolidated Basic Hindi Vocabulary (Classes I to VIII) / Compiled by Uday Shankar and Jai Narain Kaushin. New Delhi: National, 1982.

"Vocabulary, English-Somali, Somali-English" Mogadishu: Office of the FAO Representative, 1989. It has been compiled to help foreigners who are interested in acquiring some knowledge of the language.

COMBINATION OF DICTIONARY AND OTHER REFERENCE SOURCES

With a view to capture larger market, publishers have resorted to producing dictionaries which combine in them the features of *(a)* encyclopaedia *(b)* thesaurus *(c)* or even handbooks. This has resulted in following types of publications:

(a) Dictionary-cum- Thesaurus
(b) Encyclopaedic Dictionary
(c) Dictionary-cum-Handbook

DIFFERENT TYPES OF DICTIONARIES

Though dictionaries are defined as reference books consisting of words and phrases, they cover almost every field of interest. We have a wide range and variety of dictionaries. They are divided into different categories according to their nature and scope of contents. Usually, librarians categorise them into the following four groups as it facilitates them in the organisation of the reference collection.

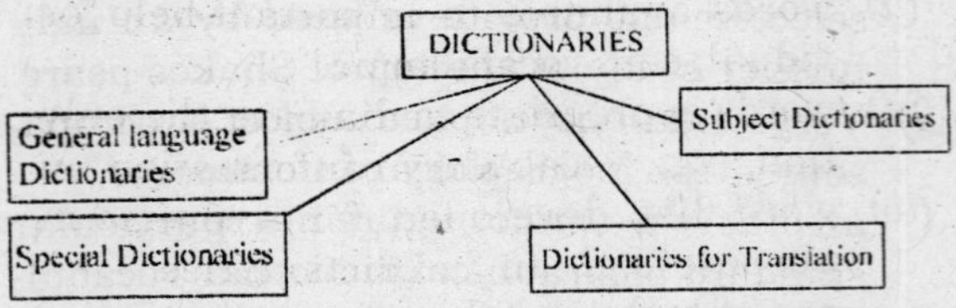

ENCYCLOPAEDIAS

Encyclopaedia has a very distinct and distant past. Man always has an inner urge to share his knowledge with his contemporaries and people of future generation by maintaining records. Though Aristotle and Plato were pioneers in systematizing all available knowledge, it was Pliny, the Elder who in 77 A.D. produced the first encyclopaedia *'Historia Naturalis'*. It contained a series of anthologies on topics such as Botany, Zoology, Metallurgy, Cosmography, Astronomy, Medicine, Magic, Fine Arts, etc. They were in thirty-seven volumes arranged in classified order. It was translated in English as *'Natural History'* in ten volumes.

During the Middle age; several scholarly and notable works of encyclopaedic nature were produced.

The encyclopaedia became a popular form of publication in 19th Century. The first edition of *'Encyclopaedia Americana'* published in 1829 is the landmark in the history of American Encyclopaedias. The advanced printing technology made publishing of encyclopaedia a potential and profitable business. *'The Metropolitana'* (1817-45) and *'The Penny Cyclopaedia'* (1833-43) were two successors to the *'Britannica'* in England.

The Great Soviet Encyclopaedia, 1926-47 appeared in sixty-five volumes.

The first two decades of the 20th Century saw *Jnanacakra Yani Gujarati Encyclopaedia* in 9 volumes (1918). Post-independent India saw a spurt in the activities of encyclopaedia compilation in various Indian languages. Hindi, Tamil, Bangali, Marathi and Malayalam languages in India and Urdu (from Pakistan) have already got general encyclopaedias. Other languages are also on their way to have an encyclopaedia of their own.

Hindi Vishwakosh. Varanasi: Nagri Pracharini Sabha, 1960-70. 13 vols.

Vigyanam. Thiruvananthapuram: Balan Prakashan, 1956-69.6 vots.

Morathi_Vishwakosh. Bombay: Maharashtra Rajyasahitya Sanskriti Mandal, 1973.

Sankshipta Odia Jnanakosha : Encyclopaedia Orissana. Cuttack: New Students Store, 1963, 65.4 vols.

TYPES OF ENCYCLOPAEDIAS

Twentieth century has seen a considerable growth in number and kind of encyclopaedia due to sudden proliferation of knowledge in all fields. In order to organise the collection in the reference section effectively, they are divided into two main categories, namely, *general* and *special* or *subject* encyclopaedias according to the scope, purpose and coverage.

The difference in scope and coverage of general and special encyclopaedia is evident. General encyclopaedia contains a collection of articles giving essential information about all the branches of knowledge. They are arranged either in alphabetical or classified order by subjects or names. They are intended for the general readers. It is a common practice to bring out supplements to encyclopaedias to keep them up-to-date but revised editions are published occasionally. It is rather a huge and highly expensive task to produce an authoritative general encyclopaedia. In contrast to this category, special or subject encyclopaedia is a collection of articles limited to a specific field of area. They are generally arranged alphabetically by subject and names. They are designed to satisfy the needs of the specialists interested in a particular subject. They are published in abundance in almost all the subject areas due to expansion of literature in every field and increasing demand from the users. The cost of publishing is comparatively less due to its limited scope and coverage.

The encyclopaedias can be further divided by using anyone of the following characteristics:

(i) Size or volume, i.e., one or two volume set or multi-volume set.
(ii) User's age, i.e., adult, junior, children.
(iii) Area covered, i.e., universal or regional national.
(iv) According to language.

USES OF ENCYCLOPAEDIAS

We have surveyed different types of encyclopaedias in above Section. In this section, we will discuss various uses of these encyclopaedias. An encyclopaedia is a store house of knowledge and provides information on all subjects. They form the backbone of the reference work in a library.

(i) Encyclopaedias are looked for concise, digested and in some cases simplified account on a topic on which otherwise there may be abundance of available literature.
(ii) Encyclopaedias also help us in such cases where the topic of enquiry is very restricted in scope and the library has no book on the topic.
(iii) Encyclopaedias generally press information in an impartial manner, giving all the view points on a subject.
(iv) They attempt to provide essential historical background to the topic of inquiry.
(v) References generally listed at the end of a brief or detailed description are selective and provide important help for further study of the topic.
(vi) Very often encyclopaedias are the only source for biographical information on an otherwise minor figure not covered in standard biographical dictionaries.
(vii) The earlier editions of encyclopaedias have their own value. They are a rich source for an account of state of knowledge at a given time on any topic that may be omitted.

The checkpoints for evaluating encyclopaedias are :

(a) Authority
(b) Scope and purpose
(c) Treatment
(d) Arrangement
(e) Format
(f) Revision
(g) Limitation
(h) Special features

DIFFERENT TYPES OF READY REFERENCE SOURCES

There are many types of ready reference sources. These sources satisfy fact-finding queries or in certain cases, material-finding queries.

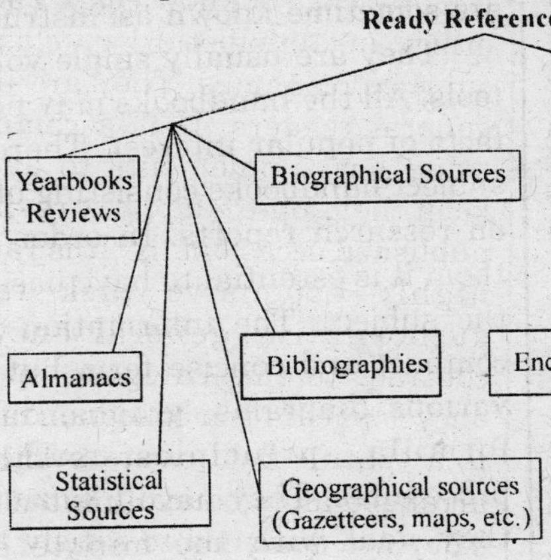

YEARBOOKS

Yearbooks are also known as annuals. As it is evident from the literal meaning of the term, a yearbook is a serial publication issued every year. It is called a compendium because it provides comprehensive account in a concise form of otherwise a vast subject. It contains current information of one or more subjects–in brief, descriptive or statistical form. Yearbooks are published as independent publications or as supplements to an encyclopaedia. Therefore, yearbooks can be divided into two major groups:

(a) Yearbooks

(b) Supplement to Encyclopaedias.

DIRECTORIES

Directories can be institutional providing information regarding the name, structure, functions, objectives, operational activities, addresses, officers, members, etc., of various types of institutions. There are directories of persons, which cover information about the name, address, status, academic qualifications, profession, experience, affiliations, etc., of individuals. The entries in the directory are systematically arranged in alphabetical or classified order. The term 'directory' is also used for a list of events, newspapers, periodicals and so on. They vary in kind, scope, purpose and size.

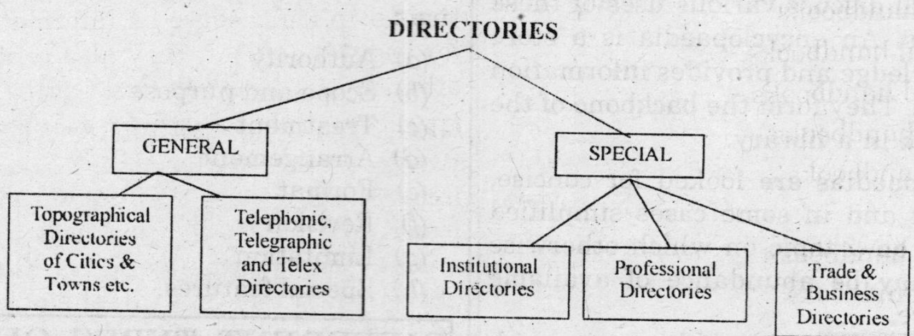

HANDBOOKS, MANUALS, GUIDE BOOKS

We have a very large group of ready reference sources consisting of handbooks, manuals. sourcebooks and guide-books. It is difficult to distinguish them from one another as they have common scope and identical purpose. These terms are used synonymously as they have similar features. They are also known as compendia as they contain concise and comprehensive account of given fields of knowledge.

The word 'handbook' is from German word 'handbuck' meaning a small book or a treatise giving useful facts. The literal meaning of the term 'handbook' is the book which is 'handy' to use as it contains all sorts of facts and 'handy' to carry it conveniently in hand. A 'manual' is a corresponding word derived from Latin term 'manuals'. It means a guide book, a compendious book, an abridged handbook or a concise treatise which can be referred for guidance in any occupation, art or study. They are essential ready reference sources consisting of 'facts to know' and 'instructions to do'. They are sometime known as 'instruction books'.

They are usually single volume reference tools. All the handbooks may not be providing facts of popular interest. There are countless subject handbooks consisting of articles based on research reports. In order to understand them it is essential to have basic knowledge of the subject. The information is provided in compact and concise form but illustrated by various diagrams, graphs, data, equations, formula, principles, symbols, tables, procedures. They have limited scope because they deal with the minute details of the specialised subjects meant for a small group of specialists. In fact, they are valuable for their depth of information in a narrow subject field.

There is a rapid increase in publishing of handbooks and manuals. There are countless handbooks on specific subjects. With the growth of knowledge, they become out of date and revised editions have to be published. They are reliable and indispensable reference tools for libraries. They can be grouped into following categories:

VARIOUS TYPES OF HANDBOOKS AND MANUALS:

(a) General handbooks
(b) Statistical handbooks
(c) Historical handbooks
(d) Literacy handbooks
(e) Official handbooks
(f) Tables
(g) Practical handbooks
(h) Subject handbooks

GEOGRAPHICAL SOURCES

Geographical sources deals with the surface of the earth including the division of the world into continents and countries. The climate, plants, animals, naturals resources, people and industries form part of the geographical studies. In recent times, it has become one of the important disciplines under social sciences. The natural result of all these is a demand for information sources in geography.

Geographical reference tools have become an important segment of basic reference collection for most libraries. The reference libraries are obliged to answer a number of questions seeking information about cities, towns, mountains, lakes, rivers, forest, etc., in connection with their description, location and other details. There are a variety of information sources that help in answering such questions. The study of all such sources becomes vital for reference work.

TYPES OF GEOGRAPHICAL INFORMATION SOURCES

We can divide geographical information sources into two categories:

(i) General Reference Sources (covering geographical information), and
(ii) Geographical Reference Sources (specific sources).

GENERAL REFERENCE SOURCES

The dictionaries, encyclopaedias, yearbooks, almanacs, etc., and sources which we have studied, can be categorised as general reference sources. All these reference books in their own right serve as information sources for geography. But, they also contain a lot of other information relating to other areas.

GEOGRAPHICAL REFERENCE SOURCES

We can sub-divide the specialised geographical information sources that are used in reference work into three categories, viz., maps, atlases and globes, gazetteers and travel guides. The obvious advantages of these specialised geographical reference tools are:

(i) they give information for smaller units not found in general reference books;
(ii) the information given often is more precise: and they are generally limited to one area,. and easier to use.

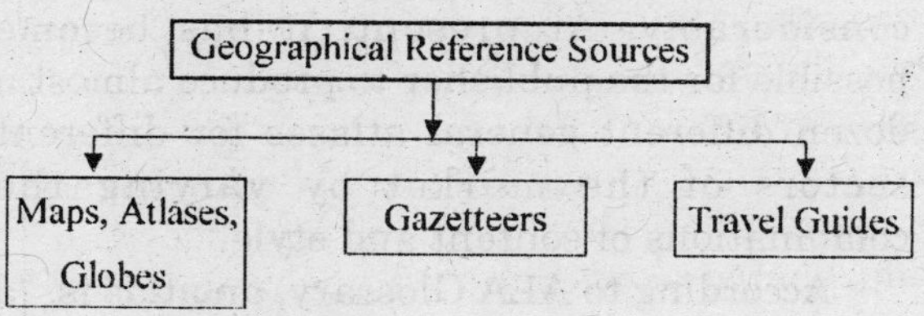

MAPS, ATLASES, GLOBES

Maps, atlases and globes are the main sources of geographical information. A map is a representation of certain boundaries of the earth on a flat surface showing countries, bodies of water, cities, etc. An atlas is a collection of maps, tables, charts, etc., whereas a globe is a spherical representation of the earth.

DEFINITION

Maps: According to ALA Glossary of Library and Information Science (1983), "a map is a representation normally drawn to a scale and on a flat medium of a selection of material or abstract features on, or in relation to, the surface of the earth or another celestial body."

The definition given by R.A. Skelton, formerly Superintendent of the Map Room of the British Museum is as under: "A map is a graphic document in which location, extent and direction can be more precisely defined than by the written word; and its construction is a mathematical process strictly controlled by measurement and calculation."

The Library of Congress defines maps in a broad way as "All forms of cartographic materials normally added to the collections of the library including flat maps and charts, collection of maps in atlas form, terrain models, globes, etc. "

Atlas: More than four hundred years have passed since Mercqator coined the term Atlas to describe a collection of maps bound up in a volume. The term became popular with the sixteenth century geographers. Since then, there has been rapid progress in this direction. At the turn of the nineteenth century the scope of atlas production was widened considerably. At present, it has become possible for the publisher to produce almost a dozen different general atlases for different sectors of the market by varying the combinations of content and style.

According to ALA Glossary, an atlas is, "a volume of maps, plates, engravings, tables etc., with or without descriptive letter press. It may be an independent publication or it may have been issued to accompany one or more volumes of that."

Globe: The difference between a map and globe is one of form. A map is any geographic image of the earth drawn to scale on a flat surface whereas a globe is a spherical representation of the earth surface. It is a hollow ball of metal, bearing a world map on its surface and is mount on an axle which permits its rotation. The term 'globe' is synonymously used for the earth. It is called in cartography as a scale model of the earth. The first model of the globe was made in Luxemberg in Germany in 1492.

USES

Maps and atlases are used by common men as well as specialists both for work and pleasure. Varied uses of maps and atlases depend on their types. We shall first describe various types of maps, and then explain their uses.

(i) A physical map is usually referred to for visual location and identification of the world, country, region, city or town, mountain, river, lake, sea, ocean, gulf, bay, desert or any other geographical formation.

(ii) Topographic maps trace details of geological, soil, forest and other basic information and for historical, economic, political or other types of development. They are used to show land use, land ownership, various methods of communications, transportation etc.

(iii) A route map shows roads, rail roads, bridges, etc.

(iv) A political map normally limits itself to political boundaries of different countries, states, cities, towns, etc.

GAZETTEERS

The term gazetteer has two meanings. It can be either the index to an atlas or a separately published reference work providing information about places of the world of a particular country or region. In this section, we shall define a gazetteer and study its scope and uses, with examples.

The scope of the gazetteers differs depending on whether they are international, national or district, etc.

	Gazetteer	Index to an Atlas
1.	The information available about each place name in the gazetteer is much more in detail.	It gives factual details about longitude, latitude at the page number of the map on which the place name is marked.
2.	It enlists many small places of less importance.	It includes only important places. However big may be the maps, they cannot accommodate all small places.
3.	It may be published in a single, handy volume or multi-volume.	It is usually available in larger size as it contains big maps to include all important places and it is heavy as maps are printed on thick art papers.

USES

Information about a place in a district or town is generally sought through gazetteers. The usual delay in their revision compared to atlases often renders them unsuitable as a source of recent information. As a reference source, a gazetteer provides historical, social, cultural, political, industrial, demographic and administrative details about a place in a count, or about a whole country.

GAZETTEER OF LNDIA

The *Indian Union*/Central Gazetteer Unit, Government of india: Delhi: Publications Division, 1965–1978. 4 volumes. Developed on the pattern of the first four volumes of the Imperial Gazetteer. The volumes are titled as:

V.I Country and People
V.II History and Culture
V.III Economic Structure and Activities
V.IV Administration and Public Welfare

All the chapters in each volume have been contributed by a team of experts in the field and carry a bibliography at the end. Volumes have been reprinted from time to time, volume 2 had its fifth printing in 1997.

District Gazetteers: Most of the districts in India have gazetteers now. They could be called miniature encyclopaedias for each district. They contain extremely useful reference materials for the administrator, the scholar and the layman alike.

After India became independent, this project caught the attention of the Government of India. A scheme was formulated in 1955 for the revision and rewriting of district gazetteers. All state governments accepted the scheme and established District Gazetteers' Departments. As a result we have now district gazetteers for most of the districts in India. They have been published under the auspices of the respective State Governments.

These district gazetteers include comprehensive information with all necessary background data, statistical particulars and ancillary details on the historical, archaeological, political, administrative, economic, commercial, industrial, agricultural, sociological, cultural and other aspects of the district and the life of the people of the area with maps, charts, tables and list of subdivision, and villages. Some examples are provided below:

(a) *Bihar District Gazetteer* / ed. by Roychaudhury.

(b) *Orissa District Gazetteers* / ed. by Nilamanisenapti. Koraput, Cuttack : Govt. Press, 1966.

(c) *Uttar Pradesh District Gazetteers. V.9.Moradabad*/ by E. B. Joshi. Lucknow: Supdt. Printing and Stationery, 1959.

(d) *Andhra Pradesh District. Gazetteers.* The Gazetteer of the District of Hyderabad by M. V. S. Prasada Rau. Hyderabad : District Gazetteers Department, Andhra Pradesh.

(e) *Gazetteer of the Bombay Presidency: Poona District* (Facsimile Reproduction) Vol. XVIII parts I, II, III. 1992. (Originally printed in 1885).

Gazetteer of Maharashtra. Bombay. Published by the Executive Editor and Secretary, Gazetteers Department, III. Population. IV. Agriculture. V. Capital. VI. Trade. VII. History. VIII. The land. IX. Justice X. Finance XI. Instruction XII. Health. XIII. Sub-divisions. XIV. Places. Appendix. Index. Maps included.

TRAVEL GUIDES

The main purpose of any travel guide is to inform the traveller as what to see, where to stay and how to reach a particular place. *Glossary of Library and Information Science* defines a travel guide "as a handbook for travellers that gives information about a city, region or a country or a similar handbook about a building, museum, etc."

Travel guides basically are meant for the people who want to visit various places in their own country or other parts of the world. They help making their journey pleasant and comfortable. Almost all important travel guides contain information on historic sites, museums and other places that are worth visiting for cultural enrichment. Information about routes and travel facilities is also included. Where to dine and what to buy all these can be found by using a travel guide.

USES OF STATISTICAL INFORMATION SOURCES

Statistical Information Sources provide: *(i)* readymade compiled statistics in all the fields or in one of the fields of specialisation; *(ii)* Authentic data in all sorts of subjects from official data records collected, checked and rechecked by expert statisticians; *(iii)* population statistics regarding births, deaths, age wise, sex wise information in various fields; *(iv)* history statistics of multiple aspects in last centuries, decades or years; *(v)* and comparative statistics of various countries in several aspects over a time span of few years.

TYPES OF STATISTICAL INFORMATION SOURCES

(a) Dictionaries and encyclopaedias
(b) Yearbooks, directories and atlases
(c) Govt. reports
(d) Special statistical sources.

MULTIPLE CHOICE QUESTIONS

1. Grogan divided reference sources in how many parts:
A. 2 B. 3
C. 4 D. 5

2. Grogan divided reference sources in—
A. Conventional & Non-Conventional
B. Primary & Secondary
C. Primary, Secondary & Tertiary
D. All of the above

3. Which is a Primary source of information?
A. Bibliography B. Patent
C. Dictionary D. Directory

4. Materials which are most authentic & original and usually take the form of a journal article, report or a patent are—
A. Primary sources
B. Secondary sources
C. Tertiary sources
D. Bibliography

5. The original information is selected, modified and rearranged in a suitable format for the purpose of easy location by users is—
A. Primary sources
B. Secondary sources

C. Tertiary sources
D. Patent

6. Information that is a distillation and collection of primary and secondary sources is—
A. Tertiary sources
B. Year books
C. Almanacs
D. All of above

7. The service that is the establishing of contact between Reader & Book by personal service is—
A. Online services
B. Reference services
C. Teletex services
D. Combination of A & C

8. Books & other library materials which may not be borrowed for use out of the library, either because of their nature is such that they are prepared for brief consultation rather than for continuous reading are—
A. Reference books
B. Reference materials
C. Online materials
D. All of above

9. The main types of reference & information sources are:—
A. Documentary
B. Mass Media
C. Non-Documentary
D. A & B

10. The main difference(s) between a reference book and a simple book is/are—
A. it is meant chiefly for consultation
B. it is mainly not for continuous reading
C. Both of the above
D. None of the above

11. The printed books existed in—
A. 16th century B. 18th century
C. 17th century D. 19th century

12. The newspapers & periodicals became visible in—
A. 16th century
B. Later part of 18th century
C. After 18th century
D. It could not indicated in dates

13. The Documentary reference sources are—
A. Dictionaries & Encyclopaedias
B. Bibliographies & Geographical sources
C. Ready reference sources & Patents, Indexes, Biographies
D. All of the above

14. A book which explains the words of any language, or terms of a subject, arranged in some definite order with explanation of their meanings & use is—
A. Index B. Patent
C. Dictionary D. None of all

15. The science of compiling a dictionary is known as—
A. Oxiography B. Lexicography
C. Lexiography D. Calligraphy

16. *'Dictionarium'* means—
A. a patent B. a dictionary
C. a lexion D. a lexicon

17. Types of dictionaries is/are—
A. abridged & unabridged
B. bilingual
C. multi-lingual
D. All of above

18. It is a systemic summary of the knowledge & work containing information on all subjects or limited to a special field or subject arranged in systematic order—
A. Dictionary B. Encyclopaedia
C. Lexicon D. Bibliography

19. The difference(s) between a dictionary and an encyclopaedia is/are—
A. a dictionary tells "what" about a word
B. an encyclopaedia tells "what", "when", "how", "where", and "why" of an idea, a person, a place, an event or things
C. Both of above
D. None of above

20. Which reference of sources referred to as "Backbone of reference services in libraries"?
A. Dictionaries B. Encyclopaedias
C. Biographies D. Bibliographies

21. The ancient Greek philosopher, who is referred as "father of encyclopaedia"—
A. Aristotle B. Alexander
C. John Harris D. Hippocrates

22. First known encyclopaedia was written by—
A. Paul Otlet
B. Aristotle
C. Hippocrates
D. Not written but published by a publisher

23. The first encyclopaedia to be published in English was the work of—
A. John Harris (*Laxion Technicum*, 1704)
B. A.I. Serille (*Etymologiarum libri* XX, 623 A.D.)
C. Oxford encyclopaedia
D. I.B.E. encyclopaedia (UNESCO, 1914)

24. Major types of Encyclopaedia are—
A. General B. Bridged
C. Subject D. A & B

25. Examples of General encyclopaedia are—
A. Coller's Encyclopaedia (24 volumes, 1949)
B. Encyclopaedia Americana (30 volumes, 1929)
C. The New Encyclopaedia Britannica (32 vol. 1974)
D. All of the above

26. Examples of subject encyclopaedia is/are—
A. McGraw-Hill Encyclopaedia of Science & Technology (19 volumes, 1987)
B. Encyclopaedia of Library & Information Science (35 volume & in 1968)
C. Both of above
D. None of above

27. It is a well organised list of written, printed or otherwise produced record of civilization e.g. of books, articles in periodicals is—
A. Dictionary B. Encyclopaedia
C. Bibliography D. Biography

28. Which is not true for Bibliographies?
A. It is available in several forms
B. It helps in locating the needed materials in libraries
C. Its uses are selection, identification, verification
D. It is not for research workers

29. Examples of Bibliography are—
A. Indian Books in Print
B. Forthcoming books
C. Cumulative Book Index
D. All of the above

30. A large part of the literature of reference consists of works that contain information about people, is called—
A. Bibliographical sources
B. Biographical sources
C. Geographical sources
D. Indexing periodicals

31. Types of Biographical sources are—
A. Current Biographical Dictionaries
B. Retrospective Biographical Dictionaries
C. Universal & National Biographical Dictionaries
D. All of the above

32. The sources consists of information that is distilled and collection of primary & secondary sources are—
A. Directory B. Reference
C. Tertiary D. Bibliographic

33. Three distinct approaches for giving reference service are—
A. Conservative approach
B. Liberal approach
C. Moderate approach
D. All of above

34. Which supplement is the existing card catalogues and can be consulted for comprehensive searches?
A. DIALOG
B. OPAC
C. OCLC
D. MEDLARS database

35. It is a systemic summary of the knowledge that is the most significant to mankind—
A. Encyclopaedia B. Directory
C. Yearbook D. Handbook

36. Year books & Annuals are—
A. Primary sources
B. Ready reference sources
C. Tertiary sources
D. Bibliographic sources

37. The bibliography that deals with the study & detailed description of documents—
A. Enumerative B. Systematic
C. Analytical D. Descriptive

38. It is a book explaining the words of a language, or the terms of a subject, arranged in some definite order, usually arranged in alphabetical order, with explanation of their meaning & use—
A. Index B. Thesaurus
C. Dictionary D. Encyclopaedia

39. Words or phrases made by re-arranging the letter of another word or phrase is—
A. Acronym B. Angram
C. Archaism D. Antonym

40. Who is the father of Encyclopaedia?
A. Johan H. Alsled
B. Aristotle
C. John Harris
D. Seriue

41. "Indian Books in Print" is an example of which type of bibliography?
A. Trade B. National
C. Universal D. Subject

42. Which were two attempted to create a universal classified bibliography of books & important periodical articles?
A. Paul Otlet, Henri La Fontaine
B. British Library, Library of Congress
C. Dewey, Comoriani
D. Ranganathan, Bhattacharya

43. Chemical Abstracts is published—
A. fortnightly B. yearly
C. monthly D. weekly

44. Which personality is associated with the Publication of Science Citation Index, of the Institute of Scientific Information, Phaldephia, U.S.A.?
A. William A. Katz
B. Eugene Garfied
C. Paul Otlet
D. Henri La Fontaine

45. The main purpose of which source is to present consolidated information available in various forms & to repackage the same in a condensed form for users—
A. Surveys
B. Reviews
C. Trend reports
D. State-of-the-Art reports

46. The CD-ROM version of Chemical Abstracts and Indexes was started in—
A. 1994 B. 1995
C. 1996 D. 1999

47. New trends in Teaching of Different subject is a publication of—
A. UNESCO B. INSA
C. CSIR D. World Bank

48. Glossary, Lexicon, Theasures, Vocabulary are some of the alternate names for—
A. Bibliography B. Acronyms
C. Encyclopaedia D. Dictionaries

49. The first edition of Encyclopaedia Americana was published in—
A. 1920 B. 1732
C. 1829 D. 1817

50. World book Encyclopaedia is an example of—
A. General encyclopaedia
B. Subject encyclopaedia
C. Universal encyclopaedia
D. Children encyclopaedia

51. Encyclopaedia of Library & Information Science is published by—
A. Bowker & Saur
B. Dekker
C. Cambridge University Press
D. McGraw Hill

52. World of Learning is an example of—
A. Handbook B. Directory
C. Yearbook D. Encyclopaedia

53. Dictionary of Synonyms & Antonyms fall under the category of dictionaries covering—
A. specific linguistic aspects of words

B. a special type of class or words
C. literary aspects
D. special group of concepts

54. The first modern subject encyclopaedia became available in the subject of—
A. Science & Technology
B. Language & Arts
C. Political Science & History
D. Philosophy & Religion

55. Famous First Facts is an example of—
A. Handbook B. Encyclopaedia
C. Yearbook D. Directory

56. Universities Handbook : India is published by—
A. UGC
B. AIU
C. University of Delhi
D. Ministry of HRD

57. BIS Handbook is a catalogue of how many Indian standards with alphabetical index—
A. 2000 B. 20000
C. 13000 D. 1,70,000

58. Almanacs are grouped into three categories namely Astronomical, Informational and—
A. Local B. Topical
C. Statistical D. International

59. The Patent Information System (PIS) of India was set up in 1980 at—
A. Pune B. Nagpur
C. Chennai D. New Delhi

60. The International Patent Documentation Centre (INPADOC) is situated in—
A. Vienna B. UK
C. USSR D. Australia

61. Standards World Over is a publication of
A. ASTM B. BIS
C. ISO D. IEO

62. The maps which trace the details of geological, soil, forest and other basic information for historical, economic, political or other types of development—
A. Physical B. Topographic
C. Route D. Political

63. Gazetteer of India: The Indian Union is in how many volumes?
A. 3 B. 2
C. 4 D. 5

64. Current Geographical Publications is published by—
A. Royal Geographic Survey, London
B. American Geographical Society
C. British Library
D. Bowker–Saur

65. Source Book of Global Statistics is an example of—
A. Bibliographic sources for statistical information
B. Adhoc sources of statistical information
C. Directory of statistical information
D. Handbook for statistical information

66. International Who's Who is published by—
A. Europa B. Wilson
C. Marquis D. Bowker–Saur

67. World Tables is a publication of—
A. UNESCO B. UN
C. IMF D. World Bank

68. Social Indicaters of Development is a publication of—
A. World Bank B. UN
C. UNESCO D. UNDP

69. The New York Time Index is published—
A. monthly B. weekly
C. annually D. semi-monthly

70. Facts on File is a service of—
A. Current awareness
B. S.D.I.
C. Loose leaf
D. Statistical

71. Asian Recorder is a publication of—
A. monthly period
B. annual
C. bi-monthly
D. weekly

72. Keessing's Record of World Events is published—
A. weekly B. monthly
C. half-yearly D. yearly

73. Data India is published by—
A. P.T.I.
B. Times of India
C. IWFA
D. Hari Sharan Chhabra

74. Which organisation was established to provide referral service globally, for all sources of environmental information?
A. UNEP B. UNESCO
C. UNCTAD D. UNICEF

75. Global Information Referral System of which agency provides comprehensive and up-to-date information of skills & capabilities available in developing countries?
A. World Bank B. UNDP
C. UNEP D. UNESCO

76. Summary of World Broadcasts is published by—
A. BBC
B. Chadwyek-Healey
C. Doordarshan
D. CBS television

77. These are engaged in activities such as translation, printing, publishing etc.—
A. Information gatherers
B. Information processors
C. Information recorders
D. Information generators

78. The information systems that reflect mostly government sponsored projects/programmes such as nuclear energy missions, space research and the like—
A. Discipline-oriented
B. Mission-oriented
C. Problem-oriented
D. Information-oriented

79. The highly specialised information institutions that emerged to provide critical, analytical & evaluated support services to institutions involved in high level—
A. Referral centres
B. Information Analysis centres
C. Documentation centres
D. Problem-oriented Information systems

80. Which source of print media carries contents of mass communication?
A. Daily Newspaper
B. Journals
C. Books
D. Pamphlets

81. The centre that deals with the enquiries for information that could be answered through non-documentary sources, is—
A. Bibliography
B. Information
C. Reference
D. Referral

82. Which dictionary can combine text, images and sound in one package & can make cross referencing a very simple process?
A. Print format B. Traditional format
C. Multi-volumes D. CD-ROM

83. ORACLE & CEEFAX are systems of broadcast on—
A. Online access B. Videotex
C. Teletext D. Computer

84. The state-of-the art reports can be grouped into three categories namely reviews & survey, advances & progress and—
A. Trend reports
B. Yearbooks
C. Research reports
D. Current Awareness Bulletins

85. Annual review of Information Science & Technology is a good example of—
A. Bibliographical reviews
B. Reading list
C. Reference list
D. Subject index

86. Reviews are of two types namely—
A. subject oriented & focusing on particular scientific or technical problem on its solution
B. topical & subject oriented
C. research oriented & subject oriented
D. chronological & topical oriented

87. New Trends in Teaching of Different subject is publication of—
A. UNESCO B. INSA
C. CSIR D. World Bank

88. Oxford English Dictionary & Webster's Third New International Dictionary fall under the group of—
A. Prescriptive dictionaries
B. Adult dictionaries
C. Descriptive dictionaries
D. Unabridged dictionaries

89. Census Atlas National Volume is an example of—
A. Local atlas
B. Historical atlas
C. Demographic atlas
D. Anthropological atlas

90. Statistical Abstract of India supersedes—
A. Indian Statistical Abstracts
B. Statistical Abstracts of British India
C. Abstract of Indian Statistics
D. Annual Statistical Abstracts of India

91. National Biographical Dictionary of India is published by—
A. S.P. Sen B. Durga Das
C. Times of India D. Jagdish S. Sharma

92. Which is a pervasive part of modern culture, a medium to build up images of a society?
A. Mass media B. Public relation
C. Advertisements D. Multimedia

93. Social Indicator of Development is a publication of—
A. World Bank B. UNESCO
C. FAO D. ILO

94. Commercial publishers come under the category of—
A. referral institutions
B. institutions that service knowledge & information
C. knowledge creating institutions
D. information processing & disseminating institutions

95. Which is an example of an Indian news digest service on the net?
A. Indian News
B. Indian World Samachar
C. Bharat Samachar
D. Bhartiya Samachar

96. Which forms of communication involve creativity, persuasion & impact of the message carried by them?
A. Multimedia B. Public relation
C. Mass media D. Advertisements

97. Which group of experts includes computer hardware & software specialists involved in many aspects of system design, maintenance & similar other services?
A. Information Recorder
B. Information Retrievers
C. Information Disseminators
D. Information Technologists

98. Asian Recorder is a weekly and a news sheet of the news digest. How many countries it cover?
A. 40 B. 45
C. 50 D. 55

99. The Universal Bibliographic Control (UBC) programme sponsored by I.F.L.A. in the year—
A. 1974 B. 1931
C. 1981 D. 1973

100. The primary function(s) of indexing & abstracting periodicals is/are—
A. current use
B. retrospective search function
C. comprehensive use
D. All the above

101. Indian Science Abstract is published by—
A. NISCAIR–fortnightly
B. DESSIC–monthly
C. DESIDOC–Weekly
D. McGraw Hill company

102. Who was the first person to use the term "Encyclopaedia"?
A. Plato
B. Aristotle
C. Johann Heinrich
D. N.P. Sabha

103. The example(s) of National & Regional Encyclopaedia is/are—
A. Encyclopaedia of India
B. Oxford Encylopaedia of Modern Islamic World
C. Dictionary of Art
D. A & B

104. Which statement(s) is/are NOT true for encyclopaedia?
A.. These are looked for concise literature
B. They attempt to provide essential historical background to the topic of inquiry
C. They generally present information in an impartial manner, giving all the view points on a subject
D. All are true

105. The checkpoints for evaluating encyclopaedia are—
A. Authority of publisher/editor
B. Scope & purpose
C. Treatment of subjects
D. All of the above

106. The different types of Ready reference sources are—
A. Yearbooks & Almanacs
B. Directories & Handbooks
C. Manuals & Guide-books
D. All of the above

107. The basic purpose of yearbooks is to—
A. record annual developments in a geographical area, in a subject discipline or in an organisation
B. provide information of a particular area
C. Both of above
D. None of above

108. The basic objective(s) of bringing annual supplements to Encyclopaedia is/are—
A. to update basic set
B. to summarise the year's major events
C. to promote their sale by updating them
D. All of the above

109. The types of special Directories are—
A. Institutional Directories
B. Professional Directories
C. Trade & Business Directories
D. All of the above

110. International Directory of Marine Scientists is published by—
A. I.L.O. B. F.A.O.
C. W.H.O. D. C.S.I.R.

111. Directories of Libraries & Who's Who in Library Profession in Delhi is published by—
A. Indian Library Association
B. Delhi Library Association
C. University of Delhi
D. University Grants Commission

112. Guiness Book of World Records is an example of—
A. General Handbooks
B. Official Handbooks
C. Historical Handbooks
D. Practical Handbooks

113. The different types of Practical Handbooks is/are—
A. Family health, First aid
B. Home Maintenance
C. Cooking recipes & Handicraft
D. All of the above

114. Match the "A" with "B"

Column A	Column B
1. Family health Handbooks	(a) Establishing knowledge
2. Handbooks	(b) Baking book
3. Cooking recipes Handbooks	(c) Where there is no doctor
4. Official Handbooks	(d) Knit to fit
	(e) Staff car rules

Codes:-
A. 1–c, 2–a, 3–b, 4–e
B. 1–a, 2–b, 3–c, 4–d
C. 1–e, 2–a, 3–b, 4–c
D. 1–a, 2–c, 3–b, 4–e

115. The term "handbook" is derived from language—
A. Latin B. Indian
C. German D. Russian

116. Rules & regulations for Government servants can be located from—
A. Health Handbooks
B. Official Handbooks
C. Government Manuals
D. None of the above

117. Math the "A" with "B"—

Column A	Column B
1. Arrangement	(a) Accuracy, Reliability
2. Authority	(b) Clear & Legible type faces
3. Index	(c) Alphabetical or Classified
4. Typography	(d) 'see' & 'see also' references

Codes :-
A. 1–c, 2–a, 3–b, 4–d
B. 1–a, 2–b, 3–c, 4–d
C. 1–c, 2–b, 3–a, 4–d
D. 1–b, 2–c, 3–d, 4–a

118. Directories are called ready reference sources because—
A. they are an annual calender covering information
B. they summarise the year's events
C. they are referred to locate short and factual information
D. all of the above

119. There are special features for assessing the value of ready reference sources—
A. Recency & Brevity
B. Indexes & Bibliographies
C. Methods of Compilation & Trends in Development
D. All of the above

120. The criteria of format to evaluate ready reference sources is/are—
A. size & paper
B. typography & binding
C. physical appearance
D. All of above

121. The first recorded patent was recorded in the year—
A. 1591 B. 1617
C. 1945 D. 1974

122. The International Patent Documentation Centre (INPADOC) is located at—
A. Geneva B. Vienna
C. Yorkshire D. New York

123. The Patent Information System (PIS) was set up in 1980 at—
A. Delhi B. Pune
C. Kolkata D. Nagpur

124. The advantage(s) of Geographical reference sources is/are—
A. they give information for smaller units not found in general reference books
B. the information given in them, often is more precise
C. they are generally limited to one area & easier to use
D. All of the above

125. Geographical sources are—
A. Maps, Atlases, Globes
B. Gazetteers
C. Travel Guides
D. All of the above

126. Maps & Atlases may be—
A. General
B. Topographic & Thematic
C. Local & Special
D. All of above

127. Who coined the term "Atlas" first?
A. Heinrich B. Bacquarrel
C. Mercquator D. None of these

128. The first model of the globe was made in 1492 at—
A. Luxemberg in Germany
B. Mexico
C. Sydney in Australia
D. Not known till now

129. Which maps give the details of geological, soil, forest and other basic information?
A. Physical maps
B. Topographic maps
C. Route maps
D. Political maps

130. The official mapping organisation(s) in India is/are—
A. Survey of India

B. National Atlas & Thematic Mapping Organisation
C. Geological Survey of India
D. All of the above

131. National Atlas of India is published by—
A. Survey of India
B. Geological Survey of India
C. National Atlas & Thematic Mapping Organisation
D. None of these

132. Census Atlas : National Volume in India is published by—
A. Auditor General
B. Registrar General & Census Commissioner
C. President
D. Any one of the above

133. A Geographical dictionary is—
A. Index B. Gazetteer
C. Atlas D. Directory

134. District Gazetteers could be called as—
A. Miniature encyclopaedia
B. Bridged encyclopaedia
C. Titled Indexes
D. None of these

135. The most important tool for evaluation of travel guides is—
A. Topography B. Currency
C. Coverage D. None of these

136. Travel guides are—
A. One-time guides
B. Series guides
C. Ecology guides
D. A & B only

137. International Who's Who is an example of
A. Biographical sources
B. Bibliographical sources
C. Gazetteers
D. All of these

138. The main important steps involved in the process of rendering biographical reference service are—
A. Reference review
B. Nature of Question
C. Knowledge of Biographical sources
D. All of these

139. A person who is the subject of biography—
A. Employee B. Biographee
C. Biographer D. Historian

140. A person who writes a biography of another is—
A. Autobiographer B. Biographer
C. Portraiter D. Any of these

141. Adhoc publications of statistical information sources are published on—
A. Specific subjects
B. Geographical sources
C. General subjects
D. Serial publications

142. Which is the problem associated with the statistical sources?
A. The sources are never up-to-date
B. Non-availability of statistics
C. Statistics provided may not be in the form of the user needs
D. All of these

143. Which is not a type of statistical sources?
A. Yearbooks
B. Government reports
C. Encyclopaedias
D. Biographies

144. Main types of sources of information on current events are—
A. Indexes to newspaper
B. News summaries & news digests
C. Summaries to TV & Radio Broadcasts
D. All of the above

145. Asian Recorder is an example of—
A. Continental Digest
B. Regional Digests
C. Country Digest
D. A & B only

146. Summary of World Broadcasts is a work of—
A. P.T.I.
B. B.B.C.
C. Oxford University
D. U.G.C.

147. The most time consuming job in any reference section is to—
A. search for current material on recent events
B. collect historial reviews on specific subjects
C. store the current events
D. Any of the above

148. Kessing's Record of World Events is a News Digests consist of—
A. news summary providing records of national & international current affairs with updates
B. factual, objective reference source based on press, broadcasts, official & other sources
C. main texts which contains coherent & systemic coverage of a particular country or topic tracing recent developments
D. All of the above

149. The line of type at the end of a newspaper or magazine article indicating its authorship is—
A. Durondline
B. Byline
C. Topographic line
D. Simple line

150. World of Learning is a—
A. Primary sources
B. Secondary sources
C. Tertiary sources
D. None of the above

151. National Bibliography is an example of—
A. Documentary sources
B. Primary sources
C. Secondary sources
D. Tertiary sources

152. Universities are example of—
A. Non-documentary sources
B. Documentary sources
C. Primary sources
D. Secondary sources

153. The I.N.B. is—
A. International Bank
B. Indian National Bureau
C. Indian National Bibliography
D. International Bibliography

154. I.N.B. is published by—
A. INSDOC, New Delhi
B. National Library, Kolkata
C. Central Science Library, Delhi
D. Central Reference Library, Kolkata

155. I.N.B. was first published in 1957. How many languages added to it?
A. 1 B. 13
C. 16 D. 19

156. Which is NOT a part of I.N.B.?
A. Yearbooks
B. Maps
C. First issue of periodicals
D. Government publications

157. The cataloguing in British National Bibliography (B.N.B.) is done by—
A. C.C.C. B. AACR-I
C. AACR-II D. ALA Code

158. Which is the language of B.N.B.?
A. English & German
B. English only
C. Russian only
D. None of these

159. The L.I.S.A. is—
A. Local Information Science Abstract
B. Library & Information Science Abstract
C. Library Science Abstract
D. Library Science Applications

160. Which is a most famous "Yearbook"?
A. Bowker manual
B. Europa Yearbook
C. Statesman's Yearbook
D. India : a reference manual

161. L.I.S.A. was first published in 1950. Its frequency is—
A. Monthly B. Weekly
C. Yearly D. Quarterly

162. Indian Library Science Abstract is published from—
A. New Delhi B. Bangalore
C. Chennai D. Kolkata

163. Indian Library Science Abstract is published by—
A. I.L.A. B. A.L.A.
C. IASLIC D. INSDOC

164. Indian Science Abstract is published by–
A. DRTC, Bangalore
B. INSDOC, New Delhi
C. I.S.I., Bangalore
D. DESIDOC, New Delhi

165. Which is a current Reference Source?
A. Asian Recorder
B. Facts on file
C. Kessg's Record of World events
D. All of the above

166. The first edition of Encyclopaedia Bitannica published in–
A. 1758 B. 1768
C. 1868 D. 1967

167. Encyclopaedia Britannica is published from—
A. New York B. London
C. Chicago D. New Delhi

168. The number of volumes of Encyclopaedia Britannica are—
A. 30 B. 27
C. 28 D. 32

169. Encyclopaedia Americana is published from New York. It has ____ volumes.
A. 30 B. 20
C. 40 D. 50

170. In which year, the census started first?
A. 1872 B. 1891
C. 1881 D. 1901

171. Which is the best source to know the population of India?
A. Census of India
B. Asian Recorder
C. Gazetteer of India
D. Stateman's Yearbook

172. If you want to know the districts of Uttar Pradesh, in which source will you find?
A. Census of India
B. World of Learning
C. India : Mannual of refernce
D. District Gazetteer of India

173. The complete information on I.F.L.A. is given in—
A. World of Learning
B. Asian recorder
C. Europa World Year
D. None of these

174. The best source to know the climate of Himachal Pradesh is–
A. India : A Reference Annual
B. Gazetteer of India
C. Asian Recorder
D. Oxford Atlas of World

175. The best reference source to know about the education of any country is—
A. Stateman's Yearbook.
B. World of Learning
C. Europa Yearbook
D. University Handbook

176. If you want to know the birth place of Mahatma Gandhi, then which source will you choose—
A. Indian National Bibliography
B. British National Bibliography
C. India : A Reference Annual
D. Dictionary of National Biography

177. Chemical Abstract is a service of—
A. Local Leval
B. Regional Level
C. National Level
D. International Level

178. The Publisher of Books in Print is—
A. Grollier; L. B. Bowker (R.R.)
C. Whitaker; H. D. None of these

179. Who started the "reference services" in India?
A. W.A. Borden
B. A. Dickinson
C. S.R. Ranganathan
D. B.S. Qesaran

180. In which University of India, firstly the post of Reference Librarian was recognised?
A. B.H.U.
B. University of Delhi
C. University of Madras
D. J.N.U.

181. S.D.I. is—
A. Short Distance Inforamtion
B. Selective Dissemination of Information
C. State Directory of Information
D. Selective Directory Institute

182. Who discovered S.D.I.?
A. H.P. Luhn B. Calrin Moores
C. D.J. Rokison D. Dr. S.R. Pandey

183. INSDOC (NISCAIR) is a service of—
A. National Level
B. International Level
C. Local Level
D. State Level

184. When was the INSDOC (NISCAIR) established?
A. 1950 B. 1952
C. 1953 D. 1954

185. INSDOC (NISCAIR) is a part of—
A. NISSAT B. UNISIST
C. UNESCO D. CSIR

186. DESIDOC is related with—
A. Science B. Humanities
C. Electronics D. Defence Science

187. DESIDOC works under—
A. DRDO B. CSIR
C. NISSAT D. ICSSR

188. When was the DESIDOC established?
A. 1958 B. 1967
C. 1963 D. 1969

189. NASSDOC is related with—
A. Science
B. Social Science
C. Defence Science
D. Computer Science

190. The headquarters of NASSDOC is at—
A. Lucknow B. Ahmadabad
C. Mumbai D. New Delhi

191. PIS is—
A. Physical Information System
B. Patent Institute of Science
C. Patent Information System
D. Personal Information System

192. The headquarter of P.I.S. is at—
A. New Delhi B. Lucknow
C. Nagpur D. Hyderabad

193. The first Director of D.R.T.C. was—
A. C.G. Vishwanathan
B. B.S. Keshwan
C. R.S. Swaminathan
D. Dr. S.R. Ranganathan

194. "MELLARS" is a programme of—
A. I.F.L.A.
B. F.I.D.
C. National Medical Library, U.S.A.
D. Library Association – U.K.

195. Routing of Journal is—
A. S.D.I. B. C.A.S.
C. Reference service D. None of above

196. U.B.C. is—
A. Universal Bibliographic Control
B. Universal Book Centre
C. Under Bibliographic Control
D. University Book Control

197. U.B.C. is a programme of–
A. F.I.D. B. L.C.
C. I.L.A. D. I.F.L.A.

198. Which organisation give I.S.S.N. in India?
A. DESIDOC B. NISCAIR
C. NASSDOC D. I.S.O.

199. What is the name of controlled vocabulary in Indexing?
A. Lanaguage of Synonyms
B. Distionary of Synonyms
C. A Thesaurus
D. List of words

200. Who discovered the "UNITERM"?
A. H.P. Luhn B. M. Taube
C. C. Moores D. Paul Otlet

ANSWERS

1	2	3	4	5	6	7	8	9	10
B	C	B	A	A	D	B	B	D	C
11	**12**	**13**	**14**	**15**	**16**	**17**	**18**	**19**	**20**
A	B	D	C	B	B	D	C	C	B

21	22	23	24	25	26	27	28	29	30
A	B	A	D	D	C	C	D	D	B
31	32	33	34	35	36	37	38	39	40
D	C	D	B	A	B	C	C	B	B
41	42	43	44	45	46	47	48	49	50
A	A	D	B	D	D	A	D	C	D
51	52	53	54	55	56	57	58	59	60
B	B	A	D	A	B	C	B	B	A
61	62	63	64	65	66	67	68	69	70
B	B	C	B	A	A	D	A	D	A
71	72	73	74	75	76	77	78	79	80
D	B	A	A	B	A	C	B	B	A
81	82	83	84	85	86	87	88	89	90
D	D	D	A	A	A	A	C	C	A
91	92	93	94	95	96	97	98	99	100
A	A	A	D	A	D	B	B	A	D
101	102	103	104	105	106	107	108	109	110
A	B	B	D	D	D	C	D	D	B
111	112	113	114	115	116	117	118	119	120
B	A	D	A	C	B	A	D	D	D
121	122	123	124	125	126	127	128	129	130
A	B	D	D	D	D	C	A	A	D
131	132	133	134	135	136	137	138	139	140
C	B	B	A	B	D	A	D	B	B
141	142	143	144	145	146	147	148	149	150
A	D	D	D	D	B	A	D	B	C
151	152	153	154	155	156	157	158	159	160
C	D	C	D	B	B	B	B	B	C
161	162	163	164	165	166	167	168	169	170
A	D	C	B	D	B	C	A	A	A
171	172	173	174	175	176	177	178	179	180
A	D	C	B	B	D	D	B	C	C
181	182	183	184	185	186	187	188	189	190
B	A	A	B	D	D	A	A	B	D
191	192	193	194	195	196	197	198	199	200
C	C	D	C	B	A	D	B	C	B

CLASSIFICATION OF LIBRARY AND ITS CATALOGUING

CLASSIFICATION

In our present day world, we come across millions of types of books on different subjects. This immense textual diversity on several subject is the result of immense research & studies by scholars, researchers etc. "Differentiating among the books according to subject, author or title is the classification", in simple sense. The philosopher, John Dewey, said that *"knowledge is classification"*. Aristotle, Linneaus had given the concept of system classification of knowledge. Dr. S.R. Ranganathan put classification under fifth law of library science. He stated, " a library is a growing organism as knowledge and it is necessary that the classification must be comprehensive, entracing all past & present knowledge and allowing places for any possible additions to knowledge."

The word *"classification"* is derived from the Latin word *classes* which means order or rank in a particular manner. Classification is a process in which we group or separate things on the basis of common features and similarities. It means dividing into groups, grouping, sorting, arranging, ordering, ranking and relating one entity to the others.

Classification is a homonym term. Dr. S.R. Ranganathan tried to define this homonym term as:-

1. Classification is division
2. Classification is assortment
3. Classification is assortment and representation.

Library Classification:- When entities are books and other items of information, then their classification is known as Library classification.

MODES OF FORMATION OF SUBJECTS

The modes of formation of subjects that have been recognised are:

- Lamination
- Loose Assemblage
- Fission
- Fusion
- Distillation
- Clustering
- Agglomeration

Detail regarding each of the modes are as follows:—

LAMINATION

Lamination is construction by an over-layering facet, just as one makes a sandwich by layering a vegetable over a layer of bread. According to Ranganathan "when the basic layer is a basic subject and the other layers are isolate ideas, a compound subject is formed".

LOOSE ASSEMBLAGE

Loose Assemblage of Kind-1

1. General relation between political science and economics
2. Statistics for librarians
3. Influence of geography on histroy

Loose Assemblage of Kind-2: Two or more isolates taken from one and the same schedule are brought into a mutual relationship. This is called an "intra facet phase relation" and results in a complex isolate.

Examples:
1. Influence of Buddhism on Christianity
2. Difference between Lemuroidea and Anthropoidea.

Loose Assemblage of Kind-3: Two or more isolates taken from one and the same array of an order higher than 1 in one and the same schedule are brought into mutual relation. This is called an "intra array phase relation" and results in a complex array isolate.

Canonical Basic Subject: This denotes a traditional division of a main subject. The traditional division is denoted by the term "canonical constituent".

Examples:

C3 Sound
C4 Heat
C5 Radiation

Special Basic Subject: This denotes a division of a main subject (MS), in which the subject of the study is restricted in some special manner, not amounting to any of the anteriorising common isolates or any other isolate ideas. This special division is denoted by the term "special constituent" of the MS. Generally, the class number for a special BS is got by the enumeration device.

Examples:

L-9C Child medicine
L-9F Geriatrics
L-9H Female medicine

Environmented Basic Subject: This denotes a division of a MS, in which the entity of the study of the MS is within an extra normal environment, such as those enumerated in the schedule of environment divisions.

Examples:

D-9Uk2 Desert engineering
D-9Um7 Mountain engineering
D-9V4 War engineering

System Basic Subject: This denotes a division of a MS or a non-main BS expounded according to a specific system, or School of Thought, other than what is currently popular.

Examples:

B2-N Boolean algebra
L-B Ayurvedic system of medicine
S-N Gestalt psychology

Example:

Medicine–ayurvedic system–tropical environment–child

FISSION

The initial set of primary basic subjects (PBS) included in a scheme for library classification results from a division/fission of the UoS in a manner similar to the division of the UoS by scholars among themselves as convenient fields of specialisation. It may not be possible to discern a specific characteristic used in this initial division.

Fission is the process of division or splitting or breaking up into parts. This process has, until recently, been denoted by the term "dissection". However, dissection usually implies the splitting, breaking up, etc., of an entity into parts by an outside agency. On the other hand, fission is an internal process of division without the involvement of an outside agency.

Example:

In CC, the initial schedule of traditional Primary Basic Subject (PBS) was derived by a direct fission of the UoS and the following broad groups may be noted:

Primary BS covering natural sciences
Primary BS covering useful arts
Primary BS covering humanities
Primary BS covering social sciences

The term "dissection" is used to denote fission when we consider an array of divisions of an isolate or of a basic subject, resulting from fission.

FUSION

One result of interdisciplinary research, which is characteristic of present day organisation and conduct of research programmes, is the emergence of new ideas and new subjects of an interdisciplinary character. Often, an interdisciplinary subject may be deemed to go with more than one of the existing primary basic subjects (PBS). The subjects going with this PBS will usually contain the core entity whose attributes are examined by the research team. Let us call this host PBS 1. The subjects going with another PBS—that is, host PBS 2 may be related to the subjects going with the host PBS 1 in a variety of ways, e.g., phase relation (i.e., application of statistics to biology). In due course, as the field developes, there may be a number of new ideas arising out of the interdisciplinary research, such that —

- *(a)* the classification may find that they cannot be conveniently and helpfully deemed to go with the host PBI selected earlier;
- *(b)* these new ideas attract for themselves a group of specialists; and
- *(c)* a new field of specialisation concretises with normative principles / theory of its own, in addition to using the normative principles /theory of the subjects going with the host PBS 1 and 2.

DISTILLATION

In this mode, a pure discipline is evolved as a PBS from its appearance-in-action in diverse compound subjects going with either different BS or one and the same BS. It gives rise to PBS by distillation. Thus mode may be taken to be equivalent to what Boulding describes as "Multi-hybrid with common methodology". Thus, distillation may be of 2 kinds (Kind 1 and Kind 2. In Kind 1, the new PBS essentially accommodates the theory of discipline emerging or distilled out of an idea(s) occurring as a practice-in-action in subjects going with diverse BS. However, it should be remembered that, even after the formulation of a new pure discipline, the appearance of the idea as a practice-in-action will continue and should be treated as such — that is, it should be placed as an isolate idea in the subject concerned.

Examples:

In CC
Management
(PBS) 8
Management of University Library
2, J4:8

CLUSTERING

In the past, in the Universe of Documents, the general trend has been to narrow the extension of a subject embodied in a document taken as a whole. Therefore, there has been a general tendency not to bring into one and the same document, compound subjects going with the different basic subjects, except in the case of complex subjects involving phase relation and the subjects involving the use of subject device in forming or sharpening isolate facets. In recent years, however, interdisciplinary team research has often, for practical convenience, necessitated bringing together in one and the same document two or more compound subjects going with different BS.

Examples:

1. Area study, in which geogrpahical area forms the focus of the cluster, like Sinology (Chinese studies), Nippinology (Japanese studies).
2. Generalia person study, in which a multi-faceted personality forms the focus of a cluster — Gandhiana.
3. Study of entity of phenomena forming the focus of a cluster — Soil science, Surface science.

AGGLOMERATION

Agglomeration (earlier called partial comprehension) is the process of collecting together of entities into larger masses without cohesion among the components. An agglomerate can be a BS, or it can also be an isolate idea. Agglomeration may be made up of consecutive constituents or even non-consecutive constituents with respect to a classification scheme.

NOTATION

Ranganathan, in his theory of library classification, introduced the concept of three planes of work, which you are already familiar with. Of these, the notational plane is beset with several difficulties. It is in this sphere that much research has taken place and several innovations have been made. You already know the meaning of notation, its function and its kinds. We will now turn our attention to the notation in CC.

MIXED NOTATION—INDICATOR DIGITS

CC uses a mixed notation. It consists of

1. Indo-Arabic numerals, 1-9
2. Roman alphabet–both capitals and lower case, A to Z and a to z.
3. Parentheses ( )
4. Indicator digits

The following table gives the details of the indicator digits used in the 7th edition of CC.

Digit / Symbol	Name of the indicator digit	Role of the indicator digit
*	Asterisk	indicates agglomeration and interpolation
←	Backward arrow	indicates backword range
"	Double inverted comma	indicates common isolates
(The above three indicator digits have anteriorising value)		
&	Ampersand	indicates phase relation
'	Single inverted comma	indicates time facet
.	Dot	indicates space facet
:	Colon	indicates energy facet
;	Semi-colon	indicates matter facet
,	Comma	indicates personality facet
-	Hyphen	indicates speciator of kind 1
=	Equal sign	indicates speciator of kind 2
+	Plus sign	and, addition
→	Forward arrow	indicates forward range

EMPTY DIGIT

To increase the capacity of an array, CC has introduced what is called an empty digit. An empty digit has no semantic value, but it retains the ordinal value. Let us see the meaning of empty digit with the help of an example. If you are using the Indo-Arabic numerals, you can use a maximum of nine numerals (1 to 9). If a subject is to be divided, we can divide it only up to nine places and the tenth and subsequent divisions cannot be accommodated. To overcome this difficulty, CC uses numerals 1 to 8 only and 9 is left as an empty digit. It has no value by itself, but regains its full value when it is used in combination as 91, 92, 93 .... 98 or 991, 992, 993 ... 998 and so on. This method has given tremendous potential to increase arrays in any given facet. The same principle has been used while using a to z, or A to Z. In lower case letters, z is made an empty digit, and in capital letters, T, V and X are postulated as empty emptying digits and Z as empty digit. Also, CC uses a number of devices for increasing hospitality and facilitating synthesis. We will see these devices in the following section.

DEVICES

We have seen that new subjects always crop up and a classification scheme should be able to find appropriate places for such new subjects within its framework. Ranganathan provided a number of devices for this purpose. The purpose of such a device is to form a new isolate or to sharpen an existing in an array. This method has considerably reduced the size of the scheme.

The four major devices used in CC are:

1. Chronological device
2. Geographical device

3. Subject device
4. Alphabetical device

We will discuss each of these in brief as give below.

CHRONOLOGICAL DEVICE

The purpose of this device is to sharpen a facet number. It can sharpen an isolate or form a new isolate. This is done by employing a chronological number from the schedule of time isolates. All numbers for authors in the class **Literature** are derived through this device. It is impracticable to enumerate all authors. The chronological device has, however, taken care of such a contingency. To give an example, the number for Rabindranath Tagore is O, 157, 1M61. Here, M61 stands for 1861, the year of birth of Rabindranath Tagore. This device has been used in several main classes like library science, mathematics, medicine, fine arts, psychology, education, economics, etc. This device can be used wherever warranted. The basic class of systems is derived through the chronological device.

GEOGRAPHICAL DEVICE

The purpose of all these devices, as stated earlier, is to form or to sharpen an isolate number in a schedule. Employing a geographical number from the schedule of space isolates is another mechanism of doing this. It has been used in library science, fine arts, religion, linguistics, history and in several other classes. The formation of an isolate using this device is as follows:

152 = d4437 means Rajasthani Hindi, where

152 is Hindi

= is the connecting symbol

d is the symbol for dialect

4437 is Rajasthani from the schedule of space isolates.

Another example of the geographical device:

Early Egyptian religion for which the number is Q, 8677.

Here, Q,8 is other religions, and

677 is Egypt from the schedule of space isolates.

SUBJECT DEVICE

Subject device is used to form or sharpen a facet by adding to it (facet) another class number from elsewhere in the scheme. This device has been used in several main classes. The part of the number derived by the subject device should be enclosed in parenthesis (circular brackets). For example, Medical college library is 2, J3(L)

In the above example, in library science, 2,J3 represents college libraries to which is added (L) from the main class L **Medicine** to derive medical college library by subject device.

Let us take another example of subject device. Hindu Law is Z, (Q, 2) where Z is law and (Q,2) is Hindu religion from the main class Q **Religion.**

ALPHABETICAL DEVICE

Alphabetical device is also used to form or sharpen an isolate number. The device is used taking the first or the first two or three letters of the names of persons, or objects, or products widely accepted as such. The device can be used wherever warranted. The following are some examples where the device is used:

O,157,3M61,G **Gora**, a novel by Rabindranath Tagore
Here, G stands for Gora

O,157,3M61,H+W **Home and the world**, a novel by Tagore.
Here, the initial letters of the two words in the title are connected, using the plus sign (+).
(H for Home and W for World)

PHASE RELATIONS

Nowadays we come across several inter-disciplinary subjects. This is the result of interaction between two or more subjects. For this purpose, CC has provided a device called **Phase Relation.** A pahse relation may occur between two or more main classes; it may also occur within one and the same facet of a main class, or within one and the same array isolates. These three types are called inter-subject, intra-facet and intra-array phase relations respectively (see Unit 8 of Block 3).

Besides, there are six kinds of phase relations indicated in CC. These six kinds are:

1. General relation phase.
2. Bias phase.
3. Comparison phase.
4. Difference phase.
5. Tool phase.
6. Influencing phase.

The connecting symbol for a phase relation is composed of an ampersand (&) and a relation indicator as shown in the table below:

Schedule of digits (CC 7th edition)

Kind of phase relation	Inter-subject	Intra-facet	Intra-array
General	a	j	t
Bias	b	k	u
Comparison	c	m	v
Difference	d	n	w
Tool	e	p	x
Influencing	f	r	y

Following are a few examples to show the use of different kinds of phase relations in CC:

1. A general study of special and university libraries — Type: intra-facet, Kind: general, No.2,J4&jK
2. Psychology for teachers — Type: Inter-subject, Kind: bias, No.S&bT
3. Comparison of Jainism and Buddhism — Type: intra-facet, Kind: comparison, No.Q,3&m4
4. Difference between undergraduate and postgraduate education — Type: intra-array, Kind: difference, No.T,181&w2
5. Statistical analysis in library management — Type: inter-subject, Kind: tool, No.2:8&eBT
6. Influence of music on literature — Type: inter-subject, Kind: influencing, No.O&gNR.

SYSTEMS AND SPECIALS

Up to the sixth edition of CC, systems and specials were enumerated along with the concerned main classes. In the seventh edition, they have been listed in the schedule of basic subjects. However, they have been separately defined.

Systems: The term **system basic subjects** denote a division of a main class expounded after a school of thought. A school of thought is a group, or succession of persons devoted to some cause or philosophy. The class number for a system is derived by the chronological device. Some examples of system facets are:

B6-M8	Hyperbolic geometry, where B6 is geometry and M8 means the 1880s. The number stands for a system of geometry expounded in the 1880s.
L-B	Ayurveda. B is 999 to 1000 BC — a system of medicine that came into being prior to 1000 BC.

UNIVERSAL DECIMAL CLASSIFICATION

Universal Decimal Classification owes its origin to Dewey Decimal Classification (DDC). As noted in the introduction to **UDC International Medium Edition,** DDC had, even in the 19th century, "played an important part in establishing the norm of a systematic code denoting the subject as a primary means of arranging and retrieving literature in libraries". Due to this virtue of DDC, it was natural for the scheme to attract the attention of a renowned Belgian bibliographer, Paul Otlet. This was in 1895 when Otlet, in collaboration with Henri La Fontaine, was working on a Universal Bibliography under the auspices of Institute International de Bibliography in Brussels. The projected compilation with which the two Belgian bibliographers were busy was called **Universal Bibliographic Repertory,** a comprehensive classified index to all published information.

Outlet was in search of a means for arranging the entries of the planned Universal Bibliography and he found the DDC to be most useful for the purpose. He, therefore, obtained permission from Melvil Dewey to translate his classification into French. Otlet and La Fontaine were impressed by the following merits of DDC:

1. It was a classification of human knowledge;
2. It was an international language of numbers; and
3. The decimal numbers that comprised the language of DDC could be easily extended to accommodate not only new subjects, but also the details so essential for an international bibliography.

However, Otlet was not satisfied with just borrowing the DDC text and translating it into French. He must be credited with developing decimal classification further into a versatile means of arranging and retrieving literature. Several innovations were introduced into the original scheme. Thus:

1. UDC bacame a highly synthetic scheme.
2. Several relations between subjects were indentified and symbols were assigned to represent them.
3. Characteristics common to many subjects were listed separately as tables of auxiliary numbers, which could be added where required.

Due to the introduction of auxiliaries and other synthetic features, UDC achieved a higher level of detail in numbers and economy of presentation. The level of detail worked out by Otlet and La Fontaine in the French version of DDC due to their innovations served well the purpose of their **Repertory.**

The first edition of UDC, called **Handbook to the Universal Bibliographic Repertory,** in French, was published by the Institute International de Bibliography (IIB) from 1904 to 1907. The second edition was brought out during 1927 to 1933. The work of revision and expansion went on before World War 1. This was particularly so in the case of Science and Technology sections.

The expansion of these sections was the work of Donker Duyvis from the Netherlands, who was then one of the editors of UDC. The expansion of the original classification was so extensive that the number of subdivisions rose from 33,000 in the first edition to 70,000 in the second edition and 1,40,000 in the third, which were published between 1934 and 1951.

The credit for introducing and popularising UDC in the United Kingdom, and form there to the Commonwealth countries, goes to S.C. Bradford, a pioneer in the field of documen-tation. That UDC came to be regarded as perhaps the most satisfactory scheme for classifying science and technology literature is also largely due to Bradford. The responsibility for publishing a full edition of UDC in English was initially taken by the British Society for International Bibliography and ASLIB together and several parts were published by 1939. However, it was later taken over by the British Standards Institutions (BSI). The UDC and its parts have ever since been published as British Standards. The **UDC International Medium Edition** (BS 1000M: 1985) was published in 1985 in two parts — Part I : Systematic Tables (1985); and Part II.: Alphabetical Subject Index (1988). The latest is IME, English Text, Edition 2 (BS 1000M). Part I: Systematic Tables; and Part II: Alphabetical Subject Index. BSI, 1993.

English, French and German are the official languages for the maintenance of UDC. The original Institute International de Bibliography became, in 1931, the Institute International de Documentation. Another change in name came in 1937. It became the Federation International de Documentation (FID) with its headquarters at The Hague in the Netherlands. Recently, FID has added the word information to its name. It is now Federation Internationale d' Information et de Documentation / Inter-national Federation for information and Documentation. Authorised amendments to UDC appear annually in the form of **Extensions and Corrections to the UDC.** Initially, this was a six-monthly publication.

ALPHABETICAL SUBJECT INDEX

The Alphabetical Subject Index published in 1988. The entries in the index reflect the terminology used in the schedules. In most cases qualifiers have not been added under each term indicating the context in which the term is used. To tide over this problem some index entries consist of a term followed by several class numbers. For example 'Axes' is indexed and unqualified to five numbers 581.44, 621.968, 631.342, 672.719. To understand the context in which these five class numbers are used, one has to refer to the schedules.

The Index does not fully indicate the context of the terms listed. But it does indicate the range of possible locations for a particular concept. The arrangement of entries in the index is word-by-word. The users of the index are advised not to classify a document solely on the basis of index but to verify the class number in the schedules. Here is a sample entry from the index:

Lighters	629.123.15, 662.58
cigar and cigarette	662.592
electric	662.593
flint	662.592
pocket	662.59
using solar heat	662.591

PROVISION FOR FUTURE EXPANSION

The UDC notation is decimal and can accommodate emerging new concepts wherever necessary. In addition to this in-built provision, UDC has resorted to what is called **gap device**. These gaps in the notation are meant for accommodating a large number of subdivisions and are left where future expansion is envisaged. We find the following vacant numbers in the notation:

142—159.8	in Philosophy and Psychology
365—367	in Social welfare
375	in Education
4	the class Philology transferred to 8 Literature
538.1—538.8	in Physics
544—545	in Chemistry

This is how UDC has provided for future expansion.

DEWEY DECIMAL CLASSIFICATION

Melvil Dewey was born in Adams Center, New York, on December 10th, 1851. He was the son of a small storekeeper and, at the age of five, it is said that he rearranged his mother's larder — which is the place where provisions are stored — in a more systematic manner. He came to librarianship through a process of self education, a few years of teaching followed by higher studies at Oneida Seminary, Alfred University, and finally at Amherst College. He obtained a post as student library assistant in 1872 at the same college. In the following year, he put forward a plan for rearranging the library in a more systematic way. He was promoted in 1874 to the post of Assistant College Librarian. In 1876, he anonymously published his classification scheme, which had far reaching effects. Apart from the classification scheme, which bears his name, he also had many other contributions to his credit. He became the first editor of the ***Library Journal*** in 1876, a founder member of the American Library Association in 1876 and later its first Secretary. He also founded the first librarianship school in the United States (Columbia University) in 1887, promoted the standard catalogue card (12.5 ×

7.5 cm) and took an active interest in all aspects of librarianship.

FIRST EDITION

The publication of a 42-page pamphlet entitled **A classification and subject index for cataloguing and arranging the books and pamphlets of a library** in 1876, heralded the beginning of both DDC and library classification. This was the first edition, which consisted of 12 pages of preparatory matter, 12 pages of tables and 18 pages of index, a total of 42 pages. One thousand copies of this first edition were printed. It contained nearly 1000 classes. It was, however, criticised as being too minute in its subdivisions for a majority of libraries. Within a very short time it, nevertheless, became extremely popular and was soon adopted by many libraries in the United States and other countries. The original 42-page anonymous pamphlet culminated, in the course of time, in a monumental work of over 3,000 pages. According to a recent survey, over 85 per cent of all types of libraries in the USA and Canada use DDC. It has been adopted in all five continents of the world.

SPECIAL FEATURES

Dewey was not the first to introduce subject arrangement of books in libraries. He was, however, the first to introduce the following innovative features in subject arrangement:

1. The concept of relative location
2. Decimal notation
3. Detailed specification
4. Relative index

REVISION PROCESS

One other factor which has contributed to the durability of DDC has been its sustained programme of revision and updating. Revisions usually take the following forms:

- Expansion
- Reduction
- Relocation

Expansion is undertaken in order to accommodate new subjects as well as to provide more minute and specific sub-divisions under the existing subjects. This is a reasonable approach as most new subjects emerge as an outgrowth of an existing field of knowledge. With increasing specialisation, library materials also tend to be more specific and, thus, require more minute sub-divisions of the existing subjects.

Reduction consists discontinuing very rarely used existing sub-divisions. Such topics are, then, classed with the more general topic.

Relocation of a number of existing subjects takes place in every new edition.

LIBRARY CATALOGUE

The word 'catalogue' comes from the Greek phrase *Katalogos*. *Kata* means "according to" or "by", Logos has different meanings. Sometimes it means simply "words", sometimes "order" and at other times "reason". We may therefore explain "catalogue" as a work in which the contents are arranged in a "reasonable" way in a particular "order" or according to a set "plan".

Generally speaking a library catalogue is a list of books and other materials in a particular library, arranged according to a definite plan or determined order and cotaining specified items of bibliographical information for the purpose of identification and location of the materials catalogued.

The definitions of various authors are reproduced here which have historical importance and interest to the professional librarians :

A catalogue is "an explanatory, logically arranged inventory and key to the books and then contents and it is confined to the books in a particular library." (James Duff Brown)

A library catalogue is a list of books which is arranged on some definite plan. As distinguished from a bibliography it is a list of books in some library or collections.

A terminology Group at the International Conference on Cataloguing Principles (ICCP) held at Paris in 1961 defined a catalogue as "a comprehensive list of collection or collections of books, documents or similar meterial".

Dr. Ranganathan has defined the library catalogue involving three aspects;

(i) The list, -of;

(ii) Documents, -in a;

(iii) Library (single library or group of libraries).

Documents includes the books, periodicals, Microfilms, photographs, gramophone records, taperecords, etc.

Brown defined the library catalogue as one of the important key and inventory of books. Key in the sense that it indicates the location or the identification of the book and inventory in the sense that it contains the bibliographical information. But Brown has confined the catalogue limited to books while catalogue is also prepared for other reading material. Moreover, a catalogue may also be prepared for a group of libraries.

In the definition by ICCP the word "comprehensive" is controversial in the sense that by no means all the catalogues aim at comprehensiveness. But this definition brings to light the essential difference between catalogues and bibliographies.

From all the definitions, one can gather that public catalogue is the most important tool of a well equipped library. It is an inventory or a list. It is a bridge between the intellectual contents of library and the users. It is constructed or its entries are arranged according to a set plan or methodology. A library therefore always needs a systematized and well thoughtfully prepared catalogue in order to provide up to date information to the users. A library might possess sound collection of books and other reading material; but if it lacks in a good catalogue the library and the users both will be the loser. Library staff in general and reference librarian in particular always recourse to catalogue and cataloguing selection when entangled in a complicated reference/research question for the location of specific information. Librarian therefore has to consult or take help of the catalogues at every state of reference service, book selection etc. Figure given below reveals the importance of a catalogue in any library set up.

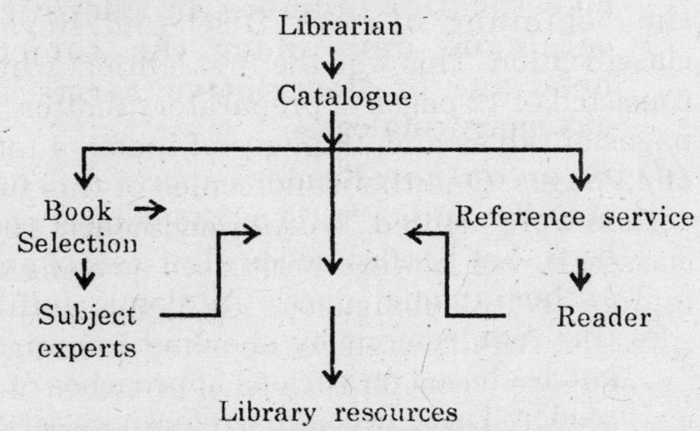

PURPOSE OF A LIBRARY CATALOGUE

The purpose of a library catalogue is to help the library user in identifying a document and also help in selecting a work or works expeditiously and exactly to his or her requirements. The library catologue helps the librarians to achieve these purposes by satisfying various approaches of a reader; giving bibliographical details for further assistance in the selection of exact documents; and bringing together other relevant information by analytical entries, cross references, etc, to sharpen the search and leading to the exact location of all relevant documents in the library.

1. LOCATE AND INDENTIFY A BOOK OF WHICH EITHER

(a) ***Author:*** Author is clearly identified by the entries made under the name of the author popularly known, or written on the title page. Needham has suggested that in case of controversial authors, the name out of the title page should be considered.

(b) ***Title:*** Title can be identified by preparing entries under title. Title entries are generally made for striking

and significant titles, i.e., for novels and other works in the "form" classes like plays and major power, and works like periodicals which have no recognized author.

(c) ***Subject:*** Subject can be identified by preparing subject entries made under a classification number in classified catalogue and under the subject headings or descriptive terms in dictionary catalogue.

(d) ***By an author:*** Reader's approach is not only the author, title or the subject of a book, but he also needs all works of one author at one place. Catalogue fulfils this requirement by showing reference entries based on various approaches of a reader. These necessary references serve the purpose and supplement the author.

(e) ***In a given kind of literature:*** There are various forms of literature: dictionary, encyclopaedia, yearbook etc. A list is prepared for the collection of one form, such a list fulfils the objective of providing information of the whole collection of a particular term of literature. The term of presentation may also be a subheading.

TYPES OF CATALOGUES

CONVENTIONAL FORMS

The conventional physical forms include:

- Bound register/Ledger form
- Printed book from
- Sheaf or Loose-leaf form, and
- Card form

We shall study these forms with reference to their features, their relative advantages and disadvantages:

(i) BOUND REGISTER OR LEDGER FORM

In this form, the entries of documents of a library are written by hand in a bound register or ledger, pages are set apart for different letters of the alphabets. These alphabet are arranged alphabetically. Minimum information about the document such as author, title, edition, accession number and class number is given for each book. There may be a separate register for authors or titles or subjects.

Typed Cyclostyled Form

Revised version of bound register form came into existence due to the typewriter and cyclostyling machine. The entries are typed. Multiple copies (up to four) can be had from the typewriter. By using a cyclostyling machine, one may get multiple copies of the catalogue. This facilitated movement of catalogue from one room to another room. All the advantages of bound register form are applicable to this form. Pages of the register are now kept in plastic jackets to increase the life of the pages. These pages re filed in separate files.

It is also difficult to provide additional entries to a document, in addition to the main entry. Hence, flexibility of different approaches to the catalogue may not be possible. Provision of cross-reference is even more difficult. All these naturally restrict the use of the catalogue. Most modern libraries have discarded this form of library catalogue.

(ii) PRINTED BOOK FORM

The printed book from of library catalogue is one of its typical forms. These types of library catalogues are prepared conforming to all the standard principles and rules of cataloguing, with cross references and multiple entries.

In the nineteenth century, the most common physical form of a library catalogue was the printed book form. Especially, some of the big libraries like British Museum Library (now renamed as the British Library), the Library of Congress, National Library Kolkata, printed their catalogues in the book form. To keep the catalogue updated, they used to issue supplements to these catalogues at regular intervals, e.g. the catalogue of

Bombay Branch of the Royal Asiatic Society of Bombay Library was kept up-to-date in this way.

(iii) SHEAF OR LOOSE-LEAF FORM

Sheaf form of library catalogue is also referred to as loose-leaf form. A sheaf form of catalogue is one in which slips of paper are put into a loose-leaf binder and bound by some mechanical device into a volume. This is a loose-leaf binder format, which provides the convenience of handling a book. In the sheaf form, each entry is made on a separate slip. But, there may also be more than one entry on each slip or page. The entries are either handwritten or typed. New slips can be inserted in appropriate places without disturbing the existing order of arrangement of entries. It is also possible to remove entries for specific documents in case such documents are withdrawn from the library stock. Roughly, each volume of a sheaf catalogue may contain about 500 to 600 leaves. The volumes so constituted may be displayed on special shelves with appropriate labels on their spines, indicating the order (either alphabetical or classified) of arrangement. At one time this form of catalogue became somewhat popular in countries like England and other European countries.

(iv) CARD FORM

Library catalogue in the card form is by far the most poopular physical form. It is widely prevalent in libraries throughout the world including India.

In this form the bibliographical elements of every document are recorded on a single card. This method of representing every document on a single card is knwon as the unit card principle. These cards stand in card-trays or cabinets with a punched hole of about half a centimetre from the bottom for inserting a locking rod. This locking system keeps the cards from falling out and also prevents unauthorised persons from removing any card from the tray. Because of its wide usage all over the world, many aspects pertaining to the card catalogue are standardised. For example, 12.5 × 7.6 cm. is the universally adopted size for a catalogue card. Similarly, the sizes of cabinets, trays for a card catalogue are all of uniform standard. Consequently, most of these items of furniture could be obtained readily from commercial vendors.

CHARACTERS OF THE BEST PHYSICAL FORM OF LIBRARY CATALOGUE

Despite the widespread use of the computer for for cataloguing, a great many catalogues in the conventional format, such as card form will continue to exist, at least in countries like India, for many years to come. Whatever physical form a catalogue may have, it should have the following features:

- It must be easy to use.
- It must be easy to keep up-to-date
- It should enable browsing on scanning over a number of entries at a time.
- Multiple copies must be easily produced
- It must occupy as little space as possible.
- It should provide multiple access tools.

INNER FORMS OF A LIBRARY CATALOGUE

The cataloguing process comprises two operations. The first is the creation of varieties of entries for documents acquired by a library. The second is the organisation of these entries in a logical and helpful order for storage and retrieval, as given below:

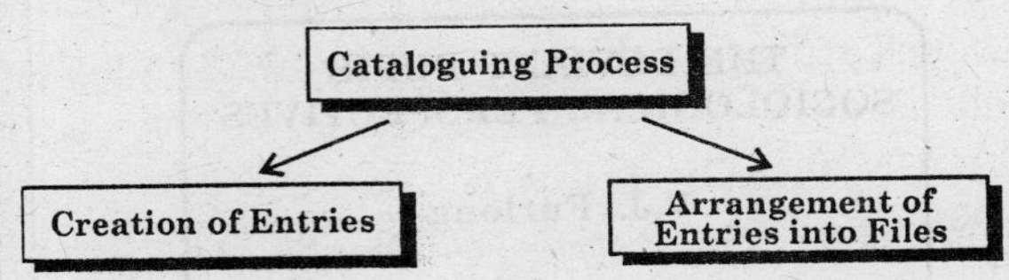

In this chapter, we are concerned only with the file organisation of catalogue entries.

While there are many ways of arranging these entries in a helpful order, the three currently existing systems are:

- Aphabetical files
- Classified files
- Alphabetico-classed files

Alphabetical catalogue can be separately designed and constructed for authors, titles, names, recording works on and by authors, subjects or all entries of authors, titles, subjects, etc. in one single alphabetical file, known as the dictionary catalogue. In classified files, the main entries are arranged according to the class number of the classification scheme chosen for the shelf organisation of documents in a library. This file is supported by an alphabetical index.

The following chart illustrates the different inner forms of a library catalogue:

INNER FORMS

Alphabetical	**Classified**	**Alphabetico-classed**
Author	Classified Part	Subject Part
Name	Alphabetical Part	Alphabetical Index
Title		
Subject		
Dictionary		

PRACTICAL CATALOGUING

Let us put that knowledge into practice. In practice, actual title page of a book will be given with as much details as are required to catalogue the book. In rendering several elements we also come across a few problems. We will discuss those problems and the solutions provided by AACR-2R.

Example

> **THE DEVIANT PUPIL**
> **SOCIOLOGICAL PERSPECTIVES**
>
> **V.J. Furlong**
>
> **Open University Press**
> **Milton Keynes**

Other Information

Call No.	371.93 Fur
Accession No.	7862
Pages	xx, 226
Date of Publication	1985
Size of the book	24 cm.
ISBN	0-335-15225-2 0-335-15126-4 (pbk.)

Main Entry

```
371.93
FUR     Furlong, V.J.
        The deviant pupil: sociological
        perspectives/ V.J. Furlong.– Milton
        Keynes: Open University Press,
        1985. xx, 226p.; 24 cm
7862    ISBN-335-15225-2
        1 Emotionally disturbed children
        I Title
```

The main entry for the book is complete. The heading for the author has been given as in the title page. The title of the book also is reproduced without any change. The name of the author is transcribed in the statement of responsibility area. Next comes the place of publication, name of the publisher and date of publication. Appropriate punctuation marks are given as already discussed. The next two paragraphs contain the physical description of the book and ISBN number. Now you may have a doubt about the ISBN number because in the other information area two ISBN numbers are given. The first ISBN number is applicable to the hardbound book and the second number is given for the paperback edition of the book. The abbreviation (pbk.) refers to paperback book. Hence you have to give only one number, whichever book you are cataloguing.

Under unit card, we have to prepare as many cards as are required and only then add the added entry information on the top line. That is why you see the subject entry card is a duplication of main entry, the only additional information transcribed is subject heading taken from **Sears List of Subject**

Headings. Subject heading is always written in capital letters. The added entry in title card is also a duplication of the main entry. The information given is only the short title of book. Sub-titles need not be given in the added entries. The complete card is not shown here **but in the library you have to write the full card.** This completes the cataloguing of the book.

The added éntries are:

Added Entry – Subject

371.93	**Emotionally Disturbed Children**
Fur	**Furlong, V. J.**
	The deviant pupil: sociological perspectives.
	(Same as in the main entry)

Added Entry – Title

371.93	**The deviant pupil**
Fur	**Furlong, V. J.**
	The deviant pupil: sociological perspectives.
	(Same as in the main entry)

SHARED WORK

The AACR-2R has defined the shared responsibility as "Collaboration between two or more persons or bodies performing the same kind of activity in the creation of the content of an item. The contribution of each may form a separate and distinct part of the item, or the contribution of each may not be separable from that of the others".

There are specific rules applicatable to shared responsibility. The AACR-2R has elaborated the scope of shared responsibility to which the rules can be applied. Rule 21.6A gives the scope of the rules as:

(i) works produced by the collaboration with two or more persons.
(ii) works for which different persons have prepared separate contributions.
(iii) works consisting of an exchange between two or more persons (like correspondent debates).
(iv) Collaboration can also be between two or more corporate bodies or between a corporate body and a person.

A. PRINCIPAL RESPONSIBILITY INDICATED

In a work of shared responsibility a particular author may have undertaken more responsibility for the creation of the work. The AACR-2R makes a distinction under two categories:

(i) Principal responsibility indicated; and
(ii) Principal responsibility not indicated.

Let us first discuss the meaning of 'Principal Responsibility Indicated'. In cases of books when there are two or more authors and if one of the authors is attributed with principal responsibility by giving prominence such as, by wording or layout etc., the rule (Rule No.21.6B1) prescribes to make the main entry under the author who has given prominence. For instance, if ther are three authors and they are printed on the title page as shown below:

Loyd Enrick
SHEPHERD B. CLOUGH
Theodore F. Marburg

Then, the indication is that the main entry heading should be made under the author Shepherd B. Clough because his name is given prominence by typography. Let us take another example of three authors.

Connie Haynes
With
Eve Kraft and John Conroy

In this case, the main entry heading should be under Connie Haynes because she has been given prominence by wording.

This is called 'Principal Responsibility Indicated'. He can be the first, second, or third author but if his name is shown distinct from other authors by wording or layout, the main entry heading has to be made under that author. In case two authors are shown as principal authors then the entry is to be made under the first named principal author.

Let us now discuss when principal responsibility is not indicated.

B. PRINCIPAL RESPONSIBILITY NOT INDICATED

Usually, when there are two or more authors and they are printed alike on the title page it means they are given equal status, or AACR-2R calls such situations as 'Principal Responsibility Not Indicated'. Under this category, it further distinguishes shared responsibility as follows:

(i) books written by two or three authors
(ii) books written by more than three authors.

BOOKS WRITTEN BY TWO AUTHORS

Example

> **William N. Dember Joel S. Warm**
>
> **Psychology of Perception**
> **Second**
> **Edition**
>
> **Holt, Rinehart and Winston**
> **New York Chicago San Francisco**

Other Information

Call No.	152.1/DEM
Accession No.	5302
Date of Publication of 2nd edition	1979
Pages	viii, 536
Size	24 cm.
ISBN	Not provided

Main Entry

> **152.1**
> **DEM** **Dember, William N.**
> **Psychology of perception/William N. Dember, Joel S. Warm. – 2nd ed. –**
> **New York: Holt, Rinehart and Winston, 1979.**
> **viii, 536.; 24 cm.**
> **5302**
> **1 Perception I Warm, Joel S. II Title**

The tracing shows what additional entries are to be prepared. There are three more entries, viz., *(i)* subject entry *(ii)* entry for the second author and *(iii)* the title entry. The three added entries are given below:

Added Entry – Subject

> **152.1** **PERCEPTION**
> **DEM** **Dember, William N.**
> **Psychology of perception**
> **(Rest as in the main entry)**

Added Entry – Second Author (also called Joint Author)

> **152.1** **Warm, Joel S.**
> **DEM** **Dember, William N.**
> **Psychology of perception**
> **(Same as in the main entry)**

Added Entry – Title

> **152.1** **Psychology of perception**
> **DEM** **Dember, William N.**
> **Psychology of perception**
> **(Same as in the main entry.**

BOOKS WRITTEN BY THREE AUTHORS

The general rule in case of three authors is to make the main entry under the name of the first author if any one the other two authors are not shown as principal author by wording or typography. In such cases, the second and third authors are given added entries. Based on this explanation two examples are given below:

Example

> **DEVELOPMENTAL PSYCHOLOGY**
> **Robert M. Liebert**
> **State University of New York at Stony Brook**
> **Rita Wicks-Nelson**
> **West Virginia Institute of Technology**
> **Robert V. Kail**
> **Purdue University**
> **Prentice-Hall, Englewood Cliffs, New Jersey**

Other Information

Call No.	155/LIE
Accession No.	6130
Date of Publication	1986
Pages	viii; 548
Size	24 cm.
ISBN	0-13-208109-1

There are three authors and all the three are given equal status. No author has been shown either by wording or layout as principal author. In such cases, the rule is to make the heading in the main entry under the first named author and to give added entries to the authors. All the pertinent entries are shown below:

Main Entry

155
LIE **Liebert, Robert M.**
Developmental psychology/Robert M. Liebert, Rita Wicks-Nelson, Robert V Kail.–4th ed. – Englewood Cliffs, New Jersey: Prentice-Hall, 986.
viii, 548.; 24 cm.
6130 **ISBN 0-13-208109-1**
1 Psychology,– Developmental I Wicks-Nelson, Rita II Kail, Robert V. III Title

The added entries are:

Added Entry – Subject

155 **Psychology–Developmental**
LIE **Liebert, Robert, M.**
Developmental Psychology
(Same as in the main entry)

Added Entry – 2nd Author

155 **Wicks-Nelson, Rita**
LIE **Liebert, Robert, M.**
Developmental Psychology
(Same as in the main entry)

The author's name is a compound surname. The entries for compound names with a hyphen should be entered as it is. Sometimes a **see reference** is given as shown below:

Nelson, Rita Wicks
See
Wicks-Nelson, Rita

We will talk about *see reference* in the later units.

Added Entry – 3rd Author

155 **Kail, Robert V.**
LIE **Liebert, Robert, M.**
Developmental Psychology
(Same as in the main entry)

BOOKS WRITTEN BY MORE THAN THREE AUTHORS

In cases of books written by more than three authors, the rule given in AACR-2R is as stated below:

"If responsibility is shared between more than three persons or corporate bodies and principal responsibility is not attributed to any one, two, or three, enter under title and make an added entry under the heading for the first person or corporate body named."

Based on this rule, we have worked out an example of a work written by more than three authors.

Example

PRINCIPLES OF PSYCHOLOGY
Richard H Price
University of Michigan, Ann Arbor
Mitehell Glickstein
Brown University
David L. Horton
University of Maryland
Ronald H. Bailey
Holt, Rinehart and Winston
New York, Chicago, San Francisco

Other Information

Call No.	150/PRI
Accession No.	5819
Date of Publication	1982
Pages	xvii, 650
Size	26 cm.
ISBN	0-03-048411-1

Main Entry

150
PRI Principles of psychology/Richard H. Price..
[et al].–New York: Holt, Rinehart and Winston, 1982.
xvii, 650p.; 26 cm.
5819 ISBN 0-03-048411-1
1 Psychology I Price, Richard H.

Added Entry – Subject

150
PRI Principles of psychology/Richard H. Price
(Same as in the main entry)

SINGLE EDITOR

Based on the above explanation two examples are worked out below:

Example

ARTIFICIAL INTELLIGENCE
The Case Against
Edited by
Rainer Born
Croom Helm
London & Sydney

Other Information

Call No.	001.535/ART
Accession No.	8245
Date of Publication	1987
Pages	xxxv, 220
Size	23 cm.
ISBN	0-7099-3293-6

Main Entry

001.535
ART Artificial intelligence: the case against/edited by
Rainer Born. – London: Croom Helm, 1987.
xxxv, 220p.; 23 cm
ISBN 0-7099-3293-6
8245
1 Artificial Intelligence I Born, Rainer

Added Entry – Subject

150 Price, Richard H.
PRI Principles of psychology/Richard H. Price
(Same as in the main entry)

COMPUTER FILES

This includes files that are encoded for manipulation by computer. These files may comprise data or programs. The chief source of information for the computer file is the title screen. If title screen is not there then information may be taken from the internal source such as main menu, program statement, etc. If information is not available from the internal source then it could be taken from:

The physical carrier or its label;
Information issued by the creator, publisher, etc.;
Information printed on the container.

In statement of responsibility give names of persons or bodies responsible for the content of the file. The names of sponsors etc. or the persons or bodies contributed in the production of the file are to be given in the notes section. The material specific details area is used in the case of computer files. This is known as 'File Characteristics Area'. The following terms may be used to designate the file characteristics:

Computer data
Computer program(s)
Computer data and program(s)

If GMD is used then the term computer may be dropped. Along with the file characteristics designation, the number of records, statements, etc. is to be given if the information is readily available. The skeletal structure for Computer Files is given below:

Call Number Creator of the item

Title [GMD] = Parallel title: other title information/1st statement of responsibility; each subsequent statement of responsibility. –Edition statement/1st Statement of responsibility. – statement of file characteristics. – 1st place of

publication, distribution etc; 1st publisher, distributor etc., date of publication etc.
Extent of item: other physical details; dimensions + accompanying material. – (series)

In the physical description the following specific material designation may be given along with number:

Computer cartridge
Computer cassette
Computer disk
Computer reel

Example

> **The Internet for Absolute Beginers**
> **Designed, written and produced by Mike Lloyd**
> **ASLIB**
> **The Association for Information Management**

Other Information

Call No.	621.385 LLO
Accession No.	4621

Contains 2 disks (double sided, double density; 31/2 in. floppy disks)

System requirement: IBM compatible PC with Windows 3.1, 4 M.B RAM, 386 or above, 7 MB hard drive space, VGA or above and a Windows Compatible mouse or other devices

Main Entry

> **621.385**
> **LLO** **Lloyd, Mike**
> **The Internet for the absolute beginners [computer file]/ designed, written and produced by Mike Lloyd. – Computer program. – London: ASLIB, 1995**
> **2 disks: double sided, double density; 3½ in.**
> **4621** **System requirements: IBM compatible PC with Windows 3.1, 4MB RAM, 386 or above, 7 MB hard drive space, VGA or above and a Windows compatible mouse or other devices.**
> **1. Internet I Title II ASLIB**

There are some physical characteristics such as number of sides, recording density sectoring which are kept optional in the rule (Rule 9.5C2).

The Added Entries for this product will include:

(i) Subject Added Entry: INTERNET
(ii) Title Added Entry: The Internet for absolute beginners
(iii) Added Entry under ASLIB.

MICROFORMS

Microforms include microfilms, microfiches, microopaques and aperture cards. The chief source of information for the microfilms, microfiches and microopaques is the title frame. In the case of aperture card it is the title card or card itself. If information is not sufficient then the accompanying material, container, etc. may be consulted. The following special data for cartographic material, music and serials needs to be added in the material specific details area:

Cartographic:	mathematical data
Music:	physical presentation of music
Serials:	numeric and/or alphabetic, chronological or other designations

In the physical description area the following terms for specific material designation may be added along with the number of physical units:

(i) Aperture card
(ii) Microfiche
(iii) Microfilm
(iv) Microopaque

MULTIPLE CHOICE QUESTIONS

1. Which terms are operative in nature & prescribe the procedure & help identify the expected quality of the operations that would result from such prescriptions?
   A. Normative B. Fundamental
   C. Associative D. Assumed
2. Third International Study Conference on Cataloguing Research held at Mumbai in—
   A. 1975 B. 1985
   C. 1995 D. None of these
3. The Indian Standards Institution, now known as ______ took up the preparation of a glossary of terms of classification.
   A. Bureau of Indian Standard
   B. Indian Standards Bureau
   C. Indian Institute of Standards
   D. Federation of Indian Standards
4. Words that are also known as technical terminology—
   A. Pre-defined B. Systematic
   C. Ordinary D. Synonyms
5. There are in all 514 technical terms used in the three editions of—
   A. Prolegomena
   B. Colon Classification
   C. Classified Catalogue Code
   D. Five laws of Library Science
6. Classification in Sense one is—
   A. Entity B. Division
   C. Universe D. Assortment
7. It is a ranked group and ranking in arranging in a definite sequence the groups formed by the division of the entities of a universe, so as to arrive at an assortment of them is—
   A. Group B. Class
   C. Entity D. Phyla
8. It is any property or quantitative measure or quality possessed by a or inherent in any entity is—
   A. Attribute B. Characteristic
   C. Universe D. Entity
9. A ______ subject is always in the context of a document, whose scope & depth are equal to the thought content of the document.
   A. main B. broad
   C. complex D. specific
10. Detailed Classification required for macro documents is known as—
    A. library classification
    B. depth classification
    C. broad classification
    D. bibliographic classification
11. A traditional subdivision of an old main class is—
    A. canonical class
    B. special main class
    C. systems main class
    D. environmental main class
12. "Fungus disease of wheat plants" is an example of—
    A. simple subject
    B. basic subject
    C. compound subject
    D. complex subject
13. A systematic or utilitarian arrangement of members of an array is—
    A. filiatory sequence
    B. helpful sequence
    C. parallel sequence
    D. evolutionary sequence
14. A person who operates classification system is—
    A. user B. expert
    C. classifier D. classificationist
15. Which number denotes that the number is used for fixing the position of an entity in a sequence?
    A. Ordinal number
    B. Cardinal number

C. Substance number
D. Ordinal number

16. In Colon Classification, 7th edition, the only Greek letter used is—
A. etah B. gamma
C. beta D. delta

17. According to Dr. S.R. Ranganathan, the terms hospitality in array & hospitality in chain represent the capacity of—
A. idea system B. practical system
C. national system D. verbal system

18. Colon Classification was a rigidly faceted scheme before—
A. 4th edition B. 5th edition
C. 6th edition D. 7th edition

19. The four canons of which plane deal with the language & terminology aspects in a scheme of classification?
A. Idea B. Verbal
C. Practical D. Notational

20. This arrangement helps bring together on the shelves documents on one & the same subject followed by those of related subjects is—
A. Title B. Author
C. Subject D. Publisher

21. Which sequence of subjects facilitates readers not only in getting documents but also helps them know the strength & weakness of the collection?
A. Filiatory B. Helpful
C. Parallel D. Evolutionary

22. It is the ordinal number whih fixes the place of a document in a library relative to other documents having the same class number—
A. Accession number
B. Year Number
C. Book Number
D. Call Number

23. The amount of literature published or likely to be published on a subject is—
A. literary warrant B. users warrant
C. collocation D. filiatory sequence

24. The total number of indicator digits used in the notational system of the 7th edition of Colon Classification is—
A. six (6) B. fourteen (14)
C. sixty (60) D. seventy-four (74)

25. Who is referred to as the first "grammarion of library classification"?
A. W.C.B. Sayers
B. E.W. Hulme
C. S.R. Ranganathan
D. E.C. Richardson

26. Which theory is a theory of library classification capable of carving out a methodology for the design of a scheme for library classification?
A. Dynamic B. Descriptive
C. General D. Special

27. Subject Classification by J.D. Brown is an example of—
A. faceted classification
B. freely-faceted classification
C. fully-faceted classification
D. freely faceted analytico-synthetic

28. Colon Classification is an excellent example of —
A. fully faceted classification
B. enumerative
C. rigidly faceted
D. freely faceted analytico-synthetic

29. Which Classification system is a very detailed, minutely divided classification, developed for a smaller area of knowledge?
A. General B. Special
C. Broad D. Unique

30. Who developed U.D.C. in 1895 taking D.D.C as its base?
A. Paul Otlet & Henri Fontaine
B. Dewey & Sayers
C. Richardson & Hulme
D. None of the above

31. Library of Congress Classification is based upon—
A. collocation B. APUPA pattern
C. users warrant D. literary warrant

32. In the Broad System of Ordering (BSO) only the punctuation marks hypen (-) & ________ are used.
A. comma (,) B. semi colon (;)
C. colon (:) D. dot (.)

33. The Broad System of Ordering was designed as a switching language in the year—
A. 1876 B. 1933
C. 1950 D. 1977

34. The process of division or splitting or breaking up into parts is—
A. fission B. fusion
C. distillation D. clustering

35. Astrophysics, Astrochemistry, Biophysics etc. are some examples of ________ mode of formation of subjects.
A. fusion B. fission
C. clustering D. distillation

36. These are certain assumptions which are helpful in carrying out the process of classification—
A. Memonics B. Postulates
C. Facets D. Isolates

37. The title that results from the analysed title by re-arrangement the Kernel terms on the basis of the postulates & principles governing the sequence—
A. Raw title B. Kernal title
C. Expressive title D. Transformed title

38. The ________ approach is a method of subject structuring.
A. title B. author
C. systems D. subject

39. Isolates such as density, quality, intensity are regarded as menifestations of—
A. matter fundamental category
B. energy fundamental category
C. property fundamental category
D. personality fundamental category

40. Isolates such as winter, night, contury, millennia etc. are the manifestations of —
A. personality fundamental category
B. matter fundamental category
C. space fundamental category
D. time fundamental category

41. In which scheme of classification the facet, relation sign double colon (::) is used when a reversal of two facets is not required?
A. C.C B. D.D.C.
C. U.D.C D. L.C.

42. "Chemistry for Biologists" is an example of—
A. intra subject phase relation
B. intra facet phase relation
C. intra array phase relation
D. inter subject phase relation

43. The phase is also referred to as "Exposition phase"—
A. Tool B. Comparison
C. Biased D. Infuence

44. Which notation of Bibliographic Classification of Mills is now generally used as a phase link?
A. Comma B. Colon
C. Hyphen D. Dot

45. It is a digit with an ordinal value but without a semantic value—
A. Indicator digit B. Empty digit
C. Emptying digit D. Empty-emptying

46. In the 7th edition of Colon Classification, for phase relation the indicator digit is—
A. dot B. colon
C. hyphen D. ampersand

47. In U.D.C. scheme, the digit 4 used for linguistics has been frozen & liguistics have been shifted to class—
A. 5 B. 6
C. 7 D. 8

48. The U.D.C. is a—
A. faceted classification
B. rigidly faceted classification
C. enumerative classification
D. fully faceted classification

49. DDC-21 on CD-ROM is ________ based LAN Compatible Microsoft System.
A. UNIX B. DOS
C. LINUX D. Windows

50. The electronic version of DDC-20th edition was issued in 1993 on CD-ROM titled—
A. Dewey online
B. Electronic Dewey
C. Dewey for windows
D. D.C.

51. The word "Catalogue" has been derived from the Greek expression—
A. cata logus B. kata logos
C. keta logus D. cata logos

52. It is a date-wise record of a library of reading and reference materials acquired by a library either by purchase, exchange or through gift—
A. self list B. accession register
C. catalogue D. bibliography

53. It is an inventory record of a library which records bibliographical data of items arranged exactly the way the items are arranged on the shelves of a library in various rooms, halls or floors—
A. Book list B. Accession list
C. Catalogue D. Self list

54. The first edition of Ranganathan's Classified Catalogue Code appeared in—
A. 1930 B. 1934
C. 1964 D. 1945

55. British Museum Cataloguing Rules is also known as—
A. Panizzi 91 Rules
B. Jewett's Rules
C. Cutter's Rules
D. A.A. Rules

56. The first part of AACR II R is denoted into how many chapters containing descri-ptive rules—
A. 10 B. 12
C. 13 D. 14

57. Loose leaf form of library catalogue is known as—
A. sheaf form B. card form
C. visible form D. cyclostyled form

58. In the 19th century the most common physical form of library catalogue was the—
A. sheaf form
B. found register form
C. printed book form
D. cyclostyled form

59. The microform catalogues are being used extensively since ________
A. 1960's B. 1970's
C. 1980's D. 1990's

60. Which form of library catalogue refers to the arrangement of catalogue entries in a logical and systematic order to fall into a helpful sequence for storage & retrieval?
A. Outer B. Inner
C. Alphabetical D. Classified

61. Name catalogue is almost used in—
A. U.S.A. B. Russia
C. Germany D. Great Britain

62. The verbal equivalents provided for class numbers in a classified catalogue are known as—
A. feature headings
B. synonyms
C. subject headings
D. key items

63. The entry that enters a document under one or other of the classes other than the dominant focus or class ________
A. Added B. Subject
C. Classified D. Cross referene

64. The function of a ________ reference is to direct the user of a catalogue from a form of the name of a person or a corporate body or the title of a work might reasonably be sought to the form that has been chosen as a name heading or a uniform title.
A. see B. see also
C. cross D. direct

65. An entry for a part of an item for which a comprehensive entry has been made is known as—
A. cross referene entry
B. analytical entry
C. see reference entry
D. see also reference

66. Which section in the C.C.C. records authorship or its substitute element?
A. Heading B. Leading
C. Title D. Author

67. AACR 2 was published in—
A. 1967 B. 1974
C. 1978 D. 1988

68. The equipment such as Chaindex & Stripdex are associated with—
A. machine readable catalogue
B. microform catalogue
C. visible index form of catalogue
D. conventional catalogue

69. Cataloguing-in-publication has been called a prenatal cataloguing by—
A. Pannizzi B. Ranganathan
C. Cutter D. Bliss

70. The International standard Bibliographic Description (ISBD) was first published in—
A. 1969 B. 1971
C. 1973 D. 1975

71. The Machine Readable Cataloguing Project was first launched by the—
A. British Library
B. Library of Congress
C. National Library
D. NISCAIR

72. The classified Catalogue consists of—
A. two parts B. three parts
C. four parts D. five parts

73. Which catalogue is a variation & extension of an author catalogue?
A. Subject B. Classified
C. Name D. Alphabetico-classes

74. The catalogue where all the entries are arranged in a single alphabetical order is—
A. author catalogue
B. dictionary catalogue
C. subject catalogue
D. title catalogue

75. ALA Filling Rules was first published in the year—
A. 1942 B. 1956
C. 1961 D. 1968

76. In Bibliographic data formats, codes used to identify different data elements in the record is known as—
A. Record label B. Directory
C. Data fields D. Content designer

77. The system in which the main entry and added entry carry the same information about the document is—
A. Unit Card system
B. Additional Card system
C. Combined Card system
D. MARC Card system

78. The first edition of CCF was published in the year—
A. 1962 B. 1974
C. 1984 D. 1976

79. In AACR-2R, the courts are entered under their—
A. name directly
B. name of chief of Justice
C. name of Govt.
D. jurisdiction

80. In CCC, the Editor of series Entry is called—
A. cross reference entry
B. cross reference index entry
C. book index entry
D. class index entry

81. The types of analytical entries in CCC is/are—
A. author analytical
B. title analytical
C. subject analytical
D. all of the above

82. In AACR–2R, the anonymous works of personal authors are to be entered under —
A. title B. editor
C. subject D. collaborator

83. According to AACR-2R, collections of treaties between two parties are to be entered under—
A. title entry B. uniform entry
C. country name D. signing parties

84. According to the needs of a document & needs of a particular library, how many levels description prescribe in AACR?
A. 1 B. 2
C. 3 D. 4

85. The list which is within its frame all bibliographic elements, which are required to describe & identify all types of materials, which are likely to appear in library collection is—

A. MARC B. CCF
C. UNIMARC D. ISBD(G)

86. Which is a cheif source of information for microforms in AACR–2R?

A. Title page B. Container fax
C. Title frame D. Container & label

87. G.M.D. is AACR–2R stands for—

A. General Material Description
B. General Material Designation
C. Geographical Material Description
D. General Monographic Designation

88. Cutter Number or Cutter Mark is used for—

A. Call Number B. Book Number
C. Class Number D. Collection Number

89. How many components are there in the structure of U.S. MARC format?

A. 2 B. 3
C. 4 D. 8

90. Which contain more than one unit concept in them & a number of terms may be used to fully describe these concepts?

A. Multi-work concept
B. Complex subject
C. Compound subject
D. Meta subject

91. Subject heading lists & thesauri are two types of ________ indexing language.

A. natural B. free
C. controlled D. uncontrolled

92. The indexing system in which coordination of terms in the index descriptions are decided before any particular request is made, is known as —

A. coordinate indexing system
B. post-coordinate indexing sytem
C. descriptive indexing system
D. pre-coordinate indexing system

93. Which type of indexing model PREÇIS & POPSI are?

A. Post-Coordinate B. Pre-Coordinate
C. Natural D. Free

94. Post-Coordinate Indexing Systems are also called as—

A. POPSI
B. KWIC
C. Coordinate Indexing System
D. Chain Indexing

95. A device for searching through a fragment of the search term so that it can match related terms starting with the same terms is called as—

A. Boolean search B. Truncation
C. Thesaurus D. Indexing language

96. Concept of Theasuro-Facet has been developed by—

A. Ranganathan
B. Jean Aitkinson
C. Derek Austin
D. Ganesh Bhattacharya

97. K.W.A.C. stands for—

A. Keyboard Associate Context
B. Keyword & Context
C. Keyboard Abbreviated Context
D. Keyword Added Context

98. Computer Added Subject System (COMPASS) was introduced for BNB in the year—

A. 1981 B. 1991
C. 1994 D. 1997

99. Which is the world's largest & most comprehensive bibliographic database?

A. First search
B. World cat
C. Prompt cat
D. O.C.L.C. Access Services

100. The World Cat Service is provided by —

A. R.L.I.N. B. L.C.
C. W.L.N. D. O.C.L.C

101. It is a system of terms used to denote the classes or ranked isolates in a scheme for classification—

A. Terminology B. Classification
C. Taxonomy D. Notion

102. The terms that define the basic concepts which are germane to the very nature of classification process are—

A. Assumed B. Fundamental
C. Normative D. Associative

103. Classification in Sense 2 is—
A. Universe B. Entity
C. Division D. Assortment

104. Any sub-aggregate of the entities formed by the division of the entities of a universe is called as—
A. Group B. Class
C. Universe D. Entity

105. When entities are books or other items of information, their classification is known as—
A. Book B. Library
C. Depth D. Broad

106. The subject that has a basic facet & one or more isolate facets—
A. Complex B. Compound
C. Basic D. Specific

107. Which sequence means placing together closely related classes?
A. Parallel B. Alphabetical
C. Filiatory D. Helpful

108. A sequence of Coordinate Classes arranged in some definite order is called —
A. an arrary B. a chain
C. a category D. a facet

109. ________ classification are contemptuously desribed as mark & park systems.
A. Facet B. Enumerative
C. Freely faceted D. Rigidly faceted

110. Numbers that are used in counting and in expressing measures are—
A. ordinary B. ordinal
C. cardinal D. indicator

111. In Colon Classification, the ordinal value of the digit "Δ" (delta) lies between the digits—
A. X and Y B. A and B
C. O and P D. M and N

112. The total number of digits in the notational system of Colon Classification is—
A. 74 B. 60
C. 14 D. 06

113. The call number for a document consists of three elements namely Class Number, Book Number and ________
A. Collection Numbers
B. Accession Numbers
C. Serial Numbers
D. Reference Numbers

114. An ordinal number, which fixes the place of a subject relative to other subjects in a scheme of classification is known as—
A. Collection Number
B. Accession number
C. Call Number
D. Class Number

115. An ordinal number which fixes the place of a document in a library relative to the documents having the same number is known as—
A. accession number
B. collection number
C. book number
D. call number

116. The amount of literature published or likely to be published on a subject is known as—
A. users warrant B. literary warrant
C. collocation D. filiatory sequence

117. A designer of a classification is ________
A. classificationist B. classifier
C. user D. expert

118. Who published the first edition of Subject Classification in 1906?
A. W.C.B. Sayers B. E.C. Richardson
C. J.D. Brown D. E.W. Hulme

119. It is one of the basic concepts of classification, propounded by Bliss which was termed by Dr. Ranganathan as the filiatory sequence is—
A. Collocation B. Consensus
C. Notion D. Subordination

120. The book *Prolegomena to Library Classification* is written by ________
A. Parkhi
B. Dr. S.R. Ranganathan
C. Bhattacharya
D. Neelameghan

121. Which system in 1971 replaced Ranganathan's Chain procedure in BNB?
A. PRECIS B. POPSI
C. COMPASS D. KWAC

122. The ________ lay down the process of work in the idea plane.
A. Principles B. Laws
C. Postulates D. Canons

123. The four canons for growing universe deal with the capacity of a ________ system for admission of newly emerging classes in the scheme of classification.
A. Cataloguing B. Classification
C. Automated D. Notational

124. Ranganathan postulated that the fundamental category ________ may manifest itself in one & the same subject more than once.
A. Personality B. Matter
C. Energy D. Time

125. Which edition of Colon Classification is an example of fully freely faceted scheme of classification?
A. 7th B. 6th
C. 5th D. 4th

126. The Library of Congress Classification is a purely—
A. enumerative classification
B. almost–enumerative classification
C. faceted classification
D. fully faceted classification

127. The Broad System of Ordering (BSO) was designed in 1977 as—
A. a switching language
B. an enumerative language
C. a dot language
D. none of these

128. Only two punctuation marks used in—
A. B.S.O. B. C.C.
C. L.C. D. All of the above

129. The process of division or splitting or breaking up into parts is—
A. lamination B. fission
C. fusion D. distillation

130. Astrophysics, Bio-physics are the examples of—
A. fusion B. fission
C. agglomeration D. loose assemblage

131. Which form of representation is the principal basis on which information systems retrieve information?
A. Books B. Subject
C. Collection D. Periodicals

132. Which title is resulted from the analysed title by rearranging the kernel terms on the basis of the postulates & principles governing their sequence?
A. Analysed B. Expressive
C. Raw D. Transformed

133. A logical arrangement of subjects, their facets and isolates which help the arrangement & display of documents on shelves in libraries is known as—
A. Logical order B. Helpful order
C. Classified order D. Alphabetical order

134. Dr. Ranganathan suggested the Method of Residues for identification of ________ isolates in the facet analysis of a compound subject.
A. Personality B. Matter
C. Energy D. Time & space

135. In the title "Works of Shakespeare", the basic subject is—
A. English B. Drama
C. America D. Literature

136. Which postulates state that any of the fundamental categories Personality & Matter may manifest more than once in one and the same round within a subject & similarlly with Space & Time in the last round.
A. Level postulates
B. Level–cluster postulates
C. Concretenss postulates
D. First facet postulates

137. Which isolates represent any kind of action, mental or physical and activities of all other entities?
A. Personality B. Energy
C. Matter D. Space

138. A phase relation is the assembling together of two or more of subject &—
A. books B. periodicals
C. isolate ideas D. collections

139. The digits a, b, c, e and g in C.C. represent—
A. intra-array phase relation
B. intra-facet phase relation
C. intra-isolates phase relation
D. inter-subject phase relation

140. Mathematics for Engineers are the examples of which phase relation?
A. General B. Bias
C. Influence D. Comparison

141. In D.D.C., the common isolates are called—
A. Special sub-divisions
B. Auxillary sub-divisions
C. Common sub-divisions
D. Standard sub-divisions

142. The connecting symbol for the time element in U.D.C. is—
A. dot (.)
B. semi colon (;)
C. plus (+)
D. double inverted comma (" ")

143. A digit with an ordinal value but without a semantic value is called—
A. special digit
B. empty digit
C. emptying digit
D. empty-emptying digit

144. Which notation is used in DDC refers to the principal of dividing each class into ten sub-divisions & each of these sub-divisions into another ten sub-divisions?
A. Decimal B. Mixed
C. Pure D. Apha-numeric

145. Which edition of DDC appeared in two formats i.e; in Print & Dewey for Windows (CD versions)?
A. 17th B. 19th
C. 20th D. 21th

146. CC versions 2 has been described a/an—
A. faceted scheme
B. almost freely faceted scheme
C. rigidly faceted scheme
D. fully freely faceted scheme

147. The A.C.I. "K"–cyclopaedia & "m"–periodical are applicable before—
A. Personality B. Energy
C. Time D. Space

148. In UDC scheme the digit 4 (linguistics) has been frozen and shifted to class—
A. 5 B. 6
C. 7 D. 8

149. The basis of the outline of main classes of __________ is said to be Bacon's chart of Learning.
A. Colon Classificaton
B. Library of Congress
C. Universal Decimal Classification
D. Dewey Decimal Classification

150. DRTC was established in Banglore in 1962 by—
A. G. Bhattacharya
B. A. Neelameghan
C. Dr. S.R. Ranganathan
D. M.A. Gopinath

151. The device/s in U.D.C. is/are—
A. Geographical devices
B. Alphabetical devices
C. Both of above
D. None of above

152. From the archaeological finds of the Assyro-Babylonian clay tablets the antiquity of the library catalogue can be easily placed around—
A. 200 B.C. B. 2000 B.C.
C. 1000 B.C. D. 400 B.C.

153. A list of documents reflecting exactly the way the documents are arranged on the shelves are called as—
A. Library catalogue
B. Shelf register
C. Accession register
D. Publisher catalogue

154. If a catalogue represents the collection of two or more libraries, it is called as—
A. Union Catalogue
B. Library catalogue
C. Bibliographies
D. Publisher's catalogue

155. The arrangement of cataloguing entries in a logical & systematic order to fall into a helpful sequence for storage & retrieval is called as—
A. Card form B. Alphabetical form
C. Classified form D. Inner form

156. Classified catalogue consists of—
A. the classified part
B. the alphabetical part
C. both of above
D. all of the above

157. Panizzi's Rules of cataloguing is also known as—
A. British Museum Cataloguing Rules
B. Jewett's Rules
C. Cutter Rules
D. AA Rules

158. Entries that go into a catalogue for parts & chapters of a book is—
A. main entries B. analytical entries
C. chapter entries D. reference entries

159. Cutter's rules for Dictionary catalogue was first published in—
A. 1876 B. 1889
C. 1904 D. 1908

160. The Classified Catalogue has two parts, the classified part and—
A. dictionary part B. alphabetical part
C. name part D. author part

161. A record of all additional entries is known as—
A. Unit Card B. Book Index Entry
C. Tracing D. Added Entry

162. Which section in the C.C.C. is that section which records authorship or its substitute element?
A. Heading B. Leading
C. Title D. Author

163. The equipments such as Chaindex and Stripdex are associated with—
A. Machine readable catalogue
B. Microform catalogue
C. Visible Index form of catalogue
D. Conventional catalogue

164. The complete catalogue record of an item, presented in the form by which the entry is to be uniformly identified & is—
A. Main Entry B. Added Entry
C. Uniform Entry D. Additional Entry

165. In CCC, the Editor of Series entry is called as—
A. Cross reference entry
B. Cross reference Index entry
C. Book Index entry
D. Class Index entry

166. The cabinet for placing catalogue cards is known as—
A. Kardex B. Chaindex
C. Stripdex D. All of the above

167. In AACR-2R under "choice of Name", there are—
A. 15 rules B. 17 rules
C. 19 rules D. 20 rules

168. The system in which the main entry and added entries carry the same information about the document is—
A. MARC card system
B. Unit Card system
C. Additional Card system
D. Combined Card system

169. In CCC, the Editor of Series entry is called—
A. Cross reference entry
B. Book Index entry
C. Class Index entry
D. Cross reference index entry

170. In CCC, Conferences & congress are entered under the—
A. name of sponser
B. name of the place
C. name by which they are known
D. under the country name.

171. Cutter Mark is used for—
A. Collection B. Book
C. Call D. Class

172. AA Code of 1908 of Cataloguing was compiled by—
A. ALA B. LC
C. ILA D. None of the above

173. Dewey Decimal Classification given by Melvil Dewey and first published in—
A. 1876 B. 1976
C. 1934 D. 1928

174. Vatican Rules of Cataloguing published in—
A. 1908 B. 1852
C. 1757 D. 1927

175. Sheaf form of library catalogue is also known as—
A. Card form B. Ledger form
C. Printed form D. Loose-leaf form

176. How many types of entries are in CCC?
A. 3 B. 4
C. 5 D. 6

177. A link in pseudo chain made of a digit group forming part of a book number is—
A. Sought link
B. Pseudo link
C. Pseudo chain
D. Tracing

178. The AACR-2 was edited by—
A. Gorman & Winkler
B. Whittaker & Bliss
C. Andrew Brown
D. None of the above

179. IInd part of AACR–2 has—
A. 13 chapters B. 6 chapters
C. 4 appendix D. All of the above

180. Which filing rules had their origins in the report of a Working Party on computer filing set up by the Library Association Cataloguing and Indexing Group?
A. LC B. ALA
C. BLAISE D. Berghoeffer

181. The internationally agreed upon number given to a book is called—
A. ISBN B. ISDN
C. ISSN D. ISMN

182. C.C.F. stands for—
A. Current Classification Format
B. Current Communication Format
C. Common Communication Format
D. Common Classification Format

183. The Machine Readable Cataloguing was firstly started by—
A. British Library B. Library of Congress
C. NISCAIR D. National Library

184. The two prominent inner forms of catalogue are—
A. Classified & Alphabetical
B. Classified & Dictionary
C. Name & Classified
D. Alphabetical & Alphetico-based

185. In Ranganathan's classified catalogue, there are five types of entries: Main entry, Cross Reference Entry, Class Index Entry, Book Index Entry and other is—
A. Name Index
B. Title Index
C. Subject Index
D. Cross Reference Index

186. The 2nd edition of *Cataloguing Practice* published in—
A. 1945 B. 1955
C. 1975 D. 1951

187. Computer Aided Subject System (COMPASS) was introduced for—
A. BNB B. C.I.P.
C. ABPR D. INB

188. The first edition of CCF was first published in—
A. 1962 B. 1984
C. 1974 D. 1976

189. A device for searching through a fragment of the search term so that it can match related terms starting with the same terms is called as—
A. Boolean Search B. Truncation
C. Thesaurus D. Indexing language

190. Post-Coordinate Indexing System are also known as—
A. POPSI
B. KWIC
C. Chain Indexing
D. Coordinate Indexing System

191. The synonymous relationship between the terms is known as—
A. Hierarchial relationship
B. Genus-Species relationship
C. Associate relationship
D. Equivalence relationship

192. ________ contain tools which till automatically create classified listing of the resource and a search mechanism for internet resources
A. Prompt Cat B. First search
C. ROADS D. World Cat

193. The concept of Thesauro–Facet has been developed by—
A. Derek Austin B. Dr. Ranganathan
C. Jean Alikison D. G. Bhattacharya

194. The universal adopted size for a Catalogue is—
A. 12.5 cm × 7.6 cm
B. 12.5 cm × 20 cm
C. Both of above
D. None of the above

195. I part of AACR-2 has—
A. 6 chapters B. 13 chapters
C. 6 appendix D. All of the above

196. Broad System of Ordering (B.S.O) was drafted by—
A. Coates & Lloyd
B. Whittaker & Whittal
C. Bliss
D. All of the above

197. B.S.O was drafted in the year—
A. 1970 B. 1971
C. 1980 D. 1981

198. Which is the bulkiest of all Classification System?
A. Library of Congress Classification
B. Colon Classification
C. Universal Decimal Classification
D. None of the above

199. Which is a book classification as well as Broad Classification?
A. Dewey Decimal Classification
B. Universal Decimal Classification
C. Colon Classification
D. Library of Congress Classification

200. A.A. code of 1908 of cataloguing was complied by—
A. A.L.A.
B. L.C.
C. I.L.A.
D. None of the above.

ANSWERS

1	2	3	4	5	6	7	8	9	10
A	A	A	A	D	A	A	D	D	D
11	**12**	**13**	**14**	**15**	**16**	**17**	**18**	**19**	**20**
A	C	B	C	A	A	C	D	D	C
21	**22**	**23**	**24**	**25**	**26**	**27**	**28**	**29**	**30**
C	D	A	B	A	A	B	D	D	A
31	**32**	**33**	**34**	**35**	**36**	**37**	**38**	**39**	**40**
D	A	D	A	A	A	B	A	C	D
41	**42**	**43**	**44**	**45**	**46**	**47**	**48**	**49**	**50**
A	B	C	C	A	B	B	A	B	C
51	**52**	**53**	**54**	**55**	**56**	**57**	**58**	**59**	**60**
B	B	D	B	A	A	A	A	B	B
61	**62**	**63**	**64**	**65**	**66**	**67**	**68**	**69**	**70**
D	A	D	A	B	A	C	C	B	B
71	**72**	**73**	**74**	**75**	**76**	**77**	**78**	**79**	**80**
B	A	C	B	A	D	A	C	C	B
81	**82**	**83**	**84**	**85**	**86**	**87**	**88**	**89**	**90**
C	A	B	C	B	A	B	B	B	B
91	**92**	**93**	**94**	**95**	**96**	**97**	**98**	**99**	**100**
C	D	A	C	A	B	B	B	D	D

101	102	103	104	105	106	107	108	109	110
C	C	D	A	B	A	C	D	C	C
111	**112**	**113**	**114**	**115**	**116**	**117**	**118**	**119**	**120**
A	B	A	D	D	B	A	A	A	B
121	**122**	**123**	**124**	**125**	**126**	**127**	**128**	**129**	**130**
A	B	C	A	B	B	B	A	B	C
131	**132**	**133**	**134**	**135**	**136**	**137**	**138**	**139**	**140**
B	C	C	D	D	D	A	C	D	B
141	**142**	**143**	**144**	**145**	**146**	**147**	**148**	**149**	**150**
B	B	A	A	D	D	A	A	B	C
151	**152**	**153**	**154**	**155**	**156**	**157**	**158**	**159**	**160**
C	D	A	A	A	C	A	C	D	B
161	**162**	**163**	**164**	**165**	**166**	**167**	**168**	**169**	**170**
A	A	C	C	A	D	C	B	A	A
171	**172**	**173**	**174**	**175**	**176**	**177**	**178**	**179**	**180**
A	A	A	D	D	C	A	A	B	C
181	**182**	**183**	**184**	**185**	**186**	**187**	**188**	**189**	**190**
A	C	C	C	D	D	C	D	A	A
191	**192**	**193**	**194**	**195**	**196**	**197**	**198**	**199**	**200**
B	A	C	C	B	A	B	A	A	A

ROLE OF INFORMATION TECHNOLOGY IN LIBRARY SCIENCE

IMPACT OF IT ON SOCIETY

The **information technology** can be defined as the technology used for processing of information on the computer system.

The information can be defined as collection of data in the formatted form such that the storage of data, retrieval of data or processing on data becomes easy. The information stored on the paper is difficult to analyse and trace. The processing of data becomes tedious when the information is stored on the paper files. The deletion of data can be done by rubbing or erasing the information on paper. The analysis of information becomes difficult and tedious on the paper system.

The computer system allows for storage of voluminous information in the storage devices. It allows for fast speed calculations even more than the speed of human brain. The use of computer system provides large number of advantages for processing of information. The advantages are

1. The data can be stored permanently.
2. Large number of calculations can be performed at very fast processing speed.
3. The degree of accuracy is very high.
4. The operations like deletion of data, modification of data can be done very easily.
5. The operation of retrieval of data can be performed and the data can be searched immediately from the stored data.
6. The operations such as indexing or arranging the data is possible.
7. The variety of functions can be utilized in the operations.
8. It allows for the decisions and logical comparisons.
9. It allows for creation of standard libraries.
10. It is possible to obtain the result in the formatted form.
11. It allows for production of graphics and aesthetics.

COMPUTER

It is an electronic machine device which carries out calculations at high speed. It has a memory to store large amount of data and it does comparisons between two values and accordingly executes the decisions.

APPLICATIONS OF COMPUTER

It is used in the field of science and engineering, defence, business, banks, hotels, hospitals, office etc. for various purposes. some of them are :

1. Inventory control
2. Production planning and control
3. Costing and budgetary control
4. Sales analysis and market research
5. Financial accounting and payroll
6. Space technology
7. Weather forecasting
8. Railway and airline reservation system
9. Crime detection
10. Applications in Engineering
11. Educational Research & Science

COMPONENTS OF A COMPUTER

It consists of three main components–

1. Input Devices
2. CPU (Central Processing Unit)
3. Output Devices

SOFTWARE

It includes operating systems, assemblers, compilers and interpreters programmes for controlling input and output devices, copying data between storage media etc.

Application software comprises the procedures and instructions which enables computer systems to do what the user requires.

SOFTWARE PACKAGES

1. Word Processing (W.P.)
2. D.T.P. programme
3. Data Base Software

Types of Computer : Computers are classified on the basis of their size & capacity:

1. Micro Computer : Single user computer.
2. Mini Computer : Multiuser computers.
3. Supermini : Multiuser having more power.
4. Mainframe : Large memory computers & connected to large number of users at different locations.
5. Super computer : High speed computers.

The Personal Computers (P.C.) are microcomputer, which are used by majority of persons. According to their memory, speed & capacity, these are :

(a) PC – XT (Extended Technology)
(b) PC – AT (Advance Technology).
(c) PC – AT–286 – Low speed.
(d) PC – AT–386 – Medium speed.
(e) PC – AT – 486 – Medium speed.
(f) PC – AT – 586 – High speed computation.

TELECOMMUNICATION

- **Transmission Media, Bandwidth**
- **Switching Systems**
- **Multiplexing, Modulation**
- **Wireless Communication**

Telecommunication is defined as the transmission of representations of information between remote locations by electronic means and this information may be in the form of voice, video or data.

The basic components of Telecommunications are:–

⇨ Data Transmission
⇨ Communication Channels
⇨ Transmission Media
⇨ Switching Mechanisms
⇨ Terminals & Networks

TRANSMISSION MEDIA

The transmission media used in telecommunications networks vary both physically and in their carrying capacity. The commonly used performance measurement of a telecommunications link is its bandwidth. This gives an indication of the range of frequencies which can be transmitted by these channels. The greater the bandwidth, the greater the rate at which data can be tansmitted.

The channels or media can be grouped into two main divisions, i.e., line and free space. In the line group, we have two metallic media, twisted pairs and coaxial cables and one optical medium – glass or optical fibres. In the free space category, we have radio propagation which includes broadcast (e.g., TV) and point to point (e.g., microwave signals).

ADVANCED NETWORKING

- **E-mail, Fax, Tele-conferencing, Videotex, Voice mail.**
- **Networking including multimedia.**
- **ISDN & OSI.**

Electronic mail (E-mail) can be defined as the exchange of messages and computer files between computers over a computer network. This network can be as small as a Local Area

Network (LAN) or it can be as large as the internet that spans the world. It is much older than the Web.

BENEFITS OF *E-MAIL*

The main benefit of e-mail when compared to other messaging mediums like fax is that it is almost instantaneous. More importantly, it directly reaches the concerned individual's electronic mail box without getting buried under a mountain of paper. In some cases, you can even confirm whether your message has been received and read by the recipient–something next to impossible with a letter or fax.

Sure the good old telephone offers advantages similar to that of a letter or fax, but what do you do when the person you are calling is not at his table or if the person is a few continents away?

With e-mail even if the recipient is not around, the message is delivered into his mailbox and is available the next time he checks in the mailbox.

E-mail also ensures a much higher degree of security & privacy. Only an authorised person can open or even know the presence of the mail. An authorised person is one who knows the login name and password to the recipient's mailbox.

Compared to other mediums e-mail is dirt-cheap. The cost of sending electronic message across the world is the same as sending one across the city—in most cases, a local telephone call. Further, as the message is in an electronic form, you save money on printing, fax paper and ink. Used correctly e-mail offers many advantages over a physical mail or message. For example, using encryption technology you could electronically deliver confidential documents, saving time and money over the standard practice of having a 'reliable' person — who could be waylaid — hand delivering a sealed document. Similarly by using digital signatures, you can even hinder forgery as digital signatures, like fingerprints can be verified and are unique for every user and message.

NETWORKING INCLUDING MULTIMEDIA:

There are different interpretations for the term 'network'. The Oxford English Dictionary states that 'a network is an interconnected chain or system of immaterial things'. On the other hand, the National Commission on Libraries and Information Science (NCLIS) USA defines network as : "Two or more libraries and/or other organisations engaged in a common pattern of information exchange, through communications, for some functional purpose. A network usually consists of a formal arrangement whereby materials, information and services provided by a variety of types of libraries and/or other oraganisations are made available to all potential users. Libraries may be in different jurisdictions but agree to serve one another on the same basis as each services its own constituents. Computers and telecommuni-cations may be among the tools used for facilitating communications among them."

TYPES OF NETWORKING

There are three types of networking, which may be said to have considerable impact on library and information services. They are: communication networks, computer networks and information networks. Although as information professionals, we are to understand the functioning of each of these types:

1. Communication Networks : Communication networks are made up of transmission lines, concentrators, switching mechanisms and non-data processing components. Due to increased competition in the communication industry, new and specialised common carriers and value-added networks with data processing equipment, is also linked to communication networks.

The current technological trend setter in communications is "packet switching technology". The greatest advantage of packet switched networks is in applications where the distance involved is great. Information services involve relatively large quantities of data for full bibliographic or full text retrieval, and therefore, the distance advantage applies more clearly to these applications. Depending upon the area of administrative jurisdiction, networks fall into three categories: Local Area Networks (LANs), Metropolitan Area Networks MANs and Wide Area Networks (WANs).

(i) **Local Area Networks (LANs) :** A Local Area Network connects a large number of different types of equipment, including computer terminals, fax, telex, CD ROM players, etc., on a single site. The majority of LANs use packet switching technology and offer very high transmission speeds—up to one hundred times faster than those available on public networks at present. Most of these are baseband that is they carry only digital computer data, but broadband LANs can carry video and voice signals as well as data. The topology of LANs can vary greatly (i.e.,linear, star, ring) affecting efficiency, reliability and costs.

(ii) **Metropolitan Area Networks MANs :** These type of networks generally cover specific metropolitan area and provide to them all the services.

(iii) **Wide Area Networks (WANs) :** Wide Area Networks (WANs) are private networks linking equipment at several different sites and have much in common with conventional large scale data networks.

In configuring a network to communicate information the focus is on minimising costs while maintaining the desired performance (or minimum desired quality) standards depend on the nature of the information to be sent. In the case of voice, quality is measured by word intelligibility or articulation index. For video, the Television Allocations Study Organisation has adopted the TASO grades ranging from excellent to poor that specify the degree of subjective acceptability of the picture displayed to viewing audiences. For both voice and video, the corresponding quantified measure of quality, signal-to-noise ratio, is used as a technical design parameter. For digital information, say from one computer to the other the quality of the transmission is expressed as the number of bit 'errors', a '1' appearing as '0' or vice versa, that occur as a fraction of the total number of bits sent.

Along with performance requirements, it is necessary to choose the channel bandwidth for analog transmission. The transmission speed of digital signals is also referred to as data rate or bit rate. These factors partly determine cost. Therefore, depending on whether the transmission is from one point to another, one point to several, or several points to a central point, a network is designed. The simplest 'network' might involve just two stations (point to point) linked for example, to transfer data from one computer to another, or it might be a complicated system where several stations are connected to a local node, several local nodes connected to a central node, and so on in hierarchical fashion.

Developments in network technology include the increasing use of computers to control switching and information flow. Most significant is the modernisation of the public network so that voice and data can be carried over a single network. This type of single network is referred to as an Integrated Services Digital Network (ISDN).

2. Open System Interconnection (ISO) : As there are many different protocols for LANs and WANs, communication betweeen two different systems can be difficult. The International Standards Oragnisation (ISO) has attempted with some success to solve the problem by the introduction of Open Systems Interconnection (OSI). OSI defines a set of procedures and standards grouped into seven layers, for the exchange of information between terminals and computers.

In theory all systems which conform to OSI specifications should be able to interconnect, but the definitions are vague in certain areas and incompatibilities do arise. To overcome this, some countries have developed their own more detailed standards.

Anyone involved in the purchase of equipment which is to be linked to a network should find out whether there are any industry specific GOSIPS (Government OSI Profiles) to which they must conform.

MULTIMEDIA

It is becoming one of the frequently used word today in the Information Industry. The Oxford English Dictionary, defined Multimedia as "an intervening substance through which impressions are conveyed to senses, e.g., through the medium of T.V.".

The second edition of Oxford English Dictionary defined multimedia as "design pertaining to a form of artistic, educational or commercial communication in which more than one medium is used."

HYPERMEDIA AND HYPERTEXT

Multimedia is a feature of changing pattern of information use, emerging through a variety of electronic media. The technologies involved are no more than *delivery methods* platforms on which new kinds of information products can be built. Hypermedia is sometimes used as a synonym for multimedia. The term hypermedia is generally used to refer to information containing high proportion of graphics and images and is almost always used where the information also included video sequences or any form of animated information.

HYPERTEXT

Hypertext is concerned with the presentation of information in a non-sequential fashion. Unlike paper texts where information is generally expected to be read in a sequential manner, hypertexts allow readers to navigate their own paths through the information. This exploits the interactive nature of the electronic medium and opens up many new possibilities, but demands careful design by the author and degree of discipline by readers. In other words, the author provides links between the related pieces of information in a manner that allows and enables readers to choose which links they wish to explore. Links maybe used to direct readers to additional information the same way that footnotes and glossaries do in paper texts, or they may provide more direct links between related pieces of information. In either case readers can view the related information simply by pointing to a 'button' or other indication on the screen. In other words, mechanisms are generally provided to allow readers to backtrack to their original position or to follow further links. If the author does not provide sufficient number of links readers are restricted and may find the information loss useful an accessible. On other hand, too many links might result in readers becoming lost in a maze of links.

INTERNET

The Internet is *"a network of networks"*. It is a global collections of high-powered computers that are connected to each other with network cables, telephone lines, microwave dishes, satellites etc.

WORLD WIDE WEB

World Wide Web and the Internet are not the same, but they are related and inter-dependent. The Web resides "on top of" the Internet. World Wide Web is a huge collection of "pages" of information linked to each other around the globe. Each page can be a combination of text, pictures, audio clips, video clips, animations and other electronically presentable material. What makes Web pages interesting is that they contain *hyperlinks* usually called links. Each link points to another web page and when you click a link, your browser program fetches the page the link connects to. Every page can have many links that take you to new destination. Web pages can be linked to other pages anywhere in the world. This system of inter linked documents is known as hypertext.

The World Wide Web is known fondly to millions as WWW, W3, or simply as the Web. The Web is actually a superset of the Internet. It can be thought of as a graphical interface to the Internet, providing a revolutionary way of accessing information scattered across millions of computers around the world.

Before the World Wide Web, the Internet was very difficult to navigate. Much of the information on it was tough to find and just as difficult to make use of. Locating and downloading files residing on the Internet needed some UNIX skills and specialised tools to get the job done.

Tim Berners-Lee is widely known as the father of the World Wide Web. Berners was a physicist at the European Organization for Nuclear Research (CERN), a highly esteemed particle physics laboratory in Switzerland. He became frustrated with the difficulty of navigating the Internet and the lack of common, easy-to-use interface for accessing the information residing on it.

As a part of his job at CERN, Berbers-Lee frequently used the Internet for research, collaboration and communicating with colleagues. He knew the problems of using the Internet and was determined to make his job easier by building a system that would make navigating easy. In 1989, he submitted a proposal for World Wide Web to the CERN Electronics and Computing for Physics Division. After receiving a feed back on the proposal he and his colleague, Robert Cailliau, revised and resubmitted it. Their revised proposal was accepted and the project was officially started. Funding was provided for the development of the Web and in 1991, the public received its first hint of what was to become a revolution on the Internet.

In February 1993, the National Center for Supercomputing Applications (NCSA) released the first public version of Mosaic for X-Windows. It was a breakthrough software product that kicked the World Wide Web into high gear. It supported a user-friendly graphical user interface that appealed to people normally uncomfortable using text based products such as Line Mode Browsers. In addition Mosaic supported the use of a mouse. You could now navigate without using your keyboard, a tremendous advance for most computer users. The Web was no longer simply a hypertext system. It had evolved into a beast that was fully functional, seamlessly integrated and hypermedia.

It was seamless because you could access all protocols and programs as a whole, without requiring a special tool for each. And it was hypermedia because these protocols delivered inter linked text, video, sound and graphics that were treated as a single coherent collection of information. The web was now a global system that allowed access to files from around the world

Since Mosaic was introduced, the Web was skyrocketed in popularity. By April 1994, just one year after the first version was released, the Web accounted for more traffic over the National Science Foundation (NSF) backbone that Gopher, an Internet protocol.

WEB SERVER

The final part of the web you will need to be concerned at this point is the server. A web server does a great deal of work in making web pages and sites available to browsers. They are the linking mechanism between you and the web; between people and pages. A large company may have its own server, but usually individuals and small companies rent or lease space on the server provided by an Internet Access company. Without servers there would be no web.

Web pages must reside somewhere on the Internet in order to be accessed with a browser and a server is where you will find them. There are literally millions of Web servers on the Internet, each of which may be home to thousands of Web pages. The server is responsible for delivering these pages to your Web browser when it asks for it: i.e., it "serves" web pages to browsers.

Web servers consist of special hardware and software that makes it possible to carry out browser requests. Pherhaps you have heard of the term client-server? This is exactly the type of relationship your browser and the server have. The browser is considered a client, since it asks to see or use certain documents located on the internet.

PROTOCOLS

The main protocol for transferring information on the Web is the Hypertext Transfer Protocol or HTTP. Web pages, both text and graphics are sent from the server to the browser using this protocol.

The web also supports most of the other popular Internet protocols, such as File Transfer Protocol (FTP), Gopher, News and Wide Area Information Service (WAIS). But you need not remember all these protocols. Your browser does all the work, dynamically switching between protocols as needed.

Uniform Resource Locators or URL's are the standard way of locating and retrieving information on the World Wide Web.

WEB PAGES

Familiarising you with the Web does not take very long, and is a fun way to prepare yourself for creating Web documents. The best place to start is with the web page, the visual part of a much larger system that people most often associate with the World Wide Web. There are many components to the Web, just as there are many pieces to the television industry. Here, there are broadcast companies, cable companies, antennae, remote controls, repair shops, satellites, and the television set itself, to name a few. The same holds true for the Web. Most people think mainly of the individual web pages, as they are the most visually captivating aspect of the entire system and what we "tune in" to see. The term "page" refers to nothing more than a World Wide Web document. A web page is much more like a word processing document than a printed page, especially the way it is viewed. When the information on a web page is not visible, you scroll either vertically or horizontally to see more.

WEB SITE

A World Wide Web site is simply a collection of inter linked web pages. Web pages need not be related. By its very nature, the Web makes it possible to link any number of items, including other pages. For instance, a page might have links to other pages containing photogrpahy, basketball, cartoons or just about anything else. Because of the inherent diversity found in the Web, to suggest that a site is a related group of documents would be big mistake. If you were to think of the Web as a giant filing cabinet, each site would be a folder inside it. The pages in turn would be documents inside the folders.

HOME PAGES

How to find a site if it is merely a collection of inter linked pages? Simple, each site has a home page, the official access point into the site. From the home page, you can get an overview of the site and begin exploring it. A properly designed home page is, in essence, like a hospitable host. It invites you in and tells you about all the things you can see and do during your visit. It is the most important page of any site, the starting point for your journey.

SEARCH ENGINES

People commonly refer to the current era as the "Information Age". The best thing about today's Internet is the enormous range of resources on it. The worst thing, of course, is that there is no guide to those resources. Finding information may be a nightmare. Fortunately, you have Web search engines to locate the information. The URL of the new site must be submitted to search engine. Keywords are built into the index page of the site. For a site to be listed after such a submission, it may take upto 7 to 10 days. SubmitAway.com helps you submit your URL to these search engines. Some search engines have a definite format and expect you to type the keywords again, while others just require the URL and take the keywords from your Web site. When you connect any of the search engines using its URL, you are asked to type one or two words in a search box. The search engine displays a list of locations that matches your search parameters.

POPULAR SEARCH ENGINES

- **www.yahoo.com** – This is one of the earliest and very popular engines. Yahoo is a preferred choice for millions surfers.
- **www.lycos.com** – An effective tool to pinpoint the site of your choice. Carnegie-Mellon University developed this site.
- **www.infoseek.com** – By far, one of the most effective search engines that will search the World Wide Web for the information you need. A good feature is the 'search within results' which will narrow down the results to a manageable number of web sites.
- **www.excite.com** – The exciting thing about this engine is the profusion of chat links ranging from the general to the very specific.
- **www.hotbot.com** – The search options are a hunter's delight. You can search in terms of words, language and time.
- **www.altavista.digital.com** – One of the few engines which lets you search across sites in many languages, ranging from Greek to Hebrew to Estonian.
- **www.isleuth.com** – It's the mother of all searches, because six engines do the work for you at once.
- **www.webcrawler.com** – Their Daily toolbox is an interesting add-on that lends it an extra edge.
- **www.goto.com** – Elegant in its simplicity, this engine does the job efficiently.
- **www.cyber411.com** – This is a meta-parallel search, which reaches across 16 engines and displays non-duplicated results.
- **www.khoj.com** – a search engine for Indian web sites. The khoj home page has links to topics of Indian interests.

TELNET

People who are in one location frequently want to use a computer in another location. Perhaps they are on a business trip and wants to read their e-mail. Perhaps they want to access data on the computer in another branch or in the main office. Telnet (short for "networking over the telephone") is the Internet tool that lets you travel from your own workstation out into cyber space to "land" on another computer.

You can also use Telnet to get services, such Gophers, line-mode Web servers and libraries, even if you do not have clients for those servers on your host system. When you are connected to a remote host via Telnet, you interact with that computer and operating system and issue commands as if you were directly connected to that computer. Your session acts as if it were a terminal session connected to the remote host. Telnet provides a command-line interface to Internet hosts running the Telnet service. With Telnet, you can establish a remote session with an Internet host. Telnet is useful for the remote administration of Internet hosts over the Internet.

USING TELNET

Telnet is one of the simplest tools on the Internet. To open a line-mode session with a remote host from a system prompt, type: **telnet hostname.**

You should see the welcome or login banner for the host.

When the Telnet program connects your computer to the remote computer, the remote computer usually asks you to enter a username and a password.

The remote computer usually displays a menu system at the top of the window. In most cases, you can select an option from the menu by typing the number that appears next to the option.

Some Telnet sites require that you type commands at the prompt. In such cases, instructions appear at the bottom of the screen telling you what to type. If the instructions do not appear, you can often view a list of commands or instructions by typing help or? at the prompt and pressing Enter.

When you first connect, look for the command to exit or quit the Telnet session. If you cannot find a command, you can exit by typing **q** or **exit** and pressing Enter. You should exit the remote computer before you shut down your Telnet program.

These sites offer products, services and/or discussions. When you Telnet to these sites, use the login name specified for the service. Be prepared to register your name, address and perhaps e-mail address on entry to these services.

WINDOWS TELNET PROGRAM

TELNET SITES

- Argonne National Laboratory in Illinois offers an educational service called Newton. To reach it, Telnet to newton.dep.anl.gov
- If you need agricultural information, try Cornell's Extension Network. To reach CENET, Telnet to empire.cce. cornell.edu
- There is a backgammon server at fraggle 165.mdstd.chalmers.se
- You can play bridge (live!) by Telnetting to Vanderbilt.okbridge.com
- MichNet and its members maintain several interesting Gophers as well as other interesting services. Telnet to hermes.merit.edu and then, at the "Which Host?" prompt, type HELP. Some of the most interesting services include UM-Weather, which has forecasts and current information as well as educational programs and curriculum ideas for teacher; the MSU Gopher, which has a library of voice recording; the libraries of many Michigan's colleges and universities; and many others.
- Telnet to books.com to find a bulletin board system (BBS) that is the bookstore Book Stacks Unlimited.
- Telnet to pac.carl.org to find book reviews and a journal article fax service.
- Telnet to classroom-earth.ciesin.org 2010 to find the Global change education bulletin board.

LIBRARY NETWORKING

Library and Information Networking is the area with a direct impact on information services, their efficiency and effectiveness. Definitions of Library Networks usually emphasise different levels of cooperation among libraries or other participating organisations in the network. According to Library of Congress (LC) the functions existing in library network are bibliographic utility and services centres. The main distinction between these functions is based on the product orientation of the bibliographic utility and the distributor orientation of the service centre. Service centres mainly function as access points to provide products and services obtained directly or derived from the bibliographic utilities. In addition to accessing the bibliographic utilities the service centres may also provide to the input data to the storage and retrieval facilities of bibliographic utilities.

It must be mentioned here that the broader world of information systems has grown over the last decade from a centralised model of terminal-based networks time-sharing a large computer, towards a decentralised view of small autonomous cooperative systems linked in a complex open network on to a peer-to-peer basis. In library information networks also, a similar type of development has taken place owing to the technological advances providing new possibilities.

THE RANGE OF NETWORK SERVICES

The range of services provided by many resource sharing networks include storage and retrieval of data such as factual, physical and bibliographic data, document ordering and delivery services, general computer and support of group communication and decision making. The most widely used networks can be described by four major types of services. They are:

- shared cataloguing;
- on-line reference;
- shared circulation;
- interlibrary loan.

Of course, cataloguing networks are, by far popular type and are often cited as examples of computer applications to library services. Even though library network systems have undergone major development since 1960s and 1970s, the central objectives of networking remain constant. They are:

- to reveal the contents of large number of libraries, especially through accessibility of catalogue databases, using OPAC interfaces;
- to make resources shown in these catalogue databases available to individual libraries and users when and where they are needed;
- to share the expense and the work involved in creating catalogue databases through the exchange of records and associated activities.
- additional functions that might be fulfilled by networks include:
- distribution and publication of electronic journals and other electronic documents;
- end-user access to other databases, such as those available on the online hosts and CD-ROM;
- value-added service such as electronic mail, directory services and file transfer;
- exchange of bibliographic and authority records usually in MARC format.

In the evolution of library networks, it will be observed that in the beginning, networks were established with limited and well-defined objectives. As the use of networking has become more pervasive due to the easy availability of the infrastructure, the scope of the networks became broader and a number of interconnected consortia of networks and members has become possible. This has enabled the end-user to choose more than one route through the maze of networks in order to locate a given document or piece of bibliographic information. In other words, access barriers have become less and less. This has resulted in the establishment of key agencies in library networking. These key agencies may be grouped into two main categories.

- Large national libraries or centralised cataloguing services which create large bibliographic databases and also occasionally provide the document delivery facility;
- Cooperatives set up by groups of libraries, who feel that they and their users can profit by resource sharing through inter library loans and also by participation in the creation of a union catalogue.

INFORMATION NETWORKS IN INDIA

1. INFLIBNET (INFORMATION AND LIBRARY NETWORK)

The University Grants Commission (UGC) in its attempt to establish networking has taken the initiative and decided to develop a network of academic libraries to effectively manage and administer the resources of these libraries and provide efficient library services to a large number of users, using modern computer and communications technologies. As a consequence of UGC's efforts INFLIBNET, a network of university and college libraries in India was established in 1988. The network became functional in 1991. As part of its development plan, INFLIBNET provided financial assistance to a large number of university libraries to modernise their operations using computer technology.

OBJECTIVES OF INFLIBNET

The main objectives INFLIBNET are as under:

- To evolve a national network of libraries and information centres in the country and to improve information handling capability;
- To provide reliable access to document collection through online union catalogue;
- To provide better access to bibliographic information sources with citation and abstracts through online accessing of international databases held by international information networks and centres;
- To provide document services by establishing resource centres around libraries having a rich collection of documents;
- To promote information resource utilisation through shared cataloguing inter-library loan service;
- To computerise operations of libraries and information centres in the country following a uniform standard;
- To facilitate communication among scientists, engineers, researchers, social-scientists, academics, faculties and students through electronic-mail.

As one of the steps towards achieving the laudable objectives mentioned above, the INFLIBNET has initiated the automation process by funding 54 university libraries. It appears that only 17 of these libraries which received financial assistance from INFLIBNET have so far acquired the hardware to commence the automation activity. Even the progress in respect of resource sharing during the period is stated to be rather slow.

INFLIBNET has also taken a number of other measures which facilitate the realisation of its objectives. Some of the significant steps in this direction are: *(i)* for the purposes of promoting resource sharing activity, it has already created a union catalogue of 50,000 records. It may mentioned here that union catalogue is one of the important tools which facilitates the resource identification, location and sharing aspects of resource sharing activity as a whole among members of the network; *(ii)* INFLIBNET has also took great initiative in the creation of databases containing 65,000 records of theses/dissertations and also a periodicals database having 30,000 records. These are some of pioneering efforts undertaken by INFLIBNET to realise its basic objectives. It is making some efforts in software development and also for the creation of suitable manpower necessary for the purpose.

If we critically examine the achievements of INFLIBNET as given in the Review Committee Report, 1996 and try to compare these with the original targets contained in original report of 1988, prepared by the Inter-agency Working Group, we notice that the achievements fall short of expectations of Inter-agency Working Group. For instance, some of the targets mentioned in the INFLIBNET report were:

(a) compilation of union catalogue of 9 million unique records of retrospective collections of 179 university libraries as against 50,000 records as mentioned above.

(b) at least 200 research and development (R & D) organisations were to be linked

to INFLIBNET. (Even this target does not seen to be realised till now)

(c) Support would be given to 170 universities and 500 college libraries for library automation. (this also remains to be achieved).

It may be stated here that UGC has drafted a new Memorandum of Association and Rules and registered the INFLIBNET Society in the year 1996. The objectives included in this Memorandum of Association are different from those recommended in the Working Group Report of 1988. However, it may be noted here that the INFLIBNET Review Committee under the chairmanship of Dr. S. Venkateshwaran in its report, submitted in 1996, also reco-mmended revision of the objectives for INFLIBNET. INFLIBNET is also engaged in the manpower development activity by undertaking some short term training programmes and workshops. These are very meagre efforts. The network must attempt to develop some standarised software, which it appears, it has not yet succeeded in achieving . Much is expected of this network. It must however be mentioned that the human resources presently engaged in this work appears to be rather inadequate if INFLIBNET is to realise its stated objectives in the near future.

2. CALIBNET (CALCUTTA LIBRARY NET-WORK)

The formation of Kolkata Library Network (CALIBNET) is the result of the efforts made by NISSAT (National Information System for Science and Technology). The DSIR (Department of Scientific and Industrial Research) initiated action for this purpose. Accordingly a feasibility study report for networking about 40 libraries in Kolkata was prepared by the CMC Limited. As per the details contained in the report, an amount Rs. 233.8 lakhs was to be spent during the two phases (Phase I and Phase II) of its implementation. The software required for this purpose was to be developed by CMC Limited based on INGRES 5.2 for CALIBNET with the financial support of NISSAT. The package named MAITRAYEE was developed and handed over to CALIBNET. It is understood that no database has been created using MAITRAYEE package in machine-readable form. It appears that no automation activity has yet been commenced utilising MAITRAYEE by any of the libraries, which were expected to be the participating members of CALIBNET. It is stated that CALIBNET is presently playing the role of a centre for CD-ROM databases which are acquired from outside sources. The other networks, namely BONET in Mumbai, BALNET in Bangalore, PUNENET in Pune, MYLIBNET in Mysore and ADINET in Ahmedabad all supported by NISSAT have not yet taken off by creating their own value-added databases and have commenced the resource sharing activity in a very effective manner. It appears that these networks are only providing E-mail and CD-ROM facilities. In other words, it may be stated that network technology usage cannot be perceived in the functioning of these networks.

3. DELNET (DELHI LIBRARY NETWORK)

India International Centre took the first initiative in the establishment of Delhi Library Network. It organised a discussion on the sharing of resources and networking in Delhi libraries in January, 1988. At this meeting a committee was constituted to study the possibilities of establishing a network of Delhi Libraries. NISSAT arranged the feasibility study through CMC Limited and provided funds for the purpose. It was established as a joint project by IIC and NISSAT in 1988.

Initially, NISSAT provided technical and financial assistance for the functioning of the network, which continued upto 1992.

DELNET was registered as a society under the Societies Registration Act of 1860, with following main objectives:

- to promote sharing of resources among the libraries by developing a network of libraries, by collecting, storing and disseminating information and by offering computerised services to the users;
- to offer guidance to the member libraries on cataloguing, database services, circulation, acquisition, serials control, online services, selection of hardware and software, etc.;
- to coordinate efforts for suitable collection development and reduce unnecessary duplication wherever possible;
- to establish a referral centre to monitor and/or facilitate catalogue search and maintain a central online union catalogue of books, serials, and non-book materials of all the participating libraries;
- to facilitate and promote delivery of documents manually and mechanically;
- to develop specialist bibliographic database of books, serials and non-book materials;
- to develop database of projects, specialists and institutions;
- to possess and maintain electronic and mechanical equipment for fast communication of information and delivery of electronic mail;
- to coordinate with other regional, national and international networks for exchange of information and documents; and
- to undertake, facilitate and provide for the publication of newsletters and/or journals devoted to networking and sharing of resources.

It may be mentioned here that DELNET made progress in several directions as the first operational library network in India.

DELNET SERVICES

DELNET offers to its member libraries the undermentioned services:

- Online and off-line access to its databases;
- Ill online: Inter-Library loan requests are entertained online for books and other documents;
- INTERNET and E-mail Services: E-mail and Internet connectivity being provided by NIC to DELNET is being extended to all the member libraries at reduced rates. ERNET E-mail is also being provided;
- DELNET-LISTSERV (INTERNET mailing list): Online information on IFLA, Library and information science jobs, happenings and Medical Clippings;
- Online information about forthcoming and new titles from publishers, book reviews, and current contents from INTERNET;
- DELNET conducts training programmes and workshops, seminars and lectures;
- Offers retro-conversion facilities to member libraries through equalised agencies; and
- DELNET has created a Web-page on INTERNET: HYPERLINK http://www.nic.in/delnet..

In addition to the above services, DELNET has a planned programme for resource sharing. The plan includes such items that have a strong potential of accelerating the pace of resource sharing activity.

The success of DELNET is reflected in the steady growth of its membership. The growth in membership can be observed most among the institutions both research oriented as well as specialised ones. Among academic libraries, it may be mentioned that all the four university libraries are active members of the network. But, the college libraries are yet to seize this opportunity. It appears only a few (i.e., 7) are members at present. The break up of the present membership of DELNET is said to be:

- Science and Technology Libraries 41
- Social Science Libraries 22

- Humanities Libraries 15
- General Libraries 25

From the statistics provided in one of the documents, it appears that there is a considerable increase in the percentage of increase in databases during the years 1996 and 1997. Also the network is striving to develop the software of its own and in the process has come out with the following:

1. **DELSIS** : An integrated modular software package developed on the basis of BASIS plus to undertake cataloguing and production of union catalogues of libraries, network and information centres:
2. **DELSERCH** : It is an offline remote database access system through E-mail. It is said to be economical and user-friendly for accessing databases remotely located.
3. **DELWINDOWS** : It is an effective tool useful for creating and retrieving bibliographic databases and catalogues.
4. **DEL-DOS** : DELNET has created a separate software for database and its retrieval on DOS platform. The software is capable of handling data inputting in Indian and European languages also using GIST.

LIBRARY AUTOMATION

LIBRARY AUTOMATION WITH COMPUTERISATION

More and more organizations began to use them, including some of the larger libraries. "Third generation" computers using something called integrated circuits began to replace the second generation units in the late 1960s. What is important about these technological developments, from the library point of view, is that integrated data systems could become a reality and computers and telecommunications could be used at a cost that many organizations could afford.

COMPUTERS AND AUTOMATION

How does a computer control library processes? Basically, all computers (maxis, minis, or micros—more about this later) function in the same manner: they can convert ("read"), store ("remember"), do arithmetic, make simple logical choices (processing), and display ("write"). "Reading" is accomplished by means of a device (input) that gives the computer its information (data). A computer "remembers" when data are put into a storage (memory) device at a specific point (storage address). Arithmetic and logical decisions are made in what is called the central processing unit (CPU). And "writing" is done by a device (output) that transforms the CPU's electronic impulses into either letters of digits that people can read. The computer is so useful because it can perform all of these functions at incredibly fast speeds, doing in seconds (or less) tasks that would take a person minutes or hours to do. (A very simplified diagram of a computer system is given in Figure 1) as people do; however, the analogy is useful to keep in mind as you first learn about computers.

	Input Unit	Central Processing Unit (CPU)	Output Unit	
U	– I.C., Typewriter terminal →	Control	→ I.C., CRT Display, →	U
S	CRT Terminal Keyboard,	Arithmetic/	Printoute (Paper,	S
E	Punch cards, Paper tape,	Logic	fiche cards, etc.)	E
R	Magnetic lape, etc.,			R

Primary Storage
↓ ↑
Secondary Storage

Fig. 1. Computer Model

MULTIPLE CHOICE QUESTIONS

1. The technology used for processing of information on the computer system may be called—
A. Information Technology
B. Networking
C. Telecommunication
D. Information Services

2. The components of Information Technology are—
A. Networking & Internet
B. DBA applications & Operating systems
C. Web page development & Multimedia systems
D. All of the above

3. Softwares in Information Technology are—
A. Application Software
B. Operating System Software
C. Operating Systems
D. All of the above

4. Softwares on payroll, Inventory control, education are the examples of—
A. Application Software
B. Operating System
C. Languages
D. Packages

5. DOS, UNIX, LAN Novell, Windows are the examples of—
A. Application software
B. Languages
C. Computer Languages
D. Operating Systems

6. Which is a multiuser system—
A. DOS B. UNIX-system
C. LAN-system D. B & C only

7. The Languages used in the Information technology—
A. BASIC & COBOL
B. PASCAL
C. JAVA
D. All of the above

8. The Packages used in the Information technology are—
A. Word Star
B. Autocad
C. Pagemaker & Corel Draw
D. All the above

9. The compilers are—
A. the programming language translators
B. Assemblers
C. Both of above
D. All of the above

10. Science of study of operational system of computer is—
A. DBA application
B. CAD
C. Operating Systems
D. None of these

11. It is an electronic machine device which carries out calculations at high speed. It has a memory to store large amount and it does comparisons between two values & executes the decisions—
A. Compuer B. Digital Diary
C. Laptop D. Calculators

12. The applications of computer are—
A. Production planning & control
B. Coasting & budgetary control
C. Market research, education, crime detection.
D. All of the above

13. The entire book-keeping is carried out with the help of ______ (w.r. to I.T.).
A. Accountants B. Secretary
C. Computers D. Tally

14. The computer helps in—
A. Space technology & weather forecasting
B. Engineering & educational, science research
C. Railway & Airline reservation system
D. All of the above

15. In mechanical engg., the computer helps by—
A. analysis of thermal, cryogenic, hydraulic system.
B. designing of machine parts.

C. designing the CNC system
D. A and B only

16. The components of a computer—
A. Input Devices
B. Central Processing Unit
C. Output Devices
D. All of the above

17. The devices used for supplying data or programme in a particular language are—
A. Input Devices B. Output Devices
C. C.P.U. D. All of the above

18. The Optical Mark Reader (OMR) and Optical Character Reader (OCR) devices can read only—
A. ready-made information
B. available information
C. primary information
D. All of the above

19. The input device for the computer which is also a primary device is—
A. Keyboard B. O.C.R.
C. O.M.R. D. All of the above

20. The physical device that controls computer operations which is also called the "BRAIN" of the computer system is—
A. Input devices
B. Output devices
C. Central Porcessing Unit (C.P.U.)
D. MICR

21. Output devices are—
A. Printers
B. Plotters
C. Visual Display Unit (V.D.U.)
D. All of the above

22. The main components of a C.P.U. are–
A. Control Unit
B. Main memory
C. Arithmetic/Logic unit
D. All of the above

23. Hardware units of a computer are—
A. C.P.U. B. Input devices
C. Output devices D. All of the above

24. The main function/s of the control unit of the C.P.U. is/are–
A. main memory and accessed by its address
B. it extracts programme instructions one at a time in required sequence from location in main storage, decodes them.
C. it contains a set of accumulators and activated through assemblers
D. All of the above

25. The largest component of the C.P.U. is—
A. Control Unit
B. A.L. Unit
C. Main memory
D. None of the above

26. Computer systems that include the digital information storage are—
A. Internal storage or core storage
B. Back up storage
C. Control Unit
D. A & D only

27. Internal storage which is never altered is—
A. Read Only Memory (ROM)
B. Random Access Memory (RAM)
C. Mega bytes
D. Control unit

28. Internal storage capacity is measured in—
A. Bits or Bytes
B. Kilobites
C. Mega & Gigabites
D. All of the above

29. The Back up storage or external storage devices are—
A. Magnetic tapes & Disks
B. Optical disk
C. Microchips, CD-ROM, WORM
D. All of the above

30. Single-user operating system/s is/are—
A. DOS B. UNIX
C. Window D. All of the above

31. It is the tansmission of representation of information between remote locations by elelctronic means and this information may be in form of voice, video or data is—
A. Communication
B. Data transmission
C. Telecommunication
D. Networking

32. The basic components of Tele-communication are–
A. Data transmission & communication channels
B. Transmission media & switching mechanisms
C. Terminals & Networks
D. All of the above

33. Which statement is TRUE regarding telecommunication?
A. In transmission media of telecommunication, the greater the bandwidth, the greater the rate at which data can be transmitted
B. Commonly used performance measurement of a telecommunications link is its bandwidth
C. The transmission media used in telecommunications networks vary both physically & in their carrying capacity
D. All of the above

34. The transmission media of telecommunication can be—
A. Line space group
B. Free space group
C. Both of above
D. None of above

35. The transmission media in telecommunication are—
A. Twisted pairs of Coaxial Cables
B. Optical Fibres & Microwave Transmission
C. Satellite Transmission
D. All of the above

36. The advantage/s of microwave trans-mission is/are—
A. it gives broad band facility able to carry several thousand channels
B. it is suitable for bulk transmission data over long distances
C. All of the above
D. None of the above

37. The commonly used transmission media is—
A. Microwave transmission
B. Satellite transmission
C. Coaxial cables
D. Circuit switching

38. The techniques which are devised to send messages in many directions at once & to ensure that these messages are received with a minimum of delay—
A. Switching systems
B. Transmission media
C. Analog transmission
D. Transmission modes

39. The different techniques used in switching systems are—
A. Circuit switching
B. Message switching
C. Packet switching
D. All of the above

40. The switching system in which a communication path is actually established before the message is accepted for transmission is—
A. Packet switching
B. Message switching
C. Circuit switching
D. None of above

41. The switching system in which the system accepts all the messages, stores them in a computer & transmits them as and when channels become available is—
A. Packet switching
B. Message switching
C. Circuit switching
D. None of the above

42. The switching system technology used in value-added network like Telenet, which provide libraries with connections to many database search services is—
A. Packet switching
B. Message switching
C. Circuit switching
D. None of these

43. The advantage/s of packet switching over circuit & message switching is/are–
A. transmission economies & shared utilisation
B. high quality & error reduced service

C. speed changing & procedures conversions
D. All of the above

44. The major pattern(s) in data transmission in telecommunication is/are—
A. Analog transmission
B. Digital transmission
C. Transmission media
D. A & B only.

45. In which type of data transmission, there is a continuous up & down pattern?
A. Media transmission
B. Analog transmission
C. Digital transmission
D. Circuit transmission

46. In which type of transmission of data, wave patterns are translated into discrete bits and are separated by intervals. Bits are the smallest unit of information in data processing is–
A. Analog transmission
B. Digital transmission
C. Circuit transmission
D. Any of the above

47. The rate at which a wave or cycle alternates between analog mode or on and digital mode or off is known as—
A. Frequency B. Amplitude
C. Attitude D. Hertz media

48. The electronic transmission frequencies for Satellite and Microwave communication respectively are—
A. 30 Gigahertz and 300 Gigahertz
B. 30 Megahertz and300 Gigahertz
C. 30 Gigahertz and 300 Megahertz
D. 30 Megahertz and 300 Megahertz

49. I.T.U. is—
A. Indian Telephone Union
B. International Telecommunication Union
C. International Telecom Unit
D. Indian Telecom Unit

50. Frequencies and bandwidth occur in telecommunication transmission from low to very high along a continuous range of frequencies is known as—
A. Frequency division
B. Spectrum
C. I.T.U.
D. F.D.N.

51. Technique to improve transmission quality and reduce the noise is Multiplexing. Its main forms are—
A. Frequency Division Multiplexing (FDM).
B. Time Division Multiplexing (TDM)
C. Internal Telecom Multiplexing (ITM)
D. A & B only

52. Which types of multiplexing protocols are mostly used by Librarians & Information scientists?
A. Simplex B. Half-Duplex
C. Full-Duplex D. B & C only

53. Which multiplexing technique is used to split a channel into several discrete narrower ones for simultaneous but separated transmission?
A. Frequency Division Multiplexing
B. Time Division Multiplexing
C. Interval Telecom Multiplexing
D. None of the above

54. In which type, the messages can be transmitted & received?
A. Simplex B. Half-Duplex
C. Full-Duplex D. All of the above

55. "MODEM" stands for—
A. Modulation-Demodulation
B. Mode of transmission
C. Modes Synchronus
D. None of the above

56. Which device function as "translators", changing the digital signals coming out of the terminal to analog so that it can travel along a voice-grade channel?
A. CCTT
B. Modems
C. "Start-Stop" signals
D. Simplex

57. Acoustic coupler, Stand-alone modems and V22, V32 are—
A. Modems B. Synchronus
C. Frequencies D. Input Devices

58. The two main components relating to W.A.N. are—
A. Media
B. Protocols
C. Both of the above
D. Standards

59. The exchange of messages and computer files between computers over a computer network is—
A. Electronic mail (e-mail)
B. Fax
C. Internet
D. O.S.I.

60. P.O.P. with respect to E-mail is—
A. Post office protocol
B. Plaster of Paris
C. Parmanent Order of Passage
D. Protocol of President

61. E-mail gets delivered instead to an incoming mail server is known as—
A. POP server B. SMTP server
C. ITs server D. Any of the above

62. E-mail works on—
A. 'Tear-Wear' theory
B. 'Natural Selection' theory
C. 'Store and Forward' principle
D. Any of the above

63. Internet's POP3 and X400 are the
A. E-mail systems
B. DOT systems
C. UNIX shell
D. T.C.P.

64. Videsh Sanchar Nigam Limited (VSNL) initially started the E-mail in—
A. Delhi & Kolkata only
B. Mumbai only
C. Bangalore only
D. All of the above

65. Gateway Internet Access Service (GIAS) was started in India on—
A. August 15, 1995
B. August 20, 1995
C. October 02, 1995
D. January 26, 1995

66. G.I.A.S. is providing the connectivity provider with—
A. Department of Telecom (D.O.T.)
B. V.S.N.L.
C. B.S.N.L.
D. M.T.N.L.

67. Before the Internet popularity, which provide e-mail service?
A. E-mail service providers (E.S.P.)
B. US-Centric Protocol
C. Hotmail.com
D. P.O.P.

68. The main advantage/s with E.S.P. is/are—
A. they offer e-mail solutions
B. they provide onsite support to both small & large organisation
C. Both of above
D. All of the above

69. The e-mail service that is specially for students free of cost—
A. Bulletin Broad systems-based e-mail
B. E-mail Service Providers
C. Web-based e-mail
D. All of the above

70. National Commission on Libraries and Information Science (NCLIS) is situtated at—
A. United States of America
B. United Kingdom
C. India
D. United Arab Emirates

71. The types of networking in libraries and information centres are—
A. Communication Networks
B. Computer Networks
C. Information Networks
D. Any of the above

72. Communication Networks are—
A. Local Area Networks (LAN)
B. Metropolitan Area Networks
C. Wide Area Networks (WAN)
D. All of the above

73. The single network in which the voice of data can be carried over a single network is—
A. Open System Interconnection (OSI)
B. Integrated Services Digital Network (ISDN).

C. International Standard Book Number (ISBN).

D. Minimum Desired Quality (MDQ).

74. A set of procedures & standards grouped into seven layers for the exchange of information between terminals & computers is—

A. OSI

B. WAN

C. ISDN

D. GOSIPS

75. The design pertaining to a form of artistic, educational or commercial communication in which more than one medium is used is called as—

A. Multimedia

B. Apple's hyper card

C. Hypertext

D. Publishing

76. Important factors in all multimedia system are—

A. they need large memory stores.

B. powerful processing technology to handle retrieval

C. delivery of both texts & images must present

D. All of the above

77. The major tool to establish Hypermedia as a practical environment for multimedia application was—

A. Hypertext

B. D.T.P.

C. Apple's Hyper Card

D. Multimedia platforms

78. The presentation of information in a non-sequential style and pattern is—

A. Hypermedia

B. Multimedia

C. Hypertext

D. Publishing

79. The importance of Hypertext is based on—

A. It offers a very powerful way of organising & accessing information technology

B. Where the information is extensive

C. It consisted of nodes or chunks of information

D. All of the above

80. The advantage/s of Hypertext as compared to computer system is/are—

A. a single framework to handle free text, semantic nets & data

B. data structures have user-oriented semantics

C. it does not require programming skills.

D. All of the above

ANSWERS

1	2	3	4	5	6	7	8	9	10
A	D	D	A	D	D	D	D	C	C
11	12	13	14	15	16	17	18	19	20
A	D	C	D	D	D	A	A	A	C
21	22	23	24	25	26	27	28	29	30
D	D	D	D	C	D	A	D	D	A
31	32	33	34	35	36	37	38	39	40
C	D	D	C	D	C	B	A	D	A
41	42	43	44	45	46	47	48	49	50
B	C	D	D	B	B	A	A	B	B
51	52	53	54	55	56	57	58	59	60
D	D	A	D	A	B	A	C	A	A
61	62	63	64	65	66	67	68	69	70
A	C	A	D	A	A	A	C	A	A
71	72	73	74	75	76	77	78	79	80
D	D	B	A	A	D	C	B	D	D

TYPES OF LIBRARIES AND U.G.C. PROGRAMMES FOR LIBRARIES

- NATIONAL LIBRARY (INDIA, USA, UK)
- ACADEMIC LIBRARY
- PUBLIC LIBRARY
- SPECIAL LIBRARY

NATIONAL LIBRARIES

The ALA Glossary of Library Terms, simply defines the National Library as "*a library maintained by a Nation.*"

A more comprehensive definition of a National Library was attempted by UNESCO, at its 16th Session of the General Conference held in 1970, when UNESCO made "Recommendations Concerning International Standardisation of Library Statistics." The following definition of the National Library occurs in this document;

"Libraries which, irrespective of the titles, are responsible for acquiring an conserving copies of all significant:

(i) publications published in the country and functioning as a

(ii) deposit library either by law or under other arrangements.

They will also normally perform some of the following functions:

(iii) produce a national bibliography.

(iv) hold and keep up-to-date a large representative collection or foreign literature, including books about the country;

(v) act as a national bibliographical information centre;

(vi) compile union catalogues;

(vii) publish retrospective bibliographies...."

This definition is quite comprehensive and covers seven of the most important functions of a National Library.

THE NATIONAL LIBRARY OF INDIA

The Constitution of India provides for the establishment of a National Library under article 62 of the VII Schedule of the Union List, and declared it as an institution of National importance.

1. HISTORICAL BACKGROUND

First Period: (1835-1903) Calcutta Public Library:

The story of our National library falls into three distinct periods. The beginning of the present National Library can be traced to the Calcutta Public Library founded by public men and scholars of Calcutta in 1835 and which was opened to public on 21st March 1836. In 1844, the Calcutta Public Library moved into a spacious building, built in honour of Lord Metcalf (Governor-General). In 1857, consequent upon the outbreak of the Indian War of Independence, the Europeans of Calcutta withdrew their support from the library and the Calcutta management of the Library in 1859.

Second Period: (1903-1947) The Imperial Library

In 1899, when Lord Curzon, the then Viceroy and Governor General of India, visited the Library, he found it in a miserable condition. Lord Curzon, who was interested in art and learning, immediately swung into action. He bought the rights of the Library from the proprietors. He later merged this Library with the Official Imperial Library consisting of government departmental libraries and the remanent of the East India Company Library. With this nucleus, Lord Curzon declared open the new Imperial Library of India on 30th January 1903 in the Metcalf Hall. John Macfarlane of the British Museum was invited to look after the new Imperial Library, as its first librarian.

Third Period : (1948-1947) The National Library of India

With the dawn of freedom, the founding fathers of the new nation transformed the former Imperial Library into the new National Library of India in 1948. One of the most pressing needs of the Library was additional space. This problem was solved by a magnanimous gesture which the then Governor-General of India, Shri C. Rajagopalachari, made by offering the Viceroy's Palace in Calcutta, namely, the Belvedere Palace, with its sprawling, lush green lawns, for housing the new National Library. Shri B.S. Kesavan, a man of vision, enthusiasm and administrative skill, was appointed the first Librarian of the new National Library. The imperial institution was transformed into a temple of knowledge of free India. The new National Library was declared open to the nation by the then Union Minister for Education, Maulana Abul Kalam Azad on 1st February 1953, in connection with the golden Jubilee celebrations of the library.

THE LIBRARY OF CONGRESS (LC)

The **Library of Congress**, Washington, D.C. which is at present considered as the **National Library of the United States of America**, was originally created to serve the U.S. Congress. It was established in 1800 with a small collection, but grew steadily. By the Copyright Law of 1870, the Library acquired the status of a depository library, getting the privilege of free delivery of two copies of printed books, charts dramatic or musical compositions, engravings, prints or photographs, etc. Today the Library ranks as one of the largest national libraries of its kind and occupies an eminent place in the world of scholarship and learning. We give below a few glimpses of this great Library. An idea of the size, magnitude and range of LC's collection and services can be had from the following facts:

- LC is the largest centre for information storage in the world, having 20 million volumes, books representing only one-fourth of its collection; the other 59 millions of stored data are on sound records, motion picture reels, computer tapes or in the form of manuscripts, maps, prints and photographs. Less than one-fourth of its collection is in English;
- It operates with a staff of about 4800, comprising professional librarians, highly trained personnel such as musicians, lawyers, chemists, computer specialists, scientists and technologists, braille specialists, etc.
- It is housed in three enormous buildings with three different architectural styles; covers a total area of over 71 acres; 3,000 readers can sit at a time in its several reading rooms; and
- It offers services to a variety of specialist groups such as Congressmen, legal community, scholars and academicians, performing artists, blind and handicapped, library and information community;

Ten million pieces of material are handled every year, twenty-seven thousand every day.

THE BRITISH LIBRARY

The British Library is the national library of the United Kingdom. It is more than just a library. It has the world's leading resources for scholarship, research and innovation, with incomparable collection, and expertise of staff. It occupies a central position in the library and information network of UK. It reflects the intellectual, cultural and socio-economic life of the country. The library aims to serve scholarship, research and development, industry, commerce and all other major users of information. Its services are based on the wealth of materials collected by the British Library System.

ACADEMIC LIBRARIES

These libraries support learning, teaching, research and other educational functions appropriate to their parent institutions. We shall explain the respective roles that these libraries play at different levels of the educational process. We shall outline the types of document collections built up in these libraries and the way in which they are processed, organised, maintained and serviced to the user communities. Nevertheless, we shall study these academic libraries in the Indian context.

SCHOOL LIBRARIES

Use of a library by a pupil must start from the primary school. The school libraries at Primary, Middle, Secondary etc.

PRIMARY SCHOOL LIBRARIES

These libraries are meant for children between five and ten or eleven years of age and the teachers who are involved in teaching and shaping them. This is the age of children when they form attitudes and habits. The school library should aim to:

- foster book mindedness;
- strengthen learning skills through kits now available in plenty;
- create a love for books and other learning resources; and
- inculcate the habit of reading in a slow but deliberate process.

In order to achieve these aims, the following aspects need careful attention on:

- building up a good stock of books and other learning and teaching materials, for the children as well as teachers;
- organising and displaying the collection to attract the attention and curiosity of children and making them easily accessible;
- designing and organising programmes and services to inculcate in children the habit of reading, learning and referring to books etc., for information;
- getting proper physical facilities in terms of building, furniture and equipment.

The foundation of the reading habits among children is well laid by providing them with graded books and other learning materials which may hold their interest and arouse their curiosity. Children like to know about space and the universe, the bottom of the sea, life in jungles and deserts, towns and villages, flora and fauna, people of other countries, general principles in science and technology. Fortunately, mankind had developed literature for children in all subject sectors.

A school library should build up collections on the following themes and use them extensively with students:

(i) Picture books depicting acts and deeds of valour and adventure, partriotism, service to fellow persons and other similar themes;

(ii) Biographies of great men and women;

(iii) Books of travel and humour;

(iv) Popular games and sports;

(v) Cultural heritage;

(vi) Reference books like Children's Encyclopaedias and illustrated Dictionaries;

(vii) Children's magazines like Children's World, Chandamama, Tinkle etc.;

(viii) Audio visual aids such as motion films, animated films, tape-slides video cassettes;

(ix) Models, charts, maps, globes, pictures, photographs, toys etc.;

Besides children's books and materials, the teaching staff would need reference books of different types such as instructional materials, books on children's psychology and other similar book. If funds do not allow acquisition of such materials, these items could be borrowed on inter-library loan from bigger libraries in the vicinity.

SECONDARY SCHOOL LIBRARIES

If primary school libraries are designed to function and operate as integral parts of the educational programme at that stage, the secondary school libraries maintain their specific educational identity in fulfilling all academic requirements of the young students for learning and of the teachers for effective teaching and their own development. Secondary school libraries support school programmes at three stage, viz. middle-classes 6 to 8, secondary classes 9 to 10, and higher secondary-classes 11 and 12, constituting a total period of seven years of the school programme. These are crucial formative years of the children and good habits formed at this stage would be everlasting. The library has a very positive educational role to play and to achieve the following aims:

- Inculcate the habit of using the school library, not only with reference to their learning for course requirements but also by learning reading for pleasure, general knowledge and recreation;
- development of learning skills for collecting information on any topic by consulting reference books and other material;
- provide opportunities to students to visit other academic, special and public libraries to get an idea of the library system in the country, as major resource for learning and use them at later stages of life.

COLLEGE LIBRARIES

College performs an important function in the educational process. College education provides a totally different environment for boys and girls who go for higher studies. usually the classes comprise a large number of students and unlike school education, the students of college get much less individual attention from the teachers. The students, therefore, have to depend much more on self-learning. Therefore, the college library is the automatic choice for students to supplement their classroom teaching.

UNIVERSITY LIBRARIES

A library is more important in a University, because a library can do without a University whereas a University cannot function without a library. The number of universities in India has gone up from a mere twenty in 1947, to more than two hundred in the nineties. This number includes conventional universities, professional universities and deemed universities. The growth is signified by the total number of students' enrolments, creation of a number of new departments, a number of mission oriented projects of research and by many other social and intellectual factors. Institutions like the Indian Institutes of Technology, (IITs), the Indian Institutes of Management, Agricultural Universities have also innovated a number of new educational practices. The open university concept for distance education is yet another new experiment at the university level. All these factors have affected university libraries in a great measure. Today, university libraries have a very large and difficult role to play in order to meet a variety of demands of information and knowledge by far larger number of people on far larger number of subjects at far higher prices and negligible grants. The clients of higher education must contribute toward the cost of learning materials because the state (any state) can never provide all required funds.

PUBLIC LIBRARIES

UNESCO'S DEFINITION

However, the most widely accepted definition of a public library was formulated by

UNESCO in 1949, which was revised in 1972 and again revised in 1994, and is known as the UNESCO Public Library Manifesto. The definition of a public library according to this manifesto is as follows:

- it is a public library which being the local gateway to knowledge, provides a basic condition for lifelong learning, independent decision-making and cultural development of the individual and social groups;
- a living force for education, culture and information, an essential agent for the fostering of peace and spiritual welfare through the minds of men and women;
- the local centre of information, making all kinds of knowledge and information readily and freely available to its users.

This definition is exhaustive, covering all the facets of public library services.

KEY MISSIONS OF PUBLIC LIBRARY

The UNESCO, in its public library manifesto, for the first time spelled out the key missions which relate to information, literacy, education and culture and should be at the core of public library services:

- creating and strengthening reading skills and habits in children from an early age;
- supporting both individual and self-conducted education as well as formal education;
- providing opportunities for personal creative development;
- stimulating the imagination and creativity of children and young people;
- providing access to cultural expressions of all performing arts;
- fostering inter-cultural dialogue and favouring cultural diversity;
- providing adequate information services to local enterprises, associations and interest groups.

MULTIPLE CHOICE QUESTIONS

1. Library plays a very important role in fostering the ________ development of the students.
A. physical B. psychological
C. spiritual D. intellectual

2. Public libraries have a responsibility to support—
A. extension education
B. formal education
C. continuing education
D. independent education

3. Dr. Thomas Bray was associated with—
A. Parish library
B. Monastic library
C. Private library
D. Cathedral library

4. Public library development in India was started from—
A. Kolkata B. Pune
C. Ahmedabad D. Baroda

5. In which year, the first general library law was enacted in USA at national level?
A. 1946 B. 1956
C. 1966 D. 1976

6. National Medical Library is located at —
A. New Delhi B. Pune
C. Banglore D. Imphal

7. The Library of Congress is the National library of—
A. UK B. USA
C. USSR D. Switzerland

8. Which department controls the public libraries in Mizoram?
A. Education B. Library
C. Culture D. Welfare

9. INFLIBNET is established by UGC and located at—
A. New Delhi B. Ahmedabad
C. Pune D. Kolkata

10. P.V. Verghese Prize is awarded by Indian Library Association for—
A. best article B. best book
C. best library D. best service

11. Who founded FID?
A. Paul otlet & La Fontaine
B. Dewey & Ranganathan
C. Otlet & Melvil Dewey
D. None of the above

12. IFLA's headquarters is located at—
A. Paris B. Chicago
C. London D. The Hague

13. Which association contributed a lot in preparing Public library Manifesto?
A. UNICEF B. UNESCO
C. UNO D. UNISIST

14. Curriculum Development Committee on Library Information Science has been constituted by—
A. UGC
B. INSDOC (NISCAIR)
C. Ministry of Education
D. University of Delhi

15. UGC National Information Centre in Social Sciences & Humanities is established at—
A. Goa University
B. M.S. University, Baroda
C. J.N.U.; Delhi
D. J.M.J.; New Delhi

16. Which library association played a major role in preparing a NAPLIS Document?
A. RRRLF B. NASSDOC
C. UGC D. NISSAT

17. AGRIS is sponsored by—
A. NLM B. FAO
C. ICAR D. CSIR

18. NISSAT sectoral centre in marine science is hosted by—
A. National Institute of Oceanography, Goa
B. National Maritine Institute, Delhi
C. Central Maritine Institute
D. National Institute of Marine Engineering, Dehradun

19. Non-formal education is supported by—
A. research libraries
B. public libraries
C. university libraries
D. special libraries

20. The earlier name of National Library, Calcutta was—
A. Central Public library
B. The Imperial library
C. Nation Imperial library
D. National Public library

21. ALA Glossary of library terms defines the National, library as "a library maintained by—"
A. Province B. Nation
C. Country D. State

22. Which has been decalared as an institution of National importance by govt. of India?
A. National Library, Kolkata
B. Delhi Public Library, Delhi
C. Canamera Public library, Chennai
D. Asiatic Society Library, Mumbai

23. A school library inculcates ________ among the school children.
A. saving habits B. competing habits
C. reading habits D. writing habits

24. Which Committee recommended 20% of the college budget for the maintenance & development of the library?
A. Prof. K.N. Raj
B. Prof. S. Radhakrishan
C. Prof. S.R. Ranganathan
D. Prof Lakshaaswamy

25. Information and Library Network (INFLIBNET) centre is established by—
A. UGC B. RRRLF
C. NBT D. NISSAT

26. Which states, public libraries Act provides on independent minister for library services?
A. Kerala B. Manipur
C. Mizoram D. West Bengal

27. One of the pioneering efforts in the direction of user studies was conducted

in 1956 on behalf of National Science Foundation by—
A. S.R. Ranganathan
B. R.R. Shaw
C. T.S. Eliot
D. J.S. Mills

28. One the methods for conducting user studies is—
A. Citation Analysis
B. Per Captia Method
C. Statistical Method
D. Research Design

29. User studies are conducted in order to know—
A. information requirements of the users
B. material requirements of the users
C. financial requirements of the users
D. all of the above

30. Which department controls the Public libraries in Mizoram?
A. Education
B. Culture
C. Library
D. Science & Technology

31. Making the users acquainted with the library's usage & services is—
A. feed back
B. user education
C. user orientation
D. library assessment

32. User education is concerned with providing instruction to the users how to make use of the—
A. information resources of library
B. human resources of library
C. physical resources of library
D. financial resources of library

33. Which agency's information policy lay stress on User education?
A. UNISIST B. AGRIS
C. INIS D. NISSAT

34. Which organisation has organised a number of seminars & workshops for promotion of user education specially in India?
A. DRTC B. NIC
C. CSIR D. INFLIBNET

35. The process of supplying the relevant documents on a specific topic to a user is—
A. Document Delivery Service
B. Current Awareness Service
C. SDI service
D. All of the above

36. India Library Association (ILA) was founded in—
A. 1925 B. 1930
C. 1933 D. 1940

37. Association for Information Management is located at—
A. London B. USA
C. Paris D. Mexico

38. Indian Science Abstract is published by—
A. DRTC B. ISIA
C. INSDOC D. NBTA

39. There are three methods usually used for evaluation of "User education" programme. One is—
A. studies behaviour
B. evaluational package
C. psychometric evaluation
D. congnitive evaluation

40. UNESCO attempted to make user education programmes through—
A. UNISIST B. NISSAT
C. INIS D. AGRIS

41. Seminar on the Development of National Library in Asia & Pacific area of 1964 held at—
A. Manila
B. New York
C. The Hague
D. None of the above

42. The new name of the "British Museum Library of Great Britiain" is—
A. Library of Congress
B. British Library
C. National Library
D. None of the above

43. National Diet Library is located at—
A. China B. Japan
C. USA D. UK

44. National Library for the Blind is located at—
A. India B. UK
C. Japan D. USA

45. National Library of Canada does functions related to—
A. lending sections
B. sharing functions
C. science, agriculture, technical etc.
D. all of the above.

46. Which article of VII schedule of Union List of Constitution of India declared "National Library" is an Institution of National importance?
A. Article 45 B. Article 42
C. Article 62 D. Article 92

47. Calcutta Public Library was opened to public on—
A. 12 Sept; 1933 B. 13 Sept; 1933
C. March 21; 1836 D. March 12; 1863

48. Which Governor-General of India opened "Imperial Library" on Jan. 30; 1903 in Metcalf Hall?
A. Lord Curzon B. Lord Cornwallis
C. Lord Irwin D. Lord Mountbatton

49. The first Librarian of "National Library" of India was—
A. Sh. B.S. Kesaran
B. Sh. B.C. Pal
C. Sh. K.M. Asadullah
D. R.R. Shaw

50. The "National Library" was declared open to the nation on Feb. 01; 1953 after the inaugration by union minister of education. The Minister was—
A. C. Rajagopalachari
B. Maulana Abul Kalam Azad
C. Sardar Patel
D. P.Chandra Mitra

51. The books of National Library of India are classified by—
A. UDC
B. DDC
C. AACR–I
D. All of the above

52. The books of "Delhi Public Library" are classified by—
A. UDC
B. DDC
C. Cutter's classification
D. Ranganathan's classification

53. A National Library for Blind & the Physically Handicapped is located at—
A. Dehradun, India
B. Ottawa, Canada
C. Delhi, India
D. None of the above

54. Which is not a function of school library?
A. generating curiosity & interest among students & teachers about the material available in library
B. to generate confidence interest in libraries for getting information
C. lending & keeping track of books and other documents to the needs & interests of teachers & students
D. to serve as a central & comprehensive collection of national output, acquired through legal deposits, gifts or exchange.

55. Which is not a collection of primary school libraries?
A. Folktales
B. Panchatantra, Arabian nights
C. Stories of animals & birds
D. Legal books

56. Which is a function of secondary school libraries?
A. Information & Reference services
B. Lending
C. Guidance & Advice services
D. All of the above

57. The main function/s of a University Library is/are—
A. development of a collection in a wide variety for learning, teaching, research
B. getting the stock of knowledge materials organised & maintained for use
C. organise & provide a variety of library,

documentation & information services, both responsive & anticipatory
D. all of the above

58. The University library is governed by statutory law of the—
A. Central Govt. B. University
C. Parliament D. None of the above

59. In University of Delhi, the Chief Librarian is a special member of—
A. Executive Council
B. Academic Council
C. Governing Council
D. None of the above

60. The "Current Awareness Services (CAS)" of university library include the services of—
A. Current contents of journals
B. SDI & Newspaper clipping services
C. Altering services to important literature in select fields
D. All of the above

61. The "specilised services" of University libraries include—
A. user education & user oriented seminars
B. special lectures & demonstration
C. exhibition & special displays
D. All of the above

62. The University Grants Commission developed "INFLIBNET" in the year—
A. 1933 B. 1955
C. 1977 D. 1988

63. The libraries associated in the educational institutions are ______
A. Academic Libraries
B. Browsing Libraries
C. Effective Libraries
D. Public Libraries

64. The arts of collection, recording, preserving & making use of the documents quickly is—
A. Networking B. Documentation
C. Browsing D. Organising

65. The interlinking of library resources and services by means of computer & communication technologies is—
A. Tape-slide kit
B. Library Network
C. Inter-Library Loan
D. Ramification

66. The main factor/s behind the evaluation of Public library" is/are—
A. Urge for knowledge & Literacy
B. Universal Public Education
C. Rapid advancement in Science & Technology
D. All of the above

67. The function/s of Public Library is/are—
A. a centre for information & culture.
B. a centre for self-education
C. a centre for Local Cultural materials
D. Any of the above

68. The correct definition of "Public Libraries" is—
A. "it is living force of education, information & culture"
B. "it is a life long learning institution"
C. "it is free to all sections of the community"
D. All of the above

69. A "special library" provides the services—
A. issue of documents & reference services
B. literature search & current awareness
C. SDI & document supply & refrral services
D. All of the above

70. A technical document containing descriptions of an invention & rating properly right to the inventor by Government is—
A. Product B. Digest
C. Patent D. Report

71. The main activities of an Information Analysis Centre are ______
A. analysis & interpretration of information
B. synthesis & evaluation of information
C. repacking of information for the purpose of enabling the users to assimilate better information
D. All of the above

72. National information Centre for Drugs & Pharmaceuticals (NICDAP) is located at—
A. Chennai B. Lucknow
C. New Delhi D. Mumbai

73. National Information Centre for Crystallography (NICRYS) in located at—
A. University of Delhi
B. University of Chennai
C. Jawaharlal Nehru University
D. Pondicherry University

74. National Information Centre for Food Science & Technology (NICFOS) is located at—
A. Mysore B. Mumbai
C. Chennai D. Lucknow

75. Indian National Scientific Documentation Centres (INSDOC) was established in 1952 as a constituent of—
A. ICAR B. CSIR
C. AIIMS D. ASI

76. The National Library of United States of America is—
A. Library of Congress (LC)
B. Librarian Congress
C. NICDS
D. NLUSA

77. Which is the largest centre for information storage in the world?
A. Library of Congress
B. British Library
C. Imperial Library
D. Delhi Public Library

78. The national library of United Kingdom is—
A. Library of Congress
B. British Library
C. National Library
D. Science Library

79. The activities of the Library of Congress which aid professional library & bibliographical services are—
A. National Union Catalogue of Printed Books & Cataloguing in Publication
B. MARC project & Library Automation Programmes
C. Both of the above
D. None of the above

80. Which Academic institution has large number of libraries?
A. Primary schools
B. Middle schools
C. Secondary schools
D. Higher secondary schools

81. Library facilities in school has been started by—
A. NIC B. IAC
C. NCERT D. DBT

82. The main function/s of a College Library is/are—
A. giving young men & women a wider & deeper understanding of various subjects
B. providing adequate & comfortable physical facilities for study
C. training young persons for various profession like law, medicine, engineering & technology
D. All of the above

83. Which is a hardcore & central part of College arch?
A. Canteen B. Library
C. Laboratory D. Auditorium

84. Which is a true statement regarding College library finance & budget?
A. No country in the world is able to provide 100% subsidy to higher education
B. No College can afford to provide all books needed by students pursuing higher level courses
C. Raj Commission recommended 20% of the college budget for the maintenance & development of library
D. All of the above

85. Who was the chairman of "UGC Library Committee Report" of 1959?
A. Dr. S.R. Ranganathan
B. Prof. K.N. Raj

C. Prof. R. Mudaliar
D. Dr. Rani N. Pandey

86. Which state Government levies a library cess on house tax and property tax as "Library fund"?
A. Pondicherry B. Andhra Pradesh
C. New Delhi D. Kolkata

87. Library of the National Institute of Nutrition is situated at—
A. Mysore B. New Delhi
C. Hyderabad D. Kolkata

88. Which kind of libraries have largest number of current periodicals?
A. Academic libraries
B. Public libraries
C. University libraries
D. Special libraries

89. Which library established the Centre for Research on User Studies (CRUS) in 1975 at University of Sheffield?
A. Library of Congress
B. British Library
C. National Library
D. No such organisation is present

90. A user is—
A. clientele B. patrons
C. a person who utilises the information resources of a library, the services & products of an information system & dervies benefit from them
D. All of the above

91. The factors in users of information that affect—
A. their perception of the problem faced & their definition of needed information
B. the specific ways they are most likely to use information & their capacity to use a given type of information
C. both of the above
D. None of the above

92. The demand for specific type of information requirements expressed by different categories of users is—
A. user studies
B. user warrant
C. user education
D. use categories

93. The systematic efforts undertaken to obtain information on the manner in which information is obtained & used by different categories of users—
A. user studies
B. user education
C. user warrant
D. user information

94. The general method/s of user studies is/are—
A. Questionnaire
B. Interview & Observation by self
C. Operations research study
D. All of the above

95. It is a process or programme through which the potential users of information are motivated to use information resources—
A. user warrant
B. user education
C. user study
D. library education

96. Who developed the concept of "User Education"?
A. Dr. S.R. Ranganathan
B. Louis Shores
C. Paul Otlet
D. Girija Kumar Jha

97. The objective/s of user education is/are —
A. creating awareness of the resources available in library
B. acquainting a series of skills which can be made use of in connection with different academic studies
C. Both of these
D. None of these

98. Which organisation/s is/are promoting user education in India?
A. INSDOC, New Delhi & DRTC, Banglore
B. BIS, New Delhi & DRTC, Banglore
C. INSDOC, New Delhi & BIS
D. IARI, New Delhi & BIS

99. "User Education" has main two components—
A. Orientation & Instruction
B. Orientation & Classification
C. Classification & Instruction
D. None of the above

100. Which Association organised the seminar on "Users & Library and Information Service"?
A. INSDOC B. IASLIC
C. ISAC D. IARI

ANSWERS

1	2	3	4	5	6	7	8	9	10
D	D	A	D	B	A	B	A	B	A
11	**12**	**13**	**14**	**15**	**16**	**17**	**18**	**19**	**20**
A	D	B	A	B	D	B	A	B	A
21	**22**	**23**	**24**	**25**	**26**	**27**	**28**	**29**	**30**
B	A	C	A	A	D	B	A	D	A
31	**32**	**33**	**34**	**35**	**36**	**37**	**38**	**39**	**40**
C	A	A	A	A	C	A	B	A	A
41	**42**	**43**	**44**	**45**	**46**	**47**	**48**	**49**	**50**
A	B	B	B	D	C	C	A	A	B
51	**52**	**53**	**54**	**55**	**56**	**57**	**58**	**59**	**60**
B	B	A	D	D	D	D	B	A	D
61	**62**	**63**	**64**	**65**	**66**	**67**	**68**	**69**	**70**
D	D	A	B	B	D	D	D	D	C
71	**72**	**73**	**74**	**75**	**76**	**77**	**78**	**79**	**80**
D	B	B	A	B	A	A	B	C	D
81	**82**	**83**	**84**	**85**	**86**	**87**	**88**	**89**	**90**
C	D	B	D	A	B	C	D	B	D
91	**92**	**93**	**94**	**95**	**96**	**97**	**98**	**99**	**100**
C	B	A	D	B	B	C	A	A	B

MANAGEMENTS IN LIBRARIES

Koontz defines "management" as, "the process of designing and maintaining an environment in which individuals, working in groups, accomplish efficiently selected aims."

To achieve the functions and objectives of a library, a librarian or Director of library has to undertake the following functions with 100% efforts and manpower:—

(i) Planning
(ii) Organising.
(iii) Staffing
(iv) Direction & Leading
(v) Controlling

PRINCIPLE OF MANAGEMENT

PRINCIPLES OF LIBRARY MANAGE MENT

1. TAYLOR'S PRINCIPLES

The fundamental principles that Taylor saw underlying the scientific approach to management may be summarized as follows:

1. Replacing rules of thumb with science (organized knowledge);
2. Obtaining harmony in group action, rather than discord;
3. Achieving cooperation of human beings, rather than chaotic individualism;
4. Working for maximum output, rather than restricted output; and
5. Developing all workers to the fullest extent possible for their own and their company's highest prosperity.

2. FAYOL'S PRINCIPLES

Noting that the principles of management are flexible, not obsolete and must be usable regardless of changing and special conditions, Fayol listed fourteen principles based on his experience. They are summarised below:

1. **Division of work:** Specialization allows workers and managers to acquire an ability, sureness, and accuracy which will increase output. More and better work will be produced with the same effort.
2. **Authority:** The right to give orders and the power to exact obedience are the essence of authority. Its roots are in the person and the position. It cannot be conceived of apart from responsibility.
3. **Discipline:** Discipline is composed of obedience, application, energy, behaviour and outward marks of respect between employers and employees. It is essential to any business. Without it no enterprise can prosper. It is what leaders make it.
4. **Unity of command:** For any action whatsoever, an employee should receive orders from one superior only. One person, one boss. In no case is there adaptation of a social organism to a duality of command.
5. **Unity of direction:** One head and one plan should lead a group of activities having the same objective. One head, one plan.
6. **Subordination of individual interest to general interest:** The interest of one person or group in a business should not prevail over that of the organization.
7. **Remuneration of personnel:** The price of services rendered should be fair and should be satisfactory to both employees and employer. A level of pay depends on an employee's value to the organization and on factors independent

of an employee's worth—such as cost of living, availability of personnel and general business conditions.

8. **Centralization:** Everything that serves to reduce the importance of an individual subordinate's role is centralization. Everything that increases the subor-dinate's importance is decent-ralization. All situations call for a balance between these two positions.
9. **Scalar Chain:** The chain formed by managers from the highest to the lowest is called a scalar chain or chain of command. Managers are the links in the chain. They should communicate to and through the links. Links may be skipped or circumvented only when superiors approve and a real need exists to do so.
10. **Order:** This principle is the simple advocacy of a place for everyone, and everyone in his or her place; a place for everything, and everything in its place. The objective of order is to avoid loss and waste.
11. **Equity:** Kindliness and justice should be practised by persons in authority to extract the best that their subordinates have to give.
12. **Stability of tenure of personnel:** Reducing the turnover of personnel will result in more efficiency and fewer expenses.
13. **Initiative:** People should be allowed the freedom to propose and to execute ideas at all levels of an enterprise. A manager who is able to permit the exercise of initiative on the part of subordinates is far superior to one who is unable to do so.
14. **Esprit De Corps:** In unity there is strength. Managers have the duty to promote harmony and to discourage and avoid those things that disturb harmony.

3. BARNARD'S PRINCIPLES

Alongwith scientific management and the manager's tasks, many scholars and practitioners were thinking about experimenting with, and writing on, industrial psychology and on social theory both of which, in many instances, were stimulated by the scientific management movement. We can get the flavour of these developments by looking briefly at the emergence of industrial psychology, the growth of personnel management, and the development of a sociological approach to human relations and management.

MANAGERIAL FUNCTIONING

FUNCTIONS OF LIBRARY MANAGEMENTM

1. PLANNING

Planning is the process of determining in advance what should be accomplished and how to do it. In other words, it is an analytical process of establishing goals, objectives and targets, assessing the future, premising, generating and evaluating alternatives, selecting programs, projects or courses, estimating resources, preparing the plan document with derivative plans and implementing the plan.

Four important characteristics of planning are *(i)* The purpose of every plan and all derivative plans is to facilitate the accomplishment of enterprise purposes and objectives; *(ii)* Planning is the "first" function and logically preceedes the execution of all other managerial functions; *(iii)* Managers at all levels are involved in planning *(iv)* The efficiency of a plan is measured by the amount it contributes to the purpose and objectives as offset by the costs of other unsought consequences required to formulate and operate. In other words, planning is characterised by its primacy, efficient contribution to purpose and objectives and all pervasiveness. Some types of plan usually developed and operated include objectives (or goals), strategies (or grand plans), policies, procedures, rules, programs and budgets.

The significance and advantages of planning are:

(a) it offsets uncertainty and change;
(b) provides a framework for execution and direction;
(c) focuses attention on objectives;
(d) improves services, leads to operations and facilities control;
(e) ensures rational and effective development;

2. ORGANISING

Organising is the process of prescribing formal relationships among people and resources (i.e., personnel, raw materials, tools, capital, etc.) to accomplish the goals.

Organising involves:

- analysing the entire activities of an organisation into homogeneous types of works and jobs;
- sorting and grouping the resulting works and jobs into a logical structure;
- assigning these activities to specific positions and persons; and
- providing a means for coordinating the efforts of individuals and groups.

Some basic principles of organising are listed below:

(a) The key activities should be clearly defined;
(b) The activities should be grouped on some logical basis;
(c) The responsibilities of each division, department, unit and job should be clearly defined;
(d) Authority should be delegated as far down in the organisation as possible;
(e) The number of persons reporting to each manager should be reasonable.

3. STAFFING

If organisational structure creates positions at different levels for performing various functions, staffing deals with providing the right type of persons to man them. Indeed persons are the key to the effective functioning of any organisation. In fact, the real strength of an organisation is its personnel; they can make or mar the organisation.

Staffing is the formal process of ensuring that the organisation has qualified workers available at all levels to meet its short and long term objectives. This function includes *(i)* Human resources planning *(ii)* Recruitment and selection *(iii)* Training and development *(iv)* Rewards and compensations *(v)* Health and safety *(vi)* Career planning and management *(vii)* Employee assistance, coaching and orientation, *(viii)* Performance appraisal. Some important basic concepts of staffing are job analysis, job description, job specification, job enlargement and job enrichment.

4. DIRECTING

Directing is the managerial function concerned with the interpersonal aspect of managing by which subordinates are led to understand and contribute effectively and efficiently to the attainment of enterprise objectives. It is aimed at getting the members of the organisation to move in the direction that will achieve its objectives. In other words, directing is the managerial function that enables managers to get things done through persons, both individually and collectively. Directing is related to staffing in the sense that these two functions are concerned with the employees of the organisation. While staffing is concerned with providing and maintaining human resources, directing deals with leading and motivating the human resources to give out the best. It is the most interpersonal aspect of management. Directing is closely related to the communicating function and motivating, actuating and leading are sub-functions of directing.

5. CONTROLLING

Another important aspect of directing is exercise of control over the system. Control does not merely mean restrictions or restraints to be forced on the system, but they are guidelines for the organisation to perform according to set standards of efficiency and quality. What is implied in this is, accountability, and the obligation of the staff at all levels, of reporting to a higher authority on their productivity both in terms of quality and quantity. But these would need yardsticks and measurement tools and techniques for evaluating performance. Thus, both directing and reporting are closely related to the controlling function.

In simple terms, controlling can be defined as the process of comparing actual performance with standards and taking any necessary corrective action. Hence, the control process consists of *(i)* establishment of standards *(ii)* measurement of performance, and *(iii)* correction of deviations. The standards may be physical standards, cost standards, revenue standards or even intangible standards. Some of the common traditional control measures are budgets, statistical data, special reports, breakeven point analysis, internal audit and personal observation.

MANAGEMENT IN LIBRARY

The management of a library means, in simple terms, efficient and effective management of material (information resources), machinery, men and money to meet the objectives of the library.

It is very important for us to note that libraries are basically paternalistic, service-oriented and not-for-profit organisations. As a matter of fact, it is that part of management which is called "service management" which is more important to libraries than the management of industrial and profit-oriented organisations.

At this juncture, it is necessary for us to have a quick look at some of the basic characteristics of service and not-for-profit organisations. Four important characteristics of service are:

1. **Intangibility:** Services often may not directly appeal to the senses of customers.
2. **Inseparability** (i.e., customer participation in service production): Service is usually produced in the presence of customers and service production and consumption are inseparable.
3. **Heterogeneity:** Service rendered cannot be fully standardised and as a result there will be variations in the quality of service rendered to different customers.
4. **Perishability:** Many times service cannot be stored and an inventory developed for later physical distribution.

Management of a library (as a service organisation) is accomplished by a combination of basic management functions and skills discussed earlier as well as management of roles. We can think of three important roles for a library manager.

(a) **Interpersonal role:** *(i)* library manager as a figurehead with duties of a ceremonial nature, *(ii)* leading role, *(iii)* liaison role.

(b) **Informational role:** *(i)* perpetually scanning and monitoring information: *(ii)* disseminator role, *(iii)* specific role of informing and satisfying various groups.

(c) **Decisional role:** *(i)* As entrepreneur looking out for new ideas and adopt them for change *(ii)* solving unanticipated problems and handling disturbances, *(iii)* resources allocation role of dividing work and delegating authority, *(iv)* negotiator role.

ORGANISATIONAL STRUCTURE

It is mainly of two types which are discussed below:

1. Formal organisational structure
2. Informal organisational structure

1. Formal organisations are social units formed for the purpose of accomplishing some objective or objectives. Two basic characteristics of formal organisations are: *(i)* they are formed to accomplish a goal, and *(ii)* the goal may be changed many times during the lifetime of the organisation. As an organisation becomes more complex and adds new objectives, frequently one objective will come into conflict with another objective. A major source of conflict in service organisations, particularly libraries, is the competition for resources. Other conflicts include line-versus-staff conflict (e.g. IT personnel and library professional staff), differences in work orientation and needs (e.g., requirement of bibliographic details by acquisition unit and cataloguing unit), etc.

A formal organisation is the result of explicit decision-making, decideing how people and activities should be related to one another. However, there is no such decision-making involved in an informal organisation which may simply evolve spontaneously or over time.

2. Informal organisation: An important aspect of the informal organisation is the informal communication network, or "grapevine" as it is more commonly known. The amount of information gathered through official circulars, memos and speeches is rather insignificant compared to what are unofficially learnt from colleagues and subordinates. The grapevine constitutes an extremely important component of the organisational information system.

TOTAL QUALITY MANAGEMENT (TQM)

Total Quality Management (TQM) is focussed on the requirements of the customer. A library patron or user is a customer. He or she is demanding a service and expects that service. Total Quality Management offers an approach for an organisation to design processes, policies, and jobs so that they are the best, most effective methods for serving users' needs, eliminating inefficiencies and assuring quality service. TQM is an important strategic management tool and a systematic approach with strong internal and external customer orientation. "Quality as a management tool especially for non-profit organisations like libraries". The service is defined by library users in the TQM context. Since users' need will continue to change, quality service will require a continuous improvement process. Libraries will continue to:

* identify customers' – who matters?
* translate customers expectations into operational process – what do we need to do to meet users' expectations?
* conduct evaluation of services based on established performance measures – what processes should we continue or change?

Simply defined, TQM is "a system of continuous improvement employing participative management and centred on the needs of customers."

T.Q.M. IN LIBRARY & INFORMATION CENTRE (IN INDIA)

Total Quality Management (TQM) as a management tool needs to radically rethink the way in which a library is organised and performs its functions. Susan and Barnard presents a model for the implementation of TQM in the library setting. It outlines a ten-step process divided into four stages shown in figure given on next page. The approach is a flexible one that can be applied in different ways to a variety of situations depending on the level of support for implementing TQM both within and outside the library.

It emphasises on organising quality once the commitment to TQM and the decision on the TQM methodology and structure is made. Quality/service awareness, various aspects of library automation training should be given to all employees.

It involves an extensive evaluation of current work processes and the relationship of these processes to customer needs and expectations. Laying heavy emphasis on team activity, team members will need extensive training on the customer service dimension of the quality process including how customers judge services. While implementing TQM in library services, a different set of skills is required of the staff. Training is a key component in TQM which upgrades the skills of the staff. Implementation of TQM provides a library organisation with the opportunity to update and enhance the abilities of the staff to work effectively and collectively. Of course there are many factors or issues that need to be addressed on the road to a successful implementation of TQM. These include:

1. IDENTIFICATION OF CUSTOMERS

As a starting point, libraries should focus their efforts on identifying the customers and determining their expectations. The objective is to provide excellent service to existing customers. Satisfied customers bring new customers, dissatisfied customers discourage new and existing coustomers. Of course improved customer service and satisfaction is a long-term strategic initiative. It requires commitment from the head of the organization, staff, funds and time. Identification of customers, and providing customer service and satisfaction work as effective management tools to help libraries to achieve their goals.

T.Q.M. in Library

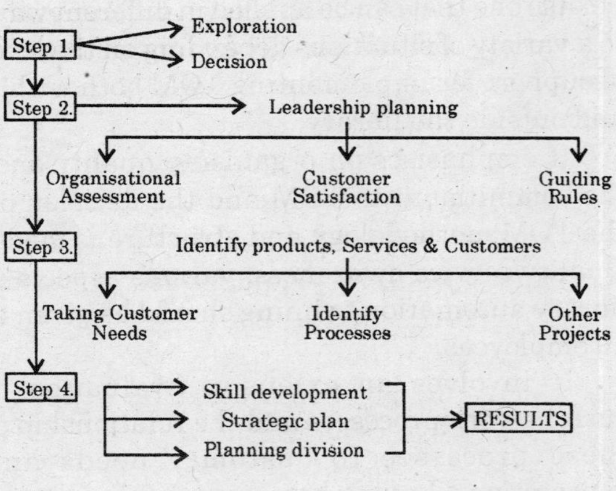

2. STANDARDIZATION OF WORK

The interrelated processes of an organization need to be standardized which help to determine how work is organized and how customer needs are met. A process is a "flow of work that progresses from one person or one activity to another." A critical process is "an important process, defined by customer need, that is a major part of the mission of the organization. Identifying and evaluating the critical processes that drive an organization are vital to the continuous improvement of systems fundamental to TQM. In selecting processes for pilot projects, consideration should be given to:

(*a*) importance of the process to primary cutomers,
(*b*) whether the process is experiencing difficulty and is recognised as needing attention, and
(*c*) likelihood of eliminating waste (by saving money, staff time, etc.)

3. QUALITY MEASUREMENT PROCEDURE

Quality as a strategic issue implies (*i*) acceptance of the importance of customer requirements throughout the organization, (*ii*) the identification of continuous improvement as a key organizational objective, and (*iii*) the introduction of meaningful performance indicators. There are a number of different approaches to measuring quality such as (*i*) complaints from customers (*ii*) customer surveys (*iii*) benchmarking or comparing the organization with its competitors, (*iv*) employee surveys and suggestion boxes.

4. IMPROVEMENT IN INTERNAL ORGANIZATION SYSTEM

If Total Quality Management is to be successful it requires a culture that actively promotes customer requirements, continuous improvement, creative problem solving and a team ethos. Organizations considering the implementation of TQM need to indentify and take into account their organisational cultures.

5. HUMAN RESOURCE MANAGEMENT

Total Quality Management is very much a people centred approach to management. A central concern is employee commitment. Successful TQM depends upon employee commitment. De Cotiis and Summers have identified a number of processes which impact upon commitment:

(a) Leader behaviour in relation to subordinates;

(b) The challenge, responsibility, and influence offered by the job;

(c) Participation in decision making; and

In implementing TQM in a library and information service environment, it is necessary to establish some basic definitions by answering questions such as "what is quality?" "who are our customers?" "how can quality be measured". The establishment of quality as a strategic issue is central to successful implementation and top management commitment will be necessary. Full employee commitment will only be achieved by appropriate human resource management structures.

MULTIPLE CHOICE QUESTIONS

1. Managerial skill are—
A. Technical skill B. Conceptual skill
C. Human skill D. All of the above

2. An acronym for seven management functions is—
A. POST CoRB B. POSD CoRB
C. POST CaRB D. PASD CoRT

3. It is the process of prescribing formal relationship among people & resources to accomplish the goals—
A. Planning B. Leading
C. Commanding D. Organising

4. Modern management uses different techniques for improving—
A. Profit B. Quality
C. Quantity D. Research

5. Planning, scheduling, monitoring and evaluation of systems for management is called—
A. Marketing technique
B. Network analysis
C. System analysis
D. System design

6. The command authority of supervisors over their subordinates—
A. Line authority
B. Personnel authority
C. Functional authority
D. Simplicity authority

7. The process of grouping related activities into manageable units is—
A. Coordination D. Decentralisation
C. Centralisation D. Departmentation

8. Being answerable for the results on one's actions is—
A. Regularity B. Functionality
C. Responsibility D. Accountability

9. Management Information System (MIS) provides all sorts of information required for—
A. Decision-making
B. Administration
C. Proper direction
D. Preparation of Budget

10. A system which allows the users to get the answer quickly by interacting with a computer is—
A. Decision Support System
B. Local Library Network
C. System Design
D. M.I.S.

11. A good library building is an outcome of librarian and—
A. Registrar
B. Building Corporation
C. Finance Officer
D. Architect

12. The storage area for the various types of documents kept in a library is—
A. Tasks B. Desks
C. Stacks D. Racks

13. Study carrels are exclusive areas meant for—
A. students B. public
C. investment D. researchers

14. Library catalogue cards are filed in especially designed drawers named—
A. Catalogue cabinet
B. Charging tray
C. Display rack
D. Filing equipment

15. Information gatekeepers come under—
A. Human sources
B. Documentary sources
C. Institutional sources
D. Neo-Conventional sources

16. Who categorises documents into three types such as primary, secondary and tertiary sources?
A. Skeltor B. Grogan
C. Ranganathan D. Hansan

17. It is a legal document and can be used as a source of industrial information—
A. Report B. Law Review
C. Patent D. Specification

18. In Encyclopaedia Britannica, which acts as an index to macropaedia?
A. Bibliography B. Propaedia
C. Micropaedia D. Introduction part

19. One of the book selection principles states that "the best reading for the largest number at _______ cost."
A. maximum B. medium
C. least D. zero

20. Payments for the books purchased can be made only after—
A. accessioning B. classification
C. cataloguing
D. arrangement in shelve

21. The standard size of an accession register is—
A. 15" × 13" B. 16" × 13"
C. 12" × 5" D. 5" × 3"

22. I.S.B.N is—
A. International Standard Book Number
B. Indian Standard Book Number
C. Integrated Service Book Number
D. None of the above

23. PRECIS was developed by—
A. Grogan B. Derek Austin
C. Ranganathan D. None of these

24. Three card system was introduced by—
A. Grogan B. Austin
C. Ranganathan D. Derek

25. PRECIS used in—
A. BNB B. INB
C. ISBD D. ISBN

26. Technical section performs mainly two functions namely classification and—
A. accessioning B. fills payment
C. shelving D. cataloguing

27. Three cards system incude—
A. Register Card B. Check Card
C. Classified Index Card
D. All of the above

28. Which is one of the records of circulation section?
A. Accession register
B. Day book
C. Catalogue Card
D. AACR-2(R)

29. Getting books back from the users and releasing the borrower's ticket is—
A. charging B. holding
C. reserving D. discharging

30. While intering the library, the personal belongings of a reader are kept in—
A. Cloak room B. Property counter
C. Gaber counter D. Store room

31. Physical condition of the books should be properly maintained by the process of
A. collation B. conservation
C. organisation D. shelf-arrangement

32. It is an important record of books, which shows the position of any book on the shelves—
A. Shelf list B. Bay Guide
C. Authority list D. Accession list

33. Books misplaced on the shelves by readers are restored. It is the process of—
A. Shelf rectification
B. Shelving
C. Shifting
D. Stock verification

34. Books lost from the library are known through—
A. Shelf list
B. Accession register
C. Charging & discharging
D. Stock verification

35. Outdated & seldom used books are withdrawn from the library, it is otherwise known as—
A. Shelving B. Weeding
C. Circulating D. Guiding

36. The objective of library binding is ______ of the library materials.
A. durability B. humidity control
C. proper organisation
D. accessibility

37. All parts and pages of a volume are correctly sequenced in first stage of binding process which is known as—
A. Collation B. Serving
C. Guard D. Pulling

38. Sheets before and after the texts of a book are called—
A. End papers B. Attach papers
C. Head bands D. Gilding

39. The strongest leather being used as one of the binding materials is—
A. Roan B. Imitation
C. Pig skin D. Sheep skin

40. Who prescribed certain standards for library building?
A. I.L.A. B. A.L.A.
C. B.L.A. D. N.B.T.

41. It is a process of helping employees in an organisation to achieve new skills & competence on a continuing basis—
A. Total Quality Management
B. Management Information System
C. Financial Resources Development
D. H.R.D.

42. A skillful method of providing means of mechanism & structural elements to streamline organisational work is called—
A. Role analysis
B. Work culture
C. Strategic planning
D. Autonomus planning

43. Posting the right person at the right place is—
A. Induction B. Coaching
C. Deploying D. Recruitment

44. T.Q.M. is a system of continuous improvement employing participative management and centred on needs of the—
A. Staff B. Customers
C. Organisation D. Government

45. Financial support given to libraries are of—
A. Recurring B. Ad-hoc
C. Non-recurring D. A & C only

46. Principle of maximum aggregate benefit is connected with—
A. Library use B. Library service
C. Library fee D. Growth of library

47. Which method take items of expenditure for libraries as the working data for allocation of funds?
A. Methods of details
B. Per captia methods
C. Principal of Economy
D. Library Budget

48. A budget which mainly covers items of current revenue & expenditure is—
A. Programme budget
B. Welfare Economics
C. Current budgeting
D. Capital budgeting

49. Which budgeting does not take into account what happened in the past but emphasis on current activities?
A. Formula B. Performance
C. Programme D. Zero-base

50. The library budget of a university is passed by the—
A. Senate
B. Executive Council
C. Academic Council
D. Research Council

51. In fund accounting, which fund cannot be used for other purposes?
A. Recurring B. Non-recurring
C. Restricted D. Encumbering

52. Scrutiny of financial transactions is known as—
A. Budgeting B. Programming
C. Accounting D. Auditing

53. One of the characteristics of scientific management is ______
A. Sufficient budget
B. System approach
C. Personnel
D. Adequate physical facilities

54. Management is a process that bring together several varied resources like physical, human and ______ along with required tools or techniques to accompolish a task.
A. technical B. financial
C. managerial D. infrastructure

55. System approach inriches ______ to achieve a common goal.
A. behaviour of staff
B. proper working condition
C. physical facilities
D. management operations

56. Managerial skills consist of human skill, technical skill and—
A. executive skill B. conceptual skill
C. operational skill D. None of these

57. Planning is an ______ process of determining in advance the procedure of accomplishing a task.
A. organised B. analytical
C. arranged D. advanced

58. Staffing is concerned with providing and maintaining—
A. financial resources
B. human resources
C. technical resources
D. physical resources

59. Directing deals with ______ the human resources to give out the best.
A. forcing B. motivating
C. pleasing D. communicating

60. Esprit De Corps means—
A. Books are for use.
B. Live or die
C. Unity is strength
D. Survival of the fittest

61. The hierarchical order of the managers from highest to the lowest is—
A. Equality B. Centralisation
C. Decentralisation
D. Scalar Chain

62. Which system improves the planning & control of operations by providing better information for decision making?
A. System Analysis (SA)
B. Management Information System (MIS)
C. Cost and Benefit System (CAB)
D. Zero-based Budgeting System

63. In which type of rack, the popular magazines are usually displayed?
A. Mehra & Co. B. Step
C. Stack D. Pigeon

64. The standard size of a card catalogue is—
A. 6.5 × 11.5 cm B. 7.5 × 12.5 cm
C. 5.5 × 8.5 cm D. 10.5 × 7.5 cm

65. Which is used in periodicals control system?
A. Lindex B. Microfilm
C. Kardex D. Charging desk

66. Pamphlets provide—
A. Statistical information
B. Political information
C. Geographical information
D. Biographical information

67. Conference proceeding are considered as—
A. primary documents
B. secondary documents
C. tertiary documents
D. conventional documents

68. 'India: A reference annual' is an example of—
A. Serial publication
B. Quarterly publication
C. Conventional publication
D. Political publication

69. Bureau of Indian Standards (BIS) is located at—
A. New Delhi B. Kolkata
C. Mumbai D. Dehradun

70. Atlases form an important source of—
A. Geographical information
B. Political information
C. Biographical information
D. None of the above

71. Which source provides information on the process and materials involved in the manufacture of a product?
A. Patents B. Specifications
C. Standards D. Trade literature

72. Encyclopaedia of Library & Information Sceince is edited by—
A. Allen Kent B. Melvil Dewey
C. J.S. Mill D. Aristotle

73. Which type of information sources are government documents?
A. Primary B. Secondary
C. Tertiary D. Non-parliamentary

74. Which is the non-print material?
A. Book B. Journal
C. Thesis D. CD-ROM

75. Institutional & human resources are considered as—
A. Documentary sources
B. Non-documentary sources
C. Tertiary sources
D. Secondary sources

76. Who gave the priciple, "The best reading for the largest number at least cost"?
A. Drury B. Melvil Dewey
C. Melvil Calvin D. None of the above

77. "Principle of book selection" is given by—
A. Drury B. Dewey
C. John Oblet D. J.H. Shera

78. His Majesty's Stationery Office (HMSO) is a publisher of—
A. Govt. of USA B. Govt. of Britain
C. Govt. of Russia D. Govt. of India

79. Micro images printed on a sheet or film is called—
A. Microfilm B. Opaque card
C. Microfiche D. Patent

80. Acquisition work in a library consists of—
A. selection & procurement
B. procurement & checking
C. checking & placing order
D. selection, procurement & assessioning

81. Who decided upon the commission rates of foreign currencies to be applied in the case of books & periodicals, and the rate of discount applicable to Indian libraries?
A. Indian Library Association
B. Good Offices Committee
C. Planning Commission
D. Publishers & Book Seller's Association

82. Requesting a borrower to return the book before its due date is—
A. Holds B. Reserve
C. Recall D. Lending

83. Which record decision taken on practices of the library relating to classification & cataloguing?
A. Authority file B. Work diary
C. Shelf-list D. Catalogue Cards

84. Shelf list facilitates—
A. Classification
B. Weeding out
C. Stock verification
D. Documentation

85. A user who seeks extension of time for books is—
A. Issue B. Reminder
C. Renewals D. Binding

86. Popular charging system/s in Indian libraries is/are—
A. Browne Charging System
B. Newark Charging System
C. Dewey Charging System
D. A & B only

87. Which is an oldest form of library cooperation?
A. Library Network
B. Internet
C. Inter-Library Loan
D. Library Automation

88. Which provide instructions to the users to locate the documents according to its class number?
A. Shelf-Guide B. General-Guide
C. Tier Guide D. Gangway Guide

89. How many books per thousand is an accepted practice to write off the lost books in a library?
A. 3 B. 4
C. 5 D. 10

90. A place where books are found in Library is—
A. Binding section B. Bindery
C. Buckram D. Hollow

91. The periodical evaluation of an employee is done by—
A. Job rotation B. Work Guide
C. Performance Appraisal
D. Refreshers Course

92. The process of introducing new entrants into the organisation is known—
A. Appraisal B. Induction
C. Deployments D. Communication

93. Which provide both matching & non-matching grants to public libraries in India?
A. N.B.T.
B. R.R.R.L.F.
C. I.L.A.
D. Planning Commission

94. One of the methods of financial estimation is—
A. Programme method
B. Zero-base method
C. Performance method
D. Per captia method

95. The principle of maximum aggregate benefit allows ______ to desire maximum benefit of library use.
A. Readers
B. Employees
C. Adequate spending
D. Library staff

96. Which organisation face the difficulty of measuring the quantity & quality of services rendered?
A. Commercial B. Service-oriented
C. Corporate D. Government

97. A regular budgeted grants given every year is—
A. Ad hoc grant B. Permanent grant
C. Non-plan grant D. Non-recurring

98. The library budget is approved by ______ before it is sent to higher authorities for final approval.
A. Executive Committee
B. Library Committee
C. Reader's Committee
D. Programme Committee

99. In performance budgeting, which is used to measure the performance and establish norms?
A. Survey method
B. Programme effectiveness
C. Interview method
D. Cost-Benefit analysis

100. UGC Library committee suggest that ______ of library budget should be spent on books.
A. 10 % B. 20 %
C. 25 % D. 30 %

101. Communicating the budget allocations to each division & department of the library is—
A. Sanction B. Notification
C. Approval D. Office order

102. Scrutiny of financial transactions of a government or non-government body is—
A. Budgeting B. Casting
C. Auditing D. According

103. The HRD function/s in a Library and Information Unit is/are—
A. Customer satisfaction & RD
B. Quality of products & services
C. Personnel planning & productivity
D. All of the above

104. The element/s of personnel planning & policy is/are—
A. Induction & development
B. Recruitment & selection of persons
C. Development of knowledge & skills
D. All of the above

105. It is a system of continuous improvement employing participative management and centred on the needs of customers is—
A. Total Quality Management (TQM)
B. Management Information System (MIS)
C. Zero-Base Budgeting (ZBB)
D. None of the above

106. The involvement of staff in the making process of the organisation & having increased awareness of organisation purpose, depend upon two important factors—
A. Leadership & Organisational style
B. Work process & Leadership
C. Organisational style & Work process
D. Any of the above

107. The main element/s of Total Quality Mangement is/are—
A. Error free process & Employee involvement
B. Continuous improvement & Quality
C. Internal, external customers & Performance measurement
D. All of the above

108. What is/are the barrier/s in implementing Total Quality Management in a Library & information unit?
A. Vocabulary barrier
B. Commitment barrier
C. Process barrier & Professional barrier
D. All of the above

109. The Universities libraries receive their funds from—
A. U.G.C. B. State Governments
C. Both of above D. None of the above

110. The main source/s of public library revenues is/are—
A. Subscriptions & endowments
B. Library cess
C. Government grants
D. All of the above

111. Major characteristic/s in the nature of library expenditure is/are—
A. Library is a spending institution
B. Library is a growing organism
C. Library expenditure is recurring
D. All of the above

112. According to the principle of equitable allocation, how many percentage of publication grant is allowed for periodicals?
A. 50% B. 70%
C. 60% D. 80%

113. Zero-Base Budgeting method was developed by—
A. Peter Phyrr B. Melvil Calvin
C. Melvil Dewey D. None of the above

114. When neither gold nor any colouring matter is used in finishing process of binding, it is called as—
A. Gold tooling B. Blind Tooling
C. Tooling D. None of the above

115. The standard size of pigeon hole type display rack is—
A. 225 cm × 180 cm B. 30 cm × 6 cm
C. 180 cm × 30 cm D. 150 cm × 30 cm

116. Flat transparencies, usually 10 × 15 cm size which can accommodate 60 or more reduced page images is—
A. Microfiche B. Duplicating method
C. Charging Desk D. Batten racks

117. Recommended ratio of lighting for visual task: table: background is—
A. 10 : 3 : 1 B. 1 : 3 : 10
C. 400 : 2 : 10 D. 10 : 2 : 3

118. POS DCORB is—
A. Planning, Organising, Staffing, Directing, Coordinating, Reporting & Budgeting
B. Planning of Staffing and Decision of Record Board
C. Planning, Coordination, Controlling and Budgeting
D. None of the above

119. The important characteristic/s of Library management is/are—
A. Impalpability & Inseparability
B. Variability & Perishability
C. All of the above
D. None of the above

120. The basic feature/s of formal organisation is/are—
A. they are formed to achieve a goal
B. the goal may be changed many times during the lifetime of the organisation
C. Any of the above
D. A & B both

121. The important feature/s of quality information from an effective Management Information System in a library is/are—
A. Timelinese & Accuracy
B. Precision, Completeness & Relevance
C. Conciseness & Appropriateness
D. All of the above

122. The entire university budget is passed by—
A. Executive Council
B. Academic Council
C. Parliament
D. Planning Commission

123. Budget excess is done by—
A. adjustment of excess amount in next year's budget
B. additional allocation subject to agreement by the authorities
C. All the above
D. None of the above

124. Financial records of a library may be—
A. Cash book, ledger
B. Allocation register
C. Monthly expenditure statement
D. All of the above

125. The cost of cataloguing a single book is —
A. Unit cost
B. Entry cost
C. Unrestricted cost
D. Profit cost

ANSWERS

1	2	3	4	5	6	7	8	9	10
D	B	D	B	A	A	C	C	A	D
11	12	13	14	15	16	17	18	19	20
D	C	D	A	C	B	D	C	C	A
21	22	23	24	25	26	27	28	29	30
B	A	B	C	C	D	D	A	D	B
31	32	33	34	35	36	37	38	39	40
A	A	A	B	B	A	D	A	D	B
41	42	43	44	45	46	47	48	49	50
A	D	A	C	D	A	B	A	B	B
51	52	53	54	55	56	57	58	59	60
A	D	B	A	D	B	A	B	B	A
61	62	63	64	65	66	67	68	69	70
B	B	C	B	D	A	D	C	A	A
71	72	73	74	75	76	77	78	79	80
D	A	A	D	C	B	A	B	C	A
81	82	83	84	85	86	87	88	89	90
C	B	A	C	C	D	C	C	B	B
91	92	93	94	95	96	97	98	99	100
C	A	B	D	A	B	B	B	D	B
101	102	103	104	105	106	107	108	109	110
A	A	D	D	A	A	D	D	A	D
111	112	113	114	115	116	117	118	119	120
D	C	A	B	A	A	A	A	C	C
121	122	123	124	125					
D	A/D	C	D	A					

LIBRARY SCIENCE: RESEARCH

INTRODUCTION

It is very essential for librarians and information scientists to have knowledge on research methodology. The vigorous growth of research in sciences as well as social sciences has **posed** three needs in the instruction and training of students.

First: Students must learn the basic elements of careful and systematic inquiry. They must understand the guiding rules and procedures that ensure setting (formulation) of problems, collection of relevant data and making of meaningful and careful analysis.

Second: They must comprehend clearly the nature of each of the major techniques of social research. The problems in social sciences are diverse and the data needed for their solution vary significantly. This diversity in problems and subject matter has in its turn contributed immensely to a deepening of the agenda for research, marked by development of new and different techniques, each with its own set of steps and its own body of safeguarding rules.

Third: Students should understand both the differences and the relations among these different techniques–when a particular technique should be used, which one should be used and how they may be employed in combination.

Research Definitions: Research is any such activity which helps to gain fresh insight into something. It is an investigation to find answers to questions. It is the way to acquire knowledge. The term 'research' has different connotations in different contexts. It is, therefore essentail to study and examine various definitions of research given by different authorities. The webster's International Dictionary defines Research as "a careful critical enquiry or examination in seeking facts for principles, diligent investigation in order to ascertain something." The Advanced Learner's Dictionary of current English defines it as "an investigation undertaken in order to discover new facts get additional information etc." According to charles H. Busha, research is a "systematic quest for knowledge that is characterised by disciplined inquiry. Efficient and effective approach to expand knowledge is the conduct of special, planned and structured investigations—a process known as research." Oxford English Dictionary defines research as:–

(*i*) The act of searching (closely or carefully) for or after a specified thing or person.

(*ii*) A search or investigation directed to the discovery of some fact by consideration of study of a subject or course of critical or scientific inquiry.

Encyclopaedia of the Social Sciences defines research as "the manipulation of things, concepts or symbols for the purpose of generalization to extend correct or verify knowledge whether that knowledge aids in the construction of a theory or in practice of an art. The mechanic or physician is a research worker only when he attempts to generalize about all automobiles or all patients of a given class". The Oxford Encyclopaedia English Dictionary (2001) defines research as:" The systematic investigation into and study of materials, sources etc. in order to establish facts and reach new conclusions and an endeavour to discover new or collate old facts etc. by the scientific study of a subject or by a course of critical investigation." P.M. cook outlines the term "Research" in a popular way. To him, "research" is an honest, exhaustive intelligent searching for facts and their meanings or implications, with reference to a problem. In an easy to remember method, he lists the attributes of "research" taking the clue from each initial alphabet of the word:

R – Rational way of thinking
E – Expert and Exhaustive Treatment
S – Search for solution
E – Exactness
A – Analysis
R – Relationship of facts
C – Critical observation, careful recording, constructive attitude and condensed generalizations
H – Honesty and Hard Working

According to DR. S.R. Ranganathan a doyen of Library and Information Science the term "research" represents a critical and exhaustive investigation to discover new facts, to interpret them in the light of known ideas, theories and laws, to revive the current laws and theories in the light of the newly discovered facts to apply the conclusion to practical purpose.

RESEARCH METHODS

Broadly speaking, there are three major research methods:

1. Historical
2. Survey
3. Experimental

— through which research is usually conducted.

Historical Method

History is said to be the story of humankind understood in a social context. An inquiry into the past in a systematic manner, is what we call historical research. It helps us to understand why, how and when past events occurred, which in turn aids anticipation of future developments in any field of activities affecting decision making in the present set up. In Library and Information Science, the study of history or an application of the historical research method is usually called "Library History". Library history, as defined by several researchess "is the systematic recounting of past events pertaining to the establishment, maintenance and utilization of systematically arranged collections of recorded information or knowledge". Historical research for its successful implementation depends highly on the sources of information, which may range from official records, newspapers, annual reports, manuscripts, etc. to eye witness and oral history records. The data collection phase in historical research requires a high level of competency to establish the authenticity of the sources of information.

Historical method in Library and Information science can be applied to write the biography of a person (e.g. Ranganathan, Dewey, Cutter, Poole and others) or in the development of a Library during a particular perion (e.g. Bollean Library, Library of Congress, National Library), or to record the history of libraries in a country, or history of development of a library technique (e.g. indexing, classification), etc. Though the historical method is often criticised for its heavy reliance on secondary sources, it is one of the methods best suited to look into the social, economic, political and cultural environment in which libraries and library science have been instituted. Pierce Butler in his *Introduction to Library Science* emphasizes that librarianship can be fully appreciated only though an understanding of its historical origins.

Survey Method

Survey research has been widely used in Social and Behavioural Sciences. It deals mainly with collection, analysis and presentation of data relating to the present time reflecting the present state of affairs in social, economic and political activities. The most commonly used survey method is the 'Opinion Poll' during election periods. Similarly an inquiry into the T.V. watching habits, newspaper reading habits and consumer behaviour might fall into the category of survey research. Another kind of survey research can be study of psychological phenomenon of a group of individuals (e.g. attitude, behaviour, motivation, etc.). Survey research is a method of gathering empirical data regarding certain phenomenon, process or object in a systematic way so as to interpret them in a broader perspective for generalizations.

Survey research is commonly used in Library and Information Science. However, it is used differently in different contexts.

Experimental Method

This is the most rigorous of all research methods and this method has its origin in science, where the researcher has the power to control the variables/ factors for conducting experiments. In social sciences, the experimental method is an extension of survey research having character-istics of an experiment. Control is one of the differental method uses a control group and one or more experimental groups (subjects). In social sciences, the subjects of investigation are usually individuals and the control group is kept under observation for comparison and contrast with the experimental groups. It is highly essential however that the control group and experimental groups possess almost equivalent characteristics though complete equivalence is impossible due to the nature of the subjects (i.e. the individuals in society). Experimental research may lead to establish casual relationships and can provide an answer as to why certain phenomena occur or what would happen if a particular factor changes.

In Library and Information Science, experimental method can be used to investigate the following: efficiency of classification schemes, effect of book display on use, impact of bibliographic instruction on library use and student's performance, innovative methods of collection developments, uses of catalogue and the extent of retrieval success in the shelf, etc.

RESEARCH METHODS AND SCIENTIFIC METHOD

Having discussed various research methods, it is very important now to understand their relationship with 'Scientific Method'. Scientific method is a philosophy, thinking or a guideline to the whole realm of research. Unless a research is based on scientific methodology, the result is not considered reliable and valid. There is a ladder of steps which make up a scientific methodology. These logical steps in scientific investigation are:

1. Identification of problem;
2. Formulation of hypothesis;
3. Collection of data;
4. Analysis and testing of hypothesis; and
5. Broad generalisation or formulation of laws.

If the laws thus formulated, hold good through a period of time they are accepted and theories are constructed. Scientific method is concerned with verification of acquired knowledge.

Scientific research is always open for refutation. In other words, the research is considered complete as if holding the final say on the topic in question. The hall-mark of scientific research, therefore, lied in providing for the necessary scope and direction in the body of the research, so that the methods adopted and conclusions drawn can be further checked. The researcher should always suggest the direction in which future research on the topic itself and its related aspects can be carried out. Scientific research is thus verifiable, refutable and therefore, always open-ended.

SURVEY ANALYSIS

Before entering into the core content of survey analysis proper, it is essential to understand some related topics such as:

(*i*) Survey: Meaning and Definition
(*ii*) Principles of Survey Research
(*iii*) Survey Research in L.I.S.

PRINCIPLES OF SURVEY RESEARCH:

Purpose of Survey

The important purpose of a survey is collection of research data. The purpose of any survey should be specified at the beginning of the research. Clear identification of the problem indicates the purpose of the survey.

Analogy: "Students are drawn to the live example of census operation", which is a comprehensive survey. It brings various facts to the knowledge of administrators, and to those engaged in socio-economic planning. It provides information relating the rate of growth of population, complexities of growth, methods of control, maintain and access factors of optimum growth.

Planning of a Survey

First determine the purpose and scope of the survey. The collection of data involves expensive Time and Money.

The following items of information may be observed in planning any survey:

(*i*) What is research problem or hypothesis?

(*ii*) What results are expected?

(*iii*) Nature and extent of population to be covered in the survey

(*iv*) Type and size of the sample.

(*v*) Techniques to be used for data collection.

(*vi*) Identification of variables-Independent and dependent.

DESCRIPTION ON VARIABLES

Variables are often used interchangeably with factors. While discussing empirical investigations, these influence the research processes as well as the end result. Different types of variables are discussed below.

(A) By Nature

(*i*) Qualitative Variables: Research factors which cannot be quantified e.g., Sex, Profession, Religion etc.

(*ii*) Quantitative Variables: The variables that can be expressed in quantitiy or can be quantified, e.g. Age, Income etc.

(B) By Relationship

(*i*) Dependent variables are factors whose changes are explained during or after the research as cause effect relationship e.g. Attitudes.

(*ii*) Independent variables are factors that can be manipulated by the researcher and may influence the dependent variable (s). e.g. Age.

SAMPLING

Sampling is one of the vital steps in survey research. The process of selecting a sample out of the population is called 'sampling'. Population is a group of individual or objects having at least one common characteristic e.g. Librarians of degree colleges, women Librarians etc.

Sample is a unit of the population to be investigated. The sample should be representative of its population. A sample is preferred to conduct a study because it is less expensive and time consuming.

From a 'population' we can draw several samples depending upon the size of the population and size of the sample. For example if the population comprises three units, viz, A, B, and C and we have to draw a sample of size two there can be three possible sample. We may note that from each sample we get a different value for the statistic e.g. the arithmetic mean of samples drawn from the same population may vary from sample to sample. These statistics for all possible samples can be arranged as a frequency distribution. Such frequency distribution is termed as sampling distribution. The standard deviation of the sampling distribution is termed as standard error. Since we can have sampling distribution for any statistic like mean, median, variance, etc. we can have standard error for the respective statistic like mean, median or variance as the case may be.

SAMPLING METHODS

There are different kinds of sampling techniques. Some of the major and popular methods are: Systematic Sampling, Simple Random sample and Stratified Random sample.

(a) *Systematic Sampling* involves selection of every element from the list of population. Suppose the size of the population is 500 and the researcher decides to select every 5th element for the sample then, it would generate of a sample 100. The process is sample, if there is a list of the population. However, in doing so, not every element gets an equal opportunity to represent the population.

(b) *Simple Random Sampling* technique is commonly used in survey research. Here, the probability for all elements of the population to enter the sample is equal. One very common random sampling is lottery type approach. A more scientific way of drawing random sample is the use of a table of random numbers.

(c) *Stratified Random Sampling* is a improved version of quota sample, where different sections of a population are proportionately represented in the sample in a random fashion. Suppose a researcher is conducting a survey of an academic library users, where the population includes teachers, students and office staff in different proportion. If the researcher decides on stratified random sampling then the sample will represent all those graphs of population proportionately.

(d) *Sample size Determination*: The size of the sample is very important, as the generation of the result depends on the representativeness and the size of the sample. Collection of data on a large sample requires much time and money. So, the sample size should generally be small, and essential to research scientific generalization. Use of formula to determine the sample size has been developed.

One such formula is:

$$n = \frac{s^2}{\left[SE(x)\right]^2}$$

where n = Sample size;

s = Standard deviation of the population

$SE(x)$ = Standard error of the mean

The only problem in this formula is the determination of standard deviation of the population. A simpler method of sample size determination is use of table.

DATA COLLECTION TECHNIQUES

The data collection techniques are:

(*i*) Observation;
(*ii*) Questionnaire;
(*iii*) Interview.

These are discussed below in brief.

(A) OBSERVATION

Observation is a well established technique for collection of data. The observation method is normally employed in measuring, testing characterising human behaviour. Observation methods go into past events and then study the present, hence it has historical orientation.

Guidelines for Making Observations:

Reamanel has suggested following guidelines:

(*i*) Obtain prior knowledge of what to observe.
(*ii*) Examine the general and specific objectives of research problem to determine what to observe.
(*iii*) Device a method of recording results.
(*iv*) Establish and define the various levels of proficiency categories and ratings used.
(*v*) Observe carefully and critically.
(*vi*) Rate specific phenomena independently.
(*vii*) Become well acquainted with the recording instrument and the procedures of its use, before making observations.

Observation Devices

1. Diaries
2. Note books
3. Schedules
4. Photograph
5. Maps

Types of Observation

1. Unstructured observation
2. Structured observation
3. Non-controlled observation
4. Controlled observation.
   (*i*) Control over the phenomena
   (*ii*) Control over observation

5. Participant observation
6. Mass observation.

Recording Techniques in Observation

The devices used in recording observation, are written, audio-visual aids, measuring and counting devices.

Characteristics of Observation Research

The observation is a method that enables specificity to the research process and provides a systematic procedure. Quantitativeness is easily attain by this method. Recording of the findings is to be done on an immediate basis for achieving better results. The method needs trained persons to adopt it. It is very scientific in approach and leads to reliable results.

(B) QUESTIONNAIRE

Questionnaire is most common and widely used survey method. It is a primary data collection method. The important step in this method is to take care in the design of questions. The questions should be specific to hypothesis and direct to the purpose of research.

Questionnaire is a tool to collect data from diverse large and widely scattered population groups.

Goode and Halt state "Questionnaire refers to a device for securing answers to questions by using a form which the respondent filles himself.

(C) INTERVIEW

Interview method, as a social research tool is used by contemporary researchers. The interview method is more direct and has greater flexibility. Young defines "Interview as a systematic method by which a person enters more or less imaginatively into the life of a "Comparative stranger". Goode and Hatt amplify if by saying "Perhaps no research technique is as close to the researchers problem as the interviewer".

The interview method is unique because the collection of data is through direct verbal interaction between individuals. Interviews stand out distinct from questionnaires; and more original, because verbal communication with interviewee, by investigator. The limitations of the questionnaire method can be eliminated supplementing it with interview method.

THE INTERVIEW PROCESS:

Interviews must be conducted in more informal and relaxed manner. Interviewer must get himself well prepared to ask relevant questions, before the actual process of interview begins. Skilled interviewers carefully frame their questions well in advance.

The following are some tips for conducting a successful interview:

1. fix an appointment with the interviewee,
2. inform him/her about the mechanical gadgets to be used by you. Such as video camera, tape recorder, etc.
3. prepare questions to be asked inadvance
4. be courteous and put friendly questions at the beginning of the interview.
5. don't use suggestive questions.
6. don't dispute with the respondent or express your emotions.
7. express thankfulness at the end of the interview.

SURVEY RESEARCH IN LIBRARY & INFORMATION SCIENCE:

Survey methods are widely used in many disciplines including Library and Information Science. Busha and Harter state that "Librarians have long conducted surveys". Usually in Library and Information Science, community surveys are conducted to gather information about Libraries and their clientele. "**Community Surveys** are conducted to gather recorded or unrecorded data about social, political and economic factors of the Libraries community". It is used in decision making, in planning, developing and conducting library services.

Library Surveys on the other hand are concerned with systematic in-depth examination of libraries, library systems, library networks, etc.

PRESENTATION OF DATA

The data collected through survey must be transformed into data files (for computer analysis) or complied into tables. This operation is considered as presentation of analysed data.

STEPS IN PRESENTATION

As stated already presentation is a step before analysis. Sometimes, it is also considered as part of analysis. In fact, it is stated that, "Analysis involves many steps" such as:

(*i*) Categorization
(*ii*) Coding
(*iii*) Tabulation
(*iv*) Statistical Analysis and Inference.

USE OF COMPUTERS IN SURVEY ANALYSIS:

Since the late 1960's computers and desk calculators are employed in the analysis of data collected on a large scale. The speed of the computer now enables the analysis of data to be performed in a faster manner. Computers, using punched cards, and other optical devices, were employed in various methods of presentation of data, particularly they were used to tabulate the data with the advent of mini and micro-computers, and pre-programmed calculators, statistical analysis became much more easier and faster. Now ready-made programs (software) are available for conducting and analysis - regression, construction of graphs, testing of hypothesis. Therefore, researchers should know how to commnunicate the data to the computer and how to select a relevant technique of statistical analysis.

The Statistical Package for social sciences (SPSS) is a software for analysis of quantified data. Another common package is the Biomedical Computer Program (BMD). Though developed essentially for medical research, it can also be used in other disciplines.

CONTENT ANALYSIS

Content analysis is a technique of research for the systematic, objective and quantitative description of the content of research data procured through interviews, schedules, questionnaries and other methods. It is also an attempt to convert symbolic behaviour into scientific data. It is a device of categorising and classifying research data according to the purpose of the study.

Content Analysis is used in social sciences, particularly as one of the means of studying communication-its nature, its underlying meanings, its dynamic processes and the people, who are engaged in talking, writing, conveying meaning to one other.

Busha and Harter have discussed the significance of content analysis in the context of libraries. They contend that many library science studies have focussed on the users of various media of communication, including books, periodicals, news papers, films and government documents, etc Less frequently, however inquiries is in the yield of library science are made regarding the actual content of the media. Among useful methods in the field of communication that can be employed by librarians to investigate internal (content) features of media is content analysis, a procedure designed to facilitate the objective analysis of the appearance of words, phrases, concepts, themes, characters, even, sentences and paragraph contained in printed or audio-visual materials.

TECHNIQUES OF CONTENT ANALYSIS:

Content Analysis involves marking the significant words, phrases, they are indicated by 'codes' as present or absent; or "yes or "no". This is known as classifying or categorising data; these form a "category set". The category of such codes may be two or more. So these categories can be generalized as, very high, high, medium, low and very low. This categorisation is simple. In the analysis, the technique used is to transform the observations from media into symbols. i.e.

(*i*) Words
(*ii*) Themes

(*iii*) Phrases
(*iv*) Concepts
(*v*) Motives

Techniques of content analysis are diverse. Describing the importance of content analysis of documents, Nicholas and Ritchie state that "bibliographic description (of documents) seldom go further than mapping the outward features of documents". Their value relies and depends upon the extent to which the documents "exterior features divulge, the inner-self after all the content of the documents is what is of great importance".

STEPS IN CONTENT ANALYSIS:

(a) Formulation of research problems.
(b) Definition and establishment of hypothesis and categories of analysis that are required to test the hypothesis.
(c) Identification and selection of methods to be analysed: the target documents, messages and media.
(d) Analysis of relevant documents and the measurement of contents according to pre-determined well defined Categories.
(e) Quantification and ordering of the categorized units.
(f) Analysis and comparison of obtained data with respect to independent variables.

USE AND APPLICATION:

Content Analysis can be used to study attitudes of persons or the press on certain important issues.

For example, certain individual documents, like diaries, intimate letters, files, autobiographies and speeches addressed to a wide audience may reveal the structure, dynamics and functioning of an individual. This is a general approach to use Content Analysis outside librarianship. Content analysis has been found useful in the study of psychological variables in political decision making.

Content Analysis can be applied to different variety of material. Documents, records, published or unpublished can be subjected to content analysis. Typically this is the "Modus Operandi" of the historical researcher, and historical research methods. In Library and Information Science, content analysis can be utilised to write biography of eminent librarian, developments in librarianship, contributions of an institute and association through the study of communication media like, diaries, reports, articles, etc.

SOCIOMETRIC TECHNIQUE

INTRODUCTION

Sociometry is traditionally identified with analysis of data collected from sociometric test tools. This test is a typical questionnaire through which each member of the group is asked with which one of the areas would he most likely carry out some activity. Sociometry thus deals with social relations among groups and individuals in a group.

Definitions

1. Sociometry is the study of patterns of communication among numbers in a group.
2. Sociometry is a method used for the discovery and manipulation of social configuration by measuring attraction and repulsion between individuals and groups.
3. Sociometry is concerned with the measurement of social distance and also the institutional behaviour.
4. Jennings has defined sociometry as "means of presenting simply and graphically the entire structure of relations existing at a given time among members of a given group.

SOCIOGRAM:

The data collected from different sources can be represented in a graphic form known as "Sociogram". A sociogram is some geometric figure which indicates each person and the connecting lines and arrows, showing the direction of choices.

Let us consider another example to draw a sociogram to know about communication amongst scientists in the industry and outside for discussing a test on research activities. Suppose the scientists were asked to list atleast 4 persons whom they usually contact for discussing latest research in their field. The result of this when drawn in a sociogram may look like this.

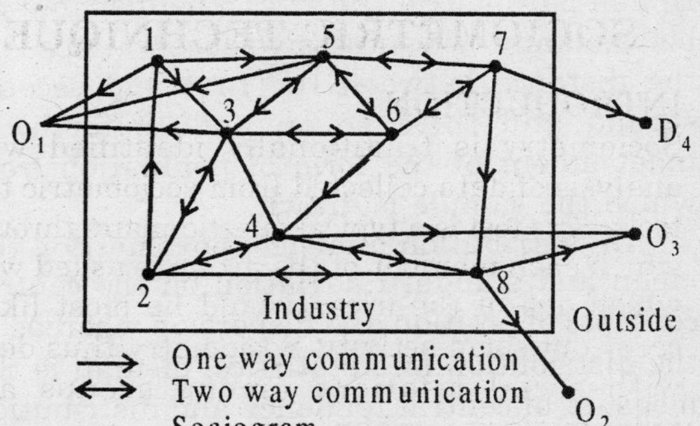

Sociogram

The above sociogram reflects that scientists no. 3 and 4 are much informed on the latest research in their field. Similarly O, has a strong relationship with the scientists of the industry depicted in the sociogram. The result of such a study could be utilised for referral purpose. For example, if somebody wants new information in the same subject which is not available in the library, then it is most likely that scientist 3 or 4 might be knowing something about it and hence may be referred for consultation.

Sociometric methods have been used with advantages in the studies of leadership, friendship patterns, group structures, social adjustments, minority prejudices, morale, public opinion etc. Sociometry has proved to be a fruitful technique of social analysis in the fields of psychology and sociology.

STATISTICAL STUDY

MEANING

It is a method which deals with data obtained by counting or measuring properties of common natural phenomena. It tries to derive reults by enumeration and by analysis.

Horace States "Statistics are aggregates of facts affected to a marked extent by multiplicity of causes numerically expressed, enumerated, or estimated according to a reasonable standard of accuracy, collected in systematic manner, for pre-determined purposes and placed in relation to each other". In other words, statistical method of research lays stress on facts, figures and nothing beyond that.

STEPS IN STATISTICAL STUDY

Statistical Study includes the application of statistics for presentation, analysis and interpretation of numerical data. These are briefly described in the following sections.

PRESENTATION OF DATA

The data collected should be suitably classified for presentation. This involves preparation of tables, graphs and diagrams to compare and study relationships among variables.

Statistical methods are applicable where enquiry and investigations are essential to arrive at the truth. The use of statistical methods can be helpful in extending human experience and knowledge. They are techniques required for handling multitudes of numerical results in such a way that the significant relationships between properties can be studied.

Statistical techniques belong to two domains as per the purpose they serve viz, "Descriptive statistics" and "Inferential Statistics". The former consists of methods and procedures for summarising, simplifying, reducing and presenting raw data, to communicate the essence of the data to another. The purpose of such methods is essentially reporting, as with presenting survey data to an administrator. However, the procedures used in the second category relate mostly to decision-making and are represented by those techniques which make it possible to use small samples with confidence as basis for decisions for a population some of the techniques used for data presentation are: tables, histogram, pi-chart, etc. The table should be properly designed to reflect all variables and a title to the table is essential for information regarding the content of the table. A proper representation of data is an asset to a research report and enchances its usefulness.

ANALYSIS OF DATA

Data analysis part is a skillful exercise and should be carried out with extreme care. The sheer beauty and elegance of methods/ techniques involved may divert attention from the main topic under analysis. It involves, application of different statistical tools like averages, dispersion, correlation. Usually it is mechanically done, but every researcher should have knowledge and appropriate statistical techniques.

Statistical inference seldom can produce certainity but it is on normal distribution of data. It is also so because some non-normal distributions can be transformed into a normal distribution. However, a large part of the data especially concerning human behaviour is not distributed normally or uniformly that is to say, the distance between the first unit and the second, the second and third etc. is not uniform/normal and we observe the distribution mostly in the form of an "array of the elements of the variable" existing independent of the form of the population from which the sample has been drawn. The aim of statistics is to enable the user to summarise with best and most accurate manner a complex (usually highly complex) phenomenon under study. When we take, for instance all the cases in the Universe/ population and derive, let us say, arithmetic means, it will not be difficult to see that such an exercise will give use a near perfect measure of this kind is known as a parameter and the value of a summarizing measure of this kind is known as a statistic. In parametric statistics therefore, the underlying assumption is of a normal distribution of data which when plotted would yield a normal distribution of data which when plotted would yield distribution curve. Recent advances in statistical estimates and testing of hypotheses have shown than no such assumption of a form of distribution curve. Recent advances in statistical estimates and testing of hypothesis have shown that no such assumption of a form of distribution (i.e. normal distribution of population) is actually required. In non-parametric statistics, the distribution between any two successive observations (i.e. the distance between the first and second, second and third so on and so forth) is independent of the form of population from which the sample is drawn.

In distribution analysis (parametric), the mean and standard deviation on the central concepts of position and dispersion whereas in the distribution free statistics, median is the measure of central tendency and distribution is measured in terms of various ranges (decile, quartile etc.) A distribution free measure of association is the spearman P. (Greek letter rho) or rank difference co-efficient of correlation.

Despite an array of techniques used, statistical inference cannot produce certainity; that only help us in ascertaining the most probable hypothesis. This exercise is usually undertaken through an accepted level of rejectability of a nul hypothesis which is the most common form of a statistical hypothesis. Such rejections are made (or as they say in statistics, the extent of error risked) within a level of significance. If the level of significance is .01, it only means that one in 100 cases rejection of hypothesis in question will be a mistake. Yet another probability expression is confidence limits which gives the probability of a parametric measure occurring within a given interval expressed by those confidence limits.

According to Pauline V.Young, "the rules and techniques of statistical inference are so designed that it is not possible to be certain about the correctness of any particular of decision, but in the long run the proportion of correct decisions is known in advance".

INTERPRETATION OF DATA

It is a step to draw inferences and conclusions. The interpretation should be commensurate with data. The prime task of interpretation is to bring to the surface the real importance of the findings. Interpretation serves two fold purpose:

(*i*) it gives an understanding of the general factors that seem to explain what has been studied in the course of the study.

(*ii*) it provides theoretical conception which can serve in turn as a guide for further research studies.

MEASUREMENT AND SCALING

The data collected by a method of counting has a finite number. Such data are termed as discrete.

Example: Number of boy and girl students sit in a exam, circulation data, acquisition data.

A second type of data is obtained by measurement, which involves the application of "scales". A "scales" is characterised by the use of an arbitrary unit of measurement, against which the phenomenon in question is compared. Thus, data obtained by measurement are by nature approximate, whereas data obtained by counting are theoretically exact. Measurement of data can take on any value, from an infinite number of possibilities between given limits on a scale. Such data are referred to as continuous.

Example: Height and weight of persons Relevance of Library materials to users (Relevant and non-relevant)

Stevens mentions four types of scales which are discussed below:

(*i*) **Nominal:** The nominal scale is qualitative in nature and not quantitative. It is commonly used to determine quality and is of yes/no type.

(*ii*) **Ordinal:** It possesses an inbuilt characteristic of order and enables to determine greater than, less than etc types of comparison with reference to quality measurement. For example, user's satisfaction in a library can be expressed in ordinal measures.

(*iii*) **Interval:** It also provides a ranking of positions as that of ordinal scale. But the distance between the limits of an interval is equal. It has also a zero point.

(*iv*) **Ratio:** Ratio scales are like that of interval scales having an absolute zero, below which no value occurs e.g., temperature scales.

APPROACHES TO EVALUATION RESEARCH

Powell (1985) has considered evaluative research as basic research because the design and measurement used in basic research can be easily employed in evaluative research.

Powell classifies the evaluative research into the following types:

(i) Summative (ii) Formative
(iii) Performance measurement

Summative evaluation is related with the effects of a programme. It is used as a basis of decide the **continuation** of the programme.

Formative is used to decide the quality of the programme and also used for improving and revising the programme.

Performance measurement is a specific type of evaluation research. According to Powell, this type of research determines what was accomplished as a result of a specific programme, services and resources being available performance measures focus on indications of library output; effectiveness of the library services. Some of the examples of performance measurement are: reference service, level of use of library facilities and equipment, circulation statistics, etc. The techniques used in performance measurements are collection of statistics, questionnaires, interviews, observation, reference questions, etc. The following table gives you information regarding the different approaches of evaluation research.

TABLE: Different Approaches of Evaluation Research

Method	Emphasis	Application	Strengths	Weaknesses
Objectives Based Evaluation	Assessment of Student attainment of pre-established goals and objectives	primarily summative	Relatively easy to understand and apply	Does not reveal unintended outcomes; Tendency oversimplify by measuring only what is easily measurable; concentrates on program content, without means for determining the value of the content.
Discrepancy Evaluation	Assessment on the basis of performance standards for educational decision-making	formative and summative	Provides constant feedback on program progress: Expands and improves on objectives based methods	Does not reveal unintended outcomes; Lengthy process requiring time and expertise.
Responsive Evaluation	Description of program processes and outcome according to values of key people	formative and summative	Reveals unintended as well as intended results; comprehensiveness of findings	Requires expertise in variety of formal methods; may be a lengthy and involved process.
Decision-oriented Evaluation	Collection and analysis of information for decision-making	formative and summative	Reveals unintended as well as intended results; comprehensiveness of findings	May concentrate too much on the value perspectives of decision makers; Not all activities are clearly evaluative
Goal-Free Evaluation	Collection and analysis of information related to actual results rather than pre-established objectives	formative and summative	Reveals unintended as well as intended results; Reveals the value of program as a whole	Requires expert evaluator of high credibility with a variety of skills.
Adversary Evaluation	Evaluation should present two competing interpretations of a Program's value	primarily summative	Pros and cons of a program discussed in strongest manner	Requires more people with sufficient skills in both evaluation and presentation may be too subjective; Not all arguments may be based on true judgement.
Illuminative Evaluation	To illuminate the acceptability of program processes and content	primarily formative	Relatively easy to implement	Kinds of information obtained may not address needs of all audiences; May be open to bias; May be too subjective for many audiences.
Evaluation Research	Assessment of educational effects for validity, reliability and generalizability	summative	Objectively demonstrated effects	Requires strict controls; only one or two effects can be evaluated at a time; Little information provided for program improvement.
Naturalistic Evaluation	Use of case study, anthropological and sociological methods to comprehensively describe program processes and results	formative and summative	Full expertise and sensitivities of evaluator employed; Comprehensiveness of results	Usually requires an expert evaluator from outside the program; Highly subjective results which may not be acceptable to all audiences.
Professional Judgement	Assess program on basis of normative and comparative standards.	formative and summative	Assures that minimum standards are met or that program has value comparable to similar programs	Consists almost entirely of judgements of merit; Little attention to program performance or outcomes

TESTING THE HYPOTHESIS

Hypothesis in scientific research may not be considered as valid unless and untill a satisfactory test of its validity has been completed. It is a mistake to consider hypotheses which are only hunches and provisional ideas-as facts, no matter how cleverly and systematically they have been arrived at.

Consider the following hypothesis: that high school students who study a unit of instruction in library skills in connection with course work in other subjects such as History or English literature (i.e. in an integrated approach) learn library skills more effectively than high school students who study an equivalent unit independently of other school subjects. To test this hypothesis, there are certain variables that need to be controlled. The two groups of students should be roughly equivalent in levels of motivation, intelligence, socio-economic status, age and perhaps other qualities as well. It is easy to see why this is so; anyone of these variables might have a differential effect on otherwise equivalent students. For example, if the students of Group A manifest more collective intelligence than Group B, then that factor itself may cause students in Group A to learn library skills more effectively than those in Group B. But by designing an experiment in such a way that the two groups are roughly equivalent in intelligence, this variable is controlled, and thus the effect will be the same for both groups. Because of the careful control that is exercised in its use, the experimental method is the most appropriate technique to test hypothesis which involve causal relationships.

Robert Bales lists the following pertinent questions which should be asked about hypotheses before they are adopted for testing:

1. Are the terms empirically specific, so that the concepts or variables can be distinguished in concrete situations?
2. Is the posited relationship between variables such that it could be verified or nullified by means of empirical operations?
3. Is there any prior evidence as to the truth or falsehood of the posited relationship?
4. Can an appropriate study design be accomplished?
5. Are the variables "context-bound" (e.g. restricted to the play group or gang), or could they be equally well applied to other interaction situation (e.g., work group or family)?
6. Are the generalization "culture-bound" (e.g. valid only in the U.S. or western Europe)?
7. Can they also be applied realistically in other cultures?
8. If other relevant factors are subject to change in the course of the observations, are they adequately specified and enumerated, so that the observers can ascertain whether they have changed during the period of observation?
9. Is the generalization part of a theoretical system from which it could be deduced as well as subsequently verified by the proposed empirical introduction?
10. Is the empirical system (that is constructed) sufficiently precise and articulate to permit predictions in concrete situations?

John Stuart Mill, a renowned English philosopher and political economist advocated two methods of arriving at logical conclusions in the testing of hypothesis:

1. "the method of agreement"
2. "the negative canon of agreement"

MANAGEMENT OF DATABASE

Data is an important resource for any organisation. Many organisations/enterprises irrespective of their nature are concerned with collection and manipulation of data. Data can be defined as the raw numbers or letters stored in a computer, which represents facts about things. Data has little meaning in its stored state, whether we think of data in the physical form in which it is stored or in its logical form, since facts without context are unusable. A store of data is referred to as a database.

Ideally, data must be accessible to any authorised person in an organisation for whatever application in whatever format desired. But, traditional computer files maintained in different organisations do not facilitate the access of this nature. In other words, computer files are designed to be of use for just one application and the set of programs associated with that application. They generally have little or no relation to other data used and required within the same organisation because they are initiated and developed independently. Such files are often unrelated to user's requests for information, particularly when these requests change in un-predictable ways.

DATABASE APPROACH

Traditionally, data accessed through computers has been stored on different storage media in the form of individual files. Files proved to be quite satisfactory so long as computerisation was limited to a few application areas and use of computers is restricted. However, as the actual users grew in number, with the advent of online sharing systems, the file systems gave rise to many serious problems. The discipline of database systems evolved in response to these problems.

Database approach is diagrammatical represented in the following figure:

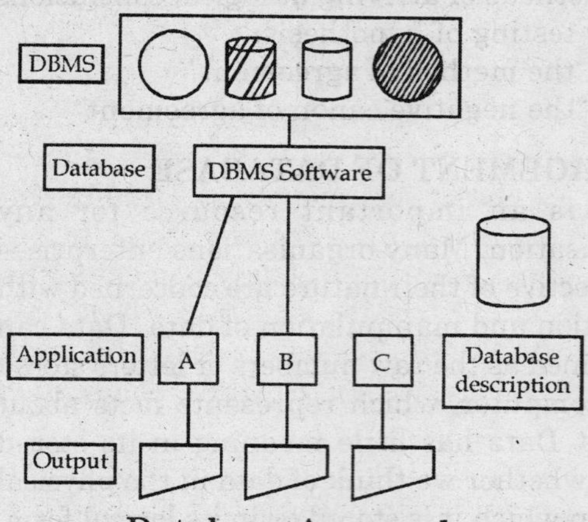

Database Approach

DATABASE MANAGEMENT SYSTEM (DBMS)

Database Management System

It is a collection of software that is used to store, delete, modify and retrieve data that is stored in a database. DBMS acts as an interface between the user and the data as in figures.

The degree of correctness, timeliness and relevance of data stored in a database indicates data integrity. Data integrity can be ensured by certain checks and validation procedures carried out whenever an update operation is attempted and also by elimination of data redundancy.

Some database management systems have features, which support data validation. For example, in ORACLE (a relational database management system) triggers can be used for this purpose.

Data independence is a property by which data files are insulated from application programs that use those files. The close link between the data and the access program is weakened and the database made more flexible to user requirements. With data independence, a programmer can write programs in FORTRAN, PASCAL, or any other language of his choice without bothering what language programs originally created the files that he wants to access.

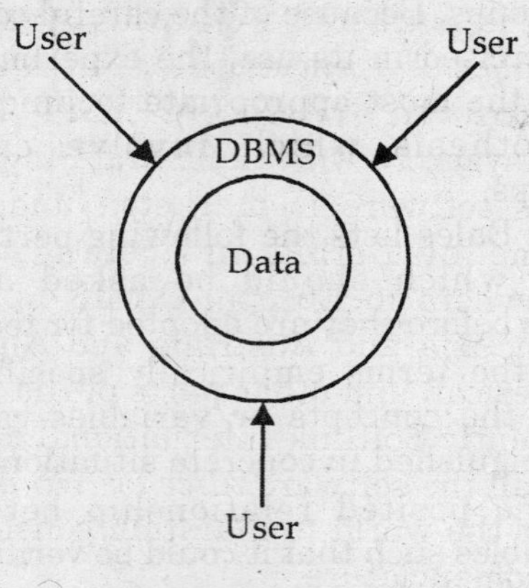

Data, DBMS and Users

Database
↓
File
↓
Record
↓
Field
↓
Character
↓
Byte
↓
Bit

Data Hierarchy

LIBRARY AUTOMATION SOFTWARE PACKAGES

The automation of library activities in India started in full swing with the introduction of CDS/ ISIS is a menu-driven generalised information storage and retrieval system designed by a team of experts under UNESCO/ PGI programme. It is specifically meant for the structured non-numerical databases. In India, NISSAT with the help of other professional bodies organised a number of training courses on application of CDS/ ISIS (DOS and Windows versions) in information organisation activities. As a result a large pool of trained manpower developed in the country.

1. **ALICE FOR WINDOWS** : This LMS developed by Softlink International, Australia, is a global software package and is marketed worldwide through a number of agencies based in America, Australia, Britain, ICEland, India, Malaysia, New Zealand and Singapore. This software is marketed under the name of Embla in Iceland, Alice elsewhere in Europe, OASIS in South East Asia and Australia and Annie in American and other parts of the world. Recently Softlink International decided to call the software *Alice for Window* all over the world to maintain consistency in nomenclature.
2. **BASISPLUS AND TECHLIB PLUS :** BASIS plus an TECHLIB plus are products of Information Dimensions Inc. (IDI), USA and National Informatics Centre (NIC), New Delhi. NIC is the value-added reseller of the packages in India.
3. **KOHA** : Koha is an intergrated library management system that was originally developed by Katipo Communications Limited of Wellington, New Zealand for the Horowhenua Library Trust (HLT), a regional library system located in Levin never Wellington. The major features of Koha are:
4. **VIRTUAILS** : Virtua ILS (Integrated Library System) is a sophisticated, internationalised library automation solution that addresses the full spectrum of library activities. This LMS is designed and developed by VTLS Inc., Virginia, USA. It uses off-the-shelf UNIX hardware and the Oracle RDBMS to guarantee continued availability and support.
5. **LAMP**: Library Automation and Management Package (LAMP) is a freeware and available for downloading from Internet at no cost. The package, developed jointly by Netherlands Library Association, Pakistan-Library Association and UNESCO, is based on CDS/ ISIS (version 3.07)
6. **NG-TLMS. NET** : NG-TLMS. net is state of the art library automation software based on TLMS (Total Library Management Service). TLMS has developed in Germany by TRANCE group. The route of development for this LMS is TLMS-NGTLMS->NGTLMS. net. NG- TLMS. net is designed on the top of TLMS by Web OPAC Applications Pvt. Ltd.
7. **WINSANJAY** : This LMS is originated from SANJAY. SANJAY is based on

CDS/ ISIS (version 2.3). It was developed by DESIDOC under a NISSAT project to meet the requirements of library management activities. It includes a set of 35 Pascal programs and 25 special menus.

8. **AUTOLIB :** Autolip is fully integrated multi-user software on Windows environment, designed to automate various activities of university libraries, college libraries, public libraries and special libraries. The software is developed by Autolib Software Systems Chennai and the product range includes the following LMS:
   - MS- Access with
     MS-SQL server with
     VB Version
     VB and web version
   - MS-Access with VB and W version
   - MS-SQL server with VB version
   - MS-SQL server with VB (public library version)

9. **E-GRANTHALAYA :** This LMS was developed by National Informatics Centre (NIC) Bangalore Center to suit the requirements of small and medium sized libraries. It is an easy to use software package and supports all the routine library operations.

10. **GRANTHALAYA :** This CUI based (DOS and UNIX) modular LMS developed in FoxPro by NISCAIR for medium range libraries. It includes all the modules required for day-to-day library operations. The package has seven modules-Library administration; Query; Circulation; Acquisition; Serials Control; Technical Processing and Data Administration.

11. **LIBSUITE :** The LMS, developed by SOFT-AID Computer Ltd., Pune, is based on web-centric architecture and designed to work with different media-LIBSUITE is based on three-tire web centric architecture in which server machine uses Windows NT/2000 and Internet Information Server (IIS)- as web server.

12. **LIBSYS :** LIBSYS is a fully integrated multi-user LMS based on client-server model and supports open system architecture, web-based access and GUI. This indigenous software package is designed and developed by LibSys Corporations, New Delhi. LIBSYS has seven basic modules-Acquisition: Cataloguing; Circulation; Serials: OPAC; Web-OPAC and Article Indexing.

13. **NEWGENLIB :** New GenLib is the result of collaboration between a charitable trust called Kesavan Institute of Information and Knowledge Management (KIIKM), Hyderabad and Venus Solutions Pvt. Ltd.

14. **NEXLIB :** The window based LMS was designed and developed by NexEvolve Logic Solutions Pvt. Ltd. It provides a simple point-and-click navigation interface backed by a powerful database engine capable of maintaining millions of records. Nexlib provides all the basis utilities required for the management of libraries, namely, Acquisition, Cataloguing, Circulation, Serials Control and OPAC.

15. **SLIM :** SLIM (System for Library Information Management), a software suit from Algorhythems Consultants Pvt. Ltd., Pune is a module-based LMS that offers wide range of functionality for library management. SLMS 21 is the latest product of the series that succeeded SLIM, SLIM ++, SLIMEX and SLIMLX. SLMS 21 supports multiple operating systems and backend databases.

NEWS SERVICES

A lot of news is generated in printed newspapers, newsletters, electronic news wires, magazines, trade journals, etc. Some companies called

News Aggregators routinely gather and scan all news and supply only what the end – user needs-highly selected and filtered. Such services are called Filtered News Services. Reuters, Desktop Data, Point Cost, Dow. Jones are some examples of such companies. In India, we have http://www. securities. com.

One might think of five different sources of news – based services:

(*a*) Individual websites of newspapers and newsletters

(*b*) Popular portals like Yahoo, Sify, Rediff, Lycos, etc

(*c*) Google News Altering Service

(*d*) News Aggregators-fee based

These sources are discussed below :

REPORT WRITING

The production of an effective report depends upon a combination of factors such as the ability and skill of the investigators for analysis, synthesis and exposition, the perceptiveness and evaluative powers of journal editors and referees. They are being discussed under the following heads:

(a) selection of an appropriate audience

(b) major components of completed research reports

(c) fundamentals of style and grammar, and

(d) preparation of manuscripts.

SELECTION OF AN APPROPRIATE AUDIENCE

Research reports can be prepared for a variety of audiences and are intended to serve to scholars or research-minded readers. A major factors in the selection of an audience is the chosen communication vehicle. For example, a research article written for a scholarly journal such as the Library Quarterly, should differ appreciably from a similar article prepared for a professional journal published by the university of Chicago and its audience comprises primarily of scholars, students and erudite specialists. In contrast, Library journal is a popular, widely read professional periodical published by R.R. Bowker Co. and is directed towards all practicing librarians. Thus, both these journals differ as far as emphasis, detail and style are concerned. Therefore selection of audience and a publication vehicle to communicate a research report is the primary requirement of report writing.

GRAPHICS IN REPORT WRITING

Words alone cannot always explain the event fully. At times details are cumbersome for the text to accommodate them. Besides on occasions, there is need for emphasis, summarization and visual effect. Graphics are the answer to these eventualities. A report writer often supplements his text with graphics to enhance its effectiveness Graphics make the text more attractive and the reading of it more interesting. Graphics are a desirable component in report writing. There are several kinds of graphic materials, e.g., tables, charts, graphs, diagrams, maps, drawings and pictures or photographs. We may record these different kinds as different techniques of presentation. All techniques do not fit in all situations. For each situation, an appropriate technique has to be selected and exploited. These are as follows:—

Situation-1 (Tables):

Suppose the manpower developments over the past few decades in librarianship is being researched into. The relevant processed data can best be presented in the form of tables which can be grasped instantly. Comparisons are possible between the various levels of education and at various points of time.

Situation-2 (Bar Charts):

Imagine a comparative study which is undertaken to ascertain the utilization of plan and non-plan grants in acquiring backruns of serials in university libraries. Bar charts can instantly display the relative contribution in this respect by the University Grants Commission and the parent institutions.

Situations 3 (pie charts):
An investigator who has completed a study in user preferences can effectively demonstrate it in the shape of pie charts, also called circular graphs, the measure of use of different publication forms.

Situation-4 (Graphs):
Use of graphs in bibliometric studies and in retrieval systems evaluation cannot be exaggerated.

The above four situations are examples of communicating large statistical information or cumbersome details effectively through tables, charts and graphs. They are also instances of summarization.

Following are the examples of other kinds of graphic material:

Situation-5 (Diagrams):
A library may recognize the need for improvement in the existing interval layout which does not facilitate unimpeded movement of staff, users and study material. The problem is studied and an alternative layout is workout. Here the investigator may describe the situation and the solution with the help of diagrams.

Situation-6 (Maps):
A researcher attempting to study the problems of mobile library service of a city public library system, will be required to supplement his description of service points with map(s).

Situation-7 (Drawings):
Drawings are rarely used in the field of librarianship. However, there exists scope for their inclusion in dissertations on library architecture. Without using drawings, no worthwhile discussion on library buildings is conceivable.

Situation-8 (Pictures):
Maximum scope exists for using pictures or photographs in the field of preservation and conservation.

MULTIPLE CHOICE QUESTIONS

1. Research is
   A. an activity to discover truth and to add new knowledge
   B. the knowledge acquired by observation
   C. the nature of an experiment
   D. none of the above
2. The benefit/s of the Research is/are
   A. research contribute to material adromcemat of society
   B. research inhances faculty development of individual researches
   C. both of above
   D. none of above
3. Librarian must know the process of research because
   A. the librarian have to guide the readers or users of the library–
   B. the library is a storehouse books and documents
   C. both of above
   D. none of above
4. The basic purpose of undertaking any research work is
   A. to discover the truth
   B. to update the knowledge of understanding of a concerned subject
   C. to give positiveness in the assertion in matter of opinion
   D. all the above
5. Research Methodology means
   A. a system of methods used for collecting data, information for the solution of problems identified for investigation
   B. a nature of an experiment, trial or attempt made or done provisionally
   C. the science of method
   D. all the above

6. Which is a *wrong* statement?
A. Basic research is defined as pure research
B. Applied research is progmatic research
C. science of method is methodology
D. The Librarian should not have the knowledge of the process of research

7. Dogmatism is
A. the process of tenative research
B. the object to rationalise research
C. the science of method
D. positiveness in the assertion in matters of opinion

8 Match the following:–

Match A
(*a*) Science
(*b*) Truth
(*c*) Objective
(*d*) Social research
(*e*) Research Methodology

Match B
1. Knowledge acquired by observation and testing of facts
2. Brief agreement with reality
3. It is rationalistic unbiased
4. Any research activity which directly deal with human beings in the context of the society

Codes:	(*a*)	(*b*)	(*c*)	(*d*)	(*e*)
A.	1	2	3	4	-
B.	-	1	2	3	4
C.	1	-	2	3	4
D.	1	2	-	3	4

9. The purpose/s of applied research is/are
A. directly at solving practical problems
B. the discovery of new knowledge that can be utilised immediately in real work situations
C. both of above
D. none of above

10. Research method/s is/are
A. census method & sampling
B. observation & interview method
C. schedule & questionnaire methode
D. all of these

11. Which is the comprehensive method of research?
A. Questionnaire method
B. Census method
C. Schedule method
D. Interview method

12. The method by which all the units of universe of research are surveyed and investigated is
A. Sampling method
B. Census method
C. Interview method
D. Schedule method

13. The method in which only chosen units of the universe of the research are surveyed is
A. Interview method
B. Sampling method
C. Observation method
D. any of these

14. Which is of the following method implies personal meetings and discussions between the researchers and the persons living in the area or society chosen for research?
A. Interview method
B. Schedule method
C. Questionnaire method
D. any of these

15. Which methods are used to elicit data & information from the respondents on the basis of a properly wooded, arranged, condified & duly pretested?
A. Interview & Schedule method
B. Schedule & Questionnaire method
C. Questionnaire & Census method
D. None of the above

16. Preparation of the periodical report on the livestock including the mankind of a country is an example of
A. Sampling method
B. Census method
C. Questionnaire method
D. Interview method

17. Which is *not* a prominent research centres in India?
A. CSIR B. ICSSR
C. ICHR D. NISCAIR

18 Match the following:–

Column A

(*a*) Formatted

(*b*) Methodology

(*c*) Tenative

Column B

1. the shape, size & general make-up
2. the science of method
3. the nature of an experiment, trial or attempt made or done provisionally

Codes:	(*a*)	(*b*)	(*c*)
A.	1	3	2
B.	2	3	1
C.	1	2	3
D.	2	1	3

19. Which is/are an essential ingredients of any research problem?

A. data B. researcher

C. resources D. all of above

20. A candidate should do before finalising a topic of research is/are

A. the topic selected is relevant to the society

B. it is likely to add to the existing stock of knowledge

C. the topic should be innovative at least in part if not as whole

D. all of the above

21. What is a collective term denoting the various processes by the aid of which the sciences are built-up?

A. Scientific method B. Knowledge method

C. Hypothesis D. Procedure

22. A tenative outline of a researcher proposal and a guideline to keep the researcher on the right track is

A. Research Methodology

B. Data collection

C. Research Design

D. Hypothesis

23. Which is *not* a component of a Research plan?

A. Title, problem, area and scope of the study

B. Hypothesis, concepts, Methodology, data collection

C. Analysis, Interpretation, Report and Bibliography

D. Zero-base planning, Hyperaction and finance

24. The important feature/s of Research design is/are

A. Regularity & Verifiability

B. Universality & Objectivity

C. Systematization & Predictability

D. all of these

25. A smaller representation of a larger whole on the basis of which a judgement or inference about aggregate or totality is made, is –

A. Scientific method

B. Sampling

C. Research process

D. all of these

26. When the whole group is taken for the study, from which the sample has been drawn is

A. Population B. Universe

C. Both of these D. None of these

27. The person who conducts public opinion polls is

A. Poller B. Pollster

C. Repollar D. Any of these

28. Which is *not* a random sampling?

A. Lottery method

B. Grid-system

C. Numbers method

D. Census method

29. The criteria which are adopted to choose a sample is/are

A. sample must represent the universe

B. sample must be of adequate size and efficient

C. sample must be representative, reliable and unbiased

D. All of the above

30. Which of the following applies to a Universe with many strata are constructed scientifically giving due weightage to

considerations of homogeneity, exclusivity and comprehensive coverage?
A. Random sampling
B. Stratified sampling
C. Representative sampling
D. Any of these

31. Universe can be
A. Definite and Indefinite universe
B. Real and Hypothetical universe
C. Both of above
D. None of above

32. The main element/s of Research design is/are
A. the problem & scope
B. purpose & limitation of study
C. Hypothesis & Methodology
D. All of these

33. Which is *not* a correct statement?
A. External & Internal criticism are unique to Historical research
B. Data for historical research are collected in the form of material evidence
C. Research design is a blue-print of the research activity
D. Null hypothesis is one of the great method of IRS

34. Delphi is a
A. survey design
B. opinion for future situation
C. both of these
D. none of these

35. Linguistic analysis of a text is
A. Textual Criticism
B. External criticism
C. Internal Criticism
D. None of above

36. Match the following:–

Match A
(*a*) A written or spoken statement
(*b*) Numerical values assigned to precoded pairs of positive & negative replies
(*c*) Analysis of the already existing data collected initially for some other purpose

Match B
1. Testimony
2. Scaling
3. Secondary analysis
4. Rating scale

Codes:	(*a*)	(*b*)	(*c*)
A.	2	3	1
B.	3	2	1
C.	1	4	3
D.	2	1	3

37. The selections of a panel of experts, preparation of a statement of value judgement; first round of questionnaire are the steps of
A. Content analysis
B. Delphi design
C. Comprehensive method
D. None of these

38. User studies and Evaluation studies are most suitable for
A. Delphi design B. Survey research
C. Budget research D. Budget research

39. A study preceding the main study usually to check the viability of the study design is
A. Consensus opinion
B. Rating study
C. Value judgement
D. Pilot study

40. The main purpose/s of Explaratory studies is/are
A. to satisfy curiosity
B. to help build a set of methodology which can be used for rigorously design research
C. to make recommendation regarding the likelihood of continuing with additional research on the topic
D. all of the above

41. Diagnostic research design has the steps of
A. identification of a problem
B. diagnosis of the causes leading to the problem
C. formulation and recommendation of a possible solution
D. all of the above

42. Which is/are the example/s of diagnostic studies used in the field of Library and Information Science?
A. User behaviour in On-Line Interactive Information Retrieval Systems

B. User attitude to microforms
C. Impact of technology on Information services
D. All of the above

43. Experimental formulation may be
A. Panel study
B. Ex-post facto experimental design
C. Both of above
D. None of above

44. Which is *not* a correct about experimental formulation?
A. It is not more accurate and precise
B. The cause & effect relation is more clearly determined in it
C. It is an ideal method for testing a causal hypothesis
D. None of the above

45. Observation is the most widely used to technique of
A. Scientific investigation
B. Scientific method
C. User studies
D. Random poll method

46. The process of selecting example from a population to obtain empirical evidence of a contemporary nature to solve problem is
A. Survey research
B. Nature research
C. Sociometric research
D. Random research

47. The basic steps of data representation are
A. Coding B. Tabulation
C. Both of these D. None of these

48. The research technique for the objective systematic and quantitative description of manigest content of communications is
A. Survey design
B. Content analysis
C. Coding
D. Library survey

49. The measurement of interrations amongst individuals and also the institutional behaviour is
A. Sociometry B. Bibliometry
C. Sociomatrix D. Sampling

50. Sociometric scale is regarded as
A. a tool of observation
B. a instrument of observation
C. a method of interview
D. A & B both

51. Formulation of research problems, definition and establishment of hypothesis; identification and selection of methods to be analysed are the steps of
A. Sociometry B. Content analysis
C. Survey D. Descriptive Survey

52. A good sociometric scale should have
A. Reliability & Validity
B. Simplicity & Practibility
C. Wide applicability
D. All of these

53. Interview is
A. research tool
B. used by contemporary researcher
C. both of these
D. None of these

54. In sampling size determination, a sampling method, in which n is the sample size, s is the standard deviation of the population and SE (x) is the standard error of the mean , then the formula to determine the sample size will be

A. $n = \dfrac{SE(x)^2}{S}$ B. $n =$

C. $n = \dfrac{S^2}{[SE(x)]^2}$ D. $n = \dfrac{S^2 \times (x)^2}{SE}$

55. The data collection technique involves
A. Interview B. Questionnaire
C. Observation D. All of the above

56. Diaries, Notebooks, Schedules, Photographes and Maps are the devices of
A. Interview B. Observation
C. Questionnaire D. All of these

57. Which is a process of content analysis in Library & Information Science?
A. Context classification
B. Subject indexing
C. Study of newspaper articles
D. All of these

58. A collection of types having certain common features which are however sufficiently different to be distinguishable from one another is

A. Typology B. Observation
C. Construction D. Indexing

59. Which is *not* a correct variable of type construction polarities?

A. Ideal-Extracted
B. General-specific
C. Scientific-Historical
D. Universal-Famous

60. Case study method is an important technique in Library & Information Science research because

A. it is intensive in nature
B. helps in formulate hypothesis
C. very comprehensive and of immense value in making questionnaires & schedules
D. all of these

61. Powell (1985) has classified "Evaluative Research" into

A. Summative evaluation
B. Formative evaluation
C. Performance measurement
D. all of these

62. Determination of the object and reason for evaluation; setting the level of performance according to the objective and selection of technique are the steps of

A. Evaluation studies
B. Environment studies
C. Statistical Studies
D. Summative Studies

63. The difficulties and problems in the Case study technique are

A. false sense of confidence
B. lack of quantitative study
C. unorganised & unsystematic
D. all of these

64. Match the following:–

Column A

(*a*) Based on metric concept
(*b*) Based on quantification
(*c*) Internal scale in which an absolute zero point exists

Match B

1. sociometric
2. Quantitative
3. Interval scale
4. Ratio scale

Codes:	(*a*)	(*b*)	(*c*)
A.	1	2	4
B.	1	3	2
C.	4	3	2
D.	3	2	4

65. Selection of cases, identification of situation, recording of data, interpretation of data are the steps of

A. Case study technique
B. Evaluation Studies
C. Survey design
D. sampling Servey

66. Application of statistical methods in Library management is

A. Sociometry B. Bibliometry
C. Librametry D. Thesaumetry

67. An indirect method of data collection used as an approach to obtain information from respondents is

A. Case study technique
B. Projective technique
C. Acentuation
D. Delphi technique

68. The need & purpose of statistical study is to

A. undertake a comparative study of the phenomena
B. analyse the relationship between data
C. deal exclusively with quantitative phenomena
D. all of above

69. The process that involves the application of different statistical tools like averages, dispersion, correlation etc. is

A. presentation of data
B. Analysis of data
C. Scale study
D. Sample Study

70. Which is not a properly matched?
A. condensation–act of making a book, speech, report etc
B. Acentuation–to emphasize something in any contest
C. Abstraction–an idea of a quality as separate from object
D. Typology–a collection of wrong fonts and alphabets

71. The statistical techniques can be used in a Library as a tool for
A. the preparation of Annual Report
B. planning its services as recruitment of staff
C. acquisition of books and to know the efficiency of staff working in library.
D. all of the above

72. The steps in statistical study is/are
A. Presentation of data
B. Analysis of data
C. Interpretation of data
D. All of these

73. Inkblot tests, story telling tests, Graphic techniques are the techniques of
A. Case study survey
B. Projective technique
C. Survey design
D. Objective technique

74. Which of the technique/s is/are used to select candidates for training in Library and Information Science?
A. Inkblot tests
B. Graphic techniques
C. A & B both
D. Thomatic Appreciation test

75. A tenative generalisation and a statement temporarily accepted as true, the validity of which remains to be tested is
A. specific study B. Hypothesis
C. Project design D. Interview method

76. The technique/s involved in delimiting the problem is/are
A. statement of the problem in a general way
B. understanding the nature of the problem
C. surveying the available literature
D. all of the above

77. The application of statistical techniques to economic theories is
A. Empirical B. Econometric
C. Presumption D. Formulation

78. The criteria involved in selecting a research problem is
A. clarity & unambiguity
B. empirical verification
C. experience & creativity
D. all of these

79. Which of the following is used to establish the validity in testing of hypothesis?
A. Defining the problem
B. Analysis of data
C. Interpretation of data
D. any of these

80. Which is *not* in the general model of the Scientific Method of Inquiry?
A. Design methodology
B. Report results
C. Analyse data
D. Catalogue use

81. Scientific research involves
A. Problem definition
B. Research design
C. Data collection
D. All of these

82. Match the following:–
Column A
(*a*) The positive square root of variance
(*b*) Middle most observation in series
(*c*) Most frequent observation in series
(*d*) Geometric Mean
Match B
1. Standard deviation
2. Median
3. Mode
4. $n\frac{S \times x}{[SE(x)]^{\frac{1}{2}}}$

Codes:	(*a*)	(*b*)	(*c*)	(*d*)
A.	4	1	2	3
B.	1	4	2	3
C.	1	2	3	4
D.	2	1	3	4

83. In the equation $Y = a + bx$, b is
A. Regression coefficient
B. Variable
C. a constant
D. cyclical coefficient

84. The periodical fluctuation in the data, spanning less than a year is
A. secular trend
B. seasonal variation
C. cyclical variation
D. all of these

85. Which is not a correct graph?

$\sqrt{f_1 x_1 \times f_2 x_2 \times \cdots f_n x_n}$.

High degree of +ve correlation

B.

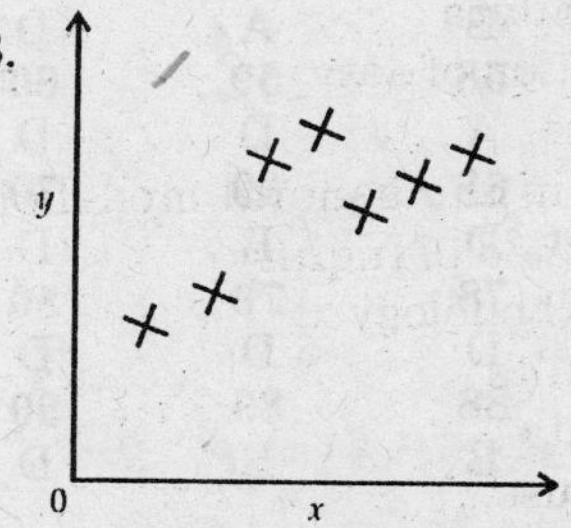

High degree of –ve correlation

C.

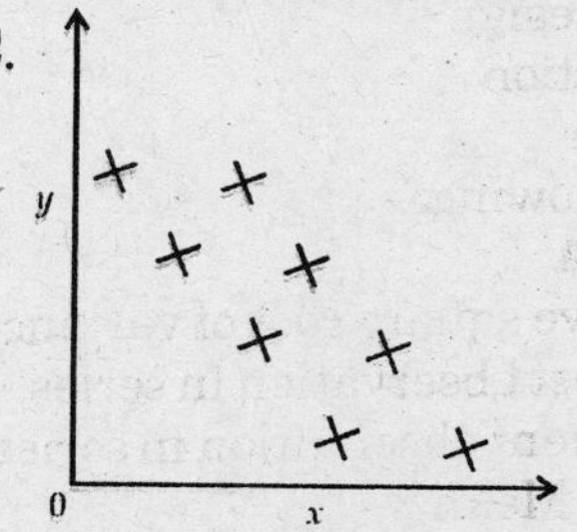

No correlation

D.

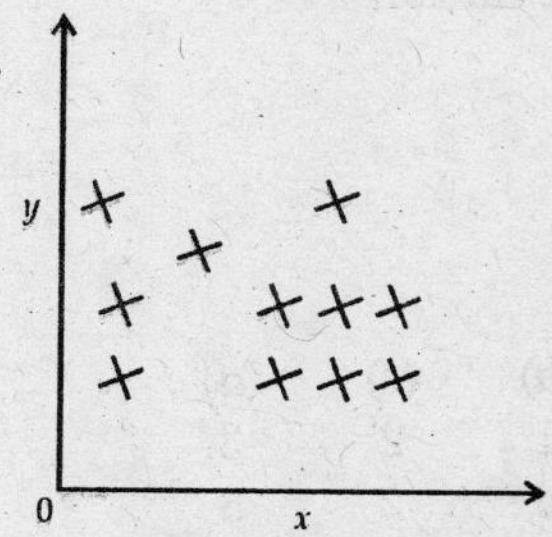

Perfect +ve correlation

86. The process of describing future possibilites and alternatives and a descriptive technique in future research is
A. Report writing B. Scenario writing
C. Juxtapose D. Appropriability

87. Match the following:–

Column A
(*a*) The test of a thesis
(*b*) Explanation of a theory
(*c*) A printed scholarly study of one theme
(*d*) Art of writing

Column B
1. rhetoric
2. monograph
3. exposition
4. dissertation

Codes:	(*a*)	(*b*)	(*c*)	(*d*)
A.	1	2	3	4
B.	4	3	2	1
C.	4	2	3	1
D.	1	3	2	4

88. A library that retires as many books as it add is
A. Weeding library
B. Self-renewing library
C. Research library
D. Technical library

89. The process that place side by side is
A. Weeding
B. Juytapose
C. Rhetorics
D. Sidametry

90. The major components of Report writing is/are–
A. selection of an appropriate audience
B. complete research report taking
C. preparation of manuscripts
D. all of the above

91. Which is a *wrong* statement?
A. A research report consists of the preliminaries, the middle and the end
B. The core is preceded by preliminaries comprising the title page, acknowledgements table of contents and introduction.
C. End part contains the appendices and bibliography

D. A pie chart can be used for bar graph representation of data in Library and Information Services.

92. Which is *not* method of Graphics in Report writing?
A. Bar Charts B. Tables
C. Graphs D. Film strips

ANSWERS

1	2	3	4	5	6	7	8	9	10
A	C	A	B	A	D	D	A	C	D
11	12	13	14	15	16	17	18	19	20
B	B	B	A	B	B	D	C	A	D
21	22	23	24	25	26	27	28	29	30
A	B	D	D	B	C	B	D	D	B
31	32	33	34	35	36	37	38	39	40
C	D	D	C	A	C	B	B	D	D
41	42	43	44	45	46	47	48	49	50
D	D	C	A	A	A	C	B	A	D
51	52	53	54	55	56	57	58	59	60
B	D	C	B	D	B	D	A	D	D
61	62	63	64	65	66	67	68	69	70
D	A	D	D	A	B	B	D	B	D
71	72	73	74	75	76	77	78	79	80
D	D	B	C	B	D	B	D	D	D
81	82	83	84	85	86	87	88	89	90
D	C	A	B	D	B	B	B	B	D
91	92								
D	D								

MISCELLANEOUS QUESTIONS

PART—I

1. Indexing and Abstracting Services come under which services?
A. CAS B. SDI
C. General D. Common

2. "Index to the Times of India" is published how many time in a year?
A. 3 B. 6
C. 4 D. 2

3. The first edition of "*Encyclopedia Britannica*" was published in how many volumes?
A. 5 B. 6
C. 2 D. 3

4. "Data India" is published by:
A. NIC B. Times of India
C. Press Institute of India D. INFLIBNET

5. Multilingual dictionaries are also known as:
A. Many language dictionary
B. Bilingual
C. Polygots
D. Translation dictionaries

6. "World of Learning" is a:
A. Annual Bibliography B. Dictionary
C. Directory D. Bibliography

7. The first encyclopaedia "*Historia Naturalis*" was published in the:
A. 77 AD B. 1024 AD
C. 1810 AD D. 1425 AD

8. "British Book News" is an example of a which kind of bibliography?
A. Trade B. National
C. Author D. Textual

9. In the classified part of INB, the entries are arranged according to:
A. CC 6th and 7th edition
B. DDC 19th edition
C. DDC 16th edition
D. UDC 3rd abridged edition

10. "Ulrich International periodical Directory" is a which kind of source of information?
A. Tertiary B. Secondary
C. Reference D. Primary

11. The three important characteristics of presentation of topic in an encyclopaedia are read ability, objectivity and
A. Style B. Format
C. Arrangement D. None of these

12. The librarians and scholars are primarily concerned with which kind of bibliograhy:
A. Enumerative B. Regional
C. Descriptive D. Historical

13. ERIC database sponsored by the Department of Health Education and Welfare, Government of USA, deals with:
A. Economics B. Energy
C. Ethics D. Education

14. Dictionary, Glossary, Lexicon, Thesaurus, Vocabulary, etc. deal with:
A. Definition
B. Concepts
C. Words and their meaning
D. Opposite words

15. New York Times Index, Indian Press Index and News paper Index are the examples of Indexing service devoted to:
A. Journal B. Periodical
C. Newspaper D. Report literature

16. Which kind of bibliography is a systematic list of all the books published all over the world?
A. Author B. Universal
C. Trade D. Title

17. "Subject Guide to Books in print" selects its subject headings from:
A. Chain procedure
B. ALA list
C. Sears list of subject heading
D. POPSI

18. "Fodors Guides" is an example of :
A. Biographical Sources
B. Encyclopaedia
C. Travel Guide
D. Directory of Institutions

19. A physical map is usually referred to:
A. Trace details of minerals resources
B. Shows roads only
C. Indicate location of a country
D. None of above

20. Encyclopaedias are of two types i.e.
A. Local and National
B. Private and Government
C. Common and General
D. General and Special/Subject

21. Year books can be divided into how many major groups?
A. General year books and supplement to encyclopaedia
B. National year books and directory
C. Gazetteer and supplement of encyclopaedia
D. None of above

22. "Indian Ephemeris and Nautical Almanac" is a type of almanac:
A. Informational B. Indicational
C. General D. Astronomical

23. The UNESCO conference on the improvement of Bibliographical service was held at ..... in .....
A. London, 1950 B. New York, 1961
C. Paris, 1961 D. Paris, 1950

24. The publication of British National Bibliography started in the year.
A. 1954 B. 1950
C. 1957 D. 1963

25. The publisher of India: Who's who is:
A. INFA Publication
B. Ministry of Finance
C. Publication Bureau
D. Sahitya Academy

26. ..... objectivity and style are the three important criteria of topics in encyclopaedia.
A. Readability B. Scope
C. Format D. Arrangement

27. "Guinees Book of world records" is a:
A. Directory B. Hand book
C. Statistics D. General publication

28. Almanacs are of three types: Astronomical, Informational and:
A. Special B. Teleyraphical
C. Artifical D. Topical

29. "Current Biography" is published by:
A. R.R. Beroker
B. H.W. Wilson
C. Europa Publication
D. Gale Research

30. "Chemical Abstract" started its publication in
A. 1876 B. 1933
C. 1907 D. 1905

31. "Directory of American Research and Technology" (DART) is published by:
A. Whitakers B. R.B. Bowker
C. Sterling D. None of these

32. "Catalogue of Books" is a publication of:
A. NISSAT
B. ILA
C. NISCAIR
D. India, Ministry of Information & Broadcasting, Publication Division

33. Classified part of ABPR is classified by:
A. UDC B. LC
C. DDC D. CC

34. "Publishers weekly" was started in the year:
A. 1876 B. 1871
C. 1972 D. 1872

35. Book Review Digest (BRD) was started in:
A. 1927 B. 1910
C. 1905 D. 1895

36. Funk and Wagnals dictionary is published from:
A. India B. Pakistan
C. New York D. None of these

37. INSDOC (NISCAIR) was merged into NISCOM in year:
A. 2002 B. 1999
C. 1997 D. 2003

38. "International Political Science Abstracts" is published from:
A. New York B. Tokyo
C. London D. Delhi

39. Psychological Abstracts was started in:
A. 1937 B. 1945
C. 1827 D. 1927

40. AIU Stands for:
A. All India Union
B. American Information Union
C. Association of India Universities
D. None of above

41. Who used the word "Bibliography" first:
A. Melvil Deway
B. Ranganathan
C. Louis Jacob de Saint Charles
D. Margret Maan

42. S.T.C. Stands for:
A. Sales Tax Company
B. Sayers Translation Council
C. Short-Title Catalogue
D. Special Training Centre

43. An Analytical Bibliography deals with the:
A. Physical aspects of the book
B. Analysis of subject
C. Classified study
D. Error

44. Bibliography deals with the art of writing, printing, illumination and binding etc. called:
A. Textual Bibliography
B. Historical Bibliography
C. Title Bibliography
D. Trade Bibliography

45. What is the new title of "Economic Abstracts"?
A. Science of Economic Abstract
B. Economic Science
C. Economic Science Abstract
D. Key to Economic Science

46. Ranganathan used the term "librametry" for the first time in ..... in his talk before the ASLIB at Leamingtion Spa (U.K.)
A. 1948 B. 1976
C. 1979 D. 1972

47. Who is a bibliothecar?
A. Author of Articles
B. Translator
C. Librarian
D. Computer Operator

48. Planning, Organising, Staffing, Directing, Coordinating, Reporting and Budgeting are ..... of management.
A. Elements B. Principles
C. Subsystems D. Structure

49. Critical Path Method (CPM) and programme Evaluation and Review Technique (PERT) are used for improving the quality of:
A. Budgeting
B. Reporting
C. Modern Management
D. None of above

50. The Library Statistics usually pertains to library resources, technical services and:
A. Finance B. Staff
C. User's services D. Revenue

ANSWERS

1	2	3	4	5	6	7	8	9	10
D	C	D	C	C	C	A	A	C	B
11	12	13	14	15	16	17	18	19	20
A	C	D	C	C	B	C	C	C	D
21	22	23	24	25	26	27	28	29	30
A	D	D	B	A	A	B	C	B	C
31	32	33	34	35	36	37	38	39	40
B	D	C	D	C	C	A	C	D	C
41	42	43	44	45	46	47	48	49	50
C	C	A	B	D	A	A	A	C	C

PART—II

1. H.E. Bliss, a great classificationist of the world wrote a book of poems titled:
A. Classification and society
B. Two lovers
C. Better late than never
D. Crimes and books
2. The first school of librarianship in the world was started by Dewey in:
A. 26th January, 1876
B. 25th January, 1887
C. 24th June, 1887
D. 5th January, 1887
3. Date of establishment of UNESCO is :
A. 4th November, 1956
B. 30th June, 1936
C. 24th November, 1948
D. 4th November, 1946
4. Establishment of Raja Ram Mohun Roy foundation at Kolkatta on:
A. 22nd May, 1972
B. 30th May, 1982
C. 22nd April, 1972
D. None of above
5. On 18th August 1962, DRTC, Bangalore was inaugurated by:
A. T. Vishwanathan
B. B.S. Keshavan
C. Dr. C.D. Deshmukh
D. P.C. Mahalanobis
6. INPADOC (2nd May 1972, Vienna) stands for:
A. International Public Administration Documentation Centre
B. Institue of Pharma and Documentation Centre
C. A Software Package
D. International Patents Documenttion Centre
7. *Hints on Library Administration in India*, is first book on Library Science, written by:
A. S.P. Mehta B. Ranganathan
C. B.H. Mehta D. S.R. Bhatia
8. Isak Collijn was a Swedish National Librarian (1927) and was first president of:
A. ALA B. FID
C. IFLA D. UNESCO
9. Who is the first "*Emeritus Fellow*" professor of library and information science appointed by UGC (India)?
A. S.R. Ranganathan
B. P.N. Kaula
C. P.B. Mangala
D. B.S. Keshavan
10. In which university the first full time diploma course in library science was started in India?
A. Delhi University B. B.H.U
C. A.M.U D. Madras University
11. Fujio is called "Dewey" of:
A. Nepal B. Japan
C. Kenya D. Russia
12. In which university of India, Dickinson, an American was appointed for the first time as university librarian?
A. A.M.U., Aligarh
B. B.H.U., Varanasi
C. University of Bombay
D. Punjab University, Chandigarh
13. The PGI is framed out of merging:
A. UNISIST and FID
B. UNISIST and UNESCO
C. UNISIST and IFLA
D. UNISIST and ALA
14. The first concept of "Library Co-operation" put to practice is traced to:
A. OCLC
B. Fermington Plan
C. Dealer Library Plan
D. None of these
15. The Universal Availability of Publications (UAP) is a programme launched by:
A. UNESCO B. FID
C. IFLA D. UNO
16. When a library or information centre provides documents from its own resources or from other sources it is known as:
A. Inter-Library Loan Service
B. Document Delivery service

C. Reprography Service
D. Reference Service

17. The UGC library committee has suggested per capita expenditure formula for:
A. Purchase of books and other reading materials
B. Periodical subscription
C. Building maintenance
D. Salaries of all staff

18. Which of the following institutes in India provides technical and other related information services to small scale industry?
A. DESIDOC B. NISSAT
C. NISCAIR D. SENDOC

19. The official agency assigning ISSN in India is
A. NISCAIR
B. NASSDOC
C. ILA
D. National Library of India

20. A latest revision of UNESCO manifesto of public library was issued in the year:
A. 1992 B. 1996
C. 1994 D. 1998

21. JOCLAI Includes:
A. ILA, IASLIC and IATLIS
B. ILA and IASLIC
C. IASLIC, GILA and ILA
D. The National and State Library Associations

22. Which of the following statements can be considered as advantages of class libraries in a school?
A. They limit the number of books a child to select from.
B. They increase the number of copies required.
C. They do not require cataloguing and classification.
D. They permit a better integration of books into teaching.

23. A college library in India differs from a university library in the following ways:
A. It is usually smaller than the university library B. It has fewer research materials
C. Both A and B
D. Neither of the above

24. International Standard Book Description does not standardise:
A. The points of access
B. Type of Information to be included in the catalogue entry
C. The punctuation markes to be followed
D. Order in which the information is to be recorded

25. Which of the following statements about national libraries is **correct**? National Libraries are expected:
A. To bring out a national bibliography
B. To function as depository library
C. To participate in universal bibliographic control
D. All of the above

26. Zero-growth libraries are that:
A. Libraries do not get more space
B. Libraries must not buy books
C. Libraries do not get more funds
D. Libraries must weed out as many books as they add

27. A library has the following section, children section, periodicals section, audio-visual section and braille section. Which of the following criteria have been used for departmentalization?
A. Function, Product and Customer
B. Function and Product
C. Function and Customer
D. Customer and Product

28. Headquarter of ILA is moved from Calcutta to Delhi in
A. 1933 B. 1965
C. 1964 D. 1953

29. In which of the following Public Libraries Acts, provision for "Library Cess" is not provided:
A. Tamil Nadu B. Maharashtra
C. Karnataka D. Andhra Pradesh

30. Special Library Association (SLA) was founded in year:
A. 1908 B. 1909
C. 1933 D. 1910

31. *Directory of Special and Research Libraries in India* was published by:
A. NISCAIR B. DESIDOC
C. IASLIC D. SENDOC

32. Which was the **first** university that changed diploma course of library science to the degree of B.Lib. Sc. in India?
A. BHU
B. Delhi University
C. Aligarh Muslim University
D. Madras University

33. On the basis of user's approach to information, it can be categorised into:
A. Potential, Expected, Actual and Beneficiary User
B. Potential, Non-potential, Actual and Research User
C. Expected, Actual, Interested and Beneficiary User
D. Potential, Expected, Technologist and Working User

34. Reading Habit, Information Gathering Habit service and ..... are the different category of user studies.
A. Communication Behaviour studies
B. Flow of Information among Users
C. Citation studies
D. None of above

35. The General Method of user studies includes
A. Questionnaire, Interview and Diary
B. Diary and Citation analysis
C. Citation analysis and Analysis of library records
D. Operational research and Computer feed back

36. Indirect method of user education includes:
A. Library Guides, Display and Documentation List
B. Orientation Lecture, Library Tour and Display
C. Audio-Visual Aids, Orientation Lecture and Internal Meeting
D. Library Tours, Reader-Librarian Dialogue and Display

37. "Recruitment Procedure & Revision of Pay Scale" is the main concern of which of the following committee:
A. Punnaya Committee (1992-94)
B. Mehrotra Committee (1983)
C. CDC (1990-93)
D. Review Committee on LIS (1961)

38. "Book Bank" scheme of UGC was introduced in:
A. 1965-66 B. 1961-63
C. 1963-64 D. 1959-61

39. Inter-University Centre for Astronomy and Astrophysics is located at:
A. Poona University, Pune
B. JNU, New Delhi
C. Devi Ahilya University, Indore
D. University of Delhi, Delhi

40. RRRLF is providing assistance to library in the form of:
A. Matching and non-matching assistance
B. Full funding
C. Assistance of Books
D. None of the above

41. There are mainly three components of digital libraries. These are:
A. Document, Information, Information Retrieval
B. Technology, Storage of Information and Information
C. Document, Technology and Operations
D. None of the above

42. SIS stands for:
A. Society for Information Science
B. Society of Information Scientists
C. Specialised Information Services
D. Services for Information Scientists

43. The four functional phase of SDI system are selection, notification, feedback & ..... .
A. classification B. readjustment
C. modification D. arrangement

44. The direct method of electrostate photocopy is also knows as:
A. Xerography
B. Diazography
C. Electrical Reproduction
D. Electrofax

45. The Diazo process is extensively used for making copies of:
A. Microfilm B. Microfile
C. Micro document D. All of these

46. Notification to user for receipt of new arrival of documents in the library comes under the category of which service:
A. Reference service
B. Inter-library loan
C. CAS
D. SDI service

47. Which of the following contains the concerned class numbers and their verbal headings?
A. Gangway B. Bay
C. General D. Shelf

48. Monthly catalogue published by controller of publications division, provides information on the current publications of:
A. Government of India
B. Delhi
C. Oxford University Press
D. Kolkata

49. Ranganathan has suggested that per capita expenditure on university and college libraries should be per student Rs. 20 and per teacher:
A. Rs. 300 B. Rs. 500
C. Rs. 100 D. Rs. 400

50. When computerised data is reproduced on microfilm/microfile without first being produced in paper print form, is called:
A. MARC B. Mircrochip
C. COM D. Microform

ANSWERS

1	2	3	4	5	6	7	8	9	10
C	D	D	A	C	D	C	C	B	D
11	**12**	**13**	**14**	**15**	**16**	**17**	**18**	**19**	**20**
B	D	B	B	C	B	B	D	A	C
21	**22**	**23**	**24**	**25**	**26**	**27**	**28**	**29**	**30**
D	D	C	A	D	D	A	C	B	B
31	**32**	**33**	**34**	**35**	**36**	**37**	**38**	**39**	**40**
C	C	A	B	A	A	B	A	A	A
41	**42**	**43**	**44**	**45**	**46**	**47**	**48**	**49**	**50**
C	A	C	D	C	C	D	A	A	C

PART—III

1. Indian Books in print is published in ..... volumes.
A. 2 vol. B. 3 vol.
C. 4 vol. D. 5 vol.
2. *Ulrich's International Periodical Directory* first published in year:
A. 1930 B. 1931
C. 1932 D. 1933
3. The European Translation Centre is located at:
A. London B. Vienna
C. Delhi D. Paris
4. "*Current Library & Information Science*" is a publication of:
A. NISSAT B. AGRIS
C. IASLIC D. AGLIS
5. Index is derived from latin word:
A. Indices B. Indicare
C. Indicate D. Indic
6. The author of "Systematic Indexing" is:
A. J. Kaiser
B. Warwick Sayer
C. S.R. Ranganathan
D. J.E.L. Farradane
7. *Sear's list* was first published in:
A. 1937 B. 1923
C. 1925 D. 1927
8. During Vedic Period, universe of knowledge is divided into:
A. Dharma, Karma, Darshan and Lalit Kala
B. Dharma, Karma, Kama and Moksha
C. Dharma, Karma, Kama and Darshan
D. Karma, Kama, Vigyana and Sahitya
9. Herbert Spencer, a well known english philosopher, divided universe of knowledge on the basis of:
A. Logic and mathematics
B. Inductive and deductive
C. Abstract and concrete
D. None of the above
10. Epistemology is derived from ... language.
A. Latin B. French
C. Greek D. English
11. In KWIC Index, the keyword is:
A. Derived from the title
B. Taken from the abstract
C. Selected from the full text
D. Assigned by the author
12. Which of the following is considered as key attribute in a bibliographic database?
A. ISBN
B. Title
C. Author
D. Main entry access point
13. The term "Subject Reference Code" (SRC) is related to:
A. Library of Congress Classification
B. Universal decimal classification
C. Broad system of ordering
D. Bibliographic classification
14. Management is an example of how knowledge grown by:
A. Fusion B. Lamination
C. Distillation D. Loose Assemblage
15. Bar Code Technology is useful for:
A. Circulation B. Acqusition
C. Stock Taking D. All of these
16. The term "Lexicography" is associated with:
A. Compilation of Encyclopaedia
B. Compilation of Abstract
C. Compilation of Dictionaries
D. None of the above
17. In CC, the principle that helps in the identification of personality category of:
A. Cow-Calf principle
B. Whole organ principle
C. Neti-Neti principle
D. Later in the principle
18. Citation Indexing was first developed in the field of:
A. Science B. Social Science
C. Law D. Literature
19. Uniterm Index was given by:
A. M. Taube B. Decrela Austin
C. S.R. Ranganathan D. Eugine Garfield

20. Medical Jurisprudence is found by which modes of formation of subject:
A. Fission B. Cluster
C. Lamination D. Fusion

21. "Natural Sciences" can be formed by which of the following modes:
A. Cluster
B. Agglomeration
C. Loose Assemblage
D. Lamination

22. C.C.F. stands for:
A. Common Catalogy Format
B. Common Communication Form
C. Common Classification Form
D. Common Communication Format

23. In "Search Engine" which device is automatically log on web pages and index their content?
A. Crowler B. Spiders
C. Indexer D. Invented file searcher

24. Who credited for designing thesaurus?
A. Morle, Roget B. Helen Browson
C. Eugine Garfield D. M. Taube

25. Relationship among concept form of component of subject may be categorised as:
A. Hierarchical relationship and Non-hierarchical relationship
B. Equivalence and associative relationship
C. General and specific relationship
D. Concept and component relationship

26. "Thesaurus of English Word & Phrases" appeared in:
A. 1872 B. 1952
C. 1869 D. 1852

27. "BLAISE" becomes operation since:
A. 1967 B. 1978
C. 1977 D. 1975

28. CODEN was developed by:
A. American Society of Information
B. American Chemical Society
C. American Society for Testing and Materials
D. National Service Foundation

29. Chemical abstract uses which of the following for standardisation purpose:
A. ISSN B. CODEN
C. ISBN D. TSBD

30. BNB adopted which of the following for preparing subject index:
A. POPSI B. Chain Indexing
C. PRECIS D. KWIC

31. Indexing & Abstracting services comes under which services?
A. CAS B. Documentation
C. General D. SDI

32. Third step of POPSI is known as:
A. Short Display
B. Display of Component
C. Selection of Approach Term
D. Display of Subject Index Term

33. Citation analysis help in:
A. Selective Cataloguing
B. Subject Cataloguing
C. Descriptive Cataloguing
D. Indentification of Document

34. "Systematic Indexing" was developed by:
A. E.J. Coats B. H.P. Luhn
C. J.E.L. Farradane D. Derek Austin

35. Uniterm Indexing was developed in:
A. 1950 B. 1955
C. 1952 D. 1953

36. Prenatal cataloguing is synonyms with:
A. Selective Cataloguing
B. Descriptive Cataloguing
C. Cataloguing in Publication
D. Subject Cataloguing

37. There are a total of 40 document in a collection. In response to a query, only 24 document are retrived, out of which only 8 were relevant. What is recall percentage?
A. 20% B. 33%
C. 40% D. 60%

38. Which of the following is ROM memory?
A. EEPROM B. PROM
C. EPROM D. All the these

39. Main memory is:
A. Volatile as well as non-volatile
B. Non-volatile
C. Volatile
D. None of the above

40. An impact printer used:
A. Thermal technology
B. Electro-mechanical mechanism

C. Ink-jet technology
D. None of the above

41. A laser printer uses:
A. Camera lens
B. Roster scan
C. Heat sensitive paper
D. None of the above

42. Library software '*Suchika*' is devised by:
A. NISCAIR B. DESIDOC
C. INFLIBNET D. UNESCO

43. Library software "*Granthalaya*" is devised by:
A. NASSDOC B. DRTC
C. NISCAIR D. DESIDOC

44. In DOS, RENAME command is used:
A. Name the file to another directory
B. Move the file to same directory on another drive
C. Change the name of the file in directory
D. None of the above

45. Which is **not true** for LAN?
A. LANs are public networks
B. LANs are designed to work in a restricted geographical area
C. LANs operate at higher speed than WANs
D. LAN and WAN are same

46. Which of the following language is not suited for the computation?
A. PASCAL B. FORTRAN
C. MACHINE D. All of these

47. Vatican library officially founded on—
A. 15 – 06 – 1475. B. 15 – 06 – 1575.
C. 30 – 05 – 1475. D. 15 – 04 – 1475.

48. Match the following : (w.r. to relation)

Column A	**Column B**
1. Librarian	(*a*) Bibliothecar
2. Dr. Ranganathan of Pakistan	(*b*) Dr. Annis Khursid
3. Official Publication of RRRLF	(*c*) Granthana
4. "Silence Please"	(*d*) General instruction

Code:	**1**	**2**	**3**	**4**
A.	*a*	*b*	*c*	*d*
B.	*d*	*c*	*b*	*a*
C.	*a*	*b*	*d*	*c*
D.	*c*	*a*	*b*	*d*

49. Match the following :

Column A	**Column B**
(*a*) Total notational sysmbols in CC-7	1. 14
(*b*) Set up of RRRLF	2. 1972
(*c*) Chairman of National Library Review Committee (1967)	3. Edward Edwards
(*d*) Father of Library Movement in U.K.	4. V.S. Jha

Code:	(*a*)	(*b*)	(*c*)	(*d*)
A.	1	2	4	3
B.	1	2	3	4
C.	4	3	2	1
D.	1	4	2	3

50. Security of Password involves :
A. Identification B. Authentication
C. Authorisation D. All of these

ANSWERS

1	2	3	4	5	6	7	8	9	10
B	C	A	D	B	A	B	B	C	C
11	**12**	**13**	**14**	**15**	**16**	**17**	**18**	**19**	**20**
A	D	A	C	D	C	C	C	A	D
21	**22**	**23**	**24**	**25**	**26**	**27**	**28**	**29**	**30**
B	D	B	A	A	D	D	C	B	C
31	**32**	**33**	**34**	**35**	**36**	**37**	**38**	**39**	**40**
B	A	A	B	B	C	D	D	C	B
41	**42**	**43**	**44**	**45**	**46**	**47**	**48**	**49**	**50**
B	B	C	C	A	B	A	A	A	D

PART—IV

1. Information technology has four components computer technology, communicaion technology, printing and publishing technology and :
   A. Documenting technology
   B. Software technology
   C. Telecommunication technology
   D. Reprography and micrography
2. UNIX is developed by :
   A. Blaise Pascal
   B. Ken Thompson and Denis Richie
   C. AT & T
   D. Stephen R. Boume
3. In computer terminology 'C' refers to :
   A. CPU
   B. Console
   C. Memory
   D. Programming Language
4. Which agency used computer first time in India?
   A. DRTC
   B. INSDOC (NISCAIR)
   C. National Library Calcutta
   D. Indian Statistical Institute, Kolkata
5. Who is the father of Computer?
   A. Blaise Pacal B. Charles Babbage
   C. John Napier D. Herman Hollerith
6. The Babbage's Analytical Engine was proposed in :
   A. 1835 AD B. 1836 AD
   C. 1832 AD D. 1830 AD
7. Which language is low level language in computer terminology?
   A. LISP B. Machine language
   C. COBOL D. BASIC
8. Popular operating system for PCs :
   A. CP/M B. UNIX
   C. MS-DOS D. All of these
9. When the power is switch on the file which automatically executed is?
   A. DOS. EXE B. SYSTEM. EXE
   C. BOOT. EXE D. AUTOEXEC. BAT
10. GUI stands for :
    A. Graphical User Interaction
    B. Graphical User Interface
    C. Graphical Universal Interface
    D. Graph User Interface
11. A LAN is owned by :
    A. Administrator B. Computer
    C. User D. All of these
12. The layer which identify destination of data?
    A. Physical layer B. MAC
    C. Serial layer D. Parallel layer
13. Password security involves :
    A. Identification B. Authentication
    C. Authorisation D. All of these
14. The Headquarter of NIC is situated at :
    A. Bangalore B. New Delhi
    C. Hyderabad D. Kolkata
15. Which of the following has funded ERNET?
    A. UNESCO B. UNDP
    C. UNICEF D. ICSU
16. The tree topology is a modified form of :
    A. Internet topology B. Bus topology
    C. Ring topology D. None
17. Internet is a :
    A. MAN
    B. Govt. Network
    C. Commercial Network only
    D. Globalisation of Network
18. SOUL is introduced by :
    A. CNIC Ltd. B. INFLIBNET
    C. NICNET D. OCLC
19. Pentium-4 is introdced by .... corporation :
    A. Computer B. Advanced computer
    C. Intel D. CNIC Ltd.
20. MPEG stands for :
    A. Motion Picture Expert Group
    B. Motion Picture Exchange Grade
    C. Motion Picture Exchange Graph
    D. Motion Picture Expert Graph
21. Internet is owned by :
    A. ARPANET
    B. National Science Foundation, USA
    C. Microsoft Ltd.
    D. Not owned by anyone

22. Who was the chairmain of NAPLIS committee appointed in October 1985?
A. P.N. Kaula
B. K.A. Issac
C. D.P. Chattopadhyaya
D. A. Neelameghan

23. National Union Catalogue of Scientific Serials in India (NUCSSI) is published by .....
A. NISCAIR B. SENDOC
C. INIS D. AGRIS

24. The first president of IASLIC was .....
A. Dr. Ranganathan B. Dr. Chattopadhyaya
C. Dr. S.L. Hora D. Shri Krishna Joshi

25. IASLIC is co-operating with .....
A. NISSAT B. UNISIST
C. INIS D. AGRIS

26. "*Journal of Librarianship*" is the publication of .....
A. ILA B. IFLA
C. ASLIB D. LA (UK)

27. The National Library launched quarterly publication. "The National Library News Letter" in the year .....
A. 1948 B. 1964
C. 1984 D. 1995

28. Lancaster's book 'Towards Paperless Information System' appeared in .....
A. 1978 B. 1987
C. 1968 D. 1957

29. "Sociometry" introduced by ....
A. Ranganathan B. Sayers
C. Jennings D. None of these

30. Which is an international storage and retrieval system for Nuclear science and Technology :
A. NUCSSI B. INTERNET
C. AGRIS D. INIS

31. "Cataloguing-in-Publication" programme was first introduced by :
A. British Library
B. National Library of India
C. Library of Congress
D. State Lenin Library

32. National Library of India uses .... to catalogue books.
A. AACR–I and II B. AACR–I
C. CCC D. AACR–II and CCC

33. The basic role of the library is to .....
A. Collect and dissemination of information
B. Collect only
C. Collect and preserve it
D. Only dissemination of information to the users

34. Who said, "Ranaganathan is to Library Science what Einstien is to Physics"?
A. Paul Otlet B. P.N. Kaula
C. C.A. Cutter D. Eugene Garfield

35. Who recommended that 6.5% of the university's budget would be a reasonable expenditure on library?
A. Ranganathan Committee
B. Radha Krishnan Commission
C. Sinha Commission
D. Kothari Commission

ANSWERS

1	2	3	4	5	6	7	8	9	10
D	B	D	D	B	A	B	A	D	B
11	12	13	14	15	16	17	18	19	20
C	B	D	D	D	C	D	B	C	A
21	22	23	24	25	26	27	28	29	30
D	C	A	C	A	A	C	A	C	D
31	32	33	34	35					
C	B	A	D	B					

GENERAL AWARENESS

NATIONAL SYMBOLS

STATE EMBLEM

State Emblem of India is an adaptation from the Sarnath Lion Capital of Ashoka. It was adopted by he Government of India on January 26, 1950. In the adapted form, only three lions are visible, the fourth being hidden from the view. The wheel (Dharma Chakra) appears in relief in the centre of the abacus with a bull on the right and a horse on the left.

The bell-shaped lotus has been omitted. The words ''Satyameva Jayate'' meaning ''Truth alone riumphs'' are inscribed below the Emblem in Devanagari script.

NATIONAL FLAG

The National Flag of India is a horizontal tricolour of leep saffron (Kesari), white and dark green in equal proportion. In the centre of the white band there is a wheel in navy blue colour. It has 24 spokes. The ratio of the length and the breadth of the flag is 3 : 2. Its lesign was adopted by the Constituent Assembly of ndia on July 22, 1947.

NATIONAL ANTHEM

Rabindranath Tagore's song 'Jana-gana-mana' was dopted by the Constituent Assembly as the National Anthem of India on January 24, 1950.

Jana-gan-mana-adhinayaka jaya he, Bharata-bhagya-vidhata
Punjab-Sindh-Gujarat-Maratha-Dravida-Utkala-Banga
Vindhya-Himachala-Yamuna-Ganga Uchhala-jaladhi-taranga.
Tava subha name jage, Tava subha asisa mange, Gahe tava jaya gatha.
Jana-gana-mangala-dayak, jaya he Bharata bhagya vidhata,
Jaya he, jaya he, jaya he, Jaya jaya jaya, jaya he.

ATIONAL SONG

Bankim Chandra Chatterji's 'Vande Mataram' which vas a source of inspiration to the people in their truggle for freedom, has been adopted as National ong. It has an equal status with the National Anthem.

Vande Mataram
Sujalam, suphalam, malayaja-shitalam,
Shasya shyamalam, Mataram
Shubhrajyotsna,pulkita yaminim,
Phulla kusumita drumadalashobhinim,
Subhasinim sumadhura—bhashinim,
Sukhadam, Varadam, Mataram.

NATIONAL CALENDAR

It is based on the Saka era with Chaitra as its first month and a normal year of 365 days. It was adopted from March 22, 1957. Dates of the national calendar have a permanent correspondence with dates of Gregorian calendar as Chaitra I falls on March 22 in a normal year and March 21 in a leap year. In official communications, both Saka and Gregorian calendar dates are written. Months of the national calendar are Chaitra, Vaishakha, Jaishtha, Ashada, Shravan, Bhadra, Ashvina, Kartika, Margashirsha, Pausha, Magha and Phalguna.

NATIONAL ANIMAL

The magnificent tiger — Panthera tigris (Linnaeus) is the national animal of India. Tiger is found in several parts of the country and is known for its grace, strength, agility and enormous power. 'Project Tiger' was launched in 1973 to check their dwindling population in India.

NATIONAL BIRD

The Indian Peacock — Pavo Christatus (Linnaeus) is the national bird of India. It is a colourful, swan-sized bird with a fan-shaped crest of feathers on its head and a long-slander neck. The male species is more colourful with blue breast and a spectacular bronze-green train of around 200 elongated feathers.

National Flower—Lotus

National Tree—Banyan

National Fruit—Mango

National Currency—Rupee '₹'

(One Rupee = 100 Paise)

National Aquatic Animal—Dolphin

BOOKS AND AUTHORS

Name of Book	Author
Ain-e-Akbari	Abul Fazal
Anand Math	Bankim Chandra Chatterjee
An Unknown Indian	Nirad C. Chaudhuri
Arthshastra	Kautilya
Coolie	Mulk Raj Anand
Das Kapital	Karl Marx
Discovery of India	Jawaharlal Nehru
Eternal India	Mrs. Indira Gandhi
Godan	Prem Chand
Gitanjali	Rabindranath Tagore
Gora	Rabindranath Tagore
Geet Govinda	Jayadeva
Harsha Charit	Bana Bhatta
Hindu View of Life	Dr. S. Radhakrishnan
India Wins Freedom	Maulana Abul Kalam Azad
Jobs of Millions	V.V. Giri
Jungle Book	Rudyard Kipling
Kamayani	Jai Shankar Prasad
Kadambari	Bana Bhatta
Life Divine	Sri Aurobindo
Last days of Netaji	G.D. Khosla
Les Miserables	Victor Hugo
Mahabharat	Veda Vyas
Macbeth	William Shakespeare
Mein Kempf	Hitler
Meghduta	Kalidas
Mother (Maa)	Maxim Gorky
Mother India	Katherine Mayo
My Experiments with Truth	Mahatma Gandhi
My Presidential Years	R. Venkataraman
Neeti Shatak	Bhartrihari
Nehru and His Vision	Dr. K.R. Narayanan
Old Man and the Sea	Ernest Hemingway
One World	Wendell Wilkie
Panchtantra	Vishnu Sharma
Paradise Lost	John Milton
Ramayana	Valmiki (in Sanskrit)
Raghuvansham	Kalidas
Rajtarangini	Kalhan
Ram Charit Manas	Tulsi Das
Abhijnan Shakuntalam	Kalidas
Satanic Verses	Salman Rushdie
Saket	Maithili Sharan Gupta
Speed Post	Shobha De
The God of Small Things	Arundhati Roy
Treasure Island	R.L. Stevenson
Twelfth Night	William Shakespeare
Train to Pakistan	Khuswant Singh
Uttara Ram Charitra	Bhava Bhuti
Vanity Fair	W.M. Thackeray
War and Peace	Leo Tolstoy
Wealth of Nations	Adam Smith
Wake up India	Annie Besant

INVENTIONS AND DISCOVERIES

Geographical Discoveries

Discovery	Discoverer
America	Columbus
Brazil	Cabral
North Pole	Robert Peary
Everest (Conquered)	Tabie Junko
Planetary Motion	Kepler
Hawaiian Islands	Captain Cook
South Pole	Amundsen
Solar System	Copernicus

Chemistry and Physics

Discovery	Discoverer
Atom Bomb	Otto Hahn
Atomic Theory	Dalton
Atomic Numbers	Moseley
Cosmic Rays	R.S. Millikan
Dynamite	Alfred Nobel
Electrons Theory	Bohr
Electricity (current)	Volta
Electric Telegraphy (Code)	S. Morse

Discovery	Discoverer
Gravitation	Newton
Gas Light	Murdock
Oxygen	J. Priestly
Photography	L. Daguerre
Printing for the blind	Louis Braille
Radium	Madame Curie
Telegraph	Samuel Morse
Television	J.L. Baird
Telephone	Graham Bell
Wireless	G. Marconi
X-rays	W.K. Roentgen
Mechanical	
Aeroplane	Wright Brothers
Bicycle	Macmillan
Computer	Charles Babbage
Dynamo	Michal Faraday
Diesel Engine	Rudolf Diesel
Engine (Railway)	Stephenson
Fountain Pen	Waterman
Gramophone	Edison
Locomotive Power of Steam	James Watt
Helicopter	Brequet
Life Boat	Henry Greathead

Discovery	Discoverer
Microscope	Z. Jansen
Printing Press	Gutenberg
Revolver	Colt
Sewing Machine	Elias Howe
Thermometer	Fahrenheit
Transistor	W. Shockley
Typewriter	Sholes
Telescope	Hans Lippershey
Tank (Military)	Swinton
Medical	
Antiseptic Surgery	Lord Joseph Lister
Bacteria	Leeuwenhock
Circulation of Blood	William Harvey
Homoeopathy (Discovered)	Hahnemann
Insulin	F. Banting
Penicillin	Alexander Flemming
Malaria Parasite	Dr. Ronald Ross
Stethoscope	Laennec
Vitamins	Funk
Anti-Rabies Treatment	Pasteur
General	
Nylon	Carouthers
Science of Geometry	Euclids

WORLD'S GEOGRAPHICAL SURNAMES

City of Sky-scrapers—New York • City of Seven Hills—Rome • City of Dreaming Spires—Oxford City of Golden Gate—San Francisco • City of Magnificent Buildings—Washington D.C. • City of Eternal Springs—Quito (S. America) • China's Sorrow—Hwang Ho • Cockpit of Europe—Belgium Dark Continent—Africa • Emerald Isle—Ireland Eternal City—Rome • Empire City—New York Forbidden City—Lhasa (Tibet) • Garden City—Chicago • Gate of Tears—Strait of Bab-el-Mandeb Gift of the Nile—Egypt • Granite City—Aberdeen (Scotland) • Hermit Kingdom—Korea • Herring Pond—Atlantic Ocean • Holy Land—Jerusalem Island Continent—Australia • Islands of Cloves—Zanzibar • Isle of Pearls—Bahrein (Persian Gulf) Key to the Mediterranean—Gibralter • Land of Lakes—Scotland • Land of Golden Fleece—Australia • Land of Maple Leaf—Canada • Land of Morning Calm—Korea • Land of Midnight Sun—Norway • Land of the Thousand Lakes—Finland • Land of the Thunderbolt—Bhutan • Land of White Elephant—Thailand • Land of Thousand Elephants—Laos • Land of Rising Sun—Japan • Loneliest Island—Tristan De Gunha (Mid-Atlantic) • Manchester of Japan—Osaka • Pillars of Hercules—Strait of Gibraltar • Pearl of the Antilles—Cuba • Playground of Europe—Switzerland • Quaker City—Philadelphia • Queen of the Adriatic—Venice • Roof of the World—The Pamirs, Central Asia • Sugar bowl of the world—Cuba • Venice of the North—Stockholm • Windy City—Chicago • Whiteman's grave—Guinea Coast of Africa • Yellow River—Huang Ho (China) • Sickman of Europe—Turkiye

CAPITALS AND CURRENCIES OF COUNTRIES

Country	*Capital*	*Currency*
Afghanistan	Kabul	Afghani
Algeria	Algiers	Dinar
Angola	Luanda	New Kwanza
Argentina	Buenos Aires	Peso
Armenia	Yeravan	Dram
Australia	Canberra	Dollar
Austria	Vienna	Euro
Azerbaijan	Baku	Monat
Bahrain	Manama	Dinar
Bangladesh	Dhaka	Taka
Barbados	Bridgetown	Dollar
Belgium	Brussels	Euro
Bhutan	Thimphu	Ngultrum
Bolivia	La paz	Boliviano
Brazil	Brasilia	Cruzeiro
Bulgaria	Sofia	Lev
Byelorussia	Minsk	Zaichik
Cambodia	Phnom-Penh	Riel
Canada	Ottawa	Dollar
Chile	Santiago	Peso
China	Beijing	Yuan
Colombia	Bogota	Peso
Congo	Brazzaville	Franc
Croatia	Zagreb	Kuna
Cuba	Havana	Peso
Cyprus	Nicosia	Euro
Czech Republic	Prague	Crown
Denmark	Copenhagen	Krone
Egypt	Cairo	Pound
Estonia	Tallinn	Kroon
Ethiopia	Addis Ababa	Birr
Fiji	Suva	Dollar
Finland	Helsinki	Euro
France	Paris	Euro
Georgia	Tbilisi	Lari
Germany	Berlin	Euro
Ghana	Accra	Cedi
Greece	Athens	Euro
Guatemala	Guatemala City	Quetzal
Hong Kong	Victoria	Dollar
Hungary	Budapest	Forints
	Reykjavik	Krona
	New Delhi	Rupee

Country	*Capital*	*Currency*
Indonesia	Jakarta	Rupiah
Iran	Teheran	Rial
Iraq	Baghdad	Dinar
Ireland	Dublin	Euro
Israel	Jerusalem	Shekel
Italy	Rome	Euro
Jamaica	Kingston	Dollar
Japan	Tokyo	Yen
Jordan	Amman	Dinar
Kazakhstan	Akmola	Tenge
Kenya	Nairobi	Shilling
Korea (S)	Seoul	Won
Korea (N)	Pyongyang	Won
Kyrgyzstan	Bishkek	Som
Kuwait	Kuwait City	Dinar
Laos	Vientiane	Kip
Latvia	Riga	Lat
Lebanon	Beirut	Pound
Libya	Tripoli	Dinar
Lithuania	Vilnius	Litas
Malaysia	Kuala Lumpur	Ringgit
Maldives	Male	Rufiyya
Mauritius	Port Louis	Rupee
Moldavia	Chisinau	Leu
Mexico	Mexico City	Peso
Morocco	Rabat	Dirham
Mozambique	Maputo	Metical
Myanmar (Burma)	Nay Pyi Taw	Kyat
Nepal	Kathmandu	Rupee
Netherlands	Amsterdam	Euro
New Zealand	Wellington	Dollar
Nigeria	Abuja	Naira
Norway	Oslo	Krone
Oman	Muscat	Rial
Pakistan	Islamabad	Rupee
Philippines	Manila	Peso
Poland	Warsaw	Zloty
Portugal	Lisbon	Euro
Qatar	Doha	Riyal
Romania	Bucharest	Leu
Russia	Moscow	Ruble
Saudi Arabia	Riyadh	Rial

Country	*Capital*	*Currency*
Slovakia	Bratislava	Euro
Spain	Madrid	Euro
Sri Lanka	Colombo	Rupee
Sudan	Khartoum	Dinar
Sweden	Stockholm	Krona
Switzerland	Berne	Swiss Francs
Syria	Damascus	Pound
South Africa	Capetown (Legislative) Pretoria (Administrative)	Rand
Tajikistan	Dushanbe	Somoni
Taiwan	Taipei	Dollar
Tanzania	Dodoma	Shilling
Thailand	Bangkok	Baht
Turkiye	Ankara	Turkish Lira
Turkmania	Ashikabad	Manat
Uganda	Kampala	Shilling
Ukraine	Kiev	Hyrvna
United Arab Emirates	Abu Dhabi	Dirham
U.K.	London	Pound Sterling
U.S.A.	Washington	Dollar
Uzbekistan	Tashkent	Som
Vietnam	Hanoi	Dong
Yemen	Sana'a	Rial/Dinar
Zimbabwe	Harare	Dollar
Congo (Democratic Republic)	Kinshasa	Franc
Zambia	Lusaka	Kwacha

INDIAN CITIES AND THEIR RIVERS

City	State	River
Agra	U.P.	Yamuna
Ahmedabad	Gujarat	Sabarmati
Alwaye	Kerala	Periyar
Kolkata	West Bengal	Hooghly
Cuttack	Odisha	Mahanadi
Delhi	Delhi	Yamuna
Haridwar	Uttarakhand	Ganga
Kanpur	Uttar Pradesh	Ganga
Ludhiana	Punjab	Sutlej
Lucknow	Uttar Pradesh	Gomati
Nasik	Maharashtra	Godavari
Patna	Bihar	Ganga
Prayagraj	U.P.	Confluence of the Ganga, Yamuna and invisible Saraswati
Srinagar	J & K	Jhelum
Surat	Gujarat	Tapti
Tiruchirapally	Tamil Nadu	Kaveri
Ujjain	Madhya Pradesh	Shipra
Vijayawada	Andhra Pradesh	Krishna
Varanasi	Uttar Pradesh	Ganga

WONDERS OF THE WORLD

Seven Wonders of the Ancient World: (1) the Pyramids of Egypt, built in approximately 2700 BC; (2) the Hanging Gardens at Babylon; (3) the temple of Artemis at Emphesus; (4) the statue of Zeus at Olympia; (5) the tomb of Mausolus at Halicarnassus, built in nearly 350 BC; (6) the Colossus of Rhodes, built in nearly 280 BC; (7) the Pharos Lighthouse at Alexandria.

Seven Wonders of the Medieval World: (1) the Colosseum of Rome; (2) the Great Wall of China; (3) the Porcelain Tower of Nanking; (4) the Mosque at St. Sophia (Constantinople); (5) Stonehenge; (6) the Catacombs of Rome; (7) the Leaning Tower of Pisa.

Seven New Wonders of the World: (1) Taj Mahal of Agra (India); (2) Pyramid at Chichen Itza (Mexico); (3) Machu Picchu (Peru); (4) Statue of Christ The Redeemer (Brazil); (5) Great Wall of China; (6) Roman Colosseum, Italy; (7) Ruins of Petra, Jordan.

STATES & UNION TERRITORIES OF INDIA (CAPITALS, PRINCIPAL LANGUAGES)

States & Union Territories	*Capitals*	*Principal Languages*
■ Andhra Pradesh	Amravati	*Telgu and Urdu*
■ Arunachal Pradesh	Itanagar	*Monpa, Adi, Nissi etc.*
■ Assam	Dispur	*Assamese and Bengali*
■ Bihar	Patna	*Hindi and Maithili*
■ Chhattishgarh	Raipur	*Hindi*
■ Goa	Panaji	*Konkani*
■ Gujarat	GandhiNagar	*Gujarati*
■ Haryana	Chandigarh	*Hindi*
■ Himachal Pradesh	Shimla	*Hindi and Pahari*
■ Jharkhand	Ranchi	*Hindi*
■ Kerala	Thiruvananthpuram	*Malyalam*
■ Karnataka	Bengluru	*Kannada*
■ Madhya Pradesh	Bhopal	*Hindi*
■ Maharashtra	Mumbai	*Marathi*
■ Meghalaya	Shillong	*Khashi, Jayantia and Garo*
■ Manipur	Imphal	*Manipuri*
■ Mizoram	Aizawl	*Mizo and English*
■ Nagaland	Kohima	*Naga, Assamese and English*
■ Odisha	Bhubaneshwar	*Odiya*
■ Punjab	Chandigarh	*Punjabi*
■ Rajasthan	Jaipur	*Hindi, Rajasthani*
■ Sikkim	Gangtok	*Sikkimese and Gorkhali*
■ Tamil Nadu	Chennai	*Tamil*
■ Tripura	Agartala	*Bengali, Tripuri*
■ Uttar Pradesh	Lucknow	*Hindi*
■ Uttarakhand	Dehradun	*Hindi*
■ West Bengal	Kolkata	*Bengali*
■ Telangana	Hyderabad	*Telgu and Urdu*
■ Jammu & Kashmir	Srinagar/Jammu	*Kashmiri, Dongri, Urdu, Dardi and Pahari*
■ Andaman and Nicobar Islands	Shri Vijaya Puram	*Hindi, Nicobarese, Bengali, Malayalam, Tamil, Telugu*
■ Chandigarh	Chandigarh	*Hindi, Punjabi, English*
■ Dadar and Nagar Haveli and Daman and Diu	Daman	*Gujarati, Hindi*
■ Delhi	Delhi	*Hindi, Punjabi*
■ Lakshadweep	Kavaratti	*Malayalam*
■ Puducherry	Puducherry	*Tamil, Telugu, Malayalam, English and French*
■ Ladakh	Leh	*Ladakhi*

HIGH COURTS IN INDIA

Name	*Territorial Jurisdiction*	*Seat*
Allahabad	Uttar Pradesh	Prayagraj (Bench at Lucknow)
Andhra Pradesh	Andhra Pradesh	Amaravati
Bombay	Maharashtra, Goa, Dadar and Nagar Haveli and Daman and Diu	Mumbai (Benches at Nagpur, Panaji, and Sambhaji Nagar)
Calcutta	West Bengal and Andaman & Nicobar Islands	Kolkata (Circuit Benches at Shri Vijaya Puram and Jalpaiguri)
Chhattisgarh	Chhattisgarh	Bilaspur
Delhi	New Delhi	NCT of Delhi
Gauhati	Assam, Nagaland, Mizoram and Arunachal Pradesh	Guwahati (Benches at Kohima, Aizawl and Itanagar)
Gujarat	Gujarat	Sola (Ahmedabad)
Himachal Pradesh	Himachal Pradesh	Shimla
Jammu & Kashmir and Ladakh	Jammu & Kashmir/Ladakh	Srinagar and Jammu
Jharkhand	Jharkhand	Ranchi
Karnataka	Karnataka	Bengaluru (Circuit Benches at Dharwar and Gulbarga)
Kerala	Kerala & Lakshadweep	Kochi
Madhya Pradesh	Madhya Pradesh	Jabalpur (Benches at Gwalior and Indore)
Madras	Tamil Nadu & Puducherry	Chennai (Bench at Madurai)
Orissa	Odisha	Cuttack
Patna	Bihar	Patna
Punjab and Haryana	Punjab, Haryana and Chandigarh	Chandigarh
Rajasthan	Rajasthan	Jodhpur (Bench at Jaipur)
Sikkim	Sikkim	Gangtok
Uttarakhand	Uttarakhand	Nainital
Tripura	Tripura	Agartala
Meghalaya	Meghalaya	Shillong
Manipur	Manipur	Imphal
Telangana	Telangana	Hyderabad

FAMOUS HILL STATIONS

Hill Station	State/UT
1. Almora, Mussoorie, Nainital	Uttarakhand
2. Cherrapunji (Shillong), Khasi Hills (Shillong)	Meghalaya
3. Ooty, Kodaikanal, Yercaud	Tamil Nadu
4. Dalhousie, Kassauli	Himachal Pradesh
5. Darjeeling	West Bengal
6. Gulmarg, Srinagar	Jammu and Kashmir
7. Mahabaleshwar	Maharashtra
8. Mt. Abu	Rajasthan
9. Pachmarhi	Madhya Pradesh

FAMOUS NATIONAL PARKS

1. Corbett National Park	Nainital, Uttarakhand
2. Dudhwa National Park	Lakhimpur Kheri, Uttar Pradesh
3. Kaziranga National Park	Jorhat, Assam
4. Kanha National Park	Jabalpur, Bhedaghat
5. Gir National Park	Rajkot, Junagarh, Gujarat
6. Guindy National Park	Guindy, Chennai, Tamil Nadu
7. Nagairhole National Park	Coorg, Karnataka
8. Bandipur National Park	Mysore, Karnataka

FAMOUS NATIONAL WILDLIFE SANCTUARIES

1. Dachigam Wildlife Sanctuary	Srinagar, Jammu and Kashmir
2. Sariska	Alwar, Rajasthan
3. Hazaribagh Wildlife Sanctuary	Hazaribagh, Jharkhand
4. Tiger Project	Sawai Madhopur, Rajasthan
5. Mudhumali Wildlife Sanctuary	Mudhumalia, Nilgiri, Tamil Nadu
6. Periyar Wildlife Sanctuary	Idukki, Kottayam, Kerala

HOLY PLACES IN INDIA

1.	Amarnath	Jammu and Kashmir
2.	Ayodhya	Uttar Pradesh
3.	Badrinath	Uttarakhand
4.	Dwarka	Gujarat
5.	Haridwar	Uttarakhand
6.	Kancheepuram	Tamil Nadu
7.	Kedarnath	Uttarakhand
8.	Mathura	Uttar Pradesh
9.	Puri	Odisha
10.	Rameswaram	Tamil Nadu
11.	Tirupati	Andhra Pradesh
12.	Ujjain	Madhya Pradesh
13.	Varanasi	Uttar Pradesh
14.	Bodh Gaya	Bihar

SPORTS

Terms Associated With Sports :

Cricket : Ashes, Bye, Bodyline, Bowling, Break, Cover-point, Creases, Chinaman, Chucker, Drive, Duck, Follow on, Googly, Hit-Wicket, Hat-trick, Leg-before-wicket, Leg break, Leg-bye, Maiden over, No ball, Night-watchman, Runner, Run-out, Stumped, Silly-point, Slip.

Football : Handball, Corner kick, Dribble, Free Kick, Hat-trick, Off-side, Penalty Kick, Try, Throw in, Wembley.

Hockey : Bully, Carry, Corner kick, Corner, Penalty stroke, Off-side, Penalty, Roll in scoop, Sticks, Sudden death, Striking circle, Short Corner, Scoop, Tie-breaker, Under-cutting, Hat-trick.

Tennis : Backhand drive, Deuce, Fault, Half-volley, Net, Let, Volley, Smash, Service.

Billiards : Break, Cannons, Cue, Pot, Jigger, Scratch, In Bauk, In, Off.

Bridge : Dummy, Finesse, Grand-slam, Little Slam, Revoke, Ruff slam, Trump, Tricks, Vulnerable.

Volley Ball : Booster, Love, Service, Volley, Smasher.

Badminton : Smash, Drop, Let.

Chess : Check, Checkmate, Gambit, State-mate.

Golf : Bogy, Caddie, Hole, Links, Stymie, Tee, Put.

Polo : Chukker, Mallet, Bunder.

Baseball : Bunting, Diamond, Pitcher, Put-out, Strike, Home.

Boxing : Knockout, Punch, Upper-cut, Jab, Hook.

FAMOUS TROPHIES

Agha Khan Cup	Hockey
Beighton Cup	Hockey
Corbillion Cup	World Table Tennis (Women)
Davis Cup	Lawn Tennis
Duleep Trophy	Cricket
Durand Cup	Football
Ezra Cup	Polo
I.F.A. Shield	Football
Irani Cup	Cricket (India)
Jayalaxmi Cup	Table Tennis (Women)
Lady Rattan Tata Trophy	Hockey (Women)
Nehru Cup	Hockey (India)
Obaidullah Cup	Hockey
Ranji Trophy	Cricket (India)
Rangaswamy Cup	Hockey (India)
Rovers Cup	Football (India)
Santosh Trophy	Football (India)
Subroto Cup	Football
Thomas Cup	Badminton
Uber Cup	Badminton (Women)
Wellington Trophy	Rowing (India)

BIGGEST, LARGEST, TALLEST OF THE WORLD

Airport, *Largest*—King Fahd International Airport, Dammon (Saudi Arabia)

Animal, *Tallest*—Giraffe (Average height 6.09 m); *Largest and Heaviest*—Blue Whale (190 tonnes)

Longest recorded Animal—Boot lace Worm (55 m); *Fastest*—Cheetah (Approximately 100 km/hr)

Bay, *Largest*—Bay of Bengal

Continent, *biggest*—Asia (31,845,872 km^2); *Smallest*—Australia Mainland (Area 76,17,930 km^2)

Desert, *Largest*—Sahara (N. Africa; maximum length 5,150 km EW; maximum width 3,200 km NS)

Dome, *Largest*—Singapore National Stadium (310 m)

Fish, *Largest fresh water*—Plabeuk (China, Laos and Thailand); *Most abundant*—Bristle mouth; *Most venomous*—Stone Fish (Indo-Pacific Waters)

Fountain, *Tallest*—King Fahd's Fountain (Jeddah, Saudi Arabia)

Gulf, *Largest*—Gulf of Mexico (1,544,000 sq. km)

Island, *Biggest*—Greenland (Kalaatdlit Nunaat-2,175,000 sq km)

Lake, *Largest*—Caspian Sea (Azerbaijan, Russia, Iran border: 37.18 lakh km^2); *Deepest*—Baikal (Siberia); *Largest (fresh water)*—Superior Lake (USA---Canada border: 82,350 km^2)

Mountain, *Highest peak*—Mt. Everest (8848 m; Nepal); *Highest range*—Himalayas, Asia (upto 4200 m); *Greatest mountain range*—Himalaya-Karakoram (96 out of 109 peaks over 7315 m are here)

Museum, *Largest*—American Museum of Natural History, New York

Ocean, *Largest and Deepest*—The Pacific (Area: 166,240,000 km^2; Depth: 10,924 m)

Platform, *Longest (rail)*—Shri Siddharoodha Swamiji Railway Station, Hubballi (Karnataka; India, 1507 m. long)

Railway Station, *Largest*—Grand Central Terminal (New York City; 19 hc)

Rivers, *Longest*—(i) Nile (6650 km) (ii) Amazon (6437 km)

Sea, *Largest*—Philippine Sea (5,695,000 sq. km)

Star, *Brightest*—Sirius A (also called Dog Star)

Temple, *Largest*—Angkor Vat (Cambodia: 402 acres)

Tunnel, *Longest (railway)*—Gotthard Base Rail Tunnel (Switzerland; 57.1 km); *Largest (road)*—Laerdal, Norway (24.51 km)

FIRST IN INDIA

Governor General of Independent India — Lord Mountbatten

Cosmonaut — Sq. Ldr. Rakesh Sharma

Field Marshal — S.H.F.J. Manekshaw

Indian Governor General of Indian Union — C. Rajagopalachari

Indian I.C.S. Officer — Satyendra Nath Tagore

Indian to swim across English Channel — Mihir Sen

Indian Women to swim across English Channel — Miss Arti Saha

Man to climb Mount Everest — Tenzing Norgay

Man to climb Mount Everest without Oxygen — Phu Dorjee

Man to climb Mount Everest twice — Nwang Gombu

Nobel Prize Winner — Rabindra Nath Tagore

President of Indian National Congress — W.C. Banerjee

President of Indian Republic — Dr. Rajendra Prasad

Talkie Film — Alam Ara (1931)

Test Tube Baby (Documented) — Indira

Viceroy of India — Lord Canning

Woman Minister of Indian Union — Rajkumari Amrit Kaur

Woman Governor — Mrs. Sarojini Naidu

Woman President of Indian National Congress — Dr. Annie Besant

Woman Prime Minister — Mrs. Indira Gandhi

Woman Speaker of a State Assembly — Mrs. Shanno Devi

Prime Minister of India — Pt. Jawaharlal Nehru

Muslim President of Indian Union — Dr. Zakir Hussain

Speaker of Lok Sabha — G.V. Mavlankar

Women to Climb Mount Everest — Bachhendri Pal

Woman Judge in Supreme Court — Mrs. Meera Sahib Fatima Biwi

Women Chief Justice of a High Court — Smt. Leela Seth

The First Indian Weightlifter to Win bronze medal in Olympics — Karnam Malleshwari (Sydney, in 2000)

Chief of Defence Staff (CDS) —General Bipin Rawat

World Chess Champion — Vishwanathan Anand

India's First Woman Merchant Navy Officer — Sonali Banerjee

The First Woman Air Vice-Marshal — P. Bandopadhyaya

The First Indian to be appointed as United Nations Civilian Police Advisor — Ms. Kiran Bedi

The First Women to be appointed Deputy Governor of Reserve Bank of India — K.J. Udeshi

The First Indian Lady to win a medal in World Athletic Championship — Anju Bobby George

The First Sikh Prime Minister of India — Dr. Manmohan Singh

IMPORTANT DAYS

15th January — Army Day
26th January — Republic Day
30th January — Leprosy Eradication Day/ Martyr's Day
28th February — National Science Day
8th march — International Women's Day
15th March — World Consumer's Day
21st March — World Disabled Day
5th April — National Marine Day
7th April — World Health Day
18th April — World Heritage Day
22nd April — International Earth Day
Ist May — Worker's Day
3rd May — International Sun Day
21st May — Anti-Terrorism Day
24th May — Commonwealth Day
31st May — World No Tobacco Day
5th June — World Environment Day
21st June — World Yoga Day
26th June — International Day against Drug Abuse
11th July — World Population Day
15th August — Independence Day
24th August — Sanskrit Day
5th September — Teacher's Day
8th September — World Literacy Day
27th September — World Tourism Day
1st October — World Elder's Day
4th October — World Animal Day
8th October — Air Force Day
10th October — National Solidarity Day
16th October — World Food Day
24th October — U.N. Day
14th November — World Diabetes Day
14th November — Children's Day
19th November — National Integration Day
26th November — Law Day
1st December — World AIDS Day
4th December — Navy Day
7th December — Flag Day
10th December — Human Rights Day

PARLIAMENTS OF IMPORTANT COUNTRIES

Afghanistan — Shora
Britain — Parliament House of Commons, House of Lords
Denmark — Folketing
The Netherlands — States General
India — Sansad
Israel — Knesset
Iran — Majlis
Ireland — Airetann
Iceland — Althing
Japan — Diet
Norway — Storting
Russia — Supreme Soviet
Spain — Cortes
Sweden — Riksdag
U.S.A. — Congress Senate
Germany — Bundestag

MINERAL RESOURCES OF THE WORLD

Mineral	Largest Producers
Iron Ore	China, Japan, Russia
Tin	China, Indonesia, Peru
Lead	China, Australia, U.S.A.
Zinc	China, Australia, Peru
Manganese	South Africa, Brazil, Australia
Aluminium	China, Russia, Canada
Petroleum	Saudi Arabia, Russia, USA
Silver	Peru, Mexico, China
Coal	China, USA, India

WORLD'S LARGEST PRODUCERS

Articles	Producers	Articles	Producers
Carpets	Iran	Cheese	USA
Cocoa	Cote d'Ivoire	Coffee	Brazil
Copper	Chile	Cotton	China
Diamonds	Russia	Jute	India
Rice	China	Rubber	Thailand
Silk	China	Steel	China
Sugar	Brazil	Tea	China
Tin	China	Wheat	China
Wool	Australia		

TEN LARGEST COUNTRIES BY AREAS

Rank by Area	Country	Area (sq. km.)
1.	Russia	17,075,400
2.	Canada	9,976,139
3.	China	9,561,000
4.	U.S.A.	9,363,123
5.	Brazil	8,511,965
6.	Australia	7,686,848
7.	India	3,287,263
8.	Argentina	2,776,889
9.	Kazakhstan	2,724,900
10.	Algeria	2,381,741

PRESIDENT OF INDIA

He is the constitutional head of the Republic but not the real executive.

Qualifications: (1) Indian citizen; (2) age not less than 35 years; (3) should have qualifications for election to Lok Sabha; (4) should not hold any office of profit; (5) should not be a Member of Parliament or State Legislature.

Election: He is elected by the elected Members of Parliament and State Legislative Assemblies in accordance with the system of proportional representation by means of single transferable vote.

Powers: He makes appointment to all the Constitutional posts. He can address either House of Parliament and send message to them. He can summon and prorogue either House of Parliament and dissolve Lok Sabha. All Bills passed by Parliament must receive his assent to become an Act. He issues Ordinance when Parliament is not in session. No money Bill can be introduced in Lok Sabha without his recommendation. He can grant pardon, reprieve or remit punishment and he can commute death sentences. He can declare national emergency, state emergency and financial emergency.

VICE-PRESIDENT OF INDIA

The Vice-President acts as the ex-officio Chairman of Rajya Sabha and acts as the President when the latter is unable to discharge his functions due to illness, absence or any other reason, or till the election of a new President when a vacancy is caused by the death, resignation or removal of the President.

The Vice-President is elected by an electoral college consisting of the members of both Houses of Parliament in accordance with the system of proportional representation by means of the single transferable vote. He must be a citizen of India, not less than 35 years of age, and should be eligible for election as a member of the Council of States.

PRIME MINISTER OF INDIA

The Prime Minister is the leader of the majority party in the Parliament and the President cannot exercise his discretion in the appointment of the Prime Minister. He stays in office till the majority of the members of Lok Sabha has confidence in him. He occupies an important posi-tion in relation to the council of Ministers. He recommends the names of the persons to be included in the Council of Ministers. He allocates portfolios among them and can ask any minister to tender resignation. He can drop a minister while reshuffling the ministry. He coordinates the administration of various departments. He is the chief link between the President and the Council. He is the leader of the majority party and so, he has a great influence on the Parliament and the party. The Prime Minister enjoys such extensive powers as have been described as the virtual ruler of the country.

THE SOLAR SYSTEM: SOME FACTS

Number of Planets: 8—Mercury, Venus, Earth, Mars, Jupiter, Saturn, Uranus and Neptune.

Largest most
Massive planet .... Jupiter
Brightest planet .... Venus
Brightest star .... Sirius
Fastest orbiting planet .... Mercury
Longest (Synodic) day .... Mercury
Planet with largest moon .... Jupiter
Greatest average density .... Jupiter
Tallest mountain .... Earth
Strongest magnetic fields .... Jupiter
Most circular orbit .... Venus
Shortest (synodic) day .... Jupiter
Hottest planet .... Venus
No moons .... Mercury, Venus
Planet with moon with most eccentric orbit .... Neptune
Lowest average density .... Saturn
Deepest Oceans .... Jupiter
Greatest amount of liquid on the surface .... Earth

THE EARTH: FACTS AND DATA

Composition of the Earth: Aluminium (0.4%), Sulphur (2.7%), Silicon (13%), Oxygen (28%), Calcium (1.2%), Nickel (2.7%), Magnesium (17%), Iron (35%)

Surface area	: 510100500 sq km
Land Surface (29.1%)	: 148950800 sq km
Ocean Surface (70.9%)	: 361149700 sq km
Type of water	: 97% salt, 3% fresh
Total area of water	: 382672000 sq km
Equatorial diameter	: 12753 km
Equatorial Circumference	: 40066 km
Polar Circumference	: 39992 km
Polar diameter	: 12710 km
Equatorial radius	: 6376 km
Polar radius	: 6335 km
Mass (estimated weight)	: 594×10^{19} metric tons
Mean distance from the Sun	: 149407000 km

Earth's orbit speed (around sun)	: 107320 kmph	Time of Rotation (on its axis)	: 23 hrs 56 min 4.09 seconds
Period of Revolution (round the sun)	: 365 days 5 hrs 48 min. 45.51 seconds	Inclination of the axis (to the plane of the ecliptic)	: 23°27'

PRINCIPAL MOUNTAIN PEAKS OF THE WORLD

	Mountains	Height in Metres	Range	Date of First Ascent
1.	Mount Everest	8,848	Himalayas	May 29, 1953
2.	K-2 (Godwin Austen)	8,611	Karakoram	July 31, 1954
3.	Kanchenjunga	8,597	Himalayas	May 25, 1955
4.	Lhotse	8,511	Himalayas	May 18, 1956
5.	Makalu I	8,481	Himalayas	May 15, 1955
6.	Dhaulagiri I	8,167	Himalayas	May 13, 1960
7.	Mansalu I	8,156	Himalayas	May 9, 1956
8.	Chollyo	8,153	Himalayas	Oct. 19, 1954
9.	Nanga Parbat	8,124	Himalayas	July 3, 1953
10.	Annapurna I	8,091	Himalayas	June 3, 1950
11.	Gasherbrum I	8,068	Karakoram	July 5, 1958
12.	Broad Peak I	8,047	Karakoram	June 9, 1957
13.	Gasherbrum II	8,034	Karakoram	July 7, 1956
14.	Shisha Pangma (Gosainthan)	8,014	Himalayas	May 2, 1964
15.	Gasherbrum III	7,952	Karakoram	Aug. 11, 1975

POPULAR NICK NAMES OF SOME FAMOUS PERSONALITIES

Andhra Kesari	T. Prakasam
Anna	C.N. Anna Durai
Bang Bandhu	Sheikh Mujibur Rehman
Bapu	Mahatma Gandhi
Bard of Avon	William Shakespeare
Chachaji	Jawaharlal Nehru
Desh Bandhu	C.R. Das
Frontier Gandhi	Khan Abdul Gaffar Khan
Fuhrer	Adolf Hitler
G.B.S.	George Bernard Shaw
Grand Old Man of India	Dadabhai Naoroji
Grand Old Man of Britain	Gladstone
Guru Dev	Rabindra Nath Tagore
Guruji	M.S. Golwalkar
Iron Man of India	Sardar Patel
Lok Nayak	Jayaprakash Narayan
Lady with the Lamp	Florence Nightingale
Lal, Bal, Pal	Lala Lajpat Rai, Bal Gangadhar Tilak, Bipin Chandra Pal
Little Corporal	Napoleon Bonaparte
Lokmanya	Bal Gangadhar Tilak
Mahamana	Pt. Madan Mohan Malaviya
Maid of Orleans	Joan of Arc
Maiden Queen	Queen Elizabeth I
Missile Man	A.P.J. Abdul Kalam
Man of Destiny	Napoleon Bonaparte
Netaji	Subhash Chandra Bose
Nightingale of India	Sarojini Naidu
Panditji	Jawaharlal Nehru
Punjab Kesari	Lala Lajpat Rai
Shastriji	Lal Bahadur Shastri
Uncle Ho	Ho Chi Minh
Wizard of the North	Walter Scott

FAMOUS INTERNATIONAL ORGANISATIONS, HEADQUARTERS

International Organisations	*Headquarters*
United Nations Organisations (U.N.O.)	New York
International Monetary Fund (I.M.F.)	Washington D.C.
World Health Organisation (W.H.O.)	Geneva
Food & Agricultural Organisation (FAO)	Rome
International Labour Organisation (ILO)	Geneva
UNESCO	Paris
International Court of Justice	The Hague
Universal Postal Union (UPU)	Berne
International Civil Aviation Organisation (ICAO)	Montreal
UNIDO	Vienna
International Atomic Energy Agency (IAEA)	Vienna
International Finance Corporation (IFC)	Washington
United Nations Development Programme (UNDP)	New York
UNICEF	New York
International Maritime Organisation (IMO)	London
World Meteorological Organisation (WMO)	Geneva
International Telecommunication Union (ITU)	Geneva
Arab League	Cairo
Commonwealth of Nations	London
World Trade Organisation (WTO)	Geneva
International Development Association (IDA)	Washington D.C.
International Bank for Reconstruction and Development (IBRD)	Washington D.C.
World Intellectual Property Organisation (WIPO)	Geneva
Organisation of Islamic Conference (OIC)	Jeddah (Saudi Arabia)
European Union	Brussels
Red Cross	Geneva
Interpol	Lyons (France)
Asian Development Bank (ADB)	Manila
North Atlantic Treaty Organisation (NATO)	Brussels
Association of South East Asian Nations (ASEAN)	Jakarta

AWARDS

NOBEL PRIZES

- These Prizes were instituted in 1901 by a Swedish scientist, Dr. Alfred Nobel; the discoverer of Dynamite.
- Six prizes are awarded annually for (*i*) Chemistry, (*ii*) Physics, (*iii*) Medicine, (*iv*) Literature, (*v*) Peace and (*vi*) Economics —started since 1969.
- The following Indians so far have been awarded these prizes: (*i*) Dr. Rabindra Nath Tagore (1913) for his "Geetanjali". (*ii*) Dr. C.V. Raman for Physics in 1930, (*iii*) Mother Teresa for Peace in 1979, (*iv*) Prof. Amartya Sen in 1998 for Economics and (*v*) Kailash Satyarthi in 2014 for Peace.
- In addition, four non-resident Indians have also been awarded the Nobel Prize. They are: (*i*) Hargobind Khurana for Medicine in 1968, (*ii*) Subramanian Chandrasekhar for Physics in 1983, (*iii*) Venkatraman Ramkrishnan for Chemistry in 2009, (*iv*) Abhijit Vinayak Banerjee for Economics in 2019.

BHARAT RATNA

- Bharat Ratna is India's highest Civilian Award. It was first awarded in 1954.
- The actual award is designed in the shape of a *peepal* leaf with Bharat Ratna inscribed in Devanagri script in the Sun Figure.
- This is India's highest civilian award. It is given for exceptional work on art, literature, science and recognition of public service of the highest order.
- The emblem, the Sun and the rim are of platinum. The inscriptions are in burnished bronze.
- Government servants are not eligible for it

ART AND CULTURE

☞ Classical Dances

Dance	*State*	*Famous Artists*
Bharat Natyam	Tamil Nadu	Yamini Krishnamurthy, Rukmini Devi Arundale, Swapna Sundari, Sonal Mansingh, Vaijanti Mala, Mrinalini Sarabhai, Chandralekha, Indrani, Ram Gopal, Bal Saraswati
Kathakali	Kerala	Gopinath, K.K. Nayar, Kunju-Kurup, T.K. Chandu
Kuchipudi	Andhra Pradesh/ Telangana	Sapna Sundari, Raja Reddy, Shobha Nayar, Radha Reddy, Vedantam Satyanarayan, Vimpanti Chinna Satyam.
Kathak	North India	Birju Maharaj, Gopi Krishna, Shambhu Maharaj, Sitara Devi, Vishnu Sharma, Durga Lal, Shobhana Narayan
Odissi	Odisha	Kelucharan Mahapatra, Indrani Rehman, Madhavi Mudgal, Pratima Bedi, Samyukta Panigrahi, Sonal Mansingh, Debudas
Manipuri	Manipur	Uday Shankar, Bipin Singh, Suryamukhi, Darohra Jhaveri

☞ Famous Folk Dances

State/UT	*Folk Dance*	*State/UT*	*Folk Dance*
Andhra Pradesh/ Telangana	Dandari, Banjara	Kerala	Mohini Attam, Padayuni
Assam	Bihu, Keli Gopal, Sataria	Madhya Pradesh	Lota Nritya, Jawara
Bihar	Chhau, Magahi, Durga dance	Maharashtra	Tamasha, Dahi Handi, Gof Deepak Dindi
W. Bengal	Kirtan, Kalatri, Asweabadh, Brita, Kalidance	Manipur	Dhol Cholam
Chhattisgarh	Saila, Karama, Bhagoria	Meghalaya	Nongakarem
Gujarat	Garba, Rasalila, Tippani, Dandia,	Nagaland	Bamboo dance
		Odisha	Chhau, Maya Shabari, Dalachai
Haryana	Damyal, Lahoor	Punjab	Gidda, Bhangra, Panihari
Himachal Pradesh	Dussehra dance, Hikat, Notio	Rajasthan	Thumar, Kathaputali, Tera Tali
Jammu & Kashmir	Dumhal	Tamil Nadu	Terukalathu, Kabalatam, Kargam, Pulivesham
		Tripura	Hazagiri
Jharkhand	Jhau, Ghumakudia, Jadur, Sarhul, Soharai, Karama, Vaima, Loojhari, Jat-Jatin, Vidayat	Uttar Pradesh	Rasalila, Nautanki, Thali, Dhurang, Jhumela, Huraka, Bol.
		Uttarakhand	Kajari, Karan
Karnataka	Yakshagan, Dolu Kunitha	Goa	Dhode Modini

MUSIC

Main Schools of Classical Music

- There are two main schools of classical music, namely, the Hindustani and the Carnatic. The Hindustani school of classical music is in vogue in north-western India, eastern India and northern parts of the South India.

Musical Instruments

- ***They are:*** Tabla, Mridangam, Pakhawaj, Chandai, Dholak, Veena, Sitar, Sarod, Gootuvadhyam, Sarangi, Flute, Nadaswaram, Shehnai, Shringi and Turahi.

FAMOUS INTERNATIONAL AIR SERVICES

Air Service	*Name of Country*	*Air Service*	*Name of Country*
Air India	India	Lufthansa Airlines	Germany
British Overseas Airways Corporation	Britain	Iraqi Airways	Iraq
		National Airlines	Iran
Trans World Airlines	America	Quantas Airlines	Australia
Russian Airlines	Russia	Hong-Kong Airlines	Hong-Kong
Japan Airlines	Japan	Egypt Airlines	Egypt
Pakistan International Airlines	Pakistan	Slovak Airlines	Slovakia
Malaysia Airlines	Malaysia	S.I.A.	Singapore
Royal Nepal Airlines	Nepal	Garuda Airways	Indonesia
Swiss Airways	Switzerland	Bangladesh Viman Sewa	Bangladesh
Air France	France	Air Lanka	Sri Lanka
Kuwait Airways	Kuwait	Elitalia Airlines	Italy
Pan American World Airways	America	Air Canada	Canada
K.L.M. Royal Airlines	The Netherlands (Holland)		

FAMOUS RELIGIONS, FOUNDERS, HOLY BOOKS & PLACES OF WORSHIP

Religion	*Founder*	*Holy Books*	*Place of Worship*
Hinduism	Hinduism has no one Founder. (This religion is based upon the religion of original Aryan Settlers)	Ramayan, Vedas, Puranas and Geeta	Temple
Sikh	Guru Nanak Dev	Guru Grantha Sahib	Gurdwara
Christianity	Jesus Christ	Bible	Church
Islam	Prophet Mohammed	Koran (Quran)	Mosque
Parsi	Zoroaster	Zend Avesta	Fire Temple
Jainism	Adinath Rishavdev	Jain Granth	Jain Temple
Buddhism	Gautam Buddha	Tripitaka	Buddha Temple
Jew	Moosa	Torah	Synagogue

INTELLIGENCE AGENCIES OF SOME PROMINENT COUNTRIES

Country	*Intelligence Agency*	*Country*	*Intelligence Agency*
India	Research & Analysis Wing (RAW), Intelligence Bureau (I.B.), Central Bureau of Investigation (C.B.I.)	Russia	K.G.B. (Komitel Gosudarstvennoy Bezopasnosty) (Committee for State Security)
Pakistan	Inter Service Intelligence (I.S.I.)	Canada	Security Intelligence Service
U.S.A.	Central Intelligence Agency, Federal Bureau of Investigation	S. Africa	Bureau of State Security
		Iran	Sabak
Britain	Military Intelligence (M.I.)-5 and 6, Special Branch, Ultra, Joint Intelligence Organisation	Iraq	Al-Mukhabarat
		Australia	Australian Security and Intelligence Organisation
Israel	Mosad	France	S.D.E.C.E.
Egypt	Mukhabarat	Spain	C.E.S.I.D.
Japan	Nicho	Cuba	D.G.I.

SOME PROMINENT RACES OF THE WORLD

Races	Country/Area	Races	Country/Area	Races	Country/Area	Races	Country/Area
Veddas	Sri Lanka	Pygmy	Congo Basin	Eskimo	Canada, Tundra Region	Bushman	Kalahari Desert
Somaid	West Siberia	Bantu	Central and South Africa	Lapps	European Tundra	Red Indian	North America
Masai	East Africa	Tartars	Siberia	Hausa	Nigeria		
Muree	New Zealand	Baddu	Arab's Desert	Kirghiz	Steppes (Russia)		
Yakoot	Russian Tundra	Semang	Malaysia				
Papuans	New Guyana						

FAMOUS STRAITS OF THE WORLD

Strait	Between	Country
Malacca Strait	Andaman Sea and South China Sea	Indonesia
Palk Strait	Mannar and Bay of Bengal	India-Sri Lanka
Magellan Strait	Pacific and South Atlantic Ocean	Chile
Dover Strait	English Channel and North Sea	England-France
Berring Strait	Berring Sea and Chukasi Sea	Alaska-Russia
Sugaroo Strait	Japan Sea and Pacific Ocean	Japan
Sunda Strait	Java and Indian Ocean	Indonesia
Gibralter Strait	Mediterranean Sea and Atlantic Ocean	Spain
Harmuj Strait	Persia and Bay of Oman	Oman-Iran
Hudson Strait	Bay of Hudson and Atlantic Ocean	Canada

FAMOUS NEWSPAPERS OF THE WORLD

Newspaper	Place of Publishing	Language
Daily News	New York (America)	English
Guardian	London (Britain)	English
Pravada	Moscow (Russia)	Russian
Al-Ahram	Cairo (Egypt)	Arabic
Merdeca	Jakarta (Indonesia)	Indonesian
Times	London (Britain)	English
People's Daily	Beijing (China)	Chinese
New Statesman	Britain	English
Daily Mirror	Britain	English

Newspaper	Place of Publishing	Language
Hindu, Hindustan, Times of India, Tribune, Statesman, Indian Express, Economic Times	India	English
Hindustan, Nav Bharat Times, Dainik Bhaskar, Dainik Jagaran, Punjab Kesari	India	Hindi

IMPORTANT BOUNDARY LINES

Boundary Line	Countries
Durand Line	Pakistan and Afghanistan
Hindenberg Line	Germany-Poland
Maginot Line	France and Germany
Mannerhein Line	Russia-Finland
Mc Mahon Line	India-China
Order Niesse Line	Germany-Poland
Radcliff Line	India-Pakistan
Seigfrid Line	Germany-France
24th Parallel	India-Pakistan

Boundary Line	Countries
17th Parallel	The line which defined the boundary between North Vietnam and South Vietnam before the two were united.
38th Parallel	North Korea and South Korea
49th Parallel	U.S.A. and Canada

SIGNALS/SIGNS AND MEANING

Signal/Sign	*Meaning*	*Signal/Sign*	*Meaning*
Red Triangle	Family Planning	White Flag	Treaty or Surrender
Red Cross	Medical Help	Yellow Flag	Vehicles with patients of contagious diseases
Red Light	Danger, 'Stop' for the movement of vehicles	Two Bones across with a Skull	Danger of electricity
Green Light	Go	Half mast flown Flag	National mourning
Olive Branch	Peace	Lotus and culture	Sign of civilization
White Pigeon or Dove	Peace	Wheel (Chakra)	Sign of Progress
Black Strip on Arm	(i) Opposition (ii) Sorrow	A blind folded woman with scale in hand	Sign of Justice
Black Flag	Opposition	Reversed flown	National calamity flag
Red Flag	(i) Danger (ii) Revolution		

NATIONAL EMBLEMS OF IMPORTANT COUNTRIES

Country	*National Emblem*	*Country*	*National Emblem*
America	Golden Rod	New Zealand	Kiwi, Fern Southern Cross
Australia	Kangaroo	Norway	Lion
Ireland	Shamrock	Nepal	Kukri
Italy	White Lily	Pakistan	Crescent
Israel	Candelabrum	Poland	Eagle
Iran	Rose	France	Lily
Canada	White Lily	Belgium	Lion
Great Britain	Rose	Bangladesh	Water Lily
Chile	Candor and Huemul	Mongolia	The Soyombo
Germany	Corn Flower	Russia	Double headed eagle
Japan	Chrysanthemum	Lebanon	Cedar Tree
Zimbabwe	Zimbabwe Bird	Sudan	Secretary Bird
Denmark	Beach	Syria	Eagle
Turkiye	Crescent and Star	India	Lioned Capital
The Netherlands	Lion		

THE CONTINENTS OF THE WORLD

Name	*Population (2021) (In million)*	*Per cent of the world's population*
Asia	4,584	59.1
Africa	1,375	17.4
Europe	747	9.8
North America	373	4.8
South America	651	8.4
Australia	41.66	0.5
Antarctica	NA	NA

COMPUTER

The computer is the system of that electronic device through which various informations are processed on the basis of a definite set of instructions called program and mathematical (numerical) and non-mathematical both types of informations are processed.

The first mechanical computer was composed or fabricated by Blaise Pascal in 1642 and it is called Pascalene. But in 1833, Charles Babbage first time conceived an automatic calculator or computer. Charles Babbage is called the father of modern computer. Herman made an electronic tabulating machine based on punch cards which operates automatically.

In 1937, first mechanical computer mark-I was fabricated by Howard Akeen. The most outstanding contribution in the development of modern computer goes to John Wan Newmaan who brought the 2nd revolution in the area of computer in 1951. He discovered EDVAC (Electronic Discrete Variable Automatic Computer) and utilised the stored program and the binary number system in the computer.

FUNCTIONS OF COMPUTER

1. Collection and composition (input) of datas;
2. Storage of datas.
3. Processing of datas.
4. Retrieval or output of the proccessed informations and datas.

UNITS OF COMPUTER

1. Input unit.
2. Central processing unit–CPU.
3. External Memory unit.
4. Output unit.

The CPU of the computer is called brain of the computer and sometimes CPU is also called Micro Processor of the computer. The data is entered through the input unit in the computer and through the central processing unit with the help of External Memory Unit datas are arranged and processed. Ultimately by the output unit these datas or informations are issued or released.

PARTS OF COMPUTER

- **Monitor :** The monitor of the computer is like a television in which the picture appears in the form of doted points on the screen and these are called pixcels.
- **Hard Disc and Floppy Disc :** The Hard Disc is the permanent disc in the computers while the Floppy Disc is the disc utilised when datas or informations are to be transferred from one computer to another.
- **Mouse :** The mouse of the computer is like the remote control of TV through which computer is directly regulated or controlled without utilising the key-board.
- **Printer :** The printer is a device which prints any documents or processed informations of the computer.

SOME HIGH LEVEL LANGUAGES

1. **FORTRAN :** This language was developed for solving the mathematical formulae very quickly and conveniently.
2. **COBOL :** This language was developed for the commerical purposes. For the processing of this language a group of sentences is selected called paragraph and all paragraphs composed are called a section, while all sections composed are called a division.
3. **BASIC :** In basic a definite part of the prescribed instruction is only inserted in the computer.
4. **ALGOL :** This was basically fabricated and designed for the complex algebraic calculations.
5. **PASCAL :** It is an amplified and modified form of ALGOL.
6. **COMAL :** This computer language is used for the students of secondary level.
7. **LOGO :** This language is used for children and kids for drawing Graphic line diagrams.
8. **PROLOG :** This language is developed in 1973 in France and this language is used for Artificial Intelligence which is capable and equivalent to the logical program.

9. **FORTH :** This language was invented by Charles Mure which is frequently used in all types of the works in the computer.

COMPUTER VIRUS

The computer virus is an electronic code which is used to abolish or erradicate the inclusive informations or programs of the computer. Some important computer viruses are Micheleanjalo, Dork Avangor, kilo, filip, Macmug, Scores, Casecade, Jeruslem, Date crime, Coloumbs crime, Internet virus, Pachcom, Pach EXE, COM-EXE, Marizuana, C-brain, bloody, Chenge Mungu and Desi etc.

COMPUTER NETWORKING

There are two types of networkings which are usually occur—Local Area Networking (LAN) and Wide Area Networking (WAN). By LAN all the computers of the same buildings are connected like the computers of university premises, computers of offices etc.

By WAN all the comptuers of a large area are connected like the computers of all the offices of a city or town etc. In India a very large computer network namely INDONET has been installing through which all the main towns and cities has to be interlinked.

COMPUTER TERMINOLOGY

- **Bit :** The bit is a unit of measurement of the electronic data. One bit is either 0 or 1 but not both. On composing 8 bits, 1 byte is formed.
- **Bug :** The Bug is the error in the computer program or system and its eradication is called Debug.
- **Byte :** Total eight bits compose a byte. Thus 8 bits = 1 byte.
- **CD-ROM :** A CD like of music CD in which data can be stored substantially called CD-ROM. In a CD with comparison to floppy extremely more datas can be stored but one problem in it is that one time recorded data can not be deleted or modified.
- **Chip :** It is a thin slice on which by a special mechanism a circuit is designed which is normally made from Silicon.
- **Memory System :** The place where computer data and program are temporarily kept is called Memory system. Usually memory is implied from RAM.
- **Modem :** The device which converts digital signals into analogue signals and vice-versa is called Modem.
- **RAM :** It is Random Access Memory (a place) where datas to be processed are kept temporarily and it is unstable memory.
- **ROM :** It is Read Only Memory and it is stable or Non-valatile memory which doesn't ended after power off.
- **Scanner :** It is a device through which graphic image is transformed to digital image and the scanners are of usually two types one desktop and another hand operating.

PROGRAMING

Computers perform phenomenal feats of calculation, but they do not do so in a complicated way. They actually carry out very simple operations, such as addition and subtraction. They achieve their fantastic computing power by carrying out these operations at incredible speed.

The programme, or set of instructions for operating the computer, is therefore written as a sequence of very simple steps. (See box below) Several computer languages have been developed for different applications, including BASIC, COBOL, FORTRAN and PASCAL. Writing programmes is very skilled and time-consuming work. But for most typical computer applications ready-written programmes are available, called "packages".

☞ **How A Programme Works**

Without a programme to tell it what to do and how to do it, a computer is unable to function. If, for example, you wanted to know how many times the word 'the' appears in this paragraph, or in the whole book, it would not be enough merely to put the text into a computer and then ask it how many times the word appears. For the computer to accomplish the calculations it has to be told what to do in simple steps. The instructions might be:

1. Scan the text until a space followed by 'T' or 't' is found.
2. If the next letter is not 'h', go back to step 1.
3. If the letter is 'h', is the next letter 'e'?
4. If not, go back to step 1. If it is, go to step 5.
5. If 'e' is followed by a space, add 1 to the total.
6. Go back to step 1.

A full computer programme for this operation would need to be broken down into even more simple steps, but a series of such programmes could enable a computer to analyse any amount of text in great detail.

DEFENCE

The Supreme Command of the Armed Forces is vested in the hands of the President of the Country. The responsibility for national defence, however, rests with the Cabinet. All important questions having a bearing on defence are decided by the Cabinet Committee on Political Affairs, which is presided over by the Prime Minister. The Defence Minister is responsible to Parliament for all matters concerning the Defence Services. All the administrative and operational control of Armed Forces are exercised by the Ministry of Defence. The three services – Army, Navy and Air Force function through their respective service headquarters headed by the chief of Staff.

COMMISSIONED RANKS IN DEFENCE SERVICES

Army	*Navy*	*Air Force*
General	Admiral	Air Chief Marshal
Lieutenant-General	Vice-Admiral	Air Marshal
Major-General	Rear-Admiral	Air Vice-Marshal
Brigadier	Commodor	Air Commodor
Colonel	Captain	Group Captain
Lieutenant-Colonel	Commander	Wing Commander
Major	Lt.Commander	Squadron Leader
Captain	Lieutenant	Flight Lieutenant
Lieutenant	Sub-Lieutenant	Flying Officer

INTERNAL SECURITY ORGANISATIONS OF INDIA

S. No	*Name of Organisation*	*Year of Creation*	*Headquarters*
1.	Assam Rifles (A.R.)	1835	Shillong
2.	Central Reserve Police Force (C.R.P.F.)	1939	New Delhi
3.	National Cadet Corps (N.C.C.)	1948	New Delhi
4.	Territorial Army	1948	In different States
5.	Indo-Tibetan Border Police	1962	New Delhi
6.	Home Guard	1962	In different States
7.	Coast Guard	1978	New Delhi
8.	Border Security Force (B.S.F.)	1965	New Delhi
9.	Central Industrial Security Force (C.I.S.F.)	1969	New Delhi
10.	National Security Guard	1984	New Delhi
11.	Police	—	In different States

COMMANDER-IN-CHIEFS OF INDIA

1. General Sir Rob Lockhart	Aug. 15, 1947 — Dec. 31, 1947
2. General Sir Roy Bucher	Jan. 1, 1948 — Jan. 14, 1949
3. General K. M. Kariappa	Jan. 15, 1949 — Jan. 14, 1953
4. General Maharaj Rajendra Sinhji	Jan. 15, 1953 — March 31, 1955

FIRST INDIAN CHIEFS OF STAFF OF INDIAN FORCES

1. General Maharaj Rajendra Sinhji (Army Staff)	April 1, 1955 — May 14, 1955
2. Vice Admiral R.D. Katari (Naval Staff)	April 22, 1958 — June 4, 1962
3. Air Marshal S. Mukherjee (Air Staff)	April 1, 1954 — Nov. 8, 1960

ARMY INSTITUTES

1. Sainik Schools upto +2 Level	33 places in India
2. Rashtriya Indian Military College (prepare for entrance to N.D.A)	Dehradun
3. National Defence Academy (three services)	Khadakwasla, Pune
4. Indian Military Academy (Army)	Dehradun
5. Officers Training Academy (3 services) Short Courses	Chennai
6. National Defence College	New Delhi
7. The College of Combat	Mhow
8. The College of Military Engineering	Kirkee
9. Military College of Telecommunication Engineering	Mhow
10. The armoured Corps Centre and School	Ahmed Nagar
11. The School Artillery	Deolali
12. The Infantry School	Mhow and Belgaum
13. College of Material Management	Jabalpur

AIR FORCE INSTITUTIONS

Air Force Academy	Hyderabad
Helicopter Training School	Hakimpet
Flying Instructors School	Tambaram, Chennai
The College of Air Warfare	Secunderabad
Air Force Administrative College	Coimbatore
Air Force Technical College	Jalahalli

DEFENCE PRODUCTION UNITS

1. Bharat Dynamites Ltd.	Hyderabad
2. Praga Tools	Hyderabad
3. Mishra Dattu Nigam	Hyderabad
4. Bharat Electronics Ltd.	Bangalore
5. Bharath Earthmovers Ltd.	Bangalore
6. Heavy Vehicles Ltd.	Avadi, Chennai
7. Garden Reach Ship Builders and Engineers Ltd.	Kolkata
8. Mazagaon Dock	Mumbai
9. Goa Shipyard	Marmugao
10. Hindustan Shipyard Ltd.	Vishakhapatnam
11. Hindustan Aeronautics Ltd.	Bangalore, Hyderabad, Nasik, Koraput, Kanpur, Lucknow

☞ Indian Army Commands

Command	HQ Location	Command	HQ Location
Eastern Command	Kolkata	Western Command	Chandigarh
Northern Command	Udhampur	Southern Command	Pune
Central Command	Lucknow	Training Command	Shimla
South-Western Command	Jaipur		

☞ Indian Air Force Commands

Command	HQ Location	Command	HQ Location
Western Air Command	New Delhi	South-Western Air Command	Gandhinagar
Central Air Command	Prayagraj	Eastern Air Command	Shillong
Southern Air Command	Thiruvananthapuram	Training Command	Bengaluru

☞ Indian Navy Commands

Command	HQ Location	Command	HQ Location
Eastern Naval Command	Vishakhapatnam	Western Naval Command	Mumbai
Southern Naval Command	Kochi		

☞ Missile and Other Weapons

Name	Class	Range
✶ Agni I	SRBM	850 km
✶ Agni II	MRBM	2500 km
✶ Agni III	IRBM	3500 km-5500 km
✶ Agni IV *or* Agni II Prime	IRBM	4000 km
✶ Agni V	ICBM	5000 km-6000 km
✶ Agni VI	ICBM	8000 km-10000 km
✶ Agni 3SL	ICBM	5200 km-11600 km
✶ Dhanush	SRBM	350 km
✶ Nirbhay	Subsonic Cruise Missile	1000 km

Name	Class	Range
✶ Brahmos	Supersonic Cruise Missile	290 km
✶ Brahmos 2	Hypersonic Cruise Missile	290 km
✶ Prithvi I	SRBM	150 km
✶ Prithvi III	SRBM	350 km
✶ Sagarika	SLBM	700 km-2200 km
✶ Shaurya	TBM	700 km-2200 km
✶ Astra	Air to Air Missile	80 km-100 km
✶ Barak-I	SRSAM	12 km
✶ Barak-8	SRSAM	90 km

☞ Chief of Defence Staff (CDS)

To bring in reform in higher defence management in the country, the post of Chief of Defence Staff (CDS) was created in the rank of a four-star General with salary and prerequisites equivalent to a Service Chief. The Chief of Defence Staff will also head the Department of Military Affairs (DMA), to be created within the Ministry of Defence and functions as its Secretary. Gen. Bipin Rawat was the first CDS of the country from January 1, 2020 to December 08, 2021. Gen. Anil Chauhan assumed the charge of the second CDS on September 30, 2022.

MULTIPLE CHOICE QUESTIONS

1. Match List-I with List-II and select the correct answer from the codes given below the lists:

List-I

(*a*) Napoleon Bonaparte
(*b*) Jean Jacques Rousseau
(*c*) Croce
(*d*) Madame Roland

List-II

1. 'A history is contemporary history'
2. 'Liberty what crimes are committed in thy name'
3. 'Man is born free but everywhere he is in chains.'
4. 'I am the Child of Revolution'

Codes :

	(*a*)	(*b*)	(*c*)	(*d*)
A.	1	2	3	4
B.	4	3	1	2
C.	3	4	2	1
D.	3	4	1	2

2. Abraham Lincon was elected the President of United States in:
A. 1862 B. 1860
C. 1875 D. 1855

3. Who was known as the 'Prince of Humanists'?
A. Francisco Petrarch B. Dante
C. Boccacio D. Erasmus

4. D-Day is the day when:
A. Germany declared war on Britain
B. US dropped the atom bomb on Hiroshima.
C. Allied Troops landed in Normandy
D. Germany surrendered to the allies

5. Whose teachings inspired the French Revolution?
A. Locke
B. Rousseau
C. Hegel
D. Plato

6. At a time when empires in Europe were crumbling before the might of Napoleon which one of the following Governor-Generals kept the British flag flying high in India?
A. Warren Hastings B. Lord Cornwallis
C. Lord Wellesley D. Lord Hastings

7. Which one of the following statements regarding Fascism in Italy is *not* true?
A. The Fascists came to power as a result of popular uprising
B. In 1926, all political parties except Mussolini's party were banned
C. The Fascists suppressed the Socialist movement
D. The Fascists were hostile to the Communists

8. The fall of Czar Nicholas-II is known as:
A. Bloody Sunday
B. Bolshevik Revolution
C. February Revolution
D. October Revolution

9. Industrial Revolution took place first in:
A. France B. Germany
C. United Kingdom D. Japan

10. The British Prime Minister at the outbreak of World War II was :
A. Churchill B. Baldwin
C. Attlee D. Chemberlain

11. The 'Great Depression' (1929) economic crisis was met by adopting the policy of
A. Stimulus B. Marshall Plan
C. New Deal D. Open Door

12. The slogan "No taxation' without representation" was raised during the:
A. American War of Independence
B. Russian Revolution
C. French Revolution
D. Indian Freedom struggle

13. In the nineteenth century the people of Europe started moving from the villages to the cities due to the impact of :
A. Epidemics
B. War
C. Industrialisation
D. Population explosion in villages

14. The important cause of the Civil War in America was:
A. Abolition of slavery
B. Quest for freedom
C. Industrialisation
D. Rebellion by the native Americans

15. Industrial Revolution could not have come about without:
A. Merchant capitalism
B. The Enclosure Movement
C. The services of the proletariat class
D. An agricultural revolution

16. Consider the following statements :
The French Revolution came about mainly due to the :
1. Extreme poverty of the people
2. Impact of the works of great writers
3. Cruelty of the rulers
4. Impact of impulsive reaction
Which of the above statements are correct?
A. 1, 2 and 4 B. 2 and 3
C. 1, 3 and 4 D. 1, 2, 3 and 4

17. Asia's oldest and largest Buddhist monastery is situated in :
A. Tawang (Arunachal Pardesh)
B. Lhasa (Tibet)
C. Trincomallee (Sri Lanka)
D. Ulan Bator (Mongolia)

18. Who was the main architect of the Russian Revolution?
A. Karl Marx B. Lenin
C. Stalin D. Tolstoy

19. V.I. Lenin is associated with :
A. Russian Revolution of 1917
B. Chinese Revolution of 1949
C. German Revolution
D. French Revolution of 1789

20. Which one of the following statements is *not* correct?
A. Voltaire believed in Natural Religion
B. Rousseau wrote *Social Contract*
C. Montesquieu authored *The Spirit of Laws*
D. Necker believed in 'General Will'

21. 6th April, 1930 is well known in the history of India because this date is associated with..........
A. Dandi March by Mahatma Gandhi
B. Quit India Movement
C. Partition of Bengal
D. Partition of India

22. Which ruler enforced the system of 'Price Control' in India?
A. Mohammad Tughlak
B. Razia Begum
C. Alauddin Khilji
D. Sher Shah Suri

23. The concept of 'Din-e-Elahi' was founded by which king?
A. Dara Shikoh B. Akbar
C. Sher Shah Suri D. Shahjahan

24. Who are supposed to be the earliest inhabitants of India? Where did they come from?
A. Aryans from Central Asia
B. Dravidians from Mediterranean
C. Negroids from Africa
D. Bhils and the Santhals from West Asia

25. The one chief characteristic of temple architecture of the Gupta Age was :
A. Absence of dome
B. Huge size
C. Beautiful carvings
D. absence of a covered courtyard for the gathering of worshippers

26. The Rigveda consists of :
A. 1000 hymns B. 2028 hymns
C. 1028 hymns D. 1038 hymns

27. The central point in Ashoka's dharma was :
A. royalty to kings
B. peace and non-violence
C. respect to elders
D. religious tolerance

28. The social evil which was conspicuously absent during ancient India was

A. *Sati*-System B. *Devadasi*-System
C. Polygamy D. *Purdah*-System

29. Which, among the following, can be accepted as a novelty introduced by Mughal emperors to their buildings?

A. Domes B. Minarets
C. Arches D. Attached gardens

30. The first ruler of India who defeated Muhammud of Ghur was :

A. Mularaja II of Gujarat
B. Prithviraja Chauhan of Delhi
C. Jayachand of Kannauj
D. Parmaldeva of Bundelkhand

31. What important event happened in India in 1911?

A. Bengal was partitioned
B. Non-Cooperation movement was launched
C. India's capital was shifted from Calcutta to Delhi
D. Mahatma Gandhi presided over the Congress session

32. The first phase of the Congress Party (1885-1905) was characterized by its efforts to secure:

A. limited independence
B. complete freedom
C. Indianization of services
D. constitutional reforms

33. The Muslim League demanded a separate homeland for the Indian Muslims openly for the first time at its annual session held in Lahore in the year :

A. 1931 A.D. B. 1936 A.D.
C. 1940 A.D. D. 1941 A.D.

34. Under whose governorship did the East India Company secure the Diwani Rights in Bengal, Bihar and Odisha from Emperor Shah Alam?

A. Lord Cornwallis
B. Lord William Bentinck
C. Lord Clive
D. Lord Wellesley

35. The Simon Commission was generally boycotted by the Indian political parties. What was the reason for this general non-cooperation?

A. the Commission aimed at dividing the people
B. it was an 'all white' Commission
C. it came after the Jallianwala Bagh carnage
D. it was an eye wash

36. Aligarh Muslim University was founded by :

A. Dr. Saifuddin Kitchlu
B. Mohammad Ali Jinnah
C. Sir Syed Ahmed Khan
D. Maulana Mohammad Ali

37. Ibn Batutah was an African traveller visiting India during the time of :

A. Alivardi Khan
B. Ala-ud-din Khalji
C. Iltutmish
D. Mohammad-bin-Tughlaq

38. The battle of Wandiawash was fought in :

A. 1726 B. 1760
C. 1818 D. 1857

39. The abolition of *Sati* by government regulation was at the time of :

A. Warren Hastings B. Lord Wellesley
C. Lord Bentinck D. Lord Ahmerst

40. Pick out the wrong combination :

A. Dilwara Temple : Mt. Abu
B. Pashupati Temple : Kathmandu
C. Padmanabh Temple : Bangalore
D. Minakshi Temple : Madurai

41. Match the following:

(a) Chanhudaro *(b)* Kalibangan
(c) Lothal *(d)* Surkotada

1. Alleged discovery of the skeleton of horse.
2. Bead making.
3. Traces of a dock and ship on seal.
4. Evidence of ploughing the fields.

The Correct code is :

	(a)	*(b)*	*(c)*	*(d)*
A.	2	4	3	1
B.	2	1	3	4
C.	1	2	3	4
D.	2	1	4	3

42. Match the Harappan settlements with the banks of rivers on which they were located :

(*a*)	Harappa	1.	Ravi
(*b*)	Mohenjodaro	2.	Indus
(*c*)	Ropar	3.	Sutlej
(*d*)	Kalibangan	4.	Ghaggar
(*e*)	Lothal	5.	Bhogava

Codes :

	(*a*)	(*b*)	(*c*)	(*d*)	(*e*)
A.	1	2	3	4	5
B.	1	2	3	5	4
C.	2	1	3	5	4
D.	2	1	4	3	5

43. The Goddess 'Kannagi' whose many temples were erected during the 'Sangam Age' was the goddess of :

A. Chastity B. Love
C. Prowess D. Wisdom

44. The Jain goal of life is to attain deliverance from the fetters of mudane existence, the way to which lies through three jewels. Which one of the following was not included among the 'three jewels' of Jainism?

A. Right faith B. Right action
C. Right knowledge D. Right conduct

45. The most striking feature of the Ashokan pillar is polish. Name the Ashokan pillar which is considered to be the most graceful of all Ashokan pillars.

A. Sarnath
B. Rampurva
C. Laurya-Nandangarh
D. Rummindei

46. Which are the correct statements?

1. The land grants, started in Satavahana period, paved the way for feudal developments in India.
2. Silk and spices were the Chief Indian export articles of Indo-Roman trade.
3. The Guptas issued the largest number of gold coins in ancient India.
4. The first memorial of a 'SATI' dated 510 A.D. is found at Eran in Madhya Pradesh.

A. 1 and 2 B. 1, 3, and 4
C. 1 and 4 D. 1, 2, 3 and 4

47. Who among the following patronised the 'Gandhara' (Indo-Greek style) School of Art?

A. Ashoka, the Great
B. Harsha Vardhana
C. Kanishka
D. Chandragupta Vikramaditya

48. The Sultanate of Delhi had five ruling dynasties. The dynasty having longest and shortest period were :

A. Ilbari and Khalji
B. Tughlaq and Khalji
C. Tughlaq and Sayyid
D. Ilbari and Lodis

49. Which one of the following events took place at the last during reign of Muhammad-bin-Tughlaq?

A. Introduction of token currency
B. Increase of land-revenue in Doab
C. Transfer of Capital from Delhi to Devagiri.
D. Conquest of Khurasan and Iraq

50. The most learned medieval Muslim ruler who was well versed in various branches of learning including astronomy, mathematics and medicine was :

A. Jalaluddin Khilji
B. Sikander Lodi
C. Ghiyasuddin Tughlaq
D. Muhammad-bin-Tughlaq

51. The 'Sufis' had 12 silsilas. They propounded the idea of Union with God through:

A. Love B. Rituals
C. Fasts D. Prayers

52. Match the following:

(*a*)	Peshwa	1.	Foreign affairs
(*b*)	Panditrao	2.	Audit and accounts
(*c*)	Amatya	3.	Providing grants to scholars
(*d*)	Sumant	4.	General supervision
		5.	Military affairs

Select the correct code :

	(*a*)	(*b*)	(*c*)	(*d*)
A.	2	3	4	5
B.	4	1	2	3
C.	4	3	2	1
D.	3	1	4	2

53. The Regulating Act of 1773 can be regarded as the first measure to :
A. assert the right of British Parliament to legislate for India
B. separate the legislature from the executive
C. separate the judiciary from the executive
D. centralise law-making

54. What was the exact constitutional status of the Indian Republic on 26th January, 1950?
A. A Democratic Republic
B. A Sovereign, Democratic Republic
C. A Sovereign, Secular, Democratic Republic
D. A Sovereign, Socialist, Secular, Democratic Republic

55. When the British obtained the grant of Diwani of Bengal, Bihar and Odisha they acquired the right to :
A. maintain law and order in these territories
B. administer civil justice and collect revenue in these territories
C. collect revenue and establish revenue administration in these territories
D. militarily defend these territories

56. Which of the following were responsible for the growth of nationalism in India during the British rule?
1. Economic exploitation of India.
2. Impact of western education.
3. Role of the Press.
Select the correct answer using the codes given below :
Codes:
A. 1, 2 and 3 B. 1 and 2
C. 2 and 3 D. 1 and 3

57. Which one of the following nationalist leaders has been described as being radical in politics but conservative on social issues?
A. G.K. Gokhale
B. B.G. Tilak
C. Lala Lajpat Rai
D. Madan Mohan Malviya

58. Provincial Autonomy in British India was envisaged by the :
A. Act of 1909 B. Act of 1919
C. Act of 1935 D. Act of 1947

59. Dyarchy means :
A. double government
B. a government in which the centre is very powerful
C. a government based on division of power between centre and provinces
D. None of the above

60. The Indian National Congress observed 'Independence Day' for the first time on 26th January in :
A. 1920 B. 1925
C. 1930 D. 1947

61. ....is situated near the banks of Sabarmati River
A. Bhavnagar B. Aurangabad
C. Ahmedabad D. Rajkot

62. Sericulture is:
A. science of the various kinds of serum
B. artificial rearing of fish
C. art of silkworm breeding
D. study of various cultures of a community

63. The most abundant constituents of earth's crust are:
A. Igneous rocks
B. Sedimentary rocks
C. Metamorphic rocks
D. Granite

64. Indian Standard Time is based on:
A. 80°E longitude B. 82½°E longitude
C. 110°E longitude D. 25°E longitude

65. Tides in the oceans are caused by :
A. Gravitational pull of the moon on the earth's surface including sea water
B. Gravitational pull of the sun on the earth's surface only and not on the sea water
C. Gravitational pull of the moon and the sun on the earth's surface including the sea water
D. None of these

66. Nagarjunasagar Project is situated on the river:
A. Tungabhadra
B. Cauvery
C. Krishna
D. Godavari

67. The difference between the Indian Standard Time and the Greenwich Mean Time is:
A. – 3½ hours B. + 3½ hours
C. – 5½ hours D. + 5½ hours

68. Which of the following dams is not on Narmada river?
A. Indira-Sagar Project
B. Maheshwar Hydel Power Project
C. Jobat Project
D. Koyna Power Project

69. Which of the following statements is **not true** about the availability of water on the earth, the crisis for which is going to increase in the years to come?
A. About 97.5 per cent of the total volume of water available on the earth is salty
B. 80 per cent of the water available to us for use comes in bursts as monsoons
C. About 2.5 per cent of the total water available on the earth is polluted water and cannot be used for human activities
D. Possibility is that some big glaciers will melt in the coming ten-fifteen years and sea level will rise by 3-4 metres all over the earth

70. Which of the following is **not** a cash crop?
A. Jute B. Paddy
C. Cashewnut D. Sugarcane

71. Through which States does Cauvery River flow?
A. Gujarat, M.P., Tamil Nadu
B. Karnataka, Kerala, Tamil Nadu
C. Karnataka, Kerala, Andhra Pradesh
D. M.P., Maharashtra, Tamil Nadu

72. Indian Standard Time is the local time of 82½ºE which passes through :
A. Guntur B. Delhi
C. Allahabad D. Kolkata

73. The 17th parallel defines the boundary between:
A. North and South Korea
B. USA and Canada
C. North and South Vietnam
D. China and Russia

74. During the period of south-west monsoon, Tamil Nadu remains dry because:
A. the winds do not reach this area
B. there are no mountains in this area
C. it lies in the rain shadow area
D. the temperature is too high to let the winds cool down

75. Which country does top in producing cocoa?
A. Cote d'Ivoire B. Brazil
C. Croatia D. Nigeria

76. The biggest reserves of thorium are in :
A. India B. China
C. The Soviet Union D. U.S.A.

77. The Girnar Hills are situated in which of the following states?
A. Gujarat B. Karnataka
C. Madhya Pradesh D. Maharashtra

78. During December 22nd the sun is vertically over:
A. Tropic of Cancer
B. Tropic of Capricorn
C. The Equator
D. None of the above

79. Photosphere is described as the :
A. Lower layer of atmosphere
B. Visible surface of the sun from which radiation emanates
C. Wavelength of solar spectrum
D. None of the above

80. Broadly, there are three layers of the earth of the crust, the mantle and the core. The crust forms what percentage of the volume of the earth?
A. 0.5% B. 2.5%
C. 7.5% D. 12.5%

81. The grassland of Argentina is known as :
A. Pampas B. Campos
C. Savanna D. None of the above

82. Different seasons are formed because :
A. Sun is moving around the earth
B. of revolution of the earth around the Sun on its orbit
C. of rotation of the earth around its axis
D. All of the above

83. Eskers and Drumlins are features formed by:
A. underground water
B. running water
C. the action of wind
D. glacial action

84. Match List-I and List-II and select the correct answer using the codes given below the Lists :

List-I *(Rivers)*	**List-II** *(Towns)*
(*a*) Ghaghara	1. Lucknow
(*b*) Brahmaputra	2. Hoshangabad
(*c*) Narmada	3. Ahmedabad
(*d*) Sabarmati	4. Guwahati
	5. Ayodhya

	(*a*)	(*b*)	(*c*)	(*d*)
A.	4	5	1	2
B.	5	4	2	3
C.	5	4	3	1
D.	3	5	2	1

85. Which of the statements as regards the consequences of the movement of the earth is not correct?
A. Revolution of the earth is the cause of the change of seasons.
B. Rotation of the earth is the cause of days and nights.
C. Rotation of the earth causes variation in the duration of days and nights.
D. Rotation of the earth effects the movement of winds and ocean currents.

86. The world is divided into :
A. 12 time zones
B. 20 time zones
C. 24 time zones
D. 36 time zones

87. The 'Kiel' canal links the :
A. Pacific and Atlantic Oceans
B. Mediterranean Sea and Red Sea
C. Mediterranean Sea and Black Sea
D. North Sea and Baltic Sea

88. Match the following :

List-I	**List-II**
(*a*) Himadri	1. Outer Himalayas
(*b*) Shivalik	2. Inner Himalayas
(*c*) Himanchal	3. Middle Himalayas
(*d*) Sahyadri	4. Western Ghats

Codes:

	(*a*)	(*b*)	(*c*)	(*d*)
A.	1	2	3	4
B.	4	2	3	1
C.	2	1	3	4
D.	1	2	3	4

89. The term 'Regur' refers to:
A. Laterite soils
B. Black Cotton soils
C. Red Soils
D. Deltaic Alluvial Soils

90. Location of sugar industry in India is shifting from north to south because of:
A. cheap labour
B. expanding regional market
C. cheap and abundant supply of power
D. high yield and high sugar content in sugarcane

91. Consider the following statements :
1. Ozone is found mostly in the Stratosphere.
2. Ozone layer lies 55-75 km above the surface of the earth.
3. Ozone absorbs ultraviolet radiation from the Sun.
4. Ozone layer has no significance for life on the earth.

Which of the above statements are correct?
A. 1 and 3 B. 2 and 4
C. 2 and 3 D. 1 and 4

92. Match List-I with List-II and select the correct answer using the codes given below the Lists :

List-I *(Crops)*	**List-II** *(Producer)*
(*a*) Banana	1. Brazil
(*b*) Cocoa	2. Cote d'Ivoire
(*c*) Coffee	3. India
(*d*) Tea	4. China

Codes :

	(*a*)	(*b*)	(*c*)	(*d*)
A.	2	3	1	4
B.	3	2	1	4
C.	3	2	4	1
D.	2	3	4	1

93. Darjeeling and Dharamsala would be the right places to visit if one wanted to get a clear view respectively of :
A. Kanchanjunga and Dhauladhar ranges
B. Nandadevi and Dhauladhar ranges
C. Kanchanjunga and Nandadevi ranges
D. Nandadevi and Nanga Parvat

94. Atmosphere exists because:
A. The Gravitational force of the Earth
B. Revolution of the Earth
C. Rotation of the Earth
D. Weight of the gases of atmosphere

95. Victoria lake is located in the continent:
A. Africa
B. Asia
C. North America
D. South America

96. The famous Lagoon Lake of India is :
A. Dal Lake B. Chilka Lake
C. Pulicat Lake D. Mansarover

97. Where are most of the earth's active volcanoes concentrated?
A. Indian Ocean B. Pacific Ocean
C. Aral Sea D. Atlantic Ocean

98. Through which of the following states does the river Chambal flow?
A. U.P., M.P., Rajasthan
B. M.P., Gujarat, U.P.
C. Rajasthan, M.P., Bihar
D. Gujarat, M.P., U.P.

99. Which country is called the sugar bowl of the world?
A. Cuba B. India
C. Argentina D. USA

100. The area covered by forest in India is about:
A. 46% B. 33%
C. 23% D. 21.76%

101. A closed economy is the one which :
A. does not permit emigration or immigration
B. permits emigration but no immigration
C. engages in no foreign trade
D. engages in no foreign and domestic trade or transit

102. In a developed economy the major share of employment originates in the :
A. primary sector B. tertiary sector
C. secondary sector D. any of the above

103. The Economic and Social Commission for Asia and Pacific (ESCAP) is located at :
A. Bangkok B. Kuala Lumpur
C. Manila D. Singapore

104. Commercial vehicles are not produced by which of the following companies in India?
A. TELCO B. Ashok Leyland
C. DCM Daewoo D. Birla Yamaha

105. In India, the Public Sector is most dominant in:
A. transport
B. steel production
C. commercial banking
D. organised term-lending financial institutions

106. The main argument advanced in favour of small scale and cottage industries in India is that:
A. cost of production is low
B. they require small capital investment
C. they advance the goal of equitable distribution of wealth
D. they generate a large volume of employment

107. The most serious economic problems of India are:
A. Poverty and unemployment
B. Stagnation, not poverty
C. Unemployment, not poverty
D. Underdevelopment, not poverty

108. Which of the following is not one of the three central problems of an economy?
A. What to produce
B. How to produce
C. When to produce
D. For whom to produce

109. If saving exceeds investment, the national income will:
A. fall B. rise
C. fluctuate D. remain constant

110. In which of the following industries in India are the maximum number of workers employed?
A. Sugar B. Jute
C. Textiles D. Iron and Steel

111. Terrace Cultivation is practiced mostly:
A. in urban areas
B. on slopes of mountains
C. on tops of hills
D. in undulating tracts

112. Which of the following is a Selective Credit Control method?
A. Bank Rate
B. RBI directives
C. Cash Reserve Ratio
D. Open market operations

113. Which of the following taxes is not shared by the Central Government with the States?
A. Union excise duties
B. Customs duty
C. Income tax
D. Estate duty

114. ICICI is the name of a:
A. Financial Institution
B. Chemical Industry
C. Cotton Industry
D. Chamber of Commerce and Industry

115. Structural Unemployment arises due to
A. Deflationary conditions
B. Heavy industry bias
C. Shortage of raw material
D. Inadequate productive capacity

116. Which Commission replaced the Planning Commission in 2015?
A. NIYAM Aayog
B. NAGRIK Aayog
C. NITI Aayog
D. Jan Aayog

117. The largest public sector bank in India is:
A. Central Bank of India
B. Punjab National Bank
C. State Bank of India
D. Indian Overseas Bank

118. Which of the following statements best explains the term contraband goods?
A. Goods produced only for exports
B. Goods produced in joint sector only
C. Goods for the trading of which licence is not required
D. Goods that are forbidden, from export, import or even possession, by law

119. Price in the market is fixed by:
A. Stock exchange rates
B. The demand and supply ruling in the market at a particular time
C. The Finance Minister
D. None of the above

120. Devaluation of currency helps to promote:
A. National Income
B. Savings
C. Imports at lower cost
D. Exports

121. Balanced economic growth can be achieved only if:
A. All the sectors of economy grow at the same rate
B. Population growth is arrested
C. All the inter dependent sectors grow in harmony
D. Basic and heavy industries are assigned highest priority

122. P.V. Sindhu is associated with which of the following sports?
A. Badminton
B. Weightlifting
C. Swimming
D. Tennis

123. 'MODVAT' stands for:
A. Modified Value Added Tax
B. Deduction of cost of inputs from the value of output
C. Reduction in import duties
D. Imposition of tax on professions

124. Who among the following is the first to receive 'Dada Saheb Phalke' award?
A. Shivaji Ganeson B. Devika Rani
C. Dr. Raj Kumar D. None of the above

125. The term 'devaluation' means:
A. Reducing the value of a currency in terms of another currency
B. Increasing the value of a currency
C. Revising the value of a currency
D. None of the above

126. Per capita net availability of pulses has shown a tendency of:
A. Increase over time
B. Decrease over time
C. Constant over time
D. First increase then decrease

127. National Income is the same as:
A. Net national product at market price
B. Net domestic product at market price
C. Net national product at factor cost
D. Net domestic product at factor cost

128. Which one of the following is not an example of indirect tax?
A. Sales tax B. Excise duty
C. Customs duty D. Expenditure tax

129. The major aim of devaluation is to:
A. encourage imports
B. encourage exports
C. encourage both exports and imports
D. discourage both exports and imports

130. Structural unemployment arises due to:
A. deflationary conditions
B. heavy industry bias
C. shortage of raw materials
D. inadequate productive capacity

131. When was the Family Planning Programme officially started in India?
A. 1950 B. 1952
C. 1956 D. 1962

132. When was the Reserve Bank of India nationalised?
A. 1947 B. 1949
C. 1950 D. 1951

133. Which of the following is *not* a feature of the Indian economy?
A. High rate of population growth
B. Disguised unemployment
C. Lowest rate of adult literacy
D. High rate of exports

134. The 'Relative Deprivation' approach for measuring poverty has been adopted by:
A. developing countries
B. developed countries
C. under-developed countries
D. None of the above

135. One of the main factors that led to rapid expansion of Indian exports is:
A. Imposition of import duties
B. Liberalisation of the economy
C. Recession in other countries
D. Diversification of exports

136. Sustainable economic development means an increase in the rate of growth of real:
A. total and per capita product
B. total and per capita product and level of literacy rate
C. total and per capita product and life expectancy at birth
D. total and per capita product, taking into account the cost of degradation of the quality of environment in this process

137. Functional unemployment occurs when:
A. unemployed have no qualification for job
B. people frequently change their job
C. people were thrown out from job due to recession
D. None of these

138. Which among the following does **not** have a 'free trade zone'?
A. Kandla B. Mumbai
C. Visakhapatnam D. Thiruvanantpuram

139. Sun Belt of USA is important for which one of the following industries?
A. Cotton textile
B. Petrochemicals
C. Hi-tech electronics
D. Food Processing

140. Commercial banking system in India is
A. unit banking B. branch banking
C. mixed banking D. None of the above

141. Who gives recognition to political parties in India?
A. Parliament

B. President
C. Supreme Court
D. Election Commission

142. The Quorum of the Legislative Council is :
A. one-fourth of its total membership
B. one-third of its membership
C. one-tenth of its membership
D. 25

143. The Indian Constitution is:
A. federal
B. unitary
C. a happy mixture of the federal and unitary
D. federal in normal times and unitary in times of emergency

144. Universal adult franchise implies a right to vote to all:
A. adult residents of the State
B. adult male citizens of the State
C. residents of the State
D. adult citizens of the State

145. When a resolution prefering a charge against the President has been passed by a specified majority in the House, it is sent to the other House for investigation. If, as a result of such an investigation, a resolution is passed through a specified majority by the other House, declaring that the charge has been sustained, the President shall leave his office. The specified special majority must not be less than :
A. two-third of the members present and voting
B. one-third of the members present and voting
C. three-fourth of the members present and voting and two-third of the total membership
D. two-third of the total membership

146. Which one of the following judicial powers of the President of India has been *wrongly* listed?
A. he appoints the Chief Justice and other judges of the Supreme Court
B. he can remove the judges of the Supreme Court on grounds of misconduct
C. he can consult the Supreme Court on any question of law or fact which is of public importance
D. he can grant pardon, reprieves and respites to persons punished under Union Law

147. The Vice-president of India can be removed from his office before the expiry of his term if :
A. the Rajya Sabha passes a resolution by a majority of its members and the Lok Sabha agrees with the resolution
B. if the Supreme Court of India recommends his removal
C. the President so desires
D. None of the above

148. The Chief Justice of a High Court in India is appointed by the :
A. Governor of the State
B. Prime Minister of India
C. Chief Justice of the Supreme Court
D. President of India

149. Which of the following statements is constitutionally not true about the passing of the Union Budgets, Railway Budgets and Finance Bill in India?
1. Under the law, Finance Bill should be adopted by both the Houses of the Parliament within 45 days of its introduction.
2. If the Finance Bill is not adopted within specified period, the government loses its authority to levy the taxes proposed in the budgets.
3. In the absence of full budget, a vote-on-account gives the power to the government to spend.
4. Government cannot raise revenues without a proper approval of the Finance Bill

A. Only 2 B. Only 3
C. Only 4 D. Only 1, 2 and 3

150. Normally, on whose advice the President's Rule is imposed in a State?
A. Chief Minister
B. Legislative Assembly
C. Governor
D. Chief Justice of High Court

151. Which Article of the Indian Constitution deals with Amendment procedure?
A. Article 368 B. Article 358
C. Article 367 D. All of these

152. Government is the agency through which the will of :
A. the state is expressed
B. the people is expressed
C. the head of the state is expressed
D. the majority is expressed

153. In a unitary system of government :
A. The centre is all powerful
B. The centre is weaker than the states
C. The centre and states stand at par
D. The states and centre are supreme in their respective spheres

154. In Cabinet System of Government the real executive authority rests with :
A. The Council of Ministers
B. The Prime Minister
C. The Constitution
D. The Parliament

155. The Head of the State under a parliamentary government:
A. is an elected representative
B. is a hereditary person
C. is a nominated person
D. may be any one of the above

156. In the event of a ministerial proposal being defeated on the floor of the legislature, under the parliamentary system :
A. the government waits for a general no-confidence motion
B. the minister concerned is taken to task by the Prime Minister
C. the minister is forced to resign
D. the whole Council of Ministers resign

157. The "due process of law" is an essential characteristic of the judicial system of:
A. UK B. France
C. USA D. India

158. Under the Constitution it is :
A. obligatory for the President to accept the advice of the Council of Ministers but is not obliged to follow it
B. obligatory for the President to accept the advice of the Council of Ministers
C. not obligatory for the President to seek or accept the advice of the Council of Ministers
D. obligatory for the President to seek the advice of the Council of Ministers if his own party is in power

159. Which one of the following statements is correct?
A. the Presiding Officer of Rajya Sabha is elected every year
B. the Presiding Officer of Rajya Sabha is elected for a term of two years at a time
C. the Presiding Officer of Rajya Sabha is elected for a term of six years
D. the Vice-President of India is the ex-officio Presiding Officer of Rajya Sabha

160. The introduction of "no confidence" motion in the Lok Sabha requires the support of at least:
A. 50 members B. 70 members
C. 60 members D. 80 members

161. The High Court comes under :
A. State List B. Union List
C. Concurrent List D. None of the above

162. Which one of the following has been wrongly listed as a Fundamental Duty of the Indian citizens?
A. to develop scientific temper, humanism and spirit of inquiry and reform
B. to work for raising the prestige of the country in the international sphere
C. to protect and improve the natural environment
D. to strive towards excellence in all spheres of individual and collective activity

163. Which one of the following is not a Fundamental Duty as outlined in Article 51A of the Constitution?
A. to abide by the Constitution and respect its ideals
B. to defend the country and render national service when called upon to do so

C. to work for the moral upliftment of the weaker sections of society
D. to preserve the rich heritage

164. The main characteristics of the Directive Principles of State Policy given in the Indian Constitution are :
A. not enforceable by any court
B. fundamental in the governance of the country
C. 'Like instruments, instructions, political manifesto and a code of moral precepts which have to guide governors of the country'
D. no law can be passed, which is opposed to these principles

165. Of the following which are true?
A. In a State, the Legislative Council is dominant with regard to non-financial bills and the Legislative Assembly with regard to financial (money) bills
B. Vidhan Parishad can virtually block legisla-tion even if the same is passed by the Vidhan Sabha
C. In case of a tie between the two Houses, the Governor is duty-bound to call a joint session of the two Houses to have the issue settled on a majority verdict
D. If a Bill is twice approved by the Vidhan Sabha, it becomes law even if rejected by the Vidhan Parishad

166. Which one of the following types of emergency can be declared by the President?
A. Emergency due to threat of war and external aggresion
B. Emergency due to break-down of constitu-tional machinery in a State
C. Financial emergency on account of threat to the financial credit of India
D. all the three emergencies

167. The chairman of which of the following parliamentary committees is invariably from the members of ruling party?
A. Committee on public undertakings
B. Public accounts committee
C. Estimates committee
D. Committee on delegated legislation

168. Which of the following is not a formally prescribed devic‿ available to the members of parliament?
A. Question hour
B. Zero hour
C. Half-an-hour discussion
D. Short duration discussion

169. Which of the following is not a tool of executive control over public administration?
A. Power of appointment and removal
B. Line agencies
C. Appeal to public opinion
D. Civil services code

170. If the Speaker of the State Legislative Assembly decides to resign, he should submit his resignation to the:
A. Judges of the High Court
B. Deputy Speaker
C. Chief Minister
D. Finance Minister

171. Who was the first Home Minister of Independent India?
A. Rajendra Prasad
B. Jawahar Lal Nehru
C. B.R. Ambedkar
D. Sardar Vallabh Bhai Patel

172. India is a Federal State because of:
A. dual judiciary
B. dual citizenship prevalent here
C. share of power between the Centre and the States
D. rigid Constitution

173. Residuary Subjects are those subjects which are:
A. contained in the State list
B. contained in the Union list
C. contained in the Concurrent list
D. not covered by any of the three lists

174. Which of the following writs can be issued, by the Supreme Court, to enforce Fundamental Rights?
A. Writ of Habeas Corpus
B. Writ of Mandamus
C. Writ of Quo Warranto
D. All of these

175. When the offices of both the President and the Vice-President of India are vacant, who will discharge their functions?
A. Prime Minister
B. Home Minister
C. Chief Justice of India
D. The Speaker

176. The Supreme Court tenders advice to the President of India on a matter of law or fact:
A. on its own
B. only when such advice is sought
C. only if the matter relates to some basic issue
D. only if the issue poses a threat to the unity and integrity of the country

177. Six months shall **not** intervene between two sessions of the Indian Parliament because :
A. it is the customary practice
B. it is the British convention followed in India
C. it is an obligation under the Constitution of India
D. None of the above

178. The States of the Indian Union can be recognised or their boundaries altered by:
A. the Union Parliament by a simple majority in the ordinary process of legislation
B. two-thirds majority of both the Houses of Parliament
C. two-thirds majority of both the Houses of Parliament and the consent of the legislatures of concerned States
D. an executive order of the Union government with the consent of the concerned State governments

179. The Basic Feature theory of the Constitution of India was propounded by the Supreme Court in the case of :
A. Minerva Mills Vs. Union of India
B. Golaknath Vs. State of Punjab
C. Maneka Gandhi Vs. Union of India
D. Keshavananda Vs. State of Kerala

180. Which one of the following writs is issued by a court in case of illegal detention of a person?
A. Habeas corpus B. Mandamus
C. Certiorari D. Quo-warranto

181. Name the instrument with the help of which a sailor in a submarine can see the objects on the surface of the sea.
A. Telescope B. Periscope
C. Gycroscope D. Stereoscope

182. 'HEMOPHILLIA' is the disease of ....
A. liver B. blood
C. brain D. bones

183. Vitamin A is abundantly found in ....
A. Brinjal B. Tomato
C. Carrot D. Cabbage

184. .... is not soluble in water.
A. Vitamin A B. Vitamin B
C. Vitamin C D. None of these

185. The blood vessels with the smallest diameter are called ....
A. capillaries B. arterioles
C. venules D. lymphatics

186. Out of the following .... has the greatest elasticity.
A. steel B. rubber
C. aluminium D. annealed copper

187. Cooking gas is a mixture of which of the following two gases?
A. Carbon Dioxide and Oxygen
B. Butane and Propane
C. Carbon Monoxide and Carbon Dioxide
D. Methane and Ethylene

188. The substance most commonly used as a food preservative is:
A. sodium carbonate B. tartaric acid
C. acetic acid D. benzoic acid

189. Normally, the substances that fight against diseases in human systems are known as:
A. dioxyribonucleic acids
B. carbohydrates
C. enzymes
D. antibodies

190. The SI unit of temperature is ....
A. Kelvin B. Celsius
C. Fahrenheit D. None of the above

191. One of the common fungal diseases of man is :
A. plague B. ringworm
C. cholera D. typhoid

192. A clear sky is blue because:
A. red light is scattered more than blue
B. ultraviolet light has been absorbed
C. blue light is scattered more than red
D. blue light has been absorbed

193. Jenner introduced the method of making people immune to :
A. small pox B. rabies
C. cholera D. polio

194. The largest cell in the human body is :
A. Nerve cell B. Live cell
C. Muscle cell D. Kidney cell

195. What is the device that steps up or steps down the voltage?
A. Dynamo B. Conductor
C. Inductor D. Transformer

196. The protein deficiency disease is known as :
A. Kwashiorker B. Cirrhosis
C. Eczema D. Clycoses

197. Iron deficiency causes :
A. rickets B. anaemia
C. cirrhosis D. goitre

198. Blood group of an individual is controlled by :
A. Haemoglobin B. Shape of RBC
C. Shape of WBC D. Genes

199. In a normal man the amount of blood pumped out by the heart per minute is about :
A. 1 litre B. 3 litres
C. 4 litres D. 5 litres

200. Red/green colour blindness in man is known as :
A. Protanopia
B. Deutetanopia
C. Both A and B above
D. Marfan's syndrome

201. The blue colour of the water in the sea is due to :
A. Reflection of the blue light by the impurities in sea water
B. Reflection of the blue sky by sea water and scattering of blue light by water molecules
C. Absorption of other colours by water molecules
D. None of the above

202. The image formed on the retina of the eye is:
A. upright and real
B. larger than the object
C. small and inverted
D. enlarged and real

203. Unit of loudness of sound is:
A. bel B. decibel
C. phon D. none of these

204. Oil rises up the wick in a lamp :
A. because oil is volatile
B. due to the capillary action phenomenon
C. due to the surface tension phenomenon
D. because oil is very light

205. The 'stones' formed in human kidney consist mostly of :
A. calcium oxalate
B. sodium acetate
C. magnesium sulphate
D. calcium

206. We hear the sound later, while the light is seen earlier:
A. because light's speed is more than that of sound
B. because lights travel in a straight direction while sound in a zigzag direction
C. because sound's frequency is lower than light
D. All of the above

207. Which part of an eye is transplanted?
A. Cornea B. Retina
C. Iris D. Sciera

208. The Universal donor group of blood is:
A. O B. A
C. B D. AB

209. The green colour of the leaf is due to :
A. Presence of Chloroplast
B. Presence of Chromium
C. Presence of Nicoplast
D. Presence of excess of oxygen

210. Voice of a child is more shrill than that of an elderly person because:
A. the pitch of the child's voice is higher than that of the person
B. the pitch is lower
C. the child is more energetic
D. None of the above

ANSWERS

1 B	2 C	3 D	4 C	5 B	6 C	7 A	8 C	9 C	10 D
11 C	12 A	13 C	14 A	15 A	16 D	17 A	18 B	19 A	20 D
21 A	22 C	23 B	24 C	25 D	26 C	27 B	28 D	29 D	30 B
31 C	32 D	33 C	34 C	35 B	36 C	37 D	38 B	39 C	40 C
41 A	42 A	43 A	44 B	45 C	46 D	47 C	48 B	49 B	50 D
51 A	52 C	53 A	54 B	55 B	56 A	57 B	58 C	59 A	60 C
61 C	62 C	63 B	64 B	65 C	66 C	67 D	68 D	69 D	70 B
71 B	72 C	73 C	74 C	75 A	76 A	77 A	78 B	79 B	80 A
81 A	82 B	83 D	84 B	85 C	86 C	87 D	88 C	89 B	90 D
91 A	92 B	93 A	94 A	95 A	96 B	97 B	98 A	99 A	100 D
101 C	102 B	103 A	104 D	105 D	106 D	107 A	108 C	109 D	110 C
111 B	112 B	113 B	114 A	115 D	116 C	117 C	118 D	119 B	120 D
121 C	122 A	123 A	124 B	125 A	126 D	127 C	128 D	129 B	130 D
131 B	132 B	133 D	134 A	135 B	136 D	137 B	138 D	139 D	140 C
141 D	142 C	143 D	144 D	145 D	146 B	147 A	148 D	149 C	150 C
151 A	152 B	153 A	154 A	155 A	156 D	157 C	158 B	159 D	160 A
161 B	162 B	163 C	164 B	165 D	166 D	167 C	168 B	169 B	170 B
171 D	172 C	173 D	174 D	175 C	176 B	177 C	178 A	179 D	180 A
181 B	182 B	183 C	184 A	185 A	186 A	187 B	188 D	189 D	190 A
191 B	192 C	193 A	194 A	195 D	196 A	197 B	198 D	199 D	200 A
201 B	202 B	203 B	204 B	205 A	206 A	207 A	208 A	209 A	210 A